COMMONHOLD

COMMONHOLD

Guy Fetherstonhaugh QC
Mark Sefton
Edward Peters
Barristers, Falcon Chambers

OXFORD
UNIVERSITY PRESS

Great Clarendon Street, Oxford OX2 6DP

Oxford University Press is a department of the University of Oxford.
It furthers the University's objective of excellence in research, scholarship,
and education by publishing worldwide in

Oxford New York

Auckland Bangkok Buenos Aires Cape Town Chennai
Dar es Salaam Delhi Hong Kong Istanbul Karachi Kolkata
Kuala Lumpur Madrid Melbourne Mexico City Mumbai Nairobi
São Paulo Shanghai Taipei Tokyo Toronto

Oxford is a registered trade mark of Oxford University Press
in the UK and in certain other countries

Published in the United States
by Oxford University Press Inc., New York

First published 2004

British Library Cataloguing in Publication Data
Data available

Library of Congress Cataloging in Publication Data
Data available

ISBN 0-19-927224-7

1 3 5 7 9 10 8 6 4 2

Typeset by Hope Services (Abingdon) Ltd
Printed in Great Britain
on acid-free paper by
Ashford Colour Press Limited, Gosport, Hampshire

Acknowledgements

To Ronald Bernstein QC, great friend and former head of our Chambers, without whose wisdom and good cheer this project might have remained a pipe dream.

To Peter Jackson, our Chambers librarian, without whose resourcefulness, ingenuity and industry this project might have been a lot shorter than it is.

And to Alexia, Rosie, Tom and Ned, without whose forbearance and love the senior author would have taken longer holidays and built more sandcastles.

Foreword

By the Honourable Mr Justice Lewison

In Thomas Love Peacock's *The Misfortunes of Elphin*, the modernisers propose to rebuild the great embankment which protects the plain of Gwaelod against the sea. The embankment evolved piecemeal over the years. A conversation takes place between Tiethrin, one of the commissioners of the embankment, Elphin, the prince, and Seithenyn, the Lord High Commissioner. The latter, of course, has a vested interest in the way things are.

> 'The stonework,' said Tiethrin, 'is sapped and mined: the piles are rotten, broken and dislocated: the floodgates and sluices are leaky and creaky.'
>
> 'That is the beauty of it,' said Seithenyn. 'Some parts of it are rotten, and some parts of it are sound.'
>
> 'It is well,' said Elphin, 'that some parts of it are sound: it were better that all were so.'
>
> 'So I have heard some people say before,' said Seithenyn; 'perverse people, blind to venerable antiquity: that very unamiable sort of people, who are in the habit of indulging their reason. But I say, the parts that are rotten give elasticity to those that are sound: they give elasticity, elasticity, elasticity. If it were all sound, it would break by its own obstinate stiffness: the soundness is checked by the rottenness, and the stiffness is balanced by the elasticity. There is nothing so dangerous as innovation.'

Many people perceive similar rottenness in the leasehold system of property ownership, at least as regards the acquisition of capital assets. The perceived problems are threefold. First the asset is a wasting asset. Secondly, some landlords are perceived as having interests that are adverse to those of the leaseholders. Thirdly, leasehold is seen as an unacceptable hangover from the feudal system. It is true that, historically, the leasehold system enabled the orderly and planned development of many of our treasured urban landscapes. But these planning functions are now, for the most part, carried out by public bodies rather than private interests. It is true, also, that Parliament has intervened to combat the worst imbalances between leaseholder and freeholder. Forfeiture and service charges, to take only two examples, are now highly regulated. But this is perceived not to be enough. Shakespeare's question:

> Why so large cost, having so short a lease,
> Dost thou upon thy fading mansion spend?

is still politically charged. On the other side of the coin, for reasons buried in the venerable antiquity of the common law, positive covenants cannot easily be made to bind successive owners of a freehold. So the current system could not accommodate the aspirations of flat dwellers to have the advantages of freehold ownership without the disadvantages. The Seithenyns have lost the argument for retaining the system as it is.

The legislators have now indulged their reason and innovated. The result is commonhold. It has been the best part of quarter of a century in gestating; and even now the infant has not yet fully emerged into the light of day. Much detail is still to be supplied by statutory instrument.

However, the lawyer will need to be prepared in advance of the finalisation of the details. The authors of this work, all experts in property law, have thoroughly researched not only the black letter law laid down by the commonhold legislation, but also the policy that underpins it, the likely shape of future regulations, and lessons to be learned from other jurisdictions that have condominium legislation of their own. They explain how to set up, run and terminate a commonhold, and conclude with a description of best practice. Their treatment, is thorough, informative and, above all, accessible.

Is innovation dangerous? The authors conclude that, in the case of commonhold, it is not. They believe that commonhold will prove to be workable, practical and popular. Their impressive volume gives every reason to share their confidence.

Kim Lewison

Royal Courts of Justice
September 2003

Preface

It is exciting, but difficult, to be given the privilege of producing a work on an entirely new form of land ownership. Exciting, because although models in overseas jurisdictions have established good track records for many decades, the Government has selected a rather different path upon which to embark with its own commonhold model. Difficult, because forecasting the likely success of this model involves guesswork quite as much as the application of established legal precedent.

So why bother with this rather uncertain project? To whom should it appeal? Is leasehold not good enough as a property-owning vehicle, given the host of recent amendments made to it (ironically enough by the same Act)? Will commonhold be a roaring success or a damp squib?

Although we cannot pretend that the sample is remotely representative, we the authors give commonhold our vote of confidence. Offered the chance between owning a property as a freehold unit in a commonhold or as a long leasehold, we would unhesitatingly plump for commonhold. We are particularly impressed by the comparative clarity and standardisation of documentation in commonhold; the sense that commonholders will have a community of interest in running a successful system; the constructive, courteous, open and honest relations that are more likely to characterise commonhold than leasehold; the emphasis in commonhold on dispute resolution that is likely to encourage complaints to be resolved rapidly and painlessly rather than being allowed to fester; and the fact that the unit in commonhold is not a wasting asset.

For those reasons, prospective owners should find commonhold more attractive; their mortgagees should be more ready to lend money against it, given the greater security and the cheaper cost of investigating documentation; and developers should find commonhold easier to sell than leasehold. As time goes by, we would expect existing long leaseholders to wish to convert to commonhold to realise the same benefits. We would also expect that commercial occupiers will want to be represented.

These are early days in the life of commonhold: the commonhold parts of the Act are not yet in force, and the regulations that will set out the bulk of the operational detail have not even progressed to final draft. But it is not too early to start the familiarisation process: we have striven to set out our understanding of how the Act will operate when in force once the regulations have been made. We have written a work that aims to set out in clear logical steps what must be done in order to ensure that commonhold will be a familiar working vehicle and not merely the name of a volume gathering dust on a shelf. The work is aimed not merely at lawyers and other professionals, but also at the commonhold association which will want a practical working guide to commonhold in one up-to-date volume.

Conscious that there is not much planning time available for those who might be contemplating setting up a commonhold as soon as the Act comes into force, we have aimed to provide as full an account as possible at this stage of the actual or apprehended procedures which will govern the creation and operation of commonhold. Our task has not been assisted by the lack of any detailed guidance regarding the extent and likely substance of the proposed commonhold regulations which will contain the detailed guidance. We have attempted nevertheless to provide as full a set of forms and precedents as possible, and will aim to revise and update those documents and details of procedure generally as soon as the material becomes available. In due course, a companion website will also be made available containing the latest updates along with additional helpful materials. It will be revised on a regular basis: http://www.oup.com/uk/booksites/practitionerlaw

Guy Fetherstonhaugh QC
Mark Sefton
Edward Peters

Falcon Chambers
Falcon Court
London EC4Y 1AA

September 2003

Contents—Summary

Contents

Table of Cases

Tables of Statutory Materials

A. STATUTES

United Kingdom

Australia

Australian Capital Territory

New South Wales

Northern Territory

Queensland

South Australia

Tasmania

Victoria

Western Australia

Bahamas

Barbados

Bermuda

Canada

Grenada

Jamaica

New Zealand

St Vincent and the Grenadines

Singapore

Trinidad and Tobago

USA

B. STATUTORY INSTRUMENTS, REGULATIONS, AND RULES

United Kingdom

C. COMMONHOLD COMMUNITY DOCUMENTS

PART A
COMMONHOLD

Chapter 1
INTRODUCTION TO COMMONHOLD

1.1 GENERAL

1.1.1 The Commonhold and Leasehold Reform Act 2002

Royal assent to the Commonhold and Leasehold Reform Act 2002 (referred to throughout this work as 'the Act') was given on 1 May 2002. As its title suggests, the Act deals with two topics.

Part 1 contains 70 sections and five associated schedules, and enacts a new form of land ownership known as commonhold. It is likely that Part 1 will be brought into force in the first half of 2004.

Part 2 of the Act deals with amendments to leasehold law, and in particular with enhancements of the means by which long residential leaseholders may require the freehold of their building to be transferred to a company set up on their behalf.

There is no overlap between the two topics, and leasehold reform is not considered in this work.

1.1.2 The aim of this work

The aim of this work is to provide a complete guide to commonhold for actual or prospective property owners, be they property developers or existing lessees, who might be contemplating setting up a commonhold; and for those professionals (lawyers, surveyors and accountants) who might be asked to assist in the creation, operation or termination of a commonhold.

In line with that aim, the authors have attempted to explain the structures and principles of commonhold in sufficient detail to provide the material with which working systems may be set up and problems may be solved. They have endeavoured equally, however, to satisfy the interests of the small commonhold association and its non-professional directors, who will wish to take advantage of the straightforward Best Practice Guide in Chapter 8; the Frequently Asked Questions in Chapter 7; and the Forms and Precedents which provide templates for dealing with all situations that may arise.

1.1.3 What is commonhold?

The term 'commonhold' was, it is said,[1] coined by Sir Brandon Rhys Williams MP, who in 1978 introduced a 'Co-Ownership of Flats Bill' under the Ten Minute Rule. The Bill proposed that disadvantaged residential lessees might compulsorily acquire their freehold reversion through the medium of a company which would be known as a 'commonhold company', in which all the participating lessees would hold shares. This mechanism has little, however, to do with the form of commonhold to be introduced by Part 1 of the Act, having more in common with the 'Right to Manage' company scheme introduced by Part 2 of the Act.

The term 'commonhold' now describes a new form of land ownership within registered freehold land. The commonhold scheme ensures that the occupants of a development are entirely in control, with no landlord or other third party able to exercise influence. Unit-holders in a commonhold building or other development will own the registered freehold estate in commonhold land in their respective units. The unit-holders will also be the exclusive members of a private company limited by guarantee which will own the registered freehold estate in commonhold land of the common parts.

1.2 THE SCOPE OF COMMONHOLD

1.2.1 Introduction

Throughout the passage of the Commonhold Bill through the Houses of Parliament, the Government steadily resisted the blandishments of those on its own benches as well as of the Opposition who sought to have the scope of commonhold applied on the widest possible basis. Instead, commonhold is to be made available only to those who vote for it unanimously, and will not be available at all in certain circumstances.

1.2.2 Those for whom commonhold will not be available

Conversion to commonhold from leasehold will be possible, but only where all those with a substantial interest in the land consent. Most obviously, this will mean obtaining the consent of all the leaseholders (whose leases will be extinguished on conversion) and of the landlord, who is likely to be resistant to a change which will remove an income-producing asset. Although Lord Williams of Elvel stated during the Committee Stage that the Government was 'trying to encourage commonhold to become something other than a formula for new

[1] The authors are indebted in this respect to the research carried out by Mr N Roberts for his 2002 paper in The Conveyancer, 'Commonhold: a new property term—but no property in a term!' [2002] 66 Conv 341.

builds',[2] it was acknowledged by the Minister responsible for promoting the Bill in the House of Commons that this might cut down drastically the numbers of those for whom the Act would present the greatest prize:

I should stress that although we envisage that the primary take-up of commonhold in the short term will be in new-build development, that will not necessarily be exclusively the case. We believe that existing leaseholders will occasionally convert to commonhold.[3]

Moreover, commonhold will not apply at all to agricultural land; to flying freeholds (ironically for the reason that the Government lacked the time or the inclination to tackle the recommendations of the Wilberforce Report—see paragraph 1.3.3 below); and to specified cases of statutory reverter.[4]

1.2.3 Those for whom commonhold will be available

In principle, commonhold will work as well for a house containing two flats as it will for a large development containing many units of residential or commercial accommodation.

The Government's prognosis is that commonhold:

. . . will be most commonly used for residential flats, but it is equally applicable to houses and to mixed-use and commercial developments.[5]

Because areas of land in a commonhold need not be geographically proximate, it is quite possible that commonhold developments may comprise not merely housing estates and blocks of flats, but 'even a complete town'.[6]

1.2.4. Criticisms of commonhold

Although the Bill commanded all party support, it attracted detailed criticism during its passage through Parliament. The following were the main criticisms:

(a) the requirement for unanimous agreement for any conversion from leasehold;

(b) the exclusion of flying freeholds;

(c) the omission of a 'sunset clause' providing for mandatory conversion from leasehold after a limited period;

(d) the absence of any requirement rendering commonhold a mandatory form of property holding for new communal developments; and

(e) the absence of effective sanction against defaulting unit-holders.

[2] *Official Report, House of Lords*, 16 October 2001; col 484.
[3] *Official Report, House of Commons*, 8 January 2002; col 431.
[4] See Schedule 2 to the Act and the discussion of this topic in paragraph 2.3.7.
[5] Paragraph 6 of the Consultation Paper published by the Lord Chancellor's Department on 10 October 2002.
[6] *Official Report, House of Commons*, 8 January 2002; vol 377, col 430.

1.2.5 Answers to the criticism

The Government's retort to these and similar criticisms was to insist on maintaining a relatively simple code that would attract developers and others. As the Minister said during the Second Reading in the House of Commons:

> . . . we believe that commonhold offers enormous attractions, but it would be wrong of us to prescribe it at this stage. The property market is complex and fluid, and we think that the scheme should have time to bed in. We want to see how the market responds to commonhold, so the answer . . . is, in short, 'Let the market decide.' We believe that it will make the appropriate decision and recognise the full advantages of commonhold.[7]

The authors share the Minister's optimism.

1.3 THE NEED FOR COMMONHOLD

1.3.1 The rule regarding the burden of positive covenants

The common law of England and Wales has over the course of time developed a rule that the burden of a positive covenant—an obligation to do something—which affects land does not bind successors in title of the original covenantor. To use the shorthand familiar to property lawyers, the burden of such a covenant 'does not run with the land'. This rule derives from the decision of the Court of Appeal in *Austerberry v Oldham Corporation* (1885) 29 Ch D 750. In that case, the owners of a site of a road covenanted that they and their successors in title would construct the road and keep it in repair. The road was sold to the defendants and it was held that the repair covenant could not be enforced against them. Cotton LJ expressed the reasons of the court as follows:

> . . . undoubtedly, where there is a restrictive covenant, the burden and benefit of which do not run at law, Courts of Equity restrain anyone who takes the property with notice of that covenant from using it in a way inconsistent with the covenant. But here the covenant which is attempted to be insisted upon on this appeal is a covenant to lay out money in doing certain work upon this land; and, that being so . . . that is not a covenant which a Court of Equity will enforce: it will not enforce a covenant not running at law when it is sought to enforce that covenant in such a way as to require the successors in title of the covenantor, to spend money, and in that way to undertake a burden upon themselves. The covenantor must not use the property for a purpose inconsistent with the use for which it was originally granted; but in my opinion a Court of Equity does not and ought not to enforce a covenant binding only in equity in such a way as to require the successors of the covenantor himself, they having entered into no covenant, to expend sums of money in accordance with what the original covenantor bound himself to do.

In *Rhone v Stephens* [1994] 2 AC 310, the House of Lords was invited to overrule this rule, but declined to do so. Lord Templeman said:

[7] *Official Report, House of Commons*, 8 January 2002; col 428.

Equity cannot compel an owner to comply with a positive covenant entered into by his predecessors in title without flatly contradicting the common law rule that a person cannot be made liable upon a contract unless he was a party to it. Enforcement of a positive covenant lies in contract; a positive covenant compels an owner to exercise his rights. Enforcement of a negative covenant lies in property; a negative covenant deprives the owner of a right over property.

. . . For over 100 years it has been clear and accepted law that equity will enforce negative covenants against freehold land but has no power to enforce positive covenants against successors in title of the land. To enforce a positive covenant would be to enforce a personal obligation against a person who has not covenanted. To enforce negative covenants is only to treat the land as subject to a restriction.

. . . [Y]our Lordships were invited to overrule the decision of the Court of Appeal in the *Austerberry* case. To do so would destroy the distinction between law and equity and to convert the rule of equity into a rule of notice. It is plain from the articles, reports and papers to which we were referred that judicial legislation to overrule the *Austerberry* case would create a number of difficulties, anomalies and uncertainties and affect the rights and liabilities of people who have for over 100 years bought and sold land in the knowledge, imparted at an elementary stage to every student of the law of real property, that positive covenants affecting freehold land are not directly enforceable except against the original covenantor. Parliamentary legislation to deal with the decision in the *Austerberry* case would require careful consideration of the consequences. Moreover, experience with leasehold tenure where positive covenants are enforceable by virtue of privity of estate has demonstrated that social injustice can be caused by logic.

The rule that the burden of positive covenants does not run with the land may therefore be regarded as settled.

1.3.2 The effect of the rule regarding the burden of positive covenants

In practice, the rule which prevents the transmission of the burden of positive covenants means, for example, that an obligation by freeholder A to keep in repair the boundary wall between his property and that of his neighbour will not be enforceable against the purchaser of the land of freeholder A. Although there are conveyancing procedures available which provide solutions to this problem in certain circumstances, they are cumbersome, sometimes difficult and expensive to implement, and unpopular with purchasers.

The problems are even more acute, of course, where one property depends upon another in some way, and where it is therefore of critical importance that the covenant be enforceable. The obvious example is that of flats in a building, which depend on each other for shelter and support, and which have a common need for insurance and maintenance. Although the courts have shown themselves ready to imply duties of care in such situations (see, for example, *Abbahall Ltd v Smee* [2003] 1 All ER 465), those duties fall some way short of the absolute obligations which a freeholder might desire.

1.3.3 The Wilberforce Report

In 1965, a committee appointed by the Lord Chancellor and under the chairmanship of Lord Wilberforce delivered a report[8] which referred to the difficulties caused by the decision in the *Austerberry* case and recommended legislation to provide that positive covenants which related to the use of land and were intended to benefit specified other land should run with the land.

The recommendations of the Wilberforce Report were never taken further, although a Law Commission working paper in 1971[9] described the present law on positive rights as being illogical, uncertain, incomplete and inflexible. A further Law Commission Report[10] laid before Parliament in 1984 made recommendations for the reform of the law relating to positive and restrictive obligations and submitted a draft Bill for that purpose. Nothing was, however, done.

1.3.4 Leasehold as remedy

The rule preventing the transmission of the burden of positive covenants has only a very restricted application as between the landlord to a lease and the successors in title of the original tenant. In the case of leases granted prior to 1996, covenants by tenants which 'touch and concern' the land are enforceable by the landlord against the successors in title of the tenant. In the case of leases granted after 1995, the Landlord and Tenant (Covenants) Act 1995 provides that all covenants between landlord and tenant are enforceable by and against their successors in title, save those which are expressed to be personal.

It might therefore seem as if a leasehold structure would afford a remedy where it is desirable for the burden of positive covenants to bind successors in title of the covenantor. Leases of residential premises have long been favoured in this country for that reason. There are estimated to be approximately one million houses and one million flats held in long leasehold ownership in England and Wales. However, while short-term leases of commercial premises do indeed provide a useful mechanism for the transmission of covenants, longer leases, particularly of residential premises, introduce problems of their own.

1.3.5 The problems with leases

The chief problems associated with long leases of residential premises are as follows:

(a) A long lease is a wasting asset: the investment in the tenant's home steadily loses value as the lease approaches the end of its term.

[8] The Report of the Committee on Positive Covenants Affecting Land (1965) Cmnd 2719.
[9] No 36: Transfer of Land: Appurtenant Rights, published on 5 July 1971.
[10] Transfer of Land: The Law of Positive and Restrictive Covenants (Law Com no 127).

(b) The interest of the tenant under a long lease often conflicts with that of his landlord: many leaseholders experience serious difficulties with their landlords, ranging from neglect of their obligations under the lease to outright exploitation.

(c) The defaulting tenant under a lease will usually be subject to the draconian penalty of forfeiture which, if deployed successfully, will destroy the value of his interest disproportionately to the default in question.

(d) There is generally no implied right for covenants to be enforced directly between tenants (save where it is possible to demonstrate the existence of a letting scheme, as in the case of *Williams v Kiley* [2003] 1 EGLR 46, which involved leases in a shopping parade).

(e) Leasehold documentation is not uniform.

(f) Tenants are obliged to pay a ground rent which may be considerable.

Frequent legislative attempts over a number of decades (of which Part 2 of the Act is but the most recent example) to alleviate or cure some of these problems have met with mixed success. Overall, notwithstanding those attempts, the dissatisfaction with leasehold tenure as a form of home ownership appears to have increased rather than decreased over the years.

1.3.6 Commonhold as remedy

In introducing the Second Reading of the Commonhold and Leasehold Reform Bill in the House of Commons, the Parliamentary Secretary for the Lord Chancellor's Department said:

> The problems of long leasehold provide the impetus for the Bill. They are the wrong that the provisions of this Bill are intended to put right.[11]

It is true to say that participation in a commonhold scheme will remove every single one of the problems identified in paragraph 1.3.5 above. However, it is perhaps more accurate to say in the light of the analysis above that the problems associated with the transmission of the burden of positive covenants have provided the impetus for the Act. Commonhold is a means of owning registered freehold land which gives owners of individual units in a development the security of freehold ownership but allows them to control and manage their own communal areas and applies positive obligations to every successive owner. It is thus an alternative, rather than an answer, to leasehold ownership.

1.3.7 Commonhold and Leasehold: a tabular comparison

It is instructive to compare commonhold with leasehold in its most favourable form (very long lease, with the freehold held by a company established under Part 2 of the Act) in the way illustrated in Table 1.1 below.

[11] *Official Report, House of Commons*, 8 January 2002; col 422.

TABLE 1.1

Factor	Commonhold	Leasehold	Comment
Ownership	Ownership is freehold rather than leasehold, so asset is permanent.	Being restricted to a term of years, the asset is a wasting one.	A factor of marginal importance where the term is very long—although there is some satisfaction to be had in being the only owner of your plot in commonhold.
Leasing ability	Leasing of a commonhold unit is restricted, the current proposal being that leases should either be periodic, or for terms of up to 21 years.	Leasing of a leasehold unit is not usually restricted at all.	Leasehold is clearly more advantageous as far as this factor is concerned – although query how much demand there would be to grant long leases of a commonhold unit in any event.
Assignment	Assignment of a commonhold unit is completely unrestricted.	Assignment may be restricted under some leases – although this would be unusual in very long leases.	Commonhold enjoys a clear advantage where leasehold restricts assignment.
Compliance with obligations	The methods of procuring enforcement of obligations in commonhold is graduated and well structured. Moreover, it is possible for obligations to be enforced effectively between unit-holders (through the agency of the commonhold association).	The system of obligations in leasehold remains adversarial, with landlords, with their interest in the demise, dictating compliance. Enforcement of obligations between leaseholders is usually difficult if not impossible.	Commonhold is founded upon the proposition that there is a mutuality of interest between unit-holders and their association. The adversarial perception in leasehold promises to be hard to shake off, despite the changes wrought by Part 2 of the Act.

Factor	Commonhold	Leasehold	Comment
Restrictions on Service charges	In commonhold, there are few rules to complicate the way in which necessary works are done, services supplied, and reimbursement made. The successful administration of such matters depends not upon compliance with complicated statutory regimes, but rather upon the mutuality of interest that is the hallmark of commonhold.	In leasehold, by contrast, the service charge regime is beset by complexity, symptomatic of its genesis in the adversarial relationship between landlord and tenant.	As far as the commonhold association is concerned, the service charge (or "commonhold assessment") regime is much to be preferred for its comparative simplicity. This should also work in favour of the unit-holders.
Sanctions for non-compliance	In keeping with its softer image, commonhold depends to a large extent upon the good will and responsibility of its members, and has few sanctions for non-compliance with obligations. Litigation is treated as a last resort.	By comparison, forfeiture, although much diluted, still has a vital role in leasehold. Litigation is often seen as the first resort. Even if proceedings are not brought, the landlord has a powerful weapon to deploy on the occasion of any proposed assignment.	The comparative absence of powerful sanction in commonhold may at first be seen as a disadvantage. However, the same factor may well add to the attractiveness of commonhold from the unit-holder's viewpoint.
Documentation	Commonhold documentation is largely standardised, making for common (and easily understood) rules and cheaper, quicker conveyancing.	Leasehold documentation is often idiosyncratic and couched in archaic language. It is rarely standardised, and makes for complicated and expensive conveyancing.	Commonhold is the clear winner in this respect.

1.4 THE LEGISLATIVE HISTORY OF COMMONHOLD

1.4.1 Introduction

The Act has been a long time in the making. Although Commonwealth and other jurisdictions have happily been living with strata title (to give commonhold its overseas name) for many decades (see paragraph 1.4.2 below), with or without accompanying leasehold systems, the British Government has been slow to recognise and implement the benefits that commonhold brings.

1.4.2 The first steps to reform

The genesis of commonhold can be traced back at least as far as 1965, when the Wilberforce committee on positive covenants affecting land (see paragraph 1.3.3 above) recommended the introduction of an optional basis for new, large, multiple developments of a modified strata title system, similar to that which had been introduced a few years earlier in New South Wales. 'Strata title' is, as its name implies, a means by which property consisting of numbers of individual layers belonging to different people (typically a block of flats) may be owned.

Matters developed further in 1984, when the issue was referred to the Law Commission. In its report 'The Law of Positive and Restrictive Covenants', the Law Commission recognised that the law was defective in imposing mutually enforceable property rights and obligations. The commission recommended the creation of a new interest in land—the land obligation—that would be capable of subsisting as a legal interest like an easement, and which would impose a burden on the owner of one piece of land, either for the benefit of the owner of another piece, or as part of a development scheme. Those recommendations were accepted by the Government, but then superseded to an extent by the commonhold proposals that were put forward.

The Commission recommended the adoption of some form of condominium legislation (strata title by another name—see paragraph 1.5.5 below) similar to that in America, Australia, and various other jurisdictions. In response to the report, the Government established an interdepartmental working group, under the chairmanship of a law commissioner, to produce proposals for similar legislation in England and Wales. It reported in July 1987,[12] and recommended commonhold as a new way in which to own property.

The Lord Chancellor asked the Law Commission for a report and draft bill, which were produced in 1990. After further consultation, the Lord Chancellor announced the Government's intention to bring forward the necessary legislation as soon as parliamentary time could be found for it.

[12] Commonhold—Freehold Flats and the Freehold Ownership of other Interdependent Buildings (Cm 179).

A draft bill and consultation paper on commonhold had been prepared by 1996, and the Bill was proposed in the Queen's Speech in October 1996. The general election intervened in May 1997, however, and the Bill fell by the wayside. The pressure of business with a higher priority from the new Government rendered the restoration of the Bill a distant prospect.

1.4.3 The progress of the Commonhold Bill to enactment

In December 2000, the Government finally introduced a Commonhold and Leasehold Reform Bill in the House of Lords. The Bill progressed to a Third Reading in the House of Lords, but failed to proceed further when a general election was called in May 2001.

The Bill was, however, reintroduced on 21 June 2001, shortly after the general election. In the House of Lords, it received its Second Reading on 5 July 2001;[13] had its Committee Stage on 16 and 22 October 2001;[14] its Report Stage on 13 November 2001;[15] and its Third Reading on 19 November 2001.[16] In the House of Commons, it received its Second Reading on 8 January 2002;[17] had its Committee Stage on 15, 17, 22 and 24 January 2002;[18] its Report Stage on 11 and 13 March 2002;[19] and its Third Reading on 13 March 2002.[20] The Commons Amendments were considered by the House of Lords on 15 April 2002.[21]

The Bill thus received an unusual amount of scrutiny in the House of Lords, having had two First Readings, two Second Readings, a lengthy exercise in Grand Committee, discussions during its unfinished Report Stage, and other Readings during its second round.

1.5 SOLUTIONS ADOPTED ABROAD

1.5.1 Introduction

During the Committee Stage of the Bill in the House of Lords, Baroness Scotland remarked that:

> [W]hile developing this Bill we have quite shamelessly borrowed good ideas from a number of other jurisdictions.[22]

[13] *Official Report, House of Lords*; vol 626, cols 885–924.
[14] *Official Report, House of Lords*; vol 627, cols 482–547; 562–584; 819–826; 840–894.
[15] *Official Report, House of Lords*; vol 628, cols 463–528; 542–558.
[16] *Official Report, House of Lords*; vol 628, cols 907–947.
[17] *Official Report, House of Commons*; vol 377, cols 422–515.
[18] *Official Report, House of Commons*; Standing Committee D.
[19] *Official Report, House of Commons*; vol 381, cols 640–729.
[20] *Official Report, House of Commons*; vol 381, cols 907–987.
[21] *Official Report, House of Lords*; vol 633, cols 683–725.
[22] *Official Report, House of Lords*; 16 October 2001; col 535.

A number of the former colonies in Australasia and the New World have operated systems of strata title or condominium law for many decades, and the extent of the parliamentary plunder from that experience has been considerable. Although the authors have not enjoyed the good fortune of those Members who journeyed to Honolulu and beyond in tireless pursuit of the commonhold ideal, the following is a summary of the principal systems of commonhold-type systems which have been adopted in other parts of the world.

1.5.2 Australia[23]

The Australian strata title system began in New South Wales with the Conveyancing (Strata Titles) Act 1961 (NSW). There is now strata title legislation in every State and Territory,[24] and strata title is a common form of land ownership for residential, commercial and industrial purposes. In New South Wales, for example, there are now well over 600,000 strata title lots in existence, with an average of 10–12 lots per scheme; it is estimated that almost a quarter of the population live in, own or are employed within a strata title scheme.[25]

Strata title schemes originate with the deposit at the Land Titles Office of a strata plan.[26] Upon acceptance of the plan, the existing title certificates are cancelled, and new strata titles issued for each unit and for the common property. The strata plan sets out the boundaries of each unit and any building on the unit, and establishes the liability of each unit for common expenditure through a system of unit entitlements. A majority of states require a minimum of two units and some common property. A unit must generally consist of the whole or part of a building. Parts of the common property may be reserved for the exclusive use of individual unit owners.[27] A strata corporation is registered as the proprietor of the common property, which it holds on trust for the unit holders. Each unit-holder is a member of the strata corporation, whose articles of association and regulations govern the running of the strata scheme. Corporations can generally adopt different articles and regulations, or resolve to amend them, subject to varying degrees of state legislative restrictions. The strata corporation is responsible for maintaining the common property, insuring the scheme, and enforcing the obligations of the unit-holders. Unit-holders are liable for repairing their own units.

[23] For an introduction to Australian strata title law, see *Australian Real Property Law*, by Bradbrook, MacCallum and Moore, 2nd edn, 1997, Chapter 13.

[24] The principal legislation is: New South Wales: Strata Titles Act 1973; Victoria: Subdivision Act 1988; Subdivision (Body Corporate) Regulations; Queensland: Building Units and Group Titles Act 1980; SA: Community Titles Act 1996; Western Australia: Strata Titles Act 1988; Tasmania: Conveyancing and Law of Property Act 1884; Australian Capital Territory: Unit Titles Act 1970; Northern Territory: Unit Titles Act 1970. See Bradbrook et al (above), para 13-03.

[25] Department of Fair Trading (NSW): *National Competition Policy Review: Strata Schemes Management Act 1996, Final Report 2001*, p 2.

[26] Other than in Victoria, where the strata plan has been abandoned as a concept.

[27] Bradbrook et al (above), para 13-08.

Contributions from unit-holders are enforceable as debts, and recoverable from successors in title to the unit.[28] Disputes are variably (in different States) referable to Strata Titles Boards, Commissioners, Referees or the courts.[29]

1.5.3 New Zealand

In New Zealand, the Unit Titles Act 1977 established a system of stratum estates, whereby two or more units are owned by individual proprietors, and the common property is owned by all the unit proprietors as tenants in common. A unit plan defines the extent of the units and the common property, and is deposited with the appropriate district land registry. A schedule of unit entitlements is fixed by a valuer at the commencement of a scheme, on the basis of the relative values of each unit, and that determines the percentage which each unit is liable to contribute to the common expenses, its share in the common property and its voting rights. The proprietors of all the units collectively constitute the body corporate of a scheme. The body corporate is responsible for insuring the scheme, maintaining the common property, enforcing the rules, and levying contributions from the units towards the common expenditure. Accessory units are units designed to be used with principal units, such as garages, gardens and parking spaces.

1.5.4 Singapore

Singapore has a strata title system, governed by the Singapore Land Titles (Strata) Act 1967[30] (although many developments are called 'condominiums'). The establishment and operation of strata schemes is regulated in some detail by the Act and its associated regulations. The Commissioner of Buildings must approve in advance the proposed schedule of strata units, and the share values to be allotted to those units. Upon registration of a strata title scheme, individual certificates of title are issued for the various units. The common property is owned by a management corporation. The lot owners are all members of the corporation, which governs the running of the scheme through an elected council. Disputes respecting the strata units or the strata development, including the common property, are referable to Strata Titles Boards, which also hear applications for orders for collective sales.[31] Members of the panel from which the Boards are selected have a wide range of experience, and include accountants, architects, engineers, lawyers, property consultants, surveyors and lay members.

[28] Bradbrook et al (above), paras 13.12, 13.13, 13.17.

[29] Bradbrook et al (above), paras 13.27–28.

[30] Cap 158, 1988.

[31] See Part VI of the Land Titles (Strata) Act; and Land Titles (Strata Titles Boards) Regulations 1999.

1.5.5 The United States[32]

Condominium legislation developed in the United States from the 1960s onwards, and is mainly used as a system for owning residential apartment buildings.[33] The first US condominium enabling statute was in Puerto Rico in 1958. All states now have such legislation. Many of the first generation of condominium statutes were based on the Model Statute for the Creation of Apartment Ownership, introduced by the Federal Housing Administration in 1961. The legislation of many states is now based on two more recent models drawn up by the Commission on Uniform State Laws: the Uniform Condominium Act (1977, amended 1980)[34] and the Uniform Common Interest Ownership Act (1982, amended 1994).[35]

The freehold of each unit in a condominium is individually owned, with the unit-holders owning the common elements as tenants in common. The condominium enabling legislation usually prohibits the partition of the building or the common elements by the unit owners, and prohibits the separation of a unit from the unit-holder's share in the common elements. It also makes provision for the use, management and maintenance of the common elements. Under the enabling legislation, each condominium must have a 'condominium declaration', providing for: (a) the relevant land to be submitted to the provisions of the statute; (b) the establishment of the unit-holders into a property owners' association, which must elect a board of directors; and (c) covenants, by-laws and administrative regulations adopted by the association to run with each unit and to bind all successive owners thereof. The condominium statute will usually list various specific matters which must be included in the by-laws of the condominium association, such as maintenance of the building and common elements, the assessment and collection of maintenance charges, the approval and financing of capital improvements, restrictions on the use and transfer of units, and what happens in the event of the condominium being destroyed.[36]

1.5.6 Canada

Each Canadian state has its own condominium enabling legislation,[37] and condominiums are a common system of ownership for multi-unit residential,

[32] For an introduction to US condominium law in the context of the US law of real property, see eg *The Law of Property*, Stoebuck and Whitman, 3rd edn, 2000.

[33] For what follows, see Stoebuck and Whitman (above), p 33, p 181.

[34] The model for the states of Alabama, Arizona, Maine, Missouri, New Mexico, North Carolina, Pennsylvania, Rhode Island, Texas, Virginia and Washington.

[35] The model for the states of Alaska, Colorado, Connecticut, Minnesota, Nevada, Vermont and West Virginia.

[36] See Stoebuck and Whitman (above), p 33, p 181. The control of transfers of units is often achieved by providing for pre-emptive rights of first refusal on sale or leasing. The enabling legislation often excludes the rule against perpetuities and the common law rule against restraints on alienation.

[37] See eg Ontario: Condominium Act RSO 1998; Condominium Act RSO1990; Condominium Act RSO 1979; British Columbia: Condominium Act RSBC 1996; Condominium Act RSBC 1979; Manitoba: Condominium Act RSM 1970; Nova Scotia: Condominium Property Act SNS, 1970–1.

commercial and mixed-use projects. The freehold of each unit is separately owned, each unit-holder being a tenant in common of the common elements. A condominium plan defines the boundaries of the units and the common elements. A statutory condominium corporation manages the condominium property. Governed by a Board of Directors, it has the duty to control, manage and administer the common elements and the assets of the corporation, and to ensure the unit owners comply with their obligations under statute and under the by-laws and rules of the condominium.

1.5.7 The Caribbean[38]

A number of Caribbean countries have introduced condominium legislation, largely modelled on United States systems, including the Bahamas,[39] Barbados,[40] Bermuda,[41] Grenada,[42] Jamaica,[43] Trinidad and Tobago,[44] and St Vincent and the Grenadines.[45] Condominiums are commonly used for holiday accommodation and for commercial developments.[46]

1.6 THE STRUCTURE OF COMMONHOLD

1.6.1 Introduction

In essence, the unit-holder in a commonhold development owns the registered freehold title in his unit, and also has the right to become a member of a company—the commonhold association—which owns the common parts of the area in which the unit is situated. Regulation of desired rights and obligations between the unit-holders and the commonhold association is achieved by means of various provisions of the Act; by the memorandum and articles of association of the association; and by a document regulated by the Act called the 'commonhold community statement'.

1.6.2 The commonhold unit

This will typically consist of a flat in a block of flats; a house on a housing estate which shares communal facilities with other houses on the estate; a unit on an industrial estate or a retail shop in a parade; or any combination of such features.

[38] For an introduction to Commonwealth Caribbean condominium law, see *Commonwealth Caribbean Property Law* by Professor Gilbert Kodilinye, 1st edn, 2000, Chapter 8.

[39] Law of Property and Conveyancing (Condominium) Act, Ch 124, 1965.

[40] Condominium Act, Cap 224A.

[41] Condominium Act 1986.

[42] Condominium Act, Cap 60.

[43] Registration (Strata Titles) Act.

[44] Condominium Act 1981.

[45] Condominium Act, Cap 227.

[46] See Kodilinye (above), p 129.

It will be essential in any commonhold for the exact physical boundaries of each commonhold unit to be drawn accurately in order to indicate the boundaries within which any set of rights and obligations will operate. The unit-holder, for example, will need to know precisely what part of the structure of his building he is to insure and maintain. Conversely, the commonhold association will need to be aware of the extent of its own obligations.

1.6.3 The common parts of the commonhold

The common parts of the commonhold are defined by the Act as everything else within the title that does not comprise the individual units.

1.6.4 The commonhold association

The commonhold association is a company limited by guarantee. This form of company is similar in some ways to a conventional company limited by shares. Its operations are governed by the Companies Acts, and it has a board of directors.

However, instead of shareholders it has members, and instead of buying shares and receiving dividends they offer a guarantee—usually a nominal £1—as the limit of their liability.

Since there is also generally a provision that assets of the company can only be passed to a similar company if it is wound-up, there is no way to distribute profits for private gain. Accordingly, funders and supporters of such a company can be sure that any surpluses are ploughed back into the company to meet its objectives.

1.6.5 The memorandum and articles of association of the commonhold association

The memorandum of association of the commonhold association sets out the essential attributes of the commonhold association and describes its relationship with the outside world. It is required to state the name of the commonhold association; the situation of its registered office; the objects of the commonhold association; the fact that the liability of its members is limited; and the amount of the guarantee.

The articles of association of the commonhold association regulate the relations between the officers of the commonhold association (the directors, who need not be members of the association) and its members. They deal with such matters as voting rights, frequency of meetings of the association and functions of the directors.

The form and content of the memorandum and articles of association of the commonhold association are closely regulated by the Act.

1.6.6 The commonhold community statement

The commonhold community statement controls the way in which the commonhold is run, as opposed to the formal corporate rules (the memorandum and articles of association), which control the way in which the commonhold association must operate. The commonhold community statement will define the extent of the units; it will provide for the rights and duties of the unit-holders and the commonhold association; it will regulate the use and maintenance of the common parts and the units; and it will set out how the commonhold association may levy a maintenance charge (called a 'commonhold assessment').
Again, the form and content of the commonhold community statement is regulated by the Act, although it is recognised that there are local issues peculiar to any individual development which will require dedicated rules.

1.7 THE PRINCIPLES OF COMMONHOLD

1.7.1 Introduction

The guiding principles behind the Commonhold Bill were repeatedly said during the passage of the Bill through Parliament to be:

(a) parity of interest;

(b) uniformity of structure; and

(c) standardisation of the documentation, as far as possible.[47]

To these principles might be added a fourth, which is evident from the way in which the Act has been drafted:

(d) the inclusion of the working detail of the Act in a series of easily amendable regulations.

The extent to which these principles are enshrined in the Act and are likely to be encountered in practice is examined in this Section.

1.7.2 Parity of interest

Each unit-holder will have two interests in the property of a commonhold: ownership of his unit; and the right to be a member of the commonhold association, and with it the right to vote on how the commonhold should be administered. There will therefore be a mutuality of interest in a commonhold.

[47] See eg *Official Report, House of Commons, Second Reading, Standing Committee D*, 15 January 2002; col 18.

1.7.3 Uniformity of structure

The Government's aspiration is that the structural elements of commonhold—the memorandum and articles of association and the commonhold community statement—should be uniform.

There is no reason why this aspiration should not be achieved in relation to the memorandum and articles of association, given the comparatively limited scope of those documents and the narrow range of objectives of a commonhold association. The Consultation Paper published by the Lord Chancellor's Department on 10 October 2002 seeks to put this into practice by providing that the memorandum of association should not be capable of any amendment; and that the articles of association should only be variable in part. As the Post-Consultation Report dated August 2003 establishes, it is unlikely that there will be any significant departure from these proposals.

As far as the commonhold community statement is concerned, however, the widely differing types of development suitable for commonhold that are likely to be encountered—from a converted house containing two flats to a purpose built block containing fifty; from a mixed use marina development to a holiday chalet site; from an industrial estate to a shopping centre—make it most unlikely that substantial uniformity will be achieved in practice.

When the draft Land Registration Rules supporting the Land Registration Act 2002 were published, the Land Registry put forward similar proposals for uniformity, including a proposal that all new registrable leases of registered land granted after October 2003 would have to be prepared using a single standard form. The Land Registry also suggested that all variations of leases would have to be prepared on a different standard form. The Consultation Paper introducing those proposals attracted substantial criticism, with almost 80 per cent of the responses relating to the above forms disagreeing with the Land Registry's proposals. Critics of the proposals had suggested that the introduction of a standard lease could increase their workload (and therefore legal costs). They also argued that the new forms would require in-house managers and managing agents to reprogramme their management systems to select information from different places within the lease. On 17 January 2003, the Land Registry announced that it had decided to withdraw its proposals and to study the responses with a view to bringing forward revised proposals in the second half of 2003. The revised rules were laid before Parliament on 5 June 2003, and came into force on 13 October 2003. They contain no proposals for a standard form of lease.

The authors suggest that a commonhold community statement which seeks to impose too much uniformity at the expense of flexibility will prove just as unpopular. The Post-Consultation Report dated August 2003 appends a draft commonhold community statement (see Form 2.3) which seeks to accommodate the need for flexibility by including some provisions which are intended to be mandatory with others which may be adapted or omitted to meet the particular needs, desires and contingencies of any given commonhold association.

1.7.4 Standardisation of documentation

The same theme of uniformity emerges in connection with the other documents which will be required in relation to the formation, operation and termination of a commonhold.

Most of the documents necessary to the registration of a freehold estate as a freehold estate in commonhold land (see Forms 1.1 to 1.12 and 1.15 to 1.17 in the Forms and Precedents part of this work) have been chosen to receive this standardisation treatment. The Consultation Paper published by the Lord Chancellor's Department on 10 October 2002 and the Post-Consultation Report dated August 2003 propose that a number of other forms to do with the operation of the commonhold should also be standardised (see for example, Forms 1.13, 2.9 and 2.13).

The avowed aim in drafting such documents in standard form was to avoid, so far as possible, the need for commonholders to have recourse to lawyers.[48] The authors sympathise with that aim, even if (as lawyers) they do not look forward to its successful implementation with open enthusiasm. They question, however, the need for a complex range of tailor-made forms for what may be a very small and informal organisation. Take, for example, the case of a commonhold of four flats or houses on an estate. The requirement to have a ponderous and formulaic dispute resolution procedure, for example, involving the sending of a series of notices beginning with a 'Notification of Complaint' (Form 4.1); proceeding through a 'Notice of default' (Form 4.4); and possibly culminating in an 'Indemnity notice' (Form 4.6) may appear to some to be a procedure designed to antagonise neighbours, when a successful commonhold will largely depend upon the ability of its members to coexist in an informal and friendly manner.

The standardisation initiative only goes so far, however. As the Post-Consultation Report dated August 2003 states:

> . . . there should be a strong core of standard provisions but beyond these individual commonholds should have a wide degree of flexibility. This approach supports our belief that commonholders should, as far as possible, be able to enjoy the freedoms of freeholders generally, rather than the numerous constraints traditionally associated with leases.

1.7.5 Detail in the regulations

The 70 sections of Part 1 of the Act and its five associated sections occupy just over 41 pages of text in the Queen's Printers' copy. The Consultation Paper published by the Lord Chancellor's Department on 10 October 2002 seeking views on its proposals regarding the commonhold regulations (which are not included in

[48] The Post-Consultation Report dated August 2003 stated: 'The second general theme reinforced by the response to the consultation is that the commonhold documents should, if at all possible, be in plain English and operable, in the main, without expert assistance. We want to achieve this objective but are conscious of the need to ensure that the documents are legally clear and effective.'

anything other than the sketchiest of forms) is 165 pages in extent. The Post-Consultation Report dated August 2003 taken together with its appendices extends to a further 232 pages. The draft Commonhold (Land Registration) Rules 2003 add an altogether more modest 27 pages. No draft amended Civil Procedure Rules nor dedicated Company or Insolvency Rules have yet been published. Once all those documents are available, it is reasonably clear that the sheer mass of regulations and rules will far outweigh the statutory material.

The Government has sought from the first to relegate major parts of the machinery of the Act to regulations, which may be amended comparatively easily, rather than dealing with such matters in the main body of the Act. Responding to a point made regarding the complexity of the subject matter of the Bill during the Second Reading in the House of Commons, the Parliamentary Secretary, Lord Chancellor's Department said:

> [This] is a complex matter and that is why the provisions in the Bill are simple, practical and designed to be flexible. That is why we have also made provision for the use of regulations to deal with what will inevitably be a complex and fast-evolving property market.[49]

The same theme was expanded upon a little later:

> We are aware of the scarcity of parliamentary time for amending primary legislation. Commonhold will be a completely new facet to our land law, and we recognise that despite all the hard work and extensive consultation on the Bill, when commonhold comes on line, some provisions will inevitably be found to be capable of improvement. We want to be able to react rapidly in such circumstances and secondary legislation affords us the opportunity to do so.[50]

Leaving aside the constitutional propriety of allowing delegated legislation to carry out such an important and little scrutinised function, it must be remarked that it will be critical for commonholders and those advising them to keep abreast of the emergence of new and amending rules and regulations. This work will publish details of any such provisions as soon as reasonably possible. At the time of going to press (November 2003), the Lord Chancellor has made only one commencement order relating to the commonhold provisions in Part I of the Act.[51]

[49] *Official Report, House of Commons*, 8 January 2002; col 426.

[50] *Official Report, House of Commons*, 8 January 2002; col 429.

[51] See the Commonhold and Leasehold Reform Act 2002 (Commencement No 3) Order 2003 in the Statutory Instruments section at the end of the Statutes etc part of the work, which was made on 8 September 2003, and which brought the regulation-making and other formal powers in sections 42, 62, 64, 65, 66, 67, 69 and 70 into force on 29 September 2003.

Chapter 2
CREATING A COMMONHOLD

PART 1 GENERAL

2.1 INTRODUCTION

The creation of a commonhold involves the following stages:

(a) The identification of the land which is to form the commonhold.

(b) The obtaining of the necessary consent from the persons interested in the land.

(c) The formation of the commonhold association.

(d) The preparation of the commonhold community statement.

(e) The application to the Land Registry for the registration of the land as a freehold estate in commonhold land.

These five stages are considered in turn in the next five parts of this chapter. Part 7 looks at development rights. Part 8 then considers the special considerations relevant to an application which does not relate to a new development, but which relates to land that is already occupied by long lessees. Part 9 considers the effects of registration. Part 10 considers the rules for making amendments to a commonhold. Part 11 considers the procedure for rectifying a registration which has been made in error.

PART 2 TYPES OF LAND

2.2 LAND WHICH CAN BE COMMONHOLD

2.2.1 Introduction

Any land can be registered as commonhold land, save for the following:

(a) Unregistered land;

(b) Leasehold land;

(c) Commonhold land;
(d) Flying freeholds;
(e) Agricultural land; and
(f) Contingent estates.

All the land which is to form the commonhold must be identified on a plan. The plan must be attached to the commonhold community statement. The detailed requirements for the plan are considered in Part 5 of this chapter.

2.2.2 Multiple site commonholds

A single commonhold can encompass land on two or more sites which are not contiguous. This is expressly permitted by the Act, and is called a 'multiple site commonhold'.[1] A single commonhold can therefore include, for example, two parcels of land on opposite sides of a highway. The two separate parcels must, however, be governed by a single commonhold community statement and a single commonhold association.[2]

The Act provides that regulations may be made which will set out a procedure for the separate owners of two parcels of land to make a joint application to convert the parcels into a single commonhold.[3] However, the regulations from the Land Registry[4] will require the owners first to amalgamate the two parcels of land under a single title number, with the same sole owner or joint owners registered as the proprietors of all the land that is to be converted.[5]

2.2.3 Commercial commonholds

There is no rule that a commonhold must only relate to residential property. It may be a purely commercial development, purely residential or a mixture of residential and commercial. Commercial and mixed use developments held under arrangements similar to commonhold have proven track records in many other jurisdictions.

2.3 LAND WHICH CANNOT BE COMMONHOLD

2.3.1 Introduction

The following types of land cannot be registered as commonhold:

(a) Unregistered land—see paragraph 2.3.2 below;
(b) Leasehold land—see paragraph 2.3.3 below;

[1] Section 57(1). [2] Section 57(2). [3] Section 57(3).
[4] The Land Registry (Commonhold) Rules 2003.
[5] Paragraph 68, Land Registry Consultation Paper, 2 September 2002.

(c) Commonhold land—see paragraph 2.3.4 below;
(d) Flying freeholds—see paragraph 2.3.5 below;
(e) Agricultural land—see paragraph 2.3.6 below;
(f) Contingent estates—see paragraph 2.3.7 below.

2.3.2 Unregistered land

The only person who can make an application for land to be converted into commonhold is the registered freehold owner.[6] It follows that unregistered land cannot be registered as commonhold. However, the Act's definition of the registered freehold owner includes any person who has applied to be registered as the freehold owner, provided that the Registrar is satisfied that he is entitled to the registration.[7] The result is that, although an unregistered freehold owner must apply for first registration of his title before the land can be converted to commonhold, it should in principle be possible to apply for first registration at the same time as applying for the conversion to commonhold. Rules may be made which provide for 'the order in which commonhold registration documents and general registration documents are to be dealt with by the Registrar',[8] and it is thought that the Act's intention was to allow for a simultaneous first registration and registration of the land as commonhold. However, the Land Registry (Commonhold) Rules 2003 do not contain a relevant procedure. The consequence is that the owner of unregistered land will probably need to apply separately for first registration, before he then applies to register the land as commonhold.

2.3.3 Leasehold land

The only estate that can be registered as a commonhold is a freehold estate. A developer therefore cannot create a commonhold where his interest in the land is only under a long lease. Similarly, the long lessees of the flats in an existing development cannot convert to commonhold unless they have first acquired the freehold, either by private treaty or under their rights of collective enfranchisement. The procedure for converting an existing development into a commonhold is considered in Part 8.

2.3.4 Commonhold land

A commonhold is a species of freehold estate. However, no application for registration as a commonhold can be made in relation to land of which any part is already a commonhold.[9] This is to prevent the subdivision of an existing commonhold into further subsidiary commonholds.

[6] Section 2(1)(a). [7] Section 2(3)(b). [8] Section 65(3)(d). [9] Section 2(1)(b).

2.3.5 Flying freeholds

Land cannot be registered as a commonhold if all or any part of it includes a flying freehold.[10] A flying freehold is statutorily defined for the purposes of the 2002 Act: an application to register land as commonhold cannot be made 'in relation to land above ground level ("raised land") unless all the land between the ground and the raised land is the subject of the same application'.

The consequences of this rule are that:

(a) A commonhold cannot exclude the lower storeys of a building. A commonhold of a building which has commercial units on the ground floor and residential units on the floors above must include both the commercial and the residential elements within a single commonhold.

(b) A commonhold is able to exclude the upper storeys of a building. A commonhold can exist which includes the commercial units on the ground floor of a building, but which does not include the residential units on the floors above. However, this would be difficult to achieve in practice, because the upper floors would need to become flying freeholds, and would then be practically unsaleable.

(c) A commonhold is able to exclude any premises that are below ground level. It can therefore exclude, for example, an underground car park.

The rule against flying freeholds does not prevent the addition of a flying freehold to an existing commonhold, provided that all the land between the ground level and the additional land is already within the existing commonhold. This permits, for example, the addition to a commonhold of an upper storey extension.

2.3.6 Agricultural land

Land cannot be registered as commonhold if the whole or any part of it is agricultural land.[11] Land is agricultural land for this purpose if it is any of the following:

(a) Agricultural land within the meaning of the Agriculture Act 1947.[12] The definition of agricultural land in the 1947 Act is 'Land used for agriculture which is so used for the purposes of a trade or business, or which is designated by the Minister for the purposes of this subsection, and includes any land so designated as land which in the opinion of the Minister ought to be brought into use for agriculture.'[13]

(b) Land which is comprised in a tenancy of an agricultural holding within the meaning of the Agricultural Holdings Act 1986.[14]

[10] Section 4; Schedule 2, paragraph 1.
[11] Section 4; Schedule 2, paragraph 2.
[12] Schedule 2, paragraph 2(a).
[13] Section 109(1), Agriculture Act 1947.
[14] Schedule 2, paragraph 2(b).

(c) Land which is comprised within a farm business tenancy for the purposes of the Agricultural Tenancies Act 1995.[15]

Reference should be had to specialist works for the interpretation of these statutes.

2.3.7 Contingent estates

Land cannot be registered as commonhold if the whole or any part of it is a contingent estate.[16] A contingent estate is land that is liable to revert or vest in a person other than the present registered proprietor, on the occurrence or non-occurrence of a particular event, as a result of the operation of the School Sites Act 1841, the Literary and Scientific Institutions Act 1854, the Places of Worship Sites Act 1873 or the Land Clauses Acts. Regulations can be made which add to or remove from this list of statutes.[17]

The School Sites Act 1841 is a statute enabling land which had been settled as part of an estate to be conveyed to be used for educational purposes.[18] Any land conveyed under this statutory power was liable to revert to the estate in the event that it ceased to be used for these purposes.[19] However, the Reverter of Sites Act 1987 now provides that the ownership of the land no longer reverts to the estate; the land can be sold free of the reverter, and the transferor instead holds the proceeds of sale on trust for the person to whom the land would previously have reverted.[20] It is therefore not clear why this land cannot be converted into commonhold.

The Literary and Scientific Institutions Act 1854 is a similar statute enabling settled land, land subject to a trust, and land belonging to various ecclesiastical and lay

[15] Schedule 2, paragraph 2(c).

[16] Schedule 2, paragraph 3.

[17] Schedule 2, paragraph 3(4).

[18] Many large estates in the 19th century had been settled, and the person entitled to the land for the time being did not have the power to dispose of it; section 2 of the 1841 Act conferred a power of sale for educational purposes on 'any person, being seised in fee simple, fee tail or for life, of and in any manor or lands of freehold, copyhold or customary tenure, and having the beneficial interest therein . . .', provided that 'the person next entitled to the same in remainder, in fee simple or fee tail' was also a party to the conveyance.

[19] Section 2 provides that '. . . upon the said land so granted as aforesaid, or any part thereof, ceasing to be used for the purposes in this Act mentioned, the same shall thereupon immediately revert to and become a portion of the said estate held in fee simple or otherwise, or of any manor or land as aforesaid, as fully to all intents and purposes as if this Act had not been passed'.

[20] The purpose of the 1987 Act was explained by the Lord Chancellor as follows: 'The Bill remedies problems arising under various nineteenth century statutes allowing individuals to donate land for charitable purposes on the basis that, if the land ever ceased to be used for the stated purpose, it would revert to the donor or his successors. . . . The problems arise when, once reverter occurs, the donor or his successors cannot be found or identified . . .': *Official Report, House of Lords*, 8 December 1996; cols 984–987. Section 1 of the 1987 Act provides that the 1841 Act 'shall be deemed always to have had effect, as if it provided (instead of for the reverter) for the land to be vested after that time, on the trust arising under this section, in the persons in whom it was vested immediately before that time'.

corporations and duchies, to be conveyed to literary and scientific institutions.[21] Again, the land conveyed under this statutory power was liable to revert to the transferor if it ceased to be used for these institutional purposes.[22] But, again, the Reverter of Sites Act 1987 now enables the land to be sold free of the reverter, and instead imposes a trust on the proceeds of sale.[23]

The Places of Worship Sites Act 1873 similarly permitted up to an acre of settled land to be conveyed for use as a site for religious worship or burial, or for use as a minister's residence.[24] The land was originally liable to revert to the transferor if this purpose were to cease, but it is now again simply subject to a trust of the proceeds of sale.[25]

The Land Clauses Acts that are referred to in the 2002 Act are presumably the Lands Clauses Consolidation Act 1845 and the Lands Clauses Consolidation Acts Amendment Act 1860: the various other Lands Clauses Acts were repealed by the Compulsory Purchase Act 1965. There are no vesting provisions or reverter provisions in the 1860 Act. The 1845 Act contains a procedure for the compulsory acquisition of land, under which the acquiring party is entitled to pay the purchase money or compensation into court and execute a deed poll which has the statutory effect of vesting the land in them.[26] It is thought that land which is liable to vest in this way is the land that the Act prohibits from being converted into commonhold.

PART 3 CONSENTS

2.4 GENERAL

An application to register land as a commonhold must be made by the registered proprietor of the freehold estate.[27] The application therefore cannot be made without the registered freeholder's consent, considered in Section 2.5 below.
The Act also requires consent to be obtained from:

(a) The registered proprietors of any leases granted for a term exceeding 21 years—see Section 2.6 below.

(b) The registered proprietors of any charges over the land—see Section 2.7 below.

[21] These are defined as being 'every institution for the time being established for the promotion of science, literature, the fine arts, for adult instruction, the diffusion of useful knowledge, the foundation or maintenance of libraries or reading rooms for general use among the members or open to the public, of public museums and galleries of paintings and other works of art, collections of natural history, mechanical and philosophical inventions, instruments or designs: Provided that the Royal Institution . . . shall be exempt from the operation of this Act': section 33.

[22] The reverter is imposed by section 4 of the Act.

[23] Section 7(1), section 1.

[24] Provided that it had not previously been 'part of a demesne or pleasure ground attached to a mansion house': section 1.

[25] Section 7(1), section 1.

[26] Sections 75, 77.

[27] Section 2.

(c) Any other classes of person that are prescribed by regulations—see Section 2.8 below.

Remedies available where consent cannot be obtained are considered in Section 2.9 below.

2.5 INTERESTS IN THE FREEHOLD

2.5.1 General

The consent of the registered proprietor of the freehold estate in the whole or any part of the land is required in order to apply to register the land as commonhold.[28]

2.5.2 Beneficial interest in the freehold

The Act does not require consent to be obtained from anyone claiming a beneficial interest in the freehold under a trust of the land. The Land Registry Consultation Paper does not supply any means for the owner of a beneficial interest to prevent a conversion to commonhold. However, it is possible that if the interest has been protected by an appropriate entry on the register, then the Registrar will simply refuse to process the commonhold registration without the removal of the beneficial owner's entry on the register, or without the beneficial owner's concurrence. If the Registrar does not adopt this practice, then the beneficial owner's only remedy will be to apply for an injunction against the registered freeholder to restrain the application for conversion, provided that he becomes aware of the application before it has been processed.

After the commonhold registration has been completed, a beneficial owner of the freehold cannot apply to the court for an order under section 6 that the registration be cancelled and the land shall cease to be a commonhold. This remedy is only available if there was an error in the application, and a failure to obtain the consent of the beneficial owner is not an error. It is thought, however, that a beneficial interest in the freehold estate before its conversion to commonhold will later attach to the proceeds of sale of the commonhold units.

2.6 REGISTERED LEASEHOLDERS

2.6.1 General

Consent is needed from the registered proprietor of a leasehold estate in the whole or any part of the land, provided that it was granted for a term of more than 21 years.[29]

[28] Section 3(1)(a).

[29] Section 3(1)(b). This is the same length of lease as presently makes it mandatory to complete a grant or disposition by registration.

2.6.2 Leases for more than 21 years

The following rules apply to determine whether a lease was granted for a term of more than 21 years:

(a) The term of a lease cannot as a matter of law begin any earlier than the date of its grant.[30] A lease which was granted on 1 January 2003 for a term of 21 years, expressed to commence on 25 December 2002, is therefore a lease granted for a term of only 20 years and 359 days: the term of the lease began on 1 January 2003 and will end on 25 December 2023.

(b) There must be a single term of more than 21 years. The consent of a lessee is not required where he has occupied under two consecutive leases for terms of less than 21 years, even if he has been a lessee for more than 21 consecutive years at the date of the application.[31]

(c) A lease is for a term of more than 21 years even if it contains a break clause which entitles the landlord to determine it at an earlier date.[32]

2.6.3 Other lessees

Consent is not required from the following:

(a) The owner of an equitable lease of any length. Consent is therefore not required, for example, from a person who occupies under an enforceable agreement for the grant of a lease for a term of 99 years, if the lease itself was never executed and registered.

(b) The owner of a beneficial interest in a registered lease of any length.

(c) The legal or equitable owner of any lease for a term of 21 years or less. This includes protected and statutory tenants under the Rent Act 1977 and assured and assured shorthold tenants under the Housing Act 1988, whose consent is not required.

(d) The owner of a lease for more than 21 years that has not been registered.

The effect of a conversion to commonhold is to extinguish all leases of the whole or any part of the commonhold.[33] This rule is considered further in Part 8 of this chapter.

2.6.4 Unanimity

The consequence of the requirement that consent is required from the registered long lessees of any part of the land is that the long lessees of an existing develop-

[30] *Roberts v Church Commissioners for England* [1972] 1 QB 278.
[31] *Roberts v Church Commissioners for England* [1972] 1 QB 278.
[32] *Eton College v Bard* [1983] Ch 321.
[33] Sections 7(3)(d), 9(3)(f).

ment cannot convert to commonhold unless the agreement to do so is unanimous. This was perceived by many during the passage of the Bill as a serious weakness: a unanimous agreement to convert to commonhold will be rare, so commonhold is likely to be a form of land ownership which is confined to new developments.

2.7 REGISTERED CHARGEES

2.7.1 General

Consent is needed from the registered proprietor of a charge over the whole or any part of the land in order for it to be converted to commonhold.[34]

2.7.2 Equitable chargees

It is thought that consent is required not only from registered legal mortgagees or legal chargees (whose interests can be protected by an entry in the Charges Register) but also from the owners of equitable mortgages or equitable charges (such as a charging order created under the Charging Orders Act 1979) whose interests have been protected on the Register. This is because the Act requires consent from every registered proprietor of a charge, which it is thought is a wider class of persons than simply the proprietors of a registered charge. Equitable mortgages and equitable charges cannot be protected by an entry in the Charges Register, but they are still minor interests that can be protected by the entry of a notice or a caution.[35] It follows that they are the registered proprietors of a charge, even if they are not the proprietors of a registered charge.

2.8 OTHER CLASSES OF PERSON

2.8.1 General

Consent may also be needed from such other classes of person as regulations may prescribe. These other classes were not specified in the Act in order to allow the Government the flexibility to revise the class by statutory instrument. No regulations have yet been made under this section.

[34] Section 3(1)(c).

[35] *Megarry and Wade on The Law of Real Property*, 6th edn, 2000, paragraph 6-113.

2.8.2 Suggested classes

The further classes of person proposed in the Consultation Paper are the following:

(a) The owners of unregistered leases granted for a term of more than 21 years. This category is discussed in paragraph 2.8.3 below.

(b) Proprietors of a rentcharge.

(c) A person entitled to purchase the land—see paragraph 2.8.4 below.

(d) Persons entitled to the benefit of an estate management scheme under the Leasehold Reform Act 1967, the Leasehold Reform, Housing and Urban Development Act 1993 and the Rentcharges Act 1997.

2.8.3 Unregistered leases

The Consultation Paper comments with regard to the proposal that consent should be sought from owners of unregistered leases granted for a term of more than 21 years:

> It has been argued that because such lessees and their mortgagees have as much to lose as their registered equivalents, their consent should be required. Voluntary registration of title would confer the relevant protection on them but some might consider this an unreasonable imposition, at least if only a short part of the term remains unexpired. We do, however, recognise practical problems in ensuring that the consent has been given because identifying the lessee may be difficult.

The Post-Consultation Report dated August 2003 firms up on this position by stating that the Department of Constitutional Affairs is currently considering requiring consent from the unregistered proprietor of any legal leasehold estate in the whole or part of the land granted for a term of more than 21 years.

2.8.4 Persons entitled to purchase the land

In relation to this category of person whose consent might be required, the Consultation Paper states:

> A contract or an option to purchase creates an interest in land. Such a person would clearly be interested in a proposal to convert to commonhold.

2.8.5 Other proposals

The Consultation Paper alternatively proposes that consent might be required from any person whose interest was protected on the Register by a notice or restriction under the Land Registration Act 2002, or by a caution against dealings or a notice under the Land Registration Act 1925.[36] The Paper states that:

[36] These last two forms of entry are preserved by the 2002 Act.

The inherent difficulty with this approach is that the type of protection does not necessarily gauge the importance of the interest. Consideration would also have to be given to the priority of an application for an entry made on the register received, for example, on the same day as an application for the registration of a commonhold.

The Post-Consultation Report dated August 2003 adds to the categories considered above:

(a) the unregistered proprietor of any charge over the whole or part of the land;

(b) a person entitled to the benefit of any interest that is the subject of an entry in the register of title to the land or under the Land Charges Act 1972 that will be extinguished by virtue of section 21(5) of the Act.

It remains to be seen which other classes of interested person will be specified by the regulations as people from whom consent is required.

2.9 WITHHOLDING OR UNAVAILABILITY OF CONSENT

2.9.1 Introduction

If a person from whom consent for conversion to commonhold is required is able to withhold his consent unreasonably, or cannot be found, the result would be that the land could not be converted to commonhold.

The Act deals with this potential problem by allowing regulations to be made which would entitle the court to make an order dispensing with consent in prescribed circumstances.[37] This Section examines the extent to which it is likely that such regulations will be made.

2.9.2 Unreasonable withholding of consent

In the case of a person who withholds consent unreasonably, the Consultation Paper indicates that the Government does not intend to entitle the court to dispense with consent on the ground that it is being unreasonably withheld:

> We considered, but rejected, the possibility of adding the ground that an individual was unreasonably withholding his or her consent. Defining the circumstances in which consent is unreasonably withheld may be difficult and time consuming and dispensing with consent on that ground might introduce an element of compulsion which would be inappropriate for conversion to commonhold.

[37] Section 3(2)(f).

2.9.3 Untraceable proprietors

Section 3(2)(f) of the Act allows regulations to be made which will entitle the court to make an order dispensing with consent in prescribed circumstances. It is intended that there will be regulations entitling the court to order a dispensation where it is satisfied that the proprietor from whom consent is required cannot reasonably be traced.

The Post-Consultation Report dated August 2003 adds to this:

> . . . we are currently proposing to make regulations to permit the court to dispense with a consent where all reasonable efforts to obtain the consent have been exhausted.

2.9.4 Regulations concerning consent

Regulations are to be made under section 3(2) of the Act which will provide for the following:

(a) A prescribed form for the consent.[38] The draft prescribed form does not contain a certification that the consenting party has obtained independent legal advice on the nature and effect of the consent. A sensible applicant for conversion to commonhold should insist on this addition to the form. The authors have provided their own draft including such a warning at Form 1.14 in the Forms and Precedents part of this work.

(b) The effect and duration of the consent (including provision for the consent to bind successors in title to the consenting party).[39] The proposal in the Consultation Paper was that the consent should endure for a period of three months and should be binding on successors in title. In the light of the responses received to the Consultation Paper, however, the Department of Constitutional Affairs is considering lengthening this period to 12 months (see the Post-Consultation Report dated August 2003).

(c) The withdrawal of consent (including provision about preventing withdrawal in specified circumstances).[40] The Consultation Paper does not propose to allow consent to be withdrawn within three months of the date on which it is given, even in the event that there is a significant change in the circumstances of the consenting party or in the nature of the application for conversion to commonhold.

(d) For consent that was given for the purposes of one application for registration of land as commonhold to have effect also for the purposes of another separate application.[41] There are currently no proposals for regulations to be made under this heading.

[38] Section 3(2)(a). [39] Section 3(2)(b). [40] Section 3(2)(c). [41] Section 3(2)(d).

(e) For consent to be deemed to have been given in specified circumstances.[42] There are currently no proposals for regulations to be made under this heading.

(f) Enabling a court to dispense with a requirement for consent, in specified circumstances.[43] An order made under these potential regulations may be absolute or conditional[44] and may make such other provision as the court thinks appropriate.[45] The current proposal is that the court should be permitted to dispense with the requirement for consent if the individual from whom consent is required cannot reasonably be traced. The Consultation Paper proposes that there be 'stringent tests', presumably to be set out in the regulations, that 'may include requiring evidence of details of where the person was last heard of; enquiries with family, neighbours, government departments, former employer and work colleagues, advertisements that had been placed and details of the next of kin'. The Consultation Paper has rejected a proposal that the court should be entitled to dispense with consent that is being unreasonably withheld.

2.9.5 Registration without consent

If the land is registered as commonhold without the consent of a person from whom consent was required, then an application can be made to remedy the registration.[46] The court has various powers, including a power to order that the land shall cease to be commonhold land, and a power to provide for compensation.

PART 4 THE COMMONHOLD ASSOCIATION

2.10 GENERAL

The commonhold association is a private company limited by guarantee.[47] The purpose of the company is to manage the commonhold.[48] The various obligations imposed on the unit-holders by the commonhold community statement are obligations owed to the commonhold association, and the various rights granted to the unit-holders in the statement are rights enforceable against the association. The unit-holders are entitled to be members of the company,[49] and no one else is entitled to become a member.[50]

The Companies Act 1985 applies to commonhold associations just as it does to ordinary companies, except where its provisions are expressly varied.[51]

[42] Section 3(2)(e). [43] Section 3(2)(f). [44] Section 3(3)(a). [45] Section 3(3)(b).
[46] Section 6; see Part 11 of this Chapter. [47] Section 34(1).
[48] The company has a statutory duty to manage under section 35.
[49] Schedule 3, part 2, paragraph 7. [50] Schedule 3, part 2, paragraph 10.
[51] The Consultation Paper remarks that it is 'our policy that where possible the general law should apply to commonhold land'.

2.11 NATURE AND FORMATION OF THE COMMONHOLD ASSOCIATION

2.11.1 Private company limited by guarantee

The commonhold association must be a private company limited by guarantee.[52] It cannot be either a public company or a company limited by shares. The reason for this restriction is that, where a company has no share capital, non-members cannot have any right to participate in any profits.[53]

2.11.2 Naming the commonhold association

Regulations may provide that the name of the company registered under the Companies Act 1985 must satisfy specified requirements (and that, conversely, the name of any company that is not a commonhold association must not include specified words or expressions).[54]

The Consultation Paper proposes that the name of a commonhold association should have the suffix 'Commonhold Association Limited', or the Welsh equivalent 'Cymdeithas Cydradd-Ddaliad'.[55] It was also originally proposed that the word 'commonhold' and the Welsh equivalent 'Cydradd-Ddaliad' should not be used in the names of any companies that are not commonhold associations. Given, however, the likelihood that companies wishing to supply services dedicated to commonholds would wish to convey such information in their names (for example 'Commonhold Accounting Services Limited'), the Department of Constitutional Affairs suggests in its Post-Consultation Report dated August 2003 that the naming prohibition should be confined to the words 'commonhold association' used together.

2.11.3 Procedure for formation of the commonhold association

The commonhold association is formed by sending to the Registrar of Companies:

[52] Section 34(1). A company limited by guarantee is defined as 'a company having the liability of its members limited by the memorandum to such amount as the members may respectively thereby undertake to contribute to the assets of the company in the event of its being wound up': section 1(2)(b), Companies Act 1985. By contrast, a company limited by shares is: 'a company having the liability of its members limited by the memorandum to the amount, if any, unpaid on the shares respectively held by them': section 1(2)(a), Companies Act 1985.

[53] Section 15(1), Companies Act 1985.

[54] Schedule 3, part 3, paragraph 16. Paragraph 17 of the Schedule provides that, for the purposes of section 12 of the Companies Act (which sets out requirements for registration), a company which is a commonhold association must comply with any regulations that are made under paragraph 16.

[55] Paragraphs 20–21.

(a) The memorandum of association and articles of association.[56]

(b) A statement in the prescribed form containing the name and the required particulars[57] of the people who are to be the first director or directors and the first secretary or joint secretaries of the company.[58] The particulars required of an individual director are his present name, any former name, his usual residential address, his nationality, his business occupation (if any), his date of birth, and particulars of any other directorships held by him or which have been held by him.[59] The particulars required of an individual secretary are his name, any former name, and his usual residential address. The particulars required of a corporate director or secretary are simply its corporate name and its registered office. The statement must be signed by the subscribers,[60] who are in effect the people applying for the formation of the company. They will automatically become members of the company when the registration is completed.[61] The Companies Act 1985 requires there to be at least two subscribers.[62] The statement must contain a consent from each of the persons named as a director or secretary. It must also specify the intended situation of the company's registered office.

(c) The appropriate fee.

The Registrar will then issue a certificate of incorporation, and the company exists from the date specified in the certificate.[63]

This is the ordinary procedure for the formation of a company; there is no special procedure for the formation of a company which is a commonhold association.

The requirements for the memorandum and articles of association are considered below.

2.12 MEMORANDUM OF ASSOCIATION

2.12.1 General

The memorandum of association is the fundamental constitutional document of the company. It sets out the name and status of the company, its registered office and its objects, the fact that the liability of the members is limited and the amount of their guarantee, together with various other matters of central importance.

[56] Section 10(1), Companies Act 1985.

[57] Set out in Schedule 1 to the Companies Act 1985.

[58] Section 10(2), Companies Act 1985.

[59] Except that he is not required to disclose directorships that were not held during the 5 years preceding the application, or in respect of dormant or grouped companies: see the provisions at Schedule 1 of the Companies Act 1985.

[60] Section 10(3), Companies Act 1985.

[61] Section 22(1), Companies Act 1985.

[62] Section 1(1), Companies Act 1985.

[63] Section 13, Companies Act 1985.

Copies of the memorandum of association will be freely obtainable from the Land Registry, by application in form OC2 (see Form 1.10 in the Forms and Precedents part of this work).

2.12.2 Prescribed requirements for the memorandum of association

The memorandum of association must be in a prescribed form.[64] Once the regulations prescribing the form have been made (currently forecast for the end of 2003, although considerable delays have already been encountered), the authors will make the forms available, either in a supplement to this work, or online. The current draft prescribed form for the memorandum may be found at Form 2.1 in the Forms and Precedents section of this volume. The form of memorandum that is prescribed under the normal provisions of the Companies Act 1985 does not apply to a commonhold association.[65]

The 2002 Act prescribes the following requirements for the memorandum:

(a) It must state that one of the objects of the company is to exercise the functions of a commonhold association in relation to specified commonhold land;[66]

(b) It must also state that £1 is the amount specified under section 2(4) of the Companies Act 1985;[67] this is the amount by which each member of the company undertakes to contribute to the payment of the company's debts and liabilities in the event that it is wound up.

The requirements that are to be prescribed by regulations are being finalised. It has not yet been decided to what extent the contents of the prescribed form of memorandum will be mandatory, or to what extent some of the provisions will be optional. The provisional view expressed in the October 2002 Consultation Paper was that all the provisions of the memorandum should be mandatory (but that some of the provisions in the articles of association should be optional or variable).[68] The Post-Consultation Report dated August 2003 adds to this by providing:

> our current intention is that the 'model' document will be in short form without a secondary objects and powers clause. Individual commonholds will be able to add such a clause if they wish. We classify such clauses as optional.

[64] Section 34(2); Schedule 3, paragraph 2(1).

[65] The usual form of memorandum is prescribed under section 3 of the Companies Act 1985; Schedule 3, paragraph 4(1) of the 2002 Act states that this section does not apply to a commonhold association.

[66] Section 34(1)(a).

[67] Section 34(1)(b).

[68] Paragraph 35. The debate is summarised as follows: 'We consider that total prescription is likely to lead to difficulties where a commonhold has special needs or responsibilities. Total flexibility would, however, re-invent the diversity of the leasehold tradition.'

The regulations may provide that a specified provision is to have effect whether or not the subscribers include it in the memorandum.[69] A provision that is included in the memorandum but that is inconsistent with the regulations has no effect.[70]

The structure of the draft prescribed form for the memorandum is as follows.

2.12.3 Name

Paragraph 1 of the draft prescribed form states the name of the company. It is proposed that the name should contain the suffix 'commonhold association limited'.

2.12.4 Registered office

Paragraph 2 of the draft prescribed form states the address of the registered office of the company.

2.12.5 Objects

The purpose of the objects clause is to state the purposes for which the company is permitted to act.[71] Paragraph 3 of the draft prescribed form states the objects for which the commonhold association is established; the material part of the draft clause states that the objects are:

> to exercise the functions of a commonhold association in relation to [specify the name of the commonhold and its location] in accordance with the commonhold community statement, as amended from time to time, and any provision made by or by virtue of the Commonhold and Leasehold Reform Act 2002 ('the 2002 Act') and the doing of all such things as are incidental or conducive to the attainment of that object.

2.12.6 Secondary objects

As originally drafted, paragraph 4 of the draft prescribed form attached to the Consultation Paper stated the secondary objects of the company, and it comprised the majority of the memorandum. The Consultation Paper stated that it was 'intended to be comprehensive'. It stated all the various ways in which the company is permitted to act in order to further the object of carrying out the functions of a commonhold association. It included, for example, the power 'to make, administer and enforce provisions regulating or limiting the use of the Common Parts or any specified parts thereof',[72] and the power 'to insure (and use the proceeds of insurance for the purposes of rebuilding or reinstating), repair and

[69] Schedule 3, part 1, paragraph 2(3).

[70] Schedule 3, part 1, paragraph 2(4).

[71] Reference should be had to specialist works for a discussion of the true extent to which the objects clause has the practical effect of limiting the company's powers.

[72] Paragraph 4.5.

maintain the commonhold or any part or parts thereof, including the Common Parts and any of the Commonhold Units'.

As noted above, however, the Post-Consultation Report dated August 2003 proposes that the inclusion of such a clause should be optional, and the revised form supplied with it omits the clause entirely.

2.12.7 Income

Similarly, although paragraph 5 of the original draft prescribed form attached to the Consultation Paper required the commonhold association to apply all its income, from wherever it is derived, in promoting the objects of the company, and prohibited the company from making any distribution to its members, except in accordance with a termination statement or a winding-up, the revised form supplied with the Post-Consultation Report dated August 2003 omits such a clause.

2.12.8 Limited liability

Paragraph 4 of the draft prescribed form states that the liability of the members is limited.

2.12.9 Extent of liability

Paragraph 5 of the draft prescribed form states that the extent of the liability of the members is limited to £1.

2.12.10 Winding-up

Paragraph 5 of the draft prescribed form provides for the distribution of surplus assets after a winding-up. In its original form, the prescribed clause (then paragraph 8) of the draft supplied with the October 2002 Consultation Paper required the surplus to be paid to or distributed among the members of the company rateably in accordance with the percentages allocated to their units in the commonhold community statement.[73]

2.12.11 Interpretation

As originally drafted, paragraph 9 of the prescribed form contained an interpretation clause. It stated that words and expressions in the memorandum shall, unless the context otherwise requires, have the meaning given to them by the 2002 Act or by the Companies Act 1985 or any statutory modification or re-enactment

[73] This is the specified percentage of the commonhold assessment to which each unit-holder is obliged to contribute.

for the time being in force. It also contained the usual provisions that, for example, words expressed in any gender shall include any other gender. The current draft is silent on these matters.

2.12.12 Conflicts

As originally drafted, paragraph 10 of the prescribed form contained a provision that, if there was any conflict between the commonhold community statement and the provisions of the memorandum, then the memorandum should prevail. This was otiose, because the Act in any event provides that any clause in the commonhold community statement which is inconsistent with the memorandum shall be of no effect.[74] The current draft is rightly silent on this topic.

2.12.13 Subscribers

The final part of the memorandum contains a statement by the subscribers that they wish the company to be formed pursuant to the memorandum.

2.13 ARTICLES OF ASSOCIATION

2.13.1 General

The articles of association are the secondary constitutional document of the company. They contain the internal regulations for the company's management. As with the memorandum of association, copies of the articles of association will be freely obtainable from the Land Registry, by application in form OC2 (see Form 1.10 in the Forms and Precedents part of this work).

2.13.2 Prescribed Requirements

The articles of association must be in a prescribed form.[75] Once the regulations prescribing the form have been made (currently forecast for the end of 2003, although considerable delays have already been encountered), the authors will make the forms available, either in a supplement to this work, or online.

The requirement in the Companies Act 1985 that the form and content of the articles be in accordance with Tables A and C does not apply.[76] However, the current intention of the Department of Constitutional Affairs, expressed in paragraph 5 of the Summary of Responses in the Post-Consultation Report dated August 2003, is that the 'model' articles will, in general terms, continue to follow

[74] Section 31(9)(d).

[75] Schedule 3, part 1, paragraph 2(1).

[76] Schedule 3, part 1, paragraph 4(1) provides that section 8 of the Companies Act 1985 shall not apply to a commonhold association.

the content of Table F. Moreover, the following requirements in the Companies Act 1985 do apply:[77]

(a) the articles must be printed;[78]

(b) they must be divided into paragraphs numbered consecutively;[79]

(c) they must be signed by each subscriber to the memorandum in the presence of at least one witness who must attest the signature.[80]

The prescribed form for the articles of association is currently being finalised. The draft prescribed form appended to the October 2002 Consultation Paper has been revised in the form supplied with the Post-Consultation Report dated August 2003, and is set out in Form 2.2 of the Forms and Precedents section of this volume. It has not yet been decided to what extent the contents of the prescribed form of articles will be mandatory, or to what extent the provisions will be optional or open to variation. The view expressed in the Consultation Paper[81] and endorsed by the Post-Consultation Report dated August 2003 is that, unlike the memorandum, the articles should be open to variation in part. The regulations may provide that a specified provision is to have effect whether or not the subscribers include it in the articles.[82] A provision that is included in the articles but that is inconsistent with the regulations or the Act has no effect to the extent that it is inconsistent.[83]

The structure and content of the draft prescribed form is as follows.

2.13.3 Interpretation

Article 1 of the draft prescribed form defines various phrases that are used in the articles (for example, ' "the commonhold" means the land in respect of which the commonhold community statement is registered').

2.13.4 Members

Articles 2 to 5 set out a number of provisions concerning the membership of the commonhold association. Article 2 of the draft prescribed form stipulates who is entitled to be a member of the company. Article 3 recites that the company shall maintain a register of members in accordance with the regulations that are made from time to time. Articles 4 and 5 dictate the requirements for entering and removing particulars of persons from the register.

[77] Schedule 3, part 1, paragraph 4(1) disapplies the provisions of section 8 of the Companies Act 1985, but does not disapply the provisions of section 7.

[78] Section 7(3)(a).

[79] Section 7(3)(b).

[80] Section 7(3)(c).

[81] Paragraph 35.

[82] Schedule 3, part 1, paragraph 2(3).

[83] Schedule 3, part 1, paragraph 2(4).

2.13.5 General meetings

Articles 6 to 9 of the draft prescribed form deal with the calling of general meetings. One annual general meeting is compulsory (article 6), and the default position adopted by article 7 is that the company is required, in addition to its annual general meeting, to call at least one interim general meeting each year, at which the directors shall present an interim review of the commonhold association's affairs since the preceding annual general meeting. Article 9 provides that, on the requisition of members representing not less than one-tenth of the total voting rights of all the members of the company, the directors shall call an extraordinary general meeting.

2.13.6 Notice of general meetings

Articles 10 to 13 of the draft prescribed form provide that annual general meetings and extraordinary general meetings called for the purpose of passing a special resolution, a unanimous resolution, a termination-statement resolution, a winding-up resolution, or a resolution appointing a new director shall not be on less than 28 days' notice; all other extraordinary general meetings shall not be on less than 21 days' notice (unless a shorter period is agreed by the requisite majority). The notice shall specify the time and place of the meeting, and shall include an agenda and the text of any resolutions to be proposed, together with a 'brief written explanation' of the resolution.

2.13.7 Proceedings at general meetings

Articles 14 to 21 prescribe the procedure to be adopted at general meetings. In summary it is as follows:

(a) No business shall be transacted unless details relating to it were included in the notice convening the meeting.

(b) Any business that arises because the members have required it shall be transacted before any other business, so far as is practicable.

(c) No business shall be transacted unless a quorum of members is present. The proposed quorum in the case of an ordinary resolution is 20 per cent of the members entitled to vote on the business, or three members, whichever is the greater; 35 per cent or four members in the case of a special resolution; and 50 per cent or five members in the case of a unanimous resolution.

(d) The meeting shall be adjourned for a week if there is no quorum present.

(e) The meeting shall be chaired by the chairman of the board of directors, or by such other director as the directors shall nominate, or by a nominated member if no director is present or willing to act as chairman.

(f) A director who is not a member of the company shall still be entitled to attend meetings, speak and propose resolutions.

(g) The chairman may adjourn the meeting with the consent of the quorum, but no business may be transacted at the adjourned meeting save unfinished business.

2.13.8 Voting

Articles 22 to 30 govern the ways in which voting must be conducted. In summary:

(a) Article 22 defines the different types of resolution that may be passed.

(b) Resolutions shall be put to the vote by a show of hands, unless a poll is demanded. A poll may be demanded by the chairman, or by at least two members, or by a member or members representing not less than one-tenth of the total voting rights of the members having the right to vote at the meeting.

(c) Unless a poll is demanded, a declaration by the chairman that a resolution has been carried or not carried, and an entry in the minutes to that effect, shall be conclusive evidence of this fact.

(d) The demand for a poll may be withdrawn before the poll is taken, but only with the consent of the chairman.

(e) The chairman shall determine the procedure for taking a poll.

(f) As a default provision, the chairman shall have a casting vote in the event that the other votes are evenly split.

(g) A poll that has been demanded shall be taken either forthwith or at such time and place as the chairman may direct.

(h) A resolution in writing executed by a member who is not present but who would have been entitled to vote shall be effective.

2.13.9 Votes of members

Articles 31 to 43 of the draft prescribed form determine the voting rights of the members. The most important of these provisions are as follows:

(a) Every member shall have one vote, unless he is the unit-holder of more than one unit, in which case he shall have one vote for each unit. This is a default provision: the Post-Consultation Report dated August 2003 comments:

> In light of the wide range of views expressed by respondents we are now considering adopting a less prescriptive approach, using one member, one vote as a default provision but allowing commonhold associations the discretion to create their own system of voting to reflect the circumstances of the individual commonhold.

(b) Members of the commonhold association other than the developer shall not have the right to vote on a resolution for the removal of a director appointed by the developer under his rights to appoint and remove directors during the transitional period and for so long afterwards as he continues to own more than one quarter of the units in the commonhold. During this period, the developer shall likewise not have the right to vote on the appointment, removal or remuneration of any directors not appointed by him.

(c) Any objections to the qualification of any voter to vote shall be raised at the meeting, and if no objection is raised then the vote shall be valid. The chairman shall have the final and conclusive decision on whether the voter is qualified.

(d) Votes taken by poll may be given by proxy. The appointment of a proxy shall be in writing, executed by the appointor, and in a form that is specified in the articles. The appointment may either allow the proxy to vote as he sees fit, or it may specify the manner in which he is to vote.

(e) The written appointment of the proxy must be delivered to the directors in a specified manner in order for it to be valid.

2.13.10 Qualification of directors

Article 44 of the draft prescribed form provides that a director need not be a member of the commonhold association. This enables the unit-holders to appoint professional third parties to manage the company.

2.13.11 Number of directors

Article 45 of the draft prescribed form provides that the minimum number of directors shall be two. Unlike the original draft of the articles appended to the Consultation Paper, which stipulated that the maximum number of directors should be either six or the number determined by an ordinary resolution of the commonhold association, the current draft does not prescribe any maximum number.

2.13.12 Appointment and removal of directors

Articles 46 to 54 of the draft prescribed form prescribe the procedures for the appointment and removal of directors. The most important of these provisions are as follows:

(a) The developer (if permitted by the commonhold community statement) shall have the right to appoint up to two directors during the transitional period and remove or replace the directors that he has appointed; after the end of the transitional period, but while he is still the owner of more than one-quarter of the units, he shall have the right to appoint and then remove or replace a total of one-quarter of the maximum number of directors. The appointment and removal shall be effected by notice in writing, and any directors appointed by this method shall cease to hold office immediately that the developer ceases to be the owner of more than one-quarter of the units.

(b) One-third of the directors (or the number nearest to one-third) shall retire by rotation at each annual general meeting. This provision does not apply to directors appointed by the developer. A retiring director may be reappointed if he is willing to continue and if the vacancy has not been filled at the meeting.

(c) A new director cannot be appointed unless either he is recommended by the directors or notice has been given (not less than 14 nor more than 35 days before the meeting) that his appointment is to be proposed.

(d) The commonhold association may appoint directors, and determine which director or directors are to retire, by an ordinary resolution.

2.13.13 Alternate directors

In the original draft appended to the Consultation Paper, the prescribed form of the articles provided that directors may appoint alternate directors, provided they are approved by a resolution of the directors, to attend meetings in the event that the director appointing him is unable. The current draft omits this provision.

2.13.14 Disqualification and vacation of office of directors

Article 55 of the draft prescribed form provides that the office of a director shall be vacated if:

(a) an ordinary resolution of the association members is passed in favour of his removal;

(b) he ceases to be a director by virtue of any provision of the Companies Act 1985, or if he becomes prohibited by law from being a director;

(c) he becomes bankrupt or makes any arrangement or composition with his creditors generally;

(d) he is or may be suffering from a mental disorder and he is admitted to hospital for treatment under the Mental Health Act 1983, or an order is made by a court for him to be detained or for a receiver to be appointed as a result of his disorder;

(e) he resigns his office by notice to the commonhold association; or

(f) he has been absent from directors' meetings for more than six consecutive months without permission, and the directors resolve that his office shall be vacated.

2.13.15 Powers of directors

Article 56 of the draft prescribed form provides that the directors shall manage the commonhold association and may exercise all its powers, unless prohibited from doing so by a special resolution, by the memorandum and articles, or by the provisions of the Companies Act 1985. No special resolution or alteration of the memorandum or articles shall invalidate any prior act of the directors that would have been valid if the direction or alteration had not been made.

2.13.16 Managing agents

Article 57 of the draft prescribed form provides that the directors shall have power to appoint any person to be the agent of the commonhold association, for such purposes and on such conditions as they determine, including authority for the agent to delegate all or any of his powers.

As originally drafted, the articles appended to the Consultation Paper provided that the terms of the appointment or contract with the agent (including the terms as to remuneration) should have first been approved by the commonhold association in a general meeting. This restriction does not appear in the current version of article 57.

2.13.17 Delegation of directors' powers

Article 58 of the draft prescribed form allows the directors to delegate their powers to committees consisting of two or more directors, members of the commonhold association and others, provided that the majority of the members of any committee are members of the company. They may delegate powers to specified directors or to managing agents.

2.13.18 Remuneration of directors

Article 59 of the draft prescribed form provides as a default provision that directors may be remunerated, but only if a special resolution has been passed to this effect at a general meeting. A director appointed by a developer can never be entitled to any remuneration from the commonhold association, although he can obviously be remunerated by the developer himself.

2.13.19 Directors' expenses

Article 60 of the draft prescribed form provides as a default provision that the directors are entitled to be paid their reasonable expenses.

2.13.20 Director's appointments and interests

Articles 61 to 64 of the draft prescribed form set out rules permitting the director to have an interest in transactions or arrangements with the commonhold association, provided there has been proper disclosure.

2.13.21 Proceedings of directors

Articles 65 to 74 of the draft prescribed form set out a number of default provisions containing rules for the conduct of directors' meetings.

2.13.22 Secretary

Article 75 of the draft prescribed form provides that the secretary shall be appointed by the directors and may be removed by them.

2.13.23 Minutes

Article 76 of the draft prescribed form requires the directors to keep minutes of all appointments, and of all meetings of the commonhold association, of the directors and of any committees.

2.13.24 Agents

Article 77 of the draft prescribed form allows the directors of the commonhold association to enter into contracts with the association's managing agents.

2.13.25 No distribution of profits

Article 78 of the draft prescribed form recites the default provision that, save in accordance with a termination statement or in a winding-up, the commonhold association shall not make a distribution of profits or assets to its members.

2.13.26 Winding-up

Article 79 of the draft prescribed form recites as a default provision that any surplus remaining after a winding-up shall be paid to or distributed among the members in accordance with the percentages allocated to their units in the commonhold community statement.

2.13.27 Inspection and copying of books and records

Articles 80 and 81 of the draft prescribed form confer a right on the members to inspect (and, subject to a copying charge, to be provided with copies of) the books and records of the commonhold association. The directors can impose conditions on this right if the books or records contain confidential material that would harm the commonhold association if it were to be disclosed. Up-to-date copies of the commonhold community statement and the memorandum and articles of association must be kept at the office of the commonhold association, available for inspection by any unit-holder.

2.13.28 Notices

Articles 82 to 85 of the draft prescribed form require all notices to be given either in writing or using electronic communications such as e-mail, unless there is insufficient time. Article 85 contains a deeming provision in relation to the date and fact of service.

2.13.29 Indemnity

Article 86 of the draft prescribed form provides for the directors (and any other officers or auditors) to be indemnified by the commonhold association against any liability incurred in criminal or civil proceedings for negligence, default, breach of duty or breach of trust, provided that the proceedings are unsuccessful.

2.14 ALTERATIONS

2.14.1 General

This Section deals with the various alterations that the commonhold association as a company may seek to make to its memorandum and articles of association and to its registered office. Its ability to make such alterations pursuant to the Companies Acts has, however, been constrained by regulations made under the Act.

It is clear that the draftsmen of the Act envisaged that the memorandum and articles of association might be amended (more properly, 'altered'). However, in the October 2002 Consultation Paper, the Lord Chancellor's Department proposed that the scope for amendment of the memorandum and articles of association should be limited.

2.14.2 Alterations to the memorandum

Subject, in the case of a commonhold association, to the regulations considered below, a company can alter the statement of the company's objects in the memorandum by passing a special resolution.[84] The company must deliver a printed copy of the altered memorandum to the Registrar of Companies.[85]

In the case of an alteration to the memorandum of a commonhold association, there are two additional requirements:

(a) First, the alteration must be registered with the Land Registry. The alteration does not take effect until the Land Registry has registered the altered version.[86] The application for registration should be made on Land Registry Form CM3.[87] It must be accompanied by:

- (i) a printed copy of the altered memorandum;[88]
- (ii) a certificate[89] from the directors of the commonhold association that the altered memorandum complies with the regulations made under the Act about the memorandum's form and content; and
- (iii) a certified true copy of the new memorandum, for retention by the Registrar. The Registrar will return the original, and will make any consequential amendments to the register which he thinks appropriate.

(b) Secondly, draft regulations have now (September 2003) been published providing that the memorandum of association of a commonhold association must be in the form contained in Schedule 1 to the Regulations or a form to the same effect; and that further clauses may be added.[90] The draft prescribed form of the memorandum is copied at Form 2.1 of the Forms and Precedents part of this book. Unlike earlier drafts, it is short and terse, and contains provisions that cannot be amended. Other clauses may, however, be added (for example an expansion of the objects clause), apparently without limitation, provided that no other provisions are infringed.

Much of the form and content of the memorandum for a commonhold association is mandatory, and it is therefore likely that this procedure will seldom be invoked, except in the case of a change to the name of the association or its registered office.

[84] Section 4(1), Companies Act 1985.
[85] Section 18, Companies Act 1985.
[86] Schedule 3, part 1, paragraph 3(1).
[87] A copy of Form CM3 is at Form 1.3 in the Forms and Precedents section of this volume.
[88] This requirement must be implied from the duty imposed on the Land Registrar to keep a copy of the altered memorandum in his custody: Schedule 3, part 1, paragraph 3(2).
[89] Schedule 3, part 1, paragraph 3(3); a form suitable for use is at Form 2.6 in the Forms and Precedents part of this book.
[90] See regulation 12.

2.14.3 Cancellation of alterations to the memorandum

Section 5(1) of the Companies Act 1985 entitles an application to be made to the court by not less than 15 per cent of a company's members[91] or by not less than 15 per cent of the holders of the company's debentures for an alteration to the memorandum to be cancelled. An application under this section must be made within 21 days of the date on which the resolution was passed. An application to the Land Registry to register the alteration to the memorandum cannot be made unless the period for making an application under section 5(1) has expired without an application being issued, or an application which has been made has been withdrawn, or the alteration has been confirmed by the court.

2.14.4 Alterations to the articles of association

The articles of association of a company can also be altered by a special resolution of the company.[92] The company must deliver a printed copy of the new articles to the Registrar of Companies.[93]

In the case of an alteration to the articles of association of a commonhold association, there are again two additional requirements:

(a) The procedure for registration at the Land Registry in the case of an alteration of the articles of association of a commonhold association is identical to that considered in paragraph 2.14.2 above in relation to the memorandum.

(b) Secondly, draft regulations have now (September 2003) been published. Regulation 13 prescribes all the articles, which must be in the form contained in Schedule 1 to the Regulations or a form to the same effect; and provides that some of them (shown underlined on the draft at Form 2.2 in the Forms and Precedents part of this book) may be replaced by articles of the commonhold association's own making; while others must be replaced in given eventualities by specified alternatives.

The Companies Act 1985 does not contain a provision in relation to the articles (unlike in relation to the memorandum) which entitles the members or the debenture holders to apply to the court to prevent the alteration, once it has passed by a special resolution.

2.14.5 Recording the amendments

As with the case of amendments to the commonhold community statement (see paragraph 2.18.4 below), the authors suggest that it would be useful to have a

[91] Excluding those who consented to or voted in favour of the alteration: section 5(2), Companies Act 1985.

[92] Section 9, Companies Act 1985.

[93] Section 18, Companies Act 1985.

separate master table giving details of all amendments made both to the commonhold community statement and to the memorandum and articles of association. A suggested form for such a record is Form 2.8 in the Forms and Precedents part of this book.

2.14.6 Change of registered office

An ordinary company may change its registered office simply by giving notice of the change to the Registrar of Companies.[94] A commonhold association, however, must also alter the memorandum of association and the commonhold community statement. The changes must be registered with the Land Registry in addition to the Registrar of Companies. The change of address does not take effect until it is registered with the Land Registry.[95] The old registered office remains a valid address for service until 14 days after the date on which the new address is registered with the Registrar of Companies.[96]

2.14.7 Unit-holder's powers to compel alterations

A unit-holder cannot ordinarily compel alterations to the memorandum or the articles of association without securing an appropriate resolution of the commonhold association. However, a unit-holder who considers that the memorandum or articles do not comply with the regulations may apply to the court for a declaration to this effect.[97] An application of this nature will rarely have any purpose, except where there is a dispute about whether the memorandum or articles are in fact inconsistent with the regulations, because the Act provides that any provision in the memorandum or the articles which is inconsistent with the regulations has no effect.[98]

The application must be made within the period of three months beginning with the date on which the applicant became a unit-holder, or within three months of an alteration that does not comply with the regulations, or within any further period that the court might permit. (The date on which a person becomes a unit-holder is the date on which he becomes entitled to be registered as the proprietor, which will usually be the date on which contracts for the purchase are completed, and not the later date on which the transfer is registered.) If the court grants the declaration, then it can also make any other consequential order that it thinks appropriate.[99] A non-exhaustive list of the available remedies is as follows:

(a) an order requiring a director or other specified officer of the commonhold association to take steps to alter or amend a document;

[94] Section 287, Companies Act 1985.
[95] Schedule 3, part 1, paragraph 3.
[96] Section 287, Companies Act 1985.
[97] Section 40(1)(a).
[98] Schedule 3, paragraph 2(4).
[99] Section 40(2).

(b) an order requiring a director or other specified officer to take other specified steps;

(c) an award of compensation (whether or not contingent upon the occurrence or non-occurrence of a specified event) to be paid by the commonhold association to a specified person;

(d) an order providing for the land to cease to be commonhold land.

The court should ordinarily simply order that the directors take all necessary steps to effect an alteration in the offending provisions of the memorandum or the articles. The power to order that the land shall cease to be a commonhold is a draconian remedy, and it is thought that this would only be appropriate where, for example, the directors have attempted to alter the offending provisions, but the members of the company have voted against the necessary resolution. The power to award compensation should only be exercised where the applicant can demonstrate that he has suffered loss as a result of the enforcement by the association of the provisions that have been declared to be inconsistent with the regulations; the court does not have the power in proceedings of this nature to make a punitive order against the company.

2.15 MEMBERSHIP OF THE COMMONHOLD ASSOCIATION

2.15.1 General

The Act restricts who can be a member of a commonhold association.[100] The nature of the restriction depends upon the stage the development has reached. The three stages are as follows:

(a) the pre-commonhold period, which is the period beginning with the incorporation of the association and ending with the registration of the land as commonhold;

(b) the transitional period, which is the period between the registration of the land as commonhold and the date on which the first unit-holder becomes entitled to be registered as the proprietor of a unit;[101]

(c) any period after the end of the transitional period.

2.15.2 Pre-commonhold period

The subscribers are the only people entitled to be members of the company during the pre-commonhold period beginning with the incorporation of the company and ending with the registration of the land as a commonhold. The

[100] Schedule 3, part 2, paragraph 10.

[101] Sections 8(1), 7(3).

subscribers are the people who have subscribed their names to the memorandum and have applied to form the company.[102] They are deemed to have agreed to become members of the company, and their names are automatically entered in the register of members when the company is first incorporated.[103] The Companies Act 1985 requires there to be at least two subscribers: section 1(1) provides that 'Any two or more persons associated for a lawful purpose may, by subscribing their names to a memorandum of association . . . form an incorporated company . . .' There is nothing in the Commonhold and Leasehold Reform Act 2002 which disapplies this provision, so it is thought that there must be at least two subscribers at the date of incorporation. However, paragraph 5 of Schedule 3 to the Act also states that the 'members (or member)' for the pre-commonhold shall be 'the subscribers (or subscriber)'. This provision cannot mean that only one subscriber is necessary for a commonhold association, because of the terms of the Companies Act 1985; instead, it is thought to reflect the fact that the subscribers are entitled to resign their membership at any time after the company has been incorporated.

2.15.3 Transitional period

The transitional period is the period between the registration of the land as a commonhold and the date on which the first unit-holder becomes entitled to be registered as the proprietor of a unit.[104] There is no transitional period where the conversion to commonhold relates to an existing development, and there has been a request to register the ownership of the units at the same time as the registration of the land as commonhold.

The subscriber or subscribers of the company continue to be its members throughout the transitional period, unless they resign their membership.[105]

The Act also allows any person who is the developer for the time being in respect of all or part of the commonhold to become a member of the company during the transitional period.[106] The developer is either:

(a) the person who made the application for the land to be registered as a commonhold;[107] or

(b) any person to whom the freehold estate in the whole of the commonhold has been transferred during the transitional period.[108]

A person who has become the developer by transfer will usually want to become a member of the company, because it is only the company that can apply to amend

[102] Section 1(1), Companies Act 1985.
[103] Section 22(1), Companies Act 1985; this section is expressly said to apply to a commonhold association subject to Schedule 3.
[104] Sections 8(1), 7(3).
[105] Schedule 3, part 2, paragraph 6(2).
[106] Schedule 3, part 2, paragraph 5(3).
[107] Section 58(1), section 2(1).
[108] Section 59.

the memorandum and articles of association or the commonhold community statement. There is no requirement in the Act for the original developer to resign his membership: the Act only restricts who can become a member and not who can be a member. This is a matter that should therefore be dealt with in the contracts for the sale of the development.

2.15.4 After the end of the transitional period

The transitional period ends when someone other than the person who first applied to register the land as commonhold becomes entitled to be registered as the proprietor of one or more of the commonhold units, but not all of them.[109] A transfer of all of the units does not end the transitional period, because this will usually be a transfer of the entire commonhold to a new developer.

A person is entitled to be registered as a member of the commonhold association if he becomes the unit-holder of a unit in relation to which the association exercises functions. He becomes the unit-holder immediately that he is entitled to be registered as the proprietor of the freehold estate in the unit.[110] He can therefore apply to become a member without waiting for his title to the unit to be registered.

No one other than a unit-holder can become a member of the commonhold association.[111] This is to prohibit people who are not the owners of units from becoming involved in the management of the commonhold. A unit-holder or joint unit-holder who is a member of the association, but who ceases to own the unit, automatically ceases to be a member of the association.[112] This does not affect any rights or liabilities that have already accrued in relation to matters that arose during the period of his ownership.[113] A unit-holder who has become a member of the association cannot resign his membership during the period of his ownership of the unit; only a subscriber or a developer is entitled to resign.[114] There is no provision that requires the subscribers or the developer to resign their membership of the commonhold association, even if they do not retain ownership of any of the units.

A commonhold association may not be a member of itself.[115]

2.15.5 Joint unit-holders

Two or more joint owners of a unit cannot each become members of the commonhold association; only one of them is entitled to be a member. This is to ensure that the owners of a single unit do not acquire disproportionate voting rights.

[109] Sections 8(1), 7(3).
[110] Section 12.
[111] Schedule 3, part 2, paragraph 10.
[112] Schedule 3, part 2, paragraph 12(a).
[113] Schedule 3, part 2, paragraph 12(b).
[114] Schedule 3, part 2, paragraph 13.
[115] Schedule 3, part 2, paragraph 9.

The rules for determining which of the joint owners is entitled to apply for membership are as follows:

(a) The owners can nominate one of themselves to become a member.[116] The nomination must be made in writing and addressed to the commonhold association.[117] It must be received by the commonhold association before the end of a prescribed period.[118] No period has yet been prescribed. The Consultation Paper proposes that the period should be 21 days from the date of the transfer of the unit. It is not clear whether time is to run from the date on which the new owners become entitled to be registered as the proprietors of the unit, or the date on which the registration is completed. However, it would be consistent with the Act's definition of a unit-holder[119] for the time to run from the date on which the new owners become entitled to be registered.

(b) In the event that no nomination is received within the prescribed period then, by default, the person whose name appears first in the proprietorship register is the only person entitled to become a member.[120] A joint unit-holder can then apply to the court for an order that he is entitled to become a member in place of the person who has become entitled by default.

(c) After the end of the prescribed period, the joint unit-holders may nominate one of themselves to be entitled to become a member in place of either (a) a person who was nominated either within the prescribed period or afterwards; or (b) a person who became entitled to be a member as a result of the court order.[121]

There are two important restrictions in this procedure.

The first is that an application to the court by a joint unit-holder for an order that he be entitled to become a member of the commonhold association can only be made if the person who is already entitled only became entitled by default of a nomination within the prescribed period.[122] A joint unit-holder who did nominate his co-owner cannot then apply to the court to have his entitlement removed. There is no procedure in the Act for a person who is dissatisfied with the way in which his co-owner is exercising his voting rights to apply to the court to be allowed to replace him as a member of the company.

The second is that the joint unit-holders cannot nominate one of themselves to be entitled to become a member of the company in place of someone who became entitled by default of a nomination within the prescribed period.[123] The only way to replace a person who became entitled to be a member as a result of a failure to

[116] Schedule 3, part 2, paragraph 8(2).

[117] Schedule 3, part 2, paragraph 8(3)(a).

[118] Schedule 3, part 2, paragraph 8(3)(b).

[119] Section 12.

[120] Schedule 3, part 2, paragraph 8(4).

[121] Schedule 3, part 2, paragraph 8(5).

[122] The application to the court can only be made in respect of a person registered 'by virtue of sub-paragraph (4)'.

[123] The nomination procedure does not apply where the person presently entitled became so entitled by virtue of the default procedure in paragraph 8(4); it expressly only applies where the person presently entitled became so entitled by virtue of paragraph 8(2), (5) or (6).

nominate within the prescribed period is to make an application to the court. It is therefore extremely important that joint purchasers of a unit remember to make a nomination within the prescribed period from the date of the transfer.

The Act therefore does not provide satisfactorily for the means of resolving a dispute between joint owners about who should be the member of the company. The Consultation Paper considers this problem as follows:

> One solution might be to allow the vote of the unit to be split so that the vote could be cast to reflect differing views between joint unit-holders but that has the potential to become rather complicated. An alternative could be that where there are joint unit-holders their vote may only be cast if they all agree. If they fail to agree how to vote, the vote will not be cast. A further alternative could be that, if the unit-holders do not agree, the member may cast the vote anyhow.

Although this and other possible solutions were discussed in the responses to the Consultation Paper, the Department of Constitutional Affairs comments in its Post-Consultation Report dated August 2003:

> At present we do not propose any special provision for non-member joint unit-holders.

Time will tell whether this policy can be maintained.

Section 13 of the Act provides an exhaustive guide to the circumstances in the Act in which joint unit-holders are required to act jointly; may act individually; or are treated as jointly and severally liable.

2.15.6 Registration of membership

A person entitled to become a member of the commonhold association does not become a member automatically. He must apply to the company to be entered in the register of members, and his membership only runs from the date on which the company then effects the registration.[124] He does not have the right to vote until he has been entered on the register. If the company fails to register him promptly, it is in breach of its duty under section 352 of the Companies Act 1985. The company and its officers commit an offence and are liable to a fine for the breach. If they continue to default, then they are also liable for a daily default fine.[125] An officer only commits an offence if he knowingly or wilfully authorises or permits the default.[126] The offence is triable summarily in the magistrates court, and the maximum fine is £1,000 together with a further £100 per day for so long as the default continues.[127]

[124] Schedule 3, part 2, paragraph 11 provides that: 'A person who is entitled to be entered in the register of members of a commonhold association becomes a member when the company registers him in pursuance of its duty under section 352 of the Companies Act 1985 (c 6) (duty to maintain register of members).'

[125] Section 352(5), Companies Act 1985.

[126] Section 730(5), Companies Act 1985.

[127] Section 730(2), Schedule 24, Companies Act 1985.

A person aggrieved at the company's default or unnecessary delay in entering his name on the register can apply to the court for the register to be rectified.[128] This procedure can be used to determine a dispute as to the entitlement of a unit-holder to be entered on the register.[129]

Regulations may be made which specifically provide, in relation to a commonhold association, the following:

(a) The way in which the duty to enter new members in the register is to be performed.[130]

(b) The period within which the new member must be entered on the register.[131]

The liability to a fine under section 352 of the Companies Act 1985 will extend to a breach of any of the specific regulations that may be published.

A person entitled to become a member is not obliged to take up membership. He is free to choose not to become a member, although he will obviously then not have any voting rights at meetings of the commonhold association. It is thought that it would be wrong for the commonhold association to enter a new unit-holder's name on the register simply upon receipt of a notice that the ownership of the unit has been transferred.[132] A unit-holder who has become a member cannot resign his membership while he continues to be the owner of the unit.[133] A subscriber or a developer who is not also a unit-holder may resign by giving notice in writing to the association.[134]

PART 5 THE COMMONHOLD COMMUNITY STATEMENT

2.16 GENERAL

2.16.1 Definition

The commonhold community statement is the document which defines the rights and duties of the commonhold association and of the unit-holders.[135] It may also

[128] Under section 359(1) of the Companies Act 1985. The court, for these purposes, is any court having jurisdiction to wind-up the company: section 744.

[129] Section 359(1), Companies Act 1985: 'On such an application the court may decide any question relating to the title of a person who is a party to the application to have his name entered in or omitted from the register, whether the question arises between members or alleged members, or between members or alleged members on the one hand and the company on the other hand, and generally may decide any question necessary or expedient to be decided for rectification of the register.'

[130] Schedule 3, part 2, paragraph 14(1).

[131] The Act further states that 'A period specified [for this purpose] may be expressed to begin with (a) the date of notification under section 15(3), (b) the date on which the directors of the commonhold association first become aware of a specified matter, or (c) some other time.'

[132] Section 15(3).

[133] Schedule 3, part 2, paragraph 13.

[134] Schedule 3, part 2, paragraph 13.

[135] Section 31(1).

make provision about the way in which decisions are to be taken in connection with the management of the commonhold or about any other matter which concerns the commonhold.[136]

There must be a single commonhold community statement for all of the units in the development. The result is that each of the unit-holders will be bound by the same obligations and will have the same rights against the association.

As with the memorandum and articles of association, copies of the commonhold community statement will be freely obtainable from the Land Registry, by application in form OC2 (see Form 1.10 in the Forms and Precedents part of this work).

2.16.2 Prescribed form

The commonhold community statement must be in a prescribed form.[137] The standardisation of the form and much of the content of the statement is one of the features that the Government perceives will make the acquisition of a commonhold unit more attractive than the purchase of a long lease. The Partial Regulatory Impact Assessment lists the advantages of a prescribed form as follows:

(a) Advisers will become familiar with the standard form of the document, and therefore the cost of advising a potential purchaser will be lower than the cost of advising on the acquisition of a long lease.[138]

(b) The standard documentation will reduce the cost to lenders of investigating the security.[139]

(c) The similarity of the rights and duties of unit-holders between different commonholds, in contrast to the diversity of the rights and duties in different long leases, means that 'the expectations of a person coming to join a commonhold are less likely to be disappointed or frustrated by unforeseen terms and conditions'.[140]

2.16.3 Sources of rights and obligations

There are three sources for the rights and obligations that are to be contained in a commonhold community statement:

[136] Section 31(3)(c).
[137] Section 31(2).

[138] Paragraph 16 of the Assessment states that 'For advisers, the advent of commonhold should enable advice to be given more efficiently and may open some 'niche' opportunities for specialists. This should also benefit their clients.'

[139] Paragraph 17 of the Assessment states that 'the standardisation of documentation should provide a better security and reduce the cost of investigating the quality of the security. This should also benefit borrowers.'

[140] Paragraph 18.

(a) The first is the Act, which itself prescribes some of the contents of the statement. For example, the Act requires the statement to impose a duty on the commonhold association to insure the common parts of the development.[141] This duty cannot be omitted and it cannot be imposed on the unit-holders instead of the association.

(b) The second is the form that will be prescribed by regulations. Many of the terms contained in the prescribed form will be mandatory,[142] and cannot be deleted or varied. Some of the less important terms, however, are optional, and can be included, amended or deleted entirely.

(c) The third is the developer or applicant. The draftsman of the commonhold community statement can include any terms he chooses, provided that:

(i) they do not conflict with the terms that the Act and the prescribed form require to be included; and

(ii) their inclusion is not prohibited by the Act or the regulations.

The terms of the draft prescribed form are unsatisfactory in some respects. The form will require various additions in order to avoid disputes or problems.

2.16.4 Optional terms

There is no limit on the terms that can be included in the commonhold community statement, provided that they do not conflict with the requirements of the Act or the regulations. The Act provides a list of the types of duty that the statement can impose on either the association or the unit-holders. This is not an exhaustive list. The types of duty in the list are as follows:

(a) a duty to pay money; this may include a provision for the payment of interest in the case of late payment;[143]

(b) a duty to undertake works;

(c) a duty to grant access;

(d) a duty to give notice;

(e) a duty to refrain from entering into transactions of a specified kind in relation to a commonhold unit;

(f) a duty to refrain from using the whole or part of a commonhold unit for a specified purpose or for anything other than a specified purpose;

[141] Section 26(b).

[142] Section 32(2) provides that 'The regulations may permit, require or prohibit the inclusion in a statement of (a) specified provision, or (b) provision of a specified kind, for a specified purpose or about a specified matter.'

[143] Section 31(6).

(g) a duty to refrain from undertaking works (including alterations) of a specified kind;

(h) a duty to refrain from causing nuisance or annoyance;

(i) a duty to refrain from specified behaviour;

(j) a duty to indemnify the commonhold association or a unit-holder in respect of costs arising from the breach of a statutory requirement.

2.16.5 Formalities

The Act does not require the unit-holders or the association to execute the commonhold community statement in order for its terms to be enforceable.[144] A unit-holder is bound by the terms of the statement as a direct consequence of his ownership of the unit. It is binding on him as soon as he becomes a unit-holder. He becomes a unit-holder on the date on which he becomes entitled to be registered as the proprietor of the unit, not on the potentially later date on which the registration is completed.[145]

2.16.6 Inconsistent terms

A term in the commonhold community statement has no effect to the extent that it is inconsistent with the Act, the regulations, or the memorandum or articles of association of the commonhold association.[146] A term which conflicts is void only 'to the extent that' there is a conflict, and it should be given effect so far as is possible.

2.16.7 Joint unit-holders

Regulations may make provision for the construction, in the case of joint unit-holders, of a reference in the commonhold community statement to a unit-holder.[147] It is not known what specific regulations are envisaged under this provision.

[144] Section 31(7).
[145] Section 12.
[146] Section 31(9) provides that a provision in the statement shall be of no effect to the extent that '(a) it is prohibited by virtue of section 32, (b) it is inconsistent with any provision made by or by virtue of this Part, (c) it is inconsistent with anything which is treated as included in the statement by virtue of section 32, or (d) it is inconsistent with the memorandum or articles of association of the commonhold association'.
[147] Section 13(6)(b).

2.17 CONTENTS OF THE COMMONHOLD COMMUNITY STATEMENT

The form of the commonhold community statement in its most recent draft (that which accompanied the Post-Consultation Report issued by the Department of Constitutional Affairs in August 2003) is set out at Form 2.3 of the Forms and Precedents part of this work. Its terms are considered below.

2.17.1 Covering pages

The commonhold community statement commences with a covering page briefly describing its purport, together with a list of contents, extending to three Parts (subdivided into various categories) and four Annexes.

2.17.2 Part I: signatures and table of amendments

This part provides for the requisite two directors or a director and the secretary of the commonhold association to sign the statement. It also sets out a table of amendments, the purpose and format of which is considered further in Section 2.19 below.

2.17.3 Part II: factual information about the commonhold

This Part is subdivided into four separate sections, requiring factual information to be given about the commonhold. The first two sections merely require formal brief details to be given regarding the commonhold and commonhold association: the name and description of the commonhold; and the name and any previous names of the commonhold association, together with its registered number at Companies House and its date of incorporation.

The remaining two sections, entitled '3. Commonhold units and common parts'[148] and '4. Limited use areas' deal in much more detail with the commonhold units, and to a lesser extent with limited use areas, as explained in paragraphs 2.17.4 to 2.17.10 below.

2.17.4 Part II: (a) the extent of the common parts

Although the heading of section 3 refers to the common parts, no provision is in fact made for any information to be supplied regarding the common parts. That is no doubt because the Act does not require the statement to define the extent of the

[148] Although no provision is in fact made for any information to be supplied regarding the common parts.

common parts as well, because these are tersely defined in the Act itself as being every part of the commonhold which is not for the time being a commonhold unit.[149]

In contrast to the original draft which accompanied the Consultation Paper, the current draft prescribed form does not require the common parts to be identified on the plan as well. Such identification of the common parts could not have any operative effect, because if the statement defined the common parts as being anything other than all the parts of the commonhold that are not included within a unit, then it would be inconsistent with the Act, and the provisions of the Act would prevail.[150]

2.17.5 Part II: (b) the extent of the commonhold unit

The first two parts of paragraph 3 of Part II of the commonhold community statement contain tables allowing for information to be included regarding:

(a) The total number of units in the commonhold.

(b) A description of the unit, broken down into columns.

The tabular format may not be the most convenient format for displaying this information, and commonhold associations will no doubt wish to devise their own ways of conveying the requisite information.

2.17.6 Part II: (c) description of unit

The Act requires the commonhold community statement to define the extent of each of the units within the commonhold;[151] and permits the definition of the extent of a unit to:

(a) Refer to an area subject to the exclusion of specified structures, fittings, apparatus or appurtenances within the area.[152] It may therefore state, for example, that the pipes and conduits within the boundaries of the unit are not included in the unit and are therefore retained by the commonhold association.

(b) Exclude the structures which delineate an area referred to.[153] It may therefore state, for example, that the boundary walls do not form part of the unit.

(c) Refer to two or more areas, whether or not contiguous.[154] A single unit may therefore comprise, for example, a flat and a garage in separate buildings.

149 Section 25(1).

150 Section 31(9)(b).

151 Section 11(2)(b). The Act also provides that it must 'specify at least two parcels of land as commonhold units', although this requirement would seem to be otiose, because no commonhold will be created with only a single unit.

152 Section 11(3)(b).

153 Section 11(3)(c).

154 Section 11(3)(d).

The table supplied in the draft prescribed form (Table 3.2) allows for the display of this information in the following columns:

(i) an identification of the commonhold unit by reference to a plan (see paragraph 2.17.7 below);

(ii) a description of the unit, which may include or consist of its address;

(iii) the commonhold number assigned to the unit;

(iv) an indication as to whether the structure and exterior of the building containing any unit is included within the unit (see further paragraph 4.9.1);

(v) a further definition of the extent of the unit (for example, whether it includes a parking space or other structures, fittings, apparatus or appurtenances).

2.17.7 Part II: (d) the plan

The Act requires the commonhold community statement to attach a plan showing each of the units.[155] Requirements for the plan are to be prescribed by regulations. The draft requirements for the plan are as follows:

(a) It should be marked clearly with the version number and the date of the commonhold community statement to which it relates.

(b) It should be no larger than A0.

(c) It must show measurements in metric.

(d) It must have a scale of at least 1/500, unless the boundaries can be shown clearly on a plan to a scale of 1/250.

(e) It must be based on an accurate survey, plotted to the chosen scale.

(f) It must show sufficient details to enable the position of the commonhold land to be related to the boundaries of the registered freeholder's title.

(g) It must show sufficient detail to enable the position of each unit to be related to the boundaries of the common parts.

(h) It must define the extent of each commonhold unit, including any separate parking spaces or garages, which must be distinguished by means of a separate number and colour reference.

(i) It must identify the floor level of each unit.

The original draft prescribed form attached to the October 2002 Consultation Paper contained a provision that stated that, in the event of any inconsistency between the written definitions and the plans, the plans would prevail. There is no such stipulation in the current (August 2003) draft of the commonhold com-

[155] Section 11(3)(a).

munity statement, although the glossary at Annex A to the statement states that: 'The extent of each commonhold unit will be *defined* in the commonhold community statement and *shown* on the plans' (emphasis supplied). The authors consider that this wording creates a presumption in favour of the primacy of the words over the plan, although that presumption will yield if the words are vague and the plan detailed.

Rather than leave the matter open to doubt, the authors would suggest that the draftsman of the commonhold community statement and the plans should expressly stipulate that the plans are either 'for the purpose of identification only' (a time-hallowed phrase familiar to conveyancers which has the result that any inconsistency would be resolved in favour of the words); or that the boundaries are 'more particularly delineated' on the plans (another well-used phrase which has the result that any inconsistency would be resolved in favour of the plans).

The Consultation Paper does not propose that the plan must show the precise position of the boundaries of the units, rather than their general position. A developer who is drafting the commonhold community statement is free to define the precise boundaries and provide that the general boundaries rule[156] is not to apply, because at the date the statement is drafted he will be the owner of all the units as well as the common parts.

The commonhold community statement should define whether the airspace above the units on the top storey of the development is part of the unit or is part of the common parts.

2.17.8 Part II: (e) allocations

Table 3.3 of section 3 of Part II is cryptically titled 'Allocation'. In fact, it deals with two linked matters and one quite separate matter:

[156] The general boundaries rule, which was previously contained in rule 278 of the Land Registration Rules 1925, is now set out in section 60 of the Land Registration Act 2002, which provides '(1) The boundary of a registered estate as shown for the purposes of the register is a general boundary, unless shown as determined under this section. (2) A general boundary does not determine the exact line of the boundary.' If the commonhold community statement does precisely define the boundaries, then it appears likely that the boundaries will be determined on the Register under section 60 of the Act without the need for a specific application to the Land Registry for this purpose. That is because of rule 122 of the Land Registration Rules 2003, which provides as follows: 'Determination of the exact line of a boundary without application. (1) This rule applies where (a) there is (i) a transfer of part of a registered estate in land, or (ii) the grant of a term of years absolute which is a registrable disposition of part of a registered estate in land, (b) there is a common boundary, and (c) there is sufficient information in the disposition to enable the registrar to determine the exact line of the common boundary. (2) The registrar may determine the exact line of the common boundary and if he does he must—(a) make an entry in the individual registers of the affected registered titles stating that the exact line of the common boundary is determined under section 60 of the Act, and (b) subject to paragraph (3), add to the title plan of the disponor's affected registered title (whether or not the disponor is still the proprietor of that title, or still entitled to be registered as proprietor of that title) and to the title plan of the registered title under which the disposition is being registered, such particulars of the exact line of the common boundary as he considers appropriate.'

(a) the percentage allocated to each unit for the purposes of the apportionment of the commonhold assessment;

(b) the allocated percentage of the reserve fund applicable to each unit;

(c) the number of votes allocated to each member of the commonhold association.

All three of these allocations are critical to the functioning of the commonhold, and are examined in more detail in Chapter 4.

2.17.9 Part II: (f) permitted uses

Table 3.4 in section 3 of Part 4 allows for the permitted use and any restrictions on the use of commonhold units to be recorded. User restrictions are discussed in detail in Section 4.12 of the text of this work.

2.17.10 Part II: (g) limited use areas

Section 4 of Part II contains a further table (Table 3.5) allowing for the recording of which if any parts of the commonhold are limited use areas (ie parts of the common parts which may be dedicated to a particular purpose, such as the boiler room). Limited use areas are examined in paragraph 4.12.7 of the text of this work.

2.17.11 Part III: the rules—(a) general

Part III of the draft prescribed commonhold community statement sets out the main body of the rules governing behaviour in the commonhold. These are intended to bear out the following statement in the Post-Consultation Report dated August 2003:

> . . . there should be a strong core of standard provisions but beyond these individual commonholds should have a wide degree of flexibility. This approach supports our belief that commonholders should, as far as possible, be able to enjoy the freedoms of freeholders generally, rather than the numerous constraints traditionally associated with leases.

It is fair to add that the draft prescribed form of the commonhold community statement supplied with that statement contains far fewer rules than the original draft supplied with the Consultation Paper.

The rules are examined in brief detail below. Their effect on the practice of running a commonhold is explored in Chapter 4.

2.17.12 Part III: the rules—(b) dealings with the freehold

The Act requires that a commonhold community statement may not provide for the transfer or loss of an interest in land on the occurrence or non-occurrence of a specified event.[157] The statement therefore cannot contain any provision equivalent to a re-entry clause in a lease, entitling the commonhold association to forfeit the unit-holder's interest in the event of a default.

The Act further requires that a commonhold community statement may not contain any provision which prevents or restricts the transfer of a commonhold unit. A transfer is defined as the transfer of a unit-holder's estate in a unit to another person whether or not for consideration, whether or not subject to any reservation or other terms, and whether or not by operation of law.[158] The effect of the restriction in the Act is that the commonhold community statement cannot provide that the association's consent is required for the transfer of a unit, and the association cannot, for example, include a provision insisting that any arrears under the commonhold assessment are to be paid before the unit-holder is able to dispose of the unit.

The combined effect of these two prohibitions attracted significant criticism during the passage of the Bill through Parliament, because of the restrictions they impose on the availability of sanctions against a defaulting unit-holder. Various amendments were proposed, under which the commonhold association was to be entitled either to sell the unit and recoup the debt out of the proceeds of sale as a first chargee, or to prevent it from being sold or transferred until the debts had been paid. Either of these amendments would have given the association a form of security for the non-payment of debts, but the Government was implacably opposed to both of them, which were perceived as re-introducing the most unpopular elements of long leasehold ownership into the commonhold system.

The original draft of the commonhold community statement attached to the Consultation Paper simply repeated this requirement of the Act by providing that the commonhold association should not prevent or restrict the transfer of a commonhold unit. The current draft (supplied with the Post-Consultation Report dated August 2003) reacts to the critical responses received by providing:

> On transfer of a commonhold unit the new unit-holder must pay any debts incurred by the former unit-holder which remain outstanding in respect of the commonhold assessment and the reserve fund levies.

This provision is welcome: it replaces the earlier proposal that the defaulting unit-holder should remain liable after the transfer, with all the difficulties for recovery and enforcement that would result.

The draft prescribed form also requires a new unit-holder to notify the association of a transfer within the time limit prescribed by the regulations.

2.17.13 Part III: the rules—(c) restrictions on granting leases or licences of units

The Act contains various provisions which restrict the ability of a unit-holder to grant certain types of lease of a residential commonhold unit.[159] There is no need

[157] Section 31(8).
[158] Section 15(2).
[159] Section 17. These restrictions are considered in Chapter 3.

for these restrictions to be set out in the commonhold community statement in order for them to apply to a unit-holder, although they are repeated in the draft prescribed form. The statement is also expressly permitted to include provisions restricting the creation of a lease in a non-residential commonhold unit.[160] The current prescribed draft provides that a unit-holder many not grant a tenancy in a residential commonhold unit for a term of more than 21 years, and imposes obligations on the unit-holder to notify the commonhold association of the grant of any tenancy or licence for a period longer than 28 days. The commonhold association is obliged by the current prescribed draft of the statement to maintain a register of such tenancies and licences.

The provisions in the Act restricting the grant of certain types of lease do not apply to the grant of a licence to occupy the unit, or to the grant of a tenancy at will. However, the statement is able to impose equivalent restrictions. As originally drafted, the draft prescribed form contained a prohibition on granting a licence or other right over, or parting with possession of, the unit or any part of the unit, except with the prior written consent of the board of directors of the commonhold association and subject to such terms and conditions as the board of directors may specify. That restriction does not appear in the current prescribed draft, and at present it is not proposed that there should be any restrictions on the grant of licences or periodic tenancies.

There is, however, nothing preventing an individual commonhold association introducing further restrictions on leasing (for example a ban on holiday lettings). A lease of a unit which is granted in contravention of the restrictions in the Act is void.[161]

In the case of either residential or non-residential units, section 19(1) of the Act provides that regulations may enable the statement to impose obligations on the tenant of the unit in addition to the unit-holder.[162] The Act envisages that the tenants of a unit may be made liable to discharge any payments which are due from the unit-holder under the commonhold community statement, with the right to set off against the rent any payments that they are required to make. The current prescribed draft contains a number of provisions implementing these powers, including obligations upon the tenant to pay commonhold assessments in lieu of the unit-holder where his tenancy agreement so provides; and to abide by those rules of the commonhold community statement which affect his occupancy.

2.17.14 Part III: the rules—(d) use of the commonhold

The commonhold community statement must contain a provision which regulates the use of the commonhold units.[163]

[160] Section 18.

[161] Section 17(1) provides that 'It shall not be possible to create a term of years absolute in a residential commonhold unit unless the term satisfies prescribed conditions.'

[162] Section 19(1).

[163] Section 14(1).

The Act does not specify the level of detail that must be contained in this provision. All that is likely to be needed is a short provision that the use is restricted either to residential and other incidental purposes, or to non-residential purposes.[164]

The commonhold community statement must also contain a provision which regulates the use of the common parts.[165] The Act again does not specify the level of detail that must be contained in this provision. The provision in the draft prescribed form is that: 'Subject to any applicable Rules, the common parts may be used by all unit-holders and their invitees'.

It is permissible for the statement to designate an area or areas of the common parts called 'limited use areas'.[166] A limited use area is an area in relation to which there can be restrictions on either the class of person who may make use of the area, or the kind of use to which the area may be put. There can be more than one limited use area, and different restrictions may apply to each of them.[167] Restrictions can sensibly be imposed on, for example, the unit-holders' rights of access to rooms containing plant or machinery.

The current draft prescribed form contains a bare minimum of stipulations restrictive of user:

(a) confining the use of the commonhold unit to the use set out in Table 3.4 of Part II (see paragraph 2.17.9 above);

(b) confining the use of limited use areas to the uses set out in Table 4 of Part II (see paragraph 2.17.10 above);

(c) providing that the common parts must not be used in such a way as to prejudice the use of or access to a commonhold unit;

(d) prohibiting the use of any unit or the common parts in such a way as to cause a nuisance;

(e) prohibiting the unit-holder from acting in such a way as to prejudice the insurance of the commonhold association.

As originally drafted, the commonhold community statement was much more prescriptive: many of its terms appeared to have been borrowed from a standard form residential lease. For example, the draft contained a provision that: 'No commonhold unit may be used for any illegal or immoral purposes.'[168] This and

[164] This seems to be implicit in the wording of section 17, which deals with restrictions on the right to lease a residential commonhold unit, and which states in subsection (5) that 'A commonhold unit is residential if provision made in the commonhold community statement by virtue of section 14(1) requires it to be used only (a) for residential purposes, or (b) for residential and other incidental purposes.' The provision in the draft prescribed form supports this interpretation, because it states in relation to a residential commonhold simply that 'The commonhold units designated as residential units . . . shall be used only for residential purposes and other incidental purposes.'

[165] Section 26(a). [166] Section 25(2). [167] Section 25(3).

[168] It was once held in relation to a lease that a flat which was let to a mistress by a man who was to pay the rent was let for an immoral purpose: *Upfill v Wright* [1911] 1 KB 506. This is not thought still to be good law: *Woodfall's Law of Landlord and Tenant*, paragraph 11.181.

similarly restrictive provisions have been excised in line, no doubt, with the Government's aim to treat commonhold as closely as possible as freehold.

2.17.15 Part III: the rules—(e) insurance

The requirements of the Act in relation to insurance are that:

(1) The commonhold community statement must contain a provision imposing duties in respect of the insurance of each commonhold unit.[169] These duties can be imposed either on the commonhold association or on the unit-holders.[170]

(2) The commonhold community statement must contain a provision imposing a duty on the commonhold association to insure the common parts.[171] This duty cannot be imposed on the unit-holders.

The Act does not define the types of insurance that are to be maintained. It is thought that the requirement in the Act extends only to buildings insurance, and not to contents insurance or public liability insurance.

The current draft of the statement puts forward the following scheme for insurance:

(a) *Public insurance liability*: the commonhold association is obliged to take out and maintain such insurance in respect of the whole commonhold. As originally drafted, the prescribed form required the unit-holder to take out and maintain public liability insurance in relation to the unit. This change of tune is clearly sensible.

(b) *Buildings insurance*: the commonhold association is obliged to take out and maintain such insurance in respect of the common parts. There is no obligation at all regarding the buildings insurance for the units, which appears to be a mistake in view of the mandatory terms of section 14(2) of the Act.[172] In practical terms, it is likely to be more satisfactory for the buildings insurance for the units to be taken out by the commonhold association, so that a single policy covers the entire development.

(c) *Contents insurance*: again, as originally drafted, the prescribed form required the unit-holder to take out and maintain contents insurance. The current draft is silent on this topic, having clearly taken on-board the common-sense objections to this level of prescription put forward by many of the respondents to the Consultation Paper.[173]

[169] Section 14(2). [170] Section 14(3). [171] Section 26(b).

[172] Save to the extent that the commonhold unit is defined to exclude all the structure and exterior and all other fabric to which such insurance would attach.

[173] Lord Monson's remark in the House of Lords was: 'Why . . . is it made obligatory for each unit-holder to insure his or her contents? It is a sensible thing to insure one's contents, but surely it is nobody's business if one fails to do so? If your contents are stolen or burned, you are the only loser. It does not affect the other unit-holders at all.'

(d) *Level of cover*: the Act does not specify the extent of the cover that is required to comply with the buildings insurance obligation. As originally drafted, the prescribed form required the commonhold association to take out 'appropriate' insurance cover. The current draft (that supplied with the Post-Consultation Report dated August 2003) improves on this by requiring the association to insure against loss or damage by fire; to procure full rebuilding and reinstatement cover on specified terms; and to cover the cost of any necessary alternative accommodation.

(e) *Maintaining the level of cover*: finally, the current prescribed draft requires as a default provision that a professional buildings insurance valuation be obtained at least every five years.

2.17.16 Part III: the rules—(f) repair and maintenance

The Act requires the commonhold community statement to include the following:

(a) *Common parts*: the statement must contain a provision requiring the commonhold association to repair and maintain the common parts.[174] This obligation cannot be imposed on the unit-holders.

(b) *Units*: the statement must also contain a provision imposing duties in respect of the repair and maintenance of each of the commonhold units.[175] The Act expressly allows these duties to be imposed either on the commonhold association or on the unit-holders.[176]

The Act is silent on the following matters:

(a) *Standard of repair*: the Act does not require the commonhold community statement to prescribe the standard of the work required to comply with the duty to repair and maintain either the common parts or the unit. The Consultation Paper did not impose a mandatory standard. The authors suggest that the statement should include either a prescribed standard or a satisfactory method for determining whether repairs have been carried out in accordance with the duty (by providing, for example, that they are to be carried out to the reasonable satisfaction of a surveyor appointed by the board of directors).

(b) *Renewal*: the Act does not require the association to renew, reconstruct or rebuild the common parts.[177] A covenant merely to repair and maintain would not ordinarily require the reconstruction of substantially the whole of the common parts or the units, were this to become necessary as the result of, for example, a fire or a serious inherent defect in the construction. It has been held in a New South Wales case that, in relation to a strata scheme, an obligation to repair includes an

[174] Section 26(c). [175] Section 14(2). [176] Section 14(3).

[177] The difference between renewal and repair is that a renewal is the reconstruction of substantially the whole of the subject matter of the covenant: *Lurcott v Wakely* [1911] 1 KB 905.

obligation to renew if necessary;[178] but there must be doubt about whether this decision would be followed in relation to a commonhold.

As originally drafted, the prescribed form made it mandatory for the unit-holder rather than the association to repair and maintain the interior of the unit, and obliged either the association or the unit-holder to repair the exterior of the unit. The consultation paper invited the consultees to consider whether it was overly prescriptive for the unit-holder to be obliged to repair and maintain the interior of the unit, rather than simply to repair and maintain it in so far as this is necessary to prevent the other unit-holders from being adversely affected.

The current prescribed draft has veered to the opposite extreme by specifying no obligation at all regarding the repair of the commonhold unit. Even if this is thought to be an attractive proposition for prospective unit-holders, it appears to ignore the mandatory terms of section 14(2). The comment made in the Post-Consultation Report dated August 2003 on this topic is as follows:

> . . . commonholds would be able to impose obligations on unit-holders to maintain their units if they so wish but we do not consider that a general mandatory obligation to keep a unit in good repair would be appropriate for a freehold owner, or necessary for a structurally independent unit.

The authors suggest that some minimal level of obligation would be desirable in the case of most commonholds.

2.17.17 Part III: the rules—(g) alterations

The Act does not contain any mandatory requirements in relation to alterations. As originally drafted, the prescribed form contained a provision that:

> Any alterations to the structure or external appearance of a commonhold unit may only be made with the written consent of the Board of Directors, and subject to the provisions of section 23 and 24 of the Act (if applicable).[179]

A restriction on structural (as opposed to non-structural) alterations is sensible. However, the obligation in the original draft prescribed form was not qualified to the effect that the directors' consent must not be unreasonably withheld. The effect of the restriction was therefore that the unit-holder would have been bound by the qualification even if the refusal of consent were unreasonable. The unit-holder's only remedy would be to take action against the directors for a breach of their statutory duty to exercise their powers so as to permit or facilitate so far as possible his enjoyment of his freehold estate in the unit.[180] A more satisfactory clause would simply require the consent not to be unreasonably withheld: the

[178] *Proprietor of Strata Plan no 6522 v Furney* (1976) (Digest).
[179] Sections 23 and 24 are provisions that relate to a change in the size of a unit.
[180] Section 35(1).

effect of this qualification would be to release the unit-holder from the terms of the restriction in the event that the directors were to act unreasonably.

The current prescribed draft has, however, departed entirely from this restrictive regime. Alterations to commonhold units are completely unregulated, although alterations by unit-holders to the common parts are prohibited; and alterations to the common parts by the commonhold association are permitted only if a resolution to that effect is passed. The authors suggest that a prudent commonhold association will wish to have some measure of control over alterations to units, in line with the suggestion made above.

2.17.18 Part III: the rules—(h) the commonhold assessment

The Act requires the commonhold community statement to make provision for a service charge to be paid by the unit-holders.[181] This is referred to as the 'commonhold assessment'.[182]

The requirements of the Act are as follows:

(a) The provisions must require the directors of the commonhold association to make an annual estimate of the income needed from the unit-holders in order to meet the expenses of the association.[183]

(b) They must enable the directors of the association to make further estimates from time to time of any additional income that is needed from the unit-holders in addition to the income raised by the annual estimate.[184] The directors are therefore obliged to charge an annual sum, but have the power to make additional charges from time to time, should it prove necessary.

(c) The provisions must specify the percentage of the total of these estimates that is to be allocated to and paid by each unit.[185] The statement cannot simply specify that there is to be payment of a 'fair' or 'reasonable' percentage of the assessment. The sum of the percentages allocated to each of the units must total 100.[186] However, a nil percentage may be applied to particular units. This allows, for example, a caretaker's flat to be excluded from the liability to pay the assessment. The allocation of percentages must be done carefully: a dispute over payment is most likely to arise where, for example, the percentage has failed to take account of the fact that a flat is on the ground floor and therefore gains no benefit from any expenditure on the maintenance of the lift.

(d) They must oblige each unit-holder to make payments in respect of the percentage of each estimate that has been allocated to his unit.[187]

[181] Section 38.
[182] This phrase appears in the heading to section 38, but does not appear in the text of the Act.
[183] Section 38(1)(a).
[184] Section 38(1)(b).
[185] Section 38(1)(c).
[186] Section 38(2)(a).
[187] Section 38(1)(d).

(e) They must require the directors of the commonhold association to serve notices on unit-holders specifying the payments that are required and the date on which the payment is to fall due.[188]

As originally drafted, the prescribed form contained the following additional requirements:

(f) The directors were required to take into account, when making their estimate, any other income that is reasonably expected to accrue to the association. The result would have been that, for example, any sums received from hiring a garden in the common parts for a corporate function would have to have been set off against the amount of the commonhold assessment and could not have been added to the reserve fund or used for any other purpose.

(g) The estimate must include details of the income and expenditure in the previous year. It must also specify the amounts that are due from any defaulting unit-holders.

(h) The notices requiring payment must be served on the unit-holders within 28 days of the determination of the estimate of the amount required. They are to allow the unit-holders at least 28 days for payment, except where earlier payment is necessary to enable the association to pay its debts as and when they fall due. The notice may allow the unit-holders to pay by instalments on specified dates.

(i) The Consultation Paper also contained a further proposal that the estimate should be approved by a vote at a general meeting, rather than simply determined by the directors.

The current draft prescribed form omits or relaxes all of these additional stipulations. Now, the form largely follows the wording of the Act, but adds:

(j) a requirement that the directors must serve a notice on each unit-holder at least three months before payment would otherwise become due, detailing the estimate allocated to the unit;

(k) provision for each unit-holder to make representations regarding the estimate within one month of service of such a notice;

(l) a requirement that the directors must then make any adjustment thought fit in the light of such representations, with further notification to be made in the light of such adjustment.

(m) a default provision for interest to be payable upon late assessment payments.

The draft prescribed form does not contain a provision requiring the unit-holder to pay the commonhold assessment without set-off. A provision against set-off should probably be included: the association has very limited remedies against a

[188] Section 38(1)(e).

defaulting unit-holder, and a restriction on set-off would prevent the unit-holder from withholding payment on the ground that he has a cross-claim against the association. A provision against set-off is only effective if it expressly uses the words set-off; a provision requiring payment without deduction or abatement is insufficient.[189]

2.17.19 Part III: the rules—(i) the reserve fund

The Act provides that regulations may be made requiring the commonhold community statement to provide for a reserve fund. This is defined as 'one or more funds to finance the repair and maintenance of common parts . . . [and] commonhold units'.[190] In the event that regulations are made which do require the establishment of a reserve fund, then the Act will require the statement also to contain further provisions which:

(a) Entitle or require the directors of the association to set a levy from time to time.[191]

(b) Specify the percentage of any such levy which is to be allocated to each unit.[192] This percentage need not be the same as the percentage allocated in relation to the commonhold assessment. The percentages must again add up to 100, but a nil percentage may be specified in relation to a particular unit or units.[193]

(c) Require each unit-holder to make payments in respect of his percentage of the levy.[194]

(d) Require the directors of the association to serve notices on the unit-holders specifying the payments that are required and the date on which they are to fall due.[195]

(e) Require the commonhold community statement to specify the 'reserve fund activity'. This is the activity or activities which the fund may be used to finance.[196] The activities must all relate to repair or maintenance.[197] The Act prohibits the reserve fund from being used to finance the enforcement of debts other than the enforcement of a judgment debt that is referable to a reserve fund activity.[198]

[189] *Connaught Restaurants Ltd v Indoor Leisure Ltd* [1994] 1 WLR 501.
[190] Section 39(1). [191] Section 39(2)(a). [192] Section 39(2)(b).
[193] Section 39(3). [194] Section 39(2)(c). [195] Section 39(2)(d).
[196] Section 39(5)(a).
[197] Otherwise, it is not permissible for there to be a reserve fund at all in relation to the activity: section 39(1).
[198] Section 39(4); the section further provides that 'assets are used for the purpose of enforcement of a debt if, in particular, they are taken in execution or are made the subject of a charging order under section 1 of the Charging Orders Act' (subsection (5)(b)) and 'the reference to a judgment debt includes a reference to any interest payable on a judgment debt' (subsection (5)(c)). This restriction on the use of the fund ceases to apply in the event that the court makes a winding-up order in respect of the association, the association passes a voluntary winding-up resolution, or if the property ceases to be commonhold land because it was registered in error or because documents are rectified: section 56.

The current draft prescribed form requires the directors to commission a reserve study by an 'appropriate professional' at least every ten years, and to have regard to it when determining the amount of any reserve fund levy. No guidance is given as to the content or precise purpose of this study, in contrast to the following prescription in the original draft:

> At least every ten years, and at any other time as they may think necessary or appropriate, the Board of Directors shall prepare, on the basis of an inspection and with the assistance of such surveyors, engineers or other professional advisers as may be appropriate, a written study listing all of the major assets, equipment, fixtures or fittings which the Commonhold Association owns or maintains with a remaining life of less than [number] years (a 'reserve study'). The reserve study must estimate in the case of each such item, (i) the remaining life of the item, (ii) the costs of maintaining and replacing the item, and (iii) the annual contribution required to maintain such costs.

Presumably the Government now considers that such matters can safely be left to the good sense of the individual association.

If the directors determine that a reserve fund is necessary, then the procedure to be followed is identical to that set out in relation to the commonhold assessment levy (see paragraph 2.17.18 above). The draft adds, in a rare throwback to the needlessly hectoring tone of the original:

> In setting the levy the directors must endeavour to ensure that unnecessary reserves are not accumulated and where they do so accumulate they may be used for the general expenses of the commonhold.

2.17.20 Part III: the rules—(j) complaints and default procedure

The Act does not make it mandatory for the commonhold community statement to contain any provisions about a complaints procedure, default procedures or enforcement. These procedures are to be defined by regulations, which are yet to be published in their final form.

As originally drafted, the prescribed form defined procedures which were in summary as follows:

(a) *Complaints procedure*: a unit-holder who has grounds for complaining about a breach, and who cannot resolve the complaint by agreement, shall notify the directors in writing and provide them with such information as they reasonably require to enable them to take steps to enforce the breach under the default procedure. The unit-holder is required to follow the complaints procedure before either taking any legal proceedings against another unit-holder, or referring the matter to the ombudsman (rules 38 and 40).

(b) *Default procedure*: if the board of directors have reason to believe that any person is in breach, then they shall first attempt to resolve the matter informally. If they cannot resolve the matter informally, then they must serve the defaulter with a written default notice before taking any further action. The notice must specify the breach in sufficient detail for the defaulter to understand what is alleged. It must specify a reasonable period within which the breach must cease or be remedied, or within which the unit-holder must show that there has been no breach or anticipated breach. The default notice must contain a prominent warning that if the defaulter does not comply, then the commonhold association may take action without further notice, including (a) remedying the breach itself, (b) serving an indemnity notice, or (c) referring the dispute to an ombudsman or taking legal proceedings. It must also warn the defaulter that any action taken may result in orders being made against him for compensation, costs and interest (rules 41 to 45.)

(c) *Rights of access to units*: rule 46 granted the commonhold association rights of access to the units to remedy breaches. The provision in the draft prescribed form was that:

In addition to any other rights of access which may exist or be enforceable at law, every unit-holder hereby grants to the commonhold association, acting by its officers or other duly appointed agents for the purpose,

(a) the right to enter upon his commonhold unit in the event of emergency or risk of harm, whether by fire, flood, escape of noxious substances, electricity or otherwise, to the commonhold or to the health or well-being of any person upon the commonhold or in adjoining premises; and

(b) the right to enter upon his commonhold unit to carry out any repairs or maintenance in accordance with [the association's express right to do so in the event of the unit-holder's default] provided that such right of access shall only be enforceable with the consent of the unit-holder, or pursuant to the order of a court of competent jurisdiction.

(d) *Enforcement of rules relating to the parking of vehicles*: the draft prescribed form contained a provision that:

Without prejudice to its other rights to ensure compliance with the Rules, the Commonhold Association may take such lawful steps as are necessary to enforce any Rules relating to the parking of vehicles on any part of the Commonhold, including arranging for the immobilisation or removal of vehicles parked in contravention of the Rules.

The Consultation Paper proposed that this should be an optional provision. If it were to be omitted, then the commonhold association would commit a tort were it to immobilise or remove a vehicle, unless sufficiently clear notices had been displayed in the common parts which stated the consequences of parking without the permission of the association.[199]

(e) *Indemnity*: the draft prescribed form contained a provision that:

Without prejudice to any other remedy to which the commonhold association or any other unit-holder may be entitled, any unit-holder who is in breach of any provision of the

[199] *Arthur & Anor v Anker* [1997] QB 564; *Vine v London Borough of Waltham Forest* [2000] 1 WLR 2383.

articles or the rules or any statutory requirement (the 'defaulter') shall indemnify and hold harmless the commonhold association and any other unit-holder against any costs arising from such breach, including, if appropriate, the costs of remedying the breach or of acting in the stead of the defaulter as permitted by the Rules.

If the Board of Directors are of the opinion that the commonhold association or any other unit-holder has incurred costs arising from such breach as aforesaid which the defaulter ought to pay, they shall serve a notice ('an indemnity notice') on the defaulter requiring him to pay the amount of such costs to the commonhold association within a specified period of time being not less than 14 days.

This was an essential provision. Without it, the association would be unable to charge a defaulter with the costs incurred in remedying the default (except by an order of the court) and the costs would need to be recovered from all the unit-holders under the commonhold assessment in the fixed percentages allocated to each individual unit. However, the costs recoverable from the defaulter should be limited to those which were reasonably incurred and reasonable in amount. This should be stated expressly.

The current draft appended to the Post-Consultation Report dated August 2003 keeps the rough structure of (a) the complaints procedure and (b) the default procedure (but without using those confusing titles); it (c) omits the right of access to units (save for the right to enter to carry out repairs for which the commonhold association is liable—see rule 21); it (d) omits the proposed rule regarding enforcement of parking regulations; and it (e) excludes the proposed indemnity provision. The wisdom of these omissions is questionable, and the prudent commonhold association may wish to introduce rules in accordance with the original draft.

Of note are the proposed stipulations:

(a) That in their dealings with each other, the commonhold association and unit-holders have a duty 'to not be wholly unreasonable' (rule 41): it is difficult to conceive of a less onerous duty, or of a more open invitation to troublesome members to be only partly unreasonable.

(b) That tenants of unit-holders may be entitled to seek to enforce duties imposed upon other unit-holders or upon the commonhold association (rule 42).

(c) That unit-holders may only enforce commonhold duties against other unit-holders by going through the commonhold association (rule 42).

(d) That litigation may not be commenced by a unit-holder until after any dispute has been referred to an ombudsman, save in cases of emergency (rule 45).

These rules and the procedures they involve are discussed in Chapter 6 in greater detail.

2.17.21 Part III: the rules—(k) termination

A commonhold community statement is able to specify the provisions that are to be contained in the termination statement that must be approved in the event that the commonhold association is wound-up. This is not compulsory.

The current draft of the commonhold community statement (ie that appended to the Post-Consultation Report dated August 2003) proposes only that a termination statement must provide that where the commonhold association is entitled to become registered as the proprietor of the freehold estate in each commonhold unit following a termination application, a unit-holder may continue to occupy his commonhold unit until the commonhold association disposes of the commonhold land (see rule 53).

The contents of a termination statement are considered in Chapter 5.

2.17.22 Part III: the rules—(l) amendment of the commonhold community statement

The rules governing amendment of a commonhold community statement are examined in detail in Section 2.18 below.

2.17.23 Part III: the rules—(m) notices

The draft prescribed form contains a provision that:

> Any notice to be given to or by any person pursuant to these Rules shall be in writing. The commonhold association may give any notice to a unit-holder either personally or by sending it by first class post in a prepaid envelope addressed to the unit-holder at his commonhold unit or by leaving it at that address. Proof that an envelope containing a notice was properly addressed, prepaid and posted by first class post shall be conclusive evidence that the notice was given. A notice sent by first class post shall be deemed to be given at the expiration of 48 hours after the envelope containing it was posted.

The Consultation Paper proposed that this should be an optional provision. It is sensible for the statement to provide for a presumption of service from the posting of the document, because otherwise proof would need to be adduced that the document had in fact been received. However, the use of the word 'conclusive' indicates that proof of postage will here raise an irrebuttable presumption that service has been effected. The provision should be qualified to the effect either that the presumption is rebuttable or that the presumption only arises in the event that the letter is not returned undelivered.

2.17.24 Part III: the rules—(n) miscellaneous rules

As originally drafted, the draft prescribed form contained a number of other provisions regulating behaviour in a commonhold. Although it was proposed that all these rules should be optional, their very presence in the draft form invited their inclusion as a matter of prudence quite apart from anything else. In line, however, with the thinking of the Department of Constitutional Affairs that members should be free to regulate their own affairs without such intrusive drafting, the current draft is far less prescriptive, and omits many of the less important proposed rules. Some commonhold associations may nevertheless wish to include all or some of the rules originally proposed, and for the sake of completeness they are set out below.

(i) *Access*
The original draft provided:

No unit-holder or his invitees shall do any thing or leave or permit to be left any goods, rubbish or other object which obstructs or hinders lawful access to any part of the Commonhold.

(ii) *Aerials and satellite dishes*
The original draft provided:

No unit-holder or his invitees shall erect or permit to project outside his Commonhold Unit or into the Common Parts any radio or television aerial or satellite dish.

If this provision is to be included, then it should probably be combined with a corresponding obligation on the commonhold association to provide and maintain an appropriate communal radio and television aerial or satellite dish for the benefit of the unit-holders.

(iii) *Nuisance and annoyance*
The original draft provided:

A unit-holder must not, and must take reasonable steps to ensure that his invitees do not, behave in a way or create any sound or noise which causes or is likely to cause any annoyance, nuisance, injury or disturbance to other unit-holders, or to any other person lawfully on the commonhold, or to the occupiers of adjoining buildings or premises.

A nuisance has been defined as 'an inconvenience materially interfering with the ordinary comfort physically of human existence, not merely according to dainty modes and habits of living, but according to plain and sober and simple notions among the English people'.[200] An annoyance is a wider concept: it is 'a thing which reasonably troubles the mind and pleasure, not of a fanciful person or a skilled person who knows the truth, but of the ordinary sensible English inhabitant of a house—anything which disturbs his reasonable peace of mind . . . [is] an annoyance, although it may not appear to amount to physical detriment to comfort'.[201]

200 *Walter v Selfe* (1851) 4 De G & Sm 315.

201 *Tod-Heatly v Benham* (1888) 40 ChD.

(iv) *Cleaning of common parts, exterior and windows*
The original draft required the commonhold association to carry out regular cleaning of the common parts and the exterior, including the windows.

(v) *Cleaning of units*
The original draft imposed a duty on the unit-holder to clean the interior of the unit regularly. A more sensible alternative proposal would be to require the unit-holder to clean the interior of his unit in the event that a failure would materially impinge on the other unit-holders' enjoyment of their own units.

(vi) *Drainage and water pipes*
The draft prescribed form originally contained a provision that:

> Every unit-holder shall take adequate steps to prevent the leakage of pipes or escape of water from his commonhold unit, including lagging all pipes and tanks against freezing.

(vii) *Hanging of clothes*
The draft prescribed form originally contained a provision that:

> Save in the areas specifically made available for the same by the commonhold association, no unit-holder or his invitees may hang or expose any clothes or other articles outside his commonhold unit or in the common parts.

(viii) *Hazardous materials*
The draft prescribed form originally contained a provision that:

> A unit-holder or his invitees may not, without the written consent of the Board of Directors, bring onto the commonhold or store in any part thereof, any flammable, hazardous or noxious substance. This does not apply to the storage of fuel in the fuel tank of a vehicle or in a small reserve tank for use in connection with the vehicle.

(ix) *Mechanical, scientific or electrical items*
The draft prescribed form originally contained a provision that:

> Except with the written consent of the Board of Directors, no unit-holder of a residential unit or his invitees shall have or install in his commonhold unit any mechanical, scientific or electrical apparatus other than ordinary domestic appliances.

The justification for including such a rule is unclear.

(x) *Pets*
The draft prescribed form originally contained a provision that:

> No animals may be kept or brought onto the commonhold without the written consent of the Board of Directors.

It should be noted that a provision in this form would prohibit the ownership of a guide dog or a hearing dog.

(xi) *Signs*
The draft prescribed form originally contained a provision that:

No unit-holder or his invitees shall post or permit to be posted any notice or sign in the common parts, except upon any noticeboard or other facility provided for the same by the commonhold association.

The Consultation Paper rightly pointed out that in its current form this provision would prohibit the display of a for sale sign outside the unit.[202]

(xii) *Smoke detectors*
The draft prescribed form originally contained a provision that:

Each unit-holder shall install in his commonhold unit and maintain in working order a smoke detector or smoke detection system of a type specified by the Board of Directors and complying with any applicable health and safety or building regulations. The commonhold association shall install in the common parts and maintain in working order a smoke detector or smoke detection system of a type complying with any applicable health and safety or building regulations.

(xiii) *Window boxes*
The draft prescribed form originally contained a provision that:

No flower pot or other like object shall be placed outside the commonhold units or in the common parts except where provided by or with the written consent of the commonhold association.

2.18 AMENDMENT OF A COMMONHOLD COMMUNITY STATEMENT

2.18.1 General

The Act provides that regulations shall require a commonhold community statement to make provision about how it can be amended.[203] The proposals as to how this can be achieved have now evolved.

2.18.2 The original proposals for amendment

The Consultation Paper issued by the Lord Chancellor's Department in October 2002 proposed that a resolution of the commonhold association should be required for any amendment of the commonhold community statement, and it canvassed three different options:[204]

[202] Paragraph 176. [203] Section 33(1). [204] Paragraph 200.

(a) An amendment should only ever be allowed with a unanimous resolution of the commonhold association. The Paper described this option as 'somewhat over prescriptive'.

(b) Some amendments should only be allowed by a unanimous resolution of the commonhold association; others should be allowed after a special resolution.

(c) Some amendments should require a unanimous resolution; some should require a special resolution; and some should require only an ordinary resolution by the directors.

It was further proposed that the amendments should be readily identifiable from the face of the document, and that the document should contain a note of how many times it has been amended (the proposal was that it should bear a 'version number').[205]

2.18.3 The August 2003 proposals

The current draft (ie that appended to the Post-Consultation Report dated August 2003) sets out the following guide to amendment:

(a) The *mandatory* rules (ie the unchanging core of the commonhold community statement) cannot be changed, even by unanimous vote of all the members (rule 54).

(b) The *non-mandatory* rules may be changed with sufficient majority votes in accordance with the articles of association, with the size of the majority depending on the subject matter of the rule (rule 54). Thus:

- (i) a *unanimous* resolution is necessary to change the allocation of votes given to a commonhold unit (rule 55);
- (ii) a *special* resolution is necessary to—
  - (1) make a provision in place of a default provision;
  - (2) with the consent of the unit-holder, change the permitted use of a commonhold unit;
  - (3) change the percentage of the commonhold assessment or reserve fund levies allocated to a commonhold unit; and
  - (4) change the restrictions on the limited use areas (rule 56);
- (iii) an *ordinary* resolution is necessary to:
  - (1) subject to rule 56(a), add, delete or amend any rule contained in the default or optional provisions of this commonhold community statement;
  - (2) with the consent of the unit-holder and/or registered proprietor of any charge, change the size of a commonhold unit or the common parts;

[205] Paragraph 201.

(3) alter the common parts; and

(4) with the consent of the developer, amend the development rights (rule 57).

(c) There are additional rules regarding registration (see paragraph 2.18.5 below).

2.18.4 Recording the amendments

Part 1 of the current (August 2003) draft of the commonhold community statement makes provision for the amendments to the commonhold community statement to be recorded in a table, for which space is provided. In addition to this, the authors suggest that it would be useful to have a separate master table giving details of all amendments made both to the commonhold community statement and to the memorandum and articles of association. A suggested form for such a record is Form 2.8 in the Forms and Precedents part of this book.

2.18.5 Registration of the amended commonhold community statement

An amendment to the commonhold community statement has no effect until it is registered with the Land Registry.[206] This stipulation is repeated in the form of rule 58. It will therefore be essential to apply to the Land Registry to register the amended commonhold community statement. The requirements regarding such an application are set out in section 33 of the Act and in the commonhold community statement itself (which rather unsatisfactorily repeats some but not all of section 33).

The application is made by the commonhold association on Land Registry Form CM3 (see Form 1.3 in the Forms and Precedents part of this book). Such an application must be accompanied by:

(a) the original and a certified copy of the amended commonhold community statement;

(b) a certificate given by the directors of the commonhold association that (i) the rules on amendment of the commonhold community statement have been complied with (see rule 59) and (ii) the amended commonhold community statement satisfies the requirements of Part I of the Act (see section 33(5)) (see Form 2.5 in the Forms and Precedents part of this work);

(c) (where the amendment of the commonhold community statement changes the size of a commonhold unit or the common parts), the consent of the unit-holder or registered proprietor of any charge (or orders of the court dispensing with consents) (section 33(6) and (7), and rule 59).

The Registrar will keep the certified copy, return the original, and will alter the register to refer to the new statement.[207]

[206] Section 33(3). [207] Section 33(4).

2.18.6 Alterations to the extent of units

Further rules apply if the alterations to the commonhold community statement involve a change in the extent of a unit. There can obviously be no alteration to the extent of a unit without the consent of the unit-holder. The consent must be made in writing, and it must be given before the amendment is made.[208] Form 1.15 in the Forms and Precedents part of this work provides a suggested precedent for such a consent. Regulations may be made which enable a court to dispense with this requirement for consent, on the application of the commonhold association in prescribed circumstances. No regulations have yet been made, and it is not clear what circumstances are envisaged.

If the unit that is to be altered is subject to a registered charge, then the consent of the registered proprietor of the charge must also be secured.[209] The consent must again be made in writing and be given before the amendment is made.[210] Form 1.15 in the Forms and Precedents part of this work provides a suggested precedent for such a consent.

This requirement applies even if the extent of the unit is to be increased and not diminished. Regulations may again be made enabling the court to dispense with this requirement for consent on the application of the commonhold association in prescribed circumstances.[211] No regulations have yet been made. The effect of an alteration in the extent of land subject to a registered charge is that: (1) if land is removed from the unit, the charge is extinguished to the extent that it relates to the removed land,[212] and (2) if land is added, the charge is extended to relate to the land which is added.[213] This latter provision may result in an under-secured lender becoming fully secured, if the increase in the extent of the unit sufficiently increases its value. Regulations may also be made requiring notice to be given to the Registrar in the circumstances of a change in the extent of a charged unit, and requiring the Registrar to alter the register to reflect the extent of the land to which the charge relates. These provisions do not apply if the charge is unregistered.

2.18.7 Unit-holder's powers to compel alterations to the commonhold community statement

A unit-holder cannot ordinarily compel alterations to the commonhold community statement without securing an appropriate resolution of the commonhold association.

However, a unit-holder who considers that the statement does not comply with the regulations may apply to the court for a declaration to this effect.[214] The application must be made within the period of three months beginning with the date on which he became a unit-holder, within three months of the alleged failure to comply, or outside these periods with the permission of the court. If a declaration

[208] Section 23(1). [209] Section 24(2). [210] Section 24(2)(a), (b).
[211] Section 24(3). [212] Section 24(4). [213] Section 24(5). [214] Section 40(1)(b).

is granted, the court can make any other consequential order that it thinks fit.[215] A non-exhaustive list of the available remedies is as follows:

(a) An order requiring a director or other specified officer of the commonhold association to take steps to alter or amend a document.

(b) An order requiring a director or other specified officer to take other specified steps.

(c) An award of compensation (whether or not contingent upon the occurrence or non-occurrence of a specified event) to be paid by the commonhold association to a specified person.

(d) An order providing for the land to cease to be commonhold land. It is not thought that it will often, if ever, be appropriate for the court to order that the land shall cease to be commonhold land.

PART 6: APPLICATION FOR REGISTRATION

2.19 GENERAL

2.19.1 Introduction

This part of this chapter considers the procedure for registering land as commonhold. There are special considerations that relate to the conversion of an existing leasehold development to commonhold. These special considerations are discussed in Part 7.

2.19.2 Application form

The application for registration of a freehold estate as a freehold estate in commonhold land is made to the Land Registry under section 2 of the Act.[216] The application must[217] be made on Form CM1 in Schedule 1 to the Commonhold (Land Registration) Rules 2003. A copy of the form is reproduced as Form 1.1 in the Forms and Precedents part of this work. Part 8 of the form requires up to three addresses for service to be given, one of which must be a postal address. The Land Registry Consultation Paper has indicated that if this part of the form is not correctly completed, then the application will be rejected.[218] Part 13 of the form requires the applicant to certify whether section 9 of the Act applies to the application; in the case of a new development, where the units have not yet been sold, this certification does not need to be completed.

[215] Section 40(2).

[216] The application is made to the Registrar, who is defined in section 67(1) as the Chief Land Registrar.

[217] Rule 5(1) of the draft Commonhold (Land Registration) Rules 2003.

[218] Paragraph 49.

2.19.3 Supporting documents

The application must enclose the following documents:

(a) Documents relating to consents: the consent forms or any orders of the court dispensing with the requirement for consent (combined with any evidence needed to show that a conditional order has been complied with, and any evidence of deemed consent; this evidence should be provided by way of a statutory declaration).[219]

(b) Documents relating to the commonhold association: the memorandum of association and the articles of association of the commonhold association;[220] the certificate of incorporation supplied by the Registrar of Companies under section 13 of the Companies Act 1985, together with any altered certificate of incorporation issued under section 28 of that Act.[221] The original documents must be provided. In addition to these originals, a certified copy of the memorandum and articles of association must also be provided.[222] The certified copy will be retained and the originals returned to the applicant.[223]

(c) The commonhold community statement.[224] The original document must be provided. In addition to the original, a certified copy must also be provided.[225] The certified copy must contain a copy of the plan, which must not have been reduced in size, and which must be copied in colour in order to comply with all the same requirements as the original plan. The Land Registry has indicated that, if the copy of the plan does not comply with these requirements, then the application will be rejected.[226] The certified copy will be retained and the originals returned to the applicant.

(d) A certificate[227] given by the directors of the commonhold association that:

- (i) the memorandum and articles of association submitted with the application are in the prescribed form and contain the prescribed content;
- (ii) the commonhold community statement complies with the Act and the Regulations;
- (iii) the land to which the application relates is not land which cannot be commonhold land under the Act;
- (iv) the commonhold association has not traded; and

[219] Section 2(2); Schedule 1, paragraph 6.
[220] Section 2(2); Schedule 1, paragraphs 2, 3 and 4.
[221] Schedule 1, paragraphs 2, 3.
[222] Rule 5(2), draft Commonhold (Land Registration) Rules 2003.
[223] Paragraph 60, Land Registry Consultation Paper.
[224] Section 2(2); Schedule 1, paragraph 5.
[225] Rule 5(2), draft Commonhold (Land Registration) Rules 2003.
[226] Under the powers in Rule 6 of the draft Commonhold (Land Registration) Rules 2003. See paragraph 62 of the Land Registry Consultation Paper.
[227] Form 2.4 in the Forms and Precedents section contains a precedent for the certificate.

(v) the commonhold association has not incurred any liability which has not been discharged.[228]

The form and content of these various documents is considered in the preceding parts of this chapter.

2.19.4 Completion of registration

If the Registrar is satisfied as to the application, then he will complete it by:[229]

(a) entering the applicant as the proprietor of the title to each of the units;

(b) entering the applicant as the proprietor of the title to the common parts;

(c) entering notice in the property register of the register of title to the common parts of the memorandum and articles of association of the commonhold association and the commonhold community statement.

It is the Land Registry's intention to create separate titles for the common parts and for each of the individual units.[230] The commonhold community statement and the memorandum and articles of association will be referred to in the property register for the title to the common parts.[231]

On completion of the application, the applicant will receive official copies of each unit title and an equivalent number of copies of the common parts title. These can then be used by the applicant to pass on to prospective purchasers. Further official copies of the common parts title will be supplied by the Land Registry upon completion of an application in Form OC1 (see Form 1.9 in the Forms and Precedents part of this work).

2.19.5 Multiple site commonholds

It is the Land Registry's intention to make regulations in relation to multiple site commonholds. The regulations will require that the ownership of all of the sites be vested jointly in the same owners under the same title.[232] This means that, for example, if there are two sites, each owned by a different developer, and the aim is to develop the two sites together as a single commonhold, then the two titles must be amalgamated into a single title in order to make the commonhold application.

[228] Section 2(2); Schedule 1, paragraph 7.

[229] Rule 7, draft Commonhold (Land Registration) Rules 2003.

[230] Paragraphs 42–43, Land Registry Consultation Paper: 'This will mean that when purchasers come to deal with individual units those transactions will be based on the whole of a registered title. They should be less expensive for purchasers and easier to effect than if the purchase of each unit involved dealing with part of a larger title.'

[231] Paragraph 60, Land Registry Consultation Paper.

[232] Paragraph 68, Land Registry Consultation Paper.

2.19.6 Unregistered land

The only person who can apply to register land as a freehold estate in commonhold land is the registered freeholder. The Act defines the registered freehold owner as including any person who has applied to be registered as the freehold proprietor, provided that the Registrar is satisfied that he is entitled to be so registered.[233] It is thought that the intention was to allow for simultaneous applications for the first registration of unregistered land and the registration of the land as commonhold. However, the present draft Commonhold (Land Registration) Rules 2003 do not prescribe a procedure for achieving this, and it is therefore likely that consecutive applications will need to be made for the first registration of title and then for the registration of the land as commonhold. The procedure for first registration of title is outside the scope of this work, and reference should be had to specialist texts.

2.19.7 Cancellation

During the transitional period (which is the period between the registration of the land as commonhold and the date on which the first unit-holder becomes entitled to be registered as the proprietor of a unit[234]) the registered owner of the commonhold can apply for the registration to be cancelled. The land will then revert to ordinary registered freehold ownership.[235] The application must be made on Land Registry Form CM2. An application to cancel the registration as commonhold must be supported by consents from the same persons as were required to consent to the original application for registration.[236]

PART 7 DEVELOPMENT RIGHTS

2.20 GENERAL

2.20.1 Introduction

The developer of a commonhold development is obviously free to develop the land as he chooses both before it is registered as a commonhold and during the transitional period (before any of the units has been sold).

However, once he has sold or transferred the first of the units, the transitional period comes to an end, the common parts vest in the commonhold association, and the unit-holder acquires rights in relation to the use and management of the development. The association's ownership of the common parts and the rights of

[233] Section 2(3)(b).
[234] Sections 8(1), 7(3).
[235] Rule 12, draft Commonhold (Land Registration) Rules 2003.
[236] Section 8(5).

the unit-holders could potentially be used to interfere with the completion of the development, which suggests that the developer wishing to avoid interference should wait until the completion of the development before selling the first unit. However, it would be undesirable for a developer to be forced to complete the entire development before selling any of the units. The Act therefore permits a commonhold community statement to confer rights on the developer ('development rights') which are designed to enable him to complete his 'development business' without interference from the initial purchasers of the units.

2.20.2 The nature of 'development rights'

Section 58(3) of the Act specifies that the development rights may include the following:

(a) An obligation on the commonhold association or the unit-holders to co-operate with the developer for specified purposes that are connected with development business.

(b) A provision restricting the developer's right to compel co-operation except on specified terms and conditions.

(c) A provision specifying the consequences of a breach of either of these provisions.

(d) A provision disapplying the Act's requirement for the commonhold association to pass a unanimous resolution approving the addition of land to the commonhold before an application can be made to the Land Registry for the land to be added.

2.20.3 The nature of 'development business'

Development business is defined in Schedule 4 to the Act as:

(a) the completion or execution of works on a commonhold, on land which is or may be added to a commonhold, or on land which has been removed from a commonhold;

(b) transactions in commonhold units;

(c) advertising and other activities designed to promote transactions in commonhold units;

(d) the addition of land to a commonhold;

(e) the removal of land from a commonhold;

(f) the amendment of a commonhold community statement (including amendment to redefine the extent of a commonhold unit); and

(g) the appointment and removal of directors of a commonhold association.

2.20.4 Machinery in the commonhold community statement

The original (October 2002) draft of the commonhold community statement contained a number of optional provisions regarding development rights. The current (August 2003) version of the statement provides for development rights to be set out in Annex B. Otherwise, apart from defining the terms 'development rights' and 'development business' in the glossary in Annex A consistently with the definitions in the Act, it contains no machinery regarding the exercise of such rights.

However, the Department of Constitutional Affairs has drafted the following regulation 18, which is designed to deal with development rights in the commonhold community statement:

(1) Where a commonhold community statement confers development rights on the developer in accordance with section 58 it will be treated as including the following provisions unless a provision is made in place of it—

- (a) the commonhold community statement must not be amended without the consent of the developer, in so far as the proposed amendment relates to development rights;
- (b) section 41(3) does not apply where an application to add land to the commonhold is being made by the developer;
- (c) subject to paragraph (6), the commonhold association must co-operate with the developer for the purposes of amending the commonhold community statement in the event that land is added to or removed from the commonhold or the extent of a commonhold unit is redefined;
- (d) in the event of a breach of the requirement in sub-paragraph (c) a resolution of the commonhold association to amend the commonhold community statement will be deemed to have been passed; and
- (e) the developer has rights of access to the commonhold units and common parts in order to facilitate his undertaking of development business.

(2) The rights conferred on the developer in a commonhold community statement are restricted or regulated in accordance with the following paragraphs.

(3) The developer must not unreasonably interfere with a unit-holder's quiet or peaceful enjoyment of the freehold interest in a commonhold unit.

(4) The developer must not reserve the right to remove parts of the common parts from the commonhold.

(5) The developer may not remove land from the commonhold that has been transferred to a unit-holder.

(6) The developer may not add land to the commonhold unless he reserved the right to add that land to the commonhold in the commonhold community statement.

(7) The developer must specify any major works in the commonhold community statement but this will not prevent unspecified major works being undertaken in an emergency.

(8) The developer must specify in the commonhold community statement the date on which the common parts will be completed and where major works on the common parts is specified in the commonhold community statement the developer must specify the date on which this will be completed.

(9) If in the commonhold community statement the developer reserves the right to use services available to the commonhold including, but not limited to, water, sewerage, drainage, gas, electricity, oil, rubbish disposal, air conditioning and telephone, or to install additional services, that right is subject to the developer making payment for the use of such services.

(10) The standard of materials, finishes and landscaping, and the height and density of buildings on land which is to be added to the commonhold must not be inferior to, or substantially different from those of the completed buildings in the commonhold development, except to the extent set out in the development rights in the commonhold community statement (if any).

(11) The developer, in his capacity as such, must not use any part of the commonhold except to the extent necessary to carry out the permitted development or as specified in the development rights.

(12) Any damage to the common parts or a commonhold unit caused by the developer in the course of undertaking development business must—

(a) be put right by the developer; or

(b) the reasonable costs to put right the damage must be paid by the developer

as soon as reasonably practicable.

(13) The developer must minimise the disruption to other occupants of the commonhold.

(14) The development rights expire five years from the date on which the first commonhold unit is transferred except that—

(a) where work has been commenced during the five year period it may be completed notwithstanding that the five year period has expired; and

(b) the developer may reserve the right to continue marketing the development until the last commonhold unit is sold.

(15) In this regulation 'major works' includes, but is not limited to, the construction of a new building, road or sewer or the demolition of, or structural changes to, an existing building, road or sewer.

Accordingly, where the commonhold community statement contains any development rights in the first place, the rights set out above will be the default provisions unless other arrangements are made.

2.20.5 Surrender of development rights

The development rights which are conferred by the commonhold community statement will often expire automatically, if they have been expressed in the commonhold community statement to subsist only for a specified period of time.

However, section 58(6) of the Act also allows a development right to be expressly surrendered, and provides for notice of the surrender to be referred to in the register. The purpose of these provisions is, presumably, in order for a developer to be able to make it clear to any prospective purchaser what development rights do or do not continue to subsist at the date of the search. The application to surrender is made to the Registrar on Form AP1, which is the prescribed form for general applications to the Land Registry (see Form 1.6 in the Forms and Precedents part of this work). In Form AP1, it is likely to be sufficient simply to complete paragraphs 1 to 6 and 12. Paragraph 6 should state that Form SR1 is lodged with the application.

The application to surrender development rights must be accompanied by Form SR1, which is the notice of the surrender of the development rights (see Form 1.7 in the Forms and Precedents part of this work).[237] Form SR1 must state which of the development rights are being surrendered. The Form enables the developer to specify either that all the development rights contained in the commonhold community statement are to be surrendered, or that there is to be a surrender of only some of these rights. The Form must be signed by the developer. It also requires the signature of what is described as any 'lender (if applicable)'. This does not follow from any requirement that is contained in section 58(6) of the Act, or in the draft Commonhold (Land Registration) Rules 2003. It cannot mean, though, that the signature of every unsecured lender is required in order to register the surrender of development rights; equally, it is not thought that the Land Registry will require the consent of every lender who has a registered charge over any part of the commonhold, because this would then require consent to be obtained from all the secured lenders of all the unit-holders. It is thought, therefore, that the Land Registry envisages requiring only the signature of any lender who has a registered charge over the interest that is owned by the developer. The original Form SR1, together with a certified copy, should be lodged at the Land Registry.

On receipt of the application, the Registrar will enter the terms of the notice in the property register for the common parts.[238] The development rights cease to be exercisable from the time when the notice is registered.[239] The Registrar will give notice of the surrender to the commonhold association.

[237] The requirement to enclose Form AP1 with the notice of surrender on Form SR1 does not derive from the Commonhold (Land Registration) Rules 2003 themselves, but it appears likely that this is the procedure which must be followed: see the Land Registry Commonhold Consultation Paper, paragraph 26.

[238] Section 58(6)(a); Commonhold (Land Registration) Rules 2003, rule 28(2).

[239] Section 58(6)(b).

PART 8 CONVERSION OF EXISTING DEVELOPMENTS

2.21 GENERAL

2.21.1 Introduction

The long lessees of an existing development cannot convert to commonhold without first acquiring the freehold title (or persuading the freehold owner to apply for the conversion). This is because the only person who can apply for land to be registered as commonhold is the freehold owner.[240] The long lessees must first therefore purchase the freehold, either by private treaty with the landlord or under their rights to enfranchise. The procedure for collective enfranchisement is outside the scope of this work, and reference should be had to specialist texts.

The main difficulty in converting an existing long leasehold development into a commonhold is that all the lessees who hold under a lease granted for a term of more than 21 years must consent to the conversion.[241] There is power for regulations to be made which enable the court to dispense with consent.[242] However, it is not intended that regulations will be made which allow for the court to dispense with a consent that is being unreasonably withheld. The result is that, if there is a single long lessee who is not prepared to consent to the conversion, for whatever reason, then the conversion cannot proceed. This was perceived by many, during the passage of the Bill, as one of the weakest elements of the legislation. In practice, this may well mean that very few existing leasehold developments will be converted to commonhold, at least until the benefits of commonhold have been fully realised.

2.21.2 Procedure

The lessees are likely to have acquired the freehold through an RTE (Right to Enfranchise) company.[243] The company must then make an application for registration of the freehold title as a freehold estate in commonhold land. This application is made in the same way as an ordinary application for registration as commonhold, and must be supported by all the same documents.

The main difference is that the application must be accompanied by a statement from the applicant that section 9 of the Act is to apply. This is, in effect, simply a statement that the individual ownership of the units is to be registered at the same time as the conversion of the freehold estate to commonhold. In practice, the statement has been incorporated into the Land Registry Form: paragraph 13 of Form CM1 contains an appropriate certification, which must be ticked and signed by the applicant.

[240] Section 2(1)(a). [241] Section 3(1)(b). [242] Section 3(2)(f).
[243] Under the Leasehold Reform, Housing and Urban Development Act 1993.

The application must be accompanied by a list of the commonhold units, giving in relation to each one of them the prescribed details of the proposed initial unit-holder or joint unit-holders.[244] There is no space on the form for these details to be included, so they should be appended in a separate document. Regulations are to prescribe the details that are to be required, and it is not yet known what is envisaged.

The Land Registry Consultation Paper further comments that 'Where there is an application for conversion, a lessee, or anyone else involved in the conversion process, will wish to obtain an official search with priority. Rule 3(3)(f) [of the Commonhold (Land Registration) Rules 2003] therefore amends the draft Land Registration Rules 2003 in their application to commonholds to enable this to happen.'[245]

2.21.3 Mortgages

It is likely in practice that many of the long leases will be subject to a mortgage. The effect of the conversion is to extinguish the lease, and therefore to extinguish the lender's security. The long lessee will almost certainly become the freehold owner of a unit in the building, which will provide the lender with an equivalent or better security. However, there is no provision in the Act or elsewhere by which the mortgage is automatically transferred to the freehold estate in the unit which was previously let on the mortgaged long lease. The consent of the registered proprietor of a charge is required in order for the conversion to commonhold to take place, and it is thought likely that lenders will simply withhold consent unless the borrower agrees to execute a charge over the freehold estate in the unit that will be created upon the conversion. Mortgages and charges over unregistered long leases will be extinguished, not by any express provision of the Act, but as a consequence of the extinguishment of the security. The mortgagee or chargee will be required, unless the borrower agrees to grant a new charge over the freehold unit, to obtain a judgment for the loan and then to obtain a charging order over the unit under the Charging Orders Act 1979.

PART 9 EFFECTS OF REGISTRATION

2.22 GENERAL

2.22.1 Introduction

The effects of registration vary depending on whether the application was made in relation to a new development or in relation to an existing development where the unit-holders are to be registered at the same time as the commonhold registration.

[244] Section 9(2). [245] Paragraph 18.

2.22.2 New developments

The effects of registration of a new development take place in two distinct stages.

The first stage is the transitional period, which is the period between registration of the land as commonhold and the date on which the first unit is sold (the date on which 'a person other than the applicant becomes entitled to be registered as the proprietor of the freehold estate in one or more, but not all, of the commonhold units'). The transitional period is not brought to an end by the sale or transfer of all the units, only by the sale or transfer of fewer than all. This is to enable a developer to sell or transfer the whole of the development before it has been completed, without triggering the end of the transitional period. The transitional period is brought to an end when the contract for the sale of the first unit or units is completed; it does not continue until the date of registration of the purchaser as the registered proprietor of the unit.[246] However, a mere exchange of contracts for the sale of a unit will not trigger the end of the transitional period, because this does not confer an entitlement on the purchaser to be registered as the owner of the unit.

The second stage is the period that begins after the end of the transitional period.

2.22.3 Transitional period

The immediate effects of registration are minimal, and are as follows:

(a) The applicant for registration is registered as the proprietor of the freehold estate in the commonhold land.[247] He remains the sole freehold owner of all of the land, and no part of it vests in the commonhold association.

(b) The rights and obligations set out in the commonhold community statement do not come into force.[248] The Act provides that regulations may be made which provide for some provisions of the statement to come into force with specified modifications,[249] but the Consultation Paper does not indicate that any regulations are contemplated under this provision.

(c) Any leases of any parts of the land continue in force and are not extinguished.[250]

(d) The owner retains the right to apply for the commonhold registration to be cancelled.[251]

(e) The owner is able to exercise any of the special rights in relation to the commonhold association that have been granted to him by the terms of the articles of

[246] It comes to an end when a person other than the applicant 'becomes entitled to be registered' as the owner of one of the units, not when the registration itself takes place.

[247] Section 9(2)(a).

[248] Section 7(2)(b).

[249] Section 8(2)(b).

[250] Section 7(3)(d).

[251] Section 8(4).

association, and that are restricted to the transitional period (such as, for example, the right to appoint and remove up to two directors of the company[252]).

(f) Regulations may provide that any provisions of the Act, of regulations made under the Act, of the commonhold community statement or the memorandum and articles of association of the commonhold association shall either not have effect or shall have effect but with specified modifications during the transitional period.[253] There are no regulations yet contemplated under this provision.

2.22.4 After the end of the transitional period

The effects of registration once the transitional period comes to an end are more extensive, and are as follows.

(a) The commonhold association becomes entitled to be registered as the proprietor of the freehold estate in the common parts.[254] The commonhold association is then registered automatically by the Registrar, without the need for any further application.[255] This does not usually mean, however, that the developer can then carry out no further development works to the common parts; the commonhold community statement will usually have reserved the right to continue to carry out works to the development for a specified period. The developer will therefore not usually be obliged to wait until the completion of the development before selling off any of the units.

(b) The rights and obligations set out in the commonhold community statement immediately come into force.[256]

(c) The developer's right to cancel the registration of the land as commonhold is extinguished.

(d) Any lease of the whole or part of the commonhold land is extinguished.[257]

2.22.5 Existing developments

An application for registration of an existing development will usually have been accompanied by a statement requesting that section 9 of the Act applies, and the ownership will be registered at the same time as the registration of the freehold as a freehold estate in commonhold land. The result is that there is obviously no transitional period. The immediate effects of registration are as follows:

(a) The commonhold association shall be entitled to be registered as the proprietor of the freehold estate in the common parts.[258] The association will then automatically be registered as the freehold owner of the common parts, without any need for a further application to the Registrar.[259]

252 Articles 44 to 52.
253 Section 8(2), (3).
254 Section 7(1)(3)(a).
255 Section 7(1)(3)(d).
256 Section 7(1)(c).
257 Section 7(3)(d).
258 Section 9(3)(a).
259 Section 9(3)(d).

(b) The person specified in the application as the proposed initial unit-holder (or joint unit-holders) shall be entitled to be registered as the proprietor of the freehold estate in the unit.[260] Again, the proposed unit-holder will then automatically be registered as the proprietor of the freehold estate in the unit, without any need for a further application.[261]

(c) The rights and duties conferred and imposed by the commonhold community statement immediately come into force.[262]

(d) Any lease of the whole or part of the commonhold land is extinguished.[263]

Extinguishment of leases is considered in Section 2.23 below.

2.23 EXTINGUISHMENT OF LEASES

2.23.1 Introduction

The most significant feature of the conversion of land to commonhold is that any lease of the whole or part of the land is extinguished. This occurs at the end of the transitional period, if the land is a new development; and it occurs immediately on registration, in the case of an existing development. The extinguishment applies to all leases, not simply to those long leases in relation to which the lessee's consent was required for the land to be converted to commonhold.[264] The conversion of land to commonhold can therefore result in the extinguishment of a lease, against the lessee's will, and yet without his consent having ever been sought for the conversion. The Act provides for compensation for lessees whose consent was not required, but whose leases have been extinguished.

2.23.2 Date of extinguishments

In the case of a new development, the leases are extinguished at the end of the transitional period. In the case of the conversion of an existing development, where there has been a request for section 9 to apply, the leases are extinguished 'on registration'.[265] This is the date on which the registration is completed, not the date on which the application is made.

2.23.3 Date of grant of lease

The Act does not extinguish leases that were granted after the commonhold association became entitled to be registered as the proprietor of the freehold estate in the common parts.[266] So a lease granted after the entitlement to be registered first

[260] Section 9(3)(b), (c).
[261] Section 9(3)(d).
[262] Section 9(3)(e).
[263] Section 7(3)(d).
[264] Section 3.
[265] Section 9(3).
[266] Sections 7(4)(b), 9(4)(b).

arises is not extinguished, even if this precedes the date on which the commonhold association is actually registered.

2.23.4 Length of term

The Act extinguishes leases regardless of the length of the term.[267] It therefore extinguishes the long leases in relation to which consent was required for the conversion, as well as the shorter leases in relation to which consent was not required.

2.23.5 Underleases

The Act extinguishes underleases as well as leases granted immediately out of the freehold estate. This is implicit in the compensation provisions, which state that 'If the holder of a lease superior to the extinguished lease gave consent under section 3, he shall be liable for the loss suffered by the holder of the extinguished lease.'[268]

2.23.6 Security of tenure

The Act is silent on how the extinguishment provisions will affect those tenants with statutory security of tenure. Three situations may be distinguished:

(a) Protected and statutory tenancies under the Rent Act 1977: these are considered in paragraph 2.23.7 below.

(b) Assured and assured shorthold tenancies under the Housing Act 1988: see paragraph 2.23.8 below.

(c) Business tenancies under Part II of the Landlord and Tenant Act 1954: see paragraph 2.23.9 below.

2.23.7 Protected and statutory tenancies under the Rent Act 1977

A statutory tenancy under the Rent Act 1977 will almost certainly not be extinguished by these provisions. The reason is that a statutory tenant does not have any estate or property in the land; he simply has a personal right to retain possession (which has been described as a 'status of irremovability'[269]).

By contrast, a protected tenancy under the 1977 Act (where the contractual periodic or fixed term is still continuing) will almost certainly be extinguished by the conversion to commonhold, because it is a lease and it is therefore within the extinguishment provisions. However, if a statutory tenancy arises on the extinction of the protected tenancy for the reason that the tenant is residing in the

[267] Sections 7(4)(a), 9(4)(a).

[268] Section 10(2).

[269] *Roe v Russell* [1928] 2 KB 117; *Keeves v Dean* [1924] 1 KB 685.

dwelling house,[270] the tenant will still be entitled to remain by virtue of his new personal status of irremovability.

2.23.8 Assured and assured shorthold tenancies under the Housing Act 1988

There is no obvious reason why an assured or assured shorthold tenancy should not be extinguished by the conversion to commonhold: it is a lease, and the Act extinguishes 'any lease' of the land.[271]

However, section 5(2) of the Housing Act 1988 provides that:

> If an assured tenancy which is a fixed term tenancy comes to an end otherwise than by virtue of an order of the court or a surrender or other action on the part of the tenant, then . . . the tenant shall be entitled to remain in possession of the dwelling-house let under that tenancy and . . . his right to possession shall depend upon a periodic tenancy arising by virtue of this section.

The statutory periodic tenancy arises 'immediately on the coming to an end of the fixed term tenancy'.[272] There is, again, no obvious reason why the statutory periodic tenancy, which is a lease and not simply a personal status of irremovability, will not also be extinguished by the conversion to commonhold. Section 5(1) of the Housing Act 1988, which provides that 'An assured tenancy cannot be brought to an end by the landlord except by obtaining an order of the court in accordance with the following provisions of this Chapter . . .' does not prevent the extinguishment, because this only prevents the landlord from bringing the tenancy to an end except by an order of the court. It does not prevent the lease from being brought to an end, for example, by a surrender without an order of the court; and it therefore probably does not prevent the lease from being extinguished by a conversion to commonhold. Section 5(1) must also have been impliedly repealed, to the extent that it conflicts with the later provisions of the 2002 Act.

There is an argument that the statutory tenancy under section 5(2) arises after the moment of extinguishment of the preceding contractual tenancy, in which case it would survive the conversion to commonhold. However, this conclusion would result in an unsatisfactory distinction between a contractual assured tenant, who would have a right to remain as a statutory tenant, and an occupier who is already a statutory tenant, whose lease would be extinguished and who would have no right to remain. The better view is therefore that all assured and assured shorthold tenancies, whether during or after the end of contractual term, will be extinguished by the 2002 Act. It is, however, one of the most obvious shortcomings of the 2002 Act that this difficult issue appears to have been entirely ignored.

[270] Section 2(1), Rent Act 1977: 'After the termination of a protected tenancy of a dwellinghouse the person who, immediately before that termination, was the protected tenant of the dwellinghouse shall, if and so long as he occupies the dwellinghouse as his residence, be the statutory tenant of it.'

[271] Sections 7(3)(d), 9(3)(d).

[272] Section 5(3)(a).

2.23.9 Business tenancies under Part II of the Landlord and Tenant Act 1954

There is no clear reason why business tenancies under Part II of the Landlord and Tenant Act 1954 should not be extinguished by a conversion to commonhold. Section 24 of the 1954 Act prevents a business tenancy from being brought to an end except in accordance with the provisions of that Act, but it is hard to see that this provision has not been impliedly repealed to the extent that it is in conflict with the extinguishment provisions of the 2002 Act.

2.23.10 Possession

The extinguishment of the lease confers on the freehold owner of the unit (either the developer or the unit-holder) an immediate right to possession of the property. There are no provisions in the Act requiring the ex-tenant to be given a period of notice before he is required to vacate the premises. It therefore appears that it is open to the freehold owner to commence proceedings for possession immediately.

2.23.11 Compensation

The Act grants a right to compensation to those tenants whose leases have been extinguished, but whose consent was not required for the application to convert to commonhold. Tenants from whom consent was required, and who gave their consent, are not entitled to any compensation.

The person liable to pay compensation is either the freeholder or the most proximate superior lessee from whom consent was required.[273] So if premises were let on a head lease for a term of 99 years, subject to an underlease for a term of 25 years, subject to a sub-underlease for a term of 5 years, subject to a sub-sub-underlease for a term of one year, then the sub-underlessee and the sub-sub-underlessee are each entitled to compensation from the underlessee. The sub-sub-underlessee must claim compensation from the underlessee and not from his immediate landlord, because his immediate landlord is not someone from whom consent was required for the conversion. They cannot claim compensation from the head lessee, even though this is someone from whom consent had been required for the conversion, because the head lessee is not the most proximate person from whom consent was required. A person can therefore be liable to pay compensation to more than one holder of an extinguished lease of the same unit. If there is no head lessee liable to pay compensation (because the head lease was for a term of less than 21 years) then the person liable to pay compensation is the owner of the freehold estate out of which the extinguished lease was granted.[274]

The Act entitles the holder of a relevant extinguished lease to compensation 'for loss suffered'.[275] The provisions are silent on how the loss is to be calculated.

[273] Section 10(2), (3). [274] Section 10(4). [275] Section 10(2), (4).

It is thought that the correct measure of compensation is simply the open market value of the lease that has been extinguished, which will need to be determined using valuation evidence. It is not thought that the holder of the extinguished lease will be entitled to any element of the value which is attributable to the marriage of the lease and the freehold, which will therefore accrue to the owner of the freehold. This is because the holder of the extinguished lease is only entitled to compensation for his 'loss'. The attainment of the marriage value is a benefit which accrues to the freeholder as a result of the extinguishment of the lease, but it is not thought to be a 'loss' which is suffered by the tenant when his lease is extinguished. The holder of the extinguished lease should, in addition, be entitled to his reasonable removal costs.

The Act does not provide for the right to compensation to be secured. A tenant whose lease has been extinguished will therefore have very limited rights against an insolvent developer.

2.23.12 Mortgages

The extinguishment of the leases extinguishes any security that a lender may have by way of a mortgage or charge over the lease. There are no provisions for the mortgagee to receive any compensation. However, the mortgagee's consent will have been required for the conversion to commonhold, provided that the charge was correctly registered. The mortgagee is likely therefore to have made it a condition of the grant of consent that he receive a new charge over the relevant commonhold unit or the common parts.

PART 10 AMENDMENTS TO A COMMONHOLD

2.24 ADDITION OR REMOVAL OF LAND TO AND FROM THE COMMONHOLD

2.24.1 Addition of land during the transitional period

There are no provisions in the Act or in the draft Commonhold (Land Registration) Rules that allow for the addition of land to the commonhold during the transitional period. However, during the transitional period the developer has the unilateral right to cancel the registration of the land as commonhold, and cause it to revert to an ordinary freehold title. The developer should therefore simply cancel the registration, draft a new commonhold community statement and apply for a new registration as commonhold which includes the land that is sought to be added.

2.24.2 Addition of land after the transitional period

A special procedure is prescribed for the addition of land to the commonhold once the commonhold association has already begun to exercise functions in relation to the land.[276] The procedure is as follows:

(a) The commonhold association must first pass a resolution approving the addition of the land to the commonhold.[277] The resolution must be unanimous[278] and it must be made before the application to add the land is made to the Land Registry.[279] However, the commonhold community statement may contain a provision that disapplies this rule, and entitles the developer to make an application to add land without requiring a resolution of the commonhold association.[280]

(b) An application must then be made to add the land to the commonhold. The application must be made on Land Registry Form CM4 (see Form 1.4 in the Forms and Precedents part of this book).[281] It must be accompanied by:

- (i) Consent forms[282] in relation to the land that is to be added (or any orders of the court dispensing with the requirement for consent, combined with any evidence needed to show that a conditional order has been complied with, and any evidence of deemed consent; this evidence should be provided by way of a statutory declaration).[283]
- (ii) A certificate from the directors of the commonhold association (1) that the land which is to be added is land that is not prohibited from being commonhold land, and (2) that a unanimous resolution of the commonhold association has been passed approving the addition of the land to the commonhold.

(c) The application must also be accompanied by an application to vary the commonhold community statement. This application must be made on Land Registry Form CM3 (see Form 1.3 in the Forms and Precedents part of this book).[284] The alterations to the commonhold community statement must obviously contain amended plans, and must indicate whether the additional land is to form a new unit or units, or part of the common parts.

(d) The Registrar will then amend the register accordingly. If the additional land is to form part of the common parts, then it will be registered in the name of the commonhold association;[285] If it is to form a new unit, then it will be registered in the name of the applicant. If it is to be added to an existing unit, then this can simply be reflected in the amendments to the commonhold community

[276] This occurs immediately that the transitional period comes to an end.
[277] Section 41(3).
[278] Section 41(4)(b).
[279] Section 41(4)(a).
[280] Section 58(3)(d), section 41(2), (3).
[281] Rule 23, draft Land Registration (Commonhold) Rules 2003.
[282] Section 41(5)(a).
[283] Section 2(2); Schedule 1, paragraph 6.
[284] Section 41(5)(b).
[285] Sections 7, 9, 41(6), (7).

statement, provided that the unit-holder consents in writing.[286] An amendment to the size of a charged unit also requires the consent of the proprietor of any registered charge over the unit.

2.24.3 Removal of land from the commonhold

There are no provisions permitting the removal of land from the commonhold. It therefore appears that the only way to remove land is:

(a) During the transitional period, to cancel the commonhold registration and then submit a new application for registration which excludes the land that is to be removed;

(b) After the end of the transitional period, to terminate the commonhold by a voluntary winding-up.

2.25 ALTERATIONS TO THE MEMORANDUM AND ARTICLES OF ASSOCIATION

This topic is dealt with in Section 2.14 above.

2.26 AMENDMENT OF A COMMONHOLD COMMUNITY STATEMENT

This is considered in Section 2.18 above.

PART 11 REGISTRATION IN ERROR

2.27 GENERAL

2.27.1 Introduction

The Act provides a special procedure for remedying a registration of commonhold land in error in the following circumstances:

(a) The memorandum or articles of association do not comply with the Act or the regulations;[287]

[286] Section 23(1). Section 23(2) permits regulations to be made which enable a court to dispense with the requirement for consent on the application of a commonhold association, but there do not appear to be any plans to make regulations under this section.

[287] Section 6(1)(b); Schedule 1, paragraph 7(a).

(b) The commonhold community statement does not comply with the Act or the regulations;[288]

(c) The land included in the registration is wholly or partly land which cannot be commonhold because it is a flying freehold, agricultural land, land with a contingent title, or land which is already commonhold;[289]

(d) The commonhold association has traded, or has incurred a liability which has not been discharged;[290]

(e) The registration was mistakenly made on the application of someone other than the registered freeholder;[291]

(f) The registration contravened any other provision of the Act or the regulations,[292] such as the requirement under section 3 to obtain the consent of a long lessee.

2.27.2 Procedure

In these circumstances, the Chief Land Registrar's ordinary powers to rectify the register cannot be exercised.[293] Instead, an application must be made to the court for a declaration that the land should not have been registered as a freehold estate in commonhold land. The application may be granted only to an applicant who claims to be adversely affected by the registration.[294] If the court grants the declaration, it has the power to make any further order which is appropriate. The Act includes a non-exhaustive list of the types of order that might be made, which are as follows:

(a) An order providing for the registration to be treated as valid for all purposes;

(b) An order providing for an alteration of the register;

(c) An order providing for the land to cease to be commonhold land;

(d) An order requiring a director or other specified officer of a commonhold association to take steps to alter or amend a document;

(e) An order requiring a director or other specified officer of a commonhold association to take other specified steps;

(f) An award of compensation (whether or not contingent upon the occurrence or non-occurrence of a specified event) to be paid by one specified person to another;

(g) An order applying, disapplying or modifying the indemnity provisions in Schedule 8 to the Land Registration Act 2002.[295]

[288] Section 6(1)(b); Schedule 1, paragraph 7(b).
[289] Section 6(1)(b); Schedule 1, paragraph 7(c); sections 6(1)(a), 2(1)(b).
[290] Section 6(1)(b); Schedule 1, paragraph 7(d), (e).
[291] Section 6(1)(a); section 2(1)(a).
[292] Section 6(1)(c).
[293] Section 6(2).
[294] Section 6(4).
[295] Section 6(6).

2.27.3 Winding-up of the commonhold association

If the court makes an order that the land shall cease to be commonhold land, then it follows that the commonhold association must be wound-up. The court therefore has all the same powers, if it makes such an order, as it would have had if it were making a winding-up order in respect of the commonhold association.[296] In practice, this will mean the appointment of a liquidator. A person appointed as a liquidator in these circumstances shall have all the same powers and duties as a liquidator appointed following the making of a winding-up order.[297] However, the court may in addition make specific further orders that require the liquidator to exercise his functions in a particular way, impose additional rights or duties on him, or modify or remove any of his rights or duties.[298]

The assets of the reserve fund cannot ordinarily be used for the purpose of enforcing a debt, except for a judgment debt that is referable to a reserve fund activity.[299] This restriction does not apply in the event that the court has made an order that the land shall cease to be commonhold land.[300] The assets of the reserve fund are therefore available to the liquidator.

[296] Section 55(1), (2).
[297] Section 55(3).
[298] Section 55(4).
[299] Section 39(4).
[300] Section 56(c).

Chapter 3
TRANSACTIONS WITHIN COMMONHOLD

3.1 GENERAL

3.1.1 Introduction

Sections 15 to 24 of the Act circumscribe the ability of a unit-holder to deal with his commonhold unit as freely as could a freeholder. In those provisions, the Act has sought to reconcile two conflicting aims. First, a desire to give commonhold unit owners as much freedom as possible in their dealings with their units—to free them of many of the restrictions that annoy long leaseholders, and avoid commonhold being perceived as inferior to standard freehold (in the way that long leasehold has come to be perceived). As against that, there is a recognition that commonhold units, unlike standard freehold properties, are interdependent, and that some restrictions are necessary to ensure that a commonhold can operate effectively as a community.

Sections 27 to 30 perform a similar function in relation to the common parts of the commonhold. Again, the Act has sought to reconcile two conflicting aims—the desire to give commonhold communities as much freedom as possible in their dealings with the common parts; and the need to protect the rights of individual unit-holders in respect of those common parts.

The key to the understanding of those sections is to appreciate that some of the restrictions (and freedoms) are imposed or granted by the Act itself, and are inviolable, while others may be imposed by regulations in the shape of restrictions written into the commonhold community statement

3.1.2 Layout of this Chapter

Section 3.2 of this Chapter examines the extent to which a unit-holder may be restricted from transferring his unit. Sections 3.3 and 3.4 go on to deal with restrictions on letting and licensing residential and non-residential units respectively. The creation of charges and other interests in units is dealt with in Section

3.5, while charging the common parts is discussed in Section 3.6. The topic of enlargement of the commonhold is examined in Section 3.7. Finally, Section 3.8 deals with compulsory purchase.

3.2 TRANSFER OF COMMONHOLD UNITS

3.2.1 Meaning of 'transfer' of a commonhold unit

The provisions of the Act concerning the 'transfer' of a commonhold unit[1] apply to the transfer of a unit-holder's freehold estate in that unit to another person. They apply whether or not the transfer is for consideration, and will thus apply to a gift as well as the sale of a unit.[2] They apply whether or not the transfer is subject to any reservation or other terms; for instance, a transfer of the legal estate, but with a reservation of an equitable interest.[3] They apply whether or not the transfer is by operation of law; and will thus apply to the devolution of a unit to the personal representatives of a dead unit-holder, or the vesting of a unit of a bankrupt unit-holder in his trustee in bankruptcy.[4]

3.2.2 Time of transfer

It is the actual transfer of the unit which marks the effective passing of rights and responsibilities from the former unit-holder to the new, not the new unit-holder's subsequent registration as proprietor.[5]

3.2.3 Freedom to transfer units

A commonhold community statement may not prevent or restrict the transfer of a commonhold unit.[6] The policy is that a unit-holder should have the same freedom to transfer his property as any standard freehold owner, and be free of the restrictions on assignment that are resented by many tenants of long residential leases. In Commonwealth jurisdictions, the courts have rejected contentions that community rules restricting the use of units or the characteristics of the occupiers of units (for example, setting a minimum permitted age for unit occupiers, or prohibiting smoking within units) amount to restrictions on the free transfer of units.[7]

The right to transfer part only of a unit is considered in paragraph 3.2.6 below.

[1] For the meaning of a 'commonhold unit', see section 11 of the Act, and paragraph 2.17.6.

[2] Section 15(1)(a) of the Act.

[3] Section 15(1)(b) of the Act.

[4] Section 15(1)(c) of the Act; on the devolution of real estate on death, see section 1(1) of the Administration of Estates Act 1925; on vesting in a trustee in bankruptcy, see section 306(1) of the Insolvency Act 1986.

[5] Section 16(4) of the Act. For the effect of the transfer of a unit, see further paragraph 3.2.5.

[6] Section 15(2) of the Act.

[7] See eg *Marshall v. Strata Plan No. NW 2584* (1996) (Digest); *Salerno v Proprietors of Strata Plan 42724* (1997) (Digest); see further paragraph 4.12.4 of the text.

3.2.4 Formalities upon transfer of a unit

On the transfer of the whole or part of a unit, the new unit-holder must notify the commonhold association of the transfer.[8] The commonhold association needs to be kept informed of who owns which unit: for levying the commonhold assessment, enforcing the rules of the community and giving notice of meetings.[9] Regulations prescribe: (a) the form and manner of the notice; (b) the time within which it must be given; and (c) the consequences of a failure to give the appropriate notice.[10] The proposed form of prescribed notice for the transfer of a unit is Form 1 of Annex D to the Commonhold Community Statement (August 2003) (see Form 2.11 in the Forms and Precedents part of this work).[11] A form to the same effect will be valid.[12] The Notice of Transfer of a unit requires details of the commonhold unit transferred (unit number, title number, postal address) and details of the new and former unit-holders (full names and addresses for service). The notice will be required to be sent to the commonhold association within 7 days from the date on which the Land Registry gives notice to the new unit holder or his representative[13] that the registration of the transfer has been completed.[14] The short timescale is to ensure that the records of the commonhold association are as accurate and up-to-date as possible. It is anticipated that sending the transfer notice will become a standard part of the completion of a conveyancing transaction.[15] An incoming unit-holder will not be entitled to vote at meetings of the association until he has been entered in the register of members.[16] That is likely to be left as the only sanction for a failure to give notice within the prescribed period, on the basis that the alternative of a fine would prove disproportionately troublesome to collect. Individual commonholds will be able to impose a penalty if they wish.[17] See also paragraph 4.13.4 of the text.

[8] Section 15(3) of the Act.

[9] The Lord Chancellor's Department Consultation Paper, 'Proposals for Commonhold Regulations', October 2002, paragraph 131.

[10] Section 15(4) of the Act. The latter could, in theory, include the requirement to pay a fine.

[11] Commonhold Community Statement (August 2003), rule 2. See also Department for Constitutional Affairs Consultation Response (August 2003), responses to questions 90–91.

[12] Commonhold Community Statement (August 2003), rule 2.

[13] A representative includes, but is not limited to, a solicitor or licensed conveyancer.

[14] Commonhold Community Statement (August 2003), rule 2. A period of 21 days from the date of the transfer had previously been proposed by the Lord Chancellor's Department Consultation Paper, 'Proposals for Commonhold Regulations', October 2002, paragraph 133.

[15] Department for Constitutional Affairs Consultation Response (August 2003), conclusion to questions 90–95.

[16] A person only becomes a member of the association when the company enters him in the register of members: paragraph 11, Schedule 3 of the Act. Votes can only be made by members: draft articles of association clauses 31–41 (also clauses 23–30), and section 36 of the Act. See further paragraph 4.6.1.

[17] Department for Constitutional Affairs Consultation Response (August 2003), responses to questions 93–95 and conclusion to questions 90–95. The Lord Chancellor's Department Consultation Paper, 'Proposals for Commonhold Regulations', October 2002, paragraph 134.

3.2.5 Effect of the transfer of a unit

The transferor ceases to be a member of the commonhold association when he transfers his unit and ceases to be a unit-holder.[18] From the moment of transfer, the former unit-holder cannot incur any new liability or acquire any new right under the commonhold community statement, or under any transaction effected in accordance with section 20 of the Act.[19] That rule cannot be disapplied or varied by agreement.[20] Thus, the contract for sale or the transfer document cannot tie the former unit-holder to the unit beyond the transfer date. The aim is to ensure that the current unit-holder is always the person with the full range of benefits and obligations relating to his unit, and that no one has a greater interest in the unit than he does.[21] The former unit-holder is not, however, released from any liability incurred before the transfer took effect; and likewise retains any right acquired before the transfer.[22]

Regrettably, given the importance of the question, the Act itself was not clear as to the extent of the liabilities imposed on a new unit-holder following transfer. Section 16(1) of the Act provides that:

> A right or duty conferred or imposed—
>
> (a) by a commonhold community statement, or
>
> (b) in accordance with section 20,
>
> shall affect a new unit-holder in the same way as it affected the former unit-holder.

The new unit holder evidently becomes entitled, following the transfer, to the same rights as other unit-holders. He will also become subject to the same ongoing duties as other unit-holders—for example, to pay commonhold assessments falling due after transfer, and to comply with repairing obligations affecting the unit.[23]

However, the Act did not make it clear as to whether or not the new unit-holder becomes liable for duties that fell to be performed prior to the transfer. In particular, would he become liable to pay commonhold assessments which fell due prior to the transfer, but which were not paid by the transferor? The wording of section 16 was lamentably opaque in this respect. However, the proposed Commonhold Community Statement (August 2003) now provides that:

> On transfer of a commonhold unit the new unit-holder must pay any debts incurred by the former unit-holder which remain outstanding in respect of the commonhold assessment and the reserve fund levies.

[18] Schedule 3, paragraph 12(a) of the Act.

[19] Section 16(2) of the Act. For transactions under section 20 of the Act, see paragraph 4.13.5 and Section 3.5.

[20] Section 16(3)(a) of the Act.

[21] *Explanatory Notes to the Act*, Stationery Office 2002, paragraph 64.

[22] Section 16(3)(b), and Schedule 3, paragraph 12(b) of the Act.

[23] Section 16(1) of the Act. That is, of course, one of the essential differences between commonhold and a standard freehold estate, where the burden of positive covenants does not ordinarily pass to successors in title: *Austerberry v Corporation of Oldham* (1885) 29 ChD 750.

This is a welcome U-turn from the Government's previous position, when they rejected an Opposition amendment to the Commonhold Bill in similar terms.[24] It has significant practical advantages for commonhold communities. Following a transfer, it would have been difficult and disproportionately expensive for a commonhold association to trace the transferor, and recover any sums due from him.[25] Unscrupulous persons might even have transferred ownership of units between a series of shell companies, to escape, in practice, liability for commonhold assessments. If a new unit-holder were not liable for unpaid debts predating the transfer, the majority of unit-holders would, in practice, have been likely to have ended up subsidising the minority of unit-holders who from time to time sell their units and leave the community without settling their debts. On the other hand, new unit-holders should not suffer any real prejudice by being made liable for their predecessors' unpaid debts. Standard pre-contract enquiries should be made as to whether there are any outstanding liabilities in respect of the unit (such enquiries being standard in long leaseholds). The purchaser will therefore know what liability he is facing, and can decide accordingly whether or not he wishes to proceed with the transaction—perhaps negotiating a corresponding discount on the purchase price. See also paragraphs 4.13.5 and 6.3.15 of the text.

3.2.6 Transfer of part of a unit

The transfer of the freehold estate in part only of a commonhold unit is permitted, provided that the commonhold association consents in writing to the transfer.[26] The commonhold association may only give such consent if (a) it passes a resolution to do so, and (b) at least 75 per cent of those who vote on the resolution vote in favour.[27] The part being transferred will become a new commonhold unit, unless the association consents to it becoming part of another existing unit.[28] Any purported transfer of part of a unit without the consent of the association will be of no effect.[29] Where part of a unit is transferred so as to become part of another unit, both unit holders must give their prior written consent to the necessary amendments to the commonhold community statement.[30] Any amendment of a

[24] *Official Report*, *House of Lords*, vol 627, cols 504–512; *House of Commons*, Standing Committee D, cols 40–45.

[25] Mr Wills for the Government suggested that the small claims court would provide a sufficient remedy for the 'serious nuisances to the association and to other unit-holders' caused by defaulting unit-holders (*Official Report*, *House of Commons*, Standing Committee D, cols 43–44). However, that ignores, first, the fact that the majority of any legal costs incurred by the association will be irrecoverable on the small claims track (rule 27.14 of the Civil Procedure Rules), and, secondly, the practical difficulties and expense of enforcing judgment debts.

[26] Section 21(2)(c) of the Act. The consent of the commonhold association is not required in the case of compulsory purchase of part of a unit: section 60(3); but is required by a mortgagee exercising his power of sale (Schedule 5, paragraph 2), and by trustees exercising their power to partition land (Schedule 5, paragraph 8) in respect of part of a unit. See also paragraph 4.13.3 of the text.

[27] Section 21(8), applying section 20(4) of the Act.

[28] Section 21(9) of the Act.

[29] Section 21(1)–(3) of the Act.

[30] Section 23(1) of the Act; subject to regulations providing otherwise: section 23(2).

commonhold community statement which redefines the extent of a commonhold unit over which there is a registered charge must also have the prior written consent of the proprietor of the charge.[31]

The transfer of parts of units will inevitably involve changes to the boundaries, and possibly to the number, of units within the commonhold. The policy of the Act in respect of such transfers is, therefore, that they should only be possible as part of a comprehensive process involving the parallel amendment of the commonhold community statement, and only with an appropriate level of agreement from the members of the association. The requirement for parallel amendments to the community statement is intended to prevent the problems that would be caused by unilateral, unregulated dealings with part-units. Changes in the pattern of the ownership and boundaries of units will be accompanied by the necessary amendments to ensure that the rights and responsibilities of the new unit-holders are enforceable in respect of the new position. Just as the association will wish the community statement to reflect the changed pattern of the units, so the prudent unit-holder will wish to secure appropriate changes in the percentages of the commonhold assessment fixed for the respective units.[32]

Regulations will make provision, or require the commonhold community statement to make provision, about the registration of a new unit created by the transfer of part of an existing unit.[33] Regulation 11 of the draft Commonhold Regulations sets out the procedure for submitting notice of the alteration to the Registrar. Regulations will also provide for the necessary consequential amendments to the commonhold community statement, or to other provisions made by or under the Act, in their application to units created or modified by the transfer of part of a unit.[34]

As with the transfer of a whole unit, on the transfer of part of a unit, the new unit-holder must notify the commonhold association of the transfer.[35] The proposed form of prescribed notice for the transfer of part of a unit is Form 2 of Annex D to the Commonhold Community Statement (August 2003) (see Form 2.12 in the Forms and Precedents part of this work).[36] A form to the same effect will be valid.[37] The Notice of Transfer of part only of a commonhold unit requires details of the commonhold unit from which land is being transferred and details of the commonhold unit to which it is being added, or, if it is becoming a new unit in its own right, details of that unit. The notice will be required to be sent to the commonhold association within 7 days from the date on which the Land Registry gives notice to the new unit holder or his representative[38] that the

[31] Section 24(1), (2) of the Act; subject to regulations providing otherwise: section 24(3).

[32] *Official Report, House of Commons*, Standing Committee D, cols 34–35; House of Lords Consideration of House of Commons Amendments, vol 633, cols 689–690, Baroness Scotland of Asthal.

[33] Section 21(10) of the Act. [34] Section 21(10) of the Act. [35] Section 15(3) of the Act.

[36] Commonhold Community Statement (August 2003), rule 2.

[37] Commonhold Community Statement (August 2003), rule 2.

[38] A representative includes, but is not limited to, a solicitor or licensed conveyancer.

registration of the transfer has been completed.[39] Consideration is being given as to whether a chargee should be required to notify the Land Registry of any changes to the extent of a charge over a commonhold unit which is altered in size, given that a copy of the chargee's consent to the change must accompany the application to register the amended commonhold community statement.[40] See also paragraph 4.13.3 of the text.

3.3 LETTING RESIDENTIAL COMMONHOLD UNITS

3.3.1 Prohibition on leases not satisfying prescribed conditions

The creation of a tenancy, or 'term of years absolute' (which includes periodic tenancies),[41] in a residential[42] commonhold unit is prohibited, unless the tenancy satisfies the prescribed conditions.[43] That is one of the more important restrictions on the ability of a unit-holder to treat his unit as though it were a freehold unit. The policy of the Government is that residential commonhold units should not be let for long, unbroken periods, to avoid repeating the difficulties that are perceived to exist in leasehold blocks.[44]

3.3.2 Prescribed conditions for leases

The prescribed conditions will be able to relate to the length of the term, the circumstances in which the tenancy is granted, and, indeed, to any other matter.[45] The intention is to prescribe conditions that will permit units to be let, but avoid

[39] Commonhold Community Statement (August 2003), rule 2. A period of 21 days from the date of the transfer had previously been proposed by the Lord Chancellor's Department Consultation Paper, 'Proposals for Commonhold Regulations', October 2002, paragraph 133.

[40] Department for Constitutional Affairs Consultation Response (August 2003), conclusion to questions 159–161.

[41] Section 69(3) of the Act applies the definition of 'term of years absolute' in section 205(1)(xxvii) of the Law of Property Act 1925: 'a term of years (taking effect either in possession or in reversion whether or not at a rent) with or without impeachment of waste, subject or not to another legal estate, and either certain or liable to determination by notice, re-entry, operation of law, or by a provision for cesser on redemption, or in any other event (other than the dropping of a life, or the determination of a determinable life interest); but does not include any term of years determinable with life or lives or with the cesser of a determinable life interest, nor, if created after the commencement of this Act, a term of years which is not expressed to take effect in possession within twenty-one years after the creation thereof where required under this Act to take effect within that period; and in this definition the expression "term of years" includes a term for less than a year, or for a year or years and a fraction of a year or from year to year'. See also *Prudential Assurance Co Ltd v London Residuary Body* [1992] 2 AC 386.

[42] A commonhold unit is residential if the commonhold community statement requires it to be used only: (a) for residential purposes, or (b) for residential and other incidental purposes: section 17(5). (Section 14(1) of the Act requires the commonhold community statement to regulate the use of units.)

[43] Section 17(1) of the Act.

[44] *Explanatory Notes to the Act*, Stationery Office, 2002, paragraph 65.

[45] Section 17(2) of the Act.

creating within commonhold the problems associated with long leases.[46] The Government believed that if long leases of units were permitted, that would result in units being owned by absentee investors, who would take little or no interest in the running of the commonhold community. That would detract from the aim of commonhold as a form of ownership by those with a real stake in the property. On the other hand, the Government was persuaded not to impose even tighter restrictions on letting units. It recognised that although owner-occupation of units may be a desirable aim, there will be many good reasons why unit-holders will wish to let for short periods; for example, during a posting abroad, or where a retirement home is purchased a few years before retirement. The Government also accepted that 'buy-to-let' investments formed a significant part of the market in flats, particularly in London. Tighter regulation would make commonhold developments unpopular with such purchasers, and thus with developers.[47]

3.3.2.1 *Permitted length of term*

It is proposed that the regulations will prohibit long residential leases.[48] The Government is currently undecided as to whether the maximum permitted term should be 7 or 21 years. The current proposed Commonhold Community Statement (August 2003) provides that:

> A unit-holder may not grant a tenancy in a residential commonhold unit for a term of more than 21 years.[49]

The draft Commonhold Regulations provide to the same effect.[50] The previous draft Statement (October 2002) proposed a maximum of 7 years, coinciding with the ambit of the implied repairing covenant for short lettings, and with the new threshold for compulsory registration of a lease.[51] That 7-year limit received strong support in the consultation process.[52] Whichever term length is adopted, the Government envisages that if, in the future, there is evidence that developers and purchasers would find a different maximum length of term more attractive, the regulations can be adapted to meet that market need.[53] In either case, it is

[46] The Lord Chancellor's Department Consultation Paper, 'Proposals for Commonhold Regulations', October 2002, paragraph 135. On the perceived problems of long residential leases, see paragraph 1.3.5.

[47] *Official Report, House of Lords*, vol 627, cols 513–518, Lord McIntosh of Haringey; *Official Report, House of Commons*, Standing Committee D, cols 30–31, Mr Wills; House of Lords, Report Stage, vol 628, cols 476–477, Baroness Scotland of Asthal.

[48] Lord Chancellor's Department Consultation Paper, 'Proposals for Commonhold Regulations', October 2002, paragraph 135.

[49] Rule 3.

[50] Regulation 10(1).

[51] Lord Chancellor's Department Consultation Paper, 'Proposals for Commonhold Regulations', October 2002, paragraph 138; section 11, Landlord and Tenant Act 1985; section 4(2), Land Registration Act 2002. *Explanatory Notes to the Act*, Stationery Office, 2002, paragraph 69.

[52] Department for Constitutional Affairs Consultation Response (August 2003), conclusion to questions 96–111.

[53] *Official Report, House of Commons*, vol 627, col 517, Lord McIntosh of Haringey; House of Lords Report Stage, vol 628, col 477, Baroness Scotland of Asthal.

unlikely that options to renew granted before or at the same time as the lease will be permitted.[54]

The Government is aware that the current proposals may present a bar to the provision of shared ownership housing, which, in its present form, depends on the use of long leases, and are in discussions with the Housing Corporation and others to identify a solution.[55]

3.3.2.2 *Right of commonhold association to carry out repairs*

The proposed Commonhold Community Statement (August 2003) provides that a unit-holder may not grant (a) a tenancy in a commonhold unit or (b) a licence for consideration to occupy or use a commonhold unit for a period longer than 28 days, unless it reserves the right for the commonhold association to carry out repair work in accordance with the provisions of the commonhold community statement. Any provision made in a tenancy agreement will be of no effect to the extent that it is inconsistent with the commonhold community statement or the memorandum or articles of association of the commonhold association.[56] Rule 21 of the proposed Commonhold Community Statement (August 2003) provides that, in order to carry out work necessary to keep the common parts in good repair, the commonhold association has a right to enter a commonhold unit where reasonable notice of the intention to enter has been given to the unit-holder, save in an emergency, when no notice is required.[57]

3.3.2.3 *Other prescribed conditions*

As another means of encouraging unit-holders to retain an active interest in the management of tenanted units, the Government's original preference was to avoid the grant of premium or ground rent leases of units. They had therefore considered prohibiting unit-holders from letting otherwise than at the best rent reasonably obtainable.[58] Against that, however, the Government recognised that many unit-holders will have good reasons for wanting to let at a concessionary rate (for instance to friends or family), as any standard freeholder can do. The Government's current view is that avoiding such restrictions on premiums and the level of rent to be paid will create more flexibility, prevent over-regulation of letting within commonholds and provide a closer approximation to freehold ownership.[59] The proposed Commonhold Community Statement (August 2003) contains no restrictions in that respect.[60]

[54] Department for Constitutional Affairs Consultation Response (August 2003), conclusion to questions 96–111; and regulation 10(1) of the draft Commonhold Regulations.

[55] Department for Constitutional Affairs Consultation Response (August 2003), conclusion to questions 96–111.

[56] Rule 4.

[57] See further paragraph 4.9.10 of the text.

[58] Following section 54(2), Law of Property Act 1925.

[59] Department for Constitutional Affairs Consultation Response (August 2003), conclusion to questions 96–111.

[60] Lord Chancellor's Department Consultation Paper, 'Proposals for Commonhold Regulations', October 2002, paragraph 139.

The Government had also previously considered imposing requirements that: (a) any lease should take effect in possession within three months of the date of the grant;[61] (b) the lease should be in a form approved by the commonhold association; and (c) the lease should not be a holiday or student letting.[62] However, no such restrictions are contained in the proposed Commonhold Community Statement (August 2003). Nonetheless, it is expected that if individual commonholds wish to impose greater restrictions (for example prohibiting holiday lets), they will be able to do so.

3.3.3 Letting parts of residential units

A tenancy can be created in part only of a residential commonhold unit, provided that it satisfies the prescribed conditions.[63] Regulations may modify the application of the Act relating to a unit-holder or a tenant where part of the unit is held under tenancy, so that any wrinkles in day-to-day operation can be ironed out.[64] Regulation 11(4) of the draft Commonhold Regulations applies the same prescribed conditions to leases of parts of units as apply to leases of whole units.

3.3.4 Tenancy failing to comply with prescribed conditions

Any instrument or agreement purporting to create a tenancy that does not satisfy the prescribed conditions is of no effect.[65] However, a party to such a void agreement or instrument can apply to the court for an order: (a) providing for it to have effect as if it provided for the creation of a tenancy of a specified kind; (b) providing for the return or payment of money; or (c) making such other provision as the court thinks appropriate.[66] Where agreements fail to comply with the prescribed conditions in some minor respect only, the court is likely to be willing to amend them, making any necessary consequential adjustments.

Equally, where both parties to the agreement wish the court to make the necessary changes to secure its compliance, the court is likely to be willing to comply; although in those circumstances it may be easier and cheaper for the parties to enter into a new, compliant, tenancy. However, where an agreement fails to comply with the prescribed conditions in some substantial and fundamental respect (for example, purporting to grant a 999-year lease for a premium, at a ground

[61] On the basis that after three months the lease will become registrable at the Land Registry: section 4(1)(d), Land Registration Act 2002.

[62] Lord Chancellor's Department Consultation Paper, 'Proposals for Commonhold Regulations', October 2002, paragraphs 140–141.

[63] Section 21(2)(a) of the Act.

[64] Section 21(7) of the Act; *Explanatory Notes to the Act*, Stationery Office, 2002, paragraph 69.

[65] Section 17(3) of the Act. In relation to leases of part of units, see section 21(1)–(3).

[66] Section 17(4) of the Act.

rent), the court is more likely to decline to save the agreement, and instead order the return of such consideration paid under the agreement as it thinks fit.[67]

3.3.5 Lease for lives, leases terminable on marriage and perpetually renewable leases

A lease of a commonhold unit for a life or lives, or determinable with life or lives, or on the marriage of the lessee, will be treated as if it purported to be a lease for a term of 90 years determinable after the death or marriage.[68] A perpetually renewable lease of a commonhold unit will be treated as if it purported to be a lease for a term of 2,000 years.[69] Since the prescribed conditions are likely to prohibit long leases of commonhold units,[70] it is likely that in each case such a purported lease would be of no effect.

3.3.6 Notification to commonhold association and register of tenants

The proposed Commonhold Community Statement (August 2003) provides[71] that a unit-holder must notify the commonhold association that a tenancy has been granted within 7 days from the date on which it was granted. Form 3 in Annex D to the Commonhold Community Statement (see Form 2.13 in the Forms and Precedents section of this work), or a form to the same effect, must be used. The form requires the unit-holder to provide details of the commonhold unit concerned, the unit-holder(s) and tenant(s), and the tenancy (date granted, length of term and commencement date). There is no requirement to provide the association with a copy of the tenancy. The aim is to ensure that the association has sufficient information without burdening it with unnecessary documentation.[72]

Based on such information, the commonhold association must also maintain a register of tenants, and enter in it: (a) the postal address and unit number of the commonhold unit; (b) the name(s) and address for service of the unit-holder(s); (c) the name(s) and address for service of the tenant; and (d) the length of the tenancy (or a licence for a period longer than 28 days).[73] The association will not be required to approve the form of the lease in advance.[74] There is (as yet) no

[67] It is unlikely to order the return of instalments of rent where the tenant under the void agreement has already enjoyed the accommodation for the relevant period.

[68] Schedule 5, paragraph 3 of the Act, amending section 149, Law of Property Act 1925.

[69] Schedule 5, paragraph 1 of the Act, amending section 145 and Schedule 15, paragraph 5, Law of Property Act 1925.

[70] See sub-paragraph 3.3.2.1.

[71] Rule 5.

[72] Department for Constitutional Affairs Consultation Response (August 2003), conclusion to questions 96–111.

[73] Rule 6. This accords with the Lord Chancellor's Department Consultation Paper, 'Proposals for Commonhold Regulations', October 2002, paragraph 145. There may be provision for the register to be electronic.

[74] Department for Constitutional Affairs Consultation Response (August 2003), conclusion to questions 96–111.

prescribed form for such a register: the authors' suggested form is at Form 2.15 in the Forms and Precedents part of this work. See also paragraph 4.13.7 of the text.

3.3.7 Obligations imposed on tenants of commonhold units

The Act provides for regulations to impose wide-ranging obligations on tenants of commonhold units, or for such obligations to be imposed by a commonhold community statement.[75] Such regulations will be able to be of general application, or limited to specific circumstances; and will be able to make different provision in respect of different descriptions of commonhold land or commonhold units.[76] In particular, they will be able to require a tenant of a unit to make payments to the commonhold association or to a unit-holder in discharge of payments which, under the commonhold community statement, are due to be made by the unit-holder or by another tenant of the unit.[77] They can also provide for the tenant to recover such payments from the unit-holder or from the other tenant of the unit. Alternatively, they may be given the right to set the payments against any sums owed by the tenant (whether they are owed to the person by whom the payments were due, or to some other person).[78]

In drawing up regulations under those wide-ranging powers, the Government is attempting to balance two principal considerations. On the one hand, the tenant will, in practical terms, be a member of the commonhold community for the duration of his lease. Against that, enabling the commonhold association and the other unit-holders to take action directly against the tenant may adversely affect the interest of the unit-holder, and also disrupt the relations of landlord and tenant.[79]

Under the proposed Commonhold Community Statement (August 2003), a tenant of a commonhold unit, or part of a unit, will be bound by the rules of the commonhold community statement which affect his occupancy.[80] It also provides that the tenant of a commonhold unit, or part of a unit, must make payments to the commonhold association in discharge of payments which are due, in accordance with the commonhold community statement, to be made by the unit-holder or another tenant where the tenancy agreement imposes an obligation on the tenant to pay.[81] The Government is currently considering how to identify the parts of

[75] Section 19(1) of the Act.
[76] Section 19(5) of the Act.
[77] Section 19(2) of the Act.
[78] Section 19(3) of the Act.
[79] Lord Chancellor's Department Consultation Paper, 'Proposals for Commonhold Regulations', October 2002, paragraph 144.
[80] Rule 7. This rule will be compulsory: regulation 10(1), draft Commonhold Regulations 2003. Earlier proposals also provided for (i) the lessee to be required within 21 days to give notice to the commonhold association (a) of his address for service, and (b) confirming that he was bound by the terms and conditions of the appropriate parts of the commonhold community statement; and for (ii) any assignee, chargee or underlessee of the lessee's interest to also be required to give details of their interest to the commonhold association within 21 days of the relevant transaction: Lord Chancellor's Department Consultation Paper, 'Proposals for Commonhold Regulations', October 2002, paragraph 146.
[81] Rule 8. This rule will be compulsory: regulation 10(1), draft Commonhold Regulations.

the commonhold community statement which affect the occupancy of the tenant, and to which he should be bound.[82]

The Government is also examining the relationship between the tenant and the commonhold association including dispute resolution and the interaction of obligations under a lease, subject to landlord and tenant law, with the obligations under the commonhold community statement. Special provision may be made for service charge provisions.[83] It may be left to the unit-holder and his lessee to decide the extent of the lessee's involvement in the affairs of the commonhold association.[84]

The proposed Commonhold Community Statement (August 2003) requires a tenant to provide at least one and up to three addresses for service to the commonhold association, and notify the commonhold association of any change to an address for service.[85] See also paragraph 4.13.8 of the text.

3.3.8 Modification of rules of law concerning leasehold estates

Although the Act also grants very wide powers for regulations to modify *any* statutory or common law rule of law about leasehold estates in its application to a tenancy of a commonhold unit, there are currently no proposals for such regulations.[86]

3.3.9 Licences

The proposed Commonhold Community Statement (August 2003) provides[87] that a unit-holder must notify the commonhold association that a licence for a period longer than 28 days has been granted within 7 days from the date on which it was granted. Form 4 in Annex D to the Commonhold Community Statement (see Form 2.14 in the Forms and Precedents section of this work), or a form to the same effect, must be used. The Form requires the unit-holder to provide details of the commonhold unit concerned, the unit-holder(s) and licensee(s), and the licence (date granted, length of licence and nature of licence). There is no requirement to provide the association with a copy of the licence.

As with the case of a letting, details of the licence must be entered in an articles of association register kept by the commonhold association. There is (as yet) no

[82] Department for Constitutional Affairs Consultation Response (August 2003), conclusion to questions 96–111.

[83] Department for Constitutional Affairs Consultation Response (August 2003), conclusion to questions 96–111.

[84] Lord Chancellor's Department Consultation Paper, 'Proposals for Commonhold Regulations', October 2002, paragraph 147. See further paragraph 4.13.8 of the text.

[85] Rule 61.

[86] Section 19(4) of the Act; Lord Chancellor's Department Consultation Paper, 'Proposals for Commonhold Regulations', October 2002, paragraph 148.

[87] Rule 5.

prescribed form for such a register: the authors' suggested form is at Form 2.15 in the Forms and Precedents part of this work.

Licences for less than 28 days do not need to be registered, avoiding the problems which would be caused by a requirement to register short-term bare licences (for example, giving a friend permission to stay in the spare room for a night, booking housesitters, or giving the keys to the unit to a plumber or decorator[88]).

The Government has dropped its previous proposals that: (i) the commonhold community statement would only allow a unit-holder to grant a licence or other similar right with the prior written consent of the Board of Directors of the commonhold association, and (ii) parting with possession of the whole or part of a unit would be restricted to the permitted forms of leasing.[89] Such restrictions would have been unduly restrictive.[90] See also paragraph 4.13.9 of the text.

3.4 LETTING NON-RESIDENTIAL COMMONHOLD UNITS

3.4.1 Restrictions in commonhold community statements

Any instrument or agreement which creates a tenancy in a non-residential commonhold unit takes effect subject to any provisions of the commonhold community statement.[91] A tenancy can be created in part only of a non-residential commonhold unit.[92]

3.4.2 The current proposal

The current proposal is that there should be no prescribed provisions included in the commonhold community statement in respect of non-residential tenancies, and in particular no restrictions on the length of term or rent payable.[93] Such provisions can, of course, be incorporated into individual commonhold community statements.

[88] Which in each case would amount to the grant of a bare licence: see e.g. *Megarry and Wade on The Law of Real Property*, 6th edn, 2000, paragraph 17-003.

[89] Lord Chancellor's Department Consultation Paper, 'Proposals for Commonhold Regulations', October 2002, paragraph 149.

[90] Even if such draconian restrictions might have been said to have been sanctioned by section 14(1) of the Act (which provides that the Commonhold Community Statement 'must make provision regulating the use of commonhold units'), as a restriction concerning the use made of the unit, such control would have been highly impractical in the case of short-term bare licences, and an obvious source of contention. See also Lord Chancellor's Department Consultation Paper, 'Proposals for Commonhold Regulations', October 2002, paragraph 150.

[91] Section 18 of the Act.

[92] Section 21(2)(b) of the Act.

[93] Department for Constitutional Affairs Consultation Response (August 2003), conclusion to questions 96–111; Lord Chancellor's Department Consultation Paper, 'Proposals for Commonhold Regulations', October 2002, paragraph 142.

3.4.3 Obligations imposed on tenants of non-residential commonhold units

The same provisions apply as in the case of residential units, and have been considered in Section 3.3 above.

3.5 CREATION OF CHARGES AND OTHER INTERESTS IN UNITS

3.5.1 Charges

A commonhold community statement may not prevent or restrict the creation, grant or transfer by a unit-holder of a charge over the whole of his unit.[94] Thus, the unit-holder should have the same ability to borrow money on the security of his unit as a standard freeholder. Where the unit is mortgaged with full or limited title guarantee, the mortgagor will be under an implied covenant to fully and promptly observe and perform all the obligations under the commonhold community statement that are for the time being imposed on him in his capacity as a unit-holder or joint unit-holder.[95] No amendment to a commonhold community statement which redefines the extent of a commonhold unit over which there is a registered charge may be made without the prior written consent of the proprietor of the charge.[96]

3.5.2 Prohibition on charge of part of a unit

However, it is not possible to create a charge over part only of a unit, and any instrument or agreement which purports to do so is of no effect.[97] Likewise, if land which is subject to a charge becomes commonhold land or is added to an existing commonhold unit, and the effect of that would be that the charge would become a charge over part only of a commonhold unit, it will be extinguished to that extent.[98] A charge over part of a unit, if it proved necessary to enforce in due course, would result in a change being required in the commonhold community statement, but would not be under the control of the commonhold association.[99]

[94] Section 20(1)(b) of the Act. The restrictions in section 20 on the creation of certain prescribed interests in commonhold units do not apply to a charge, or an interest arising by virtue of a charge: section 20(6). A 'charge' is any appropriation of real (or personal) property for the discharge of a debt or other obligation, without giving the creditor either a general or special property in, or possession of, the subject of the security: *Re Cosslett (Contractors) Ltd* [1998] Ch 495 at 508, per Millett J; *Young v Matthew Hall Mechanical and Electrical Engineers Pty Ltd* (1988) 13 ACLR 399, SCWA.

[95] Schedule 5, paragraph 7, amending section 5, Law of Property (Miscellaneous Provisions) Act 1994.

[96] Section 21(1), (2) of the Act; subject to regulations providing otherwise: section 21(3).

[97] Section 22(1), (2) of the Act.

[98] Section 22(3), (4) of the Act.

[99] *Official Report*, *House of Lords*, vol 627, col 519, Baroness Scotland of Asthal; *Official Report*, *House of Commons*, Standing Committee D, col 33, Mr Wills.

For the same reason, a mortgagee of the whole of a unit cannot sell part thereof, in the exercise of his power of sale, without the consent of the commonhold association.[100] If land is added to a unit which is subject to a charge, the charge is extended so as to relate also to the land which is added.[101]

3.5.3 Other interests

A commonhold community statement may not, in general, prevent or restrict the creation, grant or transfer by a unit-holder of an 'interest' in the whole or part of his unit.[102] 'Interest' for that purpose does not include a tenancy, charge, or interest arising by virtue of a charge.[103]

However, it will not be possible to create an interest in a commonhold unit of a prescribed kind, unless the commonhold association is either a party to the creation of the interest, or consents in writing to its creation.[104] The commonhold association will only be able to give its consent, or be a party to the transaction, if (a) the association passes a resolution to do so, and (b) at least 75 per cent of those who vote on the resolution vote in favour.[105] Any instrument or agreement that purports to create an interest in contravention of those restrictions will be of no effect.[106]

The policy behind the restriction on prescribed interests is to prevent unit-holders creating easements and profits à prendre in their units, or any other interests which might cause nuisance or annoyance to other unit-holders, or otherwise cause problems for the commonhold association as a whole.[107] In selecting which interests should be prescribed, therefore, the guiding principle will be whether the interest created would affect any other unit-holders or the commonhold association.[108] It is not intended there should be any restriction on creating express trusts of land in a unit, nor, presumably, on constructive or resulting trusts.[109]

It is not possible to create an interest in part only of a commonhold unit, and an instrument or agreement is of no effect to the extent that it purports to do so.[110]

[100] Schedule 5, paragraph 2 of the Act, making the mortgagee's statutory power of sale under section 101(1)(i) of the Law of Property Act 1925 subject to section 21 of the Act.

[101] Section 24(5) of the Act. Similarly, where land is removed from a charged unit, the charge is extinguished to the extent that it relates to the land which is removed: section 24(4) of the Act.

[102] Section 20(1) of the Act.

[103] Section 20(2), (6) of the Act. For charges, see paragraph 3.5.1; for tenancies of residential units, see Section 3.3; for tenancies of non-residential units, see Section 3.4.

[104] Section 20(3) of the Act.

[105] Section 20(4) of the Act. For association resolutions and voting by members, see Section 4.6.

[106] Section 20(5) of the Act.

[107] *Official Report, House of Commons* Report Stage, vol 381, col 677. Mr Wills; House of Lords Consideration of House of Commons Amendments, vol 633, cols 688–689, Baroness Scotland of Asthal.

[108] Lord Chancellor's Department Consultation Paper, 'Proposals for Commonhold Regulations', October 2002, paragraph 151.

[109] *Official Report, House of Commons* Report Stage, vol 381, col 677, Mr Wills.

[110] Section 21(1), (3) of the Act. Section 21(2) of the Act provides that the prohibition does not extend to (a) the creation of a lease of part of a residential unit, provided that it satisfies the prescribed

Where land subject to an interest becomes commonhold land or is added to a commonhold unit, and the effect of that event would be that the interest would become a charge over part only of a commonhold unit, it is extinguished to that extent.[111] Again the policy is, apparently, to prevent the fragmentation of property rights in, and control of, units, in a manner that would be outside the control of the commonhold association. The integrity of the units is thereby maintained.[112]

3.6 CHARGING COMMON PARTS

3.6.1 General prohibition on charging common parts

There is a general prohibition on the creation of a charge[113] over the common parts of the commonhold.[114] Any instrument or agreement that purports to create such a charge is of no effect.[115] That prohibition is intended to protect the rights of the members in the common parts from being put at risk by the borrowing of the commonhold association. On the same principle, where land vests in a commonhold association and becomes part of the common parts, any existing charge over it is extinguished to the extent that it relates wholly or partly to the common parts. That will be the case where, during the establishment of a commonhold, a commonhold association is registered as the proprietor of common parts;[116] and also where land is added to the common parts following an amendment to the commonhold community statement.[117]

conditions (see paragraph 3.3.2); (b) the creation of a lease in part only of a non-residential unit (see paragraph 3.4.2); or (c) the transfer of part of a unit, where the commonhold association has given its written consent (see paragraph 3.2.6).

[111] Section 21(4), (5) of the Act.

[112] See similar reasoning regarding the prohibition of charges over parts of units: paragraph 3.5.2.

[113] A 'charge' is any appropriation of real (or personal) property for the discharge of a debt or other obligation, without giving the creditor either a general or special property in, or possession of, the subject of the security: *Re Cosslett (Contractors) Ltd* [1998] Ch 495 at 508, per Millett J; *Young v Matthew Hall Mechanical and Electrical Engineers Pty Ltd* (1988) 13 ACLR 399, SCWA.

[114] 'Common parts' means every part of the commonhold which is not for the time being a commonhold unit in accordance with the commonhold community statement: section 25(1). See paragraph 2.17.4.

[115] Section 28(1), (2) of the Act.

[116] Section 28(3) of the Act. That applies whether the registration is by section 7 (registration with unit-holders) or section 9 (registration without unit-holders). On the registration of land as commonhold land, see further Part 6 of Chapter 2.

[117] Section 28(4) of the Act. For additions to common parts, see section 30 of the Act , and Section 3.7.

3.6.2 Permitted mortgages of common parts

There is one exception to the general prohibition on the charging of common parts.[118] A legal mortgage[119] of common parts may be created if it is approved by a unanimous resolution[120] of the commonhold association, passed before the creation of the mortgage.[121] That would, for example, enable the association to borrow money for the improvement of the common parts, provided that none of the members vote against the idea. In many schemes, however, the common parts are unlikely to be a very attractive form of security to lenders.

3.7 ENLARGEMENT OF COMMONHOLD

3.7.1 Right to add land to the commonhold

The boundaries of a commonhold can be enlarged, if that is considered desirable by the developer or by the commonhold association. The right of a developer to add land to a commonhold as part of his development rights has been considered in Chapter 2.[122] Land may also be added to a commonhold where: (a) the registered freeholder of the land proposes to apply to the Chief Land Registrar to add it to the commonhold; (b) the commonhold association, for the purposes of the application, already exercises functions in relation to commonhold land, and (c) the freeholder's application is approved by a resolution of the commonhold association.[123] The resolution must be passed (a) before the application to add the land is made, and (b) unanimously.[124] Land may not be added to a commonhold if any part of it is already commonhold land.[125]

3.7.2 Documents required on application to add land

The application to add land to a commonhold must be made on Land Registry Form CM4[126] (the draft is Form 1.4 in the Forms and Precedents part of this work). It must be accompanied by:

[118] Section 28(5) of the Act.

[119] By section 29(3) of the Act, 'legal mortgage' has the meaning given by section 205(1)(xvi), Law of Property Act 1925: a mortgage (which includes any charge or lien on any property for securing money or money's worth) by demise or sub-demise or a charge by way of legal mortgage.

[120] For the passing of resolutions by a commonhold association, and what constitutes a unanimous resolution, see section 36 of the Act, and Section 4.6.

[121] Section 29(1), (2) of the Act.

[122] See paragraph 2.24.1. The developer can include a provision in the commonhold community statement disapplying the requirements of section 41(2), (3), considered below, entitling him to make an application to add land without requiring a resolution of the commonhold association: section 58(3)(d), section 41(2), (3).

[123] Section 41(1), (3) and section 2(1) of the Act. 'Registrar' in section 2(1) is defined as Chief Land Registrar by section 67(1) of the Act.

[124] Section 41(4) of the Act.

[125] Section 2(1)(b) of the Act.

[126] Rule 23, draft Land Registration (Commonhold) Rules.

(a) In respect of the land to be added, the consent of anyone who: (a) is the registered proprietor of a freehold estate in the land; (b) the registered proprietor of a leasehold estate in the whole or part of the land granted for a term of more than 21 years; (c) the registered proprietor of a charge over the whole or part of the land; or (d) anyone falling within any other prescribed class of persons.[127]

(b) An application for the registration of an amended commonhold community statement (under section 33 of the Act), making provision for the existing commonhold and the added land.[128] This application must be made on Land Registry Form CM3 (see the draft at Form 1.3 in the Forms and Precedents part of this work).[129] The alterations to the commonhold community statement must obviously contain amended plans, and must indicate whether the additional land is to form a new unit or units, or part of the common parts.

(c) A certificate given by the directors of the commonhold association that (i) the application to add land has been approved by the requisite resolution of the commonhold association, and (ii) the land to be added is not land which cannot be commonhold land.[130]

The application does not need to be accompanied by any of the other documents that must be lodged upon a standard first application for registration of land as commonhold.[131]

3.7.3 Registration of land added to the common parts as commonhold

Where the whole of the added land is to form part of the common parts of the commonhold, then, upon registration of the land as commonhold, the Chief Land Registrar must register the commonhold association as proprietor of the freehold estate in the added land (without the commonhold association needing to make any further application).[132] The rights and duties conferred and imposed by the commonhold community statement will come into force, in so far as they affect the added land, on registration.[133]

[127] Section 41(5)(a) of the Act; Schedule 1, paragraph 6; section 3(1). Alternatively, evidence must be supplied of deemed consent under section 3(2)(e) of the Act ; or an order of the court dispensing with the requirement for consent under section 3(2)(f): see Schedule 1, paragraph 6. On section 3(1) of the Act, see further Section 2.5.

[128] Section 41(5)(b) of the Act. On applications under section 33 of the Act, see further Section 2.18.

[129] Section 41(5)(b).

[130] Section 41(5)(c). For the resolution of the commonhold association, see section 41(3), (4) of the Act, and Section 4.6. For land which cannot be commonhold land see Schedule 2 to the Act, and Section 2.3.

[131] Section 41(5) CLRA 2002, disapplying section 2(2) and thereby the requirement to serve the other documents listed in Schedule 1.

[132] Section 41(7)(b), (c) of the Act.

[133] Section 41(7)(d) of the Act. In such a case, the provisions of section 7 of the Act , do not apply: section 41(7)(a).

3.7.4 Registration as commonhold of land added from units

Where the added land is to consist wholly or partly of commonhold units, the provisions of either section 7 or section 9 of the Act will apply, depending on whether or not a list of initial unit-holders (in prescribed form) is to be provided upon registration of the added land as commonhold.[134] If a list of initial unit-holders is provided in accordance with section 9, then, on registration of the land as commonhold, the Chief Land Registrar must register: (a) the commonhold association as the proprietor of the freehold estate in the common parts; and (b) a person specified as an initial unit-holder as the proprietor of the freehold estate in his unit (or, as the case may be, as a joint unit-holder).[135] Upon registration of the added land as commonhold: (a) the rights and duties conferred and imposed by the commonhold community statement will come into force, in so far as they affect the added land;[136] and (b) any lease of the whole or part of the added land will be extinguished on registration.[137]

If no such list of initial unit-holders is provided, then the provisions of section 7 will apply.[138] On registration: (a) the applicant will continue to be registered as the proprietor of the freehold estate in the added land; and (b) the rights and duties conferred and imposed by the commonhold community statement will not come into force in respect of the added land.[139] Once the added land has been registered as commonhold, when any person other than the applicant becomes entitled to be registered as the proprietor of the freehold estate in one or more, but not all, of the commonhold units (i.e. once the units begin to be sold off): (a) the Chief Land Registrar must register the commonhold association as the proprietor of the freehold estate in the common parts; (b) the rights and duties conferred and imposed by the commonhold community statement will come into force, in so far as they affect the added land;[140] and (c) any lease of the whole or part of the added land will be extinguished on registration.[141]

If the added land is to be added to an existing unit, then this can simply be reflected in the amendments to the commonhold community statement, provided that the unit-holder consents in writing.[142] An amendment to the size of a

[134] Section 41(6), section 7, section 9 of the Act. On registration of land as commonhold land and on the operation of section 7 and section 9, see further Chapter 2.

[135] Section 9(3)(a)–(d) of the Act. The commonhold association need not make any further application for registration of such interests: section 9(3)(d).

[136] Sections 9(3)(e), 41(6) of the Act.

[137] Sections 9(3)(f), 41(6) of the Act. For the meaning of 'lease' in this context, see section 9(4) of the Act .

[138] Section 7(1) of the Act.

[139] Sections 7(2), 41(6) of the Act .

[140] Sections 7(3)(c), 41(6) of the Act.

[141] Sections 7(3)(d), 41(6) of the Act. For the meaning of 'lease' in this context, see section 7(4) of the Act.

[142] Section 23(1) of the Act. Section 23(2) permits regulations to be made which enable a court to dispense with the requirement for consent on the application of a commonhold association, but there do not appear to be any plans to make regulations under this section.

charged unit also requires the consent of the proprietor of any registered charge over the unit.[143]

3.8 COMPULSORY PURCHASE

3.8.1 Compulsory purchase of whole or part of commonhold

Section 60 of the Act makes provision for the acquisition of the whole, or part, of a freehold estate in commonhold land by a compulsory purchaser.[144] The general rule is that where a freehold estate in commonhold land is transferred to a compulsory purchaser, it will cease to be commonhold land.[145] However, it can continue as commonhold land if the Chief Land Registrar is satisfied that the compulsory purchaser desires the land to continue to be commonhold land.[146] Where a compulsory purchaser acquires part only of a commonhold unit, the consent of the commonhold association is not required for the transfer (as it would be in the case of any other transferee).[147]

3.8.2 Regulations

Detailed provision about the transfer of a freehold estate in commonhold land to a compulsory purchaser will be made by regulations.[148] It is envisaged that the regulations will (a) make detailed provision about the acquired land ceasing to be commonhold on compulsory acquisition; (b) make detailed provision about acquired land continuing to be commonhold where that is desired by the compulsory purchaser; (c) make detailed provision about that part of the commonhold which is not transferred, where only part of the commonhold unit is acquired; (d) provide for the service of compulsory purchase notices; (e) confer relevant powers on the courts; (f) provide for the compensation payable; (g) enable the commonhold association to require a compulsory purchaser to acquire the freehold estate in the whole, or a particular part, of the commonhold; and (h) disapply or modify other enactments relating to compulsory purchase.[149]

[143] See section 24 of the Act.

[144] A compulsory purchaser is defined for the purposes of section 60 as a person acquiring land (a) either that he is *authorised* by an enactment to acquire by compulsory purchase, or (b) that he is *obliged* to acquire by a prescribed enactment or in prescribed circumstances: section 60(7) of the Act.

[145] Section 60(1) of the Act.

[146] Section 60(2) of the Act.

[147] Section 60(3) of the Act, disapplying the requirements of section 21(2)(c) (as to which, see paragraph 3.2.6). The scheme of compulsory purchase legislation would otherwise have been undermined: *Official Report, House of Commons*, Standing Committee D, col 34.

[148] See section 60(4)–(6) of the Act.

[149] Section 60(5) of the Act. There is a wide power under section 60(4) to make regulations on any other aspect of the transfer of commonhold land to a compulsory purchaser.

Chapter 4
RUNNING A COMMONHOLD

4.1 INTRODUCTION

4.1.1 Scope of this Chapter

This Chapter is concerned with the operation of the commonhold once it has been registered, developed, and units sold to individual unit-holders. It is not concerned with the creation of such a commonhold (which is covered in full in Chapter 2), with property transactions within a commonhold (covered in Chapter 3), or with the termination of a commonhold (see Chapter 5).

4.1.2 Health warning

A small commonhold association (and particularly one that has been created following conversion of a leasehold property to commonhold) may initially take the view that running a commonhold should take no more effort than running a property with leases in place. Moreover, with the benefit of the goodwill that should flow from the fact that all owners have the same interest in ensuring the success of the development, there might appear to be much to be said for a relaxed style of management.

This Chapter does not seek to indulge in doom-mongering, nor indeed to do anything to dissuade prospective commonholders from going ahead with a form of property ownership which the authors believe has great promise. It does, however, counsel prudence of approach: commonhold may be a sound vehicle, but it also needs drivers who will keep their engines tuned; who do not run out of petrol; who lay aside money for servicing and replacement; who know the rules of the road; who are sensitive to the needs of their passengers; and who are equipped to deal with back-seat drivers.

4.1.3 Non-professional directors

The health warning given above is not intended to dissuade non-professional directors from attempting to run a commonhold association. Indeed, it is easy to see that the engagement of professional directors in the case of a small commonhold association will not be an economic proposition. As this Chapter establishes, however, there are some tasks that it would be foolhardy to attempt without professional assistance (and of course freehold and leasehold ownership is no different in this regard).

4.1.4 Arrangement of this Chapter

This Chapter is divided into 5 Parts:

(a) Part 1 deals with the corporate aspects of running a commonhold association;

(b) Part 2 is concerned with land and property matters;

(c) Part 3 discusses the financial aspects of running a commonhold;

(d) Part 4 considers enforcement by the commonhold association of its rules against unit-holders and holders of derivative interests;

(e) Part 5, finally, looks at the issues that may be involved in the running of a mixed use commonhold.

4.1.5 References to drafts

On 8 October 2002, the Lord Chancellor's Department published a Consultation Paper on the commonhold regulations proposed to be made, included with which were rudimentary drafts of the memorandum and articles of association and the commonhold community statement. In August 2003, the Department of Constitutional Affairs published a Post-Consultation Report which summarised the responses to the consultation exercise, and appended revised drafts of the same documents for further comment before publication in final format later in the year.

References in this Chapter to the commonhold community statement and the memorandum and articles of association of the commonhold association are to the revised (August 2003) drafts, save where otherwise specified. Once the consultation exercise has been concluded and the regulations have been finalised and promulgated, the text will be revised to the extent necessary to accommodate any changes in those drafts.

4.1.6 Best Practice Guide

This Chapter sets out the relevant provisions that govern the running of a commonhold, together with an analysis of the way in which they are intended to work. The reader who seeks a more practical guide to how to avoid problems arising in the running of a commonhold, and how best to deal with problems which have arisen, is invited to consult the Best Practice Guide in Chapter 8. In particular, the authors hope that the principles set out in that Chapter will be of assistance to non-professional directors.

PART 1 COMPANY MATTERS

4.2 INTRODUCTION

4.2.1 The conduct of business by a commonhold association

A commonhold association is a company limited by guarantee. It therefore has members rather than shareholders. It is, however, run by directors for the benefit of the members in the same way as a company limited by shares is run by directors for the benefit of its shareholders.

A commonhold association is often referred to as a 'not-for-profit' company. This description is apt to mislead: it refers to the fact that its income must be applied solely in promoting the objects specified in the memorandum of association. Save in accordance with a termination statement or on a winding-up of the commonhold association, no distribution shall be made to its members in cash or otherwise (see article 78 of the articles of association).

That is not to say that the commonhold association cannot run activities at a profit: indeed, it may well suit the members to organise social activities which will bring in money, or to let out parts of the common parts at a healthy return. All income derived from such activities must, however, be directed towards the operation of the commonhold, and may not be paid to the members.

4.2.2 The directors of the commonhold association

The directors of the commonhold association are responsible for the management of the association. Their constitution and functions are considered in detail in Section 4.3 below.

4.2.3 Rules by which the commonhold association is governed

The internal governance of the commonhold association (compare the administration of the commonhold, which is discussed later) is primarily effected through the articles of association. These articles lay down important rules regarding such matters as the way in which decisions are made. The articles draw heavily on Table C of the standard articles of association prescribed under the Companies Acts (see the Companies (Tables A to F) Regulations 1985).

4.3 THE BOARD OF DIRECTORS OF A COMMONHOLD ASSOCIATION

4.3.1 Qualifications of directors

In the case of smaller commonhold associations, directors will ordinarily be drawn from the ranks of the members. Article 44 of the articles of association provides, however, as a default provision that a director of a commonhold association need not be a member of the association. The commonhold regulations (13(4)) add that where a commonhold contains more than six units, article 44 *must* be altered to provide that at least one director must be a member of the commonhold association. It will therefore be possible for professional directors to be appointed to run the commonhold association on behalf of its members. The articles of association also allow for directors to receive payment for their services (see paragraph 4.3.15 below).

4.3.2 Numbers of directors

Article 45 of the articles of association prescribes a lower limit of two directors to run the commonhold association. This may be reduced to one in the case of a commonhold with less than six members—see regulation 13(5) of the commonhold regulations. There is no upper limit for the numbers of directors (although the October 2002 Consultation Paper originally proposed an upper limit of six).

4.3.3 Appointment of directors

Articles 50 and 51 of the articles of association lay down restrictions on the way in which a director of a commonhold association may be appointed. There are two routes to appointment: recommendation by the directors; or proposal by a member with voting rights.

(a) In the case of *proposal by a member*, the proposal must be preceded by notice given by the member concerned not less than 14 nor more than 35 clear days[1] before the date appointed for the meeting at which the appointment is to be proposed. The notice must state the particulars which would, if the person were appointed as director, be required to be included in the commonhold association's register of directors (namely any interest in shares or debentures existing at the time of the appointment—see section 324(1) of the Companies Act 1985), together with notice executed by that person of his willingness to be appointed.

[1] Article 1 defines the expression 'clear days' in relation to the period of notice to mean that period excluding the day when the notice is given or deemed to be given and the day for which it is given or on which it is to take effect.

(b) In *either* case, not less than 7 nor more than 28 clear days before the date appointed for holding the meeting, notice shall be given to all who are entitled to receive notice of the meeting of the person proposed for appointment. The notice must again give the requisite particulars of the person for inclusion in the commonhold association's register of directors.

The procedure and rules for the initial appointment of directors after the end of the transitional period are dealt with by articles 46 to 48 of the articles of association and are discussed in Chapter 2.

4.3.4 Appointment of additional directors

The appointment of directors ordinarily takes place at annual general meetings in the way described in paragraph 4.3.3 above. Between such meetings, there may be an unforeseen need for the appointment of an additional director. An obvious example occurs where a director has died or otherwise become unable to act, or where a post needs to be filled for a particular purpose.

Article 52 of the articles of association deals with these circumstances by providing that the commonhold association may appoint a person who is willing to act to be a director, either to fill a vacancy (other than a vacancy in respect of a developer's director) or as an additional director. A director so appointed shall hold office only until the next following annual general meeting. If he is not then reappointed, he shall vacate his office at the end of the meeting. As currently proposed, this article is intended as a default provision rather than a mandatory provision.

4.3.5 Alternate directors

Articles 53 to 57 of the original draft of the articles of association allowed for a director of the commonhold association to appoint another person to act as a director in the event that he is unable to do so. Such an appointed director is known as an 'alternate' director. Some objections were made to this proposal in the responses to the October 2002 Consultation Paper.[2] Possibly for that reason, these provisions are not to be found in the current (August 2003) draft, although the Post-Consultation Report dated August 2003 suggests that alternate directors may be included in the articles as an optional provision. This paragraph therefore addresses the topic on the basis that commonhold associations may after all wish to provide for alternate directors along the lines of the original draft.

For the sake of completeness, the articles governing alternate directors are first set out in the form in which they appeared in the draft articles of association attached to the October 2002 Consultation Paper:

[2] On the grounds that provision for alternate directors would encourage absenteeism, and that while it was appropriate for a large company it was not for a residential commonhold.

53. Any director (other than an alternate director) may appoint any other director, or any other person approved by resolution of the directors and willing to act, to be an alternate director to attend meetings of directors in the event that the director is unable to do so. If the director is a member of the Commonhold Association, his alternate must also be a member of the Commonhold Association. The director may remove from office an alternate director so appointed by him.
54. An alternate director shall be entitled to receive notice of all meetings of directors and of all meetings of committees of directors of which his appointor is a member, to attend and vote at any such meeting at which the director appointing him is not personally present and generally to perform all the functions of his appointor as a director in his absence but shall not be entitled to receive any remuneration from the Commonhold Association for his service as an alternate director. But it shall not be necessary to give notice of such a meeting to an alternate director who is absent from the United Kingdom.
55. An alternate director shall cease to be an alternate director if his appointor ceases to be a director. If a director retires but is reappointed or deemed to have been reappointed at the meeting at which he retires, any appointment of an alternate director made by him which was in force immediately prior to his retirement shall continue after his reappointment.
56. Any appointment or removal of an alternate director shall be by notice to the Commonhold Association signed by the director making or revoking the appointment or in any other manner approved by the directors.
57. Save as otherwise provided in the articles, an alternate director shall be deemed for all purposes to be a director and shall alone be responsible for his own acts and defaults and he shall not be deemed to be the agent of the director appointing him.

Article 57 of this original draft provides that an alternate director is not an agent of the appointor, but a director in his own right, governed by the rules of the commonhold association, although his powers are circumscribed in some respects. The following points are worthy of note:

(a) An alternate director may not himself appoint another alternate director (article 53).

(b) The alternate director must either be an existing director, or a person approved by resolution of the directors (article 53).

(c) If the appointing director is a member of the commonhold association, his alternate must also be a member of the commonhold association (article 53).

(d) The appointing director may remove from office an alternate director so appointed by him (article 53).

(e) The alternate director may not vote at a meeting at which his appointing director is present (article 54).

(f) The alternate director shall not be entitled to receive any remuneration from the commonhold association for his services as an alternate director (article 54).

(g) Although the alternate director shall be entitled to receive notice of all meetings of directors and of all meetings of committees of directors of which his appointor is a member, to attend and vote at any such meeting at which the director appointing him is not personally present, and generally to perform all the functions of his appointor as a director in his absence, it shall not be necessary to give notice of such a meeting to an alternate director who is absent from the United Kingdom (article 54).

(h) The alternate director shall cease to be an alternate director if his appointor ceases to be a director (article 55).

(i) If a director retires but is reappointed or deemed to have been reappointed at the meeting at which he retires, any appointment of an alternate director made by him which was in force immediately prior to his retirement shall continue after his reappointment (article 55).

(j) Any appointment or removal of an alternate director shall be by notice to the commonhold association signed by the director making or revoking the appointment or in any other manner approved by the directors (article 56).

These provisions will make a suitable addition to the articles of association of a large commonhold association.

4.3.6 Retirement of directors

The articles of association distinguish between ordinary directors, who are subject to retirement by rotation; developer's directors (who do not retire by rotation, and are dealt with in Chapter 2); additional directors (who are dealt with in paragraph 4.3.4 above); and alternate directors (who are dealt with in paragraph 4.3.5 above). This paragraph deals with the retirement of ordinary directors.

Articles 47 and 48 of the articles of association lay down the rules by which ordinary directors are to retire by rotation. Article 48 deals with the order of retirement, while article 47 stipulates the numbers concerned. Under article 48, those required to retire shall be those who have been longest in office since their last appointment or reappointment. If two or more such people are eligible, because they were appointed directors on the same day, then those to retire shall (unless they otherwise agree among themselves) be determined by lot.

Under article 47, at every annual general meeting of the commonhold association, one-third of the directors who are subject to retirement by rotation or, if their number is not three or a multiple of three, the number nearest to one-third shall retire from office; but if there is only one director who is subject to retirement by rotation, he shall retire. If the retiring director is not reappointed (see paragraph 4.3.7 below), article 53 of the articles of association provides that he shall retain office until the meeting appoints someone in his place or, if it does not do so, until the end of the meeting.

Article 49 of the articles of association provides that if the commonhold association, at the meeting at which a director retires by rotation, does not fill the vacancy, the retiring director shall, if willing to act, be deemed to have been reappointed unless at the meeting it is resolved not to fill the vacancy or unless a resolution for the reappointment of the director is put to the meeting and lost.

4.3.7 Reappointment of directors

Article 54 of the articles of association provides that a director who retires at an annual general meeting may, if willing to act, be reappointed. If he is not reappointed, he shall retain office until the meeting appoints someone in his place or, if it does not do so, until the end of the meeting.

4.3.8 Disqualification of directors

Article 55 of the articles of association sets out the circumstances in which a director is disqualified (or where 'the office of a director is vacated', to use the language of the Companies Acts which the articles of association employ):

(a) Where an ordinary resolution is passed by the members in favour of removal.

(b) Where a director ceases to be a director by virtue of any provision of the Companies Act, or becomes prohibited by law from being a director.

(c) Where a director becomes bankrupt or makes any arrangement or composition with his creditors generally, or a bankruptcy restriction order is made in accordance with the provisions of Schedule 4A to the Insolvency Act 1986.

(d) Where a director is, or may be, suffering from mental disorder and is either admitted to hospital in pursuance of an application for admission for treatment under the Mental Health Act 1983, or is made subject to a court order detaining him, or for the appointment of a receiver to exercise powers with respect to his property or affairs.

(e) Where a director resigns his office by notice to the commonhold association.

(f) (As a default provision) where a director shall for more than three consecutive months have been absent without permission of the directors from meetings of directors held during that period or from three consecutive meetings (whichever is the greater), and the directors resolve that his office be vacated.

As originally drafted, the articles of association omitted the first ground for removal, although section 303(1) of the Companies Act 1985 provides that, notwithstanding anything in a company's articles to the contrary, a director may be voted out of office by ordinary resolution during the course of an ordinary meeting of the commonhold association. In order to prevent ambushes, and to allow time for proper consideration, such a resolution may *only* be made where the meeting has been called by special notice, giving 14 days notice in writing (see sections 303(2) and 369(1)(b) and (2)(b) of the 1985 Act).

The original draft provided a further circumstance for removal:

> having been a member of the commonhold association when appointed a director, he ceases to be a member of the commonhold association.

The retention of this automatic disqualification was presumably thought to serve no useful purpose.

The article concludes with the sensible provision that where there is only one or one remaining director of the commonhold association, an appointment of a new director must take place, before the director disqualified or being removed vacates his office.

4.3.9 Employment of directors

Article 61 of the articles of association allows for a director of a commonhold association to be employed by or provide services to the association beyond the range of his duties as director. This therefore allows, for example, a lawyer to advise a commonhold association of which he is a director on matters which are within his expertise, but which fall outside his duties as director.

As originally drafted, this article was subject to a proviso that the terms of any such appointment or arrangement should have been approved in advance by the commonhold association in general meeting. This safeguard is now absent, although there is no reason why (the article being a default one) the commonhold association should not reinstate it.

4.3.10 Outside interests of directors

Article 62 of the articles of association goes further than article 61 (see paragraph 4.3.9 above) in that it allows a director of a commonhold association to become directly or indirectly involved in a non-directorial capacity with any transaction or arrangement with the commonhold association or in which the commonhold association is interested. This will include, for example, a director transacting business with a commonhold association through a limited company of which he is a director or shareholder.

As in the case of employment of directors, there is no requirement that the terms of any such arrangement should first have been approved by the commonhold association in general meeting. The director must, however, have disclosed the nature and extent of any material interest of his to the other directors.

There is thus considerable scope for a director to arrange for services to the commonhold association to be provided by an organisation in which he has an interest, provided that his community of interest is disclosed to his fellow directors.

4.3.11 Avoiding conflicts of interest

It is clear from paragraph 4.3.10 above that there is considerable room for a director of a commonhold association to profit from the opportunities afforded by his links with other organisations. Article 62(c) adds as a default provision that such a director is not bound to account to the commonhold association for any benefit he derives from any such arrangement. Moreover, no arrangements in which he is involved shall be liable to be avoided on the ground of any such interest or benefit.

This protection of the interested director's position is, however, dependent on his having given notice to his fellow directors of the extent of his interest in the transaction or service in question.

A prudent director will always therefore give such notice. Of course, where he is unaware of his outside interest, and could not reasonably be expected to have known of it, then no difficulty will arise (a matter confirmed expressly by article 63(b) of the articles of association).

Where, however, the director knows of an interest which he fails to disclose, severe consequences may follow. In particular, the commonhold association might be entitled to have a transaction in which the director was involved set aside, or to sue the director for breach of duty.

A director is not entitled to vote in a matter in which he has a conflict of interest (see article 72 and paragraph 4.3.14 below).

The current (August 2003) version of article 63 adds the following provision which did not appear in the original (October 2002) draft:

> A commonhold association must keep a register of directors' interests and whenever it receives information from a director given in fulfilment of an obligation imposed on him by article 62, it is under obligation to enter in the register, against the director's name, the information received and the date of the entry. This register is open to inspection by any member of the commonhold association.

This is a sensible provision. A proposed form for such a register may be found at Form 2.16 of the Forms and Precedents part of this book.

4.3.12 Powers of directors

Article 56 of the articles of association provides that, subject to any provision to the contrary, the business of the commonhold association shall be managed by the directors, who may exercise all the powers of the commonhold association. This power may be delegated: see paragraph 4.3.13 below. The directors may also appoint agents to exercise their powers (article 57), subject to their duty to supervise the agents (article 77).

Article 20 provides that a director shall be entitled to attend, speak and propose a resolution at any general meeting of the commonhold association, even if he is not a member of the association. If the director is not a member he may not, of course, vote on the resolution, unless the director is the chairman of the meeting, when he is entitled to a casting vote even when not a member (see article 27).

4.3.13 Delegation of powers of directors

Article 58 of the articles of association provides that the directors of the commonhold association may delegate their powers to a committee consisting of two or more directors, members of the commonhold association and others as they shall think fit, provided that the majority of the members of any such committee from time to time shall be members of the commonhold association.

The directors may also delegate to any managing director or any director holding any other executive office or any managing agent such of their powers as they consider desirable to be exercised by him. Any such delegation shall be made subject to any provisions of the commonhold community statement, may be made subject to any conditions the directors may impose, may be made either collaterally with or to the exclusion of their own powers, and may be revoked or altered.

Subject to any such conditions, the proceedings of a committee with two or more members shall be governed by the articles regulating the proceedings of directors so far as they are capable of applying.

Delegation of powers does not excuse the directors of responsibility for the performance of a relevant duty: see *Lubrano v Proprietors of Strata Plan No 4038* (1993) (Digest).

The current (August 2003) draft of this article is more restrictive than the original (October 2002) version in two respects. First, it stipulates that any such delegation must be sanctioned by ordinary resolution. Secondly, it provides that a record must be kept giving details of any powers that have been delegated. A suggested form of such a record is at Form 2.17 of the Forms and Precedents part of this book.

4.3.14 Proceedings of directors

Articles 65 to 74 of the articles of association govern proceedings of directors, all of which are drafted as default provisions. The provisions may be summarised as follows:

(a) *Calling a meeting*: any director may call a meeting of the directors, either by doing so himself, or by requiring the association secretary so to do (article 65).

(b) *Notice of meetings*: it shall not be necessary to give notice of a meeting to a director who is absent from the United Kingdom unless he has given to the commonhold association an e-mail address for service (article 65). A notice calling a meeting of the directors need not be in writing nor given using electronic communications if there is insufficient time to give such notice having regard to the urgency of the matter (article 82).

(c) *Voting*: questions arising at a meeting must be decided by a majority of votes. In the case of an equality of votes, the chairman has a second or casting vote (article 65).

(d) *Quorum*: the quorum for the transaction of the business of the directors may be fixed by the directors and, unless so fixed at any other greater number, is the greater of half the number of appointed directors for the time being, or two. At least one of the persons present at the meeting must be a director other than a developer's director (article 66). Where the number of directors is less than the number fixed as the quorum, the continuing director may act only for the purpose of filling vacancies or of calling a general meeting (article 67). A director must not be counted in the quorum present at a meeting in relation to a resolution on which he is not, by reason of a conflict of interest, entitled to vote (article 72).

(e) *Entitlement of non-member director to vote*: as article 72 implies, a non-member director is entitled to vote in matters in which there is no conflict of interest. In the previous (October 2002) version of the articles, this right was left unsaid. The current (August 2003) draft makes this right express in the shape of article 69: 'A director, despite not being a member, is entitled to speak and propose a resolution at a meeting of the directors.'

(f) *Chairman*: the directors may appoint one of their number to be the chairman of the board of directors and may at any time remove him from that office. Unless he is unwilling to do so, the director so appointed must preside at every meeting of directors at which he is present. But if there is no director holding that office, or if the director holding it is unwilling to preside or is not present within 15 minutes after the time appointed for the meeting, the directors present may appoint one of their number to be chairman of the meeting (article 68).

(g) *Validity of acts of defectively appointed or disqualified directors*: all acts done by a meeting of directors, or of a committee, or by a person acting as a director are valid, even if it is discovered later that there was a defect in the appointment of any director or that any of them were disqualified from holding office, or had vacated office, or were not entitled to vote (article 70).

(h) *Resolutions without a meeting*: a resolution in writing signed by all the directors entitled to receive notice of a meeting of directors or of a committee of directors is as valid and effectual as if it had been passed at a meeting of directors or (as the case may be) a committee of directors duly convened and held. For this purpose, the resolution may consist of several identical documents each signed by one or more directors, rather than one document signed by all (article 71).

(i) *Conflict of interest*: a director who is not a member of the commonhold association must not vote at a meeting of directors or of a committee of directors on any resolution concerning a matter in which he has, directly or indirectly, an interest or duty which is material and which conflicts or may conflict with the interests of the commonhold association (article 72). For the purposes of this article, an interest of a person who is, for any purpose of the Companies Act (excluding any statutory modification thereof not in force when this regulation becomes binding on the commonhold association), connected with a director must be treated as an interest of the director. Where, by contrast, the director is a member of the commonhold association, then he may vote at any meeting of directors or of any committee of directors of which he is a member notwithstanding that it in any way concerns or relates to a matter in which he has any interest whatsoever, directly or indirectly, and if he votes on such a resolution, his vote must be counted; and in relation to any such resolution, he shall (whether or not he votes on the same) be taken into account in calculating the quorum present at the meeting (article 73).

(j) *Ruling on director's right to vote*: if a question arises at a meeting of directors or of a committee of directors as to the right of a director to vote, the question may, before the end of the meeting, be referred to the chairman of the meeting and his ruling in relation to any director other than himself shall be final and conclusive (article 74).

4.3.15 Remuneration of directors

Article 59 of the articles of association provides that the directors of the commonhold association will not be entitled to any remuneration unless a special[3] resolution proposing remuneration is passed.[4] Such a resolution should also specify the amount of the remuneration to be paid to the directors.

4.3.16 Expenses of directors

Article 60 of the articles of association provides that the directors may be paid all travelling, hotel, and other expenses properly incurred by them in connection with their attendance at meetings of directors or committees of directors or general meetings or separate meetings of the members of the commonhold association or otherwise in connection with the discharge of their duties.

Although this entitlement does not require sanction by resolution at a meeting of the association (compare remuneration, dealt with in paragraph 4.3.15 above), the requirement that the expenses should have been 'reasonably and properly incurred'[5] should discourage abuse of the system.

4.3.17 Indemnification of directors

Article 86 of the articles of association provides for a limited indemnification of the directors and officers[6] of the commonhold association out of the assets of the commonhold association.

[3] In the original (October 2002) draft, only an ordinary resolution was proposed.
[4] This article also provides that developer's directors are not entitled to any remuneration at all.
[5] The words 'reasonably and' have been added to reinforce the original (October 2002) draft.
[6] In the original (October 2002) draft, auditors were also made the subject of this indemnity.

This indemnity is limited to any liability incurred by the director or officer in defending any proceedings, whether civil or criminal, in which judgment is given in his favour or in which he is acquitted or in connection with any application in which relief is granted to him by the court in respect of alleged liability for negligence, default, breach of duty or breach of trust in relation to the affairs of the commonhold association.

This provision does not prevent a director relying upon the benefit of any other indemnity to which he might otherwise be entitled.

4.3.18 The duty to manage

The directors of the commonhold association have the duty to manage the commonhold. Section 35 of the Act, which is headed 'Duty to manage', sheds no light on the extent of this duty, save in so far as it gives the following particulars under subsection (2):

> The directors of a commonhold association shall, in particular, use any right, power or procedure conferred or created by virtue of section 37 for the purpose of preventing, remedying or curtailing a failure on the part of a unit-holder to comply with a requirement or duty imposed on him by virtue of the commonhold community statement or a provision of this Part.

So the duty to manage will include the duty to enforce the rules against unit-holders (and their tenants—see subsection (4)). What is left unsaid is the extent of the non-contentious duties. These are summarised in paragraph 4.3.19, and developed in detail in Parts 2, 3 and 4 of this Chapter.

4.3.19 The major responsibilities of the board of directors

The major responsibilities of the board of directors of a commonhold association are as follows:

(a) Keeping proper records of the members and business of the commonhold association.

(b) Holding annual meetings of the commonhold association.

(c) Ensuring that proper personnel are engaged to perform the required tasks.

(d) Ensuring the proper maintenance of the commonhold.

(e) Maintaining adequate insurance cover for the commonhold.

(f) Preparing budgets and assessments for regular expenditure and for the reserve fund.

(g) Ensuring that proper accounts of income and expenditure are prepared.

(h) Maintaining and operating a proper internal complaints procedure.

(i) Enforcing the provisions of the commonhold community statement, the memorandum and articles of association and the provisions of the Act and regulations made under it.

The first three of those duties are examined in Sections 4.4 to 4.7 below; the next two in Part 2 of this Chapter; the next two in Part 3; and the remaining two in Part 4 below.

4.4 RECORD KEEPING

4.4.1 Introduction

The Act and its regulations lay down a number of mandatory requirements regarding record keeping.

Records or documents which must be kept by the commonhold association are:

(a) a register of members;

(b) minutes of appointments of officers;

(c) minutes of meetings;

(d) copies of the original and any amended versions of the commonhold community statement;

(e) accounting records;

(f) insurance records;

(g) register of tenants;

(h) land registration documents.

Each of these is now considered in turn.

4.4.2 Register of members

Section 352 of the Companies Act 1985 imposes a duty upon a company to maintain a register of members. Paragraph 14 of Schedule 3 to the 2002 Act provides that regulations may make provision for the way in which that duty is to be carried out by the commonhold association. Articles 4 and 5 of the articles of association set out the following provisions regarding entry in and removal from the register.

Entry: Particulars of the person entitled to be entered in the register of members must be entered by the commonhold association within 14[7] days of the occurrence of the following events (as appropriate):

[7] Paragraph 72 of the October 2002 Consultation Paper proposed 21 days, but the majority of the consultees considered that this was too long.

(a) the date of incorporation of the commonhold association;

(b) the date on which the developer notifies the commonhold association of his right to be registered;

(c) the date on which the Land Registry gives notice that the registration of the land as commonhold land has been completed;

(d) the date on which the commonhold association receives notification, in writing, from the new unit-holder that the transfer of a unit has taken place.

Removal: If a member of the commonhold association ceases to be a unit-holder or resigns, the commonhold association must make the necessary alteration to the register, again within 14 days of becoming aware of those facts.

In the case of joint unit-holders, only one may be registered as a member, and specific provisions apply governing nomination, which are discussed in detail in paragraph 2.15.5.

A form devised by the authors for recording details of members is at Form 2.9 in the Forms and Precedents part of this book.

4.4.3 Minutes of appointments of officers

Article 76 of the articles of association requires the directors of the commonhold association to cause minutes to be made of all appointments of officers made by the directors or by the developer.

Such staff appointments need not (but usually would) take place during the course of meetings of the directors, in which case they might conveniently form part of the minute of the meeting (see paragraph 4.4.4 below). There is, however, something to be said for a separate book or file recording such appointments, for ease of reference.

The minutes may be made in books kept for the purpose or stored electronically on a computer system so long as they can be made available in paper form on request.

4.4.4 Minutes of meetings

Article 76 of the articles of association also requires the directors of the commonhold association to cause minutes to be made of all proceedings at meetings of the commonhold association, of members, of the directors, and of committees. The minutes must include the names of the persons present at each such meeting, the date of the meeting and any action agreed at the meeting.

As with the case of minutes of directors' appointments (see paragraph 4.4.3 above), the minutes may be made in books kept for the purpose or stored electronically on a computer system, so long as they can be made available in paper form on request.

4.4.5 Commonhold community statement

The originals of the commonhold community statement and any amended versions must be kept with the Registrar of Companies, while certified copies are required to be lodged with the Land Registry.

The original (October 2002) draft of the commonhold community statement required the commonhold association to retain and make available for inspection at its registered office a copy of the original and any amended versions of the commonhold community statement, together with a list of the date(s) upon which such documents were registered (see clause 53). This obligation is missing from the current (August 2003) version of the commonhold community statement, but is instead to be found in article 81 of the articles of association, which adds that:

> any unit-holder has the right, on reasonable notice and at a time suitable to the commonhold association, to inspect the commonhold community statement or the memorandum and articles of association.

4.4.6 Accounting records

The commonhold association is bound to keep the originals of those details of expenditure and income which will be used to prepare its annual accounts and for audit purposes.

4.4.7 Insurance records

The commonhold association should keep the relevant details of the insurance policy it has taken out for the insurance of the common parts and any other parts of the commonhold which it is obliged to insure by virtue of rules 16, 17 and 18 of the commonhold community statement.

4.4.8 Register of tenants and licensees

Paragraph 145 of the October 2002 Consultation Paper proposed, but did not require, that the details of lettings of commonhold units should be entered into a register of lettings by the commonhold association. The respondents to the Consultation Paper were largely in favour of this proposal, and provision has been made for it in the current (August 2003) draft of the commonhold community statement, in the shape of rule 6:

> The commonhold association must maintain a register of tenants and enter in it—
>
> (a) the postal address and unit number of the commonhold unit;
> (b) the name(s) and address for service of the unit-holder(s);
> (c) the name(s) and address for service of the tenant; and
> (d) the length of the tenancy or licence for a period longer than 28 days.

The authors endorse this proposal: a mandatory register of tenants makes good sense, particularly given the extent to which tenants may become involved in the running of the commonhold association (see paragraph 4.13.8 below). A suggested form for the register is provided as Form 2.15 in the Forms and Precedents part of this book.

4.4.9 Land registration documents

Like any other registered proprietor, the commonhold association will have a registered title which will be conclusive. The commonhold association should keep its official copy of the register for reference purposes, together with the title plan.

4.4.10 Company seal

Limited companies may, but need not, have a company seal. As originally drafted, the articles of association provided that any seal should only be used by the authority of the directors or of a committee authorised by the directors. The directors might determine who should sign any instrument to which the seal is affixed and unless otherwise so determined it should be signed by a director and by the secretary or by a second director (see article 80 of the October 2002 draft).

The current (August 2003) draft omits any reference to a seal. Although the Department of Constitutional Affairs indicates in its response to the October 2002 Consultation Paper that it does not intend any change to its proposals in this regard, the absence of provision for a seal presumably reflects the Department's agreement with the view of at least one respondent that seals are often mislaid. Nevertheless, the authors agree with the view of another respondent to the effect that the existence of a company seal may bring home to the directors the 'importance of the documents it is being used on', and consider that it may well be beneficial for a commonhold association to have a seal, and to include an article dealing with its use.

4.4.11 Inspection and copying of books and records

Article 80 of the articles of association requires that all books, minutes, documents or accounting records of the commonhold association must be 'kept on the site of the commonhold or a location similarly convenient to unit-holders and must be retained for a minimum period of 3 years'. The article goes on to provide that any member of the commonhold association shall have the right, on reasonable notice, at such time and place as shall be convenient to the commonhold association, to inspect such records, and to be provided with a printed copy of the same (where records are kept digitally); or with photocopies (where records are kept manually), upon payment of any reasonable charge for copying. Rule 54 of the original (October 2002) draft of the commonhold community statement extended this right to all unit-holders; this extension does not appear in the current draft.

As originally drafted, the articles provided that the rights of inspection should be subject to any resolution of the commonhold association in general meeting, and, in the case of any book, minute, document or accounting record which the directors reasonably consider contains confidential material the disclosure of which would be contrary to the interests of the commonhold association, to any reasonable conditions or redactions which the directors may impose or make (see article 83 of the draft articles of association attached to the October 2002 Consultation Paper). This safeguard (from the point of view of the directors) or unwarranted restriction (from the point of view of the unit-holders) does not appear in the current (August 2003) draft.

Article 81 extends the obligation to make documents available for inspection to the commonhold community statement and the memorandum and articles of association. In the case of these documents, however, there is no requirement to keep the documents on site or anywhere more convenient than the 'office' (presumably the registered office) of the commonhold association; and there is no obligation to provide copies.

4.5 GENERAL MEETINGS OF THE MEMBERS OF THE COMMONHOLD ASSOCIATION

4.5.1 Introduction

The articles of association require one annual general meeting and one interim general meeting to be held each year. Directors may also convene other general meetings, and are required to do so at the request of a member.

The articles of association govern the requirements for the notice to be given for the holding of such general meetings and the requirements for the business to be conducted. Those requirements are discussed in this Section. Voting procedure and requirements, which are also prescribed by the articles of association, are considered in Section 4.6 below.

4.5.2 Annual general meetings

As its name implies, an annual general meeting is a meeting of the members of the commonhold association that is held each year. Section 366(1) of the Companies Act 1985 requires a company to hold one general meeting annually, although this requirement may be relaxed in the case of a private company. Article 6 provides that the commonhold association must hold an annual general meeting; it is clearly essential that such a meeting should take place each year, because of the volume of business that there will be to transact.

Perhaps oddly, the articles of association do not prescribe the purpose of the annual general meeting.[8] Moreover, the Companies Acts do not require any particular items of business to take place at an annual general meeting. It is tolerably clear, however, that the subject matter of the annual general meeting should include:

(a) A review of the business and affairs of the commonhold association over the past year, including consideration of the accounts, balance sheets and reports of the directors and auditor.

(b) Consideration and approval of the report and budget for the forthcoming year (see paragraph 4.15.4 below).

(c) Rotational retirement and appointment or reappointment of directors (see Section 4.3 above).

4.5.3 Initial annual general meeting

Article 47 of the articles of association provides that at the first annual general meeting after the end of the transitional period, all the directors other than any developer's directors shall retire from office. There is thus a clean sweep at this stage, in readiness for the launch of the commonhold as a fully working institution.

At this stage, there will be a great deal of initial business to be dealt with: service contracts, insurance arrangements and other relevant agreements entered into by the developer will need to be assigned or replaced.

4.5.4 Interim general meetings

Article 7 of the articles of association provides as a default provision that, in addition to its annual general meeting, the commonhold association must hold at least one other general meeting each year. Such additional general meetings are called 'interim' general meetings[9] (see article 8).

In addition to any other business the commonhold association might have to transact at an interim general meeting, article 7 continues by requiring the directors to present an interim review of the business and affairs of the commonhold association since the preceding annual general meeting.

As originally drafted, the articles provided that such an interim general meeting could not be held within three months of the annual general meeting of the commonhold association. This stipulation has now been dropped.

[8] Contrast the interim general meeting required by article 7 to consider an interim review of the business and affairs of the commonhold association since the last annual general meeting.

[9] Replacing, with good reason, the old term 'extraordinary'.

4.5.5 Calling an interim general meeting

An interim general meeting may be called by:

(a) the directors, where there are sufficient directors within the United Kingdom to call a general meeting; or

(b) any director or any member of the commonhold association, where there are insufficient directors within the United Kingdom.

The directors *must* call an interim general meeting in the event that members of the commonhold association representing not less than one-tenth of the total voting rights of all the members requisition a meeting—see article 9.

4.5.6 Venue for general meetings

Article 11 of the articles of association provides that all meetings of the commonhold association shall be held on the commonhold or at a similarly convenient location.

4.5.7 Length of notice for general meetings

Article 10 of the articles of association provides that 21 clear days'[10] notice is required for general meetings. There are the following exceptions to this;

(a) *longer* notice of 28 days is required for (i) annual general meetings; and (ii) meetings called for the passing of a special resolution, a unanimous resolution, a termination-statement resolution, a winding-up resolution or a resolution appointing a person as a director;

(b) *shorter* notice of at least three clear days may be called if agreement to such shorter notice is obtained from (i) all the members entitled to attend and vote in the case of an annual general meeting; and (ii) not less than 95 per cent of the members entitled to attend and vote in the case of any other meeting.

4.5.8 Contents of notice of general meetings

Articles 11 and 12 of the articles of association provide for the contents of the notice of a general meeting:

(a) the notice must specify the time and place of the meeting (article 11);

(b) where the meeting is an annual general meeting, the notice must specify it as such (article 11);

[10] Article 2 of the articles of association defines the expression 'clear days' in relation to the period of notice to mean that period excluding the day when the notice is given or deemed to be given and the day for which it is given or on which it is to take effect.

(c) the notice shall include or be accompanied by:
  (i) a statement of the agenda of the business to be transacted at the meeting;
  (ii) the text of any resolutions to be proposed at the meeting; and
  (iii) a brief written explanation of the resolution(s) (article 12).

A suggested form of notice for an annual general meeting is at Form 2.18 in the Forms and Precedents part of this work.

4.5.9 To whom notice of general meetings must be given

Article 13 of the articles of association requires that notice of a general meeting shall be given to all the members and to the directors of the commonhold association. However, if a person to whom notice should have been given is not in fact notified, this will not invalidate the proceedings at that meeting, provided that the omission was accidental (see article 13).

Although the articles of association do not deal with this point, it presumably follows as the converse of article 13 that if notice is deliberately not given to a person entitled to receive it, then the proceedings at that meeting will be invalidated.

4.5.10 Medium of notice of general meetings

Article 82 of the articles of association (which applies generally to the service of notices) provides that any notice to be given to or by any person pursuant to the articles shall be in writing.[11]

4.5.11 Mode of service of notice of general meetings

Article 83 of the articles of association provides that the commonhold association may give any notice of a meeting to a member either (a) personally; or (b) by leaving it at an address for service given to the commonhold association; or (c) by sending it by first class post in a prepaid envelope properly addressed to the member at an address given by him to the commonhold association as his address for service; or (d) where an electronic address has been provided as an address for service, by electronic communication to that address in accordance with any terms or conditions in connection with service by electronic communication as specified by the recipient.[12]

[11] The original version of this article (article 84 of the articles of association attached to the October 2002 Consultation Paper) added that notice could also be given using electronic communications to an address for the time being notified for that purpose to the person giving the notice. In view of the reference to electronic means of communication in article 83, however (see paragraph 4.5.11), it is considered that no significance is to be attached to this omission, and that an e-mail message will count as 'writing' for the purposes of article 82.

[12] This replaces the formulation used in the original (October 2002) draft, article 85—'in accordance with any of the methods described in subsections (4A)–(4D) of section 369 of the Companies Act'.

The original version of this article (article 85 of the articles of association attached to the October 2002 Consultation Paper) added that a member whose registered address is not within the United Kingdom and who gives to the commonhold association an address within the United Kingdom at which notices may be given to him, or an address to which notices may be sent by electronic communications, shall be entitled to have notices given to him at that address, but otherwise no such member shall be entitled to receive any notice from the commonhold association. Although this stipulation is restrictive, it makes for easier administration, and commonhold associations will wish to consider whether provision to similar effect should not be included.

4.5.12 Deemed service of notice of general meetings

A number of provisions deeming service of notice of a general meeting to have been effected are set out in articles 84 and 85:

(a) Where the commonhold association can prove that an envelope containing the notice was properly addressed, prepaid and posted by first class post, that proof shall be conclusive evidence that the notice was given. The use of the word 'conclusive' suggests that this presumption is irrebuttable. Further, a notice sent by first class post shall be deemed to have been given at the expiration of 48 hours after the envelope containing it was posted. This deeming provision is aimed at time of receipt rather than the fact of service.

(b) Where the commonhold association can prove electronic confirmation of receipt of an electronic communication, that proof shall again be conclusive evidence that the notice was given.[13] The use of the word 'conclusive' likewise suggests that this presumption is irrebuttable. The notice is deemed to have been given at the expiration of 24 hours after its transmission.

(c) Finally, where the notice was simply handed to the recipient or left manually at his address for service, the notice shall be deemed to have been given immediately after it was so handed (obviously) or left (not so obviously).

As originally drafted, the articles of association attached to the October 2002 Consultation Paper added a further deeming provision to the effect that if a member is present, either in person or by proxy, at any meeting of the commonhold association, he shall be deemed to have received notice of the meeting and, where requisite, of the purposes for which it was called. There was no suggestion that this deeming provision was akin to a rebuttable presumption; it would therefore appear to have been designed to be conclusive as to service, even were the attendee

[13] As originally drafted, the articles of association attached to the October 2002 Consultation Paper referred to proof 'that the notice was contained in an electronic communication sent in accordance with guidance issued by the Institute of Chartered Secretaries and Administrators'. The simplicity of the revision is to be welcomed.

able to prove that no notice was ever received. This provision has been omitted from the current (August 2003) draft, for reasons that are unclear.

4.5.13 Restrictions on transaction of business at general meetings

Article 14 of the articles of association provides that no business may be transacted at any general meeting unless details relating to it were included in the notice convening the meeting in accordance with Article 12. The purpose of this restriction is twofold. First, it has a timetabling function: it will be possible for the commonhold association to gauge the length of the meeting according to what is known of the proposed business, and therefore to allocate resources accordingly. Secondly, it enables the directors and other officers and members of the commonhold association to prepare for the business in an efficient manner.

4.5.14 Amendment of resolutions

A proposal to amend an ordinary resolution may, however, be voted upon if the terms of the proposed amendment were received by the commonhold association at its registered office, or at any address specified in the notice convening the meeting for the purpose of receiving electronic communications, not less than 48 hours before the time for holding the meeting (see article 14 of the articles of association). The decision of the chairman as to the admissibility of any proposed amendment shall be final and conclusive and shall not invalidate any proceedings on the substantive resolution.

4.5.15 Order of business at general meetings

At any general meeting, so far as practicable and subject to any contrary resolution of the meeting, any business arising from a requisition of members shall be transacted before any other business. If there is more than one requisition, the business arising shall be transacted in the order in which the requisitions were received by the commonhold association (see article 15 of the articles of association).

4.5.16 Adjournment of general meetings

Article 21 of the articles of association stipulates as a default provision that the chairman may, with the consent of a meeting at which a quorum is present (and must if so directed by the meeting), adjourn the meeting from time to time and from place to place. However, no business may be transacted at an adjourned meeting other than business left unfinished from the earlier meeting.[14] This means

[14] To use the language of the earlier (October 2002) draft, 'business which might properly have been transacted at the meeting had the adjournment not taken place'.

that extra business may not be added merely because of the extra time afforded, unless of course a proposal to that effect has been submitted and decided to be admissible by the chairman of the meeting (see paragraph 4.5.14 above).

A general meeting must be adjourned if it is not quorate (see article 17, discussed in paragraph 4.6.15 below).

When a meeting is adjourned for 14 days or more, at least 7 clear days'[15] notice must be given specifying the time and place of the adjourned meeting and the general nature of the business to be transacted. Otherwise it is not necessary to give any such notice.

4.5.17 Chairman of general meetings

Articles 18 and 19 of the articles of association lay down the following rules governing the chairmanship of the meeting:

(a) If the board of directors has a chairman, and he is present at the meeting, then he must chair the meeting.

(b) If the board of directors does not have a chairman, or if it does, but the chairman does not attend, then some other director (previously) nominated by the directors must preside as chairman of the meeting.

(c) If neither the chairman nor such other director (if any) be present within 15 minutes after the time appointed for holding the meeting and willing to act, the directors present must elect one of their number to be chairman.

(d) If there is only one director present and willing to act, he shall be chairman.

(e) If no director is willing to act as chairman, or if no director is present within 15 minutes after the time appointed for holding the meeting, the members present and entitled to vote must choose one of their number to be chairman.

4.6 VOTING PROCEDURE AND REQUIREMENTS

4.6.1 Entitlement to vote

Broadly speaking, only those who are unit-holders will be members of the commonhold association (see Part 2 of Schedule 3 to the Act); and only those who are members will be entitled to vote at the meetings of the association. There are, however, some departures from this general rule, which are considered in this Section. In particular, the following may also be entitled to vote in certain circumstances:

[15] Article 2 of the articles of association defines the expression 'clear days' in relation to the period of notice to mean that period excluding the day when the notice is given or deemed to be given and the day for which it is given or on which it is to take effect.

(a) a receiver in the case of disability—see paragraph 4.6.3;

(b) a receiver or other representative in the case of financial difficulty—see paragraph 4.6.4;

(c) a chargee of a member's interest in a unit—see paragraph 4.6.5;

(d) proxies of members—see paragraph 4.6.6;

(e) joint unit-holders—see paragraph 4.6.10;

(f) the commonhold association itself—see paragraph 4.6.11;

(g) a non-member chairman of the meeting—see paragraph 4.6.12;

(h) a tenant of a member—see paragraph 4.6.13.

4.6.2 Objections to entitlement to vote

Where anyone wishes to object to a voter on the grounds that he is not entitled to vote, the objection must be made at the meeting at which the vote objected to is tendered (see article 37 of the articles of association). Any objection made in due time shall be referred to the chairman, whose decision shall be final and conclusive. Every vote not disallowed at the meeting shall be valid.

4.6.3 Mental health disability

Where a member otherwise entitled to vote is under a disability through mental disorder and a court has made an order accordingly, article 35 of the articles of association provides that the member's receiver or other person authorised in that behalf appointed by that court may vote on behalf of the member. The vote may be tendered on a show of hands or (if a poll is ordered) by poll; and in the case of a poll, a proxy may be used.

Before the right to vote in this fashion can be exercised, evidence to the satisfaction of the directors of the authority of the person claiming to exercise the right to vote must be deposited at the registered office, or at such other place as is specified in accordance with the articles for the deposit of instruments of proxy, before the time appointed for holding the meeting or adjourned meeting at which the right to vote is to be exercised. The evidence may also be presented to the directors at the meeting.[16]

4.6.4 Financial disability

A receiver appointed by the court or by a mortgagee, an administrator, a trustee in bankruptcy, a commissioner in sequestration or similar person may vote in place

[16] This is a much laxer version than the original (October 2002) draft, which required such evidence to be deposited at the registered office not less than 48 hours prior to the meeting.

of a member subject to the relevant financial difficulty, whether on a show of hands or on a poll (article 35). Before this right to vote can be exercised, the requisite evidence must be furnished—see paragraph 4.6.3 above.

4.6.5 Voting rights of mortgagees

The original (October 2002) draft did not give chargees of unit-holders an independent right to vote. However, paragraph 93 of the Consultation Paper proposed that a chargee should be entitled to vote if the unit-holder defaults on payment of monies due under a charge, and the chargee then takes possession of the unit. This entitlement could only be claimed by the chargee if it first gave written notice to the commonhold association of the exercise of its right to possession of the unit.

This proposal is now enshrined in article 36, which provides that a mortgagee who takes possession of a unit may vote in place of a member, whether on a show of hands or on a poll. Before this right to vote can be exercised, the requisite evidence must be furnished—see paragraph 4.6.3 above.

4.6.6 Proxy voting

Article 38 of the articles of association allows votes on a poll to be given either personally or by proxy. A proxy may only vote once on behalf of a member on each resolution, and a member may not appoint more than one proxy to attend on the same occasion, unless the first proxy is unable to attend.[17]

A member who wishes to demand a vote by poll may instruct his proxy to make that demand, since article 23 of the articles of association provides that such a demand by a person as proxy for a member shall be the same as a demand by the member.

4.6.7 Forms of proxy

Article 39 of the articles of association provides for a form of notice to be used where a member of the commonhold association intends to use a proxy to vote. A suitable form may be found at Form 2.19 in the Forms and Precedents part of this work.

Where the member wishes to limit his proxy's freedom of manoeuvre and instruct him as to the nature of the vote to be made, he should use instead a form in Form 2.20 in the Forms and Precedents part of this work, as provided for by article 40 of the articles of association.

[17] This contrasts with the original (October 2002) draft, which allowed members to appoint more than one proxy to attend on the same occasion. The purpose of this was presumably to allow a member owning more than one unit to cast the same number of votes as he has units, thus circumventing the prohibition in article 31 on one member casting more than one vote on a show of hands (see paragraph 4.6.14 below).

Members may be permitted to appoint proxies to attend a series of general meetings over a period of time (see article 41). In such cases, the member should instead use Form 2.21 (the 'Enduring Proxy') in the Forms and Precedents part of this work.

4.6.8 Provisions applicable to voting by proxy

Article 42 of the articles of association lays down a number of stipulations concerning proxy voting:

(a) The appointment of a proxy and any authority under which it is executed or a certified or approved copy of such authority must be deposited at the registered office of the commonhold association or such other place as it specifies in the notice convening the meeting.[18]

(b) Where the appointment has been made electronically, the relevant details must be sent to the specified electronic address.

A proxy appointment which is not so deposited, delivered or received will be invalid.

4.6.9 Termination of a proxy's authority

Article 43 of the articles of association provides that where the authority of a proxy is terminated by the member prior to any vote or poll demand, then any subsequent vote or poll demand by the proxy will be ineffective—*provided* that notice of the termination has by then been received by the commonhold association at the place at which the proxy details were duly deposited or received before the commencement of the relevant meeting. If such notice has not been received, then the vote or poll demand by the proxy will be effective, despite the fact of the termination of the proxy's authority.

It will therefore be critical for the member who wishes to terminate a proxy's authority not only to take the appropriate step to communicate that termination to the proxy, but also to give the requisite notice to the commonhold association.

4.6.10 Voting rights of joint unit-holders

Where a commonhold unit is owned by two or more persons, only one of them will be entitled to become a member of the commonhold association (in accordance with the procedure laid down in paragraph 8 of Schedule 3 to the Act). Even if the non-member joint unit-holder is generally content with that arrangement, there

[18] The original (October 2002) draft stipulated that the documents should be received not less than 48 hours before the time for holding the meeting. This requirement, which applied to all the specified methods of communication, has been dropped in relation to all.

will obviously be scope for a difference of view between the joint unit-holders as to the way in which votes should be cast on certain issues.

Paragraph 91 of the October 2002 Consultation Paper suggested a number of unsatisfactory solutions to this potential problem:

(a) The articles of association might be drafted so as to allow the vote of the unit to be split so that the vote could be cast to reflect differing views between joint unit-holders. This would be complicated to administer in practice.

(b) Alternatively, the member joint unit-holder could be prevented from casting a vote unless all the other joint unit-holders agree. This would discriminate against joint unit-holders.

(c) Alternatively, the member joint unit-holder could cast his vote without regard to the wishes of his non-member joint unit-holder. This would be simple to administer, but unfair to the unit-holder whose wishes would be ignored.

The responses to this topic in the Consultation Paper were mixed; the Department of Constitutional Affairs has for the time being decided that there should be no special provision giving voting rights to non-member joint unit-holders.

4.6.11 Voting rights of the commonhold association

Only members of the commonhold association are allowed to vote, and a commonhold association cannot be a member of itself (see paragraph 9 of Schedule 3 to the Act). It would seem to follow that a commonhold association cannot have a right to vote.

However, given that membership stems from unit ownership, it would perhaps be possible for a commonhold association to gain voting rights if it owned a unit (for example an office in the commonhold used for administrative purposes, or another unit used for short term tenancies to raise income for the association). Paragraph 88 of the Consultation Paper dealt with this by proposing that the articles of association should stipulate that the commonhold association may not exercise voting rights for any units it may own.

The Post-Consultation Report dated August 2003 does not address this proposal in terms. As they stand, however, the articles of association refer to the voting rights of members only (see articles 31 and 32), from which it would seem to follow that a commonhold association cannot vote, even if it does own a unit in its own right.

4.6.12 Voting rights of the chairman

Article 27 of the articles of association provides that, in the case of an equality of votes, whether on a show of hands or on a poll, the chairman is entitled to a casting vote. Where the chairman is entitled to vote himself (for example because he is a member of the association), then his casting vote will be in addition to his personal vote. Where he is not a member (say a non-member director of the association), he is nevertheless entitled to a casting vote.

4.6.13 Voting rights of tenants

Tenants of unit-holders do not have any entitlement to vote in their own right, but it makes sense to make provision for tenants to vote in the stead of the unit-holder, if that is what the unit-holder wishes. Paragraph 92 of the Consultation Paper therefore proposed that, subject to a rule that no tenant may vote on resolutions that require unanimous votes or on termination resolutions, it be a matter for decision between the unit-holder and his tenant as to who will exercise the voting rights in respect of a unit.

The most obvious place for this matter to be dealt with would be in the tenancy agreement between unit-holder and tenant, although there is no reason why it should not be set out in a separate document.

The Consultation Paper added that, if the tenant is to exercise any voting rights, the commonhold association should be formally notified of this fact and of which resolutions the tenant may vote on, before the tenant may do so. This makes good administrative sense.

The Post-Consultation Report dated August 2003 disclosed a range of responses to the proposals, prominent among which was the observation that there is nothing preventing the unit-holder making his tenant his proxy. The Department of Constitutional Affairs is currently considering the arrangements a unit-holder could make to allow the tenant to exercise the voting rights attached to the unit. At present, therefore, the articles of association make no specific provision for tenants to be able to vote.

4.6.14 Votes per member

The general principal for voting is that every member of the commonhold association has one vote. However, where a member owns more than one unit, then, subject to the point made in the next paragraph, that member has as many votes as he has units. The extra votes to which a multiple unit-holder is entitled will only count, however, where there is a poll. Where the vote is being conducted on a show of hands, members' extra votes are not counted—see articles 31 and 32 of the articles of association. The remedy for a multiple unit-holder who wishes his extra votes to be counted is to insist upon a poll—see paragraph 4.6.19 below.

Paragraph 83 of the Consultation Paper recognises that the allocation of one vote per unit owned may lead to unfairness:

> It may not . . . reflect the actual make-up of the commonhold. If we consider the example of a mixed-use commonhold, there may be one very large unit on the ground floor, perhaps

a supermarket, above this there may be ten or more smaller residential units. It may create an unfair environment if the supermarket only exercises the same voting strength as each residential unit. On the other hand, if one person owns multiple units he or she may exercise the voting rights for every unit owned, which may effectively allow one person to dominate proceedings in the commonhold.

The Consultation Paper goes on to make the following alternative proposals in an attempt to mitigate this perceived unfairness:

(a) Allocation of voting rights by size of unit (either by area or volume).

(b) Allocation of voting rights by value of unit.

(c) Restriction of voting by category of unit-holder (residential/commercial), allowing different unit-holders to vote on those matters affecting them.

(d) Prescription against excessive use of voting rights by a multiple unit-holder.

All these proposals introduce complexity, leading to mixed answers to the proposals. The Department of Constitutional Affairs comments in its Post-Consultation Report dated August 2003:

> In light of the wide range of views expressed by respondents we are now considering adopting a less prescriptive approach, using one member, one vote as a default provision but allowing commonhold associations the discretion to create their own system of voting to reflect the circumstances of the individual commonhold. We anticipate that this would lead to some commonholds adopting alternative voting structures of the kinds detailed in the Consultation Paper. Others may use the distribution of units between properties as another way of achieving the required balance in voting rights.

4.6.15 Quorum

As originally drafted, the articles of association provided that the quorum for a general meeting of the commonhold association should be 20 per cent of the members of the commonhold association entitled to vote upon the business to be transacted, or two members of the commonhold association so entitled (whichever is the greater) present in person or by proxy. This would have had the result that for commonhold associations with ten members or fewer, the quorum would always be two members; for associations with 11 to 15 members, the quorum would be three members; for associations with 16 to 20 members, the quorum would be four members; and so on. When the meeting is not quorate, it must be adjourned—see paragraph 4.6.16 below.

The 20 per cent threshold was put forward because it is one that is frequently adopted by companies. As the figures given above illustrate, however, the application of the same rule in commonhold could lead to the affairs of the commonhold being dominated by a small clique, even where the resolution required is a special or a unanimous one. In those circumstances, paragraph 95 of the Consultation

Paper suggested as a possible solution a requirement of a higher quorum where a unanimous resolution or special resolution is to be considered:

If a resolution must be passed unanimously the articles could provide that the quorum of the meeting shall be 50% of those members of the commonhold association entitled to vote. If a special resolution is to be considered the quorum at the meeting could be 35% of those members of the commonhold association entitled to vote. A further refinement could be that in a commonhold of only four units or less, the quorum required for a general meeting will be fifty percent of those members entitled to vote, with the quorum for unanimous resolution being seventy-five percent.

The default solution adopted by the current (August 2003) draft is to increase by one the minimum number of members required for a quorum, and to apply different quorums depending upon the type of resolution under discussion—see article 16. This produces the situation shown in Table 4.1 below.

TABLE 4.1

Type of resolution	Percentage of members required for quorum	Minimum number of members required to be present personally or by proxy
Ordinary	20	3
Special	35	4
Unanimous	50	5

Commonholds with fewer members than the default provision will obviously have to tailor the figures to suit themselves (see regulation 13(3) of the commonhold regulations).

4.6.16 Absence of quorum

Article 16 of the articles of association provides that no business may be transacted at any general meeting unless a quorum is present. Article 17 spells out the consequences if the requisite quorum is not present within half an hour from the time appointed for the meeting, or if during a meeting such a quorum ceases to be present: in such circumstances, the meeting must stand adjourned to the same day in the next week at the same time and place or to such time and place as the directors may determine.

Paragraph 97 of the Consultation Paper observes that the absence or loss of a quorum may hinder any progress being made by the commonhold association, and may cause financial loss for the commonhold or difficulty for unit-holders. A procedure often adopted by companies is that if a meeting is reconvened following a failure to achieve the necessary quorum or a meeting ceasing to be quorate, the quorum for the reconvened meeting will be deemed to be the number of persons attending. However, although the Consultation Paper proposed that a similar provision be included in the articles of association, no such conclusion was reached in the Post-Consultation Report dated August 2003, and no such provision has been included in the latest version of the articles of association.

4.6.17 Voting in writing

Article 30 allows for voting on a resolution in writing. Where a resolution in writing has been executed by or on behalf of each member who would have been entitled to vote upon it if it had been proposed at a general meeting at which he was present, the resolution will be as effectual as if it had been passed at a general meeting duly convened and held.

The resolution need not be executed by all the voting members; it will suffice if all the members in question execute identical documents.

4.6.18 Taking votes by show of hands

Article 23 of the articles of association provides that a resolution put to the vote of a meeting must be decided on a show of hands unless before, or on the declaration of the result of, the show of hands, a poll is duly demanded. 'Duly' in this context is explained in paragraph 4.6.19 below.

Article 24 then provides that unless a poll is duly demanded, a declaration by the chairman that a resolution has been carried or carried unanimously, or by a particular majority, or lost, or not carried by a particular majority, and an entry to that effect in the minutes of the meeting, will be conclusive evidence of the fact without proof of the number or proportion of the votes recorded in favour of or against the resolution. In other words, it will suffice, upon a show of hands, for the chairman to record the vote as 'motion carried', 'carried by a majority', 'carried unanimously' or 'defeated', as the need may be, without recording numbers of votes.

4.6.19 Taking votes by poll

There are a number of reasons why a poll might be demanded instead of a vote by show of hands. First, the show of hands might not reveal a conclusive result. Secondly, a member owning more than one unit might wish to have all his votes counted, which would not be possible on a show of hands (see paragraph 4.6.14 above). Thirdly, a member might wish to delay the outcome of the vote, and use the time to whip up more support.

There is, however, no automatic right to a poll. Article 23 of the articles of association provides that a poll may only be demanded:

(a) by the chairman; or
(b) by at least two[19] members having the right to vote at the meeting; or

[19] The original (October 2002) draft provided for at least five members to vote in favour of a poll.

(c) by a member or members representing not less than one-tenth of the total voting rights of all the members having the right to vote at the meeting.

Article 25 provides that the demand for a poll may be withdrawn before the poll is taken, but only with the consent of the chairman. If a demand is withdrawn, then the result of a show of hands declared before the demand was made remains valid. If a poll is demanded before the declaration of the result of a show of hands and the demand is duly withdrawn, the meeting must continue as if the demand had not been made (see article 28).

The demand for a poll does not prevent the continuance of a meeting for the transaction of any business other than the question on which the poll was demanded (see article 28).

4.6.20 Method of taking votes by poll

Articles 26, 28 and 29 of the articles of association deal with the way in which the poll is taken:

(a) The chairman decides the manner in which the poll is taken, having particular regard to the convenience of members.

(b) A poll demanded on the election of a chairman or on a question of adjournment must be taken forthwith.

(c) A poll demanded on any other question must be taken either forthwith or at such time and place as the chairman may direct, having particular regard to the convenience of members, and not being more than 30 days after the poll is demanded.

(d) No notice need be given of a poll not taken forthwith if the time and place at which it is to be taken are announced at the meeting at which it is demanded. In any other case at least 7 clear days' notice must be given specifying the time and place at which the poll is to be taken.

(e) The chairman may appoint scrutineers (who need not be members of the association).

(f) The result of the poll will be deemed to be the resolution of the meeting at which the poll was demanded.

4.6.21 Resolutions

The great majority of matters requiring the decision of the members of the commonhold association at general meetings will be satisfied by 'ordinary resolutions'—that is to say, resolutions requiring only a simple majority of the votes of the members present (assuming of course that there is a quorum). Other matters require a majority of a specified percentage (a 'special resolution'), or unanimity (a 'unanimous resolution'). Yet further matters require a specified majority (80 per cent or 100 per cent) of all the members (and not merely of those who cast a vote). These terms are defined in article 22.

Table 4.2 below sets out examples of the matters requiring ordinary, special majority, or unanimous resolutions. Winding-up and termination-statement resolutions, which are dealt with in Chapter 5, are not included in the table.

TABLE 4.2

A: Matters for which ordinary resolutions (ie resolutions requiring a simple majority of the votes of the members voting) only are required:	
Subject matter of vote	**Text Reference**
1. Whether a director should be voted out of office.	4.3.8
2. Whether to approve a contract with a managing agent.	4.7.5
3. Whether to appoint a committee.	4.7.2
4. Whether to add, delete or amend any rule contained in the default or optional provisions of the commonhold community statement.	2.18.3
5. Whether to change the size of a commonhold unit or the common parts with the consent of the unit-holder and/or registered chargee.	2.18.3
6. Whether to alter the common parts.	2.18.3
7. Whether (with the consent of the developer) to amend the development rights.	2.20.4
B: Matters for which a special majority (75 per cent) of the votes of the members voting is required:	
Subject matter of vote	**Text Reference**
1. Whether to authorise the transfer of part of a commonhold unit.	4.13.3
2. Whether the directors of the commonhold association should be entitled to any remuneration and, if so, the amount.	4.3.15
3. Approval of a commonhold assessment.	4.15.4
4. Approval of a reserve fund levy at an annual general meeting.	4.16.7
5. Whether to make a provision in place of a default provision in the commonhold community statement.	2.18.3
6. Whether (with the consent of the unit-holder) to change the permitted use of a commonhold unit.	2.18.3
7. Whether to change the percentage of the commonhold assessment or reserve fund levies allocated to a commonhold unit.	2.18.3
8. Whether to change the restrictions on the limited use areas.	2.18.3
C: Matters for which the unanimous votes of all the members voting is required:[20]	
Subject matter of vote	**Text Reference**
1. Whether to permit the creation of a charge over the common parts of the commonhold.	3.6.2
2. Application to add land to a commonhold.	3.7
3. Whether to change the allocation of votes given to a commonhold unit.	2.18.3

[20] Note that winding-up and termination-statement resolutions, which are dealt with in Chapter 5, require 100% or 80% of the votes of all the members of the commonhold association, and not merely of those present at the meeting.

4.7 PERSONNEL

4.7.1 Introduction

Members of small commonhold associations may wish to carry out as many of the administrative and other functions of the association as they can, in order to minimise cost and reduce formality. For larger commonhold associations, where this will not be pragmatic, the decision will have to be taken to appoint professional directors and/or managing agents.

Whether or not such a step is taken, even the smallest commonhold association will need to appoint committees of members or directors with special responsibility for the execution and supervision of the duties of the commonhold association. The appointment of committees and managing agents and the roles of such members and directors are explored in this Section.

4.7.2 Committees

Paragraphs 113 and 114 of the October 2002 Consultation Paper suggested that provision could be made in the commonhold community statement for committees to be formed by the commonhold association, while recognising that a complex committee structure would only be necessary in larger commonhold developments.

Rule 55 of the original (October 2002) draft commonhold community statement took up this proposal by putting forward for consideration an executive committee, a finance committee and a buildings committee. In the case of a mixed development, rule 55 suggested that there should also be a residents' committee and a commercial committee, consisting respectively of unit-holders of residential and non-residential units in the commonhold. Once the commonhold association had decided on its committees, the commonhold community statement should also specify the number of members each such committee should have, together with the functions of each committee.

Rule 55 of this earlier draft of the commonhold community statement also laid down the following stipulations regarding the functioning of the committees:

(a) the committees must report to, and be subject at all times to control and supervision by, the board of directors;

(b) the board of directors may impose other functions upon the committees from time to time;

(c) the board of directors may also subject the committees to other restrictions and extend their powers from time to time;

(d) The members of such committees must be elected by the members of the commonhold association at the annual general meeting in each year to serve until the conclusion of the next annual general meeting.

In its Post-Consultation Report dated August 2003, however, the Department of Constitutional Affairs noted the responses of some of the consultees to the effect that an imposition of a committee structure would be unwieldy, and proposed that any provision regarding committees should be optional to allow this to reflect the circumstances of the individual commonhold. The current (August 2003) version of the commonhold community statement omits any reference to committees.

The current (August 2003) version of the articles of association does however lay the groundwork for the appointment of committees by the directors. Article 56 provides that, where an ordinary resolution is passed in favour, the directors may delegate any of their powers to any committee consisting of two or more directors, members of the commonhold association and others as they think fit, provided that the majority of the members of any such committee from time to time are members of the commonhold association. Any such delegation is subject to any provisions of the commonhold community statement. It is therefore open to a commonhold association to institute a committee system, unless the commonhold community statement provides otherwise.

4.7.3 Company Secretary

The commonhold association is required by section 283(1) of the Companies Act 1985 to have a company secretary. Subject to that requirement, article 75 of the articles of association provides for the company secretary to be appointed by the directors for such terms, at such remuneration and upon such conditions as they may think fit; and any secretary so appointed may be removed by them.

The company secretary is the chief administrative officer of the commonhold association, and is charged, in summary, with the duty of ensuring that the affairs of the commonhold association are conducted in accordance with the provisions of the Companies Acts, the articles of association and the general law. Having regard to the complexities that may be involved in running a commonhold association, and the guidance that may need to be given to directors and members, this may well be a weighty task, and larger commonhold associations will do well to ensure that their company secretary has trained as a lawyer or accountant.

However, although the secretary is a key officer in the commonhold association, his role is exclusively administrative and ministerial: he has none of the managerial functions which are vested in the directors. If it is intended that the secretary should exercise managerial functions, then he should be made a director of the commonhold association in addition to his secretaryship. It will be possible, and may well be an attractive solution, for a small commonhold association to have two directors (the minimum requirement under paragraph 4.3.2 above), and to have one of those directors doubling as the company secretary.

The duties of the secretary, including the derivation of those duties from the Companies Act 1985, may be summarised as follows:

(a) to be present at all meetings of the commonhold association and of the directors;

(b) to monitor compliance with the memorandum and articles of association;

(c) to make proper minutes of meetings, and to make the minutes of general meetings available (section 383);

(d) to take charge of the books of the commonhold association, including the register of members and of directors, and to make those registers available for inspection (sections 169, 325–326 and 356);

(e) to certify transfers and other documents in the name of the commonhold association;

(f) to prepare all necessary returns to the Registrar of Companies;

(g) to keep the record of charges of the commonhold association, and to ensure the registration of those charges with the Registrar of Companies (sections 411–412);

(h) to sign annual returns (section 363);

(i) to sign directors' reports on behalf of the board (section 234A);

(j) to send out copies of the commonhold association's accounts and directors' reports (sections 238–239);

(k) to ensure safe custody and proper use of any company seal;

(l) to issue notices at the direction of the board of directors;

(m) to conduct correspondence with the members in the name of the commonhold association.

4.7.4 Treasurer

The board of directors will usually wish to appoint one of their number to be a treasurer, whose duties will include signing cheques; ensuring that record books are properly kept for presentation to the auditors; and to enable immediate checks on finances to be carried out.

4.7.5 Managing agents

Article 77 of the articles of association provides for the directors to have the power on behalf of the commonhold association to appoint and enter into contracts with managing agents of the commonhold on such terms as they think fit (including a term providing for cancellation of the contract and return of records and monies paid). The directors remain bound to supervise the managing agent so appointed.

The original (October 2002) draft of this article provided that this power should not be exercised unless the terms of such appointment or contract (including those as to remuneration) should first have been approved by the commonhold association in general meeting. There is no such limitation in the current (August 2003) draft.

4.7.6 Agents and other third parties

Article 57 of the articles of association provides that, subject to article 77 (see paragraph 4.7.5 above), the directors may, by power of attorney or otherwise, appoint any person to be the agent of the commonhold association for such purposes and on such conditions as they determine, including authority for the agent to delegate all or any of his powers.

As originally drafted, the scope of this provision was enlarged or illuminated by clause 4.13 of the memorandum of association, which allowed the commonhold association:

> from time to time to employ or enter into contracts with builders, decorators, cleaners, contractors, gardeners or any other such person, to consult and retain any professional advisers and to pay, reward or remunerate in any way any person, firm or company supplying goods or services to the commonhold association.

This illumination was presumably considered to be otiose, and does not appear in the current (August 2003) version. Moreover, there is no longer a stipulation that this power may be exercised only with the prior approval of the commonhold association in general meeting (see paragraph 4.7.5 above).

4.7.7 Best Practice Guide

The Best Practice Guide in Chapter 8 considers the personnel a commonhold association will be expected to need to perform its various functions, together with a full discussion of those functions.

PART 2 LAND AND PROPERTY MATTERS

4.8 GENERAL

4.8.1 Introduction

During the passage of the Commonhold Bill through Parliament, the Bill's promoters stressed repeatedly that, in order for commonhold to attract support, it would be critical to ensure that as few restrictions as possible were placed upon the freedoms of the unit-holder. The commonholder should be treated as far as possible as if he were an independent freeholder.

There are, however, limits to the extent to which this principle can be given free expression, particularly where the unit-holders are as proximate and reliant upon each other as in the case of a block of flats. A body of rules is therefore necessary to provide for the protection of the commonhold, and to regulate some aspects of behaviour within it.

This Part examines the functioning of the commonhold in practice: how the commonhold association and the unit-holders are expected to interrelate with the aim of ensuring that the fabric of the commonhold is kept in good order and properly insured; how behaviour should be kept within tolerable limits; what may or may not be done to individual units and to the common parts; and what property transactions should be restricted.

4.8.2 The commonhold community statement

The commonhold community statement sets out the body of rules governing behaviour in a commonhold. The rules govern both the commonhold association and the unit-holders (including, significantly, those unit-holders who are not members of the commonhold association, for example because they have not yet given notice of a recent transfer of the unit to them).

Much of the content of the commonhold community statement is mandatory and in standard form, and may not be changed, even with the unanimous agreement of all members of the commonhold association. Other provisions are voluntary, and will have been inserted by the originator of the commonhold, and may be changed given the necessary majority of votes of the members.

4.8.3 The approach of the current draft commonhold community statement

In October 2002, the Lord Chancellor's Department issued a Consultation Paper with a draft commonhold community statement attached for comment. The draft was long, and indistinguishable in many respects from a long lease of residential premises in a multi-occupied block.

The level of prescription was criticised by the consultees, and the criticisms were broadly accepted. As the authors of the Post-Consultation Report dated August 2003 say:

> Our current thinking in the light of the responses received and discussions with interested parties is that there should be a strong core of standard provisions but that beyond these individual commonholds should have a wide degree of flexibility. This approach supports our belief that commonholders should, as far as possible, be able to enjoy the freedoms of freeholders generally, rather than the numerous constraints traditionally associated with leases.

The current version of the commonhold community statement which was supplied with the Post-Consultation Report is less prescriptive, although it still contains 66 proposed rules (compared with the 70 rules in the original). Five of the rules are default provisions, which, it is proposed, may be replaced (although not, it seems, deleted altogether) by alternative provisions.

4.8.4 Layout of this Part

The maintenance and repair of the commonhold units and the common parts are examined in Section 4.9. Section 4.10 contains a discussion of the allied topic of alterations to the units and to the common parts. The responsibility for the insurance of the various parts of the commonhold is analysed in Section 4.11. Section 4.12 then considers the use to which a commonhold unit may be put, with a full examination of behaviour generally in commonhold. Finally, Section 4.13 looks at the extent to which transactions concerning commonhold units are permitted within commonhold.

This Section does not deal with the financial aspects of running a commonhold (which are examined in Part 3), nor with the enforcement of commonhold obligations (considered in summary in Part 4, and in detail in Chapter 6).

4.9 MAINTENANCE AND REPAIR

4.9.1 Introduction

Sections 14(2) and 26(c) of the Act require the commonhold community statement to make provision regulating respectively the maintenance and repair of the commonhold unit and the common parts. The original (October 2002) draft of the commonhold community statement contained the following provision to satisfy the Act:

(a) a stipulation that each unit-holder should be responsible for the repair and maintenance of the interior of his commonhold unit;

(b) a requirement that the commonhold association should be responsible for the repair and maintenance of the exterior of the commonhold units; and

(c) an obligation on the commonhold association to repair and maintain the common parts.[21]

The current (August 2003) version of the commonhold community statement has departed from this maintenance model by keeping the obligation for the commonhold association to maintain the common parts (rule 20: 'The commonhold association must keep the common parts in good repair'), but omitting any obligation for the commonhold association or the unit-holders to repair or maintain the commonhold units. As the Post-Consultation Report dated August 2003 explains:

> Individual commonholds would be able to impose obligations on unit-holders to maintain their units if they so wish but we do not consider that a general mandatory obligation to

[21] These provisions were contained in rules 25 and 29 of the draft commonhold community statement attached to the October 2002 Consultation Paper.

keep a unit in good repair would be appropriate for a freehold owner, or necessary for a structurally independent unit. Similarly, an obligation to keep a unit clean does not seem to be appropriate to us. Our current intention is that the common parts would, where a unit is not structurally independent, include the structure and exterior of the building of which the unit forms part. The common parts would also include service media (pipes, drains etc.) other than those within and wholly serving a unit. The effect of this division of responsibility would carry through into the obligations relating to alterations and insurance. It will bring commonhold obligations more in line with freehold expectations and will also have the advantage of minimising the number of rights that are required over units or parts of units.

This Section deals with the appropriateness of this approach, before going on to consider the factors to be taken into account in determining the standard of repair and maintenance.

4.9.2 Division of responsibility for repair and maintenance

There was much debate in Parliament regarding the correct way of dividing responsibility for the repair and maintenance of the commonhold. While the commonhold association should clearly be responsible for the repair and maintenance of the common parts of the commonhold, it was far less obvious that it should have any responsibility for the repair and maintenance of individual units.

Much will of course depend upon the nature of the commonhold development in question. If the commonhold comprises a block of flats, then it is difficult to conceive of a reason for departing from the arrangement commonly used in leasehold, whereby the tenants are responsible for the interior and non-structural parts of their demises, while the landlord is responsible for the structure and exterior of the building. If, on the other hand, the commonhold consists of a group of interrelated but structurally independent buildings (for example a holiday chalet village), then there is no reason why the unit-holders should not bear responsibility for the repair and maintenance of the whole of their units. Since the provisions of the commonhold community statement concerning repair and maintenance are likely to be optional, those responsible for drafting the document for any commonhold development will no doubt revise the standard draft to suit their individual circumstances.

4.9.3 Standard of repair and maintenance

Although the commonhold community statement allocates responsibility for repair and maintenance of the common parts to the commonhold association, it is silent on the question of the appropriate standard to be applied when it comes to be considered what is the appropriate way in which the responsibility should be discharged. The original (October 2002) draft provided that the commonhold association should be responsible for the repair and maintenance of the common parts 'in accordance with such specifications and standards as may be set by the Board of Directors and published to Unit-holders from time to time'. It was therefore envisaged that the commonhold association should be free to determine its own standard of repair. Although this proposal has now been omitted (presumably in view of the mixed responses to the October 2002 Consultation Paper), the authors concur with this approach, if only because it would be impossible to devise and apply a 'one size fits all' standard to the many different problems that could be encountered in practice.

It is, however, necessary to consider the factors that should inform the commonhold association in their consideration of the standard to be applied to any given situation. The authors suggest the following analysis as a methodical approach to any given situation where the question of repair and maintenance is raised:

(a) Does any work need doing?

(b) If so, what work needs to be done?

(c) Are there any special factors that compel the conclusion that something else should be done instead of repair and maintenance?

(d) If not, when should the work be done?

These questions are discussed in turn in paragraphs 4.9.5 to 4.9.8 below.

4.9.4 The relevance of the leasehold authorities on 'repair' and 'maintenance'

The law of dilapidations in a leasehold context has produced a substantial number of authorities on the question what constitutes repair and/or maintenance in any given case. In summary, 'repair' involves the carrying out of work to something to remedy a deterioration, while 'maintenance' describes the carrying out of work to prevent the deterioration arising in the first place.

The authors suggest that it would be wrong to apply decisions from the leasehold context into the context of commonhold, at least without considerable caution, for a number of reasons:

(a) First, it is axiomatic that a word in a document must be construed in context, and not given a meaning derived from a similar or even identical expression from a different document.

(b) Following on from that first proposition, it should be borne in mind when construing a term such as 'repair' in a commonhold community statement, by contrast to a lease, that the scale and extent of the liability is quite different. In commonhold, all owners have a freehold interest, and it is therefore to be expected that the repairing liability should be construed in a way that will favour long- rather than short-term solutions. In the case of a lease, on the other hand, where the interests of the parties are not identical, the length of the term will be a factor the court will bear in mind in determining whether it would be appropriate to require the tenant to bear liability for a more expensive long-term cure compared to a short-term patch repair. This point is illustrated by the following words of Nicholls LJ from a leasehold case, *Holding & Management Ltd v Property Holding & Investment Trust plc* [1989] 1 WLR 1313:

[T]he exercise involves considering the context in which the word 'repair' appears in a particular lease and also the defect and remedial works proposed. Accordingly, the circumstances to be taken into account in a particular case under one or other of these heads will include some or all of the following: the nature of the building, the terms of the lease, the state of the building at the date of the lease, the nature and extent of the defect sought to be remedied, the nature, extent, and cost of the proposed remedial works, at whose expense the proposed remedial works are to be done, the value of the building and its expected lifespan, the effect of the works on such value and lifespan, current building practice, the likelihood of a recurrence if one remedy rather than another is adopted, the comparative cost of alternative remedial works and their impact on the use and enjoyment of the building by the occupants. The weight to be attached to these circumstances will vary from case to case.

(c) Thirdly, a test which is applied in a leasehold context where the proposed remedial works are extensive is whether the building thus repaired at the end of the term of the lease will be different in kind: in the usual formulation, will the works amount to giving back to the landlord something different from that which existed before? Again, this part of the conventional leasehold repairs analysis is meaningless in a commonhold context, where nothing is ever 'given back'.

(d) Fourthly, while leasehold authorities on the whole refuse to impose liability upon a covenantor for the remedy of a defect of design or workmanship,[22] where the defect has not (yet) led to any deterioration in the subject matter of the covenant, it is difficult to see why this distinction should apply to commonhold, where the interests both of the unit-holders and of the commonhold association should pull in the same direction. If a defect in, say, the common parts needs remedying, all owners should want to implement the requisite remedy, without having to consider arcane questions as to origin or cause. It is comforting to note that two decisions of the Supreme Court in Australia have adopted exactly this approach: see *Proprietors of Strata Plan No 6522 v Furney* (1976) (Digest) and *Simons v Body Corporate Strata Plan No 5181* (1980) (Digest).

4.9.5 Question (a): does any work need doing?

Buildings exposed to the vagaries of the climate in England and Wales will experience deterioration in their fabric. Some elements of the fabric (the paintwork, flat roofs, exposed woodwork) will need frequent attention; others (concrete, stonework, brickwork) will only rarely need care. Individuals will differ in their attitudes to the question whether something needs to be done: the slate on the roof

[22] See, for example, the decision of the Court of Appeal in *Post Office v Aquarius Properties Ltd* [1985] 2 EGLR 105.

that has slipped will obviously need refixing if water penetration is likely to result; if the effect is only cosmetic, then the costs involved in remedial work are likely to outweigh the benefit for all but the most image-conscious owners. Paintwork, too, is an obvious candidate for difference of opinion: two years into a painting cycle, some degradation will have taken place. Some will favour a three-yearly cycle for exterior repainting; others will be content with something less frequent, at the expense of some localised deterioration in the woodwork beneath. To take another example, wood may warp and crack as it settles into a new construction, without causing any evident stress elsewhere, although the effect may be unsightly.

In the examples given above, some deterioration will have taken place. It does not follow, however, that all deterioration requires immediate, or even any, remedy. In all cases there will be a balance to be struck between the cost of the remedy and the consequences that will flow from a permanent or temporary decision not to carry out any work.

4.9.6 Question (b): what work needs to be done?

If the answer to the first question identified in paragraph 4.9.5 above is that the disrepair in question cannot simply be left as it is, then the next question to be considered will be what work needs to be done. In many cases, the answer will be obvious: the slate should be replaced; the repainting should be carried out; the cracked wood should be replaced or strengthened. In other cases, however, the answer will not present itself so readily. Consider the case of a flat roof, which has begun to leak. Should it be replaced or patched up? In answering that question, it will help to consider the following factors:

(a) The nature of the building: is it part of the living space, where water penetration will be unwelcome; or does it comprise ancillary space, such as a car-parking area, where such considerations are less important?

(b) The value of the building and its expected lifespan: it would be unsuitable to replace the roof of a shed with a covering with a 20-year lifespan if the shed is only expected to survive for another ten years.

(c) The costs of the various competing remedial options.

(d) Current building practice and compliance with building regulations: do these favour one option over another?

(e) The life of the various options, including the likelihood of a recurrence of the problem if one remedy rather than another is adopted.

(f) The extent to which one option rather than another may attract a guarantee against faulty workmanship and materials.

(g) The extent to which the area of the building in question may be out of commission while the works are being carried out if one method rather than another is selected.

Examples of the application of some of these factors in practice, albeit in a leasehold context, are provided by *Murray v Birmingham City Council* [1987] 2 EGLR 53 and *Postel Properties Ltd v Boots the Chemist* [1996] 2 EGLR 60.

4.9.7 Question (c): are there any special factors which compel the conclusion that something else should be done instead of repair and maintenance?

To take the example of the shed with the faulty roof mentioned in paragraph 4.9.6 above, the tenant who covenants to deliver up such a shed in repair is not excused from liability on the ground that the shed is ramshackle and not worth the money:[23] he is bound to comply with his covenant, or face the consequences in damages. There again, the tenant who covenants to keep underfloor heating in repair is not excused from liability for the requisite remedial work on the ground that such a system is redundant, and can be replaced far more cheaply and efficiently with surface heating.[24]

There is some room for optimism that these and similarly unattractive results, which tend to flow from the rigid application of dilapidations law in the adversarial context which regrettably typifies landlord and tenant relationships, could be avoided in commonhold—not because such works will not continue to be regarded as repair, but because there is unlikely to be anyone with an interest in prosecuting works which are of little or no benefit, particularly if they are to bear a share of the cost. It will be different, of course, if the alternative to repair is presented as the provision of a different service at the unit-holder's cost, as was the case unsuccessfully proposed in *Proprietors of Strata Plan 159 v Blake* (1986) (Digest).

This stage of the analysis, which only becomes relevant once it has been decided that there is a need for repair works of an identified kind, involves the commonhold association and its members standing back and seeing if there are alternatives to the proposed work. Should not the shed simply be left to rot, or be pulled down and replaced by a summerhouse? What about leaving the underfloor heating *in situ*, in its defective state, and installing storage heating instead?

4.9.8 Question (d): in the absence of special factors, when should the work be done?

If the decision is taken to carry out some remedial work, it will also be necessary to choose a time for the work. Again, in making this choice, a number of factors should be considered:

[23] Unless such an argument is open to him as a matter of valuation under section 18 of the Landlord and Tenant Act 1927.

[24] As was the situation in *Creska Ltd v Hammersmith and Fulham London Borough Council* [1998] 3 EGLR 35 (although in the event the tenant was able to deploy other arguments to escape from this unattractive result).

(a) The urgency of the works: can they await more clement weather?

(b) The weather conditions: it will obviously be more prudent to programme exterior works to take place in the summer.

(c) The effect upon the use and enjoyment of the building: as against the last factor, it will be best to keep to a minimum during summer those works that are likely to interfere with the enjoyment of good weather.

(d) The extent to which the works may be combined with other planned works that will make best use of set-up costs and items such as scaffolding.

(e) The need to budget for the works so far as possible to meet the means of members.

Careful consideration of those factors may result in the works being programmed to take place in months or even years, rather than in the near future.

4.9.9 Cleaning

In relation to the cleaning of the common parts, exteriors and windows and of the commonhold units, the original (October 2002) draft of the commonhold community statement provided:

> 59. The commonhold association shall be responsible for the regular cleaning of the Common Parts and the exterior of the Commonhold, including windows.
> 60. Each Unit-holder shall be responsible for the regular cleaning of his Commonhold Unit, including the exterior and windows thereof.

The proposed division of responsibility between commonhold association and unit-holder was not therefore maintained precisely when it came to cleaning. This rule would, however, no doubt have been tailored to meet individual circumstances. It would be unreasonable to expect the holder of a unit on the tenth floor of a tower block to assume responsibility for exterior window cleaning.

The current (August 2003) version of the commonhold community statement contains no reference to cleaning, for the reasons quoted in paragraph 4.9.1 above. Individual commonholds will, however, be able to insert whatever provision they consider fit.

4.9.10 The commonhold association's right of access to units for works

A commonhold unit is owned freehold by the unit-holder, and, unless provision were made in the commonhold community statement, the commonhold association would have no right of access to the unit (other than that provided by the Access to Neighbouring Land Act 1992). This might cause problems in the event that the commonhold association wished to enter a unit against the unit-holder's will in order to carry out a repair to the common parts which could not be effected in any other way, at any rate without excessive cost.

Rule 21 of the commonhold community statement contains the following provision to deal with this eventuality:

In order to carry out work necessary to keep the common parts in good repair the commonhold association has a right to enter a commonhold unit where reasonable notice of the intention to enter has been given to the unit-holder save in an emergency when no notice is required.

The extent to which it may be necessary to resort to litigation in exercise of this right, and the relevant procedure, are discussed in Section 6.3.

The limitations upon this right must be recognised. There is no right for the commonhold association to enter to carry out works to the unit itself (but see paragraph 4.9.11 below); and there is no right of access for any purpose other than repair to the common parts (for example to make an alteration, however desirable that alteration might be). The obvious answer for the commonhold association (other than to rely upon the goodwill of the unit-holders on each occasion) will be to build an appropriate right of access into the commonhold community statement.

In *Owners of Strata Plan 48754 v Anderson* (1999) (Digest), a unit-holder over whose unit there was a right of way for maintenance purposes, objected to the installation of strip lighting in the unit to facilitate that access. His objection was overruled by the Supreme Court of New South Wales on the ground that the grant of such a right of access was accompanied by such rights as were reasonably necessary for the use of the right. The same reasoning would no doubt apply to the use of a right of access sanctioned by the commonhold community statement.

4.9.11 Works in default

The original (October 2002) draft of the commonhold community statement provided that:

26. If default is made by any Unit-holder in repairing or maintaining his Commonhold Unit as required by these Rules, the commonhold association shall be entitled to effect such repairs or maintenance as the Board of Directors shall consider appropriate in respect of the Commonhold Unit and for that purpose shall be entitled to use and enforce rights of access to the Commonhold Unit . . .

This rule does not appear in the current (August 2003) version, for the reason that there is no longer any mandatory obligation on the unit-holder to repair or maintain his unit. If such an obligation is included, however, then a works in default provision of this kind will also be desirable. There are, however, a number of points to be made about this draft:

(a) The power conferred by the draft is an extensive one, and it ought to be used responsibly and sensitively. In particular, the commonhold association will wish to bear in mind section 35(3) of the Act (discussed in Section 6.3 of the text), which absolves them of the requirement to enforce unit-holders' obligations where no significant loss or disadvantage results.

(b) The existence of this rule as drafted underlines the importance of not being overly prescriptive when it comes to the ambit of the unit-holder's repairing obligation (considered in paragraph 4.9.12 below).

(c) In practical terms, if the unit-holder has not carried out the requisite repair, he is also likely to be resistant to the commonhold association carrying out the works in default. If access for that purpose is refused, or known or reasonably supposed to be unforthcoming, then the commonhold association should resort to litigation to achieve their aim—a matter considered in Section 6.3.

4.9.12 Unit-holder's repairing and maintenance liability

As has already been remarked, the current (August 2003) version of the commonhold community statement does not provide for the unit-holder to be subject to any maintenance liability whatsoever. The Department of Constitutional Affairs considers that it should be left up to individual commonhold associations to decide whether such provision is necessary.

If some form of obligation is considered necessary, then the next step is to decide how extensive and intrusive that obligation should be. The original (October 2002) draft provided that each unit-holder should be responsible for the repair and maintenance of the interior of his unit. That obligation might, however, seem unduly prescriptive, particularly where failure to comply with such an obligation would have no effect upon others. Paragraph 156 of the October 2002 Consultation Paper observed in this connection that:

> It may be preferable to provide that the unit-holder must repair and maintain the interior of the unit if the deterioration of the interior would adversely affect any other unit-holder.

The authors commend this suggestion.

4.10 ALTERATIONS

4.10.1 Introduction

In keeping with the legislative preference for confining the operational details of commonhold to the regulations rather than the main body of the statute, the Act is, with one exception, silent on the question whether alterations may be carried out to units.

The exception is provided by sections 23 and 24, which provide that alterations to a commonhold unit which lead to a difference in its size (for example the replacement of part of a garden by a communal parking area) may not be carried out without the consent of the unit-holder, unless a court dispenses with the requirement for such consent.

Alterations to a commonhold unit which would lead to an increase in its size (for example the addition of a storey into the airspace above a unit) would constitute a trespass, and could not therefore be carried out by the unit-holder without the consent of the commonhold association. Although this point seems trite, it has been responsible for a great deal of litigation in Commonwealth and other jurisdictions: see for example *Proprietors of Strata Plan No 1627 v Schultz* (1978) (Digest); *Strauss v Oyster River Condominium Trust* (1994) (Digest); *Gaffny v Reid* (1993) (Digest).

In some of these cases (*Strauss*, *Gaffny*), a prominent theme which emerges is the extent to which the strata title proprietor has been the author of the misfortune by turning a blind eye to that which it then seeks to have removed. This underlines the need for the commonhold association to be consistent in its application of the rules.

4.10.2 The standard commonhold community statement rules

The current (August 2003) version of the commonhold community statement contains two rules regarding alterations. Confusingly, one is found under the heading 'Use', while the other is found under 'repair and maintenance':

> 12. A unit-holder must not make any alterations to the common parts.
>
> . . .
>
> 22. The commonhold association must not alter the common parts unless a resolution is passed by the commonhold association.

There is no restriction upon alterations by unit-holders to individual units, although commonhold associations may wish to introduce their own restrictions, bearing in mind the factors discussed in paragraph 4.10.3 below.

4.10.3 Possible restrictions on alterations to units

The extent to which alterations to units should be restricted by an appropriate rule in the commonhold community statement is something which individual commonhold associations should consider. The following factors may assist in that determination:

(a) Where uniformity is important, for aesthetic or other reasons, there may be much to be said for a blanket prohibition on alterations to a unit, or at any rate those which affect the external appearance of the unit. This principle has informed a number of the overseas cases: see, for example, *Proprietors of Strata Plan No 464 v Oborn* (1975) (Digest) (injunction granted for replacement of window frames unlawfully altered); *Piccadilly Place Condominium Association, Inc v Frantz* (1994) (Digest) (erection of burglar bars held not to infringe prohibition); *Monday Villas Property Owners Association v Barbe* (1997) (Digest) (injunction granted for removal of prohibited radio antennas).

(b) Where peace and quiet are important (for example in a sheltered housing development), then again a blanket prohibition may be appropriate.

(c) Where units are structurally interdependent (as in the case of a block of flats), any alterations that affect the structure should be forbidden, at any rate without the consent of the commonhold association. Alternatively, the unit may be defined in such a way as to exclude the structure and exterior.

4.10.4 A possible solution

One possible compromise between complete freedom to alter units and a blanket ban on alterations would be a requirement for the unit-holder to seek the consent of the directors to any proposed alteration to a unit. This compromise informed the drafting of the original (October 2002) draft of the commonhold community statement:

> 27. Any alterations to the structure or external appearance of a Commonhold Unit may only be made with the written consent of the Board of Directors, and subject to the provisions of sections 23 and 24 of the Act (if applicable).

This draft will be a good starting point for most prospective commonhold associations. It will not go far enough for those wishing to prohibit any work at all (see (b) in paragraph 4.10.3 above), and it will be too prescriptive for some of those living in a spread out development. It may also lead to resentment if uneven treatment is permitted with changing membership of the association, as some of the Commonwealth cases illustrate (see, for example, *Strauss*, *Gaffny* cited in paragraph 4.10.1 above).

4.11 INSURANCE

4.11.1 Introduction

Sections 14(2) and 26(b) of the Act require the commonhold community statement to make provision regulating respectively the insurance of the commonhold units and the common parts. The relevant provisions of the commonhold community statement dealing with insurance are rules 16 to 19.

As with the case of repair and maintenance, the Government's preoccupation with striving to ensure that the unit-holder should be treated like a freeholder gave rise to a dilemma: how far can or should the unit-holder be trusted to arrange matters himself? As the Opposition spokesman said during the course of the Report Stage:

> My concern is that commonhold associations will enter into many different types of agreement and that there will be no consistency. As a result, what should be insured by the commonhold association for the integrity of the whole of the unit-holders may be insured by

the unit-holder who may not have adequate insurance, may not have paid the premium or may not be fully covered. Who will check on that? The Minister's final equation was that the insurance cover of the unit-holder and the commonhold will cover 100 per cent. That is exactly the problem: it may not.[25]

Although it might be thought that the owner of a stand-alone unit should be free to take out his own insurance without supervision, it will readily be appreciated that the extent of adequate insurance is a legitimate communal concern: no one will want to live next to a burnt-out, under-insured unit. The real issue, therefore, discussed in paragraph 4.11.3 below, is not whether insurance arranged by unit-holders should be vetted by the commonhold association, but whether unit-holders should be allowed to arrange their own insurance at all.

4.11.2 Responsibility for insurance of common parts

Rules 16 and 17 of the commonhold community statement provide that the commonhold association must take out and maintain public liability and buildings insurance in respect of the common parts. Rule 18 then addresses (1) the risks to be covered against; and (2) the appropriate level of cover.

As to (1), the risks to be covered against must include (a) loss or damage by fire; (b) full rebuilding and reinstatement costs of the property insured; and (c) the cost of providing alternative accommodation in the event that a property is rendered incapable of use. The commonhold association is also free to insure against any other risk that it considers appropriate. Those risks will normally select themselves or be dictated by the insurance market, having regard to the type of commonhold development. A residential development will obviously require different cover to a mixed development.

As to (2), the sum insured must be (i) based on the costs of rebuilding or reinstating the property assessed at a point 18 months in advance; (ii) properly calculated by a member of the Royal Institution of Chartered Surveyors; and (iii) index-linked. Rule 19 adds as a default provision that an assessment of the reinstatement costs of the commonhold buildings must be carried out at least every five years for the purposes of buildings insurance.

4.11.3 Responsibility for insurance of units

The current (August 2003) draft of the commonhold community statement makes no provision in relation to the insurance of individual units. This is to be contrasted with the original (October 2002) draft, which provided the following alternative provisions:

22. Every Unit-holder shall take out and maintain buildings and contents insurance, including public liability insurance, in respect of his Commonhold Unit in a form satisfactory to the

[25] *Official Report, House of Lords*, 13 November 2001; col 474.

Board of Directors. Any buildings insurance which is in a form satisfactory to the mortgagee of a Commonhold Unit shall be deemed to be in a form satisfactory to the Board of Directors.

OR

22. Every Unit-holder shall take out and maintain contents insurance, including public liability insurance, in respect of his Commonhold Unit in a form satisfactory to the Board of Directors. The commonhold association shall take out and maintain buildings insurance, including public liability insurance, in respect of the Commonhold Units.

The alternatives illustrate the Government's dilemma, referred to in paragraph 4.11.1 above, whether the commonhold association should delegate the responsibility for insuring individual units to the unit-holders themselves (as of course would be the case in non-commonhold freehold); whether it should maintain direct control by insuring units itself; or whether it should make no unit insurance provision at all. There is much to be said for the commonhold association taking the task upon itself, particularly where the units are structurally interdependent: (a) it would then know that satisfactory cover has been procured; (b) it would be saved the administrative burden of checking with unit-holders that proper insurance has been effected; and (c) it might in the process obtain block discounts from the insurer, the benefit of which would then be passed on to the members. Commonhold associations will wish to bear these points in mind in deciding how to deal with unit insurance.

4.11.4 Contents insurance

It will be noted that both the alternative formulations in the original (October 2002) draft of the commonhold community statement (see paragraph 4.11.3 above) required the unit-holder to take out and maintain contents insurance in a form satisfactory to the board of directors. This requirement was unduly prescriptive: in line with the Government's thinking, it would do no harm to leave such matters to the whim of the individual unit-holder. In its Post-Consultation Report dated August 2003, however, the Department of Constitutional Affairs noted the dissatisfaction of the consultees with the proposed insurance provisions in general and with the requirement for unit-holders to take out contents insurance in particular, and resolved to remove this requirement, as it has now done.

4.11.5 Insurance in default

Where commonhold associations decide to insert provision for unit-holders to insure their units, then it would be prudent to have a default provision. As originally drafted, the commonhold community statement provided:

23. If default is made by any Unit-holder in effecting the insurance required by these Rules, the commonhold association shall be entitled to arrange and effect such insurance as the Board of Directors shall consider appropriate in respect of the Commonhold Unit.

Thus if a unit-holder fails to insure in accordance with an obligation imposed by the commonhold community statement, the commonhold association would be entitled to step in and make the requisite default arrangements themselves. Although this provision is to be commended, it is likely that insurers will look askance at such arrangements, at least in the early days of commonhold. The commonhold association should therefore be astute to ensure both that it has a good relationship with its insurance company; and that it has a proper paper record of its attempts to procure that the unit-holder take out its own insurance.

Part 2 of Chapter 6 deals with the default procedure which the commonhold association must follow both before carrying out insurance in default and before attempting to claim reimbursement of the premium.

4.12 USE

4.12.1 Introduction

Sections 14(1) and 26(a) of the Act require the commonhold community statement to make provision regulating respectively the use of the commonhold unit and the common parts. The relevant provisions of the commonhold community statement dealing with use are rules 9 to 15.

4.12.2 Use of residential units

Rule 9 of the commonhold community statement provides:

A commonhold unit may only be used in accordance with its permitted use as stated in Table 3.4 of Part II of this commonhold community statement.

It is intended that Table 3.4 will stipulate whether the use of the commonhold unit is 'residential', 'non-residential' or 'mixed', and may go on to provide more specific restrictions. This rule will thus, for example, prevent residential unit-holders within the commonhold from being bothered by activities which go beyond residential use and which, for instance, involve a steady stream of visitors or other disturbances.

The wide formula 'residential' is to be contrasted with the narrower formula often found in leases, 'as a private dwelling house', which would arguably prevent the use of the unit for the accommodation of lodgers or paying guests.

The formula does not prohibit the use of the unit for business purposes, provided that such a use can be said to be incidental to the use of the unit for residential purposes. Common-sense rather than dictionary definitions should assist the commonhold association in knowing where the line should be drawn: a barrister preparing his brief for the next day while sitting at home would no doubt fall within the rule; a language teacher holding extra lessons at home in the evenings, or a builder storing surplus materials in his garden, probably would not.

4.12.3 Use of non-residential units

The use of the non-residential units in a mixed use or non-residential commonhold will be constrained by planning control and also by the applicable rules of the commonhold community statement.

There is no reason why the commonhold community statement should not legislate for designated units to be used for specified purposes, in much the same way as leases of modern shopping centres or retail parades aim to cater for a mix of non-competing trades. In *Sydney Diagnostic Services Pty Ltd v Hamlena Pty Ltd* (1991) (Digest), an attempt was unsuccessfully made to have a prohibition on the use of some, but not all, units for pathology purposes declared unlawful on the grounds of discrimination.

4.12.4 Confinement to restricted classes of people

It is unlawful to discriminate on the grounds of race or religion, and a commonhold community statement could not therefore contain a rule allowing units to be occupied only by, say, Christians or Caucasians. What is less clear is whether a rule restricting occupation of a unit to retired people, or those over the age of 55, would be vulnerable to be struck down. As matters stand, Article 14 of Part I of Schedule I to the Human Rights Act 1998 (which sets out the text of the European Convention on Human Rights) prohibits discrimination against the enjoyment of any of the rights and freedoms set forth in the Convention on a number of grounds. Those rights include the right to respect for an individual's home (Article 8). Age is not listed as a ground of discrimination, but the list in Article 14 concludes with a reference to 'other status', which could arguably include age.

There is therefore an argument (but the authors would put it no higher than that) to the effect that an age restriction in commonhold would conflict with Article 14, because it could lead to a situation in which a person below the requisite age to whom a unit-holder left his unit by will would be unable to live in the unit. A similar argument has been considered in at least one Commonwealth jurisdiction. In *Marshall v Strata Plan No NW 2584* (1996) (Digest) (a decision of the Supreme Court of British Columbia), a strata council passed a by-law (equivalent for the purposes of this analysis to a rule in a commonhold community statement) providing that individuals under the age of 55 years were prohibited from residing in any unit. The prohibition was challenged on the grounds, first, that it was a constraint on the right of alienation; and secondly, that it was contrary to the Canadian Human Rights legislation. The challenge was rejected on both grounds.

That decision notwithstanding, it remains open to question whether a restriction based upon age could survive a properly evidenced challenge showing that the restriction had the effect of decreasing the market for the unit, and therefore affecting the unit-holder's right to transfer without restriction (considered in paragraph 4.13.2).

4.12.5 Garages and parking spaces

As originally drafted, the commonhold community statement attached to the October 2002 Consultation Paper provided:

17. A garage included in a residential unit shall only be used as a private garage.
18. A parking space included in a residential unit shall only be used for parking vehicles and shall be for the exclusive use of the Unit-holder of that unit and his invitees.

These restrictions have not survived into the current (August 2003) draft. That is not to say, though, that their inclusion should not be carefully considered by individual commonhold associations.

Rule 17 was intended to prevent use for public purposes or purposes which are not traditionally associated with a garage. Use for the repair of vehicles belonging to others would therefore fall within the prohibition. That is not to say, however, that the garage must necessarily be used for the parking of cars: it will be recognised that many garages are used for storage or for DIY purposes, and there would seem to be no reason to prohibit such a use, unless of course the storage ceased to be private.

Support for this interpretation is lent by rule 18 which, unlike rule 17, refers specifically to 'parking vehicles'. The greater restriction was no doubt intended to control the visual impact of the parking space which, unlike a garage, will be open to public view.

4.12.6 Use of common parts

The commonhold community statement sets out the following rules in relation to the common parts:

11. The common parts must not be used in such a way as to prevent reasonable access to a commonhold unit or which may prejudice the use of a commonhold unit.
12. A unit-holder must not make any alterations to the common parts.
13. A commonhold unit and the common parts must not be used in such a way as to cause a nuisance to other unit-holders.
14. A unit-holder must not act in any way that would be likely to prejudice the insurance cover of the commonhold association or other unit-holders.
15. A unit-holder must indemnify the commonhold association in respect of costs to put right any damage caused to the common parts by a licensee or invitee of the unit-holder.

This negative approach to drafting leaves unsaid what use may positively be made of the common parts. It may safely be inferred, however, both from the lack of any other restriction and from the specific provision made in the case of those parts of the common parts that are categorised as limited use areas (see paragraph 4.12.7 below) that the unit-holders are free to make what use of the common parts they wish within the confines of rules 11 to 15, and any other dedicated rules an individual commonhold association might wish to introduce to suit its own particular requirements (no use of the swimming pool after 11pm; no walking on the grass . . .).

This approach is to be contrasted with the original (October 2002) draft, which provided:

20. Subject to any applicable rules, the Common Parts may be used by all Unit-holders (including any Unit-holder who has created or granted a lease, licence or other right in or over their Commonhold Unit or parted with possession of the same in accordance with these Rules) and their invitees.

The reference to use by 'all' unit-holders in this formula should be noted. It will not be possible for the commonhold association to decide that part of the common parts should be allocated to the use of one individual, no matter how compelling that individual's case for special treatment. The Commonwealth cases illustrate the perils associated with this sort of uneven treatment, usually in the context of two particular areas:

(a) Use of communal parking areas: see, for example, *Sawko v Dominion Plaza One Condominium Association* (1991) (Digest); *Alpert v Le'Lisa Condominium* (1995) (Digest); *Woodruff v Fairways Villas Condominium Association* (1995) (Digest).

(b) Alterations to a commonhold unit extending into the common parts: see, for example, *Proprietors of Strata Plan No 1627 v Schultz* (1978) (Digest); *Strauss v Oyster River Condominium Trust* (1994) (Digest).

The moral to be drawn from these decisions, of equal application to domestic contexts, is that the rules will have to be applied even-handedly and consistently if litigation is to be avoided.

4.12.7 Limited use common parts

Rule 10 of the commonhold community statement provides:

Limited use areas may only be used by authorised persons and in a manner consistent with the authorised use specified in Table 4 of Part II of this commonhold community statement.

This provision is designed to deal with areas of the common parts which are not general amenity areas as such. Examples of such areas will be:

(a) Ancillary space for housing machinery, such as the lift motor room or the boiler room. Such areas should obviously be kept secure, with access limited to relevant personnel.

(b) Storage lockers or parking areas, designed for letting out to individuals from time to time, rather than for use by anyone.

(c) Patios or garden areas which are designed for the visual amenity of the commonhold association as a whole, but restricted to the use of particular unit-holders.

Case law from other jurisdictions has shown that much litigation has been caused over the last category of limited use common parts: cases such as *Zwenna Buchbinder v Owners, Strata Plan VR2096* (1992) (Digest) (erection of shed on patio); *Re Peel Condominium Corp No 73 v Rogers* (1978) (Digest) (planting of trees in garden); *Gaffny v Reid* (1993) (Digest) (extension of cottage).

4.12.8 Parking

Quite apart from individual garages and parking spaces belonging to individual unit-holders, the commonhold may have common parts that include other parking spaces for members, visitors or contractors. Whether or not such facilities are provided, the commonhold association may need controls to prevent parking in areas where it is not allowed, or to regulate the use of areas where it is allowed.

As originally drafted, the commonhold community statement attached to the October 2002 Consultation Paper proposed that the commonhold association should be given the following extensive powers in the event of such parking:

47. Without prejudice to its other rights to ensure compliance with the Rules, the commonhold association may take such lawful steps as are necessary to enforce any Rules relating to the parking of vehicles on any part of the Commonhold, including arranging for the immobilisation or removal of vehicles parked in contravention of the Rules.

This provision would have enabled the commonhold association to introduce clamping as a means of parking control. It has not survived into the current (August 2003) draft. That is not to say, however, that its inclusion should not be carefully considered by individual commonhold associations.

4.12.9 Illegal or immoral user

As originally drafted, the commonhold community statement provided:

19. No Commonhold Unit may be used for any illegal or immoral purpose.

An illegal purpose would include, for example, a use in contravention of the Town and Country Planning legislation. An immoral use is more difficult to define, because the public perception of what constitutes immoral behaviour varies over time. At the beginning of the twentieth century, it was still possible for a court to hold that unmarried lovers were behaving immorally; the position now of course is different. It is probably safe to say that it is unlikely that a user would be condemned as immoral if it were not also illegal.

The current (August 2003) version of the commonhold community statement includes no such prohibition, and it is doubtful whether its absence will be regretted.

4.12.10 Obstruction of access

As has already been remarked, rule 11 of the commonhold community statement provides that:

> The common parts must not be used in such a way as to prevent reasonable access to a commonhold unit or which may prejudice the use of a commonhold unit.

This contrasts with the original proposal regarding access in the original (October 2002) draft:

> 56. No Unit-holder or his invitees shall do any thing or leave or permit to be left any goods, rubbish or other object which obstructs or hinders lawful access to any part of the Commonhold.

The new provision applies to everyone: not merely to unit-holders and their invitees, but also to the officers of the commonhold association. It may thus be used not merely to prevent unit-holders deliberately or inadvertently obstructing access to other units, but also to prevent officers of the commonhold association from having scaffolding erected in a needlessly obstructive position (compare rule 21, discussed in paragraph 4.9.10 above). There may be occasions when the commonhold association will have no alternative but to obstruct the common parts in the exercise of their repairing obligation, resulting in an apparent conflict between this provision and rule 20. The rules have to be read together to resolve this conflict: rule 11 is concerned with everyday use, and not with operations such as repairs intended to procure that the common parts are kept freely available for such use.

4.12.11 External display

As originally drafted, the commonhold community statement contained a number of optional provisions which operated so as to prevent the external display of items from or on a unit or in the common parts. Thus:

(a) Rule 57 prohibited the erection or projection of any radio or television aerial or satellite dish.

(b) Rule 62 prevented unit-holders hanging or exposing any clothes or other articles outside units or in the common parts, save in any areas specifically made available for the same by the commonhold association.

(c) Rule 67 forbade unit-holders to post or permit to be posted any notice or sign in the common parts, except upon any noticeboard or other facility provided for that purpose by the commonhold association.

(d) Rule 70 outlawed flower pots 'or other like object' (for example window boxes) save with the written consent of the commonhold association.

These optional rules do not appear in the current (August 2003) version, in line with the aim of the Department of Constitutional Affairs to free commonhold from unnecessary restriction. Commonhold associations may yet decide that such rules should be incorporated, where, for example, the external appearance of the commonhold is thought to be worthy of special treatment. It should be noted that planning controls are unlikely to be of much assistance: satellite dishes are permitted within certain constraints under the Town and Country Planning (General Permitted Development) Orders; many signs are permitted under the Town and Country Planning (Control of Advertisement) Regulations 1992; and the other matters referred to are unlikely to be covered by planning control.

4.12.12 Nuisance and annoyance

As has already been remarked, rule 13 of the commonhold community statement prohibits conduct in the commonhold that causes a nuisance to other unit-holders. This drafting contrasts with the original (October 2002) version, which provided:

58. A Unit-holder must not, and must take reasonable steps to ensure that his invitees do not, behave in any way or create any sound or noise which causes or is likely to cause any annoyance, nuisance, injury or disturbance to other Unit-holders, or to any other person lawfully on the Commonhold, or to the occupiers of adjoining buildings or premises.

There are three points to make about this earlier version of the rule:

(a) First, it is restricted to offending behaviour by unit-holders or their invitees, and does not seek to apply the same prohibition to officers of the commonhold.

(b) Secondly, it focuses upon 'sound or noise', in contrast to other types of nuisance (for example those caused by dust or vibration).

(c) Thirdly, it does not impose absolute liability upon the unit-holder for nuisance or annoyance caused by his invitee, but only a liability to take 'reasonable steps'. Although all will turn on the circumstances, that liability could be discharged by the unit-holder pointing out to the invitee the obligations in the commonhold community statement in the first place, and then taking steps to terminate the invitee's right to occupy the unit if warning letters and/or visits fail to achieve their purpose.

The new provision is simpler and fairer, and is to be commended.

4.12.13 Use of apparatus

The original (October 2002) draft commonhold community statement provided that:

64. Except with the written consent of the Board of Directors, no Unit-holder of a residential unit or his invitees shall have or install in his Commonhold Unit any mechanical, scientific or electrical apparatus other than ordinary domestic appliances.

The purport of this rule, commonly to be found as a covenant in residential leases, is presumably to prevent nuisance or annoyance arising as a result of the operation of the apparatus. If that is so, however, it is difficult to see why the general prohibition on conduct causing a nuisance (see paragraph 4.12.12 above) should not suffice. The authors suggest that in this case the interests of the commonhold are more likely to be served by less prescription rather than more—a view with which the Department of Constitutional Affairs evidently agree, for the rule is not to be found in the current draft.

4.12.14 Drainage and water pipes

The original (October 2002) draft commonhold community statement provided:

61. Every Unit-holder shall take adequate steps to prevent the leakage of pipes or escape of water from his Commonhold Unit, including lagging all pipes and tanks against freezing.

This provision, which clearly makes good sense in the case of a unit in a block of flats (although in that case it may not go far enough) is at first of questionable relevance when it comes to a stand-alone unit. If a leak from such a unit following the thaw of frozen unlagged pipes could do no damage to other units or to the common parts, then what business is it of the commonhold association to require such steps to be taken?

One answer might be that it is in the interests of the commonhold association as a whole to ensure that the possibility of damage, no matter how confined it may be to a particular unit, is kept to a minimum, for a number of reasons. First, the financial well-being of a member will or may be affected by such a leak, with whatever consequences that may have for the association as a whole. Secondly, if the unit is insured on the same policy as the common parts, then the premium for the common parts may be affected by a claim by the unit-holder. Thirdly, it is in the interests of the commonhold association as a whole that remedial works, with all the disruption they entail, be kept to a minimum.

The rule has sensibly been omitted from the current (August 2003) draft. The authors suggest that individual commonhold associations weigh up the considerations suggested above in deciding what, if any, provision should replace it.

4.12.15 Hazardous materials

The original (October 2002) draft commonhold community statement provided that:

63. A Unit-holder or his invitees may not, without the written consent of the Board of Directors, bring onto the Commonhold or store in any part thereof, any flammable, hazardous or noxious substance. This does not apply to the storage of fuel in the fuel tank of a vehicle or in a small reserve tank for use in connection with the vehicle.

This, again, is a covenant commonly found in residential leases. Although the same arguments apply as those discussed in paragraph 4.12.13 above, the authors suggest that the seriousness of the consequences that might follow from breach of the rule militate in favour of this prohibition being given separate prominence, rather than being included under the umbrella of the general prohibition of nuisance and activity likely to prejudice insurance cover in rules 13 and 14.

4.12.16 Pets

The original (October 2002) draft commonhold community statement provided the following option regarding the keeping of pets in a commonhold:

66. No animals may be kept or brought onto the Commonhold without the written consent of the Board of Directors.

The Commonwealth cases show that more litigation has been caused by rules concerning pets than almost any other topic in commonhold life (one example only being provided by the decision of the Appeals Court of Massachusetts in *Noble v Murphy* (1993) (Digest)). This provision appears to strive for fairness by subjecting any proposal to keep a pet to the decision of the board of directors. It has not survived into the redraft supplied with the Post-Consultation Report dated August 2003. If such a provision is after all to be included, it will be important both to insist upon a consistent standard being applied, and to ensure that the rules are enforced. The needs of people who own guide dogs must also be considered.

4.12.17 Smoke detectors

The current Housing Fitness Standard issued by the Housing, Health and Safety Rating System does not require all houses to have smoke detectors, although it is increasingly recognised that the installation of a detector is an advisable precaution. The October 2002 Consultation Paper put forward the following two optional provisions for inclusion in the commonhold community statement as rules governing the installation of smoke detectors in the units and the common parts:

68. Each Unit-holder shall install in his Commonhold Unit and maintain in working order a smoke detector or smoke detection system of a type specified by the Board of Directors and complying with any applicable health and safety or building regulations.

69. The commonhold association shall install in the Common Parts and maintain in working order a smoke detector or smoke detection system of a type complying with any applicable health and safety or building regulations.

This provision seems prudent, particularly where a fire in one unit may have consequences for others. It has not survived the August 2003 revision of the draft and accordingly, if its inclusion is thought desirable, commonhold associations will have to make special provision for it.

4.12.18 Smoking

The fall in the acceptability of smoking as a socially tolerable habit in recent years has been marked—to the extent that a number of governments (including those of Australia, Canada, New Zealand, France, Italy, Norway, Sweden, Iceland, the State of California, Singapore and Thailand) have introduced or are considering introducing legislation banning smoking in most public places and private places open to the public. A number of strata schemes in Commonwealth jurisdictions have followed or initiated this trend by imposing controls on smoking in the common parts and even in some cases in individual units (see the unsuccessful challenge to such a ban in *Salerno v Proprietors of Strata Plan 42724* (1997) (Digest)).

While there may be something to be said for similar controls in commonhold, members will bear in mind the warning against over-prescription in paragraph 4.12.19 below.

4.12.19 Control of other behaviour in a commonhold

The rules referred to in paragraphs 4.12.8 to 4.12.17 above represented the Government's initial attempt to guide the commonhold association as to the appropriate controls to impose upon behaviour in a commonhold. As paragraph 174 of the Consultation Paper recognised, however:

the individual commonhold association will be best placed to determine what forms of behaviour are acceptable. We would therefore anticipate a very significant degree of variation between commonholds to be possible in relation to this part of the commonhold community statement.

The same theme emerged in the Post-Consultation Report dated August 2003:

Although there may be good arguments for individual associations introducing specific restraints, we do not think this justifies prescribing a single set of restrictions for all commonholds. We are currently considering adopting a more flexible, less prescriptive approach, allowing individual commonholds to create their own rules tailored to their individual circumstances. In essence, we are now aiming for uniformity of the format, rather than uniformity of content in relation to restrictions on behaviour.

While the most obvious topics for regulation have been set out above, others will no doubt be appropriate in individual cases. It should be simple to draft a provision to be inserted into the commonhold community statement to fit each case, or to adapt the wording of the original version of rule 28:

> No Unit-holder shall do or cause to be done any of the following works in or upon his Commonhold Unit, namely [specify].

Members will wish to bear in mind, however, that although increased restrictions may make life easier within commonhold, the presence of the restrictions may well make units difficult to sell. A balance must therefore be struck.

4.13 SELLING, LETTING, OR OTHERWISE DEALING WITH A UNIT

4.13.1 Introduction

The ways in which a unit-holder is entitled to alienate his unit, and the restrictions placed upon that entitlement, are examined in full in Chapter 3. This Section summarises the most important aspects of those entitlements and restrictions in so far as they have an impact upon the running of the commonhold.

4.13.2 Transfer of unit[26]

Section 15(2) of the Act provides that the commonhold community statement 'may not prevent or restrict the transfer of a commonhold unit'. This prohibition of any impediment on transfer of the freehold estate in a unit is one of the prime hallmarks of commonhold, and one which the Government was concerned to keep during the passage of the Commonhold Bill, in order to enhance the attractiveness of the new system. It remains to be seen whether this principle will prevent the commonhold restricting itself to certain categories of resident (for example retired people): see the discussion of this point in paragraphs 3.2.3 and 4.12.4 above.

Section 16 of the Act provides that a right or duty conferred or imposed by the commonhold community statement will affect a new unit-holder in the same way as it affected the former unit-holder; and that a former unit-holder will not incur a liability or acquire a right under or by virtue of the commonhold community statement. Taken together with section 15(2), these provisions have the following significance for the running of the commonhold:

(a) Because there is no opportunity for the commonhold association to refuse consent to a proposed transfer of a unit, the commonhold association cannot use the occasion of a proposed transfer as a vehicle for requiring an outstanding commonhold assessment to be paid. This is in contrast to the position in leasehold,

[26] See further Section 3.2 of the text.

where (i) the landlord's consent to assignment may be required, and may well be reasonably withheld if there are arrears of rent or service charge; and (ii) even if there is no prohibition on assignment without consent, the prospective assignee is unlikely to wish to proceed if there are arrears owed by the assignor, because of the risk of forfeiture.

(b) Although the transferor remains liable for arrears at the time of the transfer, his liability for assessments for the future ceases.

(c) The transferee becomes liable for future assessments (see paragraph 4.13.5 below, and the more extensive discussion of this point in paragraph 6.13.13).

(d) It is questionable whether the incoming unit-holder assumes liability for the outgoing unit-holder's commonhold debts (although this question is answered by the commonhold community statement—see paragraph 4.13.5 below).

4.13.3 Transfer of part of unit

A transfer of part of a unit is only allowed with the written consent of the commonhold association (see section 21(2)(c) of the Act and the extensive discussion in paragraphs 3.2.6). A transfer without such consent 'shall be of no effect' (section 21(3)), although it may be that the law of estoppel would mitigate any unfair consequences flowing from the application of this section in the same way as estoppel has been applied by the courts in relation to section 2 of the Law of Property (Miscellaneous Provisions) Act 1989.[27]

Any permitted transfer of part of a unit will create either an entirely new unit (section 21(9)(a)), or an enlarged unit elsewhere to which the transferred part will have been added (section 21(9)(b)). In either event, the division and addition will or may require an adjustment of the percentages according to which the commonhold assessments are levied. This is a matter that will have to be weighed up by the commonhold association at the time the application for consent to the transfer is made.

Consent to the transfer of part of a unit requires a special resolution with a 75 per cent majority (see section 21(8)). Paragraph 151 of the October 2002 Consultation Paper proposed that:

> . . . the guiding principle should be that the commonhold association will be required to consent if the interest created will affect any other unit-holders or the commonhold association [*sic*].

This proposal is obscure. Presumably the commonhold association will be entitled to vote taking into account any number of considerations, provided that they do so in good faith. See further paragraph 3.2.6 of the text.

[27] See, for example, *Yaxley v Gotts* [2000] Ch 162.

4.13.4 Notification of transfer

As paragraph 4.13.5 explains, the liability of the transferee of a unit commences at the moment of transfer, and is not dependent on either registration or notification. In practice, however, the commonhold association will need early notification of the transfer in order to continue to be able effectively to transact commonhold business (the sending of notices of meetings, the demands for payment of the commonhold assessment and so forth) with the right person.

To that end, section 15(3) of the Act requires the new unit-holder to notify the commonhold association of the transfer '*on* the transfer of a commonhold unit'; while section 15(4) provides for regulations to prescribe the form, manner and timing of such notice, and to 'make provision (including provision requiring the payment of money) about the effect of failure to give notice'. This requirement is relaxed somewhat in rule 2 of the commonhold community statement:

> On transfer of a commonhold unit or of part only of a commonhold unit the new unit-holder must notify the commonhold association of the transfer within 7 days beginning with the date on which the Land Registry gives notice to the new unit-holder or his representative that the registration of the transfer has been completed.

Annex D to the commonhold community statement contains as Forms 1 and 2 the drafts that must be used (or forms to the same effect) for transfers of a commonhold unit or part of a commonhold unit respectively. Those drafts are reproduced as Forms 2.11 and 2.12 in the Forms and Precedents part of this work.

The regulations to be made under section 15(4) may make provision regarding not merely the form and timing of the notice of transfer, but also laying down sanctions ('including provision requiring the payment of money') in the event of failure to give notice. In practice, any such sanction would be likely to be ineffective or otiose: the failure to notify is more likely to harm the incoming unit-holder (who will be liable for assessments, but unable to vote in meetings until substituted as a member of the association) than the commonhold association, which will be alerted to the situation as soon as an assessment is unpaid. Perhaps for that reason, paragraph 134 of the Consultation Paper provisionally concluded:

> . . . in practice the imposition and collection of fines may prove to be disproportionately troublesome. It may be that depriving the incoming member of the right to vote will be sufficient sanction.

The Department of Constitutional Affairs added in its Post-Consultation Report dated August 2003:

> Moreover, we do not currently propose to prescribe a penalty for failure to serve a transfer notice within the specified period of time; individual commonholds will be able to impose a penalty if they wish. We think that on balance, the inability to vote is sufficiently serious and that the fear of respondents about the effect of the enforcement of fines or penalties seems well founded.

If this conclusion turns out to be optimistic, the Government will of course have the opportunity to address the point rapidly and economically through further secondary legislation. See further paragraph 3.2.4 of the text.

4.13.5 Liability of incoming unit-holder

Section 16(1) of the Act imposes liability for commonhold duties and confers entitlement to commonhold rights upon a new unit-holder 'in the same way as it affected the former unit-holder'. There is some doubt as to whether this liability was intended to be purely prospective or retrospective. The draftsmen of the commonhold community statement have resolved this doubt in favour of the liability being retrospective, at least in relation to commonhold assessments and reserve fund levies. Rule 1 provides:

> On transfer of a commonhold unit the new unit-holder must pay any debts incurred by the former unit-holder which remain outstanding in respect of the commonhold assessment and the reserve fund levies.

It is important to note that this liability of the incoming unit-holder:

(a) Arises as soon as the transfer is completed. It does not depend upon registration being completed (see paragraph 4.13.4).

(b) Does not depend upon any notice of transfer being given (although in practice the commonhold association will be unlikely to know of the completion of the transfer until notice has been given).

Although the liabilities of the incoming unit-holder to the commonhold association arise at the date of the transfer, by virtue of section 16, the corresponding benefits will not be enjoyed in full until notice of transfer is given (which will trigger membership of the association in substitution for the outgoing unit-holder). See further paragraphs 3.2.5 and 6.3.15 of the text.

4.13.6 Tenancy of unit

Throughout the passage of the Commonhold Bill through Parliament, the Government steadfastly insisted that it should not be possible to replicate the problems of the residential long leasehold system in commonhold. This would be accomplished in part by requiring that all leases should be extinguished upon conversion to commonhold (explored in Chapter 2), and by prohibiting the creation of long residential leases under a commonhold regime.

Section 17 of the Act deals with the prohibition, while leaving the detail of what short leases may be created to regulations to be made under sections 17 and 19. In the October 2002 Consultation Paper the Government provisionally proposed (see paragraph 138) that leases of residential units should be permitted for terms of up to (but no greater than) seven years. Although this proposal received much support from consultees, in its Post-Consultation Report dated August 2003, however, the Department of Constitutional Affairs suggested instead that a 21-year limit would be workable, and added:

> Whatever the limit chosen, options to renew granted before or at the same time as the lease are unlikely to be permitted. We are also considering removing the restrictions on premiums and the level of rent to be paid. These changes would create more flexibility, avoid over-regulation of letting within commonholds and provide a closer approximation to freehold ownership. Nonetheless, if individual commonholds wish to impose greater restrictions (for example holiday lets), we currently expect them to be able to do so.

The new proposal is now enshrined in rule 3 of the commonhold community statement, which provides:

> A unit-holder may not grant a tenancy in a residential commonhold unit for a term of more than 21 years.

Section 18 of the Act also provides for the commonhold community statement to be able to impose restrictions with regard to leases of non-residential units. The Government does not, however, currently propose any restrictions upon types or lengths of leases of non-residential units (paragraph 142 of the Consultation Paper). See further 3.3 of the text.

4.13.7 Notification of tenancy of unit

There is no proposal that consent will have to be obtained to a tenancy of a unit that is sanctioned by the rules: the sanction itself will be enough. It will, however, be important for the commonhold association to be given details of any such tenancy, because of the potential involvement of the tenant in the business of the commonhold (see paragraph 4.13.8 below).

Paragraph 145 of the Consultation Paper proposed for consideration that, on any letting of a commonhold unit, the unit-holder should give notice of the letting and a copy of the lease to the commonhold association within 21 days of the letting, while paragraph 146 made the same proposal with regard to any assignment or other dealing with the tenancy. The relevant details were then to be entered into a register of lettings to be kept by the commonhold association.

Following the consultation exercise, the Department of Constitutional Affairs accepted the views of many of the respondents that the commonhold association should be provided with details of the tenant and the lease, but should not be required to approve the form of the lease in advance. The proposals have been revised, with the result that rule 5 of the commonhold community statement now provides:

> A unit-holder must notify the commonhold association that a tenancy or a licence for a period longer than 28 days has been granted within 7 days from the date on which it was granted.

The requisite notification must be made using Form 3 in Annex D to the commonhold community statement, or a form to the same effect. That draft is reproduced as Form 2.13 in the Forms and Precedents part of this work.

As has already been noted (see paragraph 4.4.8 above), rule 6 provides that the commonhold association must enter such details provided in a register of tenants and licensees (see Form 2.15 in the Forms and Precedents part of this book). The rule does not anticipate what is to happen when tenants or licensees change over, and it is suggested that it would be good practice for the commonhold community statement to include provision for notification in such circumstances, so that the register may be updated. See further paragraph 3.3.6 of the text.

4.13.8 Involvement of tenant of unit in running of commonhold[28]

Section 19 of the Act provides:

(1) Regulations may—
   (a) impose obligations on a tenant of a commonhold unit;
   (b) enable a commonhold community statement to impose obligations on a tenant of a commonhold unit.

(2) Regulations under subsection (1) may, in particular, require a tenant of a commonhold unit to make payments to the commonhold association or a unit-holder in discharge of payments which—
   (a) are due in accordance with the commonhold community statement to be made by the unit-holder, or
   (b) are due in accordance with the commonhold community statement to be made by another tenant of the unit.

(3) Regulations under subsection (1) may, in particular, provide—
   (a) for the amount of payments under subsection (2) to be set against sums owed by the tenant (whether to the person by whom the payments were due to be made or to some other person);
   (b) for the amount of payments under subsection (2) to be recovered from the unit-holder or another tenant of the unit.

It is also relevant to note that section 37(2) includes provision for tenants of unit-holders to be involved in the enforcement of commonhold duties. In particular, subsection (g) allows for the regulations to make provision permitting a tenant to enforce a duty imposed on another tenant, a unit-holder or a commonhold association (see the discussion in paragraph 6.3.3).

At first, the Government did not put forward any proposals regarding the way in which these wide-ranging powers were to be exercised, apparently because of the view expressed in paragraph 147 of the October 2002 Consultation Paper:

> We consider that it is for the unit-holder and the lessee to decide the extent to which the lessee will be involved in the affairs of the commonhold association.

[28] See also paragraph 3.3.7 of the text.

If the unit-holder and the tenant agree between themselves that the tenant will be answerable to the commonhold association, then paragraph 146 of the Consultation Paper proposed that the tenant should give notice to the commonhold association within 21 days of the tenancy agreement indicating his address for service and confirming he is bound by the terms and conditions of the commonhold community statement. It is difficult, however, to see how such an apparently voluntary submission could suffice to impose liability upon the tenant as between him and the commonhold association, without regulations to the effect envisaged by section 19(1).

The Government's initial reluctance to legislate for the imposition of liability upon tenants of commonhold units appeared to stem from the consideration mentioned in paragraph 144 of the Consultation Paper:

> Enabling the commonhold association and the other unit-holders to take action directly against the tenant may adversely affect the interest of the unit-holder and disrupt the relations of landlord and tenant.

The authors fail to see what merit there might have been in this point. If the existence of the liability is explained in the tenancy agreement, the tenant will know what to expect, and will always be able to have recourse to his landlord. This makes practical sense. As paragraph 144 of the Consultation Paper also observes:

> On the other hand, the tenant will, in practical terms, be a member of the commonhold community for the duration of the lease.

It is therefore right that the mechanism should exist for a tenant to be treated like a full member, with all the advantages and disadvantages that will entail.

The Department of Constitutional Affairs has now remedied this state of affairs by the inclusion in the current (August 2003) version of these rules:

4. A unit-holder may not grant—
    (a) a tenancy in a commonhold unit; or
    (b) a licence for consideration to occupy or use a commonhold unit for a period longer than 28 days

    unless it reserves the right for the commonhold association to carry out repair work in accordance with the provisions of this commonhold community statement. Any provision made in a tenancy agreement will be of no effect to the extent that it is inconsistent with this commonhold community statement or the memorandum or articles of association of the commonhold association.

    . . .

7. The tenant of a commonhold unit or part only of a commonhold unit must make payments to the commonhold association in discharge of payments which are due, in accordance with this commonhold community statement, to be made by the unit-holder or another tenant where the tenancy agreement imposes an obligation on the tenant to pay.
8. A tenant of a commonhold unit or part only of a commonhold unit is bound by the rules of this commonhold community statement which affect his occupancy.

4.13.9 Licence of unit

Section 20(1) of the Act provides that:

A commonhold community statement may not prevent or restrict the creation, grant or transfer by a unit-holder of—

(a) an interest in the whole or part of his unit . . .

A licence does not create an interest in land, from which it follows that this provision has no application to licences to occupy land. There does not appear to be any other provision in the Act restricting such licences (see the repirtration requirements discussed in paragraph 3.3.9).

That notwithstanding, rule 13 of the original (October 2002) draft of the commonhold community statement provided:

A Unit-holder may only create or grant any licence or other right over, or part with possession of, his Commonhold Unit or any part thereof, with the prior written consent of the board of directors of the commonhold association (the 'Board of Directors') and subject to such terms and conditions as the Board of Directors may specify.

That restriction would therefore appear to be without sanction. Whether or not that is right, the authors would agree with the view expressed in paragraph 150 of the Consultation Paper:

As a licence is, generally, a personal rather than a property right, we appreciate that requiring the consent of the Board of Directors may be seen as unduly restrictive . . .

The justification given for the restriction ('but, a licensee may well still be resident in the commonhold for a considerable period') is accurate but mysterious.

The current (August 2003) version of the commonhold community statement treats residential licences in some ways equally with, and in other ways more beneficially than tenancies, and the reader is referred to the analysis of the restrictions on tenancies discussed in paragraphs 4.13.6 to 4.13.8 above. In summary:

(a) licences may be granted without restriction, and may in particular exceed 21 years;

(b) licences for more than 28 days must reserve the right for the commonhold association to carry out repair work in accordance with the provisions of the commonhold community statement;

(c) licences for more than 28 days must be notified to the commonhold association using Form 4 in Annex D to the commonhold community statement, or a form to the same effect. That draft is reproduced as Form 2.14 in the Forms and Precedents part of this work.

There is no mechanism by which a licensee might be compelled to assume obligations towards the commonhold association, apart from the obligation to allow access (compare the case of a tenant, discussed in paragraph 4.13.8

above). Such matters will therefore have to be regulated between unit-holder and licensee. See also paragraph 3.3.9 of the text.

4.13.10 Charge of unit

As with the case of the transfer of a unit, the charging of a unit by the unit-holder cannot be fettered by the commonhold association—see section 20(1)(b) of the Act. Moreover, the commonhold association is unable to obtain priority in respect of a debt owed to it by the unit-holder: all it can do in cases of non-payment is to sue and obtain judgment for the debt, and then seek a charging order, which will then rank behind existing charges (see paragraph 6.3.12). See further Section 3.5 of the text.

PART 3 FINANCIAL MATTERS

4.14 INTRODUCTION

4.14.1 The commonhold assessment and the reserve fund

Sections 38 and 39 of the Act set out the bare bones of the financing of the commonhold operation. Both are concerned with the mechanism by which the commonhold association budgets and seeks reimbursement for costs incurred or to be incurred in running the commonhold.

A distinction is drawn between the procedure for the recovery of everyday expenditure (insurance, running repairs, housekeeping and other periodic matters), which is dealt with in section 38, and which is called 'commonhold assessment'; and the procedure, similar in a number of respects, for the recovery of the major items of expenditure typically comprising renewal of the fabric of the buildings, which are budgeted for separately—the 'reserve fund'.

Commonhold assessment is dealt with in Section 4.15; the reserve fund in Section 4.16.

4.14.2 Commonhold assessment and reserve fund compared to service charges

A block of flats which is converted from leasehold to commonhold ownership will still require repairing, insuring, cleaning, heating and general servicing; and all those services have to be budgeted and paid for under the new regime in much the same way. The commonhold assessment and the reserve fund are therefore the direct equivalent of the leasehold service charge.

However, whereas a landlord's ability to demand a service charge is heavily circumscribed by, among other things, the Landlord and Tenant Acts 1985 and 1987 and the Housing Act 1986, no such controls are proposed in the Act for commonhold assessments and reserve funding. The Government's reason for this (explained in greater detail in paragraph 4.16.12 below) is in effect that tenants need such protection because the interests of their landlords are usually quite different. In commonhold, by contrast, the unit-holders and the commonhold association should work together; if they do not, the members are able to control the association in order to redress the situation.

4.14.3 Control of assessment and reserve fund

The responsibility for making and administering the commonhold assessment and reserve fund is placed upon the board of directors of the commonhold association. The members of the commonhold association are, however, to be allowed to approve budgets, and thus will be able to exercise close control over how their money is to be spent.

4.15 THE COMMONHOLD ASSESSMENT—PROCEDURE

4.15.1 The relevant statutory provision

The basis for the assessment is laid down in section 38(1) of the Act, which requires the commonhold community statement to make provision:

(a) requiring the directors of the commonhold association to make an annual estimate of the income required to be raised from unit-holders to meet the expenses of the association,
(b) enabling the directors of the commonhold association to make estimates from time to time of income required to be raised from unit-holders in addition to the annual estimate,
(c) specifying the percentage of any estimate made under paragraph (a) or (b) which is to be allocated to each unit,
(d) requiring each unit-holder to make payments in respect of the percentage of any estimate which is allocated to his unit, and
(e) requiring the directors of the commonhold association to serve notices on unit-holders specifying payments required to be made by them and the date on which each payment is due.

There are a number of ingredients to consider in this Section:

(a) the making of the annual estimate—see paragraph 4.15.3 below;

(b) to what extent the estimate ought then to be subject to the approval of the members of the commonhold association—see paragraphs 4.15.4 and 4.15.5 below;

(c) the allocation of the balance needed among those liable to contribute—see paragraph 4.15.6 below;

(d) the assessment levy—see paragraph 4.15.7 below;

(e) further and emergency assessments—see paragraph 4.15.9 below.

4.15.2 The relevant commonhold community statement rules

The provision required by section 38(1) is enshrined in Section C (rules 23 to 40) of the commonhold community statement:

- Rules 23 to 27 broadly follow section 38(1)(a) in dealing with the requirement to make an annual estimate.
- Rule 28 deals with the making of additional assessments (section 38(1)(b)).
- Rules 29 and 30 deal with payment of the assessment (section 38(1)(d) and (e)).
- Rules 31 to 40 deal with the reserve fund (considered in Section 4.16 below).

The impact of these rules is considered in this Section and Section 4.16.

4.15.3 Assessment procedure step (1): the annual estimate

Rule 23 of the commonhold community statement provides:

> The directors of the commonhold association must make an annual estimate . . . of income required to be raised from unit-holders to meet the expenses of the commonhold association.[29]

T his step will therefore oblige the directors to calculate:

(a) the anticipated routine[30] expenditure over the course of the next financial year;

(b) the income that can be expected without levy (comprising investment income, for example from rented unsold units or let parts of the common parts; income from any social fundraising events; and late payment of levies by defaulting unit-holders);

(c) the balance that will need to be made up by the levy for the forthcoming financial year.

This exercise is necessarily one that will have to take place before the end of the current financial year, particularly given the need to produce the estimate for consideration at least three months before the first payment is due (see paragraph 4.15.4 below). Full details of income and expenditure for that year will not therefore be available, so the directors will need to carry out an exercise based upon what

[29] Rule 23 also deals with the making of 'occasional and emergency estimates'. The procedure for occasional estimates is identical to that of annual estimates, considered in paragraphs 4.15.3 to 4.15.8; the making of emergency estimates is covered in paragraph 4.15.9.

[30] Non-routine expenditure—ie substantial works of replacement or renewal of the fabric of the commonhold—is dealt with in Section 4.16 below.

is known from actual contributions and costs to date for the current year, together with anticipated contributions and costs for the remainder of the year. A form devised by the authors that gives an example of the shape and content of a suitable annual estimate is at Form 3.2 in the Forms and Precedents part of this work.

The aim of this exercise will be to produce an estimate which the board will then be able to present to the members in accordance with rule 24 (see paragraph 4.15.4 below).

4.15.4 Assessment procedure step (2): approval of the assessment

Because the unit-holders who will be asked to pay the assessment will for the most part also be members of the commonhold association, fairness and common sense suggest that they should have the opportunity to scrutinise and approve or reject the directors' proposals.

Although the subject of approval is not dealt with in section 38(1) of the Act, rules 24 to 26 of the commonhold community statement appear to proceed some way towards this objective by providing:

24. At least three calendar months before the first payment will be due the directors of the commonhold association must serve notices on each unit-holder specifying—
    (a) the total amount of the estimate;
    (b) the percentage that was allocated to his commonhold unit in Table 3.3 of Part II of this commonhold community statement; and
    (c) the amount of the estimate allocated to his commonhold unit.
25. Within one calendar month beginning with the date on which the notice referred to in rule 24 was served, each unit-holder may make representations regarding the estimate, in writing, to the commonhold association.
26. Within one calendar month after the last day on which representations may be made under rule 25, the directors must make such adjustments, if any, to the estimate as they think fit, after considering any such representations, and must make a final estimate and serve further notices on the unit-holders specifying the payments required to be made by each unit-holder and the date on which each payment is due.'

This proposal is less labour intensive than the original proposal contained in the draft commonhold community statement put forward in the October 2002 Consultation Paper:

36. In addition to, and at the same time as circulating or laying before the members of the Commonhold Association in general meeting its annual accounts and its directors' report as required by the Companies Act 1985, the Board of Directors shall also circulate or lay before the members a written report comparing the results of the Commonhold Association against its estimated budget for the year and setting out an estimated budget for the forthcoming year.

Although this original rule was silent on the question whether the members should have the opportunity to debate and approve, reject or revise the directors' proposals in the estimated budget, the Government's 'provisional proposal' in that regard was that:

> . . . the commonhold assessment should be approved by a prior special resolution at a general meeting before the unit-holders become liable to pay it.[31]

The authors suggest that a major feature of the perceived success of a commonhold will be the members' ability to vote on their own expenditure. They therefore endorse the spirit of this proposal, although they welcome the greater simplicity of the revised rules, which drop the requirements for an annual report and budget and a special resolution.

Having said that, although the Department of Constitutional Affairs accepted the concerns of some of the respondents to the consultation exercise that the requirement of an annual report and budget would overburden small commonhold associations, it also considered that there would be some value in such an exercise, and left the final decision to the discretion of each commonhold association. For those commonhold associations wishing to take this step, a sample report and budget covering topics that will typically arise has been devised by the authors and may be found at Form 3.1 in the Forms and Precedents part of this work.

4.15.5 Failure to approve the assessment

It is difficult to see that there will be major disagreement over the estimate, which will be concerned with relatively mundane matters. There will of course be scope for greater disagreement when it comes to the reserve fund, discussed in Section 4.16 below.

There may, however, one would hope rarely, be cases in which the members will be unable to agree the directors' estimate. In such cases, the members concerned should make representations in writing in accordance with rule 25, and the directors will be required to take those representations into account (or, as rule 26 has it, to 'consider' them). In the event of continuing disagreement, the decision of the directors will be final. This contrasts with the Government's initial proposals, conveyed by paragraph 167 of the October 2002 Consultation Paper, for a first meeting to discuss the estimate, and in the event of disagreement:

> . . . the directors will then be required to convene a second meeting within seven days. This procedure will continue until agreement is reached, but if no commonhold assessment estimate can be agreed upon within twenty-eight days of the original meeting, the previous commonhold assessment will continue.

This proposal is a recipe for endless wrangling. The revised rule is to be commended.

[31] Paragraph 166 of the October 2002 Consultation Paper.

4.15.6 Assessment procedure step (3): the allocation

Rule 24 of the commonhold community statement (see paragraph 4.15.4 above) provides that the initial assessment notice should give details not merely (a) of the directors' estimate of the income required to be raised from unit-holders to meet the expenses of the commonhold association, but also (b) of the percentage allocated to each unit-holder's commonhold unit in Table 3.3 of Part II of the commonhold community statement, and (c) the amount of the estimate allocated to his commonhold unit.

As to (b), although section 38(1)(c) appears to cater for a free-standing approach to the determination of the amount of the assessment that each unit-holder should bear, this rule establishes that the reference to the 'relevant percentages for the units' is a reference to the figures set out in Part II of the commonhold community statement. This will be an unchanging amount (save of course to the extent that the members vote otherwise) that will have been determined at the outset of the creation of the commonhold, as Section 2.17.8 explains. The percentage in question will already therefore have been calculated and set down in the commonhold community statement, and will not vary from estimate to estimate, unless there is a special resolution changing those percentages in accordance with rule 56. The directors need therefore only apply the percentage in (b) to the estimate in (a) in order to calculate the apportioned estimate required for (c).

This part of the exercise therefore requires nothing more than the application of simple arithmetic. Indeed, any other approach which involved the recalculation of percentages on each occasion according to the amount of work done to individual units would be a recipe for continuous argument. Moreover, any attempt to allocate the burden of expenditure in any different way, no matter how meritorious or pragmatic that might appear, would be impeachable—see, for example, the decision of the Supreme Court of New South Wales in *Jacklin v Proprietors of Strata Plan No 2795* (1975) (Digest).

4.15.7 Assessment procedure step (4): the levy

Following section 38 (1)(d) of the Act, the commonhold community statement goes on to provide that, once the directors have taken any representations into account and made any necessary adjustments:

26. . . . the directors . . . must make a final estimate and serve further notices on the unit-holders specifying the payments required to be made by each unit-holder and the date on which each payment is due.
27. Subject to rule 28,[32] the notice referred to in rule 26 must not specify a date for payment of any sum that is less than 1 calendar month after the date on which the notice was served.

[32] Which deals with emergencies.

A number of points should be made about the timing in this and the other rules considered above regarding the levy:

(a) Some commonhold associations may justifiably take the view that they should be left to determine the timing of payments for themselves without being told how to run what will in some cases be a substantial business and in others a small domestic concern. However, the requirement for the specification of a date stems from section 38(1)(e) itself, and cannot be circumvented (although commonhold associations should be free to choose an earlier or later date to suit their own circumstances).

(b) Bearing in mind the various proposed delays, and the interest the association will have in ensuring that the levy is in hand before expenditure for the new financial year has to be incurred, careful thought will have to be given to the timing of the whole assessment process if there is not to be a shortfall.

The original (October 2002) draft rule regarding the levy provided that the notice could:

> . . . if the Board of Directors think fit, give the Unit-holder the option of paying the specified sum in instalments in such amounts and on such dates as shall be specified.

This, again, is something individual commonholds can consider writing into their rules if they feel so inclined.

The authors have devised a suitable form for this levy at Form 3.4 in the Forms and Precedents part of this work.

4.15.8 Assessment procedure step (5): payment

Rule 29 of the commonhold community statement provides:

> Each unit-holder must make payments in respect of the percentage of any estimate that is allocated to his commonhold unit by the date(s) specified in any notice served in accordance with these rules.

The liability of the unit-holder will therefore be to pay the sum specified by the date specified. Liability for non-payment cannot therefore arise until the day after that date, which prompts the observation that, where a transfer of a unit takes place after a levy has been served, but before the date specified for payment, the liability for payment will become that of the transferee rather than the transferor.

Rule 30 then adds as a default provision:

> Interest must be paid on any payment due in accordance with rule 29 that is late at the rate of 8 per cent per annum for the period between the date on which the payment is due and the date on which the payment is made.

The commonhold association's recourse in the event of failure to pay by the due date is addressed in full in Chapter 6 and in summary in Part 4 below.

4.15.9 Occasional and emergency assessments

Rule 23 of the commonhold community statement covers not merely annual estimates, but also '*occasional and emergency estimates*' of income required to be raised from unit-holders. What the italicised words in this rule envisage is a shortfall in the income of the commonhold association compared to the expenditure to be incurred. Such a shortfall may have a variety of causes: accidental omission of a predictable head of expenditure; failure to cater for an increase in prices of a particular product or service; the occurrence of an unforeseen event which requires expenditure; failure to collect the levy from a member. In any of these events (and there could of course be others), the commonhold association, which is unlikely to be able readily to borrow money, can only fund the shortfall by making an extra levy—sometimes more than once a year.

The making of occasional estimates is governed by the same procedure as that applying to annual estimates, considered in paragraphs 4.15.3 to 4.15.8 above. The making of an emergency estimate,[33] on the other hand, is shorn of much of that procedure. Rule 28 simply provides:

> The directors of the commonhold association must serve notices on each unit-holder specifying the amount of the emergency estimate that has been allocated to his commonhold unit and that the payment required to be made by each unit-holder must be made within 14 days of the date of the notice.

It will be noted that there is no opportunity for unit-holders to make representations. This procedure is draconian, and should only be used in proper emergencies.

A suitable form for use in making an emergency assessment estimate may be found at Form 3.3 in the Forms and Precedents part of this work.

4.16 THE RESERVE FUND

4.16.1 The relevant statutory provision

The basis for the reserve fund is laid down in section 39(1) and (2) of the Act. Section 39(1) provides that regulations 'may' require the commonhold community statement to make provision:

(a) requiring the directors of the commonhold association to establish and maintain one or more funds to finance the repair and maintenance of common parts;
(b) requiring the directors of the commonhold association to establish and maintain one or more funds to finance the repair and maintenance of commonhold units.

[33] The term 'estimate' is misleading: the procedure describes a demand, rather than the estimation process which the earlier rules deal with.

Two important points deserve to be made about this provision. First, even the diligent reader might be excused for interpreting this section as providing for funds for the finance of *all* repair and maintenance, no matter how routine or minor, leaving section 38, by omission, to deal with the funding of all other types of expenditure, despite its obvious purport. This interpretation would be wrong: section 39 is concerned only with the funding of major works that the annual assessments, with their more restricted and less fluctuating budgets, are not designed to cover.

Secondly, although the permissive language ('may') contrasts with the mandatory language of section 38(1), which directs the commonhold community statement to provide for a commonhold association procedure, there is no doubt that the commonhold community statement will in fact provide for a reserve fund or funds to be created. In that event, section 39(2) provides that the commonhold community statement 'must also make provision':

(a) requiring or enabling the directors of the commonhold association to set a levy from time to time,
(b) specifying the percentage of any levy set under paragraph (a) which is to be allocated to each unit,
(c) requiring each unit-holder to make payments in respect of the percentage of any levy set under paragraph (a) which is allocated to his unit, and
(d) requiring the directors of the commonhold association to serve notices on unit-holders specifying payments required to be made by them and the date on which each payment is due.

Section 39 goes on to deal with a number of more peripheral matters to do with the reserve fund, which are considered later in this Section.

4.16.2 The relevant commonhold community statement rules

The provisions referred to in section 39(1) and (2) are enshrined in rules 31 to 40 of the commonhold community statement:

- rule 31 introduces the 'reserve study', which is the exercise intended to guide the commonhold association on what funding will be required in the long term;
- rule 32 establishes the power for the board of directors to create reserve funds;
- rules 33 to 40 deal with the financing of the reserve fund.

When those rules are looked at together with section 39(1) and (2), a number of considerations arise as to the creation and operation of the reserve fund:

(a) the reserve study—see paragraph 4.16.3 below;
(b) should there be a reserve fund at all?—see paragraph 4.16.4 below;
(c) one fund or more?—see paragraph 4.16.5 below;
(d) calculation of the estimate—see paragraph 4.16.6 below;

(e) approval of the estimate—see paragraph 4.16.7 below;

(f) the allocation of the balance needed among those liable to contribute—see paragraph 4.16.8 below;

(g) the reserve fund levy—see paragraph 4.16.9 below;

(h) payment of the levy—see paragraph 4.16.10 below;

(i) holding the reserve fund—see paragraph 4.16.11 below;

(j) the duty of the reserve fund holder—see paragraph 4.16.12 below.

4.16.3 Reserve fund procedure step (1): the reserve study

Rule 31 of the commonhold community statement provides:

> The directors of the commonhold association must commission a reserve study by an appropriate professional at least once in every 10 years.

In contrast to the original (October 2002) draft, this rule gives no clue as to the content or purpose of the study. The omission may be ascribed to the wish of the Department of Constitutional Affairs not to be over-prescriptive, but is curious nevertheless. In the absence of guidance, it is appropriate to look to the wording of the previous draft:

> . . . a written study listing all of the major assets, equipment, fixtures or fittings which the commonhold association owns or maintains with a remaining life of less than [number] years (a 'reserve study'). The reserve study must estimate in the case of each such item, (i) the remaining life of the item, (ii) the costs of maintaining and replacing the item, and (iii) the annual contribution required to maintain such costs.

A form devised by the authors that gives an example of the shape and content of a proposed reserve study is at Form 3.5 in the Forms and Precedents part of this work.

Part of the aim of this exercise will be to produce an estimated levy (see paragraph 4.16.6 below), which the board will then be able to present to the members for their approval (see paragraph 4.16.7 below).

4.16.4 Reserve fund procedure step (2): should there be a reserve fund at all?

Rule 32 of the commonhold community statement provides:

> The directors of the commonhold association must consider the results of the reserve study and, in particular, whether it is necessary in light of the findings in the reserve study to establish and maintain one or more reserve funds to finance the repair and maintenance of the common parts.

Thus both section 39(1) of the Act and this rule appear to leave it up to the board of directors whether to have a reserve fund at all. As against that, paragraph 170 of the October 2002 Consultation Paper proposed that all commonholds will be *required* to establish and maintain a reserve fund. The reasoning put forward in support of this proposal was as follows:

> This is to enable the commonhold association to fund spending of a capital or non-recurrent nature as easily as possible. A possible alternative to such a fund would be to levy a special assessment whenever a major item needed to be replaced, but this would entail further administration and make the task of ensuring payment more complicated.

The authors suggest, however, that this is too prescriptive, and may lead to unnecessary expense. Everything should depend upon the nature of the development. If it is new, and well built, with adequate guarantees in place, then there will be no obvious need to commit funding to fabric that should not need serious attention for very many years. Unit-holders who may wish to sell their units in the near future will naturally object to having to pay money up front to benefit a successor in title when the need is neither apparent nor obvious. The retort that the commitment may be recognised in an adjustment to the purchase price is unsatisfactory. There again, if the commonhold is small, unit-holders will probably wish to organise their affairs in a way that does not involve their funds being tied up for years in a reserve fund when their ability to finance works nearer the time may never be in doubt.

It therefore remains to be seen whether the use of reserve funding will become prevalent in a form of land holding where all owners ought to have a community of interest in funding necessary works as and when they are required. It must be recognised, however, that, in the case of large developments of ageing buildings, the accumulation of a fund or funds to finance substantial expenditure on periodic replacement of the fabric will be seen by many as prudent housekeeping.

4.16.5 Reserve fund procedure step (3): one fund or more?

Rule 32 of the commonhold community statement refers not to the establishment of 'a' reserve fund, but rather of 'one or more reserve funds'. It seems clear that what is contemplated is a number of funds: 'the reroofing fund', 'the carpark resurfacing fund', and so forth. Whether the division of the financing in this way makes any practical sense is a matter which individual boards of directors will be left to decide, with the benefit of proper advice.

4.16.6 Reserve fund procedure step (4): calculation of the reserve fund levy

Once the reserve study has been carried out, if it has been determined that a reserve fund is necessary, then rule 33 provides:

> The directors of the commonhold association must set a levy from time to time in relation to the reserve fund ('the levy').

The board of directors must therefore put themselves in a position to calculate what sum it will be appropriate to put forward as the proposed levy for the members to approve.

The starting point (and often, perhaps, the end point as well) for the calculation of this sum will be the annual contribution required to maintain and replace the item or items with which the reserve study is concerned. This will not necessarily be the only determinative factor involved in producing the estimate. The board of directors may consider that it would be appropriate to take into account all or some of the following factors:

(a) the extent to which construction costs are likely to increase or decrease over time;

(b) the extent to which design or construction techniques may improve, with the resulting (upward or downward) impact on costs;

(c) the extent to which a solution other than maintenance or replacement (at higher or lower cost) may prove advantageous or popular;

(d) whether it would be appropriate for all or parts of the likely cost to be funded by an increased commonhold assessment rather than by the reserve fund.

Alternatively, the board of directors may consider it more appropriate to produce as the requisite matter to be considered the figure derived from the reserve study, and content themselves with drawing the members' attention to the factors listed above as having some possible bearing on the question.

4.16.7 Reserve fund procedure step (5): approval of the reserve fund study and proposed levy

Because the unit-holders who will be asked to pay the reserve fund levy will for the most part also be members of the commonhold association, fairness and common sense dictate that they should have the opportunity to scrutinise and approve or reject the directors' proposals.

This is recognised by rules 34 to 36, which follow the wording of rules 24 to 26 in relation to the commonhold assessment (see paragraph 4.15.4 above). Perhaps surprisingly, there is no requirement for the setting of the reserve fund levy to be discussed in a meeting of the commonhold association, let alone that it should be the subject of a special resolution. This contrasts with the following suggestion and reasoning in paragraph 172 of the October 2002 Consultation Paper:

> . . . the estimate for the levy should be approved by a special resolution at an Annual General Meeting of the commonhold association because the relevant liabilities are some way into the future. For the same reason no emergency provision should be necessary. We also propose that the unit-holder will be entitled to inspect the reserve study and the estimates proposed for the reserve fund levies.

The authors suggest that a major feature of the perceived success of a commonhold will be the members' ability to vote on their own expenditure. They therefore endorse this proposal.

4.16.8 Reserve fund procedure step (6): allocating the balance needed among those liable to contribute

Rule 34 of the commonhold community statement refers to the 'amount of the levy that is to be allocated' to each unit; while rule 38 refers to 'the percentage of any levy that is allocated'. What does not appear in relation to the rules regarding the allocation of the reserve fund levy is any reference to how this percentage is to be calculated (compare the treatment of commonhold assessment levies in rule 24). The authors assume that this is an oversight, but note from the draft of Table 3.3 in Part II of the commonhold community statement that separate columns are provided for the specification of the commonhold assessment percentages and the reserve fund assessment percentages. The need for separate percentages is nowhere explained, although the draftsmen may have been providing for units of mixed ages requiring different levels of long-term maintenance, but similar levels of short-term care.

At any rate, it seems reasonably clear that the percentages to be applied to the reserve fund levies are those set out in the relevant column in Table 3.3, despite the fact that the language of section 39(2)(c) appears to cater for a free-standing approach to the determination of the amount of the reserve fund levy that each unit-holder should bear. This will therefore be an unchanging proportion (save of course to the extent that the members vote otherwise) that will have been determined at the outset of the creation of the commonhold, as paragraph 2.17.18 explains.

This part of the exercise therefore requires nothing more than the application of simple arithmetic. Indeed, any other approach which involved the recalculation of percentages on each occasion according to the amount of work done to individual units would be a recipe for continuous argument.

4.16.9 Reserve fund procedure step (7): the reserve fund levy

The procedure for the making of the reserve fund levy is set out in rules 36 and 37, and is identical to the procedure for the making of the commonhold assessment levy described in paragraph 4.15.7 above, save that there is no procedure for the making of an emergency levy. The authors have devised a suitable form for this levy at Form 3.6 in the Forms and Precedents part of this work.

4.16.10 Reserve fund procedure step (8): payment

In accordance with section 39(2)(c), rule 38 deals with the payment of the reserve fund levy: the procedure is again identical to that applicable to the payment of commonhold assessment levies described in paragraph 4.15.8 above.

As with such levies, there is a default provision that interest is payable upon late payments (see rule 39). The commonhold association's further recourse in the event of failure by a unit-holder to pay by the date that should be specified in the levy is addressed in full in Chapter 6 and in summary in Part 4 below.

4.16.11 Reserve fund procedure step (9): holding the reserve fund payment

Neither the Act nor the commonhold community statement lay down any stipulations regarding the way in which monies in the reserve fund are to be held. Clearly, those monies should be held in a designated bank, building society or other savings account in the name of the commonhold association, in order to preserve the separation between the reserve fund monies and the fluctuating revenue and expenditure of the commonhold assessment. This separation will also enable interest earned upon the fund to be accounted for easily, which will be important in case there is a liability to tax (see paragraph 4.18.3 below).

4.16.12 Reserve fund procedure step (10): the duty of the reserve fund holder

During the course of the Report Stage, the Opposition spokesman had this to say about the extra protection that would be afforded to the money in the reserve fund if a trust were imposed upon the commonhold association similar to that devised for leasehold service charge funds under section 42 of the Landlord and Tenant Act 1987:

> We think that the establishment of trust funds is appropriate, first, to protect the unit-holders in the event of the association's insolvency and, secondly, to prevent the misuse of funds.
>
> Contrary to the Government's suggestion, these considerations apply to commonholds which may become insolvent—for example, if they find that they have a substantial uninsured liability for nuisance, such as tree root subsidence to neighbouring land. The potential creation of substantial distinct funds is important. In our view unit-holders would not want to build up a large sinking fund if they thought it might later be eroded by expenditure on other items of ordinary day-to-day expenses.[34]

The Government's view, however, was that section 42 should be limited to the control of service charges as between landlord and tenant, and not the freehold relationships which characterise commonhold. The duties regarding the monies held from time to time in the reserve fund are, in its view, adequately protected by company law rules, and do not require the superimposition of a statutory trust to protect the unit-holders. This view was expressed more than once in these terms:

> Such considerations do not apply within commonhold. The commonhold association is a company whose members are those who paid the money into the funds. They appoint and

[34] *Official Report, House of Lords*, 13 November 2001; col 478.

dismiss the directors of the company; they approve the objects of expenditure and the setting of budgets, and have absolute control over all aspects of the company under company law. The directors who act on their behalf are bound by their fiduciary duty to act honestly and bona fide in the interests of the company and are also subject to the sanctions available under both the Companies Acts and the general criminal law. They must produce accounts and answer for their contents. Commonhold association funds are funds of the company, not of the directors. Clearly, the purposes for which section 42 was included in the 1987 Act do not apply in commonhold. It is not necessary for the directors of the commonhold association to be placed under trustee duties in relation to reserve fund moneys.[35]

It will therefore suffice for the reserve fund account(s) to be administered by the directors like any other fund, without the superimposition of duties in the nature of a trust.

4.16.13 Reserve fund procedure step (11): the use of the fund

It might be thought to go without saying that the monies in the reserve fund should be used only for the purposes for which the fund was established in the first place—for the replacement of the roof; or the resurfacing of the carpark; and so on. Should the members agree, however, there is no reason why the monies should not be diverted to quite another purpose, temporarily or permanently. After all, the monies are not impressed with a trust (see paragraph 4.16.12 above).

Rule 40 deals expressly with this situation by providing:

In setting the levy the directors must endeavour to ensure that unnecessary reserves are not accumulated and where they do so accumulate they may be used for the general expenses of the commonhold.

The only express prohibition upon use of the reserve fund monies is imposed by section 39(4):

The assets of a fund established and maintained by virtue of this section shall not be used for the purpose of enforcement of any debt except a judgment debt referable to a reserve fund activity.

Section 39(5) adds to this by explaining:

(a) 'reserve fund activity' means an activity which in accordance with the commonhold community statement can or may be financed from a fund established and maintained by virtue of this section,
(b) assets are used for the purpose of enforcement of a debt if, in particular, they are taken in execution or are made the subject of a charging order under section 1 of the Charging Orders Act 1979 (c 53), and
(c) the reference to a judgment debt includes a reference to any interest payable on a judgment debt.

[35] See, for example, *Standing Committee D*, 15 January 2002; col 55.

The purpose of this provision is presumably to discourage the commonhold association from litigating with the advantage of the large-scale source of funding that the reserve fund may contain.

4.17 ACCOUNTING

4.17.1 Introduction

Although the commonhold community statement says little about accounting, like any other company subject to the Companies Acts, the commonhold association must keep proper accounts. This Section sets out the chief requirements.

4.17.2 Annual accounts and directors' report

The statutory requirement confronting the commonhold association is to file annual accounts and a directors' report. The source documents (income and expenditure details) from which the accounts will be prepared must be kept carefully by the commonhold association. For this purpose, the commonhold association should either ensure that a finance committee is tasked with the control of the requisite records, or that a treasurer is appointed and tasked with record keeping (see paragraph 4.7.4 above).

If records are kept carefully and marshalled in good order ready for the annual audit, the costs of the exercise (which will have to be budgeted for) will be kept to a minimum.

4.17.3 Annual report and budget

In addition to its duties in relation to the annual accounts and directors' report, the commonhold community statement may also require that the board of directors circulate or lay before the members an annual report and budget. Although the current (August 2003) version of the rules does not require such a document,[36] many commonhold associations will feel that the preparation of such a document will help to ensure that the commonhold is properly run.

The preparation of such a document is considered in paragraph 4.15.4 above.

[36] Contrast the former (October 2002) version of the commonhold community statement, rule 36 of which required 'a written report comparing the results of the commonhold association against its estimated budget for the year and setting out an estimated budget for the forthcoming year'.

4.18 TAX

4.18.1 The taxable status of the commonhold association

As paragraph 4.2.1 has observed, the commonhold association is entitled to run activities for profit, provided that the profits are used for the functions of the association, rather than distribution to the members, which is prohibited under its memorandum and articles of association. In this sense the commonhold association may be regarded as a not-for-profit company.

Some commonwealth jurisdictions confer favourable tax treatment on such not-for-profit companies. In this jurisdiction, such treatment is afforded only to charities, and a commonhold association will therefore not qualify (despite attempts to introduce specific legislation to the contrary effect during the passage of the Bill through Parliament). The commonhold association will therefore be subject to corporation tax on its income, in the same way as any other corporation.

4.18.2 Income from lettings

Clause 3 of the memorandum of association provides:

> The object of the commonhold association is to exercise the functions of a commonhold association in relation to [specify the name of the commonhold and its location] in accordance with the commonhold community statement, as amended from time to time, and any provision made by or by virtue of Part 1 of the Commonhold and Leasehold Reform Act 2002 and the doing of all such things as are incidental or conducive to the attainment of that object.

That rather terse clause compares with the earlier draft,[37] which entitled the commonhold association:

> to acquire, hold as registered proprietor, manage and administer, create interests in, exchange, let on lease or otherwise, mortgage, charge, sell, dispose of, turn to account, grant licences, options, rights and privileges in respect of or otherwise deal in any way with the freehold estate in any Commonhold Unit which it may be thought advantageous for the commonhold association to acquire, hold or deal with as aforesaid from time to time, and to exercise all rights and perform all duties and obligations of a unit-holder in connection therewith.

Nevertheless, the current draft will allow, for example, the letting of parts of the common parts of the commonhold (for example a vacant garage), for rental income, provided that that is in furtherance of the objects, rather than in exercise of an independent business.

[37] Clause 4.8 of the draft appended to the October 2002 Consultation Paper.

If the commonhold association does indulge in such activities, it will incur a liability to tax, although there may be ways in which this tax can be minimised. Such matters are outside the current scope of this work, and specialist advice should be sought.

4.18.3 The reserve fund

The question which arises in relation to the reserve fund is whether assessment levies resulting in accumulations to the fund are taxable. The resolution of this question will depend upon a number of factors:

(a) Are the receipts recognised as income of the commonhold association in the accounts? If so, then it would be difficult to contend that they were not taxable receipts.

(b) Is the right to retain the monies in the fund conditional upon carrying out the repair work? If so, then it may be arguable that the monies collected would not be recognised as taxable receipts, because they would not have been 'earned'.

(c) If the monies are regarded as taxable receipts, can a deduction be claimed on the basis of the future expenditure? This will depend upon whether such a provision satisfies the requirements of FRS12 and, if so, whether it falls outside the specific statutory disallowance for 'any sum expended for repairs of premises occupied for the purposes of the [Schedule A business] beyond the sum actually expended for those purposes . . .': see section 74 of the Taxes Act 1988.

In addition, if the reserve fund has been built up to a level which appears to be far in excess of the likely future outgoings, then it is possible that all or part of any interest payable upon the invested fund will be regarded as taxable investment income.

Again, such matters are outside the current scope of this work, and specialist advice should be sought.

PART 4 ENFORCEMENT

4.19 ENFORCEMENT

4.19.1 Introduction

Enforcement between and against the commonhold association, the unit-holders and tenants of commonhold is dealt with in depth in Chapter 6. This Part summarises the appropriate remedies and methods of enforcement available to a commonhold association when unit-holders fail to comply with the rules for the commonhold.

4.19.2 The approach to enforcement

Commonhold is characterised by three principles which will make enforcement in the way in which it has traditionally been understood in a leasehold context either inappropriate or impossible:

(a) First, the traditional powerful remedies available to a landlord (forfeiture; distress save in the case of certain residential premises) are simply not allowed in commonhold. Not only that—the commonhold association has no preferential position in relation to a defaulting unit-holder, but must take its chances in the courts (subject to (b) below).

(b) Secondly, alternative dispute resolution is not only encouraged, but made mandatory in most cases as a recourse before litigation can be commenced.

(c) Third, there is no automatic presumption that each and every rule should be enforced. Section 35(3) of the Act relieves the directors of the commonhold association from taking remedial action if inaction is thought to be preferable.

Those principles are designed to make commonhold less contentious, in keeping with the community of interest it is supposed to engender. The application of the principles will have important consequences for the way in which breaches of duty are sought to be policed.

4.19.3 Enforcement in cases of breach of duty

To take perhaps the most obvious example of breach, where a unit-holder has been served with an assessment or reserve fund levy, and has failed to pay within the stipulated time, the following default procedure should be used:

(a) It would be prudent first to check that the unit-holder is not on holiday, ill, or otherwise indisposed. A telephone call or visit should suffice.

(b) If payment is not then made, a notice in writing should be sent, warning of the consequences that will follow if payment is delayed further. A proposed form for this notice (the 'default notice') may be found in the Forms and Precedents part of this work at Form 4.4.

(c) The commonhold association should also consider at this stage sending a copy of the notice(s) to the unit-holder's mortgagee. However, although the involvement of a third party may prompt the unit-holder into settling the outstanding bill, the mortgagee will know that (in contrast to a leasehold situation) its security will not be put in jeopardy if payment is not made immediately. It is therefore unlikely to apply any great pressure to the unit-holder.

(d) If service of the default notice does not trigger payment, then the commonhold association will have to decide whether to proceed further by way of reference to the commonhold ombudsman, or to litigate for the recovery of the sum in question. Much will depend upon the amount in question, and the known circumstances of the default.

4.19.4 Indemnity

The original (October 2002) draft of the commonhold community statement contained the following provisions for indemnifying the commonhold association and unit-holders affected by the breaches of any unit-holder:

48. Without prejudice to any other remedy to which the commonhold association or any other Unit-holder may be entitled, any Unit-holder who is in breach of any provision of the Articles or the Rules or any statutory requirement (the 'defaulter') shall indemnify and hold harmless the commonhold association and any other Unit-holder against any costs arising from such breach, including, if appropriate, the costs of remedying the breach or of acting in the stead of the defaulter as permitted by the Rules.
49. If the Board of Directors are of the opinion that the commonhold association or any Unit-holder has incurred any costs arising from such breach as aforesaid which the defaulter ought to pay, they shall serve a notice (an 'indemnity notice') on the defaulter requiring him to pay the amount of such costs to the commonhold association or to the other Unit-holder within a specified period being not less than 14 days.

Although a majority of the respondents to the Consultation Paper were broadly in favour of these provisions, the Department of Constitutional Affairs has dropped them without comment from the current (August 2003) version. Individual commonhold associations should, however, consider their reinstatement for the relief they may bring to harassed directors and members. This topic is discussed in paragraph 6.3.7

PART 5 RUNNING A MIXED USE COMMONHOLD

4.20 MIXED USE

4.20.1 Introduction

A mixed use commonhold will be a commonhold development that includes a mix of users, the most obvious example of which will be a residential complex with some shops and leisure facilities.

It is the Government's stated intention that the Act will be as suitable for mixed use developments as it is for purely residential developments. There ought to be no greater difficulty in operating a commonhold with a mixed use element: the issues of repair and insurance will be similar, with only user requiring adjustment. The only obvious points of difficulty, discussed below, will be:

(a) the selection of a percentage to be used for the levies and other necessary financial adjustments (insurance reinstatement, termination) that will not provoke dissent; and

(b) the allocation of voting rights.

4.20.2 The appropriate percentage

If the commonhold consists, say, of a large retail unit on the ground floor and a number of much smaller residential units above, it would obviously be inequitable for the commonhold association and reserve fund levies to be divided equally between the units. The retail unit would use a disproportionately larger share of some services (fuel, rubbish removal, redecoration), and a disproportionately smaller share of others (lift, porter).

Some way will have to be found of resolving these difficulties. In practice, this is often done in existing leasehold developments, so precedents do exist. Moreover, the point is worth stressing that it will for the most part be the developer who will select the percentages (since it is wholly unlikely that existing mixed use leasehold schemes will achieve a unanimous vote for conversion). Unit-holders who then buy into such a scheme will presumably have investigated and been satisfied with the percentages. That is not to say, however, that care should not be taken in formulating a division that is likely to make for the most contented commonhold possible.

4.20.3 Voting rights

Paragraph 83 of the October 2002 Consultation Paper makes the point that a one-member-one-vote voting structure may lead to inequitable results in the case of a mixed use commonhold. To take the example of the mixed use development referred to in paragraph 4.20.2 above:

> It may create an unfair environment if the supermarket only exercises the same voting strength as each residential unit. On the other hand, if one person owns multiple units he or she may exercise the voting rights for every unit owned, which may effectively allow one person to dominate proceedings in the commonhold.

Paragraph 84 of the Consultation Paper proposes some possible solutions that will need to be considered and resolved in order for this important feature of a mixed use commonhold to work well in practice.

Chapter 5
TERMINATING A COMMONHOLD

5.1 GENERAL

5.1.1 Introduction

This Chapter considers the ways in which a commonhold can be brought to an end. In summary:

(a) The registered proprietor of the commonhold is entitled to apply for the commonhold registration to be cancelled, provided that he does so before the end of the transitional period.[1]

(b) An application can be made to the court for an order that the land shall cease to be commonhold land; this application can only be made by a person who is adversely affected by the registration, in circumstances where the registration has been made in error.[2]

(c) The commonhold association can be voluntarily wound-up.

(d) The commonhold association can be the subject of a compulsory winding-up.

(e) The commonhold may be the subject of a compulsory purchase.

This chapter considers the procedures for a voluntary winding-up, a compulsory winding-up and a compulsory purchase of a commonhold.

There are few regulation-making powers in respect of termination in the Act because, in general, the provisions of the Insolvency Act 1986 will apply to the commonhold association as they would to any other company limited by guarantee. Nevertheless, the Government is still considering, in consultation with insolvency practitioners, whether there are any further issues concerning the termination of commonholds which should be provided for in the regulations.[3]

[1] Section 8(4). [2] Section 6(1).

[3] Department for Constitutional Affairs Consultation Response (August 2003), conclusion to questions 174–179.

5.2 VOLUNTARY WINDING-UP

5.2.1 General

The procedure for a voluntary winding-up is carried out by the ordinary procedure laid down in the Insolvency Act 1986, but subject to various modifications.[4]

The procedure for a voluntary winding-up of the commonhold association is commenced by a winding-up resolution. The procedure that is followed thereafter depends on whether the resolution (and the accompanying termination statement resolution) have been approved unanimously, or only by a slightly lesser proportion of the unit-holders. The difference between the two procedures is that the court has a more extensive role in a voluntary winding-up that was not approved unanimously.

5.2.2 Winding-up resolution

The first stage in the termination of a commonhold by the unit-holders is for a winding-up resolution to be passed in respect of the commonhold association.

5.2.3 Declaration of solvency

A winding-up resolution must be preceded by a declaration of solvency.[5] A resolution has no effect if it has not been preceded by a declaration.[6]

A declaration of solvency is a directors' statutory declaration made in accordance with section 89 of the Insolvency Act 1986.[7] It must therefore comply with the following requirements:

(a) It must be made on Form 4.70 in Schedule 4 to the Insolvency Rules 1986.[8]

(b) It must be made by statutory declaration.[9]

(c) The content of the declaration must be to the effect that the directors have made a full inquiry into the company's affairs and that, having done so, they are of the opinion that it will be able to pay its debts in full, together with interest at the official rate, within such period, not exceeding 12 months from the commencement of the winding-up, as may be specified in the declaration.[10] The directors are free to fix the period within which, in their view, the company will have been able to pay its debts in full. The official rate of interest is whichever is the higher of 8 per cent[11] and the rate that is contractually applicable to the debt.[12]

[4] The Government is still considering whether to make further modifications: Department for Constitutional Affairs Consultation Response (August 2003), conclusion to questions 174–179.

[5] Section 43(1)(a). [6] Section 43(1). [7] Section 43(2).

[8] A copy of this is at form 6.1 of the Forms and Precedents section.

[9] Section 89(1). [10] Section 89(1), Insolvency Act 1986.

[11] Which is the current rate under section 17 of the Judgments Act 1838.

[12] Sections 251, 189(4), Insolvency Act 1986.

(d) The declaration must be made at a directors' meeting of the company.[13]

(e) The declaration must be made within the 5 weeks immediately preceding the date on which the winding-up resolution is passed. It can be made on the same date as the meeting at which the winding-up resolution is passed.[14]

(f) The declaration must be made by all of the directors or, if the company has more than two directors, by a majority of them.[15]

(g) The declaration must embody a statement of the company's assets and liabilities as at the latest practical date before the making of the declaration.[16]

(h) The declaration must be delivered to the Registrar of Companies before the expiration of 15 days immediately following the date on which the winding-up resolution is passed.[17] The company and its officers are liable to a fine if they do not deliver the declaration within this time period.[18]

A director who makes a declaration without having reasonable grounds for believing that it is true is liable to imprisonment, a fine or both.

5.2.4 Termination-statement resolution

The commonhold association must also pass a termination-statement resolution before it passes the winding-up resolution.[19] Again, a winding-up resolution has no effect if it has not been preceded by the termination-statement resolution.[20]

A termination-statement resolution is a resolution approving the terms of the termination statement.[21] The effect of a winding-up is that all the commonhold land, including the freehold title to each of the units, becomes vested in the commonhold association.[22] The principal function of the termination statement is to define what is to happen to the assets and how the commonhold association is to deal with the land.

The termination statement is required to specify:

(a) The commonhold association's proposals for the transfer of the commonhold land following acquisition of the freehold estate. In practice, this is likely to specify the grant of long leases to each of the unit-holders in respect of their units, and the grant of rights over the common parts, together with the transfer of the freehold reversion to a specified individual or company.[23]

(b) How the assets of the commonhold association will be distributed.[24]

[13] Section 89(1), Insolvency Act 1986.
[14] Section 89(2), Insolvency Act 1986.
[15] Section 89(1), Insolvency Act 1986.
[16] Section 89(2)(b), Insolvency Act 1986.
[17] Section 89(3), Insolvency Act 1986.
[18] Section 89(6), Insolvency Act 1986.
[19] Section 43(1)(b), Commonhold and Leasehold Reform Act 2002.
[20] Section 43(1).
[21] Section 43(2).
[22] Section 49(3) provides that where a termination application is made, then 'The commonhold association shall by virtue of this subsection be entitled to be registered as the proprietor of the freehold estate in each commonhold unit.'
[23] Section 47(1)(a).
[24] Section 47(1)(b).

The proposed Commonhold Community Statement (August 2003) also requires that a termination statement must provide that, where the commonhold association is entitled to become registered as the proprietor of the freehold estate in each commonhold unit following a termination application, a unit-holder may continue to occupy his commonhold unit until the commonhold association disposes of the commonhold land.[25]

It is possible for the commonhold community statement to have provided for all or some of the provisions of the termination statement, requiring it to make arrangements of a specified kind, or determined in a specified manner, about the rights of the unit-holders in the event of all the land to which the statement relates ceasing to be commonhold land.[26] If the commonhold community statement does contain provisions of this nature, then the termination statement must comply with those provisions unless the court orders otherwise.[27] Any member of the commonhold association can apply to the court for an order that the termination statement need not comply with the provisions in the commonhold community statement.[28] A joint unit-holder who is not a member of the association cannot make the application, and neither can a unit-holder who did not become a member. The court's order may provide either that all the provisions of the commonhold community statement are to be disregarded or, more likely, that specified matters are to be disapplied either generally or for a specified purpose.[29]

The resolution can only be passed with at least 80 per cent of the members of the association voting in favour.

5.2.5 Winding-up resolution

The winding-up resolution must be a resolution for a voluntary winding-up of the commonhold association that complies with section 84 of the Insolvency Act 1986. A resolution to wind-up a solvent company voluntarily must ordinarily only be passed by a special resolution requiring a three-fourths majority vote.[30] However, a winding-up resolution in respect of a commonhold association must be passed by a resolution with at least 80 per cent of the members of the association voting in favour.

A copy of the resolution must be forwarded to the Registrar of Companies within 15 days.[31] The company must also, within 14 days, give notice of the resolution in the Gazette.[32]

The procedure which then applies for winding-up the company depends on whether:

[25] Rule 53. Consideration is being given as to whether the commonhold community statement should contain further provisions in respect of the termination statement: Department for Constitutional Affairs Consultation Response (August 2003), responses to question 175.

[26] Section 47(2). [27] Section 47(3). [28] Section 47(5). [29] Section 47(4).

[30] Section 378, Companies Act 1985. [31] Section 84(3), Insolvency Act 1986.

[32] Section 85(1), Insolvency Act 1986.

(a) The termination-statement resolution and the winding-up resolution were each passed with 100 per cent of the members of the association voting in favour. In this case the section 44 procedure applies to the winding-up.

(b) Either of the two resolutions were passed with less than 100 per cent of the members voting in favour. In this case the section 45 procedure applies to the winding-up instead.

5.2.6 The section 44 procedure: 100 per cent agreement—(a) appointment of a liquidator

The next stage in the winding-up procedure is to appoint a liquidator under section 91 of the Insolvency Act 1986. The liquidator must be an individual rather than a company,[33] and he must be qualified to act as an insolvency practitioner.[34] The liquidator must be appointed by the company in general meeting.[35] The chairman of the meeting must certify the appointment, but not unless and until the person who is appointed has provided him with a written statement to the effect that he is an insolvency practitioner duly qualified under the Act to be the liquidator, and that he consents to act.[36] The certificate of appointment must be in Form 4.27 to Schedule 4 of the Insolvency Rules 1986 (or in Form 4.28 if there are to be two or more liquidators). The chairman must send the certificate of appointment to the liquidator forthwith.[37] The liquidator will then give notice of his appointment to the creditors.[38]

The effect of the liquidator's appointment is that the powers of the directors immediately cease, except so far as the liquidator or the company in general meeting sanctions their continuance.[39]

The directors may not exercise any of their powers between the winding-up resolution and the appointment of a liquidator, except that they may do all such things as may be necessary for the protection of the company's assets.[40]

5.2.7 The section 44 procedure: 100 per cent agreement—(b) termination application

The liquidator must make a termination application within six months of the date of the winding-up resolution. The termination application will be made to the

[33] Section 390(1), Insolvency Act 1986.

[34] Sections 388–390, Insolvency Act 1986. The current requirements are that he must either be authorised specifically by the Secretary of State (sections 390(2)(b), 393) or, more commonly, must be authorised to act under the terms of his membership of the Chartered Association of Certified Accountants, the Institute of Chartered Accountants in England and Wales, the Institute of Chartered Accountants in Scotland, the Institute of Chartered Accountants in Ireland, the Insolvency Practitioners Association, the Law Society of Scotland, or the Law Society (section 390(2)(a), the Insolvency Practitioners (Recognised Professional Bodies) Order 1986).

[35] Section 91(1).

[36] Insolvency Rules 1986, rule 4.139(1), (2).

[37] Insolvency Rules 1986, rule 4.139(3).

[38] Insolvency Rules 1986, rule 4.139(4).

[39] Section 91(2), Insolvency Act 1986.

[40] Section 114, Insolvency Act 1986.

Chief Land Registrar on Land Registry Form CM5.[41] The application must enclose the termination statement. If the liquidator does not do so within this period, then a unit-holder may make the application instead.[42] Regulations may also prescribe further classes of person who can make the application in the event of the liquidator's default.[43] It is proposed that the further classes of person entitled to make the application should be:

(a) any directors of the commonhold association who are not also members of the company;

(b) any lessee or assignee of a unit within the commonhold; and

(c) any chargee of a commonhold unit or the common parts.[44]

The liquidator must also notify the Registrar of his appointment[45] and either:

(a) notify the Registrar that he is content with the terms of the termination statement that was submitted with the termination application;[46] or

(b) apply for the court to determine the terms of the termination statement, under section 112 of the Insolvency Act 1986.[47] A copy of any order made by the court determining the terms of the statement must be sent to the Registrar of Companies[48] and to the Chief Land Registrar.[49]

The liquidator must carry out these notifications or make an application to the court as soon as possible.[50]

5.2.8 The section 45 procedure: less than 100 per cent agreement

The difference between a winding-up that has been approved unanimously and one that has less than unanimous approval is that, in the latter case, the court determines the rights of the unit-holders following the termination of the commonhold.

The first stage is again to appoint a liquidator. This is done in the same way as with a winding-up under the section 44 procedure. The liquidator must then apply to the court for an order determining:

(a) the terms and conditions on which a termination application may be made;

(b) the terms of the termination statement to accompany a termination application.[51]

[41] Commonhold (Land Registration) Rules, rule 24(1); Schedule 1. A draft of Form CM5 is at Form 1.5 in the Forms and Precedents part of this work.

[42] Section 44(3)(a).

[43] Section 44(3)(b).

[44] Department for Constitutional Affairs Consultation Response (August 2003), responses and conclusion in respect of question 176, endorsing the original proposals in the October 2002 Consultation Paper.

[45] Section 48(2).

[46] Section 49(3)(a).

[47] Section 48(3)(b).

[48] Section 112(3), Insolvency Act 1986, section 48(5), Commonhold and Leasehold Reform Act 2002.

[49] Section 48(4).

[50] Section 48(6).

[51] Section 45(2).

The application to the court must be made within three months of the date on which the winding-up resolution is passed.[52] If the liquidator does not apply within this period, then a unit-holder may make the application instead.[53] Regulations may also prescribe further classes of person who can make the application in the event of the liquidator's default.[54]

The liquidator must then make a termination application to the Chief Land Registrar. This must be done within three months of the date of the court's order determining the terms and conditions of the application and the contents of the termination statement.[55] Again, if the liquidator does not make the application within this period then a unit-holder[56] (or anyone in the prescribed further classes of person[57]) may do so instead.

The termination application must be made on Land Registry Form CM5.[58] The application must enclose a copy of the court's order and the liquidator's certificate of appointment.[59]

5.2.9 The effect of the termination application

Under either procedure, upon receipt of the termination application the Registrar will enter the commonhold association as the proprietor of the commonhold units, and will cancel the commonhold entries on every title that is affected.[60] The Act provides that the Registrar is also to take 'such action as is appropriate for the purpose of giving effect to the termination statement'.[61]

5.2.10 The reserve fund

The reserve fund cannot ordinarily be used for the purpose of enforcing a debt, except for a judgment debt that is referable to a reserve fund activity.[62] This restriction does not apply in the event that the commonhold association has passed a voluntary winding-up resolution.[63] The assets of the reserve fund are therefore available to the liquidator.

[52] Section 45(3). Regulation 19 of the draft Commonhold Regulations. The Government is considering whether this time limit should be amended in its application to commonholds: Department for Constitutional Affairs Consultation Response (August 2003), question 177.

[53] Section 45(4)(a). [54] Section 44(4)(b). [55] Section 45(3).

[56] Section 44(3)(a). [57] Section 44(4)(b).

[58] Commonhold (Land Registration) Rules, rule 24(1); Schedule 1. A draft of Form CM5 is at Form 1.5 in the Forms and Precedents part of this work.

[59] Section 48(2). [60] Commonhold (Land Registration) Rules, rule 24(2).

[61] Section 49(4). [62] Section 39(4). [63] Section 56(a).

5.3 COMPULSORY WINDING-UP: GENERAL

5.3.1 Procedure for winding-up under the Act

The ordinary procedures for compulsorily winding-up a company apply to commonhold associations just as they do to other companies. There is no moratorium on the compulsory winding-up of a commonhold association.

5.3.2 Modifications to standard insolvency procedure

Although the procedure for a compulsory winding-up is carried out by the ordinary procedures in the Insolvency Act 1986, this again is subject to various modifications. The most important modifications, in the case of a compulsory winding-up, are that (a) the court has the power to make a succession order; and (b) the liquidator has special duties to give notice to the Chief Land Registrar of various matters that arise in the course of the liquidation.

5.3.3 Succession orders

The effect of a succession order, which is discussed in detail in Section 5.4 below, is to substitute a new commonhold association for the previous insolvent association. The commonhold land which is owned by the insolvent association is transferred to the successor organisation, and is thereby put beyond the reach of the creditors.

5.4 COMPULSORY WINDING-UP: SUCCESSION ORDERS

5.4.1 General

A succession order is an order made by the court in the course of winding-up a commonhold association, under which the freehold estate in the common parts is transferred to a new commonhold association,[64] and the new association assumes all the rights and obligations of its predecessor.[65]

5.4.2 Time for making an application for a succession order

An application for a succession order may be made at the hearing of the winding-up petition.[66] There is no scope for a pre-emptive application in advance of the presentation of the petition. A succession order cannot be made in the course of a voluntary winding-up.

64 Section 52(2). 65 Section 53(2). 66 Section 51(1).

5.4.3 Those entitled to apply for a succession order

An application for a succession order can be made by:[67]

(a) the insolvent commonhold association;

(b) one or more members of the commonhold association; or

(c) a provisional liquidator for the insolvent commonhold association, who has been appointed under section 135 of the Insolvency Act 1986.

No one else is entitled to make an application for a succession order. An application cannot be made by a unit-holder who is not a member of the company.

5.4.4 Documents supporting the application

The application for a succession order must be supported by:

(a) Evidence of the formation of the successor commonhold association. Regulations are to prescribe the nature of the evidence that is to be required.[68] It is likely to include the successor commonhold association's certificate of incorporation, any altered certificate of incorporation, and the articles and memorandum of association. The Government does not envisage prescribing any further documents.[69] The procedure for forming a commonhold association is considered in Chapter 2.

(b) A certificate given by the directors of the successor commonhold association that its memorandum and articles comply with the requirements of paragraph 2 of Schedule 3 to the Act. These requirements are considered in Chapter 2.

5.4.5 The making of the succession order

There is a presumption that the court should make a succession order upon an application being made: the Act provides that 'The court shall grant an application [for a succession order] unless it thinks that the circumstances of the insolvent commonhold association make a succession order inappropriate.' The Act is silent on what circumstances might make the order inappropriate. The circumstances of the application will always be that the commonhold association is insolvent, it has failed to pay its debts, the liability of the members of the association is limited to £1, and the effect of a succession order is to put the land owned by the association beyond the creditors' reach. A succession order will therefore always be to the benefit of the unit-holders at the expense of creditors. This result has been deemed appropriate by the presumption that a succession order should

[67] Section 51(2). [68] Section 51(3)(a).

[69] Department for Constitutional Affairs Consultation Response (August 2003), responses to question 178, and conclusion, endorsing the proposals in the October 2002 Consultation Paper.

ordinarily be made. It is consequently difficult to envisage what further circumstances might arise which would render it inappropriate for an order to be made.

5.4.6 Ancillary matters to be considered for the succession order

A succession order must make provision for the treatment of any charge over all or any part of the common parts. In practice, the order will presumably require the new commonhold association to take the transfer of the common parts subject to any charge that had been granted by its predecessor. It may also require the new commonhold association to execute a new deed containing a covenant to repay the debt.

A succession order may also:[70]

(a) require the Registrar to take action of a specified kind;

(b) enable the liquidator to require the Registrar to take action of a specified kind;

(c) make supplemental or incidental provision.

5.4.7 Effects of a succession order

The effects of a succession order are as follows:

(a) The successor commonhold association shall be entitled to be registered as the proprietor of the freehold estate in the common parts.[71] An application for registration is included as Form 1.17 in the Forms and Precedents part of this work.

(b) The insolvent commonhold association shall for all purposes cease to be treated as the proprietor of the freehold estate in the common parts.[72]

(c) The successor commonhold association shall be treated as the commonhold association for the commonhold in respect of any matter that relates to a time after the making of the winding-up order.[73] The same commonhold community statement will continue to bind the unit-holders, and will bind the successor association from the date of the winding-up order.

(d) The court may require the liquidator of the insolvent commonhold association, on the making of a winding-up order, to make available to the successor association any specified records, copies of records or information.[74] The order may prescribe the time within which these documents must be made available, and can prescribe that payment is to be made for them.[75] The court's power to make an order for payment presumably cannot be used to require the successor association

70 Section 52(4)(b), (c), (d).
71 Section 52(2).
72 Section 52(3).
73 Section 53(2).
74 Section 53(3).
75 Section 53(4).

to pay sums in respect of the insolvent association's debts; the order should presumably only relate to the costs incurred in providing the information.

(e) The successor association does not become liable for the debts of the insolvent commonhold association, save that the successor association is likely to be bound by the terms of any charge over the common parts. The successor association is also not liable in respect of any claim that a unit-holder may have had against the insolvent association.

5.5 SPECIAL DUTIES OF THE LIQUIDATOR IN A COMPULSORY WINDING-UP

5.5.1 Introduction

The Act imposes special duties on the liquidator, which apply in the event that the court makes a compulsory winding-up order but does not make a succession order in respect of the commonhold association.[76] These duties are in addition to his ordinary duties under the Insolvency Act 1986. The duties all concern the notification of the Land Registrar of various matters that relate to the winding-up.

These extra duties are all set out in section 54 of the Act, and are considered separately below.

5.5.2 Notification that section 54 applies

First, the liquidator must notify the Land Registrar of the fact that section 54 of the Act applies; in other words, that a winding-up order has been made but there has been no succession order.

5.5.3 Notification of directions

Secondly, the liquidator must notify the Land Registrar of any directions that the court has given, upon the application of the liquidator, in relation to any matter arising in the winding-up, under section 168 of the Insolvency Act 1986.[77] A copy of the court's order must accompany the notification.[78]

5.5.4 Notification of final meeting

Next, the liquidator must notify the Land Registrar of any notice given by the liquidator to the court and the Registrar of Companies under section 172(8) of the Insolvency Act 1986;[79] in other words, a notice that a final meeting has been summoned by the liquidator because the winding-up is for practical purposes

[76] Section 54(1). [77] Section 54(2)(b). [78] Section 54(3). [79] Section 54(2)(c).

complete, and of any decisions that were made at the meeting. A copy of the notice must accompany the notification.[80]

5.5.5 Notification under section 174(3)

In the event that the liquidator is the official receiver, he must notify the Land Registrar of any notice given by him to the Secretary of State under section 174(3) of the Insolvency Act 1986, that the winding-up is for practical purposes complete.[81] A copy of the notice must accompany the notification.[82]

5.5.6 Notification of application for early dissolution

In the event that the liquidator is the official receiver, he must notify the Land Registrar of any application that is made to the Registrar of Companies for the early dissolution of the company under section 202(2) of the Insolvency Act 1986, where it appears to the official receiver that the realisable assets of the company are insufficient to cover the expenses of the winding-up, and the affairs of the company do not require further investigation.[83] A copy of the application must accompany the notification.[84]

5.5.7 Notification under section 205

In the event that the liquidator is the official receiver, he must notify the Land Registrar of any notice given by him to the Registrar of Companies under section 205(1)(b) of the Insolvency Act 1986, that the winding-up is complete.[85] A copy of the notice must accompany the notification.[86]

5.5.8 Notification of any other relevant matter

Finally, the liquidator must notify the Land Registrar of any other matter that in the liquidator's opinion is relevant to the Land Registrar.[87]

5.5.9 Action by Land Registry

Upon receipt by the Land Registrar of notification that the winding-up is complete[88] then he must 'make such arrangements as appear to him to be appropriate for ensuring that the freehold estate in land in respect of which a commonhold association exercises functions ceases to be registered as a freehold estate in commonhold land as soon as is reasonably practicable'.[89]

[80] Section 54(3).
[81] Section 54(2)(d).
[82] Section 54(3).
[83] Section 54(2)(e).
[84] Section 54(3).
[85] Section 54(2)(f).
[86] Section 54(3).
[87] Section 54(2)(g).
[88] Under section 54(2)(c)–(f).
[89] Section 54(4)(a).

He must also 'take such action as appears to him to be appropriate for the purpose of giving effect to a determination made by the liquidator in the exercise of his functions'.[90]

5.5.10 Treatment of the reserve fund

The reserve fund cannot normally be used for the purpose of enforcing a debt except for a judgment debt that is referable to a reserve fund activity.[91] This restriction no longer applies in the event that the court has made a winding-up order in respect of the association.[92] The assets of the reserve fund are therefore available to the liquidator.

5.6 COMPULSORY PURCHASE

5.6.1 Introduction

The Act contains special provisions relating to the compulsory purchase of commonhold land.[93]

5.6.2 Definition of compulsory purchaser

The definition of a compulsory purchaser extends to a person who is entitled to acquire the land as a compulsory purchaser, but who in fact acquires it by private treaty. The full definition in section 60(7) is as follows:

> 'compulsory purchaser' means (a) a person acquiring land in respect of which he is authorised to exercise a power of compulsory purchase by virtue of an enactment, and (b) a person acquiring land which he is obliged to acquire by virtue of a prescribed enactment or in prescribed circumstances.

5.6.3 Options open to the compulsory purchaser

A compulsory purchaser is able to indicate to the Land Registrar that he desires the land to continue to be commonhold land. In this event, the special provisions do not apply.[94] More usually, though, a compulsory purchaser's intentions for the land will be incompatible with it continuing to be commonhold land. In that event, the provisions considered under paragraph 5.6.4 below will apply.

[90] Section 54(4)(b). [91] Section 39(4). [92] Section 56(a). [93] Section 60.
[94] Section 60(2).

5.6.4 Where the compulsory purchaser wishes to bring the commonhold to an end

Where the compulsory purchaser wishes to bring the commonhold to an end, the commonhold association's consent for the transfer of the freehold estate in part only of a commonhold unit is no longer required.[95] This prevents the commonhold association from obstructing the compulsory purchase. Regulations are to be made which will provide for the way in which the transfer is to take place.

5.6.5 Regulations

The regulations to be made for the way in which the transfer is to take place as a result of the compulsory purchase may in particular provide for:[96]

(a) The effect of a transfer of the commonhold land, including what is to happen if the compulsory purchase only relates to part of the commonhold. The regulations may provide for some or all of the land to cease to be commonhold land, and for the provisions of the Act to apply to the land with specified modifications.

(b) The requirement for the service of notices.

(c) The powers of the court in relation to the purchase.

(d) The way in which compensation is to be paid.

(e) A power enabling the commonhold association to require the compulsory purchaser to acquire the freehold estate in the whole or a particular part of the commonhold.

(f) The disapplication or modification of any provisions in any enactment relating to the compulsory purchase.

No regulations have yet been made under these provisions.

[95] Section 60(3). [96] Section 60(4)–(6).

Chapter 6
DISPUTE RESOLUTION

6.1 INTRODUCTION

6.1.1 The Act's approach to dispute resolution

Although one of the aims of the draftsmen of the Act was to harmonise relationships on interdependent estates, no one was under any illusion that the new form of property holding introduced by the Act would provide a complete cure. The Act recognises that disputes may continue to arise between neighbouring owners, and contains a range of mechanisms which seek to deal with such disputes.

The preferred approach of the Act is to treat litigation as a remedy of last resort, and to encourage the parties to a dispute to engage in alternative dispute resolution, ranging from an internal complaints procedure, at the lowest level, to the engagement of an ombudsman, mediator or arbitrator. When all else fails, the parties may have recourse to the courts.

This policy is not spelt out in the Act itself, but was put in these terms by the Parliamentary Secretary, Lord Chancellor's Department, during the Second Reading of the Commonhold Bill in the House of Commons:

> The commonhold scheme will provide for the enforcement of rights and duties between unit-holders and the commonhold association. Where internal disputes arise, we intend that the commonhold association and unit-holders should undertake a three-step process, including alternative dispute resolution, to resolve any conflict.
>
> Assuming that the informal processes fail, the first formal process will be an internal complaints procedure. Secondly, under clause 41, we will prescribe the use of the commonhold ombudsman. The commonhold ombudsman will be modelled on the independent housing ombudsman, who has a wide range of dispute resolution procedures at his disposal, including arbitration, mediation and adjudication. The last recourse available will be to the courts.[1]

6.1.2 Arrangement of this Chapter

Part 1 of this Chapter reviews the duties and rights imposed and conferred on commonhold associations, unit-holders and their tenants by the Act, and goes on to deal with the sanctions the Act imposes for breach of those duties.

[1] *Official Report, House of Commons*, 8 January 2002; col 425.

Part 2 examines the internal complaints procedure which the parties may choose or be required to select to resolve disputes incapable of resolution by more informal means.

Part 3 looks at the proposals for a commonhold ombudsman scheme.

Part 4 considers other dispute resolution mechanisms which may be available.

Finally, Part 5 focuses on litigation, and deals with such matters as procedure, remedies, alteration of the register and limitation.

6.1.3 References

References in this Chapter to the memorandum and articles of association of the commonhold association and to the commonhold community statement are to the documents in their current (August 2003) draft form which are to be found in Part 2 of the Forms and Precedents part of this work.

PART 1 DUTIES AND SANCTIONS FOR BREACH OF DUTY

6.2 DUTIES

6.2.1 Introduction

The Act imposes duties on the commonhold association and its members and unit-holders (and in some cases their tenants) in three ways:

(a) through the commonhold community statement, the contents of which are prescribed by regulations;

(b) through the memorandum and articles of association of the commonhold association, the contents of which are likewise prescribed by regulations; and

(c) through other stipulations set out in the Act or in other regulations promulgated under it.

6.2.2 Duties imposed by the commonhold community statement

Section 31(3) of the Act provides:

> A commonhold community statement may—
> (a) impose a duty on the commonhold association;
> (b) impose a duty on a unit-holder;
> (c) make provision about the taking of decisions in connection with the management of the commonhold or any other matter concerning it.

This stipulation is subject to (a) any provision made by or by virtue of the Act, and (b) any provision of the memorandum or articles of the commonhold association (see section 31(4)).

Section 31(5) provides a list of what the draftsmen perceived to be the most important duties to be found in the commonhold community statement:

(a) to pay money;
(b) to undertake works;
(c) to grant access;
(d) to give notice;
(e) to refrain from entering into transactions of a specified kind in relation to a commonhold unit;
(f) to refrain from using the whole or part of a commonhold unit for a specified purpose or for anything other than a specified purpose;
(g) to refrain from undertaking works (including alterations) of a specified kind;
(h) to refrain from causing nuisance or annoyance;
(i) to refrain from specified behaviour;
(j) to indemnify the commonhold association or a unit-holder in respect of costs arising from the breach of a statutory requirement.

The content and ambit of these duties is examined in Chapter 2.

Importantly, section 31(7) stipulates:

> A duty conferred by a commonhold community statement on a commonhold association or a unit-holder shall not require any other formality.

In other words, the unit-holder and commonhold association are bound by the duties in the commonhold community statement without further ceremony. The unit-holder, in particular, need not subscribe to the commonhold community statement in order to be liable under it. All that is required is that the unit-holder be registered as the proprietor of the unit as a freehold estate in commonhold land, and the commonhold community statement be properly registered at the Land Registry.

6.2.3 Duties imposed by the memorandum and articles of association

Paragraph 2 of Schedule 3 to the Act provides for regulations to be made governing the form and content of the memorandum and articles of association of the commonhold association. Once adopted by the commonhold association, those provisions will bind the commonhold association and its members.

The memorandum and, in particular, the articles of association of the commonhold association lay down rules concerning the transaction of business by the commonhold association. A detailed examination of those rules is set out in Part 1 of Chapter 4.

6.2.4 Other duties imposed by the Act or regulations made under it

The Act itself and regulations to be made under it impose or may impose further duties upon the unit-holders and the commonhold association:

(a) Section 15(3) imposes an obligation upon the unit-holder to whom a commonhold unit has been transferred to notify the commonhold association to that effect.

(b) Section 19(1) provides that regulations may impose obligations on a tenant of a commonhold unit.

(c) Section 35(1) obliges the directors of the commonhold association to exercise their powers so as to permit or facilitate so far as possible (a) the exercise by each unit-holder of his rights, and (b) the enjoyment by each unit-holder of the freehold estate in his unit. Subsections (2) and (3) elaborate on this duty.

(d) Section 37(1) provides for regulations to make provision about the exercise or enforcement of a right or duty imposed or conferred by the commonhold community statement or the memorandum or articles of association or a provision made under or by virtue of the Act. Subsections (2) and (3) elaborate on this provision.

(e) Section 39(4) prohibits the use of the reserve fund for the purpose of enforcement of any debt save a judgment debt.

(f) Regulations to be made under section 42(1) may require a commonhold association to become a member of an approved ombudsman scheme.

(g) Regulations to be made under section 58(3) may require a commonhold association or unit-holder to co-operate with a developer for a specified purpose connected with development business.

(h) Regulations to be made under paragraph 14 of Schedule 3 may require a commonhold association to maintain a register of members.

6.3 SANCTIONS FOR BREACH OF DUTY

6.3.1 Introduction

This Section is concerned with the recourse a commonhold association, unit-holder or tenant of a unit-holder might have in the event of any breach of a provision in the commonhold community statement, the memorandum or articles of association of the commonhold association, or of any provision made under or by virtue of the Act (collectively referred to in this Section as 'a breach of duty').

Sanctions against the commonhold association are considered in paragraphs 6.3.2 and 6.3.3. Sanctions against unit-holders or their tenants are dealt with in paragraphs 6.3.4 to 6.3.14 below.

The situation where a unit-holder who is in breach of duty transfers his unit is considered in paragraph 6.3.15 below.

6.3.2 Breach of duty by the commonhold association

In the event that the commonhold association itself is in breach of a duty imposed upon it, the straightforward remedy will be to go through the internal complaints procedure (see Part 2 below), and, if that fails, to take the matter further either by referring the dispute to the ombudsman scheme (see Part 3), or by litigating. The prospects of the matter proceeding this far are expected to be remote, given the community of interest between unit-holders collectively and their commonhold association.

6.3.3 Those entitled to take action against a commonhold association for breach of duty

Section 37(2)(g) of the Act allows for the enforcement regulations under section 37(1) to include provision for the duties to be enforced not merely by and against the commonhold association and unit-holders, but also by tenants of the unit-holders.

The justification for this was given by the Government in these terms during the course of debate in the House of Lords in which an Opposition proposal to amend the Bill to remove such tenants' rights was rejected:

> [The] amendment would omit the paragraph that gives a tenant of a unit holder the right to enforce a duty imposed on another tenant, unit holder or the commonhold association. As a result, the tenant, whose lease already in effect contains the commonhold community statement and memorandum and articles of association to which he is committed as a full unit holder, would none the less be in a much worse position than the unit holder from whom he holds his lease. Presumably the [Shadow Chancellor, who had proposed the amendment] expects that a tenant in that position would rely on his unit holder to carry out any enforcement on his behalf. That, I respectfully suggest, is not a feasible proposition and is inconsistent with other areas of the Bill where reference to the term 'unit holder' is specifically taken to include reference to a tenant of a unit holder.[2]

6.3.4 Breach of duty by unit-holders: introduction to the available courses of action

Where a unit-holder is in breach of duty, either the commonhold association or another unit-holder may wish to attempt to redress the situation. In practice, because of the possible rancour that will ensue if an individual takes action against a neighbour, it is to be expected that the directors of the commonhold association will be the enforcement party.

In the event of a breach of duty by a unit-holder, the directors should take the following steps:

[2] *Official Report, House of Lords*, 16 October 2001; col 510.

(a) They should first look to their powers of enforcement under regulations made under section 37(1) of the Act. At the same time, they should consider carefully whether it would not be in the best interests of the commonhold association simply to do nothing. This is considered further in paragraph 6.3.5 below.

(b) If they decide that some form of enforcement action is appropriate, they should first attempt an informal resolution of the matter. A telephone call or letter might suffice.

(c) If the informal approach does not bear fruit, the directors should instigate the internal complaints procedure (see Part 2 of this Chapter below), unless the circumstances are such that such action would be adverse to their interests.

(d) They should then consider if the dispute is suitable for referral to the commonhold ombudsman (see Part 3 of this Chapter below).

(e) They should also consider, separately or in conjunction with the previous steps, remedying the breach themselves. This might involve taking out emergency insurance cover in the defaulter's stead; repairing a dangerous structure on the unit for which the unit-holder is liable; or some other similarly urgent step. This is considered further in paragraph 6.3.6 below.

(f) If their commonhold community statement so provides, they should consider serving an indemnity notice upon the defaulter. This is dealt with in paragraph 6.3.7 below.

(g) Only when the above steps have failed to achieve a resolution of the dispute should the directors consider the institution of legal proceedings, considered in Part 5 below. The sanctions available through litigation are considered in paragraphs 6.3.8 to 6.3.14 below.

6.3.5 Doing nothing in response to a breach

Section 35(1) of the Act provides that:

The directors of a commonhold association shall exercise their powers so as to permit or facilitate so far as possible—

(a) the exercise by each unit-holder of his rights, and

(b) the enjoyment by each unit-holder of the freehold estate in his unit.

Subsections (2) and (3) of section 35 then add that:

(2) The directors of a commonhold association shall, in particular, use any right, power or procedure conferred or created by virtue of section 37 for the purpose of preventing, remedying or curtailing a failure on the part of a unit-holder to comply with a requirement or duty imposed on him by virtue of the commonhold community statement or a provision of this Part.

(3) But in respect of a particular failure on the part of a unit-holder (the 'defaulter') the directors of a commonhold association—

(a) need not take action if they reasonably think that inaction is in the best interests of establishing or maintaining harmonious relationships between all the unit-holders, and that it will not cause any unit-holder (other than the defaulter) significant loss or significant disadvantage, and
(b) shall have regard to the desirability of using arbitration, mediation or conciliation procedures (including referral under a scheme approved under section 42) instead of legal proceedings wherever possible.

The directors would therefore be well within their rights if they refused to take any action in response to a given breach by a unit-holder. They would have to be in a position to show, however, that they carried out the balancing exercise required by subsection (3)(a), rather than simply shrugged off the problem.

6.3.6 Self-help

Many problems that will arise during the running of a commonhold may result from inadvertence rather than deliberate disobedience. Examples are likely to be a failure to renew insurance on a unit when the owner is away, or the need for cyclical repairs on a unit being overlooked.

Where the problem needs urgent remedy, and the unit-holder cannot be contacted, or is uncooperative, the directors of the commonhold association may wish to consider taking the requisite steps themselves, provided that it is lawful for them to do so. Whether it is lawful will depend upon the terms of the commonhold community statement.

As originally drafted, the commonhold community statement provided for:

(a) each unit-holder to maintain and insure his unit;

(b) the commonhold association to enter the commonhold unit in cases of emergency to carry out works and to insure the commonhold unit in default of the unit-holder so doing;

(c) the costs incurred in the course of the commonhold association exercising lawful self-help remedies to be recoverable from the unit-holder—see paragraph 6.3.7 below.

The current (August 2003) version of the commonhold community statement omits all these provisions, reflecting the aspiration of the Department of Constitutional Affairs that ownership of a commonhold unit should approximate to ordinary freehold ownership, without undue restriction. It remains to be seen whether this framework will suit all commonholds, or whether some more interdependent commonholds will not wish to replicate the original structure of rights and obligations set out above.

6.3.7 Indemnity notice

The original (October 2002) draft of the commonhold community statement included the following provision for indemnity:

48. Without prejudice to any other remedy to which the Commonhold Association or any other Unit-holder may be entitled, any Unit-holder who is in breach of any provision of the Articles or the Rules or any statutory requirement (the 'defaulter') shall indemnify and hold harmless the Commonhold Association and any other Unit-holder against any costs arising from such breach, including, if appropriate, the costs of remedying the breach or of acting in the stead of the defaulter as permitted by the Rules.
49. If the Board of Directors are of the opinion that the Commonhold Association or any Unit-holder has incurred any costs arising from such breach as aforesaid which the defaulter ought to pay, they shall serve a notice (an 'indemnity notice') on the defaulter requiring him to pay the amount of such costs to the Commonhold Association or to the other Unit-holder within a specified period being not less than 14 days.

These two Rules were not imposed directly by the Act, but were to be made pursuant to regulations under section 37(1) (see paragraphs 6.15.3 et seq below).

Rule 48 would therefore have created a liability by a defaulting unit-holder to the commonhold association or any other unit-holder put to cost or other loss as a result of his default.

Rule 49 would have provided a preliminary means of enforcing that liability in the shape of the service of an indemnity notice setting out the costs in question. Although this notice may not have achieved much with a recalcitrant defaulter, its very formality may well have served to induce the less obdurate defaulter to reimburse the amount in question.

A majority of the respondents to the October 2002 Consultation Paper agreed with the proposed indemnity notice procedure, although doubts were expressed as to its practicality and enforceability. The current (August 2003) version of the commonhold community statement, however, omits this procedure. That is not to say though that an individual commonhold could not include its own provision to similar effect. Regulation 14(9) of the Commonhold Regulations provides that a commonhold community statement 'may contain, but is not limited to, provisions about the following matters—. . . (d) complaints and default procedure'. In those circumstances, there seems to be no reason why an indemnity notice procedure should not after all be included in the commonhold community statement.

The authors' suggestion for an appropriate draft is at Form 4.6 in the Forms and Precedents part of this work.

6.3.8 Other remedies

The most common default is likely to consist of a unit-holder being unable or unwilling to pay money which is owed. This will either be a direct breach (for example failure to pay in response to an assessment levy), or indirect (failure to respond to an indemnity notice served in relation to a previous breach—see paragraph 6.3.7 above).

The primary—indeed the only—remedy for such a breach, assuming all the more informal alternative dispute resolution procedures described in paragraph 6.3.4 above have failed, is a debt action. This will involve the institution of proceedings for the recovery of the outstanding sum. The commonhold association will not be in an elevated position relative to other creditors of the defaulter for this purpose, and will not have any weapons available to it that are not available to any other ordinary creditor.

6.3.9 Criticisms of the primary remedy

The Government's proposal to confine the commonhold association's sanction against a unit-holder owing money to it to a simple debt action met with a good deal of concerted opposition in both Houses during the passage of the Bill.

This opposition is best summed up by these extracts from speeches in the House of Commons:

> With commonhold, the Government take the view that moneys owed by way of service charge should simply be enforced as normal debts. In other words, the commonhold association would have to take the defaulting unit-holder to court to obtain a judgment and then enforce that judgment. The Government envisage that a judgment will be enforced in the ordinary way. The standard method will be to put a charging order on the unit-holder's unit and then sell it if the unit-holder continues to be recalcitrant. However, the Government are ignoring the fact that a defaulting unit-holder will probably already have a mortgage on his flat and may well have a second or even a third mortgage. This means of enforcement will therefore work only if there is equity in the flat. With leaseholds, the landlord will usually be paid by the first mortgagee, who does not want to forfeit its interest in the flat. With commonhold flats, that will not apply. . . .
>
> The absence of adequate enforcement provisions will, in our view, lead to disaster sooner or later. If a block requires extensive works and the tenants are already heavily mortgaged, it will take only a small number of defaulters to make the block unmanageable.[3]
>
> . . .
>
> It cannot be right that non-payers or late payers should be able to force other members who abide by the association's rules to increase their payments because of the non-receipt of debt. A commonhold association can make a claim against a unit holder for non-payment, secure a judgment and, in due course, ask the court for a charging order, but it is a slow and expensive procedure that gives the charges due to the commonhold association no priority over other charges.
>
> . . .
>
> If a unit-holder owes money to the commonhold association, how can the association require the unit-holder to pay up? . . . The commonhold association will succeed only if unit-holders honour their obligations. Every penny that one unit-holder escapes paying is

[3] *Official Report, House of Commons*, 8 January 2002; col 444.

a penny that other unit-holders in the block will have to pay. An effective and cheap means of enforcement is therefore essential to the success of commonhold.

. . .

The Government anticipate the commonhold association taking ordinary proceedings for debt. Ordinary money judgments are typically arrived at by obtaining a charging order over the commonhold unit, but that method of enforcement works only if there is equity in the commonhold unit. If a heavily indebted unit-holder defaults—as will often be the case—there may be no equity in the property. In leasehold property, this problem is avoided because the landlord has a power of forfeiture which takes priority over any mortgage that the lessee may have granted. The practical effect is that the first mortgagee invariably pays off the arrears owed to the landlord so that the mortgagee does not lose his security.[4]

Every commonhold block needs to be kept in repair, and the only source of funds for repairs is the commonholders themselves. The efficient collection of service charges from the unit-holders will be essential to the success of commonhold. . . .

The Government do not propose any special remedy for commonhold associations against defaulting unit-holders. They propose that, if a unit-holder does not pay his service charge, the commonhold association should bring proceedings in the usual way in the county court, recover judgment and use ordinary methods of enforcement to recover the judgment debt. In particular, the Government envisage the commonhold association's obtaining just a common or garden charging order over the commonholder's unit.

Just about everything in that idea is deficient. First, county court proceedings are slow, and anything to do with service charges is particularly slow. Secondly, the commonhold association would almost certainly be out of pocket on the legal costs associated with bringing any county court proceedings. Thirdly, the association would have a remedy against only the unit-holder, not his mortgagee, although the mortgagee benefits from repairs carried out with the service charges because the value of the security is maintained.

Fourthly, unit-holders who do not pay are likely to be impecunious. A charging order is worthless if no equity exists in the property over which the charging order is granted. The commonhold association would rank lower in priority to the mortgagee. . . .

The effect of those deficiencies is significant. First, it will place an unfair burden on those unit-holders who pay their service charges. All the money for running a commonhold block comes from the commonholders. If one commonholder does not pay, the other commonholders must pay—an effective and cheap way of enforcement. Secondly, one of the questions that mortgagees always ask solicitors to confirm when someone takes out a mortgage is whether satisfactory arrangements have been made for the repair and maintenance of buildings. Any solicitor who considers the matter in relation to a commonhold development would be bound to answer no. If one unit-holder refuses to pay service charges, then . . . the commonhold association will have a job getting the money in. There is the substantial risk of a domino effect starting, when other unit-holders see the ease with which service charge obligations are avoided.

If solicitors were unwilling to confirm to mortgage lenders that there were proper procedures in place for the proper collection of service charges, that would inevitably mean that commonhold units became unmortgageable. Without being melodramatic, it can be readily seen that the consequences of that would be disastrous for the commonhold concept.[5]

[4] *Official Report, Standing Committee D*, 15 January 2002; cols 41–42.

[5] *Official Report, House of Commons*, 11 March 2002; cols 680–681.

But this and similar arguments failed to move the Government, essentially for the reason expressed during the course of the Committee Stage in the House of Lords:

> We are simply reluctant to set up a special debt collection process which would apply in the commonhold context alone.[6]

Governments in other jurisdictions have not been so prepared to restrict the range of remedies available for use against defaulting unit-holders. In New Zealand, in particular, concern with the insufficiency of available remedies against defaulting unit-holders was made the subject of a Law Commission Report in 1999.[7] It remains to be seen whether the Government has erred in this respect on the side of freedom of rights rather than performance of duties.

6.3.10 Other suggested remedies

A number of other possible remedies were suggested by Opposition and other spokesmen during the passage of the Commonhold Bill through Parliament. In descending order of effectiveness, these were:

(a) Forfeiture—see paragraph 6.3.11 below.

(b) The creation of a priority charge to secure the debt—see paragraph 6.3.12 below.

(c) The imposition of a restriction on transfer of the commonhold unit until payment of the debt—see paragraph 6.3.13 below.

(d) The imposition of a restriction on new charges until payment of the debt—see paragraph 6.3.14 below.

Each of these suggestions was dismissed by the Government.

6.3.11 Unavailability of forfeiture as a sanction

During the Committee Stage of the Bill in the House of Lords, there were a number of speeches from the Opposition and Cross Benches in support of the availability of forfeiture as a remedy against defaulting unit-holders:

> It is not clear to me why there should be no power of forfeiture in the arrangements for managing commonhold properties. Surely the most effective sanction against a unit-holder failing to discharge his financial (or other) obligations to the association is to charge the unit as security for due performance. Unless the association has such security, its only ultimate remedy is to prove in the defaulting unit-holder's bankruptcy, in which it may recover only a small dividend.[8]

[6] *Official Report, House of Lords*, 16 October 2001; col 510.
[7] Report No 59: 'Shared Ownership of Land'.
[8] *Official Report, House of Lords*, 16 October 2001; col 499.

At present, where you have landlords and tenants, the former can use the threat of forfeiture. In practice, forfeiture is very rarely enforced because the landlord has to serve a notice calling for any defects to be remedied and give time for compliance under Section 146 of the Law of Property Act. Again, where the failure is in the payment of rent, similar provisions apply enabling a tenant to obtain relief, but such relief can only be obtained on payment of what is due. Therefore, that is a powerful and effective weapon.

Of course, that weapon could be too effective. In the hands of aggressive landlords it can be used too soon, or too frequently, and can be a cause of serious concern to tenants who are faced with inappropriate use of forfeiture proceedings. Any equivalent in the case of a commonhold association is far less likely to happen because the association is also made up of the various members. They know that any threat that they use against a recalcitrant member of the association is one that can also be used against them. Quite frankly, abuse of any power equivalent to forfeiture in the case of a commonhold association is a very remote danger.[9]

But the Government spokesmen were as passionate in their condemnation of this remedy:

Forfeiture is not something that we want to import into the commonhold. It is widely hated by leaseholders.[10]

We remain firmly of the opinion that forfeiture, or any similar provision by whatever other name, is quite inappropriate for commonhold. . . . Behind every threat there must lie the possibility of action, and the possibility of a right to forfeiture being realised in the commonhold context remains for us anathema.

We are apprehensive about importing a means of prematurely terminating a lease into commonhold because one of the fundamental precepts of commonhold is freehold ownership of units by unit holders. We cannot conceive the merit of marrying together two concepts that are on the face of it so incompatible.[11]

A commonhold unit is a freehold estate in commonhold land. Forfeiture is a process used by the holder of a superior interest to prematurely terminate an inferior interest in his property. Termination of the interest by the holder of the superior interest occurs because of the failure of the holder of the inferior interest to fulfil an obligation owed to the holder of the superior interest. Such a relationship simply does not exist, and is not intended to exist, within commonhold. We are talking about unit holders who have a parity of position without superiority or inferiority. There is no one with an interest in a commonhold unit superior to that of the unit holder. The commonhold association is the registered proprietor of the freehold estate in the common parts but has no claim to the units, nor should it, we believe.[12]

The Opposition returned to the fray when the Bill moved into Standing Committee in the House of Commons, but without moving the Government on the non-availability of forfeiture as a sanction in commonhold.[13]

[9] *Official Report, House of Lords*, 16 October 2001; col 505.
[10] *Official Report, House of Lords*, 16 October 2001; col 502.
[11] *Official Report, House of Lords*, 16 October 2001; col 508.
[12] *Official Report, House of Lords*, 16 October 2001; col 509.
[13] *Official Report, Standing Committee D*, 15 January 2002; col 41.

Section 31(8) of the Act puts the unavailability of forfeiture as a remedy beyond doubt by providing expressly that:

A commonhold community statement may not provide for the transfer or loss of an interest in land on the occurrence or non-occurrence of a specified event.

6.3.12 Unavailability of priority charge as a sanction

The suggestion that a debt owed by a unit-holder to the commonhold association should be secured by a priority charge, which could then be used to procure the sale of the unit and the recovery of the debt in priority to other creditors, was put in these terms during the Committee Stage in the House of Lords:

[We] believe that a fairly draconian remedy is needed. [We] say that it is not enough to wait until there is a sale by a unit-holder and then recover debts out of the proceeds of sale. That may well be too late. In the great majority of cases, one would be dealing with a unit-holder who remains in occupation. [We propose] that a commonhold community statement should contain a right for the commonhold association to sell the property in the event of a default, and to recover the money due out of the proceeds in priority to all other interests. In practice, it is most unlikely that the power to sell would have to be exercised in any but the most extreme cases because the threat of it would be sufficient to ensure that the money was found by the unit-holder, or possibly by a unit-holder's chargee who wants to preserve his or her security.

... We believe that such an amendment is essential if commonholds are to work properly. The absence of anything giving priority and an effective weapon for enforcement of charges is a serious defect in the current proposals.[14]

During the Second Reading of the Bill in the House of Commons, the Opposition renewed the proposal for an amendment which would have the effect that any moneys owing by a defaulting unit-holder would be a first charge on the unit and take priority over any mortgage. Then:

If a unit-holder defaults, the commonhold association will apply for possession and order a sale. At that stage it is likely that the mortgagee will intervene and pay off the arrears. If not, then the commonhold association will be able to sell the unit to recover the arrears of service charge. This is a fair recognition of the interests of other unit-holders in the block. If they do not have a powerful way of enforcing service charge demands, law-abiding unit-holders will be subsidising default unit-holders.[15]

But this, like all other attempts by the Opposition, was firmly rejected by the Government:

We would not want to see this extra level of regulation in the Bill. Under present law, there are many ways in which a commonhold association can proceed against a debtor. Every extra means added to the Bill that serves to make commonhold ownership potentially more

[14] *Official Report, House of Lords*, 16 October 2001; cols 505–506.
[15] *Official Report, Standing Committee D*, 15 January 2002; col 42.

onerous than regular freehold ownership will inevitably serve also to make it less attractive as a form of tenure.[16]

6.3.13 Unavailability of restriction on transfer as a sanction

Section 15(2) of the Act puts the unavailability of a restriction on transfer as a remedy beyond doubt by providing expressly that:

A commonhold community statement may not prevent or restrict the transfer of a commonhold unit.

To this prohibition, section 20(1) of the Act adds:

(1) A commonhold community statement may not prevent or restrict the creation, grant or transfer by a unit-holder of—
  (a) an interest in the whole or part of his unit, or
  (b) a charge over his unit.

Thus the commonhold community statement may not restrict the transfer of not only a unit, but also any interest in or charge over that unit.

The practical effect of these provisions is that a commonhold association may not use the occasion of a transfer to better its position by requiring an outstanding commonhold debt owed by the unit-holder to be paid *in order for the transfer to proceed.*

During the course of the Committee Stage of the Bill in the House of Lords, an Opposition amendment was proposed that would have provided that the following stipulation be inserted into section 15 of the Act:

(5) Outstanding debts and arrears due to the commonhold association must be paid upon transfer.[17]

At the time, the Government viewed even this provision as a restriction upon transfer, and was adamant that there were to be no impediments upon the unit-holder's ability to transfer his unit without restriction, as if it were ordinary freehold land. The reason given for this was to preserve the attraction of commonhold as a new form of property ownership.

This position has now changed. The current (August 2003) version of the commonhold community statement has as its very first rule the following:

On transfer of a commonhold unit the new unit-holder must pay any debts incurred by the former unit-holder which remain outstanding in respect of the commonhold assessment and the reserve fund levies.

It is to be emphasised that this rule (which is similar in effect to the proposed section 15(5) that the Government rejected) does not prevent the transfer

[16] *Official Report, House of Commons*, 15 January 2002; col 43.
[17] *Official Report, House of Lords*, 16 October 2001; col 504.

proceeding, and may therefore be viewed as consistent, strictly speaking, with the Government's original aim. Practically speaking, however, the new rule will either compel payment by the outgoing unit-holder, or restrict the transfer to those who are content to pay the outgoing unit-holder's debts. It remains to be seen whether this consequence will allow a challenge to the rule on the basis that it is *ultra vires* section 15(2) of the Act (see further the discussion in paragraph 6.3.15 below).

This new rule materially improves the commonhold's position: no longer will it face the prospect of a unit-holder owing substantial sums to the commonhold association simply assigning to another and then disappearing, leaving the commonhold association with a new unit-holder with no liability for the debt. This was a grave shortcoming of the original proposals, and its replacement is to be welcomed.

The limitations of the new rule are to be noted: the rule applies only to debts outstanding in respect of the commonhold assessment and the reserve fund levies (although these are likely to be the main areas of dispute), and does not apply to any other sums that might be owed by the outgoing unit-holder to the commonhold association. The rule does not therefore make commonhold debts in general 'run with the land'—a topic considered further in paragraph 6.3.15 below.

6.3.14 Unavailability of restriction on new charges as a sanction

Consistently with its reluctance to countenance any restriction upon transfer of a commonhold unit, the Government also resisted the following Opposition proposal:

> One of the provisions which might properly be contained in the CCS [commonhold community statement] is one prohibiting any new charge being created over the unit unless any debts due to the association shall first have been discharged (or will be discharged simultaneously with the execution of the charge). Absence of such a sanction might make it difficult to 'sell' a commonhold scheme.[18]

6.3.15 Whether liability runs with the land[19]

During the passage of the Commonhold Bill through Parliament, the Government insisted that a freehold unit in commonhold land should be treated like any other freehold property as far as liabilities incurred by the unit-holder were concerned. It was therefore to be expected that there would be no provision in the Act for such liabilities to attach to the land upon transfer of the unit, and become the liability of the new unit-holder.

[18] *Official Report, House of Lords*, 16 October 2001; col 499.
[19] See also paragraph 3.2.5 and 4.13.5 of the text

Section 16(1) of the Act deals with this topic by providing that:

> A right or duty conferred or imposed—
> (a) by a commonhold community statement, or
> (b) in accordance with section 20
> shall affect a new unit-holder in the same way as it affected the former unit-holder.

On one reading, this subsection is doing no more than explaining that the incoming unit-holder shall become subject to the commonhold community statement regime: in other words, it provides for the *basis* of the new unit-holder's liability, without saying anything about whether that liability is *retrospective*. Support for that interpretation is added by the consideration that the duty referred to is a prospective one ('*shall* affect . . .'), which can only logically be one that will have come into being during the currency of the new unit-holder's ownership. Moreover, the choice of language in section 16(1) ('shall affect a new unit-holder *in the same way* as it affected the former unit-holder'—emphasis supplied) is indicative of an attempt to impose a similar *type* of liability, rather than the same liability. If that is the correct interpretation of section 16(1), then it would follow that the incoming unit-holder could not be rendered liable, for example, for arrears owed by the outgoing unit-holder.

The authors accept, however, that the words are capable of being construed as imposing liability for existing breaches of the rules, including the responsibility for historic arrears of assessment. It must also be recognised that commercial common sense supports that interpretation: if a unit-holder can transfer his unit without impediment (see section 15(2)), and if the transferee is not liable for the transferor's arrears, then the position of the commonhold association will be bleak, particularly if the transferor cannot easily be traced, or is impecunious. Some comfort may be gained from the fact that the prospective transferee may be deterred by the knowledge that any shortfall will have to be met by a supplementary levy to which he will be required to contribute, but this comfort falls some way short of the protection that would ensue if the transferee were rendered liable for his predecessor's breaches.

It may be that this conundrum will be one of the first issues under the Act to be litigated, although the fact that rule 1 of the commonhold community statement expressly imposes retrospective liability for commonhold assessments and reserve fund levies (see paragraph 6.3.13 above) will be likely to confine the ambit of any debate to other commonhold debts. Until then, the authors suggest that the preferable interpretation of section 16(1) is that liability does not run with the land, and that any liability of incoming unit-holders for debts incurred by their predecessors will be confined to commonhold assessments and reserve fund levies, and even that may be vulnerable to an attack based upon *vires*. It would therefore be prudent for the commonhold association to continue to seek to recover any debt due immediately before the transfer of a commonhold unit in the first instance from the outgoing unit-holder rather than the new unit-holder.

6.3.16 No liability of transferor for successor

Section 16(2) provides that:

A former unit-holder shall not incur a liability or acquire a right—
- (a) under or by virtue of the commonhold community statement, or
- (b) by virtue of anything done in accordance with section 20.

Section 16(3) adds:

Subsection (2)
- (a) shall not be capable of being disapplied or varied by agreement, and
- (b) is without prejudice to any liability or right incurred or acquired before a transfer takes effect.

The liability of the outgoing unit-holder for new matters arising under the commonhold community statement ends at the moment of the transfer itself, and does not depend upon registration (see section 16(4)). There is thus no 'registration gap'.[20]

As was observed during the examination of the Commonhold Bill in its Committee Stage in the House of Lords, it will be critical to determine when the unit-holder becomes liable to a creditor:

Would the relevant date be when the creditor obtained judgment, when the money became due, when the work commenced, when the work was completed or when the work was requested?[21]

In paragraph 4.15.8, we set out our view that the correct date for determining liability is the date by which the levy specifies the commonhold assessment must be paid. The commonhold association would be prudent to put this matter beyond doubt by a clear statement to this effect either in the commonhold community statement or in the levy itself.

PART 2 THE INTERNAL COMPLAINTS PROCEDURE

6.4 INTRODUCTION

6.4.1 Source of the internal complaints procedure

It is a curiosity of the Act that although, during the passage of the Commonhold Bill through Parliament, the Government was keen to stress the importance of dealing with disputes over commonhold by procedures other than litigation; and although one of those procedures—reference to an ombudsman—is dealt with in

[20] Compare the situation in *Brown & Root Technology Ltd v Sun Alliance and London Assurance Co Ltd* [1996] Ch 51.

[21] *Official Report, House of Lords*, 16 October 2001; col 508.

some detail in the main body of the Act (see section 42 and Part 3 below), nowhere does the Act provide any overt sign of the Government's commitment to an internal complaints procedure as part of the alternative dispute resolution process. Indeed, section 35(3)(b) of the Act (considered in Section 6.3 above) requires the directors of the commonhold association to have regard to:

> the desirability of using arbitration, mediation or conciliation procedures (including referral under a scheme approved under section 42) instead of legal proceedings wherever possible.

The omission of any reference to an internal complaints procedure is marked.

The Government's commitment to an internal complaints procedure is nevertheless not to be doubted, and has found expression via the provisions of the commonhold community statement, which imposes rights and duties upon each unit-holder and the commonhold association (see Section 6.2 above). Section 37 of the Act, considered in Section 6.3 above, is drafted in terms sufficiently wide to allow regulations to be introduced providing for the commonhold community statement to include an internal complaints procedure. Rules 42 to 52 of the commonhold community statement set out that procedure, which is examined in detail in this Part.

The internal complaints procedure detailed in the commonhold community statement differentiates between:

(a) The procedure originating with a complaint by a unit-holder, either against another unit-holder, or against the commonhold association, through the medium of a 'complaints notice'. This procedure is examined in Section 6.5.

(b) The procedure the commonhold association follows when it either initiates a complaint against a unit-holder, or takes up a complaint made to it by a unit-holder concerning another unit-holder, in each case through the medium of a 'default notice'. This procedure is examined in Section 6.6 below.

6.4.2 The internal complaints procedure is mandatory

It must be stressed that compliance by a complainant with the commonhold association's internal complaints procedure will not be an option to be selected or discarded before proceeding to air the grievance in front of an ombudsman or the courts. Rules 45 and 49 of the commonhold community statement, which will of course be binding upon unit-holders and the commonhold association, each make it clear that, save in cases of emergency:

(a) the dispute may not be litigated unless it has first been referred to the ombudsman (although the commonhold association itself is free to proceed straight to litigation); and

(b) the dispute may not be referred to the ombudsman unless the notice procedure has first been attempted and 21 days have elapsed.

Rules 46 and 50 of the commonhold community statement exempt the parties from the whole or part of these strictures where the duty in question 'is being enforced in an emergency'.

Thus, to take one example, a unit-holder who fears that alterations are imminently about to be carried out to the flat above his unit without the consent of the commonhold association, where such consent is needed, would be justified in launching proceedings without infringing the rules. In cases that do not involve similar urgency, however, the unit-holder and commonhold association will be constrained to pursue their grievances through the internal complaints procedure and (in the case of unit-holders but not the commonhold association unless it so chooses) via the commonhold ombudsman, before commencing litigation.

6.4.3 Advantages of the internal complaints procedure

Unlike the great majority of other disputes between people, a dispute between unit-holders is peculiar in that the complainant and defaulter will commonly not merely live in proximity to each other, but will also meet frequently in the course of the running of the commonhold association of which they will both be members and perhaps officers.

It is therefore critical that the unit-holders and the commonhold association should attempt to resolve their differences in the first instance without outside assistance, using the internal complaints procedure. By contrast, if the ombudsman scheme is involved, without further recourse to litigation, there are likely to be winners and losers, with all the rancour that that will entail. If litigation is resorted to, the outcome for the loser is likely to be much the worse, and even the winner may regret his participation.

6.4.4 Disadvantages of the internal complaints procedure

On the other hand, it must be said that the internal complaints procedure in the form proposed by the Post-Consultation Report dated August 2003 is very formal,[22] and likely to be expensive to administer—at least in terms of calls on the resources of the commonhold association.

The October 2002 Consultation Paper itself recognised that the internal complaints procedure requires a fair degree of paperwork for those involved, and will place a potentially considerable burden on the directors of the commonhold association. This may be disproportionately burdensome for some, particularly small, commonholds. Time will tell how often this burden will arise in practice, and whether there will be a pressing need for the regulations to be relaxed in the case of smaller commonhold associations.

[22] The mechanism proposed by the Consultation Paper published by the Lord Chancellor's Department on 10 October 2002 was if anything more formal.

6.5 PROCEDURE FOR ENFORCEMENT OF COMPLAINT BY UNIT-HOLDER OR TENANT

6.5.1 Introduction

This Section considers that part of the commonhold internal complaints procedure where the complaint is initiated by a unit-holder. The complaint may be directed at another unit-holder, or it may be against the commonhold association itself.

The aggrieved unit-holder must, usually, try to resolve the difficulty with the offending party, but on failing to do so may initiate the complaints procedure by giving notice of the dispute to the board of directors of the commonhold association in the form of a 'complaints notice' in accordance with rule 42 of the commonhold community statement.

Where the commonhold association is itself the alleged defaulter, it should respond to the complainant by serving a 'reply notice'; and may then attempt an informal resolution. Failing that, it does not appear to be bound to institute the enforcement procedure considered in Section 6.6 below by serving a 'default notice' on itself, although it may be forced to take the dispute to the ombudsman and thence to the courts.

Where another unit-holder is the alleged defaulter, the directors must consider how to respond, and may serve a 'default notice', thus again triggering the enforcement procedure considered in Section 6.6 below.

If the complainant is dissatisfied with the progress of his complaint, he may refer the dispute to an ombudsman, and subsequently to litigation.

These procedures are now examined in detail.

6.5.2 The complaint's notice

Rule 42 of the commonhold community statement provides:

> A unit-holder or tenant (the 'complainant') may seek to enforce a duty imposed on the commonhold association or a duty imposed on another unit-holder or tenant (the 'defaulter') by serving a complaints notice on the commonhold association. Form 5 of Annex D or a form to the same effect must be used.

This is drafted permissively ('*may* seek to enforce'), and there will be nothing preventing a complainant from drawing a grievance to the attention of the commonhold association in a less formal manner, particularly if he does not wish the fact of his complaint to become a matter of record. Once the commonhold association has become aware of a breach of the rules of the commonhold community statement, by whatever means, then bound to consider it further, no matter how informally the complaint has been conveyed to it. However, the complainant is barred from taking the complaint further (ie to the ombudsman or to court) if he has not first served a formal complaints notice.

The prescribed form of notice provides for the complainant to supply the board of directors with all the necessary information they may reasonably require to enable them to take appropriate steps in an effort to resolve the matter. The details include much of what was proposed in paragraph 185 of the Consultation Paper published by the Lord Chancellor's Department on 10 October 2002, omitting only provision for a statement of the action required to remedy the breach and an estimate of the period to carry out the proposed remedial action, presumably on the ground that these were over-prescriptive.

The draft complaints notice does not require a response by the commonhold association within any specified period, but makes it clear that if it fails to respond within 21 days, then the matter may be referred to the ombudsman. This should provide sufficient incentive for the board of directors to reply promptly.

The authors have taken the draft complaints form and inserted details of some complaints to illustrate how the form might be used in practice—see Form 4.1 in the Forms and Precedents part of this work.

It would be good practice (although there is no indication that this will be a prescribed requirement) for a copy of the complaints notice to be served upon the defaulting party and any other interested party.

Although it may be thought that the degree of formality described in this paragraph is inappropriate, it should be borne in mind that, for the complaint to have reached this level in the first place, more informal means of resolution should have been exhausted.

6.5.3 Reaction by the commonhold association to the complaints notice

Upon receipt of a complaints notice, the commonhold association should take the following steps:

(a) If the commonhold association has a dedicated compliance or disputes resolution officer, the complaints notice should be passed to him to deal with. If it does not, the complaints notice should be dealt with by a responsible officer on behalf of the board of directors.

(b) The officer responsible should read through the complaints notice, noting the seriousness of the allegations, the identities of the parties involved, and whether or not it is evident that a copy of the notice has been served on the defaulter. At this stage, the officer responsible should attempt to arrive at a preliminary view whether the default is such that there may be a reasonable prospect of the dispute being resolved informally—ie by letter or telephone call. He should not, however, let this preliminary view or response delay the requirement to advance to the next stage of the procedure unless that would positively harm the prospects of the dispute being resolved peacefully. At the same time, the officer should bear in mind that the duty of the board of directors under section 35 of the Act (which explains the use of the permissive 'may' instead of 'must' in rules 43 and 44) includes the proviso in subsection (3) relieving the directors of the commonhold association of the need to take further action:

> if they reasonably think that inaction is in the best interests of establishing or maintaining harmonious relationships between all the unit-holders, and that it will not cause any unit-holder (other than the defaulter) significant loss or significant disadvantage.

(c) The officer responsible should check that copies of the complaints notice have been served upon all interested parties, including the defaulter.

(d) Depending upon the preliminary view formed by him (see (b) above) the officer responsible should, within 21 days of receipt of the complaints notice, serve:

- (i) a reply notice upon the complainant, where the alleged defaulter is the commonhold association itself (see paragraph 6.5.4 below); or
- (ii) a default notice upon the defaulter, where the alleged defaulter is another unit-holder (see paragraph 6.5.5), together with an acknowledgement to the complainant (see again paragraph 6.5.4 below).

(e) In the case of a default notice, the responsible officer should then take the remaining steps explained in the default procedure under Section 6.6 below.

6.5.4 The reply notice

It is of the essence in any disputes resolution procedure that the complainant is not given the impression that his complaint is not being taken seriously, or is not being assigned the priority it deserves, or is not being attended to expeditiously.

With this injunction in mind, it is important that the commonhold association responds with despatch to any complaints notice not merely by taking the matter up with the defaulter (see Section 6.6 below), but also by replying to the complainant. The target response time of 21 days should be treated as the very outside limit of the appropriate response time.

The Consultation Paper published by the Lord Chancellor's Department on 10 October 2002 states that it would be helpful for the commonhold community statement to prescribe a form of notice for this reply, containing brief details of the following:

(a) details of the action or decision taken by the commonhold association;

(b) contact details; and

(c) an explanation of the next steps available to the unit-holder if he or she is dissatisfied.

Confusingly, however, the current (August 2003) version of the commonhold community statement replaces this proposal with this rather different reply mechanism in rule 43:

> Where the defaulter is the commonhold association the Board of Directors may respond to the complaints notice by serving a reply notice within 21 days from the date on which the

complaints notice was served. Form 6 of Annex D or a form to the same effect must be used.

What is now proposed, therefore, is that a 'reply notice' should be served where the complaint is one directed against the commonhold association itself. No separate provision is made for any acknowledgement by the commonhold association in cases where the complaint is made against another unit-holder.

Bearing in mind the considerations set out at the beginning of this paragraph, the authors consider that the commonhold association should send out a reply to the complainant in any event, and have drafted a form which they consider suitable for the task—see Form 4.2 in the Forms and Precedents part of this work. To avoid confusion, the authors have called this document an 'Acknowledgement of complaint'.

Where the complaint is made against the commonhold association, then if a reply is considered appropriate, it should take the form of the prescribed notice at Form 4.3 in the Forms and Precedents part of this work.

6.5.5 The default notice

The officer responsible may have formed the view that the matter set out in the complaints notice is either so trivial that it requires no further action to be taken with regard to the alleged defaulter, or that it raises an issue which is outside the scope of the internal complaints procedure. In that case, he need not proceed further, although, as we have suggested, it would be courteous to send a notice to the complainant acknowledging the complaint (see paragraph 6.5.4 above).

If, however, the responsible officer has formed the view that the matter set out in the complaints notice is suitable for determination under the internal complaints procedure and must therefore be taken further, his next task is to serve a default notice upon the defaulter. At this stage, the complaints procedure and the default procedure merge, and the reader is directed to the procedure set out in Section 6.6.

6.6 PROCEDURE FOR ENFORCEMENT BY THE COMMONHOLD ASSOCIATION

6.6.1 Introduction

This Section of the text describes the part of the internal complaints procedure from the service by the commonhold association of a default notice onwards. The default procedure (for want of a better expression) may either be initiated by the commonhold association, once a default has been observed by or reported to it; or it may follow from the initiation of the complaints procedure by a unit-holder (see Section 6.5 above).

It goes without saying that the board of directors of the commonhold association should first attempt to resolve the matter by informal means where they have reason to believe that any person has breached, is breaching, or may breach any of the articles of association or the rules of the commonhold community statement. This is made explicit by rule 44 of the commonhold community statement in the case of a complaint initiated by a unit-holder:

> Where the defaulter is a unit-holder or tenant the matter complained of will be considered by the Board of Directors who, having regard to the desirability of using arbitration, mediation or conciliation procedures including referral to the ombudsman instead of legal proceedings wherever possible, may—
>
> (a) resolve the matter informally with the defaulter; or
> (b) take no action; or
> (c) serve a default notice on the defaulter and follow the procedure in rules 47 to 49.

As with the complaints procedure, the default procedure commences with the service of a notice (paragraph 6.6.2), with provision for a reply to be given (paragraph 6.6.3).

6.6.2 The default notice

The original (October 2002) draft of the commonhold community statement laid down the following rules regarding the contents of the default notice:

(a) It must specify the alleged breach or anticipated breach 'in sufficient detail to enable the alleged defaulter to understand how it is contended that the Articles or Rules have been, are being or might be breached' (rule 43).

(b) It must specify 'a reasonable period within which the alleged defaulter (i) must cease and/or remedy the breach, or (ii) give assurances satisfactory to the Board of Directors that a breach will not occur, or (iii) show that there is no breach or anticipated breach as specified in the default notice' (rule 44).

(c) It must contain a prominent warning of the consequences of failure to comply with the default notice within the required period (rule 45).

The Consultation Paper published by the Lord Chancellor's Department on 10 October 2002 proposed that the default notice also provide the following additional details:

(d) the contact details for the relevant officer of the commonhold association;
(e) the date by which a reply must be received; and
(f) the form of the desired reply to the notice.

None of these stipulations appear in the current (August 2003) version of the rules. Instead, the draftsmen have provided (see rule 47) that the prescribed form supplied as Form 7 in Annex D to the commonhold community statement must be used. This form (which is reproduced as Form 4.4 in the Forms and Precedents part of this book) contains only some of the provisions formerly considered necessary, presumably because the draftsmen thought that the detail was over-elaborate. The authors consider, however, that the prescribed form is unsatisfactorily brief, and that the commonhold association may wish to supplement those details with the notes the authors have provided in italics at the bottom of Form 4.4.

It would be good practice for a copy of the default notice to be served upon the complainant and any other interested party.

6.6.3 Reply to default notice

Rule 48 of the current (August 2003) version of the commonhold community statement provides:

> The defaulter may respond to the default notice by serving a reply notice within 21 days from the date on which the default notice was served. Form 8 of Annex D or a form to the same effect must be used.

Again, the prescribed form is terse, and leaves little room for manoeuvre. This is to be contrasted with the proposal in paragraph 186 of the Consultation Paper published by the Lord Chancellor's Department on 10 October 2002 that the form of reply to the default notice should contain the following details:

- (a) agreement to the proposals or a rejection of them;
- (b) any counter proposal;
- (c) contact details of the unit-holder and/or his or her representative; and
- (d) confirmation of understanding of the procedure for resolution of dispute.

This proposal seems sensible, and the authors have added some wording at the end of the prescribed form for the reply to the default notice which they consider suitable for the task—see Form 4.5 in the Forms and Precedents part of this work.

6.6.4 Further action

If the procedure set out above does not result in a resolution of the dispute, it would be fruitless for the parties to be required to spend further time in negotiation (although there is of course nothing to prevent them doing so if that is perceived to be a promising avenue). The Consultation Paper published by the Lord Chancellor's Department on 10 October 2002 recognises that further compulsion at this stage within the internal complaints procedure would be unlikely to achieve any significant advances.

If the complainant (or the commonhold association on his behalf) wishes to take the complaint further, the next step will be to refer the dispute to the ombudsman under an 'approved ombudsman scheme'—see Part 3 below. Without taking that step, the complainant cannot proceed to litigation—see Part 5 below. Before taking any such step, the commonhold association may also consider serving an indemnity notice (see paragraph 6.3.7 above) in respect of any costs and other expenses it has borne, provided always that the commonhold community statement contains provision for such a notice.

PART 3 THE OMBUDSMAN SCHEME

6.7 THE COMMONHOLD OMBUDSMAN SCHEME

6.7.1 Introduction

Section 42(1) of the Act states that regulations 'may' provide that a commonhold association shall be a member of an approved ombudsman scheme. Notwithstanding this apparently permissive language, the Government considers that it would be beneficial for one or more such schemes to be established for the resolution of disputes within commonhold,[23] and aims to promulgate regulations to prescribe to that effect.

Such a scheme is one to be defined by regulations made by the Lord Chancellor. Section 42 has been brought into force with effect from 29 September 2003 and a very brief draft regulation requiring membership of the scheme has now been produced.[24]

6.7.2 Regulations for a commonhold ombudsman scheme

The 'approved ombudsman scheme' to which section 42(1) of the Act refers must be a scheme which is approved by the Lord Chancellor, and it must comply with the stipulations set out in section 42(2) and (3):

(a) it must provide for the appointment of one or more persons as ombudsman;

(b) it must provide for a person to be appointed as ombudsman only if the Lord Chancellor approves the appointment in advance;

(c) it must enable a unit-holder to refer to the ombudsman a dispute between the unit-holder and a commonhold association which is a member of the scheme;

(d) it must enable a commonhold association which is a member of the scheme to refer to the ombudsman a dispute between the association and a unit-holder;

[23] See paragraph 190 of the Consultation Paper published by the Lord Chancellor's Department on 10 October 2002.

[24] Both the commencement order (the Commonhold and Leasehold Reform Act 2002 (Commencement No 3) Order 2003) and the draft regulations may be found in the Statutory Instruments section at the end of the Statutes etc part of this work.

(e) it must require the ombudsman to investigate and determine a dispute referred to him;

(f) it must require a commonhold association which is a member of the scheme to co-operate with the ombudsman in investigating or determining a dispute;

(g) it must require a commonhold association which is a member of the scheme to comply with any decision of the ombudsman (including any decision requiring the payment of money); and

(h) it must contain such provision, or provision of such a kind, as may be prescribed.

Quite apart from these mandatory provisions, the ombudsman scheme 'may contain other provision' (section 42(3)(a)).

If a commonhold association fails to comply with regulations made under subsection (1), a unit-holder may apply to the High Court for an order requiring the directors of the commonhold association to ensure that the association complies with the regulations.

The majority of these stipulations are anodyne and common to any ombudsman scheme (see Section 6.8 below). Those requiring further specific comment are examined in paragraphs 6.7.3 and 6.7.4 below.

6.7.3 Membership of the commonhold ombudsman scheme

Section 42 makes it clear that only the commonhold association itself is entitled to be a member of the ombudsman scheme. That is not to say that the unit-holders (who will not be members of the scheme) will be in a disadvantageous position compared to the commonhold association: membership of the ombudsman scheme is simply a precondition to the scheme applying in the first place, and confers no benefits on the member association that are not available to those entitled to take advantage of the scheme (see paragraph 6.7.4 below).

Although section 42 does not use the language of compulsion, the Lord Chancellor's regulation-making power in subsection (1) is clearly wide enough to prescribe that all commonhold associations should become members. During the Committee Stage of the Commonhold Bill in the House of Lords (see paragraph 6.8.2 below), the Government spokesmen expressed considerable enthusiasm for a commonhold ombudsman scheme.

Although there was at one stage room for some doubt that small commonhold associations should be required to join ombudsman schemes, it is now clear that membership of a commonhold ombudsman scheme will be compulsory: regulation 16 of the Commonhold Regulations provides: 'A commonhold association must be a member of an approved ombudsman scheme.'

6.7.4 Those entitled to take advantage of the commonhold ombudsman scheme

Where a commonhold association is a member of an ombudsman scheme, those entitled to use the scheme will be:

(a) the commonhold association itself (see section 42(2)(d));
(b) any unit-holder (see section 42(2)(d));
(c) any tenant of a unit (see section 42(5)); and
(d) anyone else who is authorised by the regulations (see section 42(3)).

No regulations have yet been made providing for anyone other than the association, unit-holders and their tenants to have access to the ombudsman scheme. The Consultation Paper published by the Lord Chancellor's Department on 10 October 2002 questions whether anyone else should be included; it is difficult to think of anyone who might have sufficient standing to be included, save possibly any tenants of the common parts of the commonhold.

6.8 OTHER OMBUDSMAN SCHEMES

6.8.1 Characteristics of an ombudsman scheme

As originally conceived, an ombudsman was an official elected by Parliament or appointed by the Head of State or the Government by or after consultation with Parliament to deal with complaints from the public regarding decisions, actions or omissions of public administration. The role of the ombudsman was to protect the people against violation of rights, abuse of powers, error, negligence, unfair decision and maladministration in order to improve public administration and make the Government's actions more open and the Government and its servants more accountable to members of the public.

As time has passed and the ombudsman scheme has grown in popularity, it has also been adapted for use as a form of internal dispute resolution or to handle complaints made against a non-governmental body by its clientele. There are now ombudsman schemes for universities, private health care facilities, corporations and banks.

Common to all such schemes is the independence of the ombudsman from the parties involved in the dispute in question. In order that the ombudsman's investigations and recommendations will be credible both to the public and to those parties, the ombudsman maintains and protects the impartiality and integrity of his office. He usually has the following powers:

(a) to make an objective investigation into complaints about the administration of the relevant system;

(b) if that investigation uncovers improper administration, to make recommendations to eliminate the improper administrative conduct; and

(c) to report on his activities in specific cases to the system administrator and the complainant, and, if the recommendations made in a specific case have not been accepted, to the legislature. Most ombudsmen also make an annual report on their work to the legislature and the public in general.

The ombudsman usually does not have the power to make decisions that are binding on the participants in the scheme. Rather, the ombudsman makes recommendations for change, as supported by a thorough investigation of the complaint.

6.8.2 The Independent Housing Ombudsman Scheme

It remains to be seen whether the Government will model the proposed commonhold ombudsman scheme on an existing scheme or select a new dedicated model. During the Committee Stage of the Commonhold Bill in the House of Lords, however, the Parliamentary Secretary, Lord Chancellor's Department, expressed the following praise for an ombudsman scheme in general, and for the Independent Housing Ombudsman Scheme ('the IHO Scheme') approved by the Secretary of State under the provisions of the Housing Act 1996 (section 51 and schedule 2) in particular:

> We believe that there is real merit in keeping disputes arising in commonholds away from the courts and tribunals insofar as it is proper to do so, always with the proviso that the courts will be there in the last resort. . . . The independent housing ombudsman scheme is inexpensive, quick and flexible and has a good reputation. An ombudsman scheme seems to us to be a perfectly good model to adopt as one approach to dispute resolution.[25]

The IHO Scheme is designed to provide a fair and effective way of dealing with complaints against member landlords (mainly housing associations) from people who receive their services. The service is free, and binding on those who submit to its jurisdiction by joining the Scheme.

The ombudsman to whom a complaint is directed may, upon investigation, identify failings in the services provided by member landlords. He can then ask them to change their way of working; he can require an apology to be made; he can provide that compensation should be payable; he can reduce the amount of a service charge for work which has been poorly done by or on behalf of a landlord; and he can require that retraining be carried out.

On the assumption that the proposed ombudsman scheme will be closely modelled on the IHO Scheme, the analysis of the commonhold ombudsman scheme set out in Sections 6.9, 6.10 and 6.11 below takes the IHO Scheme as its model.

[25] *Official Report, House of Lords*, 16 October 2001; col 512.

6.9 TERMS OF REFERENCE AND POWERS OF THE OMBUDSMAN

6.9.1 The remit of the commonhold ombudsman

Section 42(2)(e) of the Act makes it clear that the commonhold ombudsman will be required to 'investigate and determine' a dispute referred to him, but reveals nothing regarding the possible ambit or class of dispute which may be capable of being so referred. The Consultation Paper published by the Lord Chancellor's Department on 10 October 2002 asks for views on 'whether the commonhold ombudsman should be restricted to specified kinds of dispute and, if so, which?'[26] Although it would obviously be premature to form any concluded views on the eventual decision to be made regarding those questions (and the conclusions of the Department of Constitutional Affairs in the Post-Consultation Report dated August 2003 do not reveal that any decision has yet been made), it seems reasonable to suppose that the commonhold ombudsman will be required to entertain complaints by the commonhold association or a unit-holder to the effect that either has done something wrong, or has failed to do something prescribed by the commonhold community statement.

Some possible examples of disputes which are likely to be within the remit of the commonhold ombudsman are:

(a) a failure by the commonhold association to carry out repairs in a reasonable time;

(b) a contested claim by the commonhold association that a unit-holder is in arrears with an assessment levy;

(c) an unreasonable refusal by the commonhold association of its consent to alterations or anything else to which the commonhold community statement provides the commonhold association may not unreasonably withhold consent;

(d) a quarrel between unit-holders in the commonhold.

6.9.2 Matters outside the remit of the commonhold ombudsman

It is unlikely to be the case that the ombudsman will be empowered to deal with:

(a) complaints directed at general policies or decisions of the commonhold association which have been made reasonably after following proper procedures;

(b) problems that are about to go to court (or have already done so), or that the ombudsman thinks would be dealt with better that way;

(c) problems that other bodies have the power to deal with;

[26] See question 158(b).

(d) complaints from contractors, consultants, employees or others who are paid by the association, about their professional or commercial relationship;

(e) complaints from people who live near the commonhold, but do not receive a service from it.

6.9.3 Powers of the commonhold ombudsman

Again, section 42 does not spell out the powers the commonhold ombudsman will have other than to make findings as a result of his investigations. Section 42(2)(g) suggests that one of the powers available to the ombudsman will be to award compensation. The regulations will no doubt detail a number of other powers. By analogy with the IHO Scheme, it is likely that the commonhold ombudsman will be empowered to require the defaulting party to:

(a) apologise to the injured party and/or

(b) (in the case of a commonhold association only) pay compensation to reflect the loss flowing from the default and/or any expense to which the complainant has been put and/or

(c) carry out repairs or other works and/or

(d) change its procedures and/or retrain its staff.

6.10 OMBUDSMAN PROCEDURE

6.10.1 Introduction

This Section details the procedure to be followed where a commonhold association, unit-holder or tenant in a commonhold wishes to refer a dispute to the commonhold ombudsman.

6.10.2 Prerequisites to a referral to the commonhold ombudsman

The ombudsman scheme is designed to avoid formality. There are nevertheless a number of prerequisites to referral to an ombudsman which are likely to be demanded if not insisted upon.

First, the ombudsman will require complainants to have at least initiated the commonhold's internal complaints procedure, unless (possibly) he forms the view that the commonhold association or the unit-holder against whom the complaint is made is not following that procedure; or that the procedure is too difficult or inadequate; or that the delay involved will be prejudicial. This topic is considered in detail in Part 2 of this Chapter.

Secondly, it is likely that the administrators of the ombudsman scheme will prefer complainants to use a standard complaint form, although it is unlikely that this will be compulsory.

Thirdly, the ombudsman will expect a complaint to be referred to him promptly—see paragraph 6.10.3 below.

6.10.3 The time limit for making a complaint

It is obviously better if complaints are made to the ombudsman as soon as the commonhold association's internal complaints procedure has failed to achieve a satisfactory outcome.

The ombudsman will normally only accept a complaint:

(a) within 12 months of the complainant becoming aware of the problem that caused it; and

(b) not more than 12 months after the outcome of the commonhold association's internal complaints procedure.

6.10.4 The procedure for making a complaint

The procedure for referring a dispute to the commonhold ombudsman is likely to be informal, with the complainant being offered the choice of completing a complaint form online, or simply writing to the ombudsman with the requisite details. A suggested form of referral may be found at Form 4.7 in the Forms and Precedents part of this work.

The details initially required by the ombudsman in order to begin his investigations are likely to include:

(a) the name, address and contact details of the complainant;

(b) the name, address and contact details of the commonhold association;

(c) the registered details (address and title number) of the commonhold;

(d) details of the complaint (incident, date, material documents);

(e) details of the use of the commonhold association's internal complaints procedure, including the reason for any failure to use that procedure;

(f) details of what, if anything, the defaulting party has done or offered to do in response to the complaint;

(g) reasons why that response is unsatisfactory;

(h) the remedy the complainant seeks.

When making enquiries, the ombudsman or his staff will tell the defaulting party about the complaint, and may also wish to tell other people who may be involved, and show them any relevant documents. Before any such step is taken, the complainant will be given the opportunity to give his consent. If he refuses, then the ombudsman may be unable to take the complaint further.

6.10.5 Preliminary investigation by the ombudsman

The ombudsman has a duty to investigate all complaints made to him. He will first consider whether the complaint falls within the terms of the commonhold ombudsman scheme. If it does not, it will be rejected at that stage and the complainant will be given the reasons. The ombudsman will also wish to see whether the complainant has completed the commonhold association's internal complaints procedure (see paragraph 6.10.2), and whether the complaint has been brought promptly (see paragraph 6.10.3).

6.10.6 Further conduct of the ombudsman's investigation

If the ombudsman decides following his preliminary consideration that the complaint should be investigated further, he will send a copy of the complaint to the commonhold association and any other relevant unit-holder for their comments. He may ask for more information from the complainant and the commonhold association, and possibly from other organisations. The ombudsman's staff will establish what has happened, and the ombudsman will decide what is fair in all the circumstances.

There are a number of different options for the conduct of his investigation which are available to the ombudsman, and he will choose that which appears most appropriate in any given case:

(a) *Local settlement*:

He may first try to resolve the complaint informally, for instance by letters or phone calls.

(b) *Preliminary determination*:

After early enquiries, the ombudsman may decide he has enough information to reach a conclusion. He will write and tell the complainant, the commonhold association and any other unit-holder involved what his preliminary determination is. He will give those parties an opportunity to provide further evidence or comments. After reviewing them, he may confirm or modify his determination, or continue his enquiries.

(c) *Formal inquiry*:

The ombudsman may decide that the best action is to carry out a formal inquiry. This is a thorough and rigorous examination to establish the facts. It may require interviewing the people involved, in which case a member of his staff may travel to meet them. At the end, the ombudsman decides what has happened and where responsibility lies. Formal inquiries are only carried out in a few cases which are complex, or which may have serious implications.

(d) *Mediation*:

The ombudsman may have an independent mediation service which will be trained to resolve problems affecting commonholds. If so, and if the ombudsman suggests mediation, it can be arranged very quickly, and will be free of charge. An independent person discusses the complaint with the parties, although not necessarily at the same time. For mediation to take place, both sides must agree to it. The mediator will help the parties to reach an agreement which is acceptable to both of them, and which will prevent the problem arising again.

(e) *Arbitration*:

This is where an independent person considers the complaint. For arbitration to go ahead, both sides must agree to it. It is an informal legal process and the arbitrator's decision is final and legally binding on both sides. Neither side can withdraw unless the other agrees. The arbitrator's decision can be enforced in a court. If the ombudsman suggests arbitration, it can be arranged very quickly and is free of charge.

6.10.7 Anonymity and confidentiality

The ombudsman cannot deal with anonymous complaints. He must, however, keep details about the complainant confidential, within the limitations described in this paragraph. He will only publish a report of his findings if there has been a formal inquiry. The report will name the commonhold association but it will not name the complainant or give details of his address. The ombudsman may also publish summaries of some of his other investigations, including mediations and arbitrations—but the person making the complaint will never be identified.

The ombudsman will not encourage nor invite anyone to send him anything in confidence. However, he will only give details of the complaint to those people or agencies who can help sort it out, such as the commonhold association and the ombudsman's mediation service. If he does so, he will require those people who receive the information to maintain its confidentiality. The complainant can object to such disclosure, but if he does so, the ombudsman may then not be able to deal with his complaint.

The ombudsman may also, with the complainant's permission, give his details to an independent research agency commissioned to do surveys of complainants and commonhold associations, to find out if they are satisfied with the commonhold ombudsman scheme.

6.11 THE OMBUDSMAN'S DECISION AND ITS AFTERMATH

6.11.1 Outcome of the ombudsman's investigation

Following the conclusion of his investigations, the ombudsman will write to the complainant and the commonhold association and anyone else involved, explaining what he has found, what his decision is, and stating what, if anything, should be done about it.

If the ombudsman finds in favour of the complainant, he has a range of remedies open to him (see paragraph 6.9.3 above). The ombudsman may also recommend other ways he considers appropriate of resolving the complaint.

6.11.2 Enforcing the ombudsman's findings

Ombudsmen under similar schemes find that nearly all their recommendations are accepted, and there is no reason to expect that the case of ombudsmen appointed to determine commonhold disputes will be any different.

If the commonhold association or unit-holder do not comply with the ombudsman's decision, a limited number of sanctions are available:

(a) First, the ombudsman may order the defaulting party to publish that they have failed to comply, in any way he sees fit.

(b) Secondly, if (as seems likely) regulations will require a commonhold association which is a member of the scheme to comply with any decision of the ombudsman,[27] and the commonhold association refuses to comply, an aggrieved unit-holder may apply to the High Court for an order requiring the directors of the commonhold association to ensure that the association complies with the regulations (see section 42(4)). No parallel sanction exists in the case of a defaulting unit-holder.

6.11.3 Complaints about the ombudsman

There is no statutory or other right of appeal against the decisions or recommendations of the ombudsman.

If the complainant believes that the ombudsman's staff have made errors of procedure in the way they have dealt with his complaint, then his recourse in the first instance will be to write to the General Manager of the ombudsman scheme. The General Manager will look at the way the complaint was handled, and consider if it should have been dealt with differently. If the complainant is unhappy with his conclusions, he should then write to the ombudsman himself. If he remains dissatisfied, he may take his complaint to the board of the administering company. The board may appoint one or more of its public interest directors to consider the matter.

[27] The note at the end of prescribed form 5 (see Form 4.1 in the Forms and Precedents part of this book) provides that the commonhold association 'will be required to comply with any order of the ombudsman', although the current draft of the commonhold community statement is silent on this point.

PART 4 OTHER FORMS OF ALTERNATIVE DISPUTE RESOLUTION

6.12 ALTERNATIVE DISPUTE RESOLUTION

6.12.1 Introduction

Section 35(3) of the Act provides that, in the event of a default by a unit-holder, the directors of the commonhold association:

> (b) shall have regard to the desirability of using arbitration, mediation or conciliation procedures (including referral under a scheme approved under section 42) instead of legal proceedings wherever possible.

Referral under 'a scheme approved under section 42'—ie an ombudsman scheme—is considered in Part 3 of this Chapter above. Added to this, section 37(2)(i) provides for regulations concerning the exercise of rights and enforcement of duties under the commonhold community statement and other provisions to include a requirement to use 'a specified form of arbitration, mediation or conciliation procedure before legal proceedings may be brought'.

Neither the Act nor the Consultation Paper have any current proposals for any other type of 'arbitration, mediation or conciliation procedures' which might be available for use, other than the internal complaints procedure described in Part 2 above. That is not to say that the parties will not be free to devise their own procedures. However, given the existence of an internal complaints procedure and an ombudsman scheme which contains within it the ability to propose arbitration or mediation if that course appears appropriate to the ombudsman (see paragraph 6.10.6 above), it is difficult to see how any independent need for an arbitration, mediation or conciliation procedure might arise.

To the extent that such schemes gain in popularity in practice, this work will provide a full explanation of the relevant procedures.

6.12.2 Commonhold commissioner

During the course of debate on the Commonhold Bill that had been introduced by the previous Government in 1996, the Minister for Local Government (then a member of the Opposition) said:

> In Australia, the strata title system has been operating for many years with considerable success. One had hoped that those responsible in the Lord Chancellor's Department for drafting proposals for the commonhold system, which operates on similar principles to strata title, would look closely at the Australian experience.
>
> One of the conclusions to be drawn from that experience is that an appropriate body to provide advice and help with the resolution of disputes about the establishment and operation of strata titles is essential. I can see no provision in the Bill for such a service, and the

only body that provides expert specialist advisory services in this field, the Leasehold Enfranchisement Advisory Service, has no guarantee of funding beyond the end of this year. I hope that the Minister will tell the House how he expects the need for advice and assistance on the resolution of disputes will be handled. I assume that his Department would neither welcome nor be equipped to handle the scale of inquiries that are likely if commonhold takes off as a viable tenure. The Australian evidence suggests a figure of about 20,000 inquiries a year on issues relating to strata title.[28]

When the Bill was resurrected in 2001, however, the Government did not take the opportunity to provide for the introduction of a post similar to that of Strata Titles Commissioner in New South Wales, despite the matter being raised expressly:

If, as the Government claim, they really want to see commonhold come in, it is important to place a provision such as this into the Bill at this stage so that if at a later time it was found that such a commissioner was needed, one could be appointed quite simply. It will be no good at all if we have to come back with further primary legislation to do this. That is the kind of thing that never happens soon enough. If we consider how leasehold and commonhold have taken years to reach this point, it would certainly be a long time before there was enough parliamentary time to come back again on this.

I do not think that it is at all parallel to the ombudsman scheme referred to in Clause 41. It is quite different to that. The idea is to make it easy for people to handle disputes and to reduce the very high cost of the legal fees involved. I was impressed in New South Wales by how simple all kinds of tenancy matters are and how minimal are the costs for both landlord and tenant compared to this country in terms of letting or sale of a lease. It was quite enlightening for me to see the difference.[29]

The Government rejected this proposal on the grounds that the expense involved in setting up the post of commonhold commissioner would outweigh the possible benefits to be gained—at least in the early stages of commonhold development:

An appropriate mixture of locally served notices, an ombudsman, tribunals and courts ought to provide all that we need to resolve any dispute arising in commonhold.[30]

At the same time, however, the Government held out the prospect that the topic might be revisited in the light of experience.

[28] *Official Report, House of Commons*, 8 March 1996; cols 615–616.
[29] *Official Report, House of Lords*, 16 October 2001; col 534.
[30] *Official Report, House of Lords*, 16 October 2001; col 536.

PART 5 LITIGATION

6.13 INTRODUCTION

6.13.1 Disputes and other matters which may be litigated

This Chapter is concerned with dispute resolution in the context of commonhold, and the Parts set out above have in the main been concerned with the disputes which may arise as between unit-holder and the commonhold association in the course of the daily life of a commonhold, and which may as a last resort be determined by litigation. This Part deals with that last resort.

Besides such litigation, other proceedings may be necessary to resolve matters arising under the Act, some of which may be less contentious, and this Part also deals with those matters.

6.13.2 Scope of this Part

The Act is unilluminating on the topics discussed in this Part of the work, and no regulations or rules have yet been made which will enable a detailed assessment to be made of all those topics. The authors have attempted, however, to provide as full an analysis as possible at this stage, with the aim of preparing the prospective unit-holder or commonhold association with the reassurance they will need regarding the protection of their civil rights in commonhold.

Sections 6.14 to 6.17 deal with the range of possible claims which may arise under the Act. Section 6.18 examines the jurisdiction of the courts and other tribunals to deal with such claims. Section 6.19 sketches out a number of matters to do with procedure. Section 6.20, finally, deals with limitation.

6.14 NON-CONTENTIOUS CLAIMS

6.14.1 Introduction

The authors use the expression 'non-contentious claims' to mean claims which are unlikely to be disputed in principle, although there may be considerable dispute as to the precise form the relief granted may take. Such claims are in contrast to claims for breach of a rule in the commonhold community statement or of an article in the articles of association of the commonhold association, which are likely to be strongly disputed, if only because such claims may only be brought once the internal complaints procedure has failed to result in a compromise. Contentious claims are considered in Section 6.15 below.

Non-contentious claims fall into the following categories:

(a) a claim under section 6(3) for relief where a freehold estate in commonhold land has been registered in error: see paragraphs 6.14.2 to 6.14.4 below;

(b) a claim under section 40 for rectification of documents: see paragraphs 6.14.5 to 6.14.7 below;

(c) a claim under sections 3, 23, 24 or 30 for consents to be dispensed with: see paragraphs 6.14.8 and 6.14.9 below;

(d) an application by joint unit-holders under paragraph 8(5) of Schedule 3: see paragraph 6.14.10 below;

(e) an application under section 17(4) regarding a non-compliant lease: see paragraphs 6.14.11 and 6.14.12 below;

(f) an application under section 42(4) for an order compelling a commonhold association to join an approved ombudsman scheme: see paragraph 6.14.13 below.

6.14.2 Claim for relief where freehold estate in commonhold land registered in error: section 6(3)

Section 6(3) of the Act provides that, where a freehold estate in commonhold land has been registered in error (as defined in subsection (1)), the court may grant a declaration that the freehold estate should not have been registered as a freehold estate in commonhold land. An application for such a declaration may only be made by a person who claims to be adversely affected by the registration (see subsection (4)).

On granting such a declaration, the court may make 'any order which appears to it to be appropriate' (subsection (5)), and may in particular (see subsection (6)):

(a) provide for the registration to be treated as valid for all purposes;
(b) provide for alteration of the register;
(c) provide for land to cease to be commonhold land;
(d) require a director or other specified officer of a commonhold association to take steps to alter or amend a document;
(e) require a director or other specified officer of a commonhold association to take specified steps;
(f) make an award of compensation (whether or not contingent upon the occurrence or non-occurrence of a specified event) to be paid by one specified person to another;
(g) apply, disapply or modify a provision of Schedule 8 to the Land Registration Act 2002 (c 9) (indemnity).

In common with all other non-contentious claims save those to do with dispensing of consents (see paragraphs 6.14.8 and 6.14.9 below) and non-compliant leases (paragraphs 6.14.11 and 6.14.12), the court's powers under this section do not need to be brought into force by regulation (apart of course from the order which will bring Part 1 of the Act generally into force).

6.14.3 Prerequisites to the application under section 6(3)

There are two points to be made concerning the making of an application under section 6(3):

(a) The application may only be made by someone who claims to be adversely affected by the registration. The stipulation 'claims to be' rather than 'is' is puzzling and, the authors suggest, cannot be read literally, for anyone could claim to be adversely affected in order to be able to launch a claim, whether or not they are genuinely so affected. The rather more pragmatic sense of the stipulation is 'claims to be, and has reasonable grounds for that claim'. So construed, the stipulation would eliminate applications by those who wish to raise vexatious technical points when no detriment has been suffered.

(b) The application may only be made where the registration was in error in one of the three respects set out in section 6(1), namely:

> (a) the application for registration was not made in accordance with section 2,
> (b) the certificate under paragraph 7 of Schedule 1 was inaccurate, or
> (c) the registration contravened a provision made by or by virtue of this Part.

The type and seriousness of the error will condition the way in which the court will exercise its discretion in relation to the application—see paragraph 6.14.4 below.

6.14.4 Considerations for the court on an application under section 6(3)

The court hearing the application under section 6(3) will have a number of matters to consider:

(a) First, if the authors' view set out in (a) in paragraph 6.14.3 above is correct, the court should determine whether the applicant has reasonable grounds for his claim to be adversely affected by the registration. If he did not, then there is much to be said for the court declining to consider the matter further. If the court finds that there were such grounds, or if it decides to go ahead in any event, the court will still need to know to what extent the applicant has been adversely affected, because that is a matter which will affect the exercise of its discretion—see (c) below.

(b) Secondly, the court will need to decide if the registration was actually made in error in one of the three specified respects—see (b) in paragraph 6.14.3 above. Only then will the court have jurisdiction to consider the matter further.

(c) Thirdly, if the court determines that the application is well founded, it will then have to consider what if any form of relief to award the applicant. This will depend upon the seriousness of the error and the adverse affect upon the applicant. In the unlikely event that the error consists of a failure to obtain the consent of a registered proprietor of a substantial interest in the commonhold land, the court might decide that it has little alternative but to set aside the registration and let the parties achieve a negotiated remedy. If, on the other hand, the error consists of a technical irregularity in the form of the commonhold community statement, the court would almost certainly allow the registration to stand, possibly upon terms that an amended commonhold community statement is lodged with the Land Registry.

(d) Lastly, where the court makes an order under section 6(6)(c) for all the land in relation to which a commonhold association exercises functions to cease to be commonhold land, section 50(2) provides that the court shall have the powers which it would have if it were making a winding-up order in respect of the commonhold association.

Forms 5.3 and 5.4 in the Forms and Precedents part of this work will deal respectively with the application to court and the order, once the relevant rules have been promulgated.

6.14.5 Claim for rectification of documents: section 40

Section 40(1) of the Act provides that a unit-holder may apply to the court for a declaration that:

(a) the memorandum or articles of association of the relevant commonhold association do not comply with regulations under paragraph 2(1) of Schedule 3;
(b) the relevant commonhold community statement does not comply with a requirement imposed by or by virtue of this Part.

This form of relief is open only to unit-holders, and not, for example, to their tenants (who presumably are taken not to have any interest in such matters); or to the directors of the commonhold association (who would have such an interest, but who would presumably be able to, but have chosen not to, remedy matters themselves).

6.14.6 Considerations for the applicant on an application under section 40

The unit-holder who wishes to apply under section 40 for a declaration that the memorandum and articles of association or commonhold community statement are non-compliant in any respect should bear in mind the following matters:

(a) First, he should be sure of his ground concerning the non-compliance: it will be expensive to discover in court that the alleged error is based upon his own misapprehension.

(b) Secondly, although there is no requirement (compare contentious proceedings, discussed in Section 6.15) to engage in the association's internal complaints procedure before embarking upon litigation, the unit-holder would be well advised to attempt to resolve his differences with the commonhold association prior to commencing the proceedings.

(c) Thirdly, the unit-holder should attempt to gain the support of as many of his fellow unit-holders as possible. Not only will this spread the cost and risk of the proceedings, it will also avoid the impression the court might otherwise gain that the non-compliance in question is of limited effect and importance.

(d) Fourthly, the unit-holder should prepare his evidence carefully to support the specific order sought (see section 40(2) and paragraph 6.14.7 below).

(e) Lastly, the unit-holder should be careful to observe the requisite time limits, and come prepared with an explanation for the delay if the application is made outside those limits (see again paragraph 6.14.7 below).

6.14.7 Considerations for the court on an application under section 40

The court hearing the application will have first to decide if the relevant documents are non-compliant. Only then will the court have jurisdiction to consider the matter further.

If the court decides that the relevant documents are non-compliant, then it may grant a declaration to that effect, whereupon it may also 'make any order which appears to it to be appropriate' (see section 40(2)). Such an order may, in particular:

(a) require a director or other specified officer of a commonhold association to take steps to alter or amend a document;
(b) require a director or other specified officer of a commonhold association to take specified steps;
(c) make an award of compensation (whether or not contingent upon the occurrence or non-occurrence of a specified event) to be paid by the commonhold association to a specified person;
(d) make provision for land to cease to be commonhold land

[subsection (3)].

The seriousness of the step (if any) ordered by the court will obviously depend upon the extent of the non-compliance and the adverse effect upon the applicant.

Where the court makes an order under section 40(3)(d) for all the land in relation to which a commonhold association exercises functions to cease to be commonhold land, section 50(2) provides that the court shall have the powers which it would have if it were making a winding-up order in respect of the commonhold association.

Time limits apply to the making of any application under section 40. The unit-holder must under section 40(4) apply for such a declaration:

(a) within the period of 3 months beginning with the day on which he became a unit-holder, or

(b) within 3 months of the commencement of the alleged failure to comply, or
(c) with the permission of the court.

On established principles, the court is unlikely to accede to an application outside the three month periods if (a) the delay is very great; and/or (b) there is no adequate explanation for the delay; and/or (c) other unit-holders or directors or the commonhold association have taken steps which cannot be reversed on the understanding that the relevant documents would not be challenged; and/or (d) the non-compliance in question is relatively trivial.

Forms 5.15 and 5.16 in the Forms and Precedents part of this work will deal respectively with the application to court and the order, once the relevant rules have been promulgated.

6.14.8 Claim for court to dispense with consent of proprietors to registration: section 3(2)

The Act provides in a number of places for regulations to be made which may allow for applications to court to dispense with certain consents required under the Act. The consent-dispensing powers in question fall into two categories. The first is dealt with in this paragraph and the second in paragraph 6.14.9 below.

First, section 3(2) of the Act requires regulations to be made which, among other things, may enable a court to dispense with the requirement in section 3(1) for the consents of registered proprietors of substantial interests in the land to be obtained to applications to register a freehold estate as a freehold estate in commonhold land. Subsection (3) adds that the court order dispensing with the requirement for consent:

(a) may be absolute or conditional, and
(b) may make such other provision as the court thinks appropriate.

The Lord Chancellor provisionally considers that it may be appropriate to permit the court to dispense with the requirement for consent if it has not been possible to trace such a proprietor despite the use of 'all reasonable efforts'.[31] Thus far, the Department of Constitutional Affairs has published draft regulations, which contain the following proposed rule 4:

The court may dispense with the requirement for consent if a person—

(a) cannot be identified after all reasonable efforts have been made to ascertain the identity of the person required to give consent; or
(b) cannot be traced after all reasonable efforts have been made to trace him; or
(c) has been sent the request for consent and all reasonable efforts have been made to obtain a response but the person has not responded.

[31] See paragraph 56(d) of the Consultation Paper published by the Lord Chancellor's Department on 10 October 2002.

Forms 5.1 and 5.2 in the Forms and Precedents part of this work will deal respectively with the application to court for such a dispensation order and the dispensation order itself, once the relevant rules and regulations have been promulgated in their final form.

6.14.9 Claim for court to dispense with consent of unit-holder and chargee to subtraction of land from unit: sections 23(2), 24(3) and 30(3)

Secondly, three separate sections of the Act deal with regulations which 'may' be made which 'may' enable a court to dispense with the requirement for the consent by a unit-holder, and, if the unit is charged, his chargee, to the registration of an amended commonhold community statement (without which the amendment cannot take effect), where the proposal is to take land from the unit by adding it to the common parts of the commonhold or elsewhere. The sections are as follows:

(a) section 23(2): this provides for the dispensing of consent from a unit-holder, where the amendment would redefine the extent of his commonhold unit;

(b) section 24(3): this has the same effect, but this time in relation to the registered proprietor of the charge over such a unit;

(c) section 30(3): this also deals with the taking of land from a unit, and deals again with the dispensing of the consent of the registered proprietor of a charge over the unit. The only difference from section 24(3) is that this section deals specifically with a proposal to add the land in question to the common parts. The reason for this otiose addition is unclear.

In each case, the application for the court to dispense with the requisite consent may only be made by the commonhold association. Other unit-holders therefore have no standing to make such an application. Forms 5.7 to 5.12 in the Forms and Precedents part of this work will deal with the requisite applications to court and orders, if the relevant rules and regulations are promulgated. At present, however, the Lord Chancellor has no proposals to make regulations under this latter group of sections.[32]

6.14.10 Application by joint unit-holder: paragraph 8(5) of Schedule 3

Paragraph 8(5) of Schedule 3 to the Act provides that:

> On the application of a joint unit-holder the court may order that a joint unit-holder is entitled to be entered in the register of members of a commonhold association in place of a person who is or would be entitled to be registered by virtue of sub-paragraph (4).

[32] See paragraphs 193 and 197 of the Consultation Paper published by the Lord Chancellor's Department on 10 October 2002.

Sub-paragraph (4) stipulates that the joint unit-holder whose name appears first in the proprietorship register of the title to the unit is entitled to be registered in the register of members unless an application to some other effect is made before the expiry of a prescribed period.

This provision does not itself require to be brought into effect by regulation, although regulations will have to prescribe the length of period referred to in sub-paragraph (4). Before that period has expired, the joint unit-holders will be able to nominate one of their number to be a member of the commonhold association by consent.

If the joint unit-holders cannot agree on which of their number is to become a member of the commonhold association (which perhaps is unlikely, given that they will only just have obtained the unit), or if they allow the period to pass through inadvertence, with the result in either case that the person first-named in the register becomes a member by default at the end of the prescribed period, their remedy will be for one of their number to apply to court under paragraph 8(5) for himself or another to be entered in the register of members instead.

The Act affords no guidance to the parties (or to the court) where the joint unit-holders cannot agree as to the identity of the unit-holder to be entered on the register of members. Moreover, it does not deal with the situation where the joint unit-holders, or one of them, decides that another of the joint unit-holders should be substituted as member.

Forms 5.19 and 5.20 in the Forms and Precedents part of this work will deal respectively with the application to court and the order itself, once the relevant rules and regulations have been promulgated.

6.14.11 Application regarding non-compliant lease: section 17(4)

Section 17(4) of the Act provides that a party to an instrument or agreement which purports to create a term of years absolute in a residential commonhold unit which does not comply with the conditions prescribed under subsection (1) may apply to the court for an order:

(a) providing for the instrument or agreement to have effect as if it provided for the creation of a term of years of a specified kind;
(b) providing for the return or payment of money;
(c) making such other provision as the court thinks appropriate.

It is almost certain that the 'conditions prescribed under subsection (1)' will include the prohibition of the grant of a residential lease for a term exceeding 21 years (see paragraph 4.13.6). The most obvious state of affairs which this subsection contemplates, therefore, is the purported grant of a lease for a term longer than 21 years.

6.14.12 Considerations for the court on an application regarding non-compliant lease

No proposals have yet been made regarding the criteria the court is to apply when weighing up an application under section 17(4).[33] The following are examples of the possible situations which might confront the court:

(a) a purported lease for a term of 25 years has just been granted at a market rent;

(b) a purported lease for a term of 25 years has just been granted for a premium of £20,000, at a reduced market rent;

(c) a purported lease for a term of 25 years has been granted; the lessee has spent £20,000 on improving the demised premises on the understanding that the cost will be amortised over the term.

Situation (a) does not present any major difficulty: the evidence before the court is unlikely to be to the effect that a lease for a term of up to 21 years would have commanded a significantly different rent, or that the lessee would not have taken such a lease. The court is therefore likely to use its powers to order that the grant should instead take effect as a lease for a term of 21 years.

Situation (b) presents a little more difficulty, because the evidence will no doubt be to the effect that the premium was the consideration for the reduction in the rent, spread over the longer term, and that a replacement of the 25-year term by a 21-year term would drastically alter that bargain. However, although there is thus far no express prohibition on the court ordering the longer term to stand, it is most unlikely that the court would arrive at that conclusion. As paragraph 4.13.6 explains, the Government was adamant during the passage of the Bill through Parliament that it should not be possible to create residential leases in commonhold for periods longer than the stipulated length (then 7 years). The regulations made under section 17(1) will reflect this, and it would be untoward for the courts to act in a contrary fashion. The court is therefore likely to use its powers to order that the grant should instead take effect as a lease for a term of 21 years, with any financial adjustment to be made to the parties that the evidence shows to be appropriate in all the circumstances.

Situation (c) offers a harsher set of facts to situation (b), and creates the circumstances in which a court could hold that the commonhold association is estopped from contending that the document should not take effect as a lease for the longer term.[34] Again, however, leaving aside the consideration that it would be

[33] The Consultation Paper published by the Lord Chancellor's Department on 10 October 2002 is silent on the matter.

[34] There are precedents for the court to sanction an estoppel taking effect even where Parliament has decreed that the declared state of affairs is not legally possible—see, for example, *Yaxley v Gotts* [2000] Ch 162 (agreement valid notwithstanding failure to comply with section 2 of the Law of Property (Miscellaneous Provisions) Act 1989).

unfair to impose such a remedy not merely on the commonhold association, but also on the other unit-holders, the harshness of the outcome if an estoppel argument is rejected should not be allowed to obscure the policy objective referred to above and explained in paragraph 4.13.6. The court is therefore likely, again, to use its powers to order that the grant should instead take effect as a lease for a term of 21 years, with any financial adjustment to be made to the parties which the evidence shows to be appropriate in all the circumstances.

Forms 5.5 and 5.6 in the Forms and Precedents part of this work will deal respectively with the application to court and the order, once the relevant rules have been promulgated.

6.14.13 Application for order compelling commonhold association to join approved ombudsman scheme: section 42(4)

Section 42(4) of the Act provides that if a commonhold association fails to comply with regulations requiring it to be a member of an approved ombudsman scheme, a unit-holder may apply to the High Court for an order requiring the directors of the commonhold association to ensure that the association complies with those regulations.

The entitlement to make an application under this subsection, and the court's power to make an order under it, do not depend upon the making of any regulation. In theory, therefore, such an application could be launched as soon as the Act is in force; the regulation requiring the commonhold association to join an approved ombudsman scheme has been made; and an attempt has unsuccessfully been made by the unit-holders under the internal complaints procedure to persuade the commonhold association to join the scheme. We say 'in theory', because it is difficult to conceive of any circumstances in which the directors of a commonhold association would wish to engage in as conspicuous a breach of the regulations as a refusal to join such a scheme. The existence of the sanction under section 42(4) should be incentive enough for even the tardiest directors. It may therefore be expected that this subsection will rarely, if ever, be called upon.

Forms 5.17 and 5.18 in the Forms and Precedents part of this work will deal with the requisite applications to court and orders, if the relevant rules and regulations are promulgated.

6.15 CONTENTIOUS CLAIMS

6.15.1 Introduction

The expression 'contentious claims' is used by the authors (but not by the Act) to include claims for breach of a rule in the commonhold community statement or of an article in the articles of association of the commonhold association.

Such claims may also, the authors suggest, include a claim to do with the commonhold which may not amount to a breach of a rule or article, but which is actionable as a breach of contract or a tort at common law. Such claims are considered further in paragraph 6.15.2 below.

6.15.2 Common law claims

The advent of commonhold may lead to a reduction in the number of neighbour disputes and other common law claims based in nuisance, negligence and trespass, as a result of the interest all unit-holders will have in seeing that disputes are resolved informally or through the use of the internal complaints procedure.

It would be over-optimistic to suppose that all such claims will be eliminated in commonhold; research in Commonwealth jurisdictions suggests otherwise (see the examples in the Digest of Cases). In order to achieve the best prospects of a harmonious solution for those who do not merely have to live in close proximity, but also have to co-operate as members in the running of their commonhold association, it will be prudent (and should perhaps be obligatory) for the rules of procedure to be made under section 66(4) of the Act to ensure that such claims be dealt with as commonhold claims—see paragraph 6.19.4 below—even if the default does not technically arise from a breach of the commonhold community statement.

6.15.3 Rules and regulations for contentious claims

Section 37(1) of the Act introduces a regulation making power for:

the exercise or enforcement of a right or duty imposed or conferred by or by virtue of—
- (a) a commonhold community statement;
- (b) the memorandum or articles of a commonhold association;
- (c) a provision made by or by virtue of this Part.

Section 37(2) adds that such regulations may, in particular, make provision:

- (a) requiring compensation to be paid where a right is exercised in specified cases or circumstances;
- (b) requiring compensation to be paid where a duty is not complied with;
- (c) enabling recovery of costs where work is carried out for the purpose of enforcing a right or duty;
- (d) enabling recovery of costs where work is carried out in consequence of the failure to perform a duty;
- (e) permitting a unit-holder to enforce a duty imposed on another unit-holder, on a commonhold association or on a tenant;
- (f) permitting a commonhold association to enforce a duty imposed on a unit-holder or a tenant;
- (g) permitting a tenant to enforce a duty imposed on another tenant, a unit-holder or a commonhold association;

(h) permitting the enforcement of terms or conditions to which a right is subject;
(i) requiring the use of a specified form of arbitration, mediation or conciliation procedure before legal proceedings may be brought.

Section 37(3) elaborates the reference to compensation in subsection (2)(a) and (b): the regulations must make provision for calculating the amount of compensation, and for interest to be payable in the case of late payment.

Finally, subsection (4) provides, obscurely, that regulations under section 37 shall be subject to 'any provision included in a commonhold community statement in accordance with regulations made by virtue of section 32(5)(b)'. Section 32 itself provides for regulations to make provision about the content of a commonhold community statement, and section 32(5)(b) provides that those regulations may include 'any matter for which regulations under section 37 may make provision'. This circle may be broken once the relevant regulations have been finalised.

There are thus a number of matters to consider in relation to section 37:

(a) The meaning of the reference in subsection (2)(a) and (b) to 'compensation': this is discussed in paragraph 6.15.4 below.

(b) Compensation where a right is exercised: this is discussed in paragraph 6.15.5 below.

(c) Compensation where a duty is not complied with: this is discussed in paragraph 6.15.6 below.

(d) The calculation of compensation: this is discussed in paragraph 6.15.7 below.

(e) The recovery of costs where work is carried out for the purpose of enforcing a right or duty or in consequence of the failure to perform a duty: this is discussed in paragraph 6.15.8 below.

(f) Interest upon late payment: this is discussed in paragraph 6.15.9 below.

(g) The nature of enforcement of duties and conditions imposed upon the exercise of a right: this is discussed in paragraph 6.15.10 below.

(h) The persons who may enforce duties: this is discussed in paragraph 6.15.11 below.

(i) The persons against whom duties may be enforced: this is discussed in paragraph 6.15.12 below.

(j) The requirement to use alternative dispute resolution before the institution of legal proceedings: this is discussed in paragraph 6.15.13 below.

6.15.4 The meaning of 'compensation' in section 37

Section 37(2) uses the term 'compensation' to refer to payment both where a right is exercised (subsection (2)(a)), and where a duty is not complied with (subsection

(2)(b)). The term is not defined by the Act, although it is used elsewhere in different contexts (see section 6(6)(f)), which deals with compensation where a commonhold title has been registered in error; section 40(3)(c), which deals with rectification of the commonhold community statement or the memorandum and articles of association; and section 60(5)(d), which deals with compulsory purchase). Those other uses do not assist in arriving at an understanding of what is meant by the use of the term in section 37.

Until the regulations have been made which define the way in which the compensation is to be calculated (see paragraph 6.15.7 below), it will be difficult to provide a definitive guide to the meaning of the term. The difficulty is compounded by the fact that the term is apparently used in two quite different senses. In subsection (2)(a), the draftsmen appear to be envisaging the exercise of a right which does not involve any corresponding breach of duty (see paragraph 6.15.5 below) from which loss (in the sense of damages) might flow.

In subsection (2)(b), by contrast, the draftsmen are dealing with the familiar concept of damages caused by breach of duty, but appear, possibly for reasons of delicacy and the desire to avoid the language of conflict, to have selected the term 'compensation' rather than 'damages'. It is also arguable that the term 'compensation' in subsection (2)(b) should include the following matters that traditionally fall outside the province of an award of damages:[35]

(a) the recovery of any costs and fees reasonably incurred in dealing with the breach of duty;

(b) interest upon such costs (in so far as this is not covered under provision expressly made under sections 31(6) and 37(3)(b)—(see paragraph 6.15.9 below)).

It is possible that difficult questions concerning causation, remoteness and the measure of loss will arise in relation to either head of compensation. The authors will attempt a resolution of such questions when the relevant regulations are promulgated.

6.15.5 Compensation where a right is exercised

Section 37(2)(a) allows for the regulations to be made under subsection (1) to make provision:

> requiring compensation to be paid where a right is exercised in specified cases or circumstances.

This provision does not, on the face of it, require there to be any accompanying breach of a duty. The proposed requirement for compensation to be paid when no

[35] But see *Blue Circle Industries plc v Ministry of Defence* [1998] 3 All ER 385, in which the Court of Appeal allowed part of a claim for legal costs associated with the planning for works to remedy the defendant's breach of statutory duty.

right has been infringed appears at first to be a novel one. The draftsmen presumably had in mind a situation in which (for example) a unit-holder is given the right to erect scaffolding to carry out repairs or permitted alterations, but only on terms that he compensates other unit-holders for any resulting loss of amenity.

The regulation which has been drafted (see paragraph 6.15.6 below) does not shed any light on this topic.

6.15.6 Compensation where a duty is not complied with

Section 37(2)(b) allows for the regulations to be made under subsection (1) to make provision:

> requiring compensation to be paid where a duty is not complied with.

The duty in question is a duty imposed by the commonhold community statement, the memorandum or articles of association of the commonhold association, or any provision of the Act.

This subsection appears to create an obligation to pay damages (if not in so many words), where there has been a breach of such a duty. There is no reference to payment of any costs incurred in connection with any such breach, but it is likely that costs properly incurred by the injured party or by the commonhold association in a bid to deal with the consequences of the breach will be recoverable:

(a) under subsection (2)(a) itself, as part of the definition of 'compensation' (see paragraph 6.15.4 above); or

(b) under subsection (2)(c) and (d) as 'work carried out'—(see paragraph 6.15.8 below).

So much was originally made apparent from the wording of the rule initially proposed regarding an indemnity notice (see paragraph 6.3.7 above).

Judging by the Commonwealth experience, the commonhold association will not be able to excuse liability for breach of its duty to manage by asserting that it delegated its duty, as it is entitled to do (see paragraph 4.3.13). Although duties may be properly delegated, that does not excuse the commonhold association from liability in the event that the delegated duty is not performed: see article 77 of the articles of association (which expressly imposes a duty to supervise managing agents) and *Lubrano v Proprietors of Strata Plan No 4038* (1993) (Digest).

The regulation that has thus far been drafted does not greatly illuminate this topic—see regulation 17(2), which provides:

> In proceedings for the exercise or enforcement of a right or duty the court may—
> (a) order compensation to be paid; and
> (b) provide for the payment of simple interest in the case of late payment of compensation for the period between the date on which the payment is due and the date on which the payment is made
>
> as the court thinks fit.

6.15.7 Calculation of compensation under section 37

Section 37(3)(a) of the Act stipulates that provision about compensation may include:

> provision (which may include provision conferring jurisdiction on a court) for determining the amount of compensation.

No proposals under this head were put forward in the Consultation Paper published by the Lord Chancellor's Department on 10 October 2002, although it is to be expected that proposals will eventually be forthcoming. The regulation that has been drafted (see paragraph 6.15.6 above) does not, however, shed any light on this topic.

It will not be possible for the Lord Chancellor to prescribe a mathematical model for the computation of compensation in any given set of circumstances, and it is therefore to be supposed instead that the forthcoming regulations will prescribe, or give guidance on, such matters as:

(a) the factors to be taken into account in determining compensation;

(b) the extent to which matters which are not monetarily quantifiable (for example hurt feelings or loss of amenity) should be compensated;

(c) the extent to which indirect losses (such as the effect of delay on turnover of a business) should be compensated; and

(d) the time by which any compensation should be paid.

6.15.8 Recovery of costs where work is carried out for the purpose of enforcing a right or duty or in consequence of the failure to perform a duty

Section 37(2) allows for the regulations to be made under subsection (1) to make provision:

> enabling recovery of costs where work is carried out for the purpose of enforcing a right or duty [or . . .] where work is carried out in consequence of the failure to perform a duty [subsections (c) and (d)].

The term 'costs' is not defined in the Act, but the phrase 'where work is carried out' which governs it, and the words which then follow in subsections (c) and (d), suggest that it is likely to be interpreted to include:

(a) professional expenses, including surveyors fees and legal costs, properly incurred in connection with the enforcement of any breach of duty;

(b) professional expenses, including surveyors fees and legal costs, properly incurred in connection with remedying any breach of duty;

(c) other expenses (for example the cost of a building contractor) properly incurred in connection with remedying any breach of duty.

It might be contended that legal fees (for example) should not be recoverable under this provision where the breach is remedied by the defaulter without any enforcement action being required save the instruction of lawyers for advice on the appropriate approach. The argument would be that no 'work' as such will have been carried out. The authors consider that such an argument would fail both as a matter of interpretation of subsection (2)(c) and (d), and also because the costs probably fall within the meaning of the term 'compensation'—(see paragraph 6.15.4 above).

Regulation 17 of the Commonhold Regulations does not provide any elucidation:

(3) Where work is carried out for the purpose of enforcing a right or duty the reasonable cost of such work may be recovered from the unit-holder or commonhold association against whom the right or duty is being enforced.

It is also worth remarking that the original (October 2002) draft of the commonhold community statement included provision to the effect that the costs to be recovered in response to the service of an 'indemnity notice' (see paragraph 6.3.7 above) would be such as to 'indemnify and save harmless' the commonhold association or unit-holder involved (see rules 48 and 49). Although those rules have not survived into the current (August 2003) version of the rules, there would appear to be no reason why a commonhold association should not reinstate them.

6.15.9 Interest upon late payment

Section 37(3)(b) allows for the regulations to be made under subsection (1) to make provision:

for the payment of interest in the case of late payment.

The 'late payment' this provision refers to is the late payment of the compensation which may result from regulations directed at subsection (2)(a) and (b). This is echoed, but not elaborated, by regulation 17(2) of the Commonhold Regulations (quoted in paragraph 6.15.6 above), which provides for interest to be payable 'in the case of late payment of compensation'. It is doubtful whether it is also apt to include late payment of the assessment levy which the unit-holders will be required to pay periodically (see Section 4.15).

However, it could justifiably be said that the loss caused by late payment of an assessment levy will consist, wholly or in part, of the interest forgone on the assessment fund, or the interest on the money which may have to be borrowed to make up the shortfall. That loss should then be considered as a loss to be compensated under section 37(2)(b) rather than as an interest payment to be made under section 37(3)(b).

The same result may be reached through section 31(6) of the Act, which provides:

Provision in a commonhold community statement imposing a duty to pay money (whether in pursuance of subsection (5)(a) or any other provision made by or by virtue of this Part) may include provision for the payment of interest in the case of late payment.

Provided accordingly that the commonhold community statement makes such provision, the interests of the commonhold association should be safeguarded. The current (August 2003) version of the statement does indeed make such provision, as default provisions, in the shape of rules 30 and 39.

6.15.10 Enforcement of duties and conditions

Section 37(2) allows for the regulations to be made under subsection (1) to make provision permitting the enforcement of:

(a) duties imposed on others (subsections (e), (f) and (g)) and

(b) terms or conditions to which a right is subject (subsection (h)).

The subsections thus deal not merely with the enforcement of duties imposed by the various provisions of the commonhold community statement, the memorandum and articles of association of the commonhold association and the Act, but also with the enforcement of terms or conditions to which a right is subject. An example might be a provision giving a unit-holder the right to use a storage locker in the common parts, subject to a condition that no inflammatory material be stored. Regulations promulgated under subsection (2)(h) will enable the commonhold association or another unit-holder to ensure that such a condition is enforced—perhaps by a termination of the right in question if the condition is repeatedly breached.

The means of enforcement are not commented upon in the Consultation Paper published by the Lord Chancellor's Department on 10 October 2002, but are likely, in view of the terms of section 37(2)(i) (discussed in paragraph 6.15.13 below), to be constrained by:

(a) the use of the internal complaints procedure (see Part 2); followed as necessary by

(b) reference under the commonhold ombudsman scheme (see Part 3); and/or

(c) the service of an indemnity notice (see paragraph 6.3.7 above); and then as a last resort

(d) litigation.

It is extremely unlikely, in view of the considerations set out in Section 6.3 above, that the regulations will allow any form of sanction to be operated by the commonhold association or the unit-holders, other than, possibly, the termination of a permission to use part of the common parts subject to a condition which is not being complied with.

6.15.11 Persons who may enforce duties and conditions

Section 37(2) allows for the regulations to be made under subsection (1) to make provision for enforcement of the relevant duties to be undertaken by:

(a) a unit-holder (subsection (2)(e)); and

(b) the commonhold association (subsection (2)(e)); and

(c) a tenant (subsection (2)(e)).

Section 37(2)(h), which deals with the enforcement of terms or conditions attached to rights, is silent on the class of potential permitted enforcers. Given the nature of the stipulation, however, it is perhaps likely in practice that only the commonhold association will be involved in such enforcement.

Rule 42 of the current (August 2003) draft of the commonhold community statement expressly provides that a unit-holder *or tenant* may seek to enforce a duty imposed on the commonhold association or a duty imposed on another unit-holder or tenant.

6.15.12 Persons against whom duties may be enforced

Section 37(2) allows for the regulations to be made under subsection (1) to make provision for enforcement of the relevant duties against:

(a) a unit-holder (subsection (2)(e), (f) and (g)); and

(b) the commonhold association (subsections (2)(e) and (g)); and

(c) a tenant (subsection (2)(e), (f) and (g)).

Again, section 37(2)(h), which deals with the enforcement of terms or conditions attached to rights, is silent on the class of those against whom the terms may be enforced. To take the example of the storage locker given in paragraph 6.15.10 above, if the right to use the locker was given to the unit-holder, and the locker is being used by the tenant of the unit-holder in breach of a user condition attached to that right, it would clearly be sensible to provide for the commonhold association to have the right to enforce the condition against the tenant, particularly given that the unit-holder may not be contactable and/or the tenancy agreement between the unit-holder and the tenant may allow the offending use.

The respondents to the October 2002 Consultation Paper Post-Consultation Report dated August 2003 strongly emphasised the need to ensure that tenants were bound by the relevant sections of the commonhold community statement. The current (August 2003) version of the commonhold community statement includes the following provisions regarding tenants which answer that need:

(a) First, rule 8 provides that:

A tenant of a commonhold unit or part only of a commonhold unit is bound by the rules of this commonhold community statement which affect his occupancy.

(b) Secondly, rule 4 requires any tenancy agreement to reserve the right for the commonhold association to carry out repair work in accordance with the provisions of the commonhold community statement.

(c) Thirdly, rule 7 renders the tenant of a unit liable directly to the commonhold association for the payment of sums due by virtue of the commonhold community statement (most obviously a commonhold assessment) *if* his tenancy agreement so provides.

(d) Fourthly, rule 47 provides that a commonhold association may seek to enforce a duty imposed on a tenant by serving a default notice on the tenant.

(e) Fifthly, rule 51 provides that:

Where a duty is enforced against a tenant, a copy of the default notice must be served on the unit-holder and the tenant. Where the duty being enforced relates to payment of the commonhold assessment or reserve fund, a copy of the default notice must also be served on any other tenants of the commonhold unit.

(f) Sixthly, rule 52 provides:

Where rule 7 applies, the commonhold association must first seek to enforce the duty against the tenant but may subsequently seek to enforce the duty against either the unit-holder or any other tenant of the commonhold unit who has been served with a copy of the default notice.

Tenants may therefore be made liable directly to the commonhold association for payment of commonhold debts, and must allow the commonhold to gain access to the commonhold unit where necessary. This drafting strikes the right balance between safeguarding the interests of the commonhold association and interference with the relationship between unit-holder-landlord and tenant.

6.15.13 The requirement to use alternative dispute resolution

Section 37(2) allows for the regulations to be made under subsection (1) to make provision:

requiring the use of a specified form of arbitration, mediation or conciliation procedure before legal proceedings may be brought.

This form of wording does not seem apt to include either the requirement for the parties to any dispute to use the internal complaints procedure which the commonhold association will be required to have (see paragraph 6.4.4 above); or the requirement that the commonhold association should belong to an ombudsman scheme, which the parties should then use to resolve any unresolved dispute (see paragraph 6.7.3 above).

The point has already been made (see paragraph 6.12.1 above) that provision for any further alternative dispute resolution procedure would seem superfluous, given the likely availability (and, at least in the case of the internal complaints procedure, compulsory use) of the internal complaints procedure and ombudsman scheme. At any rate, the Lord Chancellor's Department has not yet put forward any proposals for the referral to such alternative dispute resolution mechanisms.

6.16 COMPANY LAW CLAIMS

6.16.1 Introduction

The commonhold association will be established as a company limited by guarantee and will be subject in the ordinary way (save where the Act expressly provides otherwise) to the regime established by the Companies Acts and the rules and regulations made thereunder: see Part 1 of Chapter 4.

Some of the company documents the commonhold association will be required expressly by the Act to have are set out in the Forms and Precedents part of this work (see especially Part 2). Readers should however bear in mind that the commonhold association will be obliged to keep and file a number of other documents, in order to satisfy the Companies Acts and the relevant rules.

6.16.2 Future plans

This work does not deal in any depth with the requirements imposed by or under the Companies Acts: the requirements are many, and a full treatment of them would greatly lengthen the work and lessen its practical utility. Nevertheless, if readers would like to see any aspect of company law dealt with in this work in greater depth, they are invited to contact the authors with their suggestions at the following address:

letters: Commonhold, Falcon Chambers, Falcon Court, London EC4Y 1AA
e-mail: commonhold@falcon-chambers.co.uk

6.17 INSOLVENCY AND OTHER TERMINATION CLAIMS

6.17.1 Introduction

Sections 43 to 56 of the Act deal with the winding-up of a commonhold association and the termination of a commonhold. These topics are discussed fully in Chapter 5.

The winding-up of a solvent or insolvent commonhold association largely follows established Insolvency Act procedure, and it is outside the current scope of this work to deal with that procedure in further detail. However, if readers would like to see any aspect of insolvency law dealt with in this work in greater depth, they are invited to contact the authors with their suggestions at the following address:

letters: Commonhold, Falcon Chambers, Falcon Court, London EC4Y 1AA
e-mail: commonhold@falcon-chambers.co.uk

6.17.2 Regulations

As paragraph 216 of the Consultation Paper published by the Lord Chancellor's Department on 10 October 2002 observes in relation to the termination of a commonhold either by its members on a voluntary basis or by the court:

> There are few regulation making powers in respect of either type of termination in the Act, because, in general, the provisions of the Insolvency Act 1986 will apply to the commonhold association as they would to any other company limited by guarantee.

There are, however, a number of specific provisions in the Act itself, which are summarised in paragraph 6.17.3 below.

6.17.3 Relevant provisions of the Act

Those provisions of the Act which invoke the procedures of the court with regard to the winding-up of a commonhold association or the termination of a commonhold are as follows:

(a) Section 45(2): this enables a liquidator of a commonhold association, whose members have passed a winding-up resolution and a termination-statement resolution with at least 80 per cent voting in favour, to apply to the court for an order determining (a) the terms and conditions on which a termination application may be made, and (b) the terms of the termination statement to accompany a termination application.

(b) Section 45(4): this enables a unit-holder or any other prescribed person to apply to court for an order under section 45(2) where the liquidator has failed to do so within a period to be prescribed.

(c) Section 47(4): this provides that the court may disapply subsection (3) (which requires a termination statement to comply with the requirements of a commonhold community statement), either generally, or in respect of specified matters, or for a specified purpose.

(d) Section 48(3)(b): this provides for the liquidator to apply to the court under section 112 of the Insolvency Act 1986 where the commonhold association has passed a termination statement resolution under section 44, but the liquidator is not content with the terms of the termination statement.

(e) Section 50: this applies sections 124 and 125 of the Insolvency Act 1986 in relation to the winding-up of a commonhold association by the court.

(f) Section 51(1): this provides that at the hearing of the petition for the winding-up of the commonhold association, an application may be made to the court for a succession order in relation to the insolvent commonhold association, the terms of which shall be in accordance with section 52(4), and may include provision in accordance with section 53(3) and (4).

6.17.4 Forms

Many of the documents for use in the procedures for winding-up a commonhold association or terminating a commonhold are prescribed by regulations made under the Companies Acts and by the Insolvency Rules 1986. Some of those documents will be adapted for use under the Act by regulations and rules which have yet to be made, and by various provisions in the Act (see paragraph 6.17.2 above).

The relevant regulations and rules will be those made under:

(a) Section 31, which prescribes the form and content of the commonhold community statement. Section 47(2) provides in turn that the commonhold community statement may make provision requiring any termination statement to make certain arrangements about the rights of unit-holders in the event that all the land to which the statement relates ceases to be commonhold land.

(b) Section 45(2), which provides for a period to be prescribed for a liquidator to apply to court for an order determining the terms of a termination application and termination statement.

(c) Section 66(4), which provides generally for rules of court to make provision for proceedings brought under the Act (and which is therefore capable of applying to insolvency and termination proceedings).

For the time being, the authors have created or adapted five forms for use in termination proceedings. These can be found in Part 6 of the Forms and Precedents part of this work. As soon as the regulations have been promulgated, the remainder of the forms will be published for inclusion in this work.

6.18 JURISDICTION OF THE COURTS

6.18.1 Introduction

The Act provides for recourse to the courts in a number of different circumstances. This Section considers what fetters there might be on such recourse (paragraph 6.18.2); the jurisdiction of the High Court compared to the county courts (paragraph 6.18.3); and the possible use of tribunals rather than courts (paragraph 6.18.4).

6.18.2 Fetters on recourse to the courts

In the case of the non-contentious claims described in Section 6.14 above (save those to do with dispensing of consents (see paragraphs 6.14.8 and 6.14.9 above) and non-compliant leases (paragraphs 6.14.11 and 6.14.12)), the company law claims dealt with in Section 6.16, and the insolvency and other termination claims discussed in Section 6.17, access to the courts is unfettered, and will be available as of right as soon as Part 1 of the Act has been brought into force.

Contentious claims (see Section 6.15 above) fall into a different category. The Act does not confer any automatic right for unit-holders, their tenants, or the commonhold association to litigate concerning a right conferred or duty imposed by the commonhold community statement, by the memorandum or articles of association of the commonhold association, or by any provision made by or by virtue of the Act. Instead, section 37(1) of the Act delegates the power to make provision for access to the courts in such contentious matters to regulations which may be made by the Lord Chancellor.

Although such regulations will be made before the Act comes into force, they are overwhelmingly likely to require that, before any proceedings are launched, the claimant must have attempted to resolve his dispute using the association's internal complaints procedure (see Section 6.4 and especially paragraph 6.4.2). They may also require that the claimant should be able to demonstrate why it is not appropriate that the dispute should be referred to the commonhold ombudsman scheme (see Part 3 above).

6.18.3 Division of commonhold business between the High Court and the county courts

Section 66(2) of the Act provides:

> Provision made by or under this Part conferring jurisdiction on a court shall be subject to provision made under section 1 of the Courts and Legal Services Act 1990 (c 41) (allocation of business between High Court and county courts).

The reference to 'Provision made by or under this Part conferring jurisdiction on a court' is to the regulations that are to be made under section 37(1) of the Act in relation to contentious claims; and sections 3(2), 23(2), 24(3), 30(3) and 17(4) concerning non-contentious claims.

Section 1(1) of the Courts and Legal Services Act 1990 gives the Lord Chancellor power by order to make provision:

(a) conferring jurisdiction on the High Court in relation to proceedings in which county courts have jurisdiction;
(b) conferring jurisdiction on county courts in relation to proceedings in which the High Court has jurisdiction;
(c) allocating proceedings to the High Court or to county courts;

(d) specifying proceedings which may be commenced only in the High Court;
(e) specifying proceedings which may be commenced only in a county court;
(f) specifying proceedings which may be taken only in the High Court;
(g) specifying proceedings which may be taken only in a county court.

Thus far, the Lord Chancellor has exercised that power by making the High Court and County Courts Jurisdiction Order 1991 (SI 1991 No 724). In summary, the general principle is that, save in the case of low value financial claims, unless an enactment specifies that the county court has exclusive jurisdiction, claims may be brought in either the High Court or a county court.

In more detail, the county court has concurrent jurisdiction with the High Court to hear and determine any action:

(a) For the recovery of land (section 21(1) of the County Courts Act 1984), unless the value of the claim for ancillary relief (for example damages for trespass) makes it necessary for the claim to be brought in the High Court.

(b) In which the title to any hereditament (ie land or property right) is in question (section 21(2) of the County Courts Act 1984).

(c) In contract or tort (section 15 of the County Courts Act 1984), subject to a rebuttable presumption (having regard to such considerations as financial substance, importance, complexity and urgency) that cases involving an (actual or estimated) value of under £25,000 must be brought in the county court, while cases involving more than £50,000 should be brought in the High Court. Such claims should be brought in the High Court if, by reason of the financial value of the claim and the amount in dispute and/or the complexity of the matter and/or the public importance of the case, the claimant believes that the claim ought to be dealt with by a High Court judge (see paragraph 2.4 of the Practice Direction supplementing Part 7 of the Civil Procedure Rules). However, claims for damages or for a specified sum (for example assessment levy) may not be commenced in the High Court unless the value of the claim is more than £15,000 (ibid, paragraph 2.1).

(d) For equitable relief, where the value of the property to be dealt with does not exceed £30,000 (section 23 of the County Courts Act 1984).

The High Court will have exclusive jurisdiction to grant an order requiring the directors of a commonhold association to ensure that the association complies with regulations requiring it to join an approved ombudsman scheme (see section 42(4) of the Act).

In relation to other contentious or non-contentious matters, the Government's current thinking is that the county court should have jurisdiction. This is confirmed by Regulation 17(1) of the Commonhold Regulations:

Jurisdiction is conferred on a county court to deal with the exercise or enforcement of a right or duty imposed by—

(a) a commonhold community statement; or
(b) the articles of association; or
(c) Regulation 19.

6.18.4 Tribunal involvement

Section 66(3) of the Act provides that:

A power under this Part to confer jurisdiction on a court includes power to confer jurisdiction on a tribunal established under an enactment.

The Government has not revealed any plans it may have for creating either a new commonhold jurisdiction for the Leasehold Valuation Tribunal and/or the Lands Tribunal, or a new tribunal analogous to the Leasehold Valuation Tribunal. It is possible that the Department of Constitutional Affairs will wish to wait and see what volume of litigation results from the Act before committing funds to the creation or extension of tribunals other than the courts. The authors consider that it is rather more likely, however, that the Department of Constitutional Affairs will eventually enlarge the jurisdiction of the Leasehold Valuation Tribunal to deal with commonhold disputes.

6.19 PROCEDURE FOR CLAIMS UNDER THE ACT

6.19.1 Introduction

As Sections 6.14 to 6.17 above show, there will be a wide range of possible claims which may be brought under the Act. Those claims may be grouped together in the same way for the purposes of this Section as follows:

(a) non-contentious claims: see paragraph 6.19.4 below;

(b) contentious claims—ie claims regarding breaches of the rules in the commonhold community statement: see paragraph 6.19.5 below;

(c) company law claims: see paragraph 6.19.7 below;

(d) claims arising in connection with the termination of the commonhold and insolvency claims: see paragraph 6.19.8 below.

6.19.2 Rules of procedure

Section 66(4) of the Act provides:

Rules of court or rules of procedure for a tribunal may make provision about proceedings brought—
(a) under or by virtue of any provision of this Part, or
(b) in relation to commonhold land.

Section 66 has been brought into force with effect from 29 September 2003,[36] although no such rules have yet been made, other than a few very anodyne additions to Part 56 of the Civil Procedure Rules. It is not known whether the Lord Chancellor intends to limit the forums for such proceedings to the courts; whether he proposes to introduce a new jurisdiction for the Leasehold Valuation Tribunal and/or Lands Tribunal to hear such matters; or whether he intends to create a new tribunal analogous to the Leasehold Valuation Tribunal.

If the new procedure is to be court- rather than tribunal-based, the Lord Chancellor is likely to make further amendments to the Civil Procedure Rules dealing specifically with proceedings under the Act, in much the same way as the recent Part 56 deals with the conduct of landlord and tenant disputes.[37]

6.19.3 Before issuing proceedings

There are a number of matters the prospective litigant should check before issuing proceedings for the resolution of any matter arising under the Act:

(a) *Alternative dispute resolution*: it will be obligatory for the litigant to show that he has first exhausted the internal complaints procedure of the commonhold association, and that he has gone through the procedures of the ombudsman scheme, unless there is good reason why either or both of those procedures was inappropriate in the circumstances—see paragraphs 6.4.2 and 6.10.2 above.

(b) *Limitation*: the litigant must ensure that any claim is brought within the relevant limitation period—see Section 6.20 below.

(c) *The rules*: the litigant must comply with any stipulation of the relevant procedural rules—see paragraph 6.19.2 above.

6.19.4 Non-contentious claims

Non-contentious claims (ie claims of the sort dealt with in Section 6.14 above) are not subject to the prohibition in rule 45 of the commonhold community statement against the issue of proceedings without first using the internal complaints procedure of the commonhold association (see paragraph 6.19.5 below). Nevertheless, the courts will expect the parties to any non-contentious claim where possible to have attempted to resolve their differences by informal means before the issue of proceedings, and may stay the proceedings to allow for such resolution if it is not persuaded that satisfactory attempts were made.

[36] The commencement order (the Commonhold and Leasehold Reform Act 2002 (Commencement No 3) Order 2003) may be found in the Statutory Instruments section at the end of the Statutes etc part of the work.

[37] It does not, however, appear to be his intention to craft a separate Part dealing with commonhold: as a result of an amendment made to the Civil Procedure Rules by the Civil Procedure (Amendment No 2) Rules 2002, 'landlord and tenant claim' in Part 56 now includes a claim under the Commonhold and Leasehold Reform Act 2002.

Rules of court to be made under section 66(4) will no doubt include provision for such claims to be brought using a variant of the Part 8 procedure. When those rules have been promulgated, the authors will devise a number of sample statements of case and orders suitable for use (see Part 5 of the Forms and Precedents part of this work).

6.19.5 Contentious claims

'Contentious claims' is the expression the authors assign to claims for breach of the rules in the commonhold community statement or the articles of association, dealt with in Section 6.15 above. Save in case of emergency:

(a) a dispute between a *complainant unit-holder* and the *commonhold association* may not be litigated unless and until the internal complaints procedure of the association and ombudsman referral procedure have first been followed (rule 45);

(b) a dispute between the *commonhold association* and a *defaulter* may not be litigated *by the defaulter* unless and until the internal complaints procedure of the association and ombudsman referral procedure have first been followed; the commonhold association, however, is free to litigate without referring the dispute to the ombudsman (rule 49).

It is to be expected that the rules of court to be made under section 66(4) of the Act will prohibit contentious claims unless rules 45 and 49 have been complied with. If proceedings are taken in breach of that prohibition, it is likely that the court will have power either to strike out the proceedings; or to impose a stay of the proceedings until the proper procedures have been followed; or to impose a costs sanction. Even if it is established that the proper procedures have been followed, the court may choose to exercise its inherent jurisdiction to stay the proceedings for a specified period to allow the parties to attempt some other form of alternative dispute resolution.

The form of the proceedings will depend upon the nature of the dispute. If the complaint raises a contested issue of fact, then the form of the proceedings and the procedure are likely to be prescribed by Part 7 of the Civil Procedure Rules. If on the other hand the facts are not in dispute, but there is an issue of law which arises, then the Part 8 procedure will be more appropriate. In either case, it is likely that there will be a procedural requirement for the claimant to provide information about attempts he has made to resolve the dispute using the internal complaints procedure.

6.19.6 Defences to contentious claims

The defences to contentious claims will presumably be drawn along traditional lines—that the defendant did not do the act or omission complained of; that, even if he did, the complaint does not in fact amount to a breach; alternatively the claimant has suffered no loss.

One particular defence worth considering in more detail is that of set-off. Such a defence is available where the defendant can point to a breach on the part of the claimant which is so closely connected with the breach alleged by the claimant that the damages said to flow from it should be offset against the compensation claimed by the claimant.

Neither the Act nor any regulation proposed to be made under it thus far prevents a defendant from raising such a defence or (which has the same strategic outcome) from obtaining a stay of the enforcement of the claimant's claim until the counterclaim has been heard, as happened in *Proprietors of Strata Plan No 30234 v Margiz Pty Ltd* (1993) (Digest). While that may seem fair, the consequences for a small, tightly funded commonhold association may be severe. A commonhold association which ultimately has no alternative but to litigate for the recovery of outstanding assessment levies from a recalcitrant unit-holder may find its proceedings stalemated by a claim to offset the amount claimed against damages for a spurious breach of duty by the association. Although ultimately such a set-off claim may fail, commonhold associations with limited funds may prefer to absorb the shortfall rather than face the costs of litigating the defendant's contentions. This point serves to stress the importance both of keeping close control over the accumulation of debt and of ensuring the rapid and early use of the internal complaints procedure—matters which are stressed in the Best Practice Guide.

6.19.7 Company law claims

This category includes proceedings which are not commonhold-specific, but are concerned with acts or omissions primarily of the directors of the commonhold association which will be actionable as a matter of company law.

As the authors explain in Section 6.16 above, such claims are outside the current scope of this work.

6.19.8 Insolvency and termination claims

This category include all forms of claim and application which are governed by the Insolvency Act 1986 and the Insolvency Rules 1986.

Again, as the authors explain in Section 6.17 above, an examination of the procedure applicable to such matters is outside the present scope of this work.

6.20 LIMITATION

6.20.1 The general rule

The Limitation Act 1980 prevents certain proceedings being brought after stipulated periods (called 'limitation periods') have expired. Such proceedings are referred to as being 'time-barred'.

Examples of limitation periods of relevance or interest to commonhold are:

(a) Actions 'on a specialty' (ie an agreement made by deed), which must not be brought after the expiration of 12 years from the date on which the cause of action accrued unless a shorter period is prescribed by any other provision of the Act (section 8).

(b) Actions for damages in tort or for breach of simple contract (as opposed to a covenant made by deed), which must not be brought after the expiration of 6 years from the date on which the damage was suffered (sections 2 and 5 of the 1980 Act).

(c) Actions for rent, which must not be brought after the expiration of 6 years from the date on which the rent became due (section 19 of the 1980 Act).

(d) Actions for the recovery of possession of registered land, which cannot be brought after the expiration of 12 years from the date on which the owner was dispossessed or discontinued his possession (section 15 and schedule 1 to the 1980 Act). The acquisition of title by adverse possession will, however, be rarer under the Land Registration Act 2002. That Act substitutes a warning procedure for registered proprietors whose land has been occupied adversely for a minimum period of 10 years. Failure to heed the warning will result in the proprietor's title becoming barred after a further period of two years. Accrued rights under the 1980 Act are not affected by the 2002 Act.

Other, mainly equitable, forms of action (such as claims for an injunction or declaration) are not subject to limitation periods, although the litigant must show, in accordance with well-hallowed equitable principles, that he has acted with reasonable promptness.

Some of these rules have been altered for the purposes of the Act, as the remaining paragraphs of this Section explain.

6.20.2 Actions for breach of commonhold duty

Paragraph 4 of Schedule 5 to the Act inserts the following new section in the Limitation Act 1980:

Commonhold

19A Actions for breach of commonhold duty

An action in respect of a right or duty of a kind referred to in section 37(1) of the Commonhold and Leasehold Reform Act 2002 (enforcement) shall not be brought after the expiration of six years from the date on which the cause of action accrued.

This section serves to make clear that a 6-year limitation period will apply to contentious claims—ie claims for breach of a rule in the commonhold community statement or of an article in the articles of association of the commonhold association—(see Section 6.15 above). This will be so even if the document imposing the duty or conferring the right was made by deed.

6.20.3 Claim for rectification of documents

Section 40(4) of the Act (see paragraph 6.14.5 above) provides for the making of an application for a declaration that the memorandum or articles of association of the commonhold association or its commonhold community statement are non-compliant with a provision made under or by virtue of the Act.

Such an application must be made:

(a) within the period of three months beginning with the day on which the applicant became a unit-holder,
(b) within three months of the commencement of the alleged failure to comply, or
(c) with the permission of the court.

This section therefore imposes its own special limitation period, which will override any other provision. The circumstances in which a court may grant or refuse to extend the time for the making of such an application are discussed in paragraph 6.14.7 above.

6.20.4 Liability for loss suffered by holder of extinguished lease

Section 10 of the Act deals with liability for any loss suffered by the holder of a lease which has been extinguished by operation of section 9(3)(f) of the Act without the consent of the leaseholder.

No limitation period is specified for the claim to recover compensation for this loss, and the Limitation Act 1980 does not provide any category into which it could meaningfully be said to fall. The loss is analogous to the loss suffered when land is compulsorily purchased, for which, however, the land acquisition legislation makes special provision.

Were this point ever to arise, it is quite possible that the court would hold that there is no applicable limitation period for the loss in question.

6.20.5 Procedural limitation periods

A number of statutes or rules of court stipulate time limits for the making of applications to court. Such time limits are usually subject to extension by the court, using powers available to it under its inherent jurisdiction or in the exercise of its general case management powers under Part 3.1 of the Civil Procedure Rules.[38]

[38] See, for example, Rule 12.9 of the Insolvency Rules 1986.

Chapter 7
FREQUENTLY ASKED QUESTIONS ABOUT COMMONHOLD

7.1 INTRODUCTION

7.1.1 Common problems

The inspiration for this Chapter was the Government's website for the Commonhold and Leasehold Reform Act 2002, which has a Frequently Asked Questions page. Enquiries made by the authors, as well as their own research into this and other jurisdictions, have led to their perception that there are some common difficulties with Part 1 of the new Act and some misconceptions with the creation and intended working of the new commonhold regime. This Chapter is therefore intended as a summary of the most common problems, together with a quick fix to them.

7.1.2 Revision

The Chapter will be revised regularly in the light of experience as the new Act beds down. Some existing questions will be deleted or revised when the expected difficulties fail to materialise; others will be added as possibly unforeseen emergencies arise.

7.1.3 Readers' requests

The authors would be grateful for any questions for incorporation in this Chapter, and will acknowledge messages sent to them at the following address:

letters: Commonhold, Falcon Chambers, Falcon Court, London EC4Y 1AA
e-mail: commonhold@falcon-chambers.co.uk

7.2 ABOUT COMMONHOLD

7.2.1 What is commonhold?

Commonhold is a new form of land owning within registered freehold land. The commonhold scheme ensures that the occupants of a development are entirely in control, with no landlord or other third party able to exercise influence. Unit-holders in a commonhold building or other development will own the registered freehold estate in commonhold land in their respective units. The unit-holders will also be the exclusive members of a private company limited by guarantee which will own the registered freehold estate in commonhold land of the common parts.

7.2.2 Why has commonhold been introduced?

Because there is no wholly satisfactory way in this country of owning property where some of the facilities enjoyed by it are used in common with others. The leasehold system, which is commonly employed to overcome some of the problems associated with communal facilities, has difficulties of its own which commonhold will resolve by vesting control and ownership of the communal facilities in an association owned by the unit-holders and introducing uniformity in the form and content of the documentation required. See Section 1.3 of the text.

7.2.3 Will commonhold work?

The Government Minister said during the Second Reading of the Bill in the House of Commons:

> . . . we believe that commonhold offers enormous attractions, but it would be wrong of us to prescribe it at this stage. The property market is complex and fluid, and we think that the scheme should have time to bed in. We want to see how the market responds to commonhold, so the answer . . . is, in short, 'Let the market decide.' We believe that it will make the appropriate decision and recognise the full advantages of commonhold.[1]

The authors share the Minister's optimism.

7.2.4 Is commonhold a new estate in land?

No: it is a new mechanism for the creation of an interdependent set of rights and obligations over land, but it is not a new type of interest in land. A commonhold can only be created where land is held in freehold ownership in the first place. See Section 2.2 and 2.3 of the text.

[1] *Official Report, House of Commons*, 8 January 2002; vol 377, col 428.

7.2.5 Is commonhold mandatory for newly built interdependent units?

No. Commonhold is a voluntary code. Developers are free to sell newly built interdependent units (flats or housing with common facilities) on long leases if they wish, although they will recognise that commonhold brings a number of advantages that will attract purchasers compared with leasehold.

7.2.6 Does commonhold apply to the whole country?

No. Commonhold applies only to England and Wales.

7.2.7 When does commonhold come into force?

The Commonhold and Leasehold Reform Act 2002 received Royal Assent on 1 May 2002. Part 1 of the Act, which deals with commonhold, is heavily dependent upon regulations, the bulk of which are to be made by the Lord Chancellor. At the time of going to press (November 2003), the Lord Chancellor has made a commencement order[2] which brings the regulation-making and other formal powers in sections 42, 62, 64, 65, 66, 67, 69 and 70 of the Act into force on 29 September 2003. Part 1 cannot, however, be brought further into force until the requisite regulations have been laid before Parliament. A Consultation Paper dealing with some of the proposed regulations was issued by the Lord Chancellor's Department on 10 October 2002, inviting comments to be given by the close of the consultation period on 6 January 2003. It was originally provisionally estimated that the Rule Committee would approve all rules, regulations and orders by the end of March 2003. However, the Post-Consultation Report was only issued in August 2003, and it is clear from that document that much remains to be done. Although some regulations have been drafted,[3] it is not now expected that the finalised regulations will be laid before Parliament until the end of 2003 at the earliest.

That is not to say, however, that plans for commonhold developments should not yet be made. There is no doubt that the Act will be brought into force in the near future, and developers will therefore wish to be in a position to take advantage of the Act at the earliest opportunity.

[2] See the Commonhold and Leasehold Reform Act 2002 (Commencement No 3) Order 2003 in the Statutes etc part of the work.

[3] See the draft Commonhold Regulations at the end of the Statutes etc part of the work.

7.3 CREATION OF COMMONHOLD

7.3.1 Does my title have to be registered before I can create a commonhold?

Basically, yes: section 2 provides that an application for a commonhold registration can only be made by a registered freeholder; it cannot be made by the owner of an unregistered freehold title. In principle, it should be possible to apply for first registration of title at the same time as applying for the registration of the freehold land as commonhold. However, the draft Commonhold (Land Registration) Rules 2003 do not provide a procedure for this to be done, so it is not clear whether the Land Registry will in practice accept a simultaneous application for first registration and for registration as a commonhold (see paragraph 2.3.2 of the text). The procedure for applying for registration is dealt with in Chapter 2.

7.3.2 How long will it take for my commonhold title to be registered?

The answer to this question will depend on whether your application is supported by all the required documents (see Schedule 1 to the Act and Chapter 2 of the text); whether those documents have been correctly completed and comply with the provisions of the Act, the commonhold community statement and the memorandum and articles of association; and whether the advances in electronic conveyancing dealt with in the Land Registration Act 2002 have been implemented. The answers to preliminary enquiries of the Land Registry suggest that a period of up to some weeks should be allowed for completion of the procedure once an application has been made, assuming that all documents are in order.

7.3.3 Does each commonhold unit-holder obtain a separate registered freehold title?

Yes. The draft Commonhold (Land Registration) Rules 2003 additionally provide for the owner of the commonhold to be issued with extra official copies of the title to the common parts, so that each unit-holder will receive official copies of the unit title and also a copy of the common parts title. See Section 2.22 of the text.

7.3.4 Who owns the airspace above a unit?

The answer to this question will depend on the way in which the unit is defined in the commonhold community statement. It will be perfectly possible for that definition to allow the unit-holder to have title to the airspace, whether the unit is a free-standing house or the top flat in a block of flats. It will be more likely, however, for the airspace above the top flat to be reserved as common parts, either because the roof space houses plant servicing the units, or because there may be a prospect of redevelopment of the roof to afford extra accommodation. See paragraphs 2.17.5 to 2.17.7 of the text.

7.3.5 Can a block of flats let on long leases be converted to a commonhold?

A block of flats is eminently suitable for conversion to commonhold. However, the long leaseholders must first purchase the freehold reversion, either by private treaty or under their rights to collective enfranchisement. It is necessary then for all the long leaseholders and their mortgagees to give consent. If any one of them refuses to agree, however unreasonably, the conversion to commonhold cannot take place. This was viewed, during the passage of the Bill, as a considerable weakness in the legislation, and it was proposed that a conversion should be possible with only a majority of the long leaseholders giving their consent. However, these proposals were rejected, and the long leaseholders must be unanimously in favour of the conversion. The procedure for converting a long leasehold development into a commonhold development is discussed further in Chapter 2.

7.3.6 Can two or more people own a commonhold unit?

Yes: a commonhold unit can be owned by joint unit-holders.

7.4 TRANSACTIONS WITHIN COMMONHOLD

7.4.1 Can the transfer of a commonhold unit be prohibited or restricted?

No. The policy is that a unit-holder should have the same freedom to transfer his property as any standard freehold owner, and be free of the restrictions on assignment that are resented by many tenants of long residential leases. See paragraph 3.2.3 of the text.

7.4.2 What are the liabilities of a former unit-holder once he has transferred the unit to a new owner?

The transferor ceases to be a member of the commonhold association when he transfers his unit and ceases to be a unit-holder. From that moment, he cannot incur any new liability or acquire any new right under the commonhold community statement. He is not, however, released from any liability incurred before the transfer took effect. See paragraph 3.2.5 of the text.

7.4.3 What are the entitlements and liabilities of a new unit-holder once the unit has been transferred to him?

The new unit-holder becomes entitled, following the transfer, to the same rights as other unit-holders. He will also become subject to the same ongoing duties as other unit-holders—for example, to pay commonhold assessments falling due after transfer, and to comply with repairing obligations affecting the unit. It is now clear that he will also become liable for commonhold assessment and reserve fund levies that fell to be paid prior to the transfer. See paragraph 3.2.5 of the text.

7.4.4 Can a unit-holder transfer part of a unit?

The transfer of the freehold estate in part of a commonhold unit is permitted, provided that the commonhold association passes a resolution in favour and consents in writing to the transfer. See paragraph 3.2.6 of the text.

7.4.5 Can a unit-holder grant a tenancy of a residential unit?

Yes, but only if he satisfies certain conditions which are prescribed by regulations. The regulations prohibit long residential leases. The current proposal is that no tenancies should be granted for a term of more than 21 years. See Section 3.3 of the text.

7.4.6 Can a unit-holder grant a tenancy of part only of a residential unit?

Yes, provided that he satisfies the prescribed conditions. See paragraph 3.3.3 of the text.

7.4.7 Will a tenant of a unit be bound by the terms and conditions of the commonhold community statement?

Yes, so far as they are appropriate to the nature of his interest. See paragraph 3.3.7 of the text.

7.4.8 Can a unit-holder grant a licence of a residential unit?

Yes. See paragraph 3.3.9 of the text.

7.4.9 Can tenancies be granted of non-residential units?

Yes, subject to any restrictions in the commonhold community statement. See Section 3.4 of the text.

7.4.10 Can a unit-holder secure a mortgage over his unit?

Yes. A unit-holder should have the same ability to borrow money on the security of his unit as a standard freeholder. However, it is not possible to create a charge over part only of a unit. See Section 3.5 of the text.

7.4.11 Will the commonhold association be able to mortgage the common parts?

Yes, but only if it is approved by a unanimous resolution of the commonhold association, passed before the creation of the mortgage. See Section 3.6 of the text.

7.4.12 Can a commonhold association add further land to the commonhold?

Yes, provided that the commonhold association passes a unanimous resolution in favour of doing so. See Section 3.7 of the text.

7.5 OPERATION OF COMMONHOLD

7.5.1 Who will run the commonhold?

The directors of the commonhold association have the responsibility for running the commonhold (see section 35 of the Act). In the case of a large commonhold, the directors will be professionals, experienced in property management, and also possessing some legal or accountancy skills. In the case of a small commonhold, although some professional skills will still be needed (for example for the annual audit), in practice the management duties can be carried out by the members themselves, who are of course entitled to become directors.

7.5.2 How many directors should there be?

The commonhold association must have at least two, directives. There is no upper limit upon the number of directors.

7.5.3 Where do I find the duties of the directors spelt out?

The directors' corporate duties are laid down in the articles of association of the commonhold association. Specific property-management duties are set out in the commonhold community statement. These duties are summarised in paragraph 4.3.19 of the text.

7.5.4 Is a director allowed to become involved in the business of the association in a personal capacity?

Yes, provided that his interest is first disclosed to his fellow directors: see paragraphs 4.3.10 and 4.3.11 of the text.

7.5.5 Are the directors entitled to be paid?

Yes, provided that a resolution to that effect is passed in a general meeting: see paragraph 4.3.15 of the text.

7.5.6 How many meetings does the commonhold association have to hold each year?

The articles of association require there to be one annual general meeting and (as a default provision) one other general meeting each year: see paragraph 4.5.1 of the text.

7.5.7 What is the purpose of such meetings?

The purpose of the annual general meeting is to review the business of the commonhold association over the past year; to review the budget for the forthcoming year; and to process the retirement and appointment of directors: see paragraph 4.5.2 of the text. The further general meeting will include an interim review of the business of the association since the preceding AGM: see paragraph 4.5.4.

7.5.8 Who can vote at these meetings?

Only members of the commonhold association, or those properly standing in their stead, may vote at general meetings, with the one exception that a non-member chairman of a general meeting may make a casting vote: see paragraph 4.6.1 of the text.

7.5.9 Is a decision taken at a general meeting effective, no matter how many members turn up to vote?

No, a decision taken at a meeting is ineffective unless there is a 'quorum': that is to say, a specified sufficient proportion of the members in attendance. The specified quorum for a general meeting is 20 per cent of the members of the commonhold association who are entitled to vote upon the business in question, or three members of the association (whichever is the greater) in the case of an ordinary resolution: see paragraph 4.6.15 of the text. Special rules apply in the case of other types of resolution, including a vote for a winding-up or termination of the commonhold.

7.5.10 Do I have to vote in person, or are votes in writing permitted?

Yes, such votes are allowed in certain circumstances: see paragraph 4.6.17 of the text.

7.5.11 What sort of majority is required for a resolution at a general meeting of the commonhold association?

This varies, depending upon the resolution in question. Paragraph 4.6.21 sets out a table giving the majorities required for different types of resolution.

7.5.12 Does a commonhold association require a company secretary?

Yes, this is a requirement of company law: see paragraph 4.7.3 of the text.

7.5.13 Does the commonhold association require a treasurer?

No although, as paragraph 4.7.4 of the text suggests, it may be prudent to have one.

7.5.14 Who will be responsible for maintaining the structure and exterior of a unit?

The current proposal is that this will be left to the owner of the unit. Where this might cause problems (as in the case of a block of flats), the unit will be defined so as to exclude the structure and exterior, and the responsibility will then pass to the commonhold association. In the case of a commonhold development which comprises structurally independent units (for example chalets), however, there is no reason why this liability should not instead be assumed by the unit-holder—see the discussion of this point in paragraph 4.9.2 of the text.

7.5.15 Does the commonhold community statement lay down any guidelines as to the standard to which repair and maintenance of any part of the commonhold is to be carried out?

No. This will be a matter for individual commonhold associations to prescribe: see paragraph 4.9.3 of the text.

7.5.16 Is a unit-holder entitled to refuse the commonhold association access over his unit for the purposes of repairs?

It depends. If the reason for the work is that the unit-holder has neglected his own responsibility, then the commonhold association may be entitled to access for the purpose of executing works in default, if the commonhold community statement so provides. Secondly, if there is an emergency, then, again, the unit-holder is not entitled to refuse access. Thirdly, if the works are the commonhold association's liability, and there is no emergency, then the unit-holder is entitled to refuse access, unless there is a specific provision in the commonhold community statement requiring access to be given. These issues are discussed in paragraph 4.9.10 of the text.

7.5.17 If the unit-holder refuses access in a case where he has no right to do so, can the commonhold association obtain access without going to court?

Again, this depends. If the situation is an emergency, then the commonhold association may go ahead without a court order, although it should of course proceed lawfully (that is to say, without infringing the provisions of, for example, the Criminal Law Act 1977). If, on the other hand, the commonhold association wishes to gain access in order to exercise works in default, and the unit-holder refuses access, the commonhold association has no alternative but to obtain a court order: see paragraph 4.9.11 of the text.

7.5.18 Is a unit-holder entitled to carry out an alteration to his own unit?

Yet again, this depends on the terms of the commonhold community statement. Purely non-structural internal alterations, which do not affect the external appearance of the unit, may ordinarily be carried out without consent. Alterations to the structure, or those which affect the external appearance of the unit, may also be carried out under the current proposals, although this situation may vary depending upon the terms of individual commonhold community statements. Alterations which would have the effect of increasing the size of the unit fall into a different category, and require a special resolution: see Section 4.10 of the text.

7.5.19 Who will bear responsibility for insuring each individual unit?

This depends: the arguments for and against individual unit-holders having that responsibility are evenly balanced, as paragraph 4.11.3 of the text observes. The current proposal is that unit-holders should be allowed to make their own insurance arrangements.

7.5.20 What about contents insurance?

The current draft of the commonhold community statement is silent on this point: see paragraph 4.11.4 of the text.

7.5.21 I am a music teacher and own a residential unit. Am I entitled to hold piano lessons in my unit in the evening?

Although this result may appear to be absurdly harsh, the view of the authors is that such a use would contravene the designation of the unit: see paragraph 4.12.2 of the text.

7.5.22 Would it be lawful for the commonhold community statement to confine membership of the association to people over the age of 55?

This remains to be seen: there are formidable arguments to the effect that such a restriction would be contrary to the principle that units must be freely alienable: see paragraph 3.2.3 and 4.12.4 of the text.

7.5.23 My unit includes a garage. Am I allowed to use the garage as a workshop for my hobby?

Yes, probably, since such a use is a fairly commonplace feature of garages: see paragraph 4.12.5 of the text.

7.5.24 My unit includes a garage. Am I allowed to use the garage as a workshop for making articles for sale to the general public?

No: this would contravene the residential use requirement: see paragraph 4.12.5 of the text.

7.5.25 My unit includes a parking space. Can I use that as a store for private purposes?

This is currently unrestricted, although it is likely that individual commonhold community statements may require that parking spaces included in a residential unit may only be used for parking: see paragraph 4.12.5 of the text.

7.5.26 My unit does not include either a garage or a parking space, although communal parking is available. Is the commonhold association entitled to grant me exclusive use of one of those spaces?

No, unless the parking is designated as limited use common parts, with that specific stipulation: see paragraphs 4.12.6 and 4.12.7 of the text.

7.5.27 Am I allowed to display a satellite dish on the exterior of my unit?

No, unless the airspace into which the satellite dish projects is within the curtilage of the unit. Even then, this may still contravene a specific prohibition in the commonhold community statement: see paragraph 4.12.11 of the text.

7.6 FINANCING THE OPERATION OF COMMONHOLD

7.6.1 Are there analogous provisions in commonhold to sections 19 and 20 (for example) of the Landlord and Tenant Act 1985, which would enable me to object to payment of a commonhold assessment levy?

No: the reason for this is set out in paragraph 4.14.2 of the text.

7.6.2 What if the commonhold assessment produces a figure that falls short of the eventual expenditure?

There are two ways in which a shortfall can be covered: by a further assessment (see paragraph 4.15.9), and by borrowing.

7.6.3 Is the commonhold association entitled to borrow money?

Yes, although it may have difficulty in furnishing security for the loan.

7.6.4 Do the trust provisions of section 42 of the Landlord and Tenant Act 1987 apply to any commonhold reserve fund?

No.

7.6.5 Why do the trust provisions of section 42 of the Landlord and Tenant Act 1987 not apply to any commonhold reserve fund?

Because section 42 is limited to the control of service charges as between landlord and tenant, and not the freehold relationships which characterise commonhold. The duties regarding the monies held from time to time in the reserve fund are adequately protected by company law rules, and do not require the superimposition of a statutory trust to protect the unit-holders. This topic is discussed further in paragraph 4.16.12.

7.6.6 Why does the commonhold association have to have a reserve fund—cannot the requisite costs simply be paid for as part of the commonhold assessment?

It remains to be seen whether the Government will insist upon reserve funding. In principle, given the Government's determination that commonhold should so far as possible simulate the freedoms associated with freehold, there is much to be said for the point of view that commonholders should be free to make up their own minds about whether or not to have a reserve fund, or to pay for major expenditure as and when it falls due. This question is discussed in paragraph 4.16.4 of the text.

7.7 TERMINATING A COMMONHOLD

7.7.1 How can a commonhold be brought to an end?

A commonhold can be brought to an end in five different ways: by an application to the Land Registry by the developer, during the transitional stage of the development; by an application to the court by someone who is adversely affected by a registration that has been made without proper compliance with all the formalities; by the voluntary winding-up of the commonhold association by the unit-holders; by the compulsory winding-up of the commonhold association by a creditor; and by reason of the compulsory purchase of the land. The termination of a commonhold is discussed in Chapter 5.

7.7.2 What is the effect of a compulsory winding-up order?

The effect of a compulsory winding-up order against the commonhold is likely to be minimal. The court has the power to make a succession order, under which the land vested in the commonhold association is transferred to a successor association, and therefore put beyond the reach of the creditors.

7.7.3 How many of the unit-holders must agree in order for the commonhold association to be voluntarily wound-up?

The commonhold association can only be wound-up if at least 80 per cent of the unit-holders agree.

7.8 DISPUTE RESOLUTION WITHIN COMMONHOLD

7.8.1 I have just bought a commonhold unit, but I have not signed up to any commonhold documentation. What, if any, liability do I have to the commonhold association?

Two interlocking provisions provide the answer to this question. First, section 31(7) of the Act provides that:

> A duty conferred by a commonhold community statement on a commonhold association or a unit-holder shall not require any other formality.

Secondly, section 16 of the Act provides that a right or duty conferred or imposed by the commonhold community statement shall affect a new unit-holder in the same way as it affected the former unit-holder. Taken together, those two provisions have the effect that a transferee will become liable to the commonhold association as soon as the transfer has been completed. This topic is examined further in paragraph 4.13.2, and generally in Chapter 3.

7.8.2 What are the sources of the various duties and entitlements imposed or bestowed in commonhold?

These stem from a variety of sources: the Act itself, the memorandum and articles of association of the commonhold association; the commonhold community statement; and the various regulations made or to be made under the Act. These are examined in detail in Section 6.2.

7.8.3 Does the commonhold association have any rights of forfeiture?

No: forfeiture is anathema to commonhold, and has deliberately been excluded as a sanction: see paragraph 6.3.11.

7.8.4 Does a unit-holder remain liable for breaches of duty incurred during his ownership, once he has transferred his unit?

Yes.

7.8.5 Does a unit-holder become liable for breaches of duty committed after he has transferred his unit?

No.

7.8.6 Does the incoming unit-holder become liable for breaches of duty committed prior to his ownership?

Yes, but only for commonhold assessment and reserve fund levies. Paragraph 6.3.15 of the text discusses this topic.

7.8.7 In the event of a breach of duty by a unit-holder, is the commonhold association free to litigate?

No: prior to litigating any breach of duty, the commonhold association must go through its internal complaints procedure, unless the urgency of the matter is such that that course would be unreasonable: see paragraph 6.4.2 of the text.

7.8.8 Can the commonhold association select its own internal complaints procedure?

No: the structure of the procedure is laid down in the commonhold community statement, and must be followed. Having said that, however, there is much that each individual commonhold association can do to impress its own stamp upon the way in which the procedure is applied. The procedure is described in full in Sections 6.4, 6.5 and 6.6 of the text.

7.8.9 Are there any prescribed forms for use as part of the internal complaints procedure?

Yes, the internal complaints procedure is reliant upon the use of prescribed forms. Although this feature may lend unnecessary formality to what may be a fairly trivial complaint, it will help to crystallise the nature of the dispute, and serve as a record. The forms used are described in Section 6.5 of the text.

7.8.10 Must the commonhold association become embroiled in disputes between unit-holders?

This will depend upon whether the commonhold association is formally notified of the dispute, and asked to take action. The commonhold association need take no action, however, if the dispute does not appear to involve a breach of the rules, or if the dispute does not appear to be a matter in which the commonhold association should be involved: see paragraph 6.5.3 of the text.

7.8.11 Is the commonhold association entitled to recover any of the costs it will have incurred through its participation in the internal complaints procedure?

This will depend upon the terms of each commonhold community statement: this may provide for a formal procedure for recovery of costs, commencing with the service of an indemnity notice. This procedure is described in paragraph 6.3.7 of the text.

7.9 THE OMBUDSMAN SCHEME[4]

7.9.1 What will the ombudsman do?

He will aim to provide a fair and effective way of dealing with complaints against other unit-holders or the commonhold association. He will seek redress for complaints, where justified. He will identify failings in the services provided by the commonhold association and can ask it to change its way of working.

7.9.2 Will all commonhold associations and unit-holders belong to the ombudsman scheme?

Commonhold associations are required to belong to the ombudsman scheme. Unit-holders will not be required to belong, but will be subject to its terms.

[4] This Section of the text assumes that the proposed ombudsman scheme will be closely modelled on the Independent Housing Ombudsman Scheme established under the Housing Act 1996—see paragraph 6.8.2 of the text.

7.9.3 In what circumstances will I be able to complain to the ombudsman?

You will have the right to complain to the ombudsman if you are a unit-holder or a director of a commonhold association and you have cause to complain about the activities of another unit-holder or the commonhold association.

7.9.4 Must I go through the commonhold association's own complaints procedure first?

Yes. The ombudsman expects people complaining to him to go through their association's internal complaints procedure first. The commonhold association must have a formal complaints procedure, the details of which will be set out in the commonhold community statement. If you do not have a copy of it, you will be able to obtain a copy by writing to the directors of the commonhold association. If you are refused a copy, or told there isn't one, please inform the ombudsman.

The ombudsman may decide to accept your complaint before you complete your commonhold association's procedure if he thinks that your association or the unit-holder against whom the complaint is made is not following the procedure; or if the procedure is too difficult or inadequate; or if it is taking too long.

7.9.5 What is the time limit for making a complaint?

You should make your complaint as soon as possible to your commonhold association, and within any time period they specify in their procedures. The ombudsman will normally only accept a complaint which was made to the association within 12 months of you becoming aware of the problem that caused it.

Then, if you are not satisfied with the way it was handled, you must complain to the ombudsman as soon as possible, but no more than 12 months after you reached the end of the association's complaint procedure.

7.9.6 What can I complain about?

You can complain if you think your association or another unit-holder has done something wrong, or something they shouldn't have done, or if they have failed to do something. Some examples:

(a) failure to carry out repairs in a reasonable time;

(b) claiming you were in arrears with an assessment levy when you were not;

(c) charging you more than anybody else for the same assessment;

(d) unreasonably refusing to give you consent to alterations or anything else to which your commonhold community statement provides the commonhold association may not unreasonably withhold consent;

(e) quarrels between you and your neighbours in the commonhold.

Generally the ombudsman will not deal with:

(a) complaints because you simply don't agree with general policies or decisions of your commonhold association which have been made reasonably after following proper procedures;

(b) problems that are about to go to court (or have already done so), or that the ombudsman thinks would be dealt with better that way;

(c) problems that other bodies have the power to deal with;

(d) complaints from contractors, consultants, employees or others who are paid by the association, about their professional or commercial relationship;

(e) complaints from people who live near the commonhold, but do not receive a service from it.

7.9.7 How do I make a complaint?

The administrators of the ombudsman scheme prefer you to use their complaint form, but if you wish to write a letter you should feel free to do so. You can use either the online complaint form, or you can request a printed one. If you cannot write your complaint down, a member of the ombudsman's staff will help you, but this carries a greater risk of misunderstandings.

7.9.8 Must I make the complaint myself?

No. If you don't feel able to complain yourself, ask an advisor or helper to do it for you—for example, a member of your family, someone living with you, someone at the commonhold association, or a Citizens Advice Bureau. But you must tell the ombudsman that that person has your full authority to complain on your behalf. If the complaint is made by a letter written on your behalf, please add your signature to it.

7.9.9 Must I say who I am?

Yes. The ombudsman cannot deal with anonymous complaints.

7.9.10 Will the details of my complaint be confidential?

The ombudsman will not encourage or invite anyone to send him anything in confidence. However, he will only give details of your complaint to those people or agencies who can help sort it out, such as your commonhold association and the ombudsman's mediation service. You can object to disclosure, but the ombudsman may then not be able to deal with your complaint.

He may also, with your permission, give your details to an independent research agency commissioned to do surveys of complainants and commonhold associations, to find out if they are satisfied with his scheme.

7.9.11 How will the ombudsman deal with my complaint?

The ombudsman has a duty to investigate all complaints made to him. He will firstly consider whether the complaint falls within the terms of the Scheme. If it does not, it will be rejected at that stage and you will be given the reasons. In particular he will see whether you have completed your commonhold association's formal complaints procedure.

If he investigates further, he will send a copy of your complaint to your commonhold association and any other relevant unit-holder for their comments. He may ask for more information from you and your commonhold association, and possibly from other organisations. The ombudsman's staff will establish what has happened, and the ombudsman will decide what is fair in all the circumstances.

You will not need to travel to the ombudsman's office. A member of his staff will travel to meet you if the ombudsman thinks a meeting is necessary.

7.9.12 What can the ombudsman do?

There are a number of different options available to the ombudsman, and he will choose that which appears most appropriate in your case:

(a) *Local settlement*:

He may first try to resolve your complaint informally, for instance by letters or phone calls.

(b) *Preliminary determination*:

After early enquiries, the ombudsman may decide he has enough information to reach a conclusion. He will write and tell you, the commonhold association and any other unit-holder involved what his preliminary determination is. He will give you an opportunity to provide further evidence or comments. After reviewing them, he may confirm or modify his determination, or continue his enquiries.

(c) *Formal inquiry*:

The ombudsman may decide that the best action is to carry out a formal inquiry. This is a thorough and rigorous examination to establish the facts. It may require interviewing you and other people involved. Again, a member of his staff may travel to meet you. At the end, the ombudsman decides what has happened and where responsibility lies. Formal inquiries are only carried out in a few cases which are complex, or which may have serious implications.

(d) *Mediation*:

The ombudsman's independent mediation service is trained to resolve problems affecting commonholds. If the ombudsman suggests mediation, it can be arranged very quickly, and is free of charge. An independent person discusses the complaint with you and your commonhold association, though not necessarily at the same time. For mediation to take place, both sides must agree to it. The mediator will help you reach an agreement which is acceptable to both of you, and which will prevent the problem arising again.

(e) *Arbitration*:
This is where an independent person considers the complaint. For arbitration to go ahead, both sides must agree to it. It is an informal legal process and the arbitrator's decision is final and legally binding on both sides—this means you must both accept the decision of the arbitrator. Neither side can pull out unless the other agrees. The arbitrator's decision can be enforced in a court. If the ombudsman suggests arbitration, it can be arranged very quickly and is free of charge.

7.9.13 What happens at the end of the investigation?

The ombudsman will write to you and your commonhold association and anyone else involved, explaining what he has found, what his decision is, and stating what, if anything, should be done about it.

If the ombudsman finds in your favour, he may recommend that your commonhold association or the defaulting unit-holder:

(a) give you an apology and/or
(b) pay you compensation and/or
(c) carry out repairs or other works and/or
(d) change the way they do things.

The ombudsman may also recommend other ways he considers appropriate of resolving the complaint.

7.9.14 How long will the ombudsman take to deal with my complaint?

Resolving complaints has to be done carefully, and this cannot be done quickly, but the ombudsman will always try to deal with complaints as promptly as he can. He will acknowledge your complaint and tell you when you may expect replies to correspondence. Targets are set for each stage, and your full co-operation is needed in meeting them. However, delays sometimes happen. The ombudsman will inform you of any changes affecting progress.

7.9.15 What if my commonhold association won't do what the ombudsman says?

Ombudsmen find that nearly all their recommendations are accepted, and commonhold associations and unit-holders are expected to comply. Commonhold associations are required to comply with the finding of the ombudsman; if the commonhold association does not do as the ombudsman says, he may order them to publish that they have failed to do so, in any way he sees fit.

7.9.16 Will the investigation of my complaint be made public?

The ombudsman must keep details about you confidential. He will only publish a report if there has been a formal inquiry. The report will name the commonhold association but it will not name you or give details of your address.

The ombudsman may also publish summaries of some of his other investigations, including mediations and arbitrations—but the person making the complaint will never be identified.

7.9.17 How do I complain about the ombudsman?

There is no appeal against the decisions or recommendations of the ombudsman. But if you believe the ombudsman's staff have made errors of procedure in the way they have dealt with your complaint, please write to the General Manager. The General Manager will look at the way your complaint was handled, and consider if it should have been dealt with differently. If you are unhappy with his conclusions, write to the ombudsman himself. If you are still dissatisfied, you may take your complaint to the board of the administering company. The board may appoint one or more of its public interest directors to consider the matter.

7.10 LITIGATION

7.10.1 Will the commonhold association or unit-holders be given free access to the courts to litigate breaches of statutory duty or breaches of the rules of the commonhold community statement?

The Act itself lays down a number of circumstances in which access to the court will be allowed as of right. Outside those specified circumstances, however, commonhold litigation will be controlled by rules that are yet to be made. It is likely that these rules will prescribe, as a minimum requirement, that recourse under the internal complaints procedure should first have been had. This is discussed in paragraph 6.18.2 of the text.

7.10.2 Is there likely to be a special procedure for such litigation?

Yes, although the details have yet to be worked out. It is likely that there will be a special Part of the Civil Procedure Rules dealing with such litigation. This topic is discussed further in Section 6.19 of the text.

7.10.3 Will there be any limitation periods applicable to such litigation?

Yes: the Act has introduced a new 6-year limitation period for actions to enforce a right or duty. Beyond that specific case, normal limitation periods will apply to other causes of action in respect of commonhold. These matters are discussed in Section 6.20 of the text.

7.11 RULES AND REGULATIONS

7.11.1 What rules and regulations apply to commonhold?

Much of the detail of the operation of the Act will be contained in rules and regulations which either already exist (in the case of rules under the Companies Act 1985 and the Insolvency Act 1986) or which will be brought in under rule and regulation-making powers contained in the Land Registration Act 2002 and the Act itself.

The principal new rules and regulations are the Commonhold (Land Registration) Rules which are in advanced draft form and the Commonhold Regulations, which remain in rudimentary form (see the Statutes etc part of this work).

In addition, provision is made for rules of court or tribunal procedure to be brought in (see section 66(4)). This power is likely to be exercised, although nothing is yet known of the shape of the likely provisions (which, in the case of court procedure, will take effect as the addition of a rule or rules to the Civil Procedure Rules). It is also possible that there will be tailor-made revisions to the rules under the Companies Act 1985 and the Insolvency Act 1986.

7.11.2 When is it likely that the new rules and regulations will be brought in?

The part of the Act dealing with commonhold cannot be brought into force until all the new rules and regulations necessary for its operation have been promulgated. At the time of writing (November 2003), the Land Registry has issued its report on the Commonhold (Land Registration) Rules, and they have been delivered to the Lord Chancellor's Department for final approval. The Commonhold Regulations are not so far advanced: although a Consultation Paper on their extent and substance was issued on 10 October 2002 with a consultation period which ended on 6 January 2003, the Lord Chancellor's Department has not met its target, announced in 2002, of producing a final draft by March 2003, although the Department of Constitutional Affairs has produced a Post-Consultation Report dated August 2003, which forecasts that the final drafts will be published before the end of 2003.

Chapter 8
BEST PRACTICE GUIDE: RUNNING A COMMONHOLD

8.1 INTRODUCTION

8.1.1 The focus of this Guide

This is a guide to the best practice to be used in running a commonhold. It is aimed at the directors of the commonhold association and their agents, who are primarily responsible for managing the commonhold. Unit-holders should, however, be aware of its provisions, both in order to understand how the directors can be expected to carry out their functions, and to gain a deeper insight into the complexities of the job.

Although this Guide cautions that it will be necessary for any commonhold association, no matter how small, to seek professional help from time to time, it has been written with the non-professional director in mind. Arcane legal problems and knotty questions of procedure, with which some of the other Chapters in this work have been compelled to deal, are left firmly alone.

8.1.2 Creation of the commonhold

This Guide is aimed at the operation of the commonhold once it has been set up as a functioning commonhold with unit-holders. It does not deal with the creation of the commonhold. Readers seeking guidance on that aspect of commonhold are directed to Chapter 2 of this work.

8.1.3 Definitions

This Guide is intended to be a readily understandable source of practical guidance for everyday use, rather than a technical document. It is, however, necessary for it to use a number of terms drawn from the Act (ie the Commonhold and Leasehold Reform Act 2002, which is referred to as the Act throughout this Guide). It is assumed that readers will be familiar with such terms as 'commonhold association', 'commonhold community statement' and 'memorandum and articles of association'. The following terms, which are used throughout this Guide, may, however, require further explanation:

• 'unit-holder'	the freehold owner of a commonhold unit
• 'commonhold unit'	the area belonging to the unit-holder, the physical boundaries of which are defined in the commonhold community statement
• 'common parts'	the area of commonhold land which does not comprise the commonhold units
• 'commonhold community statement'	the body of rules binding all unit-holders which governs most aspects of communal life in the commonhold
• 'commonhold assessment'	the process commencing with the estimate of the income needed by the commonhold association for running the commonhold over the next year, and ending with the commonhold levy
• 'commonhold levy'	the making of the demand for reimbursement of the unit-holder's proportion of the cost of running the commonhold
• 'reserve fund'	the fund to be accumulated for the repair and replacement of major parts of the commonhold
• 'reserve fund levy'	the making of the demand for the unit-holder's contribution to the reserve fund

8.1.4 Further reading

A fuller explanation of the operation of a commonhold is provided by Chapter 4 of this work.

8.1.5 Revision of this Guide

Although this Guide has been written with the benefit of experience of the working of commonholds in other jurisdictions, the authors hope and expect that it will be possible to modify and improve the advice given in the light of the operation of commonholds in England and Wales as the new Act beds down. The authors would be grateful for any suggestions for incorporation in the Guide, and will acknowledge messages sent to them at the following address:

letters: Commonhold, Falcon Chambers, Falcon Court, London EC4Y 1AA
e-mail: commonhold@falcon-chambers.co.uk

8.2 THE GOLDEN PRINCIPLES

8.2.1 Introduction

It is appropriate to commence the text of this Best Practice Guide with a list of principles to be applied in running a commonhold. These principles are not rules (the commonhold community statement has enough of those), but rather guidelines as to the way in which the rules should be approached and applied. Central to these principles, most of which interrelate, is the aim to produce a commonhold that will be not merely well run, but also harmonious.

8.2.2 Principle (1): know the rules

Although the commonhold structure outlined in the Act appears simple, a great deal lies below the waterline. The rules and regulations that go to make up the remainder of the structure are to be found in a number of different places (collated in this book). It is important that an officer of the commonhold association is familiar with the various rules, for the reasons explained in Section 8.3 below.

8.2.3 Principle (2): keep proper records

The commonhold association is statutorily obliged to keep certain records. There are other records, however, which the prudent association will keep in order to assist in the smooth administration of the commonhold. As time goes by, the nature of these records will become obvious. Section 8.4 below aims to avoid trial and error by providing a full list of the records that should be kept by the commonhold association from its creation.

8.2.4 Principle (3): be consistent

As the authorities from Commonwealth and other jurisdictions which are digested in the Digest of Cases illustrate, much litigation is caused not necessarily because of any malignant intention to thwart the will of the commonhold association (or its overseas equivalents), but rather because of a sense of unfairness that a privilege that has been allowed to other unit-holders in the past is being unfairly withheld from the litigating unit-holder. Consistency of approach will avoid or at least help to reduce this type of litigation, as Section 8.5 below explains.

8.2.5 Principle (4): have clear areas of responsibility

Problems often arise in practice when a well-meaning officer of a company is asked by a member for permission to do something, and gives an informal indication which is then taken as the relevant permission, with unfortunate results. The commonhold association should avoid this by ensuring that directors act within their own spheres of responsibility, and pass on queries outside their spheres to the relevant director. This topic is discussed in Section 8.6 below.

8.2.6 Principle (5): keep members informed

Members who are left in the dark about their governance, no matter how inadvertently, and no matter how unimportant the subject, are apt to become disgruntled, and to see plots or maladministration where none exists. Section 8.7 lays down some elementary guidelines.

8.2.7 Principle (6): take advice

It will be tempting for the small commonhold association to keep costs down by carrying out as much of the running of the association as it can without outside assistance. However, the commonhold association must be astute to ensure that such laudable motives do not lead to false economies. Where expert advice is needed, it should be sought. Section 8.8 points out the main areas where such advice will be indispensable.

8.2.8 Principle (7): use qualified personnel

Similarly, although we do not suggest that the officers of the commonhold association should be expensive professionals, mistakes will be made if the key posts are occupied by personnel who are not aware of what is expected of them. In the larger commonholds, the directors will be professionals, or will delegate to professionals. In the smaller commonholds, although it is to be expected that members will want to fill the posts as far as possible, the commonhold association should be careful to ensure that the members concerned are impressed by the importance of executing their duties professionally, as Section 8.9 explains.

8.2.9 Principle (8): be flexible

The commonhold association's primary duty is of course to manage the commonhold in accordance with the rules. This duty must not be applied too rigidly: the commonhold association is excused from the need to enforce a duty if no real harm would result. At the same time, however, it will be appreciated that not everyone sees things the same way: some people regard the observance of every last rule, no matter how minor, as a question of moral obligation. The well-run commonhold association's task will be to attempt to steer an effective middle course, as Section 8.10 below explains.

8.2.10 Principle (9): be astute to avoid conflicts of interest

The commonhold community statement contains rules dealing with the avoidance of situations in which a director of the commonhold association may be involved in a conflict of interest. Section 8.11 advises further caution in this regard.

8.2.11 Principle (10): use litigation as a last resort

Finally, although the principle that litigation should only be used as a last resort is also effectively a rule, its importance is worth stressing separately, as Section 8.12 explains.

8.3 THE RULES

8.3.1 Source of the rules

In this Section, we use the term 'rules' loosely to mean all the various provisions that control behaviour in commonhold. These rules are many and various, and originate from a number of different sources, which may be summarised as follows:

(a) The Act itself, which contains a number of provisions imposing obligations directly (for example the obligation section 35 imposes upon the directors of the commonhold association to exercise their powers to permit the enjoyment by each unit-holder of the freehold estate in his unit); and a rather greater number of provisions allowing for regulations to be made which will themselves impose duties (see (b), (c) and (d) below).

(b) Commonhold Regulations, promulgated pursuant to the many regulation-making powers in the Act. These regulations are complex, and will no doubt be supplemented with other regulations from time to time once the Government has had the opportunity to observe how the Act is working in practice.

(c) Commonhold (Land Registration) Rules: as their name implies, these rules control the important land registration issues affecting commonhold.

(d) Procedure Rules, which will govern the way in which commonhold litigation should be brought.

(e) The Companies Acts, and regulations made pursuant to those Acts, which apply to the commonhold association as a limited company (save to the extent that the Act provides otherwise).

(f) The Insolvency Acts, and rules made pursuant to those Acts, which apply in the event of the insolvency of the commonhold association or the termination of the commonhold.

The breadth and scope of those various sources of reference underline the importance of the commonhold being administered either by professional directors who are thoroughly versed in the legislative background of commonhold, or by member-directors who are prepared to sacrifice the time to learn the rules thoroughly themselves (see Section 8.9 below). That task will be made easier by the fact that, in practice, the main operational rules are to be found in the memorandum and articles of association of the commonhold association, on the one hand, and the commonhold community statement, on the other.

8.3.2 The memorandum and articles of association

These two documents form the constitution of the commonhold association. The memorandum describes the essential attributes of the commonhold association and its relationship with the outside world. The articles of association regulate the internal organisation and affairs of the commonhold association. They determine how the powers conferred on the commonhold association by the memorandum of association shall be exercised, and set out the detail of such matters as voting requirements and meeting procedure.

The content of both documents is largely prescribed by regulations made under the Act, and is standard for all commonhold associations, save for a specified range of matters where the members are allowed a free hand to decide their own procedures to suit their convenience.

A more detailed explanation of the memorandum and articles of association is provided in Part 1 of Chapter 4 of this work.

8.3.3 The commonhold community statement

The commonhold community statement is a document created by regulations made under the Act. It sets out the management framework and the rules of the commonhold including the rights and duties of the unit-holders and of the commonhold association. It will be the most important source of reference for the commonhold association as it manages the commonhold.

The commonhold community statement is not entirely comprehensive and must be read in conjunction with the memorandum and articles of association and with the registers of the common parts and unit titles. In the event of any conflict between the memorandum and articles and the commonhold community statement, the provisions of the memorandum and articles will prevail.

A more detailed explanation of the content and effect of the commonhold community statement is provided in Chapter 4 of this work.

8.3.4 Knowing the rules

Quite apart from the fact that a director of a commonhold association should be expected to know the rules which inform him how to govern the company with which he has been entrusted, there are a number of practical considerations which underline the need for thorough familiarity:

(a) Knowledge of the rules will prevent mistakes arising in the conduct of applications by unit-holders, for example for permission to install satellite dishes, or keep animals. If such activities are prohibited, but the directors allow them in the mistaken belief that they are permitted, then problems are likely to arise in the future once the true position is revealed.

(b) Knowledge of the rules will lead to greater efficiency in dealing with administration.

(c) It is safe to assume that one or more members of the commonhold will acquire a thorough knowledge of the rules. If this knowledge is not matched by the directors, this may lead to a loss of confidence by the members in the directors, with unfortunate results.

Greater indulgence towards the directors is of course to be expected in the case of small commonholds, where the directors will in practice be indistinguishable from the members. Familiarity with fellow members should not, however, be used as an excuse for failure to get to grips with the elements of the commonhold community statement and the memorandum and articles of association. Experience of similar systems abroad shows that it is when a commonhold is run in loose disregard of the rules that it is at its most vulnerable, with years of expensive litigation the predictable outcome.

8.4 RECORD KEEPING

8.4.1 Introduction

In addition to the records which the commonhold association is bound to keep because of the mandatory requirements discussed in Section 4.4 of the text, prudent commonhold associations will also keep careful records of the following:

(a) Copies of all consents and other documents sent to unit-holders recording matters relating to the operation of the commonhold.

(b) Correspondence with unit-holders.

(c) Documents generated during the course of building works.

(d) Copies of notices and other documents generated during the course of disputes.

The grounds underlying this principle are straightforward. First, while the Minutes Book will show what decisions have been taken, the reasons will rarely be apparent. It will be important to show new members who may be unfamiliar with the past that the decision currently confronting them has been made for the same reasons on a number of occasions in the past. Secondly, a documented series of precedents will assist and protect the directors when an issue is raised which has been dealt with in the past. Thirdly, a written record will assist in handovers between directors (see paragraph 8.4.9 below).

The categories of document referred to above, and the particular reasons for keeping them, are examined below.

8.4.2 Consents

There will be occasions on which a unit-holder will ask the commonhold association for permission to do something that the commonhold community statement either does not allow, or allows only with the consent of the directors. If the commonhold association does not keep good records, it will be open to a unit-holder to contend, even if this is not the case, that consent was given, but has been lost. Even though it is perhaps likely that such a contention would not ultimately be sustained, the commonhold association will wish to eliminate the potential for argument. It can do this by establishing a foolproof system which records each and every consent ever given.

8.4.3 Correspondence

Similarly, it will be prudent for the commonhold association to keep copies of all correspondence received and sent relating to the operation of the commonhold. There is also much to be said for attendance notes to be kept of relevant conversations at meetings and on the telephone. This activity should not be hidden; rather it should be advertised and celebrated as a mark of the commonhold association's efficiency. Such notes need not be verbatim: it will suffice if they record the points of importance, and note the date, time, location and identities of the speakers.

8.4.4 Construction documents

Invoices for works and services should obviously be kept for the annual audit and tax return. Other non-financial documents generated by works and services that do not fall within this requirement should be carefully reviewed before destruction in order to see whether they have any residual value. Quotations from unsuccessful tenderers for a contract may be useful for later comparison purposes, or to defeat any accusation that a project was not properly costed. Design drawings and other plans will obviously come in useful if there is any later query about pipe runs or other construction details. Specifications will show what types of materials were used. Warranties may have to be called upon.

There will be many such examples of documents which will have continuing value, and which should therefore be kept. The test the directors should apply is:

would a prudent man having these works carried out or services supplied to his own home wish to keep the details?

8.4.5 Dispute resolution documents

Chapter 6 of this work analyses the various procedures open to the commonhold association in the event of a dispute with a unit-holder which cannot be resolved by informal means. Whether the dispute resolution process thereafter takes the form of the commonhold association's internal complaints procedure, a reference to the commonhold ombudsman, litigation, or any other form of alternative dispute resolution, it is clear that there will be a potential for a number of documents to be generated. At its simplest, the internal complaints procedure involves the use of standard forms, drafts of which may be found in the Forms and Precedents part of this work.

There is no formal requirement that material of this kind should be kept, but there is clearly a case for retention. Should the matter become litigious, the court will want to see what steps the commonhold association has taken to resolve the dispute by less contentious means. It will be important to be able to show the court the existence of a paper trail illustrating these steps, commencing with correspondence, continuing with the correct and timely use of the internal complaints procedure forms, and culminating with an overt consideration of other available means.

8.4.6 Keeping records

When the documents considered above are added to the categories of document that the commonhold association is bound to keep as a matter of statutory requirement, it will be seen that the storage requirement may well be considerable.

To some extent, the storage requirement may be alleviated by the use of electronic records: correspondence and other material emanating from the commonhold association could be kept on disk; other documents could also be scanned and stored on disk. It is to be expected, however, that some members will feel more comfortable with a paper record, because this is both easier to handle and read, and more easily marshalled in chronological order. At least until current habits change, therefore, it will be sensible to plan for a means of paper storage that will be secure, dry, clean and readily accessible. A filing cabinet or cabinets in one of the units or in part of the limited use common parts provides an obvious venue.

8.4.7 Updating records

A record is only valuable if it is kept up to date. The commonhold association should ensure that the way in which the commonhold is run in practice is mirrored by the contents of the commonhold community statement and the other sources of the relevant rules. Agreed departures from the rules should be recorded, and if the departures are considered to be anything other than temporary, then consideration should be given to an amendment to the commonhold community statement which will then have to be made the subject of an application to the Land Registry (see Section 2.18). Although this approach might be regarded as unnecessarily formulaic, it will help to prevent disputes arising based upon an irregular practice to which the commonhold association has traditionally turned a blind eye.

8.4.8 Inspection and copying of records

Article 80 of the articles of association extends to the members of the commonhold association the right to inspect records which the commonhold association is obliged to keep (see paragraph 4.4.11 of the text of Chapter 4). It would be sensible to allow this right to be extended to those documents discussed in this Section, save of course those documents which concern another member, and are rightly regarded as private.

A refusal to disclose records without good reason will engender suspicion, and will create the feeling that, contrary to the spirit of the commonhold legislation, which seeks to avoid the antagonistic relationship which characterises leasehold, the directors are intent on dividing the commonhold into two camps: the rulers and the ruled. That impression is one that the directors should be astute to avoid, and a ready and positive response to a request for inspection of records will do much to help in that regard.

If members are given access to records, then it would be sensible to keep the records in a location which, although secure, is freely accessible, with, ideally, adjacent facilities for inspection and copying.

8.4.9 Handover

From time to time, directors or personnel in the employ of the commonhold association will change, and records will need to be handed over. It will be important to ensure that there is a protocol to assist in this process. There may not be time for an orderly handover (by reason of incapacity or inadvertence), and the documents may be assembled in such a way as to require an explanation for which a mere oral briefing would not suffice.

We therefore suggest that a protocol be drawn up for use in the event of handovers and to serve as an aide-mémoire should the need arise. The protocol should explain the location of each category of document, both globally ('in Unit X') and specifically ('in the folder marked 'Y' in the blue filing cabinet'); it should set out the commonhold association's policy regarding inspection and copying; it should state the identities or posts of those officers of the commonhold association who are charged with the safe keeping and security of the documents; and it should state whether back-up copies or electronic versions of the documents are kept and, if so, where.

8.5 CONSISTENCY

8.5.1 The problem

A common problem that has arisen in overseas jurisdictions is that of the unit-holder who would have been content with a ban on, say, the erection of satellite dishes, but is understandably perplexed and vexed because his neighbour was in the past allowed to install his own dish. This situation often provokes litigation, either by the unit-holder (who seeks a declaration that the commonhold association is estopped by its conduct from objecting, or is taken to have waived its right), or by the commonhold association (which seeks an injunction to prevent the unit-holder going ahead with his stated intention to erect a dish regardless).

This problem often stems from inadvertence: a lack of familiarity with the rules leading to consent having been given erroneously in the past; a failure to enforce past transgressions; or an officer of the association having given approval on a matter falling outside his sphere of responsibility. But whatever the origin of the inconsistent treatment, the impression given is of an association that is at best incompetent and at worst discriminatory.

8.5.2 The remedy

The remedy to this problem of inconsistent treatment is not to allow inconsistency to arise in the first place. In practice, if principles (1) (know the rules), (2) (keep proper records) and (4) (maintain clear areas of responsibility) are carefully applied, the problem of inconsistent treatment should never arise.

This principle is highly important: litigation from the Commonwealth and elsewhere shows that unit-holders feel very strongly about discrimination of this kind, and are prepared to spend substantial sums on costs even where what is at issue (a garden shed; an aerial; a pet) may seem unimportant by any objective standard. Even if litigation is not the outcome, the bad feeling that may be engendered does not augur well for the future well-being of the commonhold.

8.6 CLEAR AREAS OF RESPONSIBILITY

8.6.1 The problem

A unit-holder approaches the treasurer for permission to keep a cat in his unit. The treasurer does not live in the commonhold; he is busy finalising the annual accounts; he is unfamiliar with the commonhold community statement (other than those aspects of it which relate to financial matters); and he is keen on dogs. He answers the request with words to the effect 'I can't see any harm in it—it's OK by me.' The unit-holder takes this to mean that he has permission, notwithstanding the standing prohibition in the commonhold community statement. He installs a catflap in his unit at some expense, buys a cat, and invests heavily in pet-care products and animal insurance. His cat proceeds to foul the gardens in the common parts, to the general outrage of the other unit-holders, who demand that the commonhold association take action to have the cat removed. The unit-holder will not be swayed, pointing to the expenditure he has incurred in reliance upon the treasurer's words.

This situation is not far-fetched. Stories like it abound in the litigation reported from overseas. At the kernel of a substantial number of the reports is a careless remark made by an officer of the association, commenting upon matters not within his expertise or knowledge, which is then treated by the unit-holder as the requisite carte blanche to proceed.

8.6.2 The remedy

Again, the solution to the problem posed above is not to let the situation arise in the first place. The treasurer of the commonhold association should decline to deal with enquiries that do not fall within his expertise, just as, to take one further example, the compliance officer (see paragraph 8.9.4 below) should pass on enquiries relating to financial matters.

This refusal to deal with enquiries may come across as pedantic and unhelpful if not courteously handled and carefully explained. All that the director in question need say is that he is not the proper officer to deal with the query, and that the appropriate officer to ask will be the treasurer (or as the case may be). If necessary, the officer approached should volunteer to pass the query on himself, although in that event he should make it clear that approval should not be assumed to have been given in the meantime. The officer should also be astute to avoid giving any impression that the unit-holder can depend upon a positive outcome. In cases where difficulty may be anticipated, it may be prudent to follow up the initial contact with a letter referring to the query, and summarising the outcome of the initial discussion. For example:

> As I explained to you, I am not authorised to deal with such proposals. If you wish to take matters further, you should take up your enquiry with X, who deals with applications of this kind on behalf of the association. You should not proceed further with your proposal in the meantime.

8.6.3 Advertising the responsibilities

It will assist if the unit-holders are aware of the commonhold association's policy regarding this principle, and are given reminders from time to time of the areas of responsibility of the various directors. Suitable opportunities for such reminders will include annual general meetings and any newsletters the commonhold association may distribute.

8.6.4 Holiday cover

The proposed separation of responsibility between directors will require careful management. The association's aim should be to maintain sufficient qualified personnel so that there is always someone available on reasonable notice to deal with the problems that may arise.

This will be particularly important in the holiday season. It will frustrate unit-holders if they find that the compliance officer, to whom all enquiries of a particular nature should be directed, has gone overseas for two months without leaving a responsible replacement. If necessary, the use of alternate directors should be considered (see paragraph 4.3.5 of the text).

8.7 DISSEMINATION OF INFORMATION

8.7.1 The problem

In the context of leasehold, the unwillingness of landlords and their agents to divulge full details of steps supposedly being taken on their leaseholders' behalf is legendary, although the opportunities for such behaviour have been much reduced by legislation in recent years.

The motive behind this unwillingness varies from landlord to landlord. Unscrupulous landlords may be seeking to hide the secret commissions earned by way of discounts on block insurance policies, or kickbacks on building contracts. Otherwise well-meaning landlords may simply wish to avoid the potential for challenge that accompanies greater dissemination of information.

8.7.2 The solution

The culture of secrecy should have no place in commonhold. Even if the directors consider that there is no need for the unit-holders to learn of the minutiae of a particular works contract, any refusal to divulge the detail upon request will come across as lofty disdain at best; as something to hide at worst.

We do not suggest that unit-holders should routinely be copied in on each and every detail of every aspect of the administration of the commonhold: that would add unnecessarily to the costs of management. But it will be important to ensure that unit-holders are informed in broad outline of the progress of major projects and of any changes to plans, with reasons; and that any reasonable request for information is met promptly. The directors should, in other words, treat such matters, within obvious limitations, as a householder would if he were running his own house.

8.7.3 Newsletter

One obvious way of disseminating information, which the authors would encourage, is a newsletter. With the advent of desktop publishing, newsletters can be made interesting, informative and inexpensive to produce.

The opportunity afforded by a newsletter can be taken to blend social news ('barbecue next month') with reminders of rules ('don't forget that parking lots should only be used for parking') and announcements of the onset of major works ('external redecoration starts next Monday; please remember to leave your window locks disengaged').

8.8 ADVICE

8.8.1 Introduction

There are many instances where a homeowner will be tempted to cut corners by, for example, constructing an extension without the assistance of an architect; or filing a tax return without consulting an accountant; or estimating the reinstatement value of his house for insurance purposes without recourse to a valuer. Although some of those decisions may come back to haunt the homeowner, the consequences of his economies will for the most part impact only on him.

Commonhold is different. Here the understandable wish to make economies must take second place to prudence. The commonhold association must feel that it is able to take professional advice when it needs to do so. In each of the examples given above, recourse to a professional would have been sensible, and in some cases essential, as this Section explains.

8.8.2 Surveyor

As paragraph 4.9.3 of the text notes, the commonhold community statement does not lay down any generalised standard for repair and maintenance of the buildings in the commonhold.

Added to this, rule 31 requires the directors to prepare a reserve fund study at least every ten years as the basis of calculation of the amount of the contributions for the reserve fund (see paragraph 4.16.3 of the text). That study should be carried out with the assistance of such surveyors, engineers or other professional advisers as may be appropriate.

In both the above respects, the authors suggest that expert advice will be essential, and counsel against the alternative of a member director with a passing acquaintance with the subject volunteering to carry out those tasks instead. The members of the association are entitled to the benefit of good, impartial advice on such important matters, particularly when the consequences of error may not merely be expensive, but may also poison relationships within the commonhold.

A valuation surveyor will also need to be involved in the calculation of the reinstatement value of the commonhold (see paragraph 8.8.5). It is unlikely in any event that major insurers would accept calculations done on any other basis.

8.8.3 Accountant

As a limited company subject to the Companies Acts, the commonhold association will be obliged to have its accounts audited annually by an accountant. Beyond this, however, there is much to be said for more frequent recourse to an accountant. There may well be ways in which the financial affairs of the association could be streamlined; there may be pitfalls to be avoided; there may be a need for general financial advice that would not be appreciated by directors without that particular expertise.

A convenient starting point for this enquiry would be the annual audit. On that occasion, the directors might like to make it their practice to seek a general review of the way in which the financing of the commonhold could be improved.

8.8.4 Legal advice

Commonhold is a vehicle designed by the Government to be user-friendly, and to be capable of running without the need for legal advice. The forms designed for its operation have been kept simple and jargon-free. The rules are written in plain English.

So long as the rules are followed and the forms are used, no particular difficulty should arise, and we lawyers will languish on the sidelines. There will be occasions, however, when the unexpected will occur, and seemingly intractable problems will arise. Where the financial flow to the commonhold association is interrupted as a result, the problem should not be left to fester. In leasehold, where services charges are unpaid, the sale of the flat belonging to the non-paying leaseholder will usually result in payment being forthcoming, if only because the incoming leaseholder will be advised not to buy a lease that might be subject to forfeiture. In commonhold, by contrast, the incentive, although present, is much reduced, because units are freely transferable: although incoming unit-holders will be liable for existing debts, forfeiture has no role to play. Without corrective action, therefore, there may be little opportunity in commonhold for long-running disputes to be resolved. Accordingly, if a dispute appears incapable of resolution, and the commonhold association's internal complaints procedure has failed to yield a satisfactory result, then the directors should ensure that legal advice is taken, if the financial health of the commonhold association is not to be compromised.

The obtaining of legal advice should not be restricted to those areas where a dispute has already become apparent. Directors should also be careful to have new ventures checked unless they are sure that there will be no adverse legal consequences. Many have cause to rue the day they entered into a so-called 'gentleman's agreement', only to find out that they have granted formidable security of tenure to a supposed licensee. A little time spent with a lawyer prior to any such agreement would have saved a great deal of time and trouble.

8.8.5 Insurance

In the case of buildings insurance, rule 18 of the commonhold community statement provides that the level of cover must be based upon the costs of rebuilding or reinstating the property properly calculated by a member of the Royal Institution of Chartered Surveyors. In this important instance, the commonhold association has no alternative but to obtain proper professional advice.

8.9 PERSONNEL

8.9.1 Introduction

The last Section has dealt with the need for the directors to have recourse to outside expertise from time to time. This Section considers the ways in which the commonhold association can organise and staff itself to make the best use of its own resources.

8.9.2 Company secretary

The commonhold association is obliged to employ a company secretary, whose role is to be its chief administrative officer (see paragraph 4.7.3 of the text). A good company secretary will be a valuable addition to the commonhold association, taking all the burden of correspondence and other routine tasks off the shoulders of the directors. There is no reason why the company secretary should not also be responsible for compliance (see paragraph 8.9.4 below).

8.9.3 Treasurer

Although it is not a legal requirement for the commonhold association to have a treasurer, there is a need for the association to have a director or committee specifically tasked with overseeing its financial management. Duties will include:

(a) Keeping proper records of income and expenditure.

(b) Preparing financial records for audit.

(c) Preparing the annual estimate for the purposes of the commonhold assessment (see paragraph 4.15.3).

(d) Preparing and disseminating the annual report and budget (see paragraph 4.15.4).

(e) Being prepared to speak on the annual report and budget at the general meeting called to approve the expenditure (see paragraph 4.15.4).

(f) Calculating the commonhold levy and sending out the demands (see paragraphs 4.15.6 and 4.15.7).

(g) Preparing for any further assessments that may be necessary (see paragraph 4.15.9).

(h) Ensuring that the reserve fund studies are carried out at the appropriate intervals, and that the correct reserve fund levies are sent out and paid (see Section 4.16).

(i) Recommending when action should be taken in respect of outstanding unpaid levies.

The treasurer's role is not therefore a mechanical one. He, or his committee, will need in particular to prepare the commonhold budgets carefully, and be prepared to defend them. Thoroughness at this stage will reduce the necessity for further assessments arising through failure to prepare for an obvious contingency. It will also contribute to the impression that the financial management of the association is in safe hands, and keep the unit-holders content.

8.9.4 Compliance officer

The Commonwealth cases and decisions from other overseas jurisdictions show that the three leading topics in commonhold litigation are sheds (whether they can be erected by unit-holder on limited use common parts), pets (whether they should be allowed) and alterations (whether they should be reversed). In most of the cases, there is little dispute over whether the offending activity is allowed—because the written rules are usually clearly to the effect that they are not. Instead, the dispute usually concentrates on the fact that the commonhold association has allowed the offending activity to go on elsewhere: it has 'turned a blind eye'. In those circumstances, the argument continues, the blind-eye policy should continue in the case of the unit-holder who wishes the same indulgence.

If the offending activity is really one the commonhold association wishes to terminate, then it will want to forestall such arguments being based upon precedent by ensuring that the precedents themselves are never allowed to arise. The best way of doing this is to have a compliance officer charged with policing the commonhold.

The compliance officer's secondary, but equally critical, role will be to respond to disputes as and when they arise, and to ensure that the commonhold association's internal complaints procedure is correctly applied (see Part 2 of Chapter 6, and in particular paragraph 6.5.3). Experience of the Independent Housing Ombudsman Scheme (see Part 3 of Chapter 6) shows that a substantial number of the complaints in the housing sphere arise not because of malfeasance on the part of housing associations, but rather because of failure to react to a grievance properly and in time. Response time is therefore critical, and it will be essential to have cover for this role if the compliance officer is on holiday or otherwise indisposed.

The compliance officer will fail strategically, even if his policing tactics are good, if he fails to bring to his job the considerable tact and charm that will be required in order to hold the ring between unit-holders who may possess very different ideas about compliance. He should not forget that it is not every incident to which the commonhold association ought to react (see Section 8.10 below), and that successful commonhold living will involve a degree of tolerance and compromise.

8.10 FLEXIBILITY

8.10.1 Introduction

The starting point for any consideration of management of a commonhold must be the body of rules applying to it, and for that reason the first golden principle above emphasises the importance of knowing those rules. Other principles in turn stress the need to apply those rules, and to apply them consistently.

All this is not to say that the commonhold association should operate an oppressive regime where every minor transgression is punished, no matter how trivial the result. Quite apart from the costs of operating such a regime, it is doubtful whether commonhold in such circumstances would have any adherents. This Section therefore counsels a certain lightness of approach when it comes to policing the commonhold.

8.10.2 The statutory basis for leniency

Section 35(3) of the Act provides that, in the event of a default (say a breach of a rule in the commonhold community statement) by a unit-holder, the directors of the commonhold association:

> (a) need not take action if they reasonably think that inaction is in the best interests of establishing or maintaining harmonious relationships between all the unit-holders, and that it will not cause any unit-holder (other than the defaulter) significant loss or significant disadvantage . . .

This section, which is considered in paragraph 6.3.5 of the text, effectively absolves the commonhold association of liability for the enforcement of the rules in appropriate circumstances.

8.10.3 Appropriate circumstances

The appropriate circumstances for the exercise of leniency rather than the insistence of rigid adherence to the rules are where *both* the (reasonable) view is taken by the directors that inaction—ie a decision not to enforce the rules—will lead to greater peace and harmony between unit-holders; *and* no unit-holder other than the defaulter will be caused significant loss or disadvantage.

In weighing up their decision, the directors will wish in addition to bear in mind the following factors:

(a) The gravity of the default. If the default is serious, then it may well be the case that it has caused significant loss or disadvantage to another unit-holder. Whether or not it has done so, the default may be so serious that it cannot be left unchallenged.

(b) The precedent value of the default. If the directors take the view that other unit-holders will wish to do the same, with the result that one comparatively minor incident will be grossed up into something unacceptable, then they may decide that it would after all be appropriate to act.

(c) The cost of taking remedial action. If litigation is the only effective means by which the transgression may be cured, then the sheer cost of taking proceedings may act as a disincentive—see Section 8.12 below.

(d) They must, above all, act reasonably. This requirement of the Act imports an objective measure: the directors must behave as anyone else would in their stead.

Much will turn on the reactions of the other unit-holders. If a substantial body support leniency, then that should condition the response of the directors.

8.10.4 Financial considerations

Finally, the relative financial strengths of the unit-holders is worth considering as part of the topic of flexibility. Commonhold binds a number of different freehold owners together, and obliges them to pay fixed percentages for work done and services supplied without regard to the individual benefit each may derive. In this respect, it is of course no different from leasehold, where service charges are payable according to percentages fixed in leases. In leasehold, an inability to pay a high service charge bill is, more often than the detractors of leasehold are prepared to acknowledge, often met by an offer by the landlord to accept payment by instalments, or some other form of funding arrangement.

It would be a shame if commonhold did not attract the same level of generosity in appropriate circumstances, particularly where the financial difficulty has come about through a commitment to a high level of funding for the reserve fund. The commonhold association may for example consider providing for payment of the commonhold assessment levy to be made by instalments (see paragraph 4.15.7 of the text). A commonhold with solvent members will be preferable to one with members struggling financially.

8.11 CONFLICTS OF INTEREST

8.11.1 Introduction

Paragraphs 4.3.10, 4.3.11 and 4.3.14 of the text set out the rules intended to prevent conflicts of interest arising, while preserving directors' rights to profit from their links with other organisations. A situation that may often arise in practice will be that of an outside director who owns a construction company, and who will naturally wish the commonhold's works contract to be awarded to that company. The rules provide that there is nothing wrong with this arrangement, provided that the interest is first disclosed to the other directors, and the interested director is banned from voting.

8.11.2 Interests of the members

When such decisions are being taken, however, the interests of the members should not be overlooked. No matter how open and honest the interested director has been, and no matter how uninfluenced his fellow directors have been in making their selection of his company, it would not be unexpected for the members to draw different conclusions. Where relations between directors and members are good, this may not matter. Where, however, relations are not harmonious, such interests will be likely to fuel members' suspicions that they are not being treated fairly. In those circumstances, the correct advice will be not to stand by the rules, but to err on the side of caution.

8.12 LITIGATION AS A LAST RESORT

8.12.1 Introduction

The text of the first page of Chapter 6 contains these words:

> The preferred approach of the Act is to treat litigation as a remedy of last resort, and to encourage the parties to a dispute to engage in alternative dispute resolution, ranging from an internal complaints procedure, at the lowest level, to the engagement of an ombudsman, mediator or arbitrator. When all else fails, the parties may have recourse to the courts.

This principle finds expression in section 35(3)(b) of the Act, which encourages the directors to:

> . . . have regard to the desirability of using arbitration, mediation or conciliation procedures (including referral under a scheme approved under section 42) instead of legal proceedings wherever possible.

This discouragement of litigation—the final golden principle—is examined in this Section.

8.12.2 Disadvantages of litigation

The evident disadvantages of litigation—the cost and the delay—can pale into insignificance when set against the rancour caused to neighbours who have then to continue living in close proximity, often divided into bitterly opposed camps of supporters. Judges hearing disputes are very aware of this, and strive to find words in their judgments which leave crumbs of comfort for the vanquished. Those who give untruthful evidence are rarely stigmatised as liars, but are referred to as being mistaken in their recollection, while struggling to grapple with the passage of time. Despite such delicate treatment, litigants (even winners) rarely leave court with a feeling of satisfaction. For that reason, litigation must be regarded as the choice that remains when all else has been tried and found wanting.

8.12.3 Alternatives to litigation

The Act is not short of alternatives to litigation for commonholders. First, the commonhold community statement contains its own internal complaints procedure, which must be used by complainants unless there are good reasons to the contrary (see Part 2 of Chapter 6). Secondly, regulations made under the Act create a dedicated commonhold ombudsman scheme, which complainants will be encouraged to use (see Part 3 of Chapter 6). Thirdly, complainants are encouraged to have resort to the full panoply of alternative dispute resolution procedures which are available to all those with an unsatisfied grievance (see Part 4 of Chapter 6).

8.12.4 Restraints on litigation

Even if the complainant tries the alternative dispute resolution procedures described in paragraph 8.12.3 above and finds them wanting, it is by no means certain that he will then be allowed to litigate without restriction. The right to litigate under the Act is made subject to regulation which circumscribes that right, as paragraph 6.19.5 explains.

PART B
DIGEST OF CASES

Digest of Cases—Contents

ALPERT v LE'LISA CONDOMINIUM

667 AR 2d 947 (1995)

Bloom, Murphy and Salmon JJ.

United States of America: Court of Special Appeals of Maryland

Condominium—common parts included parking spaces—some parking spaces covered, some open air—board assigning covered parking spaces to unit owners on basis of length of ownership—whether valid regulation of use of common areas—whether invalid exclusion of owners from common areas

The Le'Lisa Condominium contained 32 residential units. Its common elements included 20 parking spaces under the building, which were shielded from the elements, and a further 12 in the open air. From 1984, the covered parking spaces had been assigned by the condominium board to individual unit owners, based on the length of ownership in the condominium. When a unit with a covered parking space was sold, the parking space was reassigned to the most longstanding unit owner who was not currently assigned a covered space. The claimant unit owners bought their unit in the belief that it included the right to a covered parking space, and objected to the board's reassignment of the space to another, longstanding, unit owner. They claimed that the condominium board had no authority to assign individual parking spaces for the exclusive use of individual unit owners. The council of unit owners reacted by passing a new by-law, which codified the existing practice. It was passed by a majority of the unit owners at a special meeting, with the claimants objecting. The claimants claimed the by-law was invalid and sought declaratory and injunctive relief. They claimed that the assignment of parking spaces to individual owners changed the interests of other owners in the common elements, by excluding them from parts thereof, and therefore required a unanimously approved amendment to the condominium declaration.

HELD:

Under the Maryland Condominium Act, all unit owners owned the common elements as tenants in common. The common elements could only be used for the purposes for which they were intended, and were subject to mutual rights of enjoyment by all unit owners. The Act and Le'Lisa's by-laws provided for the affairs of the condominium to be governed by a board of directors. The Act gave the board the power '*to regulate the use*, maintenance, repair, replacement and modification of common elements'. The by-laws authorised the board to promulgate and enforce 'such rules and regulations and such restrictions on or requirements as may be deemed proper respecting the general and limited common elements as are designated to prevent unreasonable interference with the use and occupancy . . . of the general and limited common elements by the members . . .'.

The issue was therefore whether the assignment of parking spaces amounted to a change in the interests of the various owners in the common elements, requiring a unanimously approved amendment to the condominium declaration; or whether it was merely a regulation of the use of a common element, in which case the by-law amendment was sufficient.

'There is a distinct difference between cases in which exclusive use, control and/or ownership of the common areas is taken from some or all of the unit owners, and cases in which some reasonable restrictions or regulation of the common areas is imposed on all owners.
. . .

Inherent in the condominium concept is the principle that to promote the health, happiness and peace of mind of the majority of the unit owners, since they are living in such close proximity and using facilities in common, each unit owner must give up a certain degree of freedom of choice which he might otherwise enjoy in separate, privately owned, property. Condominium unit owners comprise a little democratic sub-society, of necessity more restrictive, as it pertains to the use of condominium property, than may be existent outside the condominium organisation.'

The condominium had restricted the use of parking spaces to avoid a chaotic free-for-all. Each unit owner was assigned a parking space, and each was able to become eligible for the preferred spaces. It was a restriction related to promoting the health, happiness and peace of mind of all the unit owners. It did not amount to the permanent grant of exclusive use of a part of the common elements to particular owners.

Digested case considered in this judgment

Sawko v Dominion Plaza One Condominium Association (1991)

Note

For rules relating to the parking of vehicles, see paragraphs 4.12.5 and 4.12.8 of the text. For restrictions on the use of the common parts, see paragraph 4.12.6 of the text. For limited use areas of the common parts, see paragraph 4.12.7 of the text.

ASHINGTON HOLDINGS PTY LTD v WIPEMA SERVICES PTY LTD (NO 2)

[97726] 9 BPR (1998)

Young J

Australia: Supreme Court of New South Wales, Equity Division

Strata title—exercise by tenant of option for grant of lease of floor of freehold building—subsequent registration of strata title scheme in respect of building—landlord proffered lease of floor of building, subject to strata title scheme—whether landlord entitled to specific performance of option agreement—whether lease of floor as strata title unit different from lease of freehold floor

It had been determined in previous proceedings that the defendant tenant had exercised its option under a lease. The option provided for the lessor to grant a new lease of the seventh floor of a building, on the same terms as the old lease apart from certain specified exceptions. A strata scheme had subsequently been registered in respect of the relevant property. The claimant proffered a new lease to the defendant, which was virtually identical to the old lease. However, although the physical area to be used by the tenant was the same, in consequence of the registration of the strata scheme the boundaries of the demise were the internal walls of the seventh floor, rather than (as under the old lease) the whole of the seventh floor of the building. All pipes and cabling entered the lot from the common property of the strata scheme. The claimant claimed specific performance.

HELD:

The claimant was not entitled to specific performance. The fact that the seventh floor was now part of a strata title scheme meant that the new lease would not be over the same land. As well as the new boundaries to the land being the internal, rather than the external, walls of the seventh floor, the nature of the land was different. The rights of a freeholder in strata are different from the rights of a standard freeholder, since they are restricted by the strata scheme and the legislation governing it. The maintenance of the building and its common parts was now to be undertaken by the body corporate of the scheme, and not by the claimant. The body corporate would be able via by-laws to restrict the activities of the tenant, whereas such regulation would previously have been under the control of the claimant. The service charge provisions under the lease were affected by the right of the body corporate to levy assessments under the strata title scheme. For all those reasons, the new lease proffered by the landlord was not in accordance with its obligation under the option, and the claimant was not entitled to specific performance.

Note

For an overview of the nature of commonhold compared to standard freehold, see Section 1.2 of the text.

DISHER v FARNWORTH

[1993] 3 NZLR 412

McKay and Robertson JJ. and Sir Gordon Bisson

New Zealand: Court of Appeal, Wellington

Unit titles—definition of unit on unit plan included upper height limit—common property defined as so much of the scheme land as was not comprised in any unit—building constructed on unit extending into airspace above upper height limit—whether airspace above upper height limit of unit was common property—whether mandatory injunction should be granted for demolition of unit above upper height limit

Mrs Disher was the owner of a stratum estate in fee simple under the Unit Titles Act 1972 (NZ) in two units designated A and C on the unit plan. She lived in unit A. Mrs Farnworth and another were the owners of unit B. The three units were contiguous in line, on a slope: A being the highest, B the lowest, with C in the middle. Unit A enjoyed a view of the sea over units B and C. The unit plan was registered in 1987 and included a schedule setting out the respective areas, unit entitlements and upper and lower height limits for each of the units A, B and C. The upper height limit for unit B was shown as 13m and the lower height limit as 7.5m, measured from a fixed point on the site. Mrs Farnworth subsequently built a residence on unit B, of which most of the first storey roof and an upper lookout room exceeded the 13m upper height limit. Mrs Disher claimed that by exceeding the upper height limit for unit B as defined on the unit plan, Mrs Farnworth's residence intruded into the common property in contravention of the rules of the body corporate. She claimed that she had suffered loss of view and diminution in the value of her property; that Mrs Farnworth had built with full knowledge that the height limit would be exceeded; and that she was entitled to a mandatory injunction requiring Mrs Farnworth to remove so much of the offending dwelling as was necessary to comply with the height limit.

HELD:

'Unit' was defined by s 2 of the Unit Titles Act 1972 as meaning 'a part of the land consisting of a space of any shape situated below, on, or above the surface of the land, or partly in one such situation and partly in another or others, all the dimensions of which are limited, and that is designed for separate ownership'. A unit was thus a space of which all the dimensions were limited, and was not defined only by reference to land surface boundaries. Its dimensions in the vertical plane must also be limited, thus enabling separate ownership of different floors in a multi-storey building. The 'Common Property' was defined as 'so much of the land [in the unit title scheme] as is not comprised in any unit'. Under s 4 of the Act it was the registration of the plan specifying the units that effected the subdivision of the scheme land and brought into existence the stratum estates. The right to use the airspace over the whole of the land was one of the incidents of ownership attaching to the registered proprietor of the original certificate of title. Applying the statutory definitions, all the rights of the original owner falling outside the limited dimensions of the units shown on the unit plan must be common property and under the control of the body corporate. The airspace above the scheme was therefore common property, and comprised the whole of the airspace above the upper height limits of the units shown on the unit plan. It extended upwards in the same way that the original freehold title included rights to airspace; it did not have any measurable upper boundary. Although it was not shown on the unit plan as common property, it did not need to be. The intrusion into the airspace above the upper height limit of unit B without the consent of the body corporate was therefore an infringement of the rights of the other unit-holders. However, to order removal of the roof and lookout room would be a draconian remedy, disproportionate to any harm suffered by Mrs Disher from the loss of some of her view. Further, Mrs Disher and Mrs Farnsworth had each inherited their units from a common testator, and the only reason they had inherited unit titles rather than standard freehold titles (which would not have had any height limit) was due to the mistakes and misunderstandings of others in implementing the terms of the will. It was clearly not a case for a mandatory injunction. Mrs Disher was entitled to damages of $15,000 in lieu of an injunction, in respect of the diminution in the value of her house.

Note

For the definition of the extent of a commonhold unit, see paragraph 2.17.3 of the text.

GAFFNY v REID

628 A 2d 155 (1993)

Wathen CJ and Roberts, Glassman, Clifford, Collins, Rudman and Dana, JJ

United States of America: Supreme Judicial Court of Maine

Condominium—by-law providing that nothing might be altered or constructed in the common areas, nor any unit enlarged, except by written consent of the board of directors of the condominium association—unit owner constructing cottage which extended two feet into limited common area without consent of board—whether court should grant mandatory injunction for removal of cottage from limited common area

The Heron Cove Condominium, along the shore of the Pemaquid River, consisted of 15 cottage units and a common area. Portions of the common area surrounding the individual cottages were designated as limited common areas, designated for the exclusive use of the owner of the particular cottage. The by-laws of the condominium provided that nothing might be altered or constructed in the common areas, nor any unit enlarged, except by written consent of the board of directors of the condominium association. R was the owner of a unit. She demolished her existing cottage, and, without the consent of the association, constructed a new cottage which extended two feet beyond her unit into her limited use common area. The owners of nine other units in the condominium claimed an injunction requiring R to remove her newly constructed cottage from the common area, and also damages. The trial judge found that the claimants had not shown that they were irreparably injured by R's actions, and refused to grant an injunction or award damages. He held that the condominium as a whole had been improved in appearance by the new cottage; R had not acted maliciously in not obtaining the association's approval, assuming that it would acquiesce in the change; whilst removal of the structure would impose a greater harm on R than any possible harm caused to the plaintiffs by its retention. The claimants appealed.

HELD:

The defendant's right to exclusive use of her limited common area was analogous to an exclusive easement. The scope of her exclusive use was subject to the power of approval of the claimants, as properly exercised through the association's by-laws and its board of directors. By extending her cottage into the limited use area, R had violated the property rights of the claimants. The judge had consequently erred in finding that the claimants were not irreparably damaged by R's actions. However, despite the irreparable injury resulting from the encroachment, the judge had an equitable discretion to refuse to award a mandatory injunction when the effect of the encroachment was negligible compared to the cost of correcting it. In weighing the equities, the judge found that the value of the condominium in its entirety had been improved, and that the benefits to the claimants from removing the cottage would be minimal or non-existent. The judge also had evidence of a history of non-exercise of control by the claimants over limited common areas, during which unit owners expanded their cottages into limited common areas without the approval specified in the by-laws. On those facts, the judge had been entitled to exercise his discretion in the way he did. The judge was wrong to conclude that the claimants had suffered no injury. Some damage was presumed to flow from a legal injury to a property right. The claimants were entitled to nominal damages of $100.

Note

For restrictions on alterations, see Section 4.10 of the text. For restrictions on the use of limited use areas, see paragraph 4.12.7 of the text.

HUNYOR AND ANOTHER v TILELLI

[97667] 7 BPR (1997)

McLelland CJ

Australia: Supreme Court of New South Wales, Equity Division

Strata title—contract for sale of unit 'off-plan'—contract conditional upon registration of strata plan by specified date—plan not registered by specified date—whether vendor entitled to rescind—whether failure to register plan caused by vendor's breaches of the contract

The claimant purchasers entered into a contract in 1994 for the purchase 'off-plan' of a unit in an intended strata title scheme. The contract was conditional upon registration by 30 June 1996 of a strata plan substantially in accordance with the preliminary strata title plan annexed to the contract. The defendant vendor covenanted to use his reasonable endeavours promptly to construct the development in accordance with the specified architects' plans, and to carry out all matters required for the registration of a new strata plan by 30 June 1996. The strata plan was not registered by 30 June 1996, and on 10 July 1996 the vendor purported to rescind the contract on that ground. The purchasers claimed specific performance of the contract. They challenged the validity of the purported rescission on the ground, among other things, that the absence of registration of the new plan resulted from the vendor acting in breach of express and implied obligations to use his best endeavours to secure registration of the strata plan by the due date.

HELD:

The purchasers were entitled to specific performance. A party to a contract is not entitled, as against the other party, to rely on an event caused or materially contributed to by the first party's own breach of the contract. The vendor was under an express obligation to use his reasonable endeavours promptly to carry out all matters required for the registration of a new strata plan by 30 June 1996. There was an implicit correlative negative obligation not to do anything inconsistent with the performance of his positive obligation. Registration of the new strata plan could not be effected without, among other things, (i) obtaining consent for the development and the endorsement of the new strata plan by the local council, and (ii) obtaining a court order terminating an old strata title scheme on the site. None of those requirements was fulfilled until after 30 June 1996. It was clear that if the vendor had used reasonable endeavours promptly to carry out those requirements, each of them could and would have been fulfilled in sufficient time before 30 June 1996 to permit registration of the new strata plan by that date. There was no legitimate reason why the vendor could not have taken the necessary steps at a much earlier stage than he did. The nonfulfillment of any one of those requirements in due time was sufficient to prevent registration of the new strata plan by the due date, and the non-fulfillment of each of those requirements could therefore be considered as multiple sufficient causes of the failure to do so. The non-registration of the strata plan by 30 June 1996 was caused by the defendant's breaches of contract, and he was therefore not entitled to rescind the contract on that basis. It followed that the purchasers were entitled to an order for specific performance.

This judgment has been cited in the following digested case

Munro and another v Bodrex Pty Ltd (2002)

Note

For applications for registration of commonhold, see section 2 and Schedule 1 of the Act, and Part 6 of Chapter 2 of the text.

JACKLIN v PROPRIETORS OF STRATA PLAN NO 2795

[1975] 1 NSWLR 15

Holland J.

Australia: Supreme Court of New South Wales, Equity Division

Strata title—duty of body corporate to administer and maintain the common property for the benefit of unit proprietors—resolution by body corporate purporting to designate some unit proprietors a separate class of proprietor and to pass on to them responsibility for maintaining part of the common property—whether resolution ultra vires—legislative purpose of dividing scheme into units and common property—right of all unit proprietors to have whole of common property administered for them—advantages of administration of common property by body corporate

A strata title scheme consisted of a tower block of 39 home units, another building some distance away comprising three town houses, and the land surrounding them. One of the duties of the body corporate was to establish a fund to meet the expenses of maintaining the common property of the scheme, which it did by levying the unit proprietors in proportion to the unit entitlement of their respective units. The owners of two of the town house units complained that the system was unfair, because they obtained no benefit from the expenditure on the common parts of the tower block, and that expenditure was greater than the expenditure on those common parts which were for the benefit of the town houses only. In an attempt to resolve the dispute, the council of the body corporate passed a resolution which purported: (a) to treat the town house unit owners as a separate class of proprietors and the town house common property as a separate class of common property; (b) to delegate to the town house unit owners responsibility for the repair and maintenance of the town house common property; (c) to limit the amount to which the town house unit owners could have recourse to the maintenance fund of the body corporate to maintain the town house common property; (d) to require the town house unit owners themselves to raise any additional monies that were required for the maintenance of the town house common property; and (e) to absolve the proprietors of the tower block units from responsibility for providing such funds. Two of the town house unit owners claimed the resolution was void.

HELD:

The resolution was void, being beyond the powers of the body corporate under the Conveyancing (Strata Titles) Act 1961 (NSW) and the Strata Titles Act 1973 (NSW). Those Acts imposed on the body corporate a duty to control, manage and administer the common property for the benefit of the unit proprietors;

properly to maintain the common property and keep it in a state of good and serviceable repair; and to establish and maintain a fund to meet the expenses, among other things, of doing so. The legislation made, in respect of the parcel of land contained in the strata plan, a distinction between common property and the property comprised in a lot.

The distinction is made for a number of purposes. One is to enable the physical content of the two classes of property, the title thereto, easements in relation thereto and proprietors' rights of use and enjoyment thereof to be defined. Another is to enable allocation of responsibility for control, management and administration, and the repair and maintenance of the two classes of property. . . . [R]esponsibility for the control management and administration and the repair and maintenance of the common property is taken out of the hands of the individual proprietors and imposed upon the body corporate [as] a matter of legal duty.

It followed from that duty that each unit proprietor had the right to have the whole administration of repairs and maintenance of the common property carried out by the body corporate, its servants and agents. The scheme adopted by the resolution was inconsistent with that. It purported to designate a separate class of common property and a separate class of proprietor in respect thereof, and to pass on to the proprietors of that class the responsibility of deciding what repairs and maintenance should be carried out, and of procuring tradesmen to perform the work. The body corporate reserved for itself only a nominal role in the administration of such repair and maintenance. The town house proprietors, but not other proprietors, were denied some of the benefits of administration by the council and its servants.

I think it must be remembered that many persons buy a lot in a strata plan to escape the responsibility of caring for what, in a strata plan, is the responsibility of the body corporate and in a private home is a personal burden, such as grounds, garden, external and structural parts of a dwelling. To such persons the relief from this personal responsibility is a valuable incident of their rights as the proprietor of a lot in a strata plan. [The claimant] is a case in point. She does not want this responsibility. Whilst others might see merit in the council's scheme and advantages to the town house owners, her attitude is: 'It is not what I bought.'

Thus, the council's scheme could not have been relied upon as a defence to a claim by a town house proprietor for breach of the body corporate's duty to maintain town house common property, if for example, essential maintenance was not carried out, because the town house owners could not agree on what should be done, or their share of the funds provided by maintenance levies had not proved sufficient for the necessary works, and they had declined to provide the balance voluntarily.

Note

For the commonhold association's duty to manage, see section 35 of the Act and Section 6.15 of the text.

For the repair and maintenance obligations of the commonhold association, see sections 14(2), 26(c) and 31–32 of the Act, rules 20 and 21 of the proposed Commonhold Community Statement (August 2003), and Section 4.9 of the text.

LUBRANO v PROPRIETORS OF STRATA PLAN NO 4038

[97457] 6 BPR (1993)

Young J

Australia: Supreme Court of New South Wales, Equity Division

Strata title—statutory duties of body corporate—unit proprietor claiming damages for breach of statutory duty—whether claim precluded by existence of statutory penalties for breach—whether claim precluded by fact statutory duty could be delegated to managing agent

The claimant was the proprietor of a unit in a strata title scheme. The defendant was the body corporate of the scheme, and was obliged under s 68 of the Strata Titles Act 1973 (NSW) to control, manage and administer the common property for the benefit of the proprietors, properly maintain the common property, and, where necessary, renew or replace any fixtures or fittings comprised in the common property. Section 78 of the Act permitted a body corporate to delegate all of its powers, authorities, duties and functions to a managing agent. The claimant, a proprietor of a unit, claimed he had a cause of action for damages for breach of statutory duty against the body corporate, since he had suffered damage as a result of their failure to comply with their duties under s 68. The defendant body corporate denied liability on the basis that (i) the Act provided specific financial penalties against a body corporate which failed in its duties, which were an entirely adequate remedy, and (ii) the body corporate was entitled to delegate its duties under s 68, which distinguished them from other statutory duties. The question whether the lot owner had an individual cause of action came before the court as a preliminary issue.[1]

HELD:

Where a statute provides for the performance by certain persons of a particular duty, and someone belonging to a class of persons for whose benefit and protection the statute imposes the duty is injured by failure to perform it, prima facie an action by the person so injured will lie against the person who has failed to perform the duty. The statute imposed a duty on the body corporate in favour of each and every unit proprietor, including the claimant. Neither the fact that a financial penalty was imposed for a breach of the duty, nor the fact that the statute entitled the body corporate to delegate its duties precluded a claim for damages for breach of that statutory duty.

[1] The judgment does not refer to the particular breaches complained of.

Digested cases considered in this judgment

Proprietors of Strata Plan No 464 v Oborn (1975)
Proprietors of Strata Plan No 30234 v Margiz Pty Ltd (1993)

Note

For the enforcement of commonhold duties, and the payment of compensation where a duty is not complied with, see section 37 of the Act and Section 6.15 of the text.

For the commonhold association's duty to manage, see section 35 of the Act and paragraphs 4.3.13 and 4.3.18 of the text.

MARSHALL v STRATA PLAN NO NW 2584

27 BCLR (3d) 70 (1996)

Henderson J.

Canada: Supreme Court of British Columbia

Condominium—statutory prohibition on by-laws operating to prohibit or restrict the devolution, transfer, lease, mortgage or other dealing with strata units—by-law providing that individuals under the age of 55 years were prohibited from residing in any unit—whether by-law was prohibited by statutory prohibition

Section 26 of the Condominium Act, RSBC, 1979, permits a strata corporation to pass by-laws providing for the 'control, management, administration, use and enjoyment of the strata lots and common property . . .'. Section 29 of the Act provides that strata corporation by-laws may not operate to prohibit or restrict the devolution, transfer, lease, mortgage or other dealing with or of a strata lot. The strata council passed a by-law providing that individuals under the age of 55 years were prohibited from residing in any unit, a unit holder being liable for a fine of $250 per week for breach of the by-law. The petitioners, aged 73 and 78, were told that their 51-year old son could no longer live with them in their unit. The petitioners argued that the by-law was an impermissible constraint on their right of alienation. They argued that the age restriction reduced the pool of potential purchasers. Although someone under the age of 55 could buy their unit, the purchaser would not be allowed to occupy it. Since most purchasers wish to occupy what they buy, the age restriction reduced demand for the unit, and therefore lessened its value.

HELD:

The age restriction was valid. The truth of the petitioners' proposition was not self-evident. It might well be that an age restriction limiting a condominium development to older people enhanced its desirability amongst that age group. That might serve to increase demand for the strata unit within that age group, and therefore increase its value. Their proposition could only have been demonstrated through expert evidence, and none was adduced.

The court also considered the interaction between the age limit, and the Canadian Human Rights legislation.

The court declined to follow *453048 British Columbia Ltd v Strata Plan KAS 1079* (1994) 43 RPR (2d) 293 (BCSC), where Harvey J had reached a different conclusion on very similar facts (holding that the by-law was 'in all practical senses intended to control who owns and lives on the property'), on the basis that it was decided *per incuriam*.

Note

Section 15(2) of the Act provides that a commonhold community statement may not prevent or restrict the transfer of a commonhold unit. See paragraphs 3.2.3 and 4.13.2 of the text.

For restrictions and regulations concerning the leasing of units, see sections 17–19 of the Act, rules 3–8 of the proposed Commonhold Community Statement (August 2003), and Sections 3.3 and 3.4 of the text.

For restrictions on the use of commonhold units, see sections 14 and 31–33 of the Act, rules 9, 13 and 14 of the proposed Commonhold Community Statement (August 2003), and paragraphs 4.12.2 and 4.12.3 of the text.

For restrictions on the use of common parts, see section 26 of the Act, rules 10, 11 and 13–15 of the proposed Commonhold Community Statement (August 2003), and paragraph 4.12.6 of the text.

MITCHELL v PATTERN HOLDINGS PTY LTD

[2001] NSWSC 199; [97927] 10 BPR

Windeyer J.

Supreme Court of New South Wales, Equity Division

Strata title—sale of land—contract to purchase unit 'off-plan' in intended strata title development—contract conditional upon the registration of a strata plan within 12 months—registered plan to be 'substantially in accordance' with draft strata plan attached to contract—vendor to make all reasonable efforts to register the plan—council's consent to development conditional upon reduction in size of balcony of another unit by 10 m^2—plan not registered within 12 months—whether vendor entitled to rescind—whether vendor's attempts to persuade council to permit larger balcony caused unreasonable delay in registration of plan—whether plan with smaller balcony substantially in accordance with draft strata plan

The claimant entered a contract on 26 July 1999 to purchase a residential unit—unit 2— 'off-plan' in an intended strata title development. The contract was conditional upon the registration of a strata plan within 12 months, that plan to be 'substantially in accordance' with the draft strata plan attached to the contract. The vendor covenanted to use all reasonable endeavours to procure the registration of the strata plan. The strata plan was not registered within the 12 month period, and on 11 August 2000 the defendant vendor purported to rescind the contract for non-fulfilment of the condition. The vendor registered an amended strata plan in September 2000. It was different from the draft strata plan attached to the contract, in that the balcony on another unit in the scheme—unit 4—was smaller: it had been reduced in depth from 4m to 1½m, and its overall area had been reduced by approximately 10 m^2 (from about 15.95 m^2 to 5.98 m^2). The reduction in the size of the balcony had been imposed by the local authority as a condition of granting an (amended) consent for the development on 27 July 1999. The vendor had spent much time and energy during 1999 and the first 6 months of 2000 trying to persuade the council to permit a balcony of the size originally planned, but without success. The purchaser claimed it was entitled to specific performance of the contract because the vendor had not made all reasonable efforts to register the plan. The vendor maintained that any delay in registering the plan resulted from its attempts to persuade the council to permit the larger balcony, and that had been a legitimate approach. Further, the plan as registered was not 'substantially in accordance' with the plan attached to the contract, because of the change in the size of the balcony for unit 4. Given the opposition of the council to the larger balcony, it would not have been possible to register a plan substantially in accordance with the draft plan.

HELD:

The vendor's rescission was valid. The strata plan as registered was not 'substantially in accordance' with the draft strata plan attached to the contract, because of the reduction in the size of the balcony on unit 4. Unit 4 was the most expensive unit in the development, and obtaining permission for the additional 10 m^2 of its balcony, with ocean views, would have substantially enhanced its value. It was not unreasonable for the vendor to pursue its attempts to obtain permission for the larger balcony. The developer/vendor was entitled to rely on the draft strata plan, and if that plan could not be registered after proper efforts to obtain consent then it was not at fault. It was clear on the facts that the council would never have granted approval for the development with the larger balcony as shown on the draft strata plan, and therefore it would not have been possible to register a strata plan substantially in accordance with the draft plan.

Note

For commonhold plans, see Part II of the proposed Commonhold Community Statement (August 2003), and paragraph 2.17.7 of the text.

For the registration of commonhold land, see sections 2 and 5 of the Act and Part 6 of Chapter 2 of the text.

MONDAY VILLAS PROPERTY OWNERS ASSOCIATION v BARBE

598 NE 2d. 1291 (1997)

Brogan, Judge

United States of America: Court of Appeals of Ohio, Montgommery County

Condominium—prohibition on 'structures'— meaning of structure—whether 'ham' radio antennas were structures

The condominium declaration, by which unit owners were bound, provided by paragraph 1.05 that: 'Except as herein provided for, there shall be no structures or enclosures above the ground of the Commons, and no public, commercial or business use of any kind shall be permitted herein.' The effect was to prohibit additional structures being built on condominium units. B installed three antennas on his unit for use in his 'ham' radio operations. Two of the antennas were situated on tripods, and one on the top of a flagpole situated on the patio of his unit. The condominium association claimed that the antennas were a breach of paragraph 1.05, and sought injunctive relief to compel the removal of the antennas, and damages. B contended, inter alia, that his antennas did not constitute 'structures'.

HELD:

The antennas were 'structures' under paragraph 1.05. Several courts had defined 'structure' broadly. The Texas Supreme Court had defined it as 'any production or piece of work artificially built up, or composed of parts joined together in some definite manner: Stewart v Welsh 17 S.W. 2d 506; Mitchell v Gaulding Tex Civ App 4 SW 2d 41 (1972). The Supreme Court of Maine had defined it as 'anything constructed or erected and used which requires more or less permanent location on ground or attachment to something having permanent location on the ground': Leavitt v Davis 153 Me 279, 1 A 2d 535 (1957). The purpose of the restriction in this case was to guarantee the uniformity and harmony in appearance that has been associated with condominium development. Even the regulations of the Federal Communications Commission concerning amateur radio users referred to antennas as 'station antenna structures'. The fact that the association had permitted television antennas to be erected for the use of condominium owners did not make its enforcement actions against B unreasonable.

Note

For restrictions on alterations, see Section 4.10 of the text.

MUNRO AND ANOTHER v BODREX PTY LTD

[97942] 10 BPR (2002)

Bryson J.

Australia: Supreme Court of New South Wales, Equity Division

Strata title—sale of land—contract for sale of unit 'off-plan'—contract conditional upon registration of plan by specified date—plan not registered by specified date – whether vendor entitled to rescind—whether failure to register plan in time caused by vendor's breaches of contract

The claimants entered into a contract on 8 October 1999 to purchase 'off-plan' a unit in an intended strata title development. By clause 21 and special condition 40.1 of the contract, the vendor agreed that he would cause the building, within a reasonable time, to be constructed in accordance with specified building plans (on the basis of which development permission had been granted), in a good and workmanlike manner, and in accordance with all approvals, consents and requirements of all relevant authorities. By clause 21 and special condition 37, the vendor undertook to use its reasonable endeavours to have the strata plan registered within a reasonable time. The contract was made conditional upon the registration of the strata plan within 24 months from the date of the contract, with an entitlement for either party to rescind if it was not. The strata plan was not registered by 8 October 2001, and on 17 October 2001 the vendor purported to rescind the contract. The strata plan was registered on 5 November 2001. The purchasers claimed specific performance of the contract on the basis that the vendor had failed to use reasonable endeavours to have the strata plan registered, and was therefore not entitled to rescind.

HELD:

The vendor was not entitled to rescind. The delay in the registration of the strata plan was caused by delays in the local council approving the completed building, their approval being a necessary precondition to registration of the plan. There were two main causes of the council's approval of the building being delayed. The building was substantially completed by July 2001. However, the roof of the building was constructed 220mm higher than the plans had shown. The council eventually decided that that non-compliance was not significant, but it caused delay which would not have been caused if the building had been constructed in accordance with the plans. Secondly, a planter box shown on the plans was not initially constructed. The vendor was aware by July 2001 that its builders had decided not to construct the planter box, and was aware by 14 September 2001 that the council considered the omission of the planter box significant. The planter box was eventually completed on 5 October 2001, and the council then approved the completed building. There was no reasonable explanation for the planter box not having been constructed long before that as part of the ordinary building process. Thus the cause of the strata title plan not being registered by the due date was the delay in obtaining the council's approval. That delay was caused by the vendor's breach of its obligation to cause the building, within a reasonable time, to be constructed in accordance with the building plans. The vendor could not rely on the failure to register the plan in time as a basis for rescission, since it was caused by the vendor's own breach of contract.

Digested case considered in this judgment

Hunyor and Another v Tilelli (1997)

Note

For the registration of commonhold land see sections 2 and 5 of the Act and Part 6 of Chapter 2 of the text.

For commonhold plans, see Part II of the proposed Commonhold Community Statement (August 2003), and paragraph 2.17.7 of the text.

NOBLE v MURPHY

612 NE 2d 266 (1993)

Fine, Jacobs and Porada, JJ

United States of America: Appeals Court of Massachusetts, Norfolk

Condominium—by-law prohibiting the keeping of pets in units or common areas –whether objectionable to public policy—whether operation of complaint-driven procedure for enforcement was capricious—whether unfairly discriminated against the type of pets which were periodically observed outside units

The Weymouthport Condominium was a 271-unit complex managed by a trust. In 1979, following several complaints about dogs and a boa constrictor, a condominium by-law was passed providing that 'no animals, reptiles or pets of any kind shall be raised, bred or kept . . . in any Unit or in the Common Elements . . . '. The by-law allowed unit owners to keep any pets predating the by-law, and to have one household pet with the written permission of the trustees. M purchased a unit in 1983. After letting the unit for a number of years, M moved into the unit in 1988 with two pet dogs. M requested but was refused permission to keep the dogs in the unit, but he failed to remove them despite several requests to do so. The trustees of the condominium imposed a penalty of $5 per day for violation of the by-law, and ultimately brought a claim for the removal of the dogs from M's unit. M questioned the validity of the pet restriction, and the enforceability of any fines and assessments based upon it. He also complained that the by-law was not consistently enforced against all types of pet.

HELD:

There was no public policy or constitutional provision guaranteeing the right to raise, breed or keep pets in a condominium.

> Central to the concept of condominium ownership is the principle that each owner, in exchange for the benefits of association with other owners, must give up a certain degree of freedom of choice which he might otherwise enjoy in separate, privately owned, property.

Unit-holders, upon purchase, may pay a premium to procure what they regard as a beneficial restrictive scheme. No authorities or investigations were required in order reasonably to conclude that the presence of pets within a condominium may interfere with the health, happiness and peace of mind of unit owners. There was nothing objectionable in the fact that the by-law prohibited pets such as goldfish and parakeets, which posed no risk of interference of any kind to other unit owners. There will be many restrictions on the use of residential units which:

> although patently designed to prevent unreasonable interference by individual owners with other owners' use of their units and common areas, will also incidentally preclude generically similar uses that may not be as likely to encroach on other owners' use.

Considerations of efficient and even-handed enforcement supported an absolute prohibition of all pets, rather than a restriction limited to certain pets. As to enforcement of the by-law, M received ample and repeated notice of the violation, and had been given a reasonable opportunity to comply with the restriction. There was no evidence of waiver of the by-law or of its capricious enforcement. The trustees had consistently and reasonably utilised a complaint-driven procedure for enforcement, albeit that that had incidentally focused on the type of pets which were periodically observed outside units, rather than any which might have been kept within. The fines were in accord with the by-laws, and properly assessed.

Note

For restrictions on pets, see paragraph 4.12.16 of the text.

OWNERS OF STRATA PLAN 48754 v ANDERSON AND ANOTHER

[97782] 9 BPR (1999)

Young J.

Australia: Supreme Court of New South Wales, Equity Division

Strata title—common property entitled to right of way through basement unit to enable access to base of common lift shaft—whether body corporate entitled to install lights in basement unit to illuminate right of way

The claimant was the body corporate of a strata title building. The defendant was the proprietor of what was effectively the basement floor of the building (lot 9 in the scheme). The common property of the scheme had the benefit of an express right of access by foot through lot 9, which enabled access for maintenance purposes to the base of the common lift shaft. The lift maintenance company required that for safety reasons the access way to the base of the lift shaft should be lighted; that requirement was supported by statutory regulations. The claimant claimed it was entitled to install three fluorescent tubes in lot 9 to provide the access way with adequate light.

HELD:

The claimant was entitled to install the lights. The grant of an easement is also the grant of such ancillary rights as are reasonably necessary to its exercise or enjoyment. There is a derogation from the grant of an easement if an ancillary right which a reasonable bystander would have expected to have passed with the grant is denied. Here there was an express grant of a right of way in what was effectively a basement. That grant could not reasonably be used unless it was illuminated.

Note

For the commonhold association's rights of access to commonhold units to carry out its repairing and maintenance obligations, see rule 21 of the proposed Commonhold Community Statement (claimant 2003), and paragraph 4.9.10 of the text.

For the commonhold association's repair and maintenance obligations in respect of the common parts, see sections 26(c) and 31–32 of the Act, rule 20 of the proposed Commonhold Community Statement (claimant 2003), and Section 4.9 of the text.

PANSDOWNE PROPERTIES PTY LTD v KERSWELL

[97180] 3 BPR (1984)

Hutley, Glass and Mahoney JJA

Australia: Supreme Court of New South Wales, Court of Appeal

Strata title—contract for purchase of unit prior to registration of strata title—contract conditional upon registration of strata title plan substantially in the form annexed to the contract—plan as registered included additional land in common property—whether plan as registered in substantially the same form as contract plan— whether addition of land was 'alteration' to the common property within the terms of a saving clause in the contract

The respondents entered into a contract to purchase a residential unit in the course of construction in an intended strata title development, for a price of $100,000. They paid a deposit of $10,000. The property was described in the contract as 'ALL THAT dwelling house now in course of erection . . . being lot 7 in the vendor's intended strata plan . . . the intended boundaries whereof are delineated on plan annexed hereto . . .'. The annexed ground plan showed the intended building and the common property surrounding it. The plan showed the site as not including an adjacent panhandle-shaped area of land, which was steep and rocky and subject to an easement in favour of adjoining land. However, the vendor subsequently altered the strata plan so that the common property included the panhandle, and registered the strata title plan in that different form. The respondents sought to rescind the contract on that basis, and claimed the return of their deposit. Special condition 1 of the contract provided that the contract was 'subject to and conditional upon the registration of a strata plan substantially in the form annexed hereto . . . on or before the expiration of five months from the date hereof . . .'. Special condition 2 provided that 'Notwithstanding the provisions of [special condition 1] the purchaser shall not be entitled to make any objection requisition or claim for compensation by reason of . . . (b) any alterations to the common property in the number size location or unit entitlement of any lot or lots in the strata plan (other than the subject lot) . . .' The vendors argued that the purchasers had no right to rescind because (1) the registered plan was substantially in the form annexed to the contract within the meaning of special condition 1; and (2) the retention of the panhandle was an alteration to the common property within the scope of special condition 2(b).

HELD:

The purchasers were entitled to rescind the contract and to the return of their deposit.

(1) The strata title plan was not substantially in the form annexed to the contract.

In construing the contract, it is, in my opinion, fundamental to remember that what is being sold is a lot in a strata plan and each lot holder has a proportionate interest . . . with other proprietors in the common property . . . The proprietor of lot 7 was, therefore, acquiring an interest in and also the concomitant burdens on land which was not in the plan annexed to the contract. When considering whether the registered plan is substantially in the form annexed, it is, in my opinion, proper to compare what the inclusion of the panhandle means to the lot holders in a unit complex with what its absence means [per Hutley JA].

The panhandle was of no apparent utility to the lot holders of the strata plan, but carried real disadvantages. There was an obligation to contribute half of the maintenance costs of the easement, the boundaries would have to be fenced, and the council rates would be higher. Significantly, the developers had originally intended to sell off the panhandle separately.

(2) (per Hutley and Glass JA, Mahoney JA dissenting) Although minor adjustments to the external boundaries of the common property would amount to alterations to which special condition 2(b) would apply, that clause did not permit the common property to be transformed. The retention of the panhandle was not an 'alteration' to the common property at all; it led to a common property substantially different to the common property as shown on the plan annexed to the contract. Further, clause 1 prevailed over clause 2(b), since the contract was 'subject to and conditional upon compliance' with clause 1.

Note

For commonhold plans, see Part II of the proposed Commonhold Community Statement (August 2003), and paragraph 2.17.7 of the text.

For the registration of commonhold land, see sections 2 and 5 of the Act and Part 6 of Chapter 2 of the text.

PICCADILLY PLACE CONDOMINIUM ASSOCIATION, INC v FRANTZ

436 SE 2d 728 (1994)

Johnson, Judge

United States of America: Court of Appeals of Georgia

Condominium—statute prohibiting change in 'the exterior appearance of any unit' without the consent of the condominium association—installation of burglar bars on the interiors of windows of unit—whether breach of statute—whether association entitled to injunction for removal of bars

The owners of units in the Piccadilly Place Condominium were bound by the terms of a statute[1] which provided that: 'Except to the extent prohibited by the condominium instruments and subject to any restrictions and limitations specified therein, the association shall have the power to grant or withhold approval of any action by one or more unit owners or other persons entitled to occupancy of any unit if such action would change the exterior appearance of any unit . . .' F, a unit owner, installed burglar bars on the interior of the windows of his unit, without the prior written approval of the architectural control committee of the association. The condominium association claimed a mandatory injunction for removal of the bars, and damages.

HELD:

The trial court found that the installation of burglar bars on the interior of the unit did not affect the unit's exterior appearance, because they were not attached or affixed to the exterior of the unit. The court compared the interior bars to blinds, shutters or curtains, which, although they may be *visible* from the outside of the unit, were not part of the exterior, and therefore were not controlled by the statute. The judgment was upheld on appeal. As with covenants, statutes restricting an owner's use of property were to be strictly construed. Although the burglar bars may have been visible from the outside, they were not an impermissible alteration of the exterior of the unit.

Note

For restrictions on alterations, see Section 4.10 of the text.

[1] OCGA, δ 44-3-106(a)(3).

PROPRIETORS OF STRATA PLAN 159 v BLAKE

[95802] 2 BPR CASENOTES (1986)

Yeldham J

Australia: Supreme Court of New South Wales

Strata title—statutory obligation on body corporate to maintain, renew or replace common property—resolution of body corporate not to repair or replace common air conditioning system serving units on ground floor of strata building—resolution invalid

The ground floor of a strata title scheme was served by an air conditioning unit which was part of the common property. In 1981–2 it ceased to work. The cost of repair would have been $41–45,000. The body corporate resolved in general meeting to discontinue the air conditioning unit on the ground floor, and told the proprietors of the ground floor units to install their own air conditioning unit if they needed one. The owners of the ground floor units claimed that the body corporate was obliged under s 68(1)(b) of the Strata Titles Act 1973 (NSW) to repair the common air conditioning unit by restoring it to a serviceable and operative condition.

HELD:

Section 68(1)(b) imposed a mandatory duty on the body corporate to maintain, renew or replace common property. In consequence, the resolution passed at the general meeting of the body corporate was beyond their power.

Note

For the commonhold association's repair and maintenance responsibilities in respect of the common parts, see sections 26(c) and 31–32 of the Act, rule 20 of the proposed Commonhold Community Statement (August 2003), and Section 4.9 of the text.

PROPRIETORS OF STRATA PLAN NO 464 v OBORN

[97068] 1 BPR (1975)

Holland J

Australia: Supreme Court of New South Wales

Strata Title—breach of by-law by proprietor of unit—mandatory injunction—by-law prohibiting variation of external appearance of unit without consent of body corporate—replacement of windows of unit with windows of very different appearance—whether injunction should be granted for removal of windows

A strata title community comprised a ten storey building with sixty units ('lots'), facing east. It was regulated by by-laws made in 1963. By-law 5(e) provided that: 'Proprietors shall not . . . do anything to vary the external appearance of their lots without the prior consent of the council of the body corporate.' Without giving any notice to the body corporate or its executive council, the defendants, proprietors of a strata title lot, took it upon themselves in May 1973, at a cost of $1500, to remove the whole of the window frames and windows in the eastern side of their lot and replace them with western red cedar frames, stained and oiled a brown colour, and fitted with fixed and sliding windows of tinted glass. The existing frames on the eastern façade of the building were plastic-coated steel of a charcoal colour. Most were fitted throughout with glass which was colourless and untinted, but a few had no glass in the upper half. The frames and windows fitted by the defendants presented an appearance distinctly different from the rest of the lots in structure, dimensions, texture, quality and colour. An observer of the eastern face of the building could hardly fail to notice that the external appearance of their lot was different from the rest, even from a considerable distance away. The body corporate, responsible for the administration and maintenance of the common property, sought a mandatory injunction requiring the defendants to remove their windows and frames and replace them with ones which conformed to the rest of the building. The defendants contended that no injunction should be granted since the body corporate had suffered no measurable damage because: (a) there was no physical damage to the fabric of the building; (b) the old windows were in need of repair or replacement, and thus a dangerous state of affairs was remedied by the defendants at no cost to the body corporate, relieving it from the performance of its duty, and the other lot proprietors from the cost thereof; and (c) the replacement was as good in quality and durability as anything that the body corporate could come up with. They also contended that any injury from the alteration of the appearance of the building was trivial because: (a) appearance is a matter of aesthetic judgment which varies with individuals and is not measurable; (b) it could not be said that the new frames and windows were unattractive in themselves; and (c) the general appearance of the building was not uniform but was made a hotchpotch of colour and texture by blinds, curtains and hangings visible through the glass of every lot.

HELD:

It was right to grant an injunction for the removal of the frames and windows and their replacement in such manner and with such materials as the body corporate, acting within its powers, might decide.

The body corporate had suffered an injury which was not trivial. The defendants' action spurned its authority and disregarded the by-laws by which all the proprietors were bound. It placed the body corporate in a difficult position: if the breach of the by-law went without challenge, their authority was undermined and their hands tied in deciding future action with respect to the preservation and appearance of the building and the performance of their duty to act in the common interest of all lot proprietors.

Decisions which affect any part of the common property are entrusted to the body corporate and the council. They cannot be left to, or dictated by, the decision of an individual proprietor with respect to his own lot. The result would be chaos. It is for the body corporate, acting within its powers, to decide whether there will be uniformity in the external appearance of the building, either total or in particular respects. If the defendants are permitted to retain the replacement they have chosen, it will be difficult to refuse any other proprietor his own individual choice. Also, proprietors may be encouraged to act first and deal with the council afterwards, as the Oborns did.

The body corporate had not been guilty of any conduct which would make it unjust to enforce the covenant. They were never consulted about the kind of replacement. They were never given the chance to replace the defendants' frames and windows if they needed replacement.

This judgment has been cited in the following digested case

Lubrano v Proprietors of Strata Plan No 4038 (1993)

Note

For restrictions on alterations, see Section 4.10 of the text.

PROPRIETORS OF STRATA PLAN NO 1627 v SCHULTZ

[97129] 2 BPR; [92402] 1 BPR CASENOTES (1978)

Holland J

Australia: Supreme Court of New South Wales

Strata title—unit holder carrying out unauthorised alterations to common property by fixing ventilation ducts and pipes to common passageway and to exterior of building—whether works also involved a change of use of common property

S was the proprietor of a shop unit ('lot') in a strata title building, which she fitted out as a laundry. Without obtaining the consent of the body corporate, she installed in and fixed to a part of the common property metal ducts, asbestos pipes and exhaust vents to provide a ventilating exhaust system and water heater flue for the laundry. The ducts and pipes passed through holes made in the rear wall of her unit and above a false ceiling in a common passageway serving the rear of the shops to the external wall of the building, where they were continued vertically by metal brackets fixed to the wall of the building to extend above the roof. S also attached an illuminated advertising sign to a common awning which was attached to the external wall of the building and overhung the various shop units. It was common ground that the installation of the ducts and pipes involved the making of openings in and alterations and attachments to parts of the building that were common property. The body corporate sought an order for the removal of the sign and the ducts. A preliminary issue arose as to which body had jurisdiction to determine the dispute. Under s 121 of the Strata Titles Act 1973 disputes concerning user of common property were within the jurisdiction of the Strata Titles Board, whilst under s 106 of the Act disputes concerning alterations to common property were within the jurisdiction of the Strata Titles Commissioner.

HELD:

The dispute was within the jurisdiction of the Strata Titles Board. The substance of what the defendant sought was permission as proprietor of the lot to use particular parts of the common property in a special manner for special purposes appertaining to the use and enjoyment of that lot. The use proposed involved alterations to the common property but those were incidental to the main purpose.

Here the primary purpose of the defendant was to use the common property to hold and support the ventilation ducts, flue pipes and advertising sign she needed for the laundromat she wished to operate on her lot. Alterations to the common property were involved but only incidentally. Her installations would take up space in and upon parts of the common property and occupy that space for an indefinite time to the practical exclusion of other proprietors from use of the space occupied. The works and installations, while affecting common property in which all proprietors had interests as tenants in common proportional to their unit entitlements, were capable of benefiting only her lot.

Note

For the use of common parts, see section 26 of the Act, rules 10, 11, and 13–15 of the proposed Commonhold Community Statement (August 2003) and paragraph 4.12.6 of the text.

For restrictions on alterations, see Section 4.10 of the text.

PROPRIETORS OF STRATA PLAN NO 6522 v FURNEY

[1976] 1 NSWLR 412

Needham J

Australia: Supreme Court of New South Wales, Equity Division

Strata title—duty of body corporate to maintain and keep in a good state of repair the common property—whether 'repair' included replacement and renewal

A strata scheme consisted of three buildings divided into numerous residential lots. The body corporate of the scheme was under a statutory duty 'to properly maintain and keep in a state of good and serviceable repair . . . the common property'. Each of the buildings suffered from defects in the common parts which permitted the penetration of water into various lots. The various defects arose from defective workmanship, or the use of bad or unsuitable materials in the construction of the buildings. The necessary remedial works included, for example, attaching waterproof flashings and other waterproofing works which had not been originally included in the building. One issue was whether the body corporate had the right to remedy such defects.

HELD:

The necessary works constituted keeping the common parts in a state of good and serviceable repair. 'Repair' in relation to the obligations of the body corporate included replacement and renewal. Whilst its primary meaning was to restore to sound condition that which had previously been sound, it also properly meant to make good, irrespective of whether the relevant article had been good or sound before. The second meaning should be applied to the word 'repair' in the Strata Titles Act 1973 (NSW), first because it was the ordinary meaning of the word, but secondly because 'if the power to make good that which was not good before does not vest in the body corporate under the legislation, there [would be] a gap in the legislation which would mean that nobody had power to perform that duty, no matter how necessary it might be in any particular case'.

This judgment has been cited in the following digested case

Simons v Body Corporate Strata Plan No 5181 [1980] VR 103

Note

For the repair and maintenance obligations of the commonhold association, see sections 14(2), 26(c) and 31–32 of the Act, rules 20–22 of the proposed Commonhold Community Statement (August 2003), and Section 4.9 of the text.

PROPRIETORS OF STRATA PLAN NO 30234 v MARGIZ PTY LTD

[97568] 7 BPR (1993)

Brownie J

Australia: Supreme Court of New South Wales, Equity Division

Strata title—claim by body corporate to wind-up company proprietor of unit for failure to pay scheme contributions—counterclaim by unit proprietor for failure of body corporate to repair common air conditioning unit—whether court had jurisdiction to award damages—whether wrong to proceed with winding-up summons until counterclaim had been determined

The claimant was the body corporate of a strata title scheme, a 10 storey building, responsible for administering and regulating the scheme and maintaining the common property. The defendant was proprietor of three units in the scheme. The claimant sought an order that the defendant be wound-up for failing to pay outstanding contributions levied under the scheme. The defendant asserted a counterclaim for an amount exceeding the amount of those contributions. The basis of the counterclaim was that the claimant was liable under the Strata Titles Act 1973 to repair and maintain the common property air conditioning unit, and was in breach of that duty in that the air conditioning was deficient.

HELD:

Once it was recognised that the Act imposed a duty on the claimant, and that the defendant was one of the class of persons for whose benefit the duty was created (namely the proprietors of the constituent units) there was no reason why the rules of the common law would not give the court jurisdiction to award the defendant damages, upon proof of breach of duty and consequential damage. The defendant had at least a substantial argument that the claimant should pay it substantial damages, and it would be wrong to allow the claimant to proceed with its winding-up summons until that claim had been determined.

This judgment has been cited in the following digested case

Lubrano v Proprietors of Strata Plan No 4038 (1993)

Note

For the enforcement of commonhold duties, and the payment of compensation where a duty is not complied with, see section 37 of the Act and Section 6.15 of the text.

For the commonhold association's duty to manage, see section 35 of the Act and paragraph 4.3.18 of the text.

RE PEEL CONDOMINIUM CORP NO 73 v ROGERS AND ANOTHER

91 DLR (3d) 581 (1978)

Howland CJO, Brooke and Wilson JJA

Canada: Ontario Court of Appeal

Condominium—limited use area of common parts—garden area reserved for exclusive use of unit-holder—prohibition against unit-holders making any additions, alterations or improvements to common parts—unit-holder planting trees in limited use area—whether prohibited addition or alteration to common parts

The defendant, one Rogers, was the owner of a unit. Adjacent to his unit was a small area of garden, which formed part of the common parts, but according to the condominium declaration was reserved for the exclusive use of his unit. The condominium declaration prohibited any unit-holder from making any additions, alterations or improvements to any part of the common parts without the prior consent of the condominium board. Rogers planted four cedar trees in the small garden area without the consent of the board. The board applied for an order requiring him to cut them down, on the basis that they were unauthorised additions or alterations to the common parts.

HELD:

Rogers had been entitled to plant the trees. Reasonable people would understand that if they were granted the exclusive use of a garden area, they could have a garden there. It was customary to plant shrubs and trees in a garden for privacy and shade. If it had been intended to restrict its use exclusively to a grassy area, the condominium declaration could have so provided. Equally, specific rules could have been passed restricting the type and height of plants and trees. The prohibition against additions, alterations or improvements contemplated more far-reaching changes than the normal planting of trees and shrubs in a garden area.

Note

For limited use areas and restrictions on their use, see sections 25(2)–(3) and 31–32 of the Act, Part II and rule 10 of the proposed Commonhold Community Statement (August 2003), and paragraph 4.12.7 of the text.

For the regulation of the use of common parts, see sections 26 and 31–32 of the Act, rules 10, 11 and 13–15 of the proposed Commonhold Community Statement (August 2003), and paragraph 4.12.6 of the text.

SALERNO v PROPRIETORS OF STRATA PLAN NO 42724

[97648] 7 BPR (1997)

Windeyer J

Australia: Supreme Court of New South Wales, Equity Division

Strata title—body corporate passing by-law by special resolution prohibiting smoking on common parts or in any unit—whether by-law restricted the right to transfer or lease a unit

The body corporate of the strata title scheme passed by special resolution an additional by-law prohibiting the proprietor or occupier of any unit ('lot') from smoking or allowing smoking within a lot or within the common property, or from allowing any invitee to his lot to smoke within the lot or upon the common property. The by-law was passed under s 58(2) of the Strata Titles Act 1973 (NSW), which permitted a body corporate, pursuant to a special resolution, to add or amend by-laws for the purpose of the control, management, administration, use or enjoyment of the lots or common property. The claimants, proprietors of two lots in the scheme, claimed that the by-law was invalid since it contravened s 58(6) of the Act, which provided that no addition to or amendment of a by-law was to be capable of 'operating to prohibit or restrict the devolution of a lot or a transfer, lease, mortgage, or other dealing therewith'. There was evidence that the pool of potential lessees of the claimants' lots was reduced as a result of the by-law.

HELD:

The by-law was valid. It did not restrict the transfer or leasing of the lots, but rather controlled, or sought to control, the conduct of persons within the lots of the strata plan. Any person was free to purchase a lease of the lots; what those persons were not free to do was to smoke or allow smoking within the lot. Albeit the by-law might limit the class of persons who might desire to purchase or lease the lots, it did not restrict the right to lease or transfer. It might well have been different if the by-law had prohibited the lease of a lot to persons who were smokers.

Note

Section 15(2) of the Act provides that a commonhold community statement may not prevent or restrict the transfer of a commonhold unit. See paragraphs 4.13.2 and 3.2.3 of the text.

For restrictions and regulations concerning the leasing of units, see sections 17–19 of the Act, rules 3–8 of the proposed Commonhold Community Statement (August 2003), and Sections 3.3 and 3.4 of the text.

For the use of commonhold units, see section 14 and 31–33 of the Act, rules 9 and 13–15 of the proposed Commonhold Community Statement (August 2003), and paragraphs 4.12.2 and 4.12.3 of the text.

For the use of common parts, see section 26 of the Act, rules 10, 11 and 13–15 of the proposed Commonhold Community Statement (August 2003), and paragraph 4.12.6 of the text.

SAWKO v DOMINION PLAZA ONE CONDOMINIUM ASSOCIATION

578 NE 2d 623 (1991)

Bowman and Maclaren JJ

United States of America: Appellate Court of Illinois, Second District

Condominium—common elements included parking spaces—condominium association allocating most convenient spaces to handicapped unit owners—whether rights of other unit owners in the common elements thereby diminished

The common elements of the condominium included parking spaces, some in the open air, others in the more convenient and secure West Garage. The board of the condominium association decided to restrict parking in the West Garage area by assigning some of the spaces to handicapped unit owners. Such allocations were to be held during the association's pleasure. The claimant unit owner claimed that the association had thereby diminished his rights in the common elements, but had not complied with the necessary procedures for modifying the provisions of the condominium declaration regarding the unit owners' ownership of the common elements. The association acknowledged that no rule or regulation that diminished the interest of any unit owner in the common elements could be adopted without the unanimous consent of all members of the condominium association. However, it maintained that the condominium declaration entitled the board to adopt reasonable rules and regulations concerning the use of the association's parking spaces; and that a rule or regulation assigning a portion of the common elements as a parking space for a particular owner did not effectively diminish individual owners' interests in the common parts. The claimant applied for summary judgment.

HELD:

The claimant was entitled to summary judgment. The condominium association had, by allocating some parking spaces to particular unit owners, granted those owners exclusive rights over parts of the common elements, albeit for an indeterminate period. The claimant and other unit owners were precluded from the use of parts of the common elements' parking to which they had previously had access. The association had thereby diminished the claimant's interest in the common elements associated with his condominium ownership. Such action was invalid without the unanimous consent of all members of the condominium association.

This judgment is considered in the following digested cases

Alpert v Le'Lisa Condominium (1995)
Woodruff v Fairways Villas Condominium Association (1995)

Note

For restrictions on the use of the common parts, see paragraph 4.12.6 of the text.
For limited use areas of the common parts, see paragraph 4.12.7 of the text.

SIMONS v BODY CORPORATE STRATA PLAN NO 5181

[1980] VR 103

Lush J

Australia: Supreme Court of Victoria

Strata title—duty of body corporate to repair and maintain common property—external cavity wall allowing entry of water and damp into unit—boundary between unit and common property was median line of wall—division of liability for repair of wall—whether repair included replacement and renewal

A strata title scheme consisted of 39 dwelling units, arranged in two three-storey groups, together with the common property. The body corporate was under a statutory duty under s 15(1) of the Strata Titles Act 1967 (Vic) 'To keep in a state of good and serviceable repair and properly maintain the common property.' The boundary between each unit and the common property (as defined by the scheme plan and s 5(4) of the Act of 1967) was the median line of its external walls. The southern boundary wall of the applicant's unit had failed to keep out water since 1977, resulting in serious damp and water ingress. It was a cavity wall. One cause of the problem was water penetration of the outer wall, which was caused by: (i) lack of hooding on ventilators; (ii) the use of poor quality mortar in the brick-work, with subnormal water resistance; and (iii) leaving putlog holes[1] in the brick-work. The other, more serious, cause was the defective installation of flashing in the cavity at the base of the interior brick wall (in particular the failure to lead it into the face of the internal brickwork of the cavity wall, and to place it across the cavity so as to deliver any water coming down it to the outside), and the formation of mortar bridges across the internal cavity during the construction of the wall. The issues for decision were, among other things: (i) whether remedying defects in the original construction was within the scope of the body corporate's duty to 'repair'; and (ii) whether the significant defect was the failure to lead the flashing into the interior brickwork, so that that defect was on the applicant's side of the median line, and therefore her responsibility, or whether the main defects were in the external wall.

HELD:

(i) 'Repair' in relation to the obligations of the body corporate included replacement and renewal. Whilst its primary meaning was to restore to sound condition that which had previously been sound, it also properly meant to make

[1] Holes left in the walls of a building during its construction, to accommodate horizontal wooden scaffolding poles used for the construction of the upper parts of the building. They are ordinarily filled with brick or plaster in the final stages of construction. Obsolete in the UK following the advent of tubular steel scaffolding, but commonly visible on medieval ruins.

good, irrespective of whether the relevant article had been good or sound before. The second meaning should be applied to the word 'repair' in the Strata Titles Act, first because it was the ordinary meaning of the word, but secondly because 'if the power to make good that which was not good before does not vest in the body corporate under the legislation, there [would be] a gap in the legislation which would mean that nobody had power to perform that duty, no matter how necessary it might be in any particular case'. *Proprietors of Strata Plan No 6522 v Furney* [1976] 1 NSWLR 412 (Digest) applied.

(ii) On the evidence it was not possible to attribute the defects in the wall to the structure on one side or the other of the median line. The realistic and practical approach was to say that there was a cavity wall which had been defectively constructed. As the wall was jointly owned by the applicant and the respondent, they had joint responsibility to repair it.

Digested case considered in this judgment

Proprietors of Strata Plan No 6522 v Furney [1976]

Note

For the definition of the extent of a commonhold unit, see section 11 of the Act, Part II of the Proposed Commonhold Community Statement (August 2003), and paragraph 2.17.3 of the text.

For the repair and maintenance of the common parts, see sections 26(c) and 31–32 of the Act, rules 20–22 of the proposed Commonhold Community Statement (August 2003), and Section 4.9 of the text.

For the repair and maintenance of the commonhold units, see sections 14(2) and 31–32 of the Act and Section 4.9 of the text.

STRAUSS v OYSTER RIVER CONDOMINIUM TRUST

631 NE 2d 979 (1994)

Wilkins, Abrams, Lynch and Greaney JJ

Supreme Judicial Court of Massachusetts, Suffolk

Condominium—condominium trustees giving purported consent for extension of units onto common area—trustees giving purported consent for landscaping works and construction of car parking areas adjacent to units—purported consents invalid—works unlawful—whether court should grant mandatory injunction requiring removal of extensions and landscaping works

The Oyster River Condominium Trust was formed in 1980, and consisted of nine free-standing dwelling units and a common area, standing on about two and two-thirds of an acre. The condominium's master deed purported to authorise each unit owner 'to construct additions to his Unit' with the written approval of a majority of the trustees. For three years the parties accepted that provision as lawfully authorising the condominium trustees to grant to a unit owner the right to construct an addition that extended into the common area of the condominium. In accordance with that belief, the dwellings on various units were extended into the common area. Some unit-holders also carried out landscaping works to parts of the common area adjacent to their units, including the construction of parking areas. In fact, the governing legislation[1] required that the expansion of any unit into the common area required the unanimous approval of the owners of all the units. In 1984 the claimant unit-holders brought a claim for declarations that the various additions had been unlawfully constructed and the landscaping changes unlawfully made in the common area of the condominium. They also claimed that another unlawful addition was threatened by R, the owner of Unit 6. They sought an injunction restraining R from carrying out his proposed addition, and mandatory injunctions requiring the removal of the extensions and the landscaping works. The trial judge held, correctly, that the expansions of units into the common areas had been unlawful, because they were not unanimously approved by the owners. He granted the injunction restraining R's proposed addition. However, he refused to order the removal of the existing additions and landscaping works, ordering instead that the master deed and other documents be amended to reflect the altered extent of the units, with an appropriate recalculation of the condominium assessment. The claimants appealed.

HELD:

The judge had been entitled to exercise his discretion in the manner he did. The physical expansion of a unit into a common area could effectively give the unit

[1] MGLA c 183A.

owner the exclusive use of that area, and prevent any other unit owner from using it. However, the judge did not err in ruling that the landscaping works, including the construction of parking spaces, undertaken by individual unit owners in the common area, need not be removed. Those improvements had made the common areas more attractive, and did not deny any unit owner access to those parts of the common area. Nor did the judge err in refusing to order the removal of the unit buildings which extended into the common area. He had been entitled to conclude that the removal of the additions would be oppressive and inequitable. The unit holders had all proceeded in good faith, believing they had obtained the necessary approval. They had each received from the condominium trust a certificate authorising their extensions. In many cases they also had what reasonably appeared to be the approval or the acquiescence of the claimants. They were innocent wrongdoers, and had been misled by circumstances created by the developer and the original trustees. The claimants' rights were not materially compromised by the misappropriation of parts of the common area.

Note

For restrictions on the use of common parts, see paragraph 4.12.6 of the text. For changes to the extent of the common parts, see paragraph 3.7.3 of the text. For changes to the extent of commonhold units, see paragraph 3.7.4 of the text.

SYDNEY DIAGNOSTIC SERVICES PTY LTD v HAMLENA PTY LTD AND ANOTHER

[97367] 5 BPR (1991)

Mahoney, Priestly and Meagher JJ.A.

Australia: Supreme Court of New South Wales, Court of Appeal

Strata title—body corporate making by-law prohibiting particular trade from particular units—whether making of by-law within powers of body corporate—whether statutory power to regulate use of lots to be construed restrictively where operated in a discriminatory manner and in restraint of trade

The second respondent was the body corporate of a strata title scheme. The first respondent was the proprietor of lots 5 and 6 of the scheme, from which it operated a pathology business. The body corporate was empowered by section 58(2) of the Strata Titles Act 1973 (NSW) to pass by-laws 'for the purpose of the control, management, administration, use or enjoyment of the lots or the lots and common property the subject of the strata scheme . . .'. In 1983 the body corporate purported to pass a by-law which provided that a proprietor or occupier of a lot: 'Shall not upon the parcel (other than Lots 5 and 6) conduct the medical practice of pathology.' The appellant subsequently became proprietor of lot 35, from which it began to operate a pathology business. The body corporate obtained an order prohibiting the appellant from conducting the practice of pathology from the lot. The appellant claimed that the statute did not authorise the making of a by-law restricting the occupation that might be carried on upon one or more but not on all of the lots in a scheme. It submitted that, properly construed, subsection 58(2) only permitted the making of non-discriminating by-laws affecting all lots; the fact that the by-law operated in restraint of trade was a reason why the statute should be given a restrictive construction.

HELD:

The by-law was valid. The words of section 58(2) bore their prima facie meaning. Parliament must have intended bodies corporate to have power to pass by-laws regulating the use of each lot in the strata plan, and it must have been apparent to Parliament that it extended to regulating what trades, avocations and activities could and could not be conducted on each lot. A general power to pass discriminating by-laws could, in some hypothetical cases, lead to unjust results. However, general company law provided some protection, since a purported exercise of power is a nullity if it can be demonstrated to have been activated by an improper purpose, that is a purpose foreign to its real purpose.

Note

For the use of commonhold units, see sections 14 and 31–33 of the Act, rules 9 and 13–15 of the Proposed Commonhold Community Statement (August 2003), and Section 4.12 of the text.

TARVAL v STEVENS

[95812] 2 BPR CASENOTES (1990)

Clarke, Meagher and Handley JJA

Australia: Supreme Court of New South Wales, Court of Appeal

Strata title—contract for purchase of strata title unit 'off-plan'—subject matter of contract defined by reference to strata title plan which showed scheme as solely residential—vendor subsequently amended scheme to include commercial units on ground floor—fundamental breach—purchaser entitled to rescind

The purchaser contracted to purchase 'off-plan' a unit in an intended strata title scheme. The definition of the subject matter of the contract included reference to a strata plan annexed to the contract, which provided for the building only of residential units. Following registration of the strata plan, the vendor obtained consent to change of use of the lower floors of the building from residential to commercial. The evidence showed that that had a detrimental effect on the character of the building and the value of the unit. The purchaser claimed he was entitled to rescind the contract.

HELD:

The subject matter of the sale was essential to the contract. The vendor in consequence of its own acts was unable to transfer what it had contracted to sell. The vendor was in fundamental breach of the contract when it gave a notice to complete, and the purchaser was entitled to rescind.

Note

For development rights, see Section 2.20 of the text.

WOODRUFF v FAIRWAYS VILLAS CONDOMINIUM ASSOCIATION

879 FED SUPP 798 (1995)

Sam H Bell, District Judge

United States of America: United States District Court, ND Ohio, Eastern Division

Condominium—request by handicapped unit owner that common parking space adjacent her dwelling be reserved for her exclusive use—whether condominium association had power to grant request—whether would interfere with right of each unit owner to use the common areas in accordance with the purposes for which they were intended—whether would amount to hindrance or encroachment upon the rights of the other unit owners

Each unit within the Fairways Villas Condominium included a private garage, standing apart from the dwelling. Residents could also park their cars on a 'first come, first served' basis in various parking spaces scattered throughout the common areas of the condominium. W was disabled, and feared she would have difficulty on occasion walking the 50 yards from her garage to her unit. She therefore asked the association to designate the single, outdoor parking space that lay in the common area near her door as a disabled parking spot. The association refused. W claimed she had been discriminated against because of her handicap, in breach of the terms of the Fair Housing Act.[1] The Act defined 'discrimination' as including 'a refusal to make reasonable accommodations in rules, policies, practices, or services, when such accommodations may be necessary to afford [a handicapped] person equal opportunity to use and enjoy a dwelling'. The association defended the claim on the basis, among other things, that they lacked the authority to grant W's request. The condominium was regulated by the Ohio Revised Code. The Code provided that the common areas of a condominium were owned by the unit owners as tenants in common, and that each owner's percentage interest in the common areas, as expressed in the original condominium declaration, could not be altered except by an amendment to the declaration unanimously approved by all unit owners affected. The Code also provided that 'Each unit owner may use the common areas and facilities in accordance with the purposes for which they are intended. No unit owner may hinder or encroach upon the lawful rights of the other unit owners.' The association argued that by requesting that a portion of the common parking area be designated for her use only, W had necessarily sought to restrict the ability of other unit owners to use that parking area.

[1] 42 USC δ 3604(f), which makes it unlawful 'to discriminate against any person . . . in the provision of services or facilities in connection with a dwelling, because of a handicap of . . . that person'.

HELD:

The association's contentions were correct. The restriction requested by W constituted an easement, albeit of conditional duration, that would have interfered with other unit owners' proprietary interests in the use of the common area. The Code only permitted common property to be converted into limited common area property, or into the property of an individual unit owner, by the amendment of the condominium declaration by the unanimous vote of all unit owners. The association had not discriminated against W by failing to allocate a parking space to her exclusive use, since it had no authority to do so.

Digested case considered in this judgment

Sawko v Dominion Plaza One Condominium Association (1991)

Note

For restrictions on the use of the common parts, see paragraph 4.12.6 of the text. For limited use areas of the common parts, see paragraph 4.12.7 of the text.

ZENNA BUCHBINDER v OWNERS, STRATA PLAN VR2096

65 BCLR (2d) (1992)

McEachern CJBC, Locke and Proudfoot JJA

Canada: Court of Appeal of British Columbia

Condominiums—by-law prohibiting visible changes to exterior of building—by-law prohibiting enclosures of common and/or limited use common property—erection of shed on patio designated as limited common property—whether patio part of exterior of building—whether shed an enclosure of limited use common property

The appellant was the owner of a residential unit in a strata title plan. Outside her unit was a patio which was designated as limited use common property. One of the by-laws of the strata plan provided that 'No visible changes to the building's exterior are permitted . . . These changes include . . .; any additions of a permanent or semi-permanent nature; enclosures of common and/or limited common property.' The appellant erected an aluminium free-standing garden shed on the patio. The strata title corporation claimed the erection of the shed was a breach of the by-law.

HELD:

The erection of the shed was not a breach of the by-law. (1) The patio was not part of 'the building's exterior'. The exterior of the building only referred to its walls: the word 'exterior' modified 'building', and did not extend to cover a patio adjacent to that building. (2) Neither was the shed an 'addition of a permanent or semi-permanent nature': it was a free-standing structure, not attached to anything. The position would have been different if the shed had been attached to the exterior wall of the building. (3) Nor was the shed 'an enclosure of common or limited property', albeit that it was arguable that the shed enclosed the portion it covered.

Note

For restrictions on alterations, see Section 4.10 of the text.

For the commonhold association's responsibility for maintenance, see Section 4.9 of the text.

For limited use areas, see section 25(2) of the Act, rule 10 of the proposed Commonhold Community Statement (August 2003), and paragraph 4.12.7 of the text.

In *Brown v Liverpool Corporation* [1969] 3 All ER 1345, the Court of Appeal held that steps and a flagstone path which were the only means of access to a terraced dwelling house were part of its 'exterior' within the meaning of what is now section 11 of the Landlord and Tenant Act 1985.

PART C
FORMS AND PRECEDENTS

Note

The forms and precedents set out in this part of this work are a mixture of (a) formal documents prescribed by various rules and regulations and (b) working documents that have not been so prescribed, but that the authors consider will form a useful part of the practitioner's or commonholder's lexicon. The forms have been designed to accord with two objectives:

(i) to accommodate the widely expressed wishes of the consultees to the October 2002 Consultation Paper that commonhold documents should, if at all possible, be in plain English and operable, in the main, without expert assistance;
(ii) to be legally clear and effective.

The forms in Part 1 are based upon the current (2003) draft version of the Commonhold (Land Registration) Rules. It is likely that the final version of these Rules (which are expected to be laid before Parliament either at the end of 2003 or early in 2004) will be identical or closely similar.

Any comments on these forms will be gratefully received by the authors at commonhold@falcon-chambers.com.

The authors intend to keep these forms under review, and propose to publish any amendments on a companion website to this book: http://www.oup.com/uk/booksites/practitionerlaw

Forms and Precedents—Contents

Form No | **Document**

Part 1. Land Registration Forms

Part 2. Commonhold Association Forms

PART 1. LAND REGISTRATION FORMS

1.1 APPLICATION TO REGISTER A COMMONHOLD

Notes

(1) The Form that follows is a reproduction of Form CM1 in Schedule 1 to the Commonhold (Land Registration) Rules, and is a prescribed (ie mandatory) form for use in applications to register a freehold estate in land as a freehold estate in commonhold land (see rule 5(1)).

(2) The application should be accompanied by the following documents listed in Schedule 1 to the Act: (a) the certificate of incorporation for the commonhold association; (b) any altered certificate; (c) the memorandum and articles of association of the commonhold association (see Forms 2.1 and 2.2 below); (d) the commonhold community statement (see Form 2.3 below); (e) all necessary consents (see Form 1.14 below) including any orders of court dispensing with the need for consent (see Form 5.2 below); (f) a certificate given by the directors of the commonhold association complying with paragraph 7 of Schedule 1 to the Act (see Form 2.4 below). Further, unless the Registrar directs otherwise (see rule 5(2) of the Commonhold (Land Registration) Rules), the application must also be accompanied by (g) certified copies of the memorandum and articles of association of the commonhold association; (h) a certified copy of the commonhold community statement. Finally, when the application is to register the commonhold with unit-holders, the application must also be accompanied by: (i) a statement requesting that section 9 of the Act should apply (see Form 2.7 below).

(3) The Form provides for the commonhold association to state up to three addresses for service, one of which must be a postal address. Any subsequent changes of address must be notified to the Land Registry.

(4) The full procedure for making such an application is discussed in Part 6 of Chapter 2 of the text of this work.

SCHEDULE 1

Application to register commonhold **HM Land Registry** **CM1**

(if you need more room than is provided for in a panel, use continuation sheet CS and staple to this form)

1. Administrative area(s) and postcode(s) *(if known)*

2. Property

3. Title Numbers *(please specify all freehold and leasehold titles (if any) affected*

Freehold	Affects whole or part	Leasehold	Affects whole or part

4. *Please complete the statement below if applicable*
If you have already delivered this application by outline application, insert reference number ☐

5. Number of units

6. Application and Fee *A fee calculator for all types of applications can be found on the Land Registry's website at www.landreg.gov.uk/fees*

Registration of commonhold Fee Paid £

FOR OFFICIAL USE ONLY
Record of fee paid

Particulars of under/over payment

7. Documents lodged with this form *(place an "X" in the boxes that apply)*

☐ Certificate of incorporation of commonhold association

☐ Memorandum and articles of association

☐ Certified copy of memorandum and articles of association

☐ Commonhold community statement ☐ Certified copy of commonhold community statement

☐ Consents ☐ Directors' certificate ☐ List of the commonhold units and unit-holders

☐ ☐ ☐

8. Full name(s) and address(es) for service of notices and correspondence **of every applicant** for entry on the register
You may give up to three addresses for service ***one*** *of which* ***must*** *be a postal address but does not have to be within the U.K. The other addresses can be a combination of either a postal address, a box number at a U.K. document exchange or an electronic address.*

9. Application lodged by
Land Registry Key No.
Name
Address/DX No.

Reference

Telephone No. Fax No.

FOR OFFICIAL USE ONLY
Codes
Dealing

Status

SCHEDULE 1

10. Where the Registry is to deal with someone else

The Registry will, if necessary, contact the person shown in panel 9 above. You can change this by placing "X" against one or more of the statements and completing the details below.

☐ Send confirmation of registration to the person shown below

☐ Raise any requisitions or queries with the person shown below

☐ Issue to the person shown below the commonhold community statement and/or memorandum and articles of association

If you have placed "X" against either statement above, complete the following name and address details:

Name

Address/DX No.

Reference	Telephone No.

11. Information in respect of any new charge

Do not give this information if a Land Registry MD reference is printed on the charge, unless the charge has been transferred.

Full name and address (including postcode) for service of notices and correspondence of the person to be registered as proprietor of each charge. *You may give up to three addresses for service **one** of which **must** be a postal address but does not have to be within the U.K. The other addresses can be a combination of either a postal address, a box number at a U.K. document exchange or an electronic address. For a company include Companies Registered Number if any; for Scottish Co. Reg. Nos., use an SC prefix. For limited liability partnerships, use an OC prefix. For foreign companies give territory in which incorporated.*

Unless otherwise arranged with Land Registry headquarters, we require a certified copy of the chargee's constitution (in English or Welsh) if it is a body corporate but is not a company registered in England and Wales or Scotland under the Companies Acts.

12. Name, address(es) and Company Registration Number of the commonhold association

13. *Please tick this box if your application is to register a conversion to commonhold. This statement must be signed by the applicant.*

☐ I/We certify that section 9 of the Commonhold and Leasehold Reform Act 2002 applies.

Signature of applicant(s) ______________________ **Date** ______________

14. Signature of person(s) lodging this form ______________________ **Date** ______________

1.2 APPLICATION FOR FREEHOLD ESTATE TO CEASE TO BE REGISTERED AS A FREEHOLD ESTATE IN COMMONHOLD LAND IN TRANSITIONAL PERIOD

Notes:

(1) The Form that follows is a reproduction of Form CM2 in Schedule 1 to the Commonhold (Land Registration) Rules, and is a prescribed (ie mandatory) form for use in applications for land to cease to be registered as a freehold estate in commonhold land during the transitional period (see rule 12(1) and section 8(4) of the Act).

(2) The application for cessation must be accompanied by the consent of all those parties who would have had to give their consent if an application to create a commonhold had been made at that time (see section 8(5) of the Act).

(3) The full procedure for making such an application is discussed in paragraph 2.19.7 of the text of this work.

SCHEDULE 1

Application for the freehold estate to cease to be registered as the freehold estate in commonhold land in transitional period

HM Land Registry

CM2

(if you need more room than is provided for in a panel, use continuation sheet CS and staple to this form)

1. **Administrative area(s) and postcode(s)** *(if known)*

2. **Title Number**

3. *Please complete the statement below if applicable*
   If you have already delivered this application by outline application, insert reference number ☐

4. **This application affects** *(place "X" in the box that applies)*

   ☐ the **whole** of the land in the title(s) *(go to panel 5 below)*
   ☐ **part** of the land in the title(s) *(if single property, give a brief description below)*
   Property description

5. Do you wish the land to be amalgamated into one title? *(place an "X" in the box that applies)*
   ☐ Yes
   ☐ No

6. **Application and Fee** *A fee calculator for all types of applications can be found on the Land Registry's website at www.landreg.gov.uk/fees*	FOR OFFICIAL USE ONLY Record of fee paid
Cessation of commonhold Fee Paid £	Particulars of under/over payment

7. **Documents lodged with this form** *(place an "X" in the boxes that apply)*
   ☐ Consents ☐ ☐ ☐

8. **Application lodged by** Land Registry Key No. Name Address/DX No. Reference		FOR OFFICIAL USE ONLY Codes Dealing Status
Telephone No.	Reference	

SCHEDULE 1

9. Where the Registry is to deal with someone else

The Registry will, if necessary, contact the person shown in panel 8 above. You can change this by placing "X" against one or more of the statements and completing the details below.

☐ Send confirmation of registration to the person shown below

☐ Raise any requisitions or queries with the person shown below

☐ Issue to the person shown below the following document(s)

If you have placed "X" against either statement above, complete the following name and address details:

Name

Address/DX No.

Reference	Telephone No.

10. Signature of person(s) lodging this form ____________ **Date** ____________

1.3 APPLICATION FOR VARIATION OF COMMONHOLD COMMUNITY STATEMENT AND/OR MEMORANDUM AND ARTICLES OF ASSOCIATION

Notes:

(1) The Form that follows is a reproduction of Form CM3 in Schedule 1 to the Commonhold (Land Registration) Rules, and is a prescribed (ie mandatory) form for use in applications to register an amended commonhold community statement (see rule 21(1)) or an altered memorandum or articles of association (see rule 22(1)).

(2) Any alterations in the extent of a commonhold unit or the common parts of a commonhold will result in a variation of the commonhold community statement. The directors of the commonhold association must apply to the Land Registry to register the amended statement (see rule 10 of the Commonhold (Land Registration) Rules).

(3) Unless and until the amended commonhold community statement or altered memorandum or articles of association are registered, they will have no effect (see section 33(3) and paragraph 3(1) of Schedule 3 to the Act).

(4) An application regarding an amended commonhold community statement should be accompanied by (a) the amended statement; (b) a certified copy of the amended statement; and (c) a certificate given by the directors of the commonhold association that the amended commonhold community statement complies with regulations (see section 33(5) of the Act and Form 2.5).

(5) An application regarding an altered memorandum or articles of association should be accompanied by (a) the altered memorandum or articles of association; (b) a certified copy of the altered memorandum or articles of association; and (c) a certificate given by the directors of the commonhold association that the altered memorandum or articles of association comply with regulations (see paragraph 3(1) of Schedule 3 to the Act and Form 2.6).

(6) Where an amendment of a commonhold community statement would have the effect of redefining the extent of a commonhold unit or changing the extent of the common parts, the application must also be accompanied by the requisite consents under sections 23(1), 24(2) or 30(2) – see Form 1.15; or by an order of a court dispensing with consent – see variously Forms 5.8, 5.10 and 5.12.

(7) The full procedure for making such applications is discussed in Sections 2.14 and 2.18 of the text of this work.

SCHEDULE 1

Application for variation of commonhold community statement and/or memorandum and articles of association

HM Land Registry **CM3**

(if you need more room than is provided for in a panel, use continuation sheet CS and staple to this form)

1. Administrative area(s) and postcode(s) *(if known)*

2. Title Number of Common Parts

3. Title Number(s) of Units affected *(if any)*

4. *Please complete the statement below if applicable*
If you have already delivered this application by outline application, insert reference number ☐

5. Document(s) to be varied *(place "X" in either or both boxes below)*

☐ Commonhold community statement

☐ Memorandum and articles of association

6. Application and Fee *A fee calculator for all types of applications can be found on the Land Registry's website at www.landreg.gov.uk/fees*	FOR OFFICIAL USE ONLY Record of fee paid
Variation of commonhold community statement and/or memorandum and articles of association — Fee Paid £	Particulars of under/over payment

7. Documents lodged with this form *(place an "X" in the boxes that apply)*

☐ Memorandum and articles of association

☐ Certified copy of memorandum and articles of association

☐ Commonhold community statement and plan (see panel 11)

☐ Certified copy of commonhold community statement and plan

☐ Consents ☐ Directors' certificate ☐

☐ ☐ ☐

8. Application lodged by Land Registry Key No. Name Address/DX No. Reference		FOR OFFICIAL USE ONLY Codes Dealing Status
Telephone No.	Reference	

SCHEDULE 1

9. Where the Registry is to deal with someone else
The Registry will, if necessary, contact the person shown in panel 8 above. You can change this by placing "X" against one or more of the statements and completing the details below.

☐ Send confirmation of registration to the person shown below
☐ Raise any requisitions or queries with the person shown below
☐ Issue to the person shown below the following document(s)

If you have placed "X" against either statement above, complete the following name and address details:
Name
Address/DX No.

10. If the application is to vary the commonhold community statement, please summarise the variation below
*NOTE 1: Where the application does not vary the extent of the units and/or the common parts, a duplicate of the original plan or a new plan must still be attached to the commonhold community statement. If you use a new plan it must conform to the detailed requirements and technical specifications contained in Practice Leaflet ** available free of charge from any district land registry.*
*NOTE 2: Where the application does vary the extent of the units and/or common parts, the variation(s) muat be summarised below and shown on a new plan attached to the commonhold community statement. The new plan must conform to the detailed requirements and technical specifications contained in Practice Leaflet** available free of charge from any district land registry.*
If the variations are not summarised below and not shown on a new plan, your application will be rejected.

12. Signature of person(s) lodging this form ______________________ **Date** ______________

1.4 APPLICATION TO ADD LAND TO A COMMONHOLD

Notes:

(1) The Form that follows is a reproduction of Form CM4 in Schedule 1 to the Commonhold (Land Registration) Rules, and is a prescribed (ie mandatory) form for use in applications to add land to a commonhold (see rule 23 and section 41(2) of the Act).

(2) The general rules governing the alteration of the register by a registered proprietor under the Land Registration Rules 2003 are disapplied by rule 3(2) of the Commonhold (Land Registration) Rules. The rules deal with the formalities to be observed where there is an amendment of the extents of either the units or the common parts of a commonhold.

(3) The full procedure for making such an application is discussed in Section 3.7 of the text of this work.

SCHEDULE 1

Application to add land to a commonhold

HM Land Registry

(if you need more room than is provided for in a panel, use continuation sheet CS and staple to this form)

1. Administrative area(s) and postcode(s) *(if known)*

2. Existing commonhold title number

3. Title number(s) of land to be added to commonhold

4. *Please complete the statement below if applicable*
If you have already delivered this application by outline application, insert reference number ☐

5. Application and Fee *A fee calculator for all types of applications can be found on the Land Registry's website at www.landreg.gov.uk/fees*

Addition of land to commonhold	Fee Paid £	FOR OFFICIAL USE ONLY Record of fee paid Particulars of under/over payment

6. Documents lodged with this form *(place an "X" in the boxes that apply)*

☐ Consents ☐ Directors' certificate ☐ ☐

7. Application lodged by
Land Registry Key No.
Name
Address/DX No.

Reference

Telephone No. | Fax No.

FOR OFFICIAL USE ONLY
Codes
Dealing

Status

8. Where the Registry is to deal with someone else
The Registry will, if necessary, contact the person shown in panel 7 above. You can change this by placing "X" against one or more of the statements and completing the details below.

☐ Send confirmation of registration to the person shown below

☐ Raise any requisitions or queries with the person shown below

☐ Issue to the person shown below the following document(s)

If you have placed "X" against either statement above, complete the following name and address details:
Name
Address/DX No.

Reference | Telephone No.

9. I/We confirm that I/we have lodged a separate application on Form CM3 varying the commonhold community statement.

Signature of person(s) lodging the form ______________________ **Date** ______________

1.5 APPLICATION FOR TERMINATION OF A COMMONHOLD REGISTRATION

Notes:

(1) The Form that follows is a reproduction of Form CM5 in Schedule 1 to the Commonhold (Land Registration) Rules, and is a prescribed (ie mandatory) form for use in applications to terminate a commonhold registration where a commonhold is being wound-up voluntarily or by the court with no succession order being made (see rules 24 and 26).

(2) The application should be accompanied by a termination statement (see Form 6.4 below).

(3) When the liquidator notifies the Land Registry that he is content with the terms of the termination statement or he has sent to the Land Registry a copy of the court order determining the terms of the termination statement (see Form 6.10 below), the Registrar must (a) enter the commonhold association as proprietor of the commonhold units; and (b) cancel the commonhold entries on every title affected (see rules 24(2) and 26(2) of the Commonhold (Land Registration) Rules).

(4) The full procedure for making such an application is discussed in paragraph 5.2.7 of the text of this work.

SCHEDULE

Application for the termination of a commonhold registration

HM Land Registry **CM5**

(if you need more room than is provided for in a panel, use continuation CS and staple to this form)

1. **Administrative area(s) and postcode(s)** *(if known)*

2. **Title Number(s)**

3. *Please complete the statement below if applicable*
   If you have already delivered this application by outline application, insert reference number ☐

4. **Property description**

5. **Application and Fee** *A fee calculator for all types of applications can be found on the Land Registry's website at www.landreg.gov.uk/fees*

   Termination of commonhold Fee Paid £

   FOR OFFICIAL USE ONLY
   Record of fee paid

   Particulars of under/over payment

6. **Documents lodged with this form when the termination is by way of voluntary winding-up** *(place "X" in the boxes that apply)*

   ☐ Termination statement ☐ Court order

   ☐ ☐ ☐

7. **Documents lodged with this form when the termination is by way of winding-up by the court (no succession order)** *(place "X" in the boxes that apply)*

   ☐ Liquidator's notification that section 54 of the Commonhold and Leasehold Reform Act applies

   ☐ ☐ ☐

8. **Full name(s) and address(es)** for service of notices and correspondence **of every applicant** for entry on the register *You may give up to three addresses for service **one** of which **must** be a postal address but does not have to be within the U.K. The other addresses can be a combination of either a postal address, a box number at a U.K. document exchange or an electronic address.*

9. **Application lodged by**
   Land Registry Key No.
   Name
   Address/DX No.

   Reference

   Telephone No. | Reference

   FOR OFFICIAL USE ONLY
   Codes
   Dealing

   Status

SCHEDULE 1

10. Where the Registry is to deal with someone else

The Registry will, if necessary, contact the person shown in panel 9 above. You can change this by placing "X" against one or more of the statements and complete the details below.

☐ Send confirmation of registration to the person shown below

☐ Raise any requisitions or queries with the person shown below

☐ Issue to the person shown below the following document(s)

If you have placed "X" against either statement above, complete the following name and address details:

Name

Address/DX No.

Reference	Telephone No

11. Signature of person(s) lodging this form ____________________ **Date** ______________

1.6 APPLICATION TO REGISTER SURRENDER OF DEVELOPMENT RIGHT(S)

Notes

(1) The Form that follows is a reproduction of Form AP1 in Schedule 1 to the Land Registration Rules 2003, and is a prescribed (ie mandatory) form for use in general applications to the Land Registry to change the register for which no other form is prescribed (see rule 13(1) of the Land Registration Rules 2003).

(2) The application must be accompanied by a Notice in form SR1 (see Form 1.7 below) together with the appropriate fee.

(3) The full procedure for making such an application is discussed in paragraph 2.20.5 of the text of this work.

Application to change the register

Land Registry

If you need more room than is provided for in a panel, use continuation sheet CS and attach to this form.

1. Administrative area and postcode if known

2. Title number(s)

3. If you have already made this application by **outline application,** insert reference number:

4. This application affects *Place "X" in the appropriate box.*

☐ the **whole** of the title(s) *Go to panel 5.*

☐ **part** of the title(s) *Give a brief description of the property affected.*

5. Application, priority and fees *A fee calculator for all types of applications can be found on Land Registry's website at www.landregistry.gov.uk/fees*

Nature of applications numbered in priority order	Value £	Fees paid £
1.		
	TOTAL £	

Fee payment method: *Place "X" in the appropriate box.*
I wish to pay the appropriate fee payable under the current Land Registration Fee Order:

☐ by cheque or postal order, amount £ ____________ made payable to "Land Registry".

☐ by Direct Debit under an authorised agreement with Land Registry.

FOR OFFICIAL USE ONLY
Record of fees paid

Particulars of under/over payments

Fees debited £

Reference number

6. Documents lodged with this form *Number the documents in sequence; copies should also be numbered and listed as separate documents. Alternatively you may prefer to use Form DL. If you supply the original document and a certified copy, we shall assume that you request the return of the original; if a certified copy is not supplied, we may retain the original document and it may be destroyed.*

7. The applicant is: *Please provide the full name(s) of the person(s) applying to change the register.*

The application has been lodged by:
Land Registry Key No. (if appropriate)
Name (if different from the applicant)
Address/DX No.

Reference
E-mail

Telephone No.	Fax No.

FOR OFFICIAL USE ONLY
Codes
Dealing

Status

8. Where you would like us to deal with someone else *We shall deal only with the applicant, or the person lodging the application if different, unless you place "X" against one or more of the statements below and give the necessary details.*

☐ Send title information document to the person shown below

☐ Raise any requisitions or queries with the person shown below

☐ Return original documents lodged with this form (see note in panel 6) to the person shown below *If this applies only to certain documents, please specify.*

Name
Address/DX No.

Reference
E-mail

Telephone No.	Fax No.

9. Address(es) for service of the proprietor(s) of the registered estate(s). The address(es) will be entered in the register and used for correspondence and the service of notice. *Place "X" in the appropriate box(es). You may give up to three addresses for service* ***one*** *of which* ***must*** *be a postal address but does not have to be within the UK. The other addresses can be any combination of a postal address, a box number at a UK document exchange or an electronic address.*

☐ Enter the address(es) from the transfer/assent/lease

☐ Enter the address(es), including postcode, as follows:

☐ Retain the address(es) currently in the register for the title(s)

10. Disclosable overriding interests *Place "X" in the appropriate box.*

☐ This is not an application to register a registrable disposition or it is but no disclosable overriding interests affect the registered estate(s) *Section 27 of the Land Registration Act 2002 lists the registrable dispositions. Rule 57 of the Land Registration Rules 2003 sets out the disclosable overriding interests. Use Form DI to tell us about any disclosable overriding interests that affect the registered estate(s) identified in panel 2.*

☐ Form DI accompanies this application

The registrar may enter a notice of a disclosed interest in the register of title.

11. Information in respect of any new charge *Do not give this information if a Land Registry MD reference is printed on the charge, unless the charge has been transferred.*
Full name and address (including postcode) for service of notices and correspondence of the person to be registered as proprietor of each charge. *You may give up to three addresses for service* ***one*** *of which* ***must*** *be a postal address but does not have to be within the UK. The other addresses can be any combination of a postal address, a box number at a UK document exchange or an electronic address. For a company include company's registered number, if any. For Scottish companies use an SC prefix and for limited liability partnerships use an OC prefix before the registered number, if any. For foreign companies give territory in which incorporated.*

Unless otherwise arranged with Land Registry headquarters, we require a certified copy of the chargee's constitution (in English or Welsh) if it is a body corporate but is not a company registered in England and Wales or Scotland under the Companies Acts.

12. Signature of applicant or their conveyancer ______________________ **Date** ______________

1.7 NOTICE OF SURRENDER OF DEVELOPMENT RIGHT(S)

Notes

(1) The Form that follows is a reproduction of Form SR1 in Schedule 1 to the Commonhold (Land Registration) Rules, and is a prescribed (ie mandatory) form for the surrender of a development right (see rule 28(1)).

(2) The Notice should be enclosed with the application to the Land Registry to register the surrender (see Form 1.6 above): it will not suffice for the relevant parts of the application to be included in the Notice.

(3) The full procedure for making such an application is discussed in paragraph 2.20.5 of the text of this work.

SCHEDULE 1

Notice of surrender of development right(s)

HM Land Registry

SR1

(if you need more room than is provided for in a panel, use continuation sheet CS and staple to this form)

1. Administrative area(s) and postcode(s) *(if known)*

2. Title Number(s)

3. Property

4. Date

5. We (1) *[developer of the land]* of *[developer's address]*

(2) *[lender (if applicable)]* of *[lender's address]*

notify the registrar that: *(Place "X" in the box that applies and complete as appropriate)*

☐ **the following development right contained in** *[insert appropriate reference from the commonhold community statement]* the commonhold community statement is surrendered: *(Specify right)*

☐ **all the development rights contained in** *[insert appropriate reference from the commonhold community statement]* the commonhold community statement are surrendered.

6. ***To be signed by all parties.***

1.8 APPLICATION FOR AN OFFICIAL SEARCH OF THE INDEX MAP

Notes

(1) The Form that follows is a reproduction of Form SIM in Schedule 1 to the Land Registration Rules 2003, and is a prescribed (ie mandatory) form for use in applications for an official search of the index map (see rule 146(2) of the Land Registration Rules 2003) relating either to a unit or to the common parts in a commonhold development.

(2) When the index map relating to a unit is searched, the search result will reveal (a) the title number of the unit; (b) any registered leasehold titles of the unit; and (c) the title number of the common parts.

(3) When the index map relating to the common parts of a commonhold is searched, the search result will reveal (a) the title number of the common parts; (b) any registered lease of the common parts; (c) the title numbers of all the units within the commonhold; (d) any registered leasehold titles of a unit; and (e) any other freehold or leasehold title not part of the commonhold. Official copies of those titles can be applied for.

Annex E: Form SIM (Search of the Index Map)

Application for an Official Search of the Index Map (Note 1)

HM Land Registry **SIM**

FOR EXPLANATORY NOTES SEE OVERLEAF
Please complete in typescript or in BLACK BLOCK LETTERS all details within the thick black lines.

To ____________________ District Land Registry

(Note 2)

For official use only

Description	Date

Fees Debited £		Record of Fees paid	

I

of

(enter name and address of person or firm making the application)

apply for an official search of the Index Map, and the list of pending applications for first registration, in respect of the land referred to below and

shown [ ] on the attached plan.

NOTE - Any attached plan must contain sufficient details of the surrounding roads and other features to enable the land to be identified satisfactorily on the Ordnance Survey Map. However, a plan may be unnecessary if the land can be identified by postal description. Nevertheless, the Chief Land Registrar reserves the right to ask for a plan to be supplied where he considers it necessary.

PAYMENT OF FEE (Note 5)

Please enter X in the appropriate box:–

☐ the Land Registry fee of £ [ ] accompanies this application,

or

☐ please debit the Credit Account mentioned below with the appropriate fee payable under the current Land Registration Fee Order.

FOR COMPLETION BY APPLICANTS WHO ARE CREDIT ACCOUNT HOLDERS

YOUR KEY NUMBER:-

YOUR REFERENCE:- (Note 6)

Signed

Date

Telephone No.

Reference

Property

Postal number or description	
Name of road	
Name of locality	
Town	
Postcode	
Administrative area (Note 3) (including district or borough if any)	
Ordnance Survey Map Reference (Note 4)	
Known Title Number(s)	

If you have received an official copy or an official search of a common parts title and are applying for the title numbers of the commonhold units, please quote the common parts title ....

Enter Name and either address including postcode OR (if applicable) DX number of the person to whom the official certificate of result of search is to be sent.

Reference	

Annex E: Form SIM (Search of the Index Map) **continued**

Explanatory Notes

1. The purpose and scope of Official Searches of the Index Map are described in Practice Leaflet 15 obtainable free of charge from any district land registry.

2. Please send this application to the appropriate district land registry. This information is contained in Explanatory Leaflet 9 obtainable free of charge from any district land registry.

3. Please enter the administrative area (county and district, county, county or London Borough etc.) in which the property is situated.

4. Please provide the Ordnance Survey Map Reference if known. Where this is not supplied by you it will be entered by the Land Registry. This reference should be quoted on any subsequent application for first registration.

5. Please ensure that the appropriate fee payable under the current Land Registration Fee Order accompanies your application. If paying fees by cheque or postal order, these should be crossed and payable to "HM Land Registry".

Where you have requested that the fee be paid by Credit Account, receipt of this certificate of result in confirmation that the appropriate fee has been debited.

6. Any reference should be limited to 25 characters (including oblique strokes and punctuation).

1.9 APPLICATION FOR OFFICIAL COPIES OF THE REGISTER OR TITLE PLAN

Notes

(1) The Form that follows is a reproduction of Form OC1 in Schedule 1 to the Land Registration Rules 2003, and is a prescribed (ie mandatory) form for use in applications to obtain official copies of the register or title plan (see rule 133(2) of the Land Registration Rules 2003).

(2) On completion of an application under section 2, a developer will receive official copies of each unit title and an equivalent number of copies of the common parts title. These can then be used by the developer to pass on to prospective purchasers.

(3) Whenever an official copy of the common parts title is requested, an official copy of the register and title plan will always be supplied. Form OC1 has been revised to include the facility to request these copies.

(4) The full procedure for making such an application is discussed in paragraph 2.19.4 of the text of this work.

Annex D: Form OC1 (Applications of Official Copies of Register/Title Plan)

Application for **Official Copies of Register/Title Plan and/or a certificate in Form CI**

HM Land Registry **OC1**

____________ District Land Registry

Please complete the numbered panels on this form in typescript or BLOCK LETTERS.
No covering letter is necessary.
Applications for official copies of specified documents must be made on Form OC2.
Use one form per title.

For official use only | Record of fees paid. | Fee Debited. £

1 Title Number (if known)

2 Flat No. if applicable — **Property Description**

Postal number or description

Name of road

Name of locality

Town

Administrative area (including district or borough if any)

Postcode

4 **PAYMENT OF FEE**

Please enter X in the appropriate box:-

☐ the Land Registry fee of £ ☐ accompanies this application.

or

☐ please debit the Credit Account mentioned below with the appropriate fee payable under the current Land Registration Fee Order.

FOR COMPLETION BY APPLICANTS WHO ARE CREDIT ACCOUNT HOLDERS

YOUR KEY NUMBER:-

YOUR REFERENCE:- (See over)

3 Application

I____________
(enter here name and address of person or firm making the application)

of____________

apply for

☐ official copy(ies) of the **register** of the above mentioned property;

☐ official copy(ies) of the **title plan** of the above mentioned property;

☐ official copy(ies) of the register of the **caution against first registration** of the above mentioned property;

☐ official copy(ies) of the title plan of the **caution against first registration** of the above mentioned property;

☐ official copy(ies) of the **register** and **title plan** of the common parts in a commonhold development.

5 Where the title number is NOT quoted in Panel 1, please enter X in the appropriate box(es):-
As regards this property, I am interested in the

☐ Freehold estate

☐ Leasehold estate

☐ Caution against first registration

6 In case there is an application for registration pending against the title, please enter X in the appropriate box :-

☐ I require an official copy back dated to the day prior to the receipt of that application, or

☐ I require an official copy on completion of that application.

3 Application (cont.)

a certificate in Form CI in which case, **either**:-

☐ an estate plan has been approved and the plot number is ☐ **or**

☐ no estate plan has been approved and a certificate is to be issued in respect of the land shown ____________ on the attached plan and copy.

Signature of applicant :- Date Daytime telephone No :-

7 Reference ____________

Please enter above using BLOCK LETTERS the name and either address (including postcode) OR (if applicable) the DX number of the person to whom the official copies are to be sent.

Where you have requested that the fee be paid by Credit Account the appropriate fee has been debited.

Annex D: Form OC1 (Application for Official Copies of Register/Title Plan) continued

For official use only	
Official Copies to be dated: Register ______	Title Plan ______
Authorised by:- ______	Date ______
Other action ______	
Despatched by ______	Date ______

Notes for the guidance of applicants

a) The application must be sent to the district land registry serving the area in which the land is situated. A list of addresses of the district land registries is set out in Explanatory Leaflet 9 which is obtainable free from any land registry office.

b) Please enter the administrative area (county and district, county, county or London borough etc.) in which the property is situated.

c) Where application is made for a certificate CI and no estate plan has been approved a plan must be lodged in duplicate. It should be drawn to a suitable scale (generally not less than 1/2500) and must show by suitable markings the extent of the land affected and, where necessary, figured measurements to fix the position of the land by tying it to existing physical features depicted by firm black lines on the plan of the registered title.

d) If there is a pending application and you are applying for an official copy in connection with a further transaction, it is possible for negotiations to proceed on the strength of a back-dated official copy of the register which can be brought up-to-date in effect by making a non-priority official search in Form OS3 in which the date of that official copy is entered as the date for the commencement of the search. The certificate of the result of search will reveal details of the pending application for registration and will state whether or not it has yet been approved for entry on the register.
If negotiations proceed on this basis, and assuming that your prospective transaction is a transfer, lease or charge, the normal search in Form OS1 or OS2 can be made as usual immediately before the completion of the transaction.

If a back dated official copy is not required, see panel 6 overleaf, your application for official copies will be returned to you and you will be informed when the pending application has been completed. You should relodge your application for official copies at that time.

e) Full information on all aspects of applications for official copies is set out in Practice Leaflet 13 which is obtainable free from any land registry office.

f) Any reference should be limited to 25 characters (including oblique strokes and punctuation).

g) Commonhold Developments

(If you are applying for official copies of the common parts title in a commonhold development, you will receive official copies of both the register and title plan.

(Further information in connection with official copies on titles within a commonhold development can be found in Practice Advice Leaflet ** "Commonhold".

1.10 APPLICATION FOR OFFICIAL COPIES OF THE COMMONHOLD COMMUNITY STATEMENT OR MEMORANDUM AND ARTICLES OF ASSOCIATION

Notes

(1) The Form that follows is a reproduction of Form OC2 in Schedule 1 to the Land Registration Rules 2003, and is a prescribed (ie mandatory) form for use in applications to obtain official copies of such documents as the commonhold community statement or the memorandum and articles of association of a commonhold association (see rule 134 of the Land Registration Rules 2003).

(2) Whenever an official copy of such documents is requested, an official copy will always be supplied.

Application for official copies of documents only

Land Registry

OC2

The correct title number must be quoted. Use one form per title. *If you need more room than is provided for in a panel, use continuation sheet CS and attach to this form.*

1. **Administrative area and postcode** if known

2. **Title number**

3. **Property description** *Please give a full property description.*

4. **Payment of fee** *Place "X" in the appropriate box.*

   ☐ The Land Registry fee of £ [ ] accompanies this application.

   ☐ Debit the Credit Account mentioned in panel 5 with the appropriate fee payable under the current Land Registration Fee Order.

For official use only
Impression of fees

5. **The application has been lodged by:**
   Land Registry Key No. (if appropriate)
   Name
   Address/DX No.

   Reference
   E-mail

Telephone No.	Fax No.

6. If the official copies are to be sent to anyone other than the applicant in panel 5, please supply the name and address of the person to whom they should be sent.

   Reference

7. I apply for official copies of the documents listed below

Documents which are referred to in the register of the above title
Applications specifying "All", "Any", etc., will be rejected.

Nature of document	Date of document	Title number under which it is filed	No. of copies

Documents which are not referred to in the register
Please supply as much detail as possible.

Nature of document	Date of document, if known	No. of copies

8. Signature of applicant ______________________ **Date** ______________

1.11 APPLICATION BY PURCHASER FOR OFFICIAL SEARCH OF WHOLE

Notes

(1) The Form that follows is a reproduction of Form OS1 in Schedule 1 to the Land Registration Rules 2003, and is a prescribed (ie mandatory) form for use in applications by purchasers for an official search, with priority, of the whole of the land in either a registered title or a pending first registration application (see rule 148(3) of the Land Registration Rules 2003).

(2) Rule 3(1)(f) of the Commonhold (Land Registration) Rules provides that rule 148 of the Land Registration Rules 2003 shall apply to proposed unit-holders in the same way as it applies to purchasers, thus enabling existing owners (eg converting lessees) to take advantage of the priority search procedure.

(3) When used in conjunction with an application for conversion to commonhold from leasehold, the name of the applicant who intends to apply for registration as a unit-holder under the Act should be noted in Box 4, and an "X" should be entered alongside "[H]" in panel 5 (see explanatory note (e)).

Annex B: Form OS1 (Official Search of Whole)

Application by Purchaser [a] for Official Search with priority of the whole of the land in either a registered title or a pending first registration application

HM Land Registry **OS1**

____________ District Land Registry [b]

Small raised letters in **bold** type refer to explanatory notes overleaf.

Complete panels as appropriate in block letters

1 Title number (one only per form) - enter the title number of the registered land or that allotted to the pending first registration.

2 Registered proprietor(s) / Applicant(s) for first registration [c] - enter FULL name(s) either of the registered proprietor(s) of the land in the above title **or** of the person(s) applying for first registration of the land specified in panel 8.

SURNAME / COMPANY NAME:

FORENAME(S):

SURNAME / COMPANY NAME:

FORENAME(S):

3 Search from date - for a search of a **registered title** enter in the box a date falling within (a) of the definition of search from date in rule 129 of the Land Registration Rules 2003.
Note: If the date entered is not such a date the application may be rejected. In the case of a **pending first registration** search, enter the letters 'FR'.

4 Applicant(s) - enter FULL name of each purchaser, **or** lessee, **or** chargee **or** person intending to convert to commonhold [e].

5 Reason for application - I certify that the applicant(s) intend(s) to:-
(enter X in the appropriate box)

- ☐ **P** purchase
- ☐ **L** take a lease of
- ☐ **C** take a registered charge on
- ☐ **H** convert to commonhold [e]

(enter X in the appropriate box)

- ☐ the **whole** of the land in the above registered title **or**
- ☐ the **whole** of the land in the pending first registration application referred to above.

6 Enter the key number [f] (if any) and the name and (DX) address of the person lodging the application (**use BLOCK LETTERS**).

Key number:

Name:

DX No: DX Exchange:

Address including postcode (if DX not used):

Reference: [g]

7 Enter, using BLOCK LETTERS, the name and either address (including postcode) OR (if applicable) the DX No and exchange of the person to whom the result is to be sent. **(Leave blank if result is to be sent to the address in panel 6.)**

Reference: [g]

8 Property details

Administrative area (including district or borough if any): [h]

Address (including postcode) or short description of the land:

9 Type of search (enter X in the appropriate box)

☐ **Registered land search**
Application is made to ascertain whether any adverse entry [i] has been made in the register or day list since the date shown in panel 3.

☐ **Pending first registration search**
Application is made to ascertain whether any adverse entry has been made in the day list since the date of the pending first registration application referred to above.

10 **PAYMENT OF FEE** [j]

Please enter X in the appropriate box.

☐ The Land Registry fee of £ _____ accompanies this application; **or**

☐ Please debit the Credit Account mentioned in panel 6 with the appropriate fee payable under the current Land Registration Fee Order.

Note: If the fee is not paid by either of the above methods the application may be rejected.

Signature

Date Telephone No.

Annex B: Form OS1 (Official Search of Whole) continued

Explanatory Notes

(a) 'Purchaser' means any person who, in good faith and for valuable consideration, acquires or intends to acquire a legal estate in land, and includes a lessee or a chargee. An official search made by any person other than a 'purchaser', as so defined, should, provided the land is registered, be made in Form OS3.

(b) The application must be sent to the district land registry that deals with the area in which the land is situated.

(c) The name(s) of the registered proprietor(s) of the land must be entered as set out in the register of title. If there are more than two registered proprietors/applicants for first registration, enter the first two only.

(d) The statement printed on an official copy of the register contains the date (subsisting entries date) and time at which the entries shown on the copy were subsisting. The statement will also show the date on which the copy was issued.

Where a person accesses a register on-line from the registrar's computer (under rule 131 of the Land Registration Rules 2003 a date (on-line subsisting entries date) is shown which has the same function as the subsisting entries date. The time the entries were subsisting will also be shown.

The search from date must be either:

(i) a subsisting entries date taken from an official copy; or

(ii) an on-line subsisting entries date shown on register entries transmitted by the registrar's computer system.

The date stated in a Land or Charge Certificate as the date on which the Certificate was officially examined with the register cannot be used.

For the definition of "search from date" see rule 129 of the Land Registration (Official Searches) Rules 1993.

(e) The name(s) of the applicant(s) intending to make an application for registration with unit-holders under the Commonhold and Leasehold Reform Act 2002 (Act) should be entered in panel 4 and an 'X' should be entered alongside 'H' in panel 5. See the Act and the explanatory notes in respect of the Act for further information.

(f) Please enter the administrative area (county and district, county, county or London borough etc.) in which the property is situated.

(g) Except as stated below the application must be accompanied by a plan (in duplicate) showing, by a suitable colour reference, the precise extent to be searched. The plan should be drawn to an acceptable scale (generally not less than 1/2500). When necessary sufficient dimensions must be shown on the plan to define the part affected and to fix its position by tying it to those existing physical features which are depicted by firm black lines on the published large scale Ordnance Survey Map. The plan submitted should be a copy of that which will be bound up in the protected instrument. The use of a plan which does not meet the above criteria may result in the application being rejected.

For official use only
Record of Fee paid

The application need **not** be accompanied by a plan in the case of a registered building estate where the estate layout plan has already been approved by the Registry for use in connection with official searches. It will then suffice if the application refers to plot number(s) shown on the approved plan and the date of approval of that plan. If the official search procedure is to operate effectively, however, it is essential that the plot number(s) are stated correctly, particularly where the property comprises two or more separately numbered plots or parcels (e.g. a house in a block of dwellings with its garage in a separate garage block).

(h) Where a key number has been allocated it should be used. If you wish the result to be issued to an address different from that associated with the key number, enter your key number and reference but otherwise leave panel 6 blank Complete panel 7 instead.

(i) Any reference should be restricted to a maximum of 25 characters including oblique strokes and punctuation.

(j) Any entry made in the register since the search from date of this application but subsequently cancelled will not be revealed.

(k) For the fee payable and the debiting of credit accounts see the current Land Registration Fee Order. Either enclose a cheque for the fee payable (made out to "H M Land Registry") or, if you hold a credit account with the Land Registry/Land Charges Department, ensure that the key number for that account has been entered in panel 7. If you hold a credit account but do not request it to be debited, and no cheque is enclosed, the registrar may nevertheless debit your account.

(l) Fuller information about the official search procedure is contained in:

Practice Advice Leaflet 5, entitled 'Searches of Registered Land and Land Subject to a Pending First Registration Application', and;

Practice Leaflet 7, entitled 'Development of Registered Building Estates'.

Practice Advice Leaflet ** 'Commonhold etc.***.

These leaflets are available free of charge from any district land registry.

1.12 APPLICATION BY PURCHASER FOR OFFICIAL SEARCH OF PART

Notes

(1) The Form that follows is a reproduction of Form OS2 in Schedule 1 to the Land Registration Rules 2003, and is a prescribed (ie mandatory) form for use in applications by purchasers for an official search, with priority, of part of the land in either a registered title or a pending first registration application (see rule 148(3) of the Land Registration Rules 2003).

(2) Rule 3(1)(f) of the Commonhold (Land Registration) Rules provides that rule 148 of the Land Registration Rules 2003 shall apply to proposed unit-holders in the same way as it applies to purchasers, thus enabling existing owners (eg converting lessees) to take advantage of the priority search procedure.

(3) When used in conjunction with an application for conversion to commonhold from leasehold, the name of the applicant who intends to apply for registration as a unit-holder under the Act should be noted in Box 4, and an "X" should be entered alongside "[H]" in panel 5 (see explanatory note (e)).

Annex C: Form OS2 (Official Search of Part)

Application by Purchaser [a] for Official Search with priority of part of the land in either a registered title or a pending first registration application

HM Land Registry **OS2**

_________________ District Land Registry [b]

Small raised letters in **bold** type refer to explanatory notes overleaf.

Complete panels as appropriate in block letters

1 Title number (one only per form) - enter the title number of the registered land or that allotted to the pending first registration.

2 Registered proprietor(s) / Applicant(s) for first registration [c] - enter FULL name(s) either of the registered proprietor(s) of the land in the above title **or** of the person(s) applying for first registration of the land specified in panel 6.

SURNAME / COMPANY NAME:

FORENAME(S):

SURNAME / COMPANY NAME:

FORENAME(S):

3 Search from date - for a search of a **registered title** enter in the box a date falling within (a) of the definition of search from date in rule 2(1). [d]
Note: If the date entered is not such a date the application may be rejected. In the case of a **pending first registration** search, enter the letters 'FR'.

4 Applicant(s) - enter FULL name of each purchaser, **or** lessee **or** chargee.

5 Reason for application - I certify that the applicant(s) intend(s) to:- (enter X in the appropriate box)

P purchase

L take a lease of

C take a registered charge on

H convert to commonhold [e] -

the land described in panel 6, being part of the land in the above title.

6 Property details

Administrative area (including district or borough if any): [f]

Part to be searched - complete either (a) **or** (b) below. [g]
(a) Where an estate layout plan has been approved:
(i) the plot number(s) is/are
(ii) the date of approval of the estate plan is

OR

(b) Address (including postcode) or short description of the land:

as shown on the attached plan
NB. A plan must be supplied when (a) above is not completed. [g]

7 Enter the key number [h] (if any) and the name and (DX) address of the person lodging the application **(use BLOCK LETTERS).**

Key number:

Name:

DX No: DX Exchange:

Address including postcode (if DX not used):

Reference: [i]

8 Enter, using BLOCK LETTERS, the name and either address (including postcode) OR (if applicable) the DX No and exchange of the person to whom the result is to be sent. **(Leave blank if result is to be sent to the address in panel 7.)**

Reference: [i]

9 Type of search (enter X in the appropriate box)

Registered land search
Application is made to ascertain whether any adverse entry [j] has been made in the register or day list since the date shown in panel 3.

Pending first registration search
Application is made to ascertain whether any adverse entry has been made in the day list since the date of the pending first registration application referred to above.

10 **PAYMENT OF FEE** [k]

Please enter X in the appropriate box.

The Land Registry fee of £ accompanies this application; **or**

Please debit the Credit Account mentioned in panel 7 with the appropriate fee payable under the current Land Registration Fee Order.

Note: If the fee is not paid by either of the above methods the application may be rejected.

Signature

Date Telephone No.

Annex C: Form OS2 (Official Search of Part) **continued**

Explanatory Notes

(a) 'Purchaser' means any person who, in good faith and for valuable consideration, acquires or intends to acquire a legal estate in land, and includes a lessee or a chargee. An official search made by any person other than a 'purchaser', as so defined, should, provided the land is registered, be made in Form OS3.

(b) The application must be sent to the district land registry that deals with the area in which the land is situated.

(c) The name(s) of the registered proprietor(s) of the land must be entered as set out in the register of title. If there are more than two registered proprietors/applicants for first registration, enter the first two only.

(d) The statement printed on an official copy of the register contains the date (subsisting entries date) and time at which the entries shown on the copy were subsisting. The statement will also show the date on which the copy was issued.

Where a person accesses a register on-line from the registrar's computer (under rule 131 of the Land Registration Rules 2003 a date (on-line subsisting entries date) is shown which has the same function as the subsisting entries date. The time the entries were subsisting will also be shown.

The search from date must be either:

(i) a subsisting entries date taken from an official copy; or

(ii) an on-line subsisting entries date shown on register entries transmitted by the registrar's computer system.

The date stated in a Land or Charge Certificate as the date on which the Certificate was officially examined with the register cannot be used.

For the definition of "search from date" see rule 129 of the Land Registration (Official Searches) Rules 1993.

(e) The name(s) of the applicant(s) intending to make an application for registration with unit-holders under the Commonhold and Leasehold Reform Act 2002 (Act) should be entered in panel 4 and an 'X' should be entered alongside 'H' in panel 5. See the Act and the explanatory notes in respect of the Act for further information.

(f) Please enter the administrative area (county and district, county, county or London borough etc.) in which the property is situated.

(g) Except as stated below the application must be accompanied by a plan (in duplicate) showing, by a suitable colour reference, the precise extent to be searched. The plan should be drawn to an acceptable scale (generally not less than 1/2500). When necessary sufficient dimensions must be shown on the plan to define the part affected and to fix its position by tying it to those existing physical features which are depicted by firm black lines on the published large scale Ordnance Survey Map. The plan submitted should be a copy of that which will be bound up in the protected instrument. The use of a plan which does not meet the above criteria may result in the application being rejected.

For official use only
Record of Fee paid

The application need **not** be accompanied by a plan in the case of a registered building estate where the estate layout plan has already been approved by the Registry for use in connection with official searches. It will then suffice if the application refers to plot number(s) shown on the approved plan and the date of approval of that plan. If the official search procedure is to operate effectively, however, it is essential that the plot number(s) are stated correctly, particularly where the property comprises two or more separately numbered plots or parcels (e.g. a house in a block of dwellings with its garage in a separate garage block).

(h) Where a key number has been allocated it should be used. If you wish the result to be issued to an address different from that associated with the key number, enter your key number and reference but otherwise leave panel 6 blank Complete panel 7 instead.

(i) Any reference should be restricted to a maximum of 25 characters including oblique strokes and punctuation.

(j) Any entry made in the register since the search from date of this application but subsequently cancelled will not be revealed.

(k) For the fee payable and the debiting of credit accounts see the current Land Registration Fee Order. Either enclose a cheque for the fee payable (made out to "H M Land Registry") or, if you hold a credit account with the Land Registry/Land Charges Department, ensure that the key number for that account has been entered in panel 7. If you hold a credit account but do not request it to be debited, and no cheque is enclosed, the registrar may nevertheless debit your account.

(l) Fuller information about the official search procedure is contained in:

Practice Advice Leaflet 5, entitled 'Searches of Registered Land and Land Subject to a Pending First Registration Application', and;

Practice Leaflet 7, entitled 'Development of Registered Building Estates'.

Practice Advice Leaflet ** 'Commonhold etc.***.

These leaflets are available free of charge from any district land registry.

1.13 APPLICATION FOR REGISTRATION OF TRANSFER OF FREEHOLD ESTATE IN PART ONLY OF COMMONHOLD UNIT OR COMMON PARTS OF COMMONHOLD

Notes

(1) This Form, which is set out above as Form 1.6, is a reproduction of Form AP1 in Schedule 1 to the Land Registration Rules 2003, and is a prescribed (ie mandatory) form for use in general applications to the Land Registry to change the register for which no other form is prescribed (see rule 13(1) of the Land Registration Rules 2003).

(2) This application must be made where the applicant has obtained a transfer of freehold estate in part only of a commonhold unit or the common parts of a commonhold. It will follow from the nature of the application that the commonhold community statement will need to be amended (see sections 23(1), 24(2) and 30(2) of the Act), and that an application for registration of an amended commonhold community statement will also have to be made by the directors of the commonhold association (see Form 1.3 above). Rules 15 and 19 of the Commonhold (Land Registration) Rules require the applications to be made together, and provide that the Registrar may reject the application for registration of the transfer if it is not accompanied by an application to amend the commonhold community statement.

(3) The full procedure for making such an application is discussed in paragraph 3.2.6 of the text of this work.

1.14 CONSENT TO THE REGISTRATION OF LAND AS COMMONHOLD LAND

Notes

(1) This document, which is currently in draft form, will be a prescribed (ie mandatory) document once the Commonhold Regulations have been promulgated. The Form is based upon the draft forming part of the Consultation Paper issued by the Lord Chancellor's Department on 10 October 2002, with modifications inserted by the authors.

(2) Section 3 of the Act provides that land may not be registered as commonhold land without the consent of the registered proprietors of various substantial legal and other interests in the land (the categories of which are set out in subsection (1) and may be extended by regulation made under subsection (1)(d)).

(3) Where there are such interests, it must be established upon application for registration either that the consents have been obtained (section 3(1)); or that they are deemed to have been given or that they have been dispensed with by a court. A registration obtained without such consents will be liable to be altered by the court (section 6).

(4) This document will record the requisite consent.

(5) Section 3(2) provides for regulations to be made governing such matters as the form, duration, effect and revocability of the consent. The Consultation Paper issued by the Lord Chancellor's Department on 10 October 2002 proposes that the consent should (a) be in a prescribed form; (b) bind successors in title of the consentor; (c) be irrevocable for a period of three months from the date given until application date (although the Post-Consultation Report dated August 2003 has since proposed that this period should be extended to 12 months); and (d) cause the Land Registry to remove any relevant entry on the register (but not so as to cause the discharge of any charge).

(6) Paragraph 2.19.3 of the text gives a full analysis of this topic.

COMMONHOLD

Consent to the Registration of Land as Commonhold Land

Commonhold and Leasehold Reform Act 2002 Section 3(1)

---

1. **Details of the freehold land the subject of the application to become commonhold ("the Land"):**

   Description:

   Title Number:

2. **Details of the Applicant for Registration:**

   Name:

   Address:

   Address for Service (if different):

3. **Details of the persons giving consent and their interest in the Land:**

   Name of person consenting:

   Address:

   Address for Service (if different):

   Interest in the Land:

4. **Consent valid until [date]**

   Signature:

   Date:

I, ..., as [registered proprietor/trustee/beneficial owner/ personal representative] of the above Interest in the Land, have read the warning set out below regarding the desirability of taking legal advice, [and have taken such advice/but understand fully the consequences of giving the consent referred to below, and have elected not to take such advice].

I hereby consent to the registration of the Land as a freehold estate in commonhold land. I undertake not to withdraw my consent until after the date specified in paragraph 4 above.

VERY IMPORTANT

This consent will bind you and any subsequent owners of the property. Before signing this form you are strongly advised to seek legal advice.

1.15 CONSENT BY UNIT-HOLDER OR CHARGEE TO THE AMENDMENT OF A COMMONHOLD COMMUNITY STATEMENT

Notes:

(1) Section 23(1) of the Act provides that an amendment to a commonhold community statement which redefines the extent of a commonhold unit may not be made without the consent of the unit-holder.

(2) Sections 24(2) and 30(2) of the Act further provide that amendments to a commonhold community statement which respectively redefine the extent of a commonhold unit and add land from that unit to the common parts of the commonhold may not be made without the consent of the registered proprietor of any charge over the unit.

(3) This document will record the requisite consent, and may be used either by the unit-holder or by the chargee. It is not a prescribed form, and contains the authors' suggestions as to the appropriate text.

(4) In each case, the Act also provides for regulations to be made enabling an application to court for an order dispensing with the need for such consent (see Forms 5.8, 5.9 and 5.10).

(5) Paragraph 2.18.3 of the text gives a full analysis of this topic.

COMMONHOLD

Consent to amendment of the commonhold community statement

Commonhold and Leasehold Reform Act 2002, sections 23(1)/24(2)/30(2)

---

1. **Details of the commonhold association:**

   Name: [Name] Commonhold Association Limited

   Registered office:

   Address for Service (if different):

2. **Details of the freehold land the subject of the application to register an amended commonhold community statement ("the Land"):**

   Description:

   Title Number:

3. **Details of the commonhold unit ("the Unit") the extent of which is to be redefined:**

   Description:

   Title Number:

4. **Details of the persons giving consent and their interest in the Unit:**

	Unit-holder	**Chargee** ***(if any)***
Name		
Interest in Unit	*(Joint) registered proprietor*	*Mortgagee pursuant to a legal charge dated* *
Address		
Address for Service (if different)		

I, ____, as registered proprietor of the above interest in the Land, hereby consent to the amendment of the commonhold community statement to record the redefinition of the Unit [and the addition of land from the Unit to the common parts of the Land], as provided for in the commonhold community statement.

Signed this ____ day of ____ 20____ by:

VERY IMPORTANT

This consent will bind you and any subsequent owners of the property. Before signing this form you are strongly advised to seek legal advice.

1.16 TRANSFER OF FREEHOLD ESTATE IN PART ONLY OF COMMONHOLD UNIT OR COMMON PARTS OF COMMONHOLD

Notes

(1) The Form that follows is a reproduction of Form TP1 in Schedule 1 to the Land Registration Rules 2003, and is a prescribed (ie mandatory) form for use where part only of a registered title is being transferred (see rule 56 of the Land Registration Rules 2003).

(2) Where such a transfer is made, an application to register must be made in Form 1.13 above.

(3) A full analysis of the transfer of part only of a commonhold unit is given in paragraph 3.2.6 of the text of this work.

Transfer of part of registered title(s)

Land Registry

If you need more room than is provided for in a panel, use continuation sheet CS and attach to this form.

1. Stamp Duty

Place "X" in the appropriate box or boxes and complete the appropriate certificate.

☐ It is certified that this instrument falls within category ☐ in the Schedule to the Stamp Duty (Exempt Instruments) Regulations 1987

☐ It is certified that the transaction effected does not form part of a larger transaction or of a series of transactions in respect of which the amount or value or the aggregate amount or value of the consideration exceeds the sum of £

☐ It is certified that this is an instrument on which stamp duty is not chargeable by virtue of the provisions of section 92 of the Finance Act 2001

2. Title number(s) out of which the Property is transferred *Leave blank if not yet registered.*

3. Other title number(s) against which matters contained in this transfer are to be registered, if any

4. Property transferred *Insert address, including postcode, or other description of the property transferred. Any physical exclusions, e.g. mines and minerals, should be defined. Any attached plan must be signed by the transferor.*

The Property is defined: *Place "X" in the appropriate box.*

☐ on the attached plan and shown *State reference e.g. "edged red".*

☐ on the Transferor's title plan and shown *State reference e.g. "edged and numbered 1 in blue".*

5. Date

6. Transferor *Give full name(s) and company's registered number, if any.*

7. Transferee **for entry on the register** *Give full name(s) and company's registered number, if any. For Scottish companies use an SC prefix and for limited liability partnerships use an OC prefix before the registered number, if any. For foreign companies give territory in which incorporated.*

Unless otherwise arranged with Land Registry headquarters, a certified copy of the Transferee's constitution (in English or Welsh) will be required if it is a body corporate but is not a company registered in England and Wales or Scotland under the Companies Acts.

8. Transferee's intended **address(es) for service (including postcode) for entry on the register** *You may give up to three addresses for service **one** of which **must** be a postal address but does not have to be within the UK. The other addresses can be any combination of a postal address, a box number at a UK document exchange or an electronic address.*

9. The Transferor transfers the Property to the Transferee

10. Consideration *Place "X" in the appropriate box. State clearly the currency unit if other than sterling. If none of the boxes applies, insert an appropriate memorandum in the additional provisions panel.*

☐ The Transferor has received from the Transferee for the Property the sum of *In words and figures.*

☐ *Insert other receipt as appropriate.*

☐ The transfer is not for money or anything which has a monetary value

11. The Transferor transfers with *Place "X" in the appropriate box and add any modifications.*

☐ full title guarantee ☐ limited title guarantee

12. Declaration of trust *Where there is more than one Transferee, place "X" in the appropriate box.*

☐ The Transferees are to hold the Property on trust for themselves as joint tenants

☐ The Transferees are to hold the Property on trust for themselves as tenants in common in equal shares

☐ The Transferees are to hold the Property *Complete as necessary.*

13. Additional provisions

Use this panel for:

- *definitions of terms not defined above*
- *rights granted or reserved*
- *restrictive covenants*
- *other covenants*
- *agreements and declarations*
- *other agreed provisions.*

The prescribed subheadings may be added to, amended, repositioned or omitted.

Definitions

Rights granted for the benefit of the Property

Rights reserved for the benefit of other land *The land having the benefit should be defined, if necessary by reference to a plan.*

Restrictive covenants by the Transferor *Include words of covenant.*

14. Execution *The Transferor must execute this transfer as a deed using the space below. If there is more than one Transferor, all must execute. Forms of execution are given in Schedule 9 to the Land Registration Rules 2003. If the transfer contains Transferee's covenants or declarations or contains an application by the Transferee (e.g. for a restriction), it must also be executed by the Transferee (all of them, if there is more than one).*

1.17 APPLICATION TO REGISTER A SUCCESSOR COMMONHOLD ASSOCIATION

Notes

(1) This Form, which is set out above as Form 1.6, is a reproduction of Form AP1 in Schedule 1 to the Land Registration Rules 2003, and is a prescribed (ie mandatory) form for use in general applications to the Land Registry to change the register for which no other form is prescribed (see rule 13(1) of the Land Registration Rules 2003).

(2) This application must be made (see rule 25(1) of the Commonhold (Land Registration) Rules) once a succession order has been made by the court (see Form 6.18 below).

(3) The application should be made against the common parts title and all the unit titles.

(4) Unless the Registrar otherwise directs, the application must be accompanied by (a) the succession order (Form 6.18); (b) the memorandum and articles of association of the successor commonhold association; (c) a certified copy of the memorandum and articles of association of the successor commonhold association; (d) an amended commonhold community statement (bearing the change of name of the successor commonhold association); and (e) a certified copy of the amended commonhold community statement (see rule 25(2) of the Commonhold (Land Registration) Rules).

(5) Once the Registrar is satisfied as to the application, he must replace the notice in the property register of the title to the common parts of the memorandum and articles of association of the insolvent commonhold association with notice of the memorandum and articles of association of the successor, and make entries to reflect the terms of the succession order on the registers of the titles affected (rule 25(3)).

(6) The full procedure for making such an application is discussed in paragraph 5.4.7 of the text of this work.

1.18 APPLICATION TO ALTER THE REGISTER

Notes

(1) This Form, which is set out above as Form 1.6, is a reproduction of Form AP1 in Schedule 1 to the Land Registration Rules 2003, and is a prescribed (ie mandatory) form for use in general applications to the Land Registry to change the register for which no other form is prescribed (see rule 13(1) of the Land Registration Rules 2003).

(2) The application should be made where the applicant has obtained a commonhold registration in error (eg because of an inaccuracy in the documents supplied pursuant to schedule 1 to the Act). The Registrar has no power to alter the register of his own motion, but can only alter the register pursuant to an order of the court under section 6 of the Act.

(3) The application should be accompanied by the court order or a sealed copy of it (see rule 8 of the Commonhold (Land Registration) Rules).

(4) Where the court orders that the land should cease to be registered as commonhold, then an application must be made to the Registrar, and, once satisfied as to the application, the Registrar must cancel the commonhold entries on the titles affected (see rule 9 of the Commonhold (Land Registration) Rules).

PART 2. COMMONHOLD ASSOCIATION FORMS

2.1 MEMORANDUM OF ASSOCIATION

Notes

(1) This Form is taken from the draft accompanying the Post-Consultation Report issued by the Department of Constitutional Affairs in August 2003. The final version is unlikely to be substantially different, but will be supplied once it is published.

(2) This document is prescribed by regulation 12 of the Commonhold Regulations, and the existing text may not be altered or modified in any way, although clauses may be added.

(3) Section 2.12 and Part 1 of Chapter 4 of the text contain a full discussion of the memorandum of association, while Section 2.14 explains how the memorandum may be altered.

THE COMPANIES ACTS 1985 & 1989

COMPANY LIMITED BY GUARANTEE AND NOT HAVING A SHARE CAPITAL

MEMORANDUM OF ASSOCIATION
OF
[*name of commonhold association*]

1. The name of the company (referred to in this document as "the commonhold association") is [insert name].
2. The registered office of the commonhold association is to be situated in *[England and Wales] [Wales]*.
3. The object of the commonhold association is to exercise the functions of a commonhold association in relation to [specify the name of the commonhold and its location] in accordance with the commonhold community statement, as amended from time to time, and any provision made by or by virtue of Part 1 of the Commonhold and Leasehold Reform Act 2002 and the doing of all such things as are incidental or conducive to the attainment of that object.
4. The liability of the members is limited.
5. Without prejudice to any further liability which he may have under or arising out of the commonhold community statement, every member of the commonhold association undertakes to contribute such amount as may be required, not exceeding £1, to the assets of the commonhold association if it should be wound up while he is a member or within one year after he ceases to be a member, for payment of the debts and liabilities of the commonhold association contracted before he ceases to be a member, and of the costs, charges, and expenses of winding up the commonhold association, and for the adjustment of the rights of the contributories among themselves.

We, the subscribers to this memorandum of association, wish to be formed into a company pursuant to this memorandum.

Names and Addresses of Subscribers

Dated

Witness to the above signatures

2.2 ARTICLES OF ASSOCIATION

Notes:

(1) This Form is taken from the draft accompanying the Post-Consultation Report issued by the Department of Constitutional Affairs in August 2003. The final version is unlikely to be substantially different, but will be supplied as soon as it is published.

(2) This document is prescribed by regulation 13 of the Commonhold Regulations, and parts of it may not be altered or modified in any way. Other parts (shown underlined) are default provisions, and are treated as included in the articles of association unless alternative provision is made in place of them. They may be altered by special resolution.

(3) Section 2.13 and Part 1 of Chapter 4 of the text contain a full discussion of the articles of association, while Section 2.14 deals with alteration of the articles.

THE COMPANIES ACTS 1985 & 1989

COMPANY LIMITED BY GUARANTEE AND NOT HAVING A SHARE CAPITAL

ARTICLES OF ASSOCIATION
OF
[*name of commonhold association*]

INTERPRETATION

1. In these articles—

"clear days" in relation to the period of a notice means that period excluding the day when the notice is given or deemed to be given and the day for which it is given or on which it is to take effect.

"the commonhold" means the land in respect of which the commonhold community statement is registered.

"the commonhold association" means the private company limited by guarantee which exercises the functions of a commonhold association in relation to the commonhold land.

"the commonhold community statement" means the document held by the Land Registry which makes provision for the rights and duties of the commonhold association and the unit-holders and defines the extent of each commonhold unit.

"communication" includes a communication comprising sounds or images or both and a communication effecting a payment.

"the Companies Act" means the Companies Act 1985 or any statutory modification or re-enactment of it for the time being in force.

"the developer" means the person who makes an application to register a freehold estate in land as a freehold estate in commonhold land, or his successor in title who is treated as the developer, and who carries on development business on the commonhold land.

"electronic communication" means a communication transmitted (whether from one person to another, from one device to another or from a person to a device or vice versa)—

(a) by means of a telecommunication system; or
(b) by other means but while in an electronic form.

"member" means a person whose name is entered in the register of members as a member but excluding any person who has ceased to be a unit-holder or joint unit-holder of a commonhold unit or who has resigned as a member.

"office" means the registered office of the commonhold association.

"pre-commonhold period" means the period beginning with incorporation of a commonhold association and ending when land specified in its memorandum becomes commonhold land.

"the Regulations" means the Commonhold Regulations 2003 and any modification for the time being in force.

"secretary" means the secretary of the commonhold association or any other person appointed to perform the duties of the secretary of the commonhold association, including a joint, assistant or deputy secretary.

"subscribers (or subscriber)" means the first members (or member) of the commonhold association.

"telecommunications system" means a system for the conveyance, through the agency of electric, magnetic, electro-magnetic, electro-chemical or electro-mechanical energy, of—

(a) speech, music and other sounds;
(b) visual images;
(c) signals serving for the impartation (whether as between persons and persons, things and things or persons and things) of any matter otherwise than in the form of sounds or visual images; or
(d) signals serving for the actuation or control of machinery or apparatus.

"the United Kingdom" means Great Britain and Northern Ireland.

"unit-holder" means a person entitled to be registered as the proprietor of the freehold estate in a commonhold unit (whether or not he is registered).

Unless the context otherwise requires, words and expressions contained in these articles bear the same meaning as in the Commonhold and Leasehold Reform Act 2002, including any statutory modification or re-enactment of it for the time being in force, or in the Companies Act.

MEMBERS

2. The persons who are entitled to be entered in the register of members of the commonhold association are—

(a) in the pre-commonhold period, the subscribers (or subscriber) to the memorandum of association of the commonhold association;
(b) where the registration is without unit-holders, during the transitional period, the subscribers (or subscriber) to the memorandum of association of the commonhold association and a person who for the time being is the developer in respect of all or part of the commonhold; and
(c) where the registration is with unit-holders or on transfer of the unit—

    (i) a person who becomes the unit-holder of a commonhold unit; or
    (ii) one of two or more joint unit-holders of a commonhold unit and where—

        (aa) the joint unit-holders nominate, in writing to the commonhold association, one of themselves to be entered in the register of members; or
        (bb) if no nomination is received by the commonhold association within seven days beginning with the date on which the Land Registry confirms that the joint unit-holders have been entered as registered pro-

prietors of the commonhold unit, the person whose name appears first in the proprietorship register at the end of the seven days; or

(cc) the court orders a joint unit-holder to be entered in the register of members in place of a person who is or who would be entitled to be registered; or

(dd) the joint unit-holders nominate one of themselves to be entered in the register of members in place of the person previously entered.

3. The commonhold association must keep a register of members and enter in it—

(a) the name, address and unit number of each member and an address for service (if different);
(b) the date on which the person was registered as a member; and
(c) the date at which the person ceased to be a member.

4. The commonhold association must enter the particulars of a person in the register where the person is entitled to be entered in the register of members of a commonhold association within fourteen days beginning with—

(a) in the pre-commonhold period, the date of incorporation of the commonhold association; or
(b) in the transitional period, the date on which the developer notifies the commonhold association of his right to be registered; or
(c) on registration with unit-holders, the date on which the Land Registry gives notice that the registration of the land as commonhold land has been completed; or
(d) on the transfer of a unit, the date on which the commonhold association receives notification, in writing, from the new unit-holder that the transfer has taken place.

5. The commonhold association must remove the particulars of a person from the register where the person ceases to be a unit-holder or joint unit-holder of a commonhold unit or on resignation within fourteen days beginning with the date on which the commonhold association becomes aware that the person had ceased to be a member.

GENERAL MEETINGS

6. The commonhold association must hold an annual general meeting.

7. In addition to its annual general meeting, the commonhold association must hold at least one other general meeting each year at which, in addition to any other business, the directors must present an interim review of the business and affairs of the commonhold association since the preceding annual general meeting.

8. All general meetings other than annual general meetings are called extraordinary general meetings.

9. The directors may call general meetings and, in the event that members of the commonhold association representing not less than one-tenth of the total voting rights of all the members requisition a meeting, must call a general meeting. The meeting must be convened on a date not later than twenty-eight days after receipt of the

requisition. If there are insufficient directors in the United Kingdom to call a general meeting, any director or any member of the commonhold association may call a general meeting.

NOTICE OF GENERAL MEETINGS

10. An annual general meeting or an extraordinary general meeting called for the passing of a special resolution, a unanimous resolution, a termination-statement resolution, a winding-up resolution or a resolution appointing a person as a director must be called by at least twenty-eight clear days' notice. All other extraordinary general meetings must be called by at least twenty-one clear days' notice but a general meeting may be called by shorter notice of at least three clear days' if it is so agreed—

(a) in the case of an annual general meeting, by all the members entitled to attend and vote at that meeting; and
(b) in the case of any other meeting, by a majority in number of the members having a right to attend and vote being a majority together holding at least 95% of the total voting rights at that meeting of all the members.

11. The notice must specify the time and place of the meeting and in the case of an annual general meeting, must specify the meeting as an annual general meeting. The meeting should take place on the commonhold or at a similarly convenient location.

12. The notice must also include or be accompanied by a statement of the agenda of the business to be transacted at the meeting, the text of any resolution or resolutions to be proposed and a brief written explanation of them.

13. The notice must be given to the members and the directors of the commonhold association; but if any person entitled to receive notice is not sent it or does not receive it, this does not invalidate the proceedings at the meeting if the failure to notify was accidental.

PROCEEDINGS AT GENERAL MEETINGS

14. Business must not be transacted at any general meeting unless details of it were included in the notice convening the meeting in accordance with article 12. A proposal to amend an ordinary resolution may, however, be voted upon if the terms of the proposed amendment were received by the commonhold association at its office, or at an e-mail address specified in the notice convening the meeting for the purpose of receiving electronic communications, not less than 48 hours before the time of the meeting. The decision of the chairman as to the admissibility of any proposed amendment will be final and conclusive and does not invalidate any proceedings on the substantive resolution.

15. At any general meeting, so far as practicable and subject to any contrary resolution of the meeting, any business arising from a requisition of members will be transacted before any other business, and if there were more than one requisition, the business arising from it will be transacted in the order in which the requisitions were received by the commonhold association.

16. Business must not be transacted at any general meeting unless a quorum is present. The quorum for the meeting is—

(a) where an ordinary resolution is to be considered, 20% of the members of the commonhold association or three members of the commonhold association (whichever is the greater) present in person or by proxy;

(b) where a special resolution is to be considered, 35% of the members of the commonhold association or four members of the commonhold association (whichever is the greater) present in person or by proxy; and

(c) where a unanimous resolution is to be considered, 50% of the members of the commonhold association or five members of the commonhold association (whichever is the greater) present in person or by proxy.

17. If the relevant quorum is not present within half an hour after the time set for the meeting, or if during a meeting such a quorum ceases to be present, the meeting is adjourned to the same day in the next week, at the same time and place, or to another day, time and place as decided by the directors.

18. The chairman, if any, of the board of directors or in his absence some other director or person nominated by the directors will preside as chairman of the meeting. If neither the chairman nor such other director (if any) is present within fifteen minutes after the time set for the meeting and willing to act, the directors present may either elect one of themselves to be chairman and, if there is only one director present and willing to act, he will be chairman.

19. If no director is willing to act as chairman, or if no director is present within fifteen minutes after the time set for the meeting, the members present and entitled to vote must choose one of themselves to be chairman.

20. A director, despite not being a member, is entitled to attend, speak and propose (but, subject to article 27, not vote upon) a resolution at any general meeting of the commonhold association.

21. The chairman may adjourn the meeting with the consent of any quorate meeting (and must if so required by the meeting), but no business is to be transacted at an adjourned meeting other than business which might properly have been transacted at the meeting had the adjournment not taken place. No notice is required of an adjourned meeting unless the meeting is adjourned for fourteen days or more, in which case at least seven clear days' notice must be given of the time and place of the adjourned meeting and the general nature of the business to be transacted.

22. The following resolutions may be passed—

(a) unanimous resolution—where 100 per cent. of such members as (being entitled to do so) vote in favour;

(b) special resolution—where not less than 75 per cent. of such members as (being entitled to do so) vote in favour;
(c) ordinary resolution—where more than 50 per cent. of such members as (being entitled to do so) vote in favour;
(d) 80% resolution—where at least 80 per cent. of the members vote in favour (needed for termination or winding-up resolution); and
(e) 100% resolution—where 100 per cent. of the members vote in favour.

23. A resolution put to the vote of a meeting will be decided on a show of hands unless a poll is demanded (before or on the declaration of the result of the show of hands). A poll may be demanded—

(a) by the chairman; or
(b) by at least two members having the right to vote at the meeting; or
(c) by a member or members representing not less than one-tenth of the total voting rights of all the members having the right to vote at the meeting;

and a demand by a person as proxy for a member is the same as a demand by the member.

24. Unless a poll is demanded, a declaration by the chairman that a resolution has been carried or lost on a show of hands, whether unanimously or by a particular majority, and an entry to that effect in the minutes of the meeting is conclusive evidence of the fact, without proof of the number or proportion of the votes recorded in favour of or against the resolution.

25. The demand for a poll may be withdrawn before the poll is taken, but only with the consent of the chairman. The withdrawal of a demand for a poll does not invalidate the result of a show of hands declared before the demand for the poll was made.

26. A poll will be taken in such manner as the chairman directs, having particular regard to the convenience of members, and he may appoint scrutineers (who need not be members). The result of the poll will be announced at the meeting at which the poll takes place and is deemed to be the resolution of the meeting at which the poll was demanded.

27. In the case of an equality of votes, whether on a show of hands or on a poll, the chairman is entitled to a casting vote in addition to any other vote he may have.

28. A poll demanded on the election of a chairman, or on a question of adjournment of a meeting, must be taken immediately. A poll demanded on any other question may be taken at such time as the chairman directs, having regard to the convenience of members, and not being more than thirty days after the poll is demanded. The demand for a poll does not prevent the meeting dealing with any business other than the business being determined by poll. If a poll is demanded before the declaration of the result of a show of hands and the demand is withdrawn, the meeting will continue as if the demand had not been made.

29. No notice need be given of a poll not taken immediately if the time and place at which it is to be taken are announced at the meeting at which it is demanded. In any

other case at least seven clear days' notice must be given of the time and place at which the poll is to be taken.

30. A resolution in writing signed by or on behalf of each member who would have been entitled to vote upon it if it had been proposed at a general meeting at which he was present is as effectual as if it had been passed at a general meeting convened and held and may consist of several instruments in similar form each signed by or on behalf of one or more members.

VOTES OF MEMBERS

31. Subject to article 33, on a show of hands, every member who (being an individual) is present in person or (being a corporation) is present by an authorised representative, not being himself a member entitled to vote, has one vote.

32. Subject to article 33, on a poll, every member has one vote, provided that a member who is a unit-holder of more than one commonhold unit has one vote for every commonhold unit in respect of which he is entitled to have his name entered in the register of members of the commonhold association.

33. At any time at which the developer is entitled to exercise the power to appoint and remove directors pursuant to article 46, the developer is not entitled to vote upon a resolution fixing the number of directors of the commonhold association, or upon a resolution for the appointment or removal from office of any director not appointed by him, or upon any resolution concerning the remuneration of any director not appointed by him, or upon a special resolution giving a direction to the directors.

34. A member in respect of whom an order has been made by any court having jurisdiction (whether in the United Kingdom or elsewhere) in matters concerning mental disorder may vote, whether on a show of hands or on a poll, by his receiver or other person authorised in that behalf appointed by that court, and any such receiver or other person may, on a poll, vote by proxy. Evidence to the satisfaction of the directors of the authority of the person claiming to exercise the right to vote may be deposited at the office, or at such other place as is specified in accordance with the articles for the deposit of an appointment of proxy, before the time appointed for the meeting or adjourned meeting at which the right to vote is to be exercised or such evidence may be presented to the directors at the meeting. In default the right to vote is not exercisable.

35. A receiver appointed by the court or by a mortgagee, an administrator, a trustee in bankruptcy, a commissioner in sequestration or similar person may vote in place of a member, whether on a show of hands or on a poll. Evidence to the satisfaction of the directors of the authority of the person claiming to exercise the right to vote may be deposited at the office, or at such other place as is specified in accordance with the articles for the deposit of appointments of proxy, before the time appointed for the meeting or adjourned meeting at which the right to vote is to be

exercised or such evidence may be presented to the directors at the meeting. In default the right to vote is not exercisable.

36. A mortgagee who takes possession of a unit may vote in place of a member, whether on a show of hands or on a poll. Evidence to the satisfaction of the directors of the authority of the person claiming to exercise the right to vote must be deposited at the office, or at such other place as is specified in accordance with the articles for the deposit of appointments of proxy, before the time appointed for the meeting or adjourned meeting at which the right to vote is to be exercised or such evidence may be presented to the directors at the meeting. In default the right to vote is not exercisable.

37. Objections to the qualification of any voter may only be raised at the meeting or adjourned meeting at which the vote objected to is tendered, and every vote not disallowed at the meeting is valid. Any objection made in due time must be referred to the chairman whose decision is final and conclusive.

38. On a poll votes may be given either personally or by proxy. A member may not appoint more than one proxy to attend on the same occasion, save that where the first proxy appointed is unable to attend, an alternative proxy may be appointed.

39. The appointment of a proxy must be in writing, signed by or on behalf of the appointor and must be in the following form (or a form to the same effect)—

‘

[Name of commonhold association]

I/We ____, of ____, being a member/members of the above-named commonhold association, appoint ____ of ____, as my/our proxy to vote in my/our name and on my/our behalf at the annual/extraordinary general meeting of the commonhold association to be held on ____, and at any adjournment of it

Signed on ____’

40. Where members are to be given the opportunity to instruct the proxy how he must act, the appointment of a proxy must be in the following form (or a form to the same effect)—

‘

[Name of commonhold association]

I/We, ____, of ____, being a member/members of the above-named commonhold association, appoint ____ of ____, as my/our proxy to vote in my/our name and on my/our behalf at the annual/extraordinary general meeting of the commonhold association, to be held on ____, and at any adjournment of it.

This form is to be used in respect of the resolutions mentioned below as follows:

Resolution No.1 for* against*

Resolution No.2 for* against*

* Delete as appropriate

Unless instructed otherwise, the proxy may vote as he thinks fit or abstain from voting.

Signed on ____'

41. Where members are to be given an opportunity to appoint a proxy to attend all general meetings held over a period of time and to vote on his behalf in any special or ordinary resolution put to the vote of the meeting, the appointment of a proxy must be in the following form (or a form to the same effect)—

'

[Name of commonhold association]

I/We, ____, of ____, being a member/members of the above-named commonhold association, appoint ____ of ____, as my/our proxy to vote in my/our name and on my/our behalf in any special or ordinary resolution put to the vote at any of the annual and/or extraordinary general meetings of the commonhold association held from until further notice.

Signed on ____'

The form in Article 39 or 40 must be used to appoint a proxy to vote on behalf of the member in any other type of resolution.

42. The appointment of a proxy and any authority under which it is signed or a copy of such authority properly certified by a solicitor or approved in another way by the directors may—

(a) in the case of an appointment in writing, be deposited at the office of the commonhold association or at such other place within the United Kingdom as is stated either in the notice convening the meeting or in any form of proxy sent out by the commonhold association in relation to the meeting; or
(b) in the case of an appointment contained in an electronic communication, where an e-mail address has been specified for the purpose of receiving electronic communications—

   (i) in the notice convening the meeting, or
   (ii) in any form of proxy sent out by the commonhold association in relation to the meeting, or
   (iii) in any invitation contained in an electronic communication to appoint a proxy issued by the commonhold association in relation to the meeting,

   be received at that e-mail address;

at any time before the meeting or adjourned meeting, at which the person named in the appointment proposes to vote, is held. Failing that it may be delivered at the meeting to the chairman, secretary or to any director. The appointment of a proxy which is not deposited, received or delivered in accordance with this article is invalid.

43. A vote given or poll demanded by a proxy for a member, or by the authorised representative of a corporation remains valid despite the previous determination of the authority of the person voting or demanding a poll unless notice of the determination was received by the commonhold association at—

(a) the office; or
(b) at such other place at which the appointment of proxy was deposited; or
(c) where the appointment of the proxy was contained in an electronic communication, at the e-mail address at which such appointment was received

before the start of the meeting or adjourned meeting at which the vote is given or the poll demanded or (in the case of a poll taken otherwise than on the same day as the meeting or adjourned meeting) the time appointed for taking the poll.

QUALIFICATION OF DIRECTORS

44. A director need not be a member of the commonhold association.

NUMBER OF DIRECTORS

45. Unless otherwise determined by ordinary resolution, the number of directors is not subject to any maximum but must not be less than two.

APPOINTMENT AND RETIREMENT OF DIRECTORS

46. This article applies if the commonhold community statement gives the developer the right to appoint and remove directors of the commonhold association. In such event,

(a) during the transitional period the developer may appoint up to two directors in addition to any directors appointed by the subscribers (or subscriber) to the memorandum of association of the commonhold association, and may remove or replace any director so appointed;
(b) after the end of the transitional period and for so long as the developer is the unit-holder of more than one quarter of the total number of units in the commonhold, he may appoint up to one quarter (or the nearest whole number exceeding one quarter) of the maximum number of directors of the commonhold association, and may remove or replace any director so appointed;
(c) a director appointed by the developer in accordance with this article is known as a "developer's director";
(d) any appointment or removal of a developer's director must be by notice in writing signed by or on behalf of the developer and will take effect immediately it is received at the office of the commonhold association or by the secretary or as and from the date specified in the notice;
(e) if at any time the commonhold association resolves to reduce the maximum number of directors, and as a consequence the number of developer's directors in office exceeds the number permitted under this article, the developer must immediately reduce the number of developer's directors accordingly. If such reduction has not been effected by the start of the next directors' meeting, the

longest in office of the developer's directors must cease to hold office immediately so as to achieve the required reduction in numbers;

(f) if the developer ceases to be the unit-holder of more than one quarter of the total number of units in the commonhold, he may no longer appoint, replace or remove a director of the commonhold association and any developer's directors previously appointed by him under this article will cease to hold office immediately; and

(g) a developer's director who is removed from office or who ceases to hold office under this article will not have any claim against the commonhold association in this respect.

47. At the first annual general meeting after the end of the transitional period, all of the directors, other than any developer's directors, must retire from office. At every subsequent annual general meeting, one-third of the directors who are subject to retirement by rotation must retire. If the number of directors is not three or a multiple of three, the number nearest to one-third must retire from office. If there is only one director who is subject to retirement by rotation, he must retire.

48. The directors to retire by rotation are those who have been in office longest since their last appointment or reappointment. Where there are directors who were appointed or reappointed on the same day, those to retire must be determined by lot, unless the directors agree otherwise among themselves. A developer's director is not subject to retirement by rotation.

49. If the commonhold association, at the meeting at which a director retires by rotation, does not fill the vacancy, the retiring director, if willing to act, is deemed to have been reappointed unless at the meeting it is resolved not to fill the vacancy or unless a resolution for the reappointment of the director is put to the meeting and lost.

50. No person other than a director retiring by rotation may be appointed or reappointed as a director at any general meeting unless—

(a) he is recommended by the directors; or

(b) at least fourteen and not more than thirty-five clear days before the date appointed for the meeting, notice signed by a member qualified to vote at the meeting has been given to the commonhold association of the intention to propose that person for appointment or reappointment and stating the particulars which would be required to be included in the commonhold association's register of directors, if he were appointed or reappointed, together with notice signed by that person of his willingness to be appointed or reappointed.

51. At least seven and not more than twenty-eight clear days before the date appointed a general meeting notice must be given to all who are entitled to receive notice of the meeting of any person who is recommended by the directors for appointment or reappointment as a director at the meeting or in respect of whom notice has been given to the commonhold association of the intention to propose him at the meeting for appointment or reappointment as a director. The notice must give the particulars of that person which would, if he were appointed or re-appointed, be required to be included in the commonhold association's register of directors.

52. Subject to these articles, the commonhold association may by ordinary resolution appoint a person, who is willing to act, to be a director either to fill a vacancy (other than a vacancy in respect of a developer's director) or as an additional director and may also determine the rotation in which any additional directors are to retire.

53. The directors may appoint a person who is willing to act to be a director, either to fill a vacancy (other than a vacancy in respect of a developer's director) or as an additional director, provided that the appointment does not cause the number of directors to exceed any number fixed by or in accordance with these articles as the maximum number of directors. A director so appointed will hold office only until the next following annual general meeting and is not taken into account in determining the directors who are to retire by rotation at the meeting. If not re-appointed at such annual general meeting, he must vacate office at the end of the meeting.

54. Subject to these articles, a director who retires at an annual general meeting may, if willing to act, be reappointed. If he is not reappointed, he must hold office until the meeting appoints someone in his place, or if it does not do so, until the end of the meeting.

DISQUALIFICATION AND REMOVAL OF DIRECTORS

55. The office of a director must be vacated if—

(a) an ordinary resolution is passed by the members in favour of removing a director;
(b) he ceases to be a director by virtue of any provision of the Companies Act or he becomes prohibited by law from being a director; or
(c) he becomes bankrupt or makes any arrangement with his creditors generally or a bankruptcy restriction order is made in accordance with the provisions of Schedule 4A to the Insolvency Act 1986; or
(d) he is, or may be, suffering from mental disorder and either:—
    (i) he is admitted to hospital in pursuance of an application for admission for treatment under the Mental Health Act 1983 or, in Scotland, an application for admission under the Mental Health (Scotland) Act 1960, or
    (ii) an order is made by a court having jurisdiction (whether in the United Kingdom or elsewhere) in matters concerning mental disorder for his detention or for the appointment of a receiver or other person to exercise powers with respect to his property or affairs; or
(e) he resigns his office by notice to the commonhold association; or
(f) he is absent for more than three consecutive months from meetings of the directors held during that period or from three consecutive meetings (whichever is the greater) without permission from the directors and the directors resolve that his office be vacated.

Where there is only one or one remaining director of the commonhold association, an appointment of a new director must take place, before the director disqualified or being removed vacates his office.

POWERS OF DIRECTORS

56. Subject to the provisions of the Companies Act, the memorandum and the articles, and to any directions given by special resolution, the directors must manage the business of the commonhold association and they may exercise all the powers of the commonhold association. No alteration of the memorandum or articles and no such direction invalidates any prior act of the directors which would have been valid if that alteration had not been made or that direction had not been given. The powers given by this article are not limited by any special power given to the directors by the articles and the directors' powers may be exercised at a meeting at which a quorum is present.

57. Subject to the article 77, the directors may, by power of attorney or otherwise, appoint any person to be the agent of the commonhold association for such purposes and on such conditions as they determine, including authority for the agent to delegate all or any of his powers.

DELEGATION OF DIRECTORS' POWERS

58. Where an ordinary resolution is passed in favour, the directors may delegate any of their powers to any committee consisting of two or more directors, members of the commonhold association and others as they think fit, provided that the majority of the members of any such committee from time to time are members of the commonhold association. They may also delegate to any managing director or any director holding any other executive office or any managing agent such of their powers as they consider desirable to be exercised by him. Any such delegation is subject to any provisions of the commonhold community statement, may be made subject to any conditions the directors may impose, may be made either collaterally with or to the exclusion of their own powers, and may be revoked or altered. Subject to any such conditions, the proceedings of a committee with two or more members are governed by the articles regulating the proceedings of directors so far as they are capable of applying. A record must be kept giving details of any powers that have been delegated.

REMUNERATION OF DIRECTORS

59. A developer's director is not entitled to any remuneration from the commonhold association. Save as the commonhold association may by special resolution determine the directors other than a developer's director are not entitled to any remuneration. A special resolution passed entitling a director other than a developer's director remuneration must specify the amount of remuneration to be paid to the director(s), and unless the resolution provides otherwise, the remuneration is deemed to accrue from day to day.

DIRECTORS' EXPENSES

60. The directors may be paid all travelling, hotel, and other expenses reasonably and properly incurred by them in connection with their attendance at meetings of directors or committees of directors or general meetings or separate meetings of the members of the commonhold association or otherwise in connection with the discharge of their duties.

DIRECTORS' APPOINTMENTS AND INTERESTS

61. Subject to the provisions of the Companies Act, the directors may appoint one or more of their number to the office of managing director or to any other executive office under the commonhold association and may enter into an agreement or arrangement with any director for his employment by the commonhold association or for the provision by him of any services outside the scope of the ordinary duties of a director. Any appointment of a director to an executive office must terminate if he ceases to be a director but without prejudice to any claim to damages for breach of the contract of service between the director and the commonhold association.

62. Subject to the provisions of the Companies Act, and provided that he has disclosed to the directors the nature and extent of any material interest of his, a director—

(a) may be a party to, or otherwise interested in, any transaction or arrangement with the commonhold association or in which the commonhold association is otherwise interested; and
(b) may be a director or other officer of, or employed by, or a party to any transaction or arrangement with, or otherwise interested in, any body corporate promoted by the commonhold association or in which the commonhold association is otherwise interested; and
(c) is not, by reason of his office, accountable to the commonhold association for any benefit which he derives from any such office or employment or from any such transaction or arrangement or from any interest in any such body corporate and no such transaction or arrangement is liable to be avoided on the ground of any such interest or benefit.

63. For the purposes of article 62—

(a) a general notice given to the directors that a director is to be regarded as having an interest of the nature and extent specified in the notice in any transaction or arrangement in which a specified person or class of persons is interested is deemed to be a disclosure that the director has an interest in any such transaction of the nature and extent so specified; and
(b) an interest of which a director has no knowledge and of which it is unreasonable to expect him to have knowledge will not be treated as an interest of his.

A commonhold association must keep a register of directors' interests and whenever it receives information from a director given in fulfilment of an obligation imposed on him by article 62, it is under obligation to enter in the register, against the director's name, the information received and the date of the entry. This register is open to inspection by any member of the commonhold association.

64. A developer's director may provide information to the developer that he receives by virtue of his being a director.

PROCEEDINGS OF DIRECTORS

65. Subject to the provisions of these articles, the directors may regulate their proceedings, as they think fit. A director may, and the secretary at the request of a director must, call a meeting of the directors. It is not necessary to give notice of a meeting to a director who is absent from the United Kingdom unless he has given to the commonhold association an e-mail address to which notices may be sent using electronic communications. In such case the director is entitled to have notices given to him at that e-mail address. Questions arising at a meeting will be decided by a majority of votes. In the case of an equality of votes, the chairman will have a second or casting vote.

66. The quorum for the transaction of the business of the directors may be fixed by the directors and unless so fixed at any other greater number, is half (or the nearest whole number exceeding half) of the number of appointed directors for the time being or two directors (whichever is the greater). At least one of the persons present at the meeting must be a director other than a developer's director.

67. The continuing directors or a sole continuing director may act despite any vacancies in their number, but, if the number of directors is less than the number fixed as the quorum, the continuing director or directors may act only for the purpose of filling vacancies or of calling a general meeting.

68. The directors may appoint one of their number to be the chairman of the board of directors and may at any time remove him from that office. Unless he is unwilling to do so, the director so appointed must preside at every meeting of directors at which he is present. But if there is no director holding that office, or if the director holding it is unwilling to preside or is not present within fifteen minutes after the time appointed for the meeting, the directors present may appoint one of their number to be chairman of the meeting.

69. A director, despite not being a member, is entitled to speak and propose a resolution at a meeting of the directors.

70. All acts done by a meeting of directors, or of a committee, or by a person acting as a director are valid even if it is discovered later that there was a defect in the appointment of any director or that any of them were disqualified from holding office, or had vacated office, or were not entitled to vote.

71. A resolution in writing signed by all the directors entitled to receive notice of a meeting of directors or of a committee of directors is as valid and effectual as if it had been passed at a meeting of directors or (as the case may be) a committee of directors convened and held and may consist of several documents in similar form each signed by one or more directors.

72. A director who is not a member of the commonhold association must not vote at a meeting of directors or of a committee of directors on any resolution concerning a matter in which he has, directly or indirectly, an interest or duty which is material and which conflicts or may conflict with the interests of the commonhold association. For the purposes of this article, an interest of a person who is, for any purpose of the Companies Act (excluding any statutory modification of it not in force when this regulation becomes binding on the commonhold association), connected with a director is treated as an interest of the director. A director must not be counted in the quorum present at a meeting in relation to a resolution on which he is not entitled to vote.

73. A director who is a member of the commonhold association may vote at any meeting of directors or of any committee of directors of which he is a member even though the resolution concerns or relates to a matter in which he has a direct or indirect interest, and if he votes on such a resolution, his vote must be counted; and in relation to any such resolution, he must (whether or not he votes on the same) be taken into account in calculating the quorum present at the meeting.

74. If a question arises at a meeting of directors or of a committee of directors as to the right of a director to vote, the question may be referred to the chairman of the meeting before the end of the meeting, and his ruling in relation to any director other than himself must be final and conclusive.

SECRETARY

75. Subject to the provisions of the Companies Act, the secretary will be appointed by the directors for such terms, at such remuneration and upon such conditions as they may think fit; and any secretary so appointed may be removed by them.

MINUTES

76. The directors must cause minutes to be made—

(a) of all appointments of officers made by the directors or by the developer; and
(b) of all proceedings at meetings of the commonhold association and of the directors, and of committees, including the names of the persons present at each such meeting, the date of the meeting and any action agreed at the meeting.

The minutes may be made in books kept for the purpose or stored electronically on a computer system so long as they may be made available in paper form on request.

AGENTS

77. The directors have the power on behalf of the commonhold association to appoint and enter into contracts with managing agents of the commonhold on such terms as they think fit including a term providing for cancellation of the contract and return of records and monies paid. The directors remain bound to supervise the managing agent so appointed.

NO DISTRIBUTION OF PROFITS

78. Save in accordance with a termination statement or in a winding up, the commonhold association must not distribute its profits or assets, whether in cash or otherwise, to its members.

WINDING UP

79. If on a winding up of the commonhold association there remains any surplus after the satisfaction of all its debts and liabilities it must be paid to or distributed to the members of the commonhold association in the same percentages as are allocated to each commonhold unit for the payment of the commonhold assessment contained in the commonhold community statement.

INSPECTION AND COPYING OF BOOKS AND RECORDS

80. All books, minutes, documents or accounting records of the commonhold association must be kept on the site of the commonhold or a location similarly convenient to unit-holders and must be retained for a minimum period of 3 years. In addition to any right conferred by statute or by the commonhold community statement, any unit-holder has the right, on reasonable notice and at a time suitable to the commonhold association, to inspect any such book, minute, document or accounting record and where such records are kept electronically on a computer system, the unit-holder is entitled to a printed copy of the record. Where the records are kept manually, the unit-holder is entitled to be provided with a copy of the same upon payment of any reasonable fee for photocopying.

81. Up-to-date copies of the commonhold community statement and the memorandum and articles of association must be kept at the office of the commonhold association and any unit-holder has the right, on reasonable notice and at a time suitable to the commonhold association, to inspect the commonhold community statement or the memorandum and articles of association.

NOTICES

82. Any notice to be given under these articles must be in writing except that a notice calling a meeting of the directors need not be in writing if there is insufficient time to give such notice having regard to the urgency of the business to be conducted.

83. Notices may be given—

(a) personally; or
(b) by leaving it at an address given to the commonhold association as an address for service; or
(c) by sending it by first class post in a prepaid envelope properly addressed to the member at an address given to the commonhold association as an address for service; or
(d) where an electronic address has been provided as an address for service, by electronic communication to that address in accordance with any terms or conditions in connection with service by electronic communication as specified by the recipient.

84. Proof that an envelope containing a notice was properly addressed, prepaid and posted by first class post is conclusive evidence that it was given to a postal address. Electronic confirmation of receipt is conclusive evidence that a notice was given to an e-mail address.

85. A notice is deemed to be given—

(a) immediately after it was handed to the recipient or left at the address for service;
(b) at the expiration of 48 hours after it was posted to the recipient; or
(c) at the expiration of 24 hours after it was transmitted by electronic communication.

INDEMNITY

86. Subject to the provisions of the Companies Act but without affecting any indemnity to which he may otherwise be entitled, every director or other officer of the commonhold association must be indemnified out of the assets of the commonhold association against any liability incurred by him in defending any proceedings, whether civil or criminal, alleging liability for negligence, default, breach of duty or breach of trust in relation to the affairs of the commonhold association, and in which judgment is given in his favour, or in which he is acquitted, or in connection with any application in which relief is granted to him by the Court.

We/I, the subscribers/subscriber to these articles of association, wish to be formed into a company pursuant to these articles.

Names and addresses of subscribers (or subscriber)

Dated

Witness to the above signature(s)

2.3 COMMONHOLD COMMUNITY STATEMENT

Notes:

(1) This Form is taken from the draft accompanying the Post-Consultation Report issued by the Department of Constitutional Affairs in August 2003. The final version is unlikely to be substantially different, but will be supplied as soon as it is published.

(2) This document is prescribed by regulation, and parts of it may not be altered or modified in any way. Other parts (shown underlined) are default provisions, and are treated as included in the commonhold community statement unless alternative provision is made in place of them.

(3) Section 2.17 and Parts 2, 3 and 4 of Chapter 4 of the text contain a full discussion of the commonhold community statement.

COMMONHOLD AND LEASEHOLD REFORM ACT 2002

COMMONHOLD COMMUNITY STATEMENT

[*INSERT NAME OF COMMONHOLD*]

This is the *commonhold community statement* of [*insert name of commonhold*]. It sets out the rights and duties of the *commonhold association* and the *unit-holders*. It is a legally binding document.

This *commonhold community statement*, the *memorandum of association* and *articles of association* of the [*insert name of commonhold association*] together govern the [*insert name of commonhold*].

Part II of the *commonhold community statement* includes factual information concerning the land, *commonhold units* and *commonhold association*. Part III presents the *rules* that bind the *unit-holders* and the *commonhold association*.

Any provision in this *commonhold community statement* which is inconsistent with or forbidden by any provision made by or by virtue of the Commonhold and Leasehold Reform Act 2002, or is inconsistent with any provision of this *commonhold community statement* which is treated as included by virtue of the Commonhold Regulations 2003, or is inconsistent with the *memorandum* or *articles of association* has no effect.

Up-to-date information about the [enter name of the commonhold] may be found in the current versions of the *memorandum* and *articles of association* of the [*insert name of commonhold association*]. These documents are registered at the Land Registry but the *commonhold association* keeps copies at [*insert address*]. Information is also contained in the relevant registers kept by the Land Registry and in records retained at Companies House.

Italicised words are defined in the glossary.

CONTENTS

PART I: SIGNATURES AND TABLE OF AMENDMENTS

This statement must be signed on behalf of the *commonhold association* by a director and the secretary or by two directors of the *commonhold association*.

Name

Address

Name

Address

on ____________________________

This Statement has been amended as set out below.

CCS Version Number	Brief details of amendments	Date of resolution amending the CCS
2		
3		
4		
5		
6		

PART II: FACTUAL INFORMATION

1. Commonhold land

Name of commonhold:

Brief description of the location and extent of *commonhold land*:

2. Commonhold association

Name of *commonhold association*:

Previous names of *commonhold association* (if any):

Registered number:

Date of incorporation:

3. **Commonhold units and common parts**

Table 3.1

Total number of *commonhold units* in the commonhold:

Table 3.2 Definition of *commonhold unit*

Plan Reference	*Building* (description or address)	*Commonhold unit* number included in or excluded from a unit	Structure and exterior of *building*	Further definition of extent of the *commonhold unit*

Table 3.3 Allocation

Commonhold unit Number assessment	% allocation of commonhold	% allocation of *reserve fund*	Number of votes allocated to member

Table 3.4 Permitted use

Commonhold unit number	Permitted use	Further restrictions on use

4. **Limited use areas**

Area	Authorised users	Authorised use

PART III: THE RULES OF THE COMMONHOLD ASSOCIATION

Part III of this *commonhold community statement* contains the *rules* of the [*insert name of commonhold association*]

A: Dealings with the Land

Transfer of commonhold units

1. On *transfer* of a *commonhold unit* the new *unit-holder* must pay any debts incurred by the former *unit-holder* which remain outstanding in respect of the commonhold assessment and the *reserve fund* levies.

2. On *transfer* of a *commonhold unit* or of part only of a *commonhold unit* the new *unit-holder* must notify the *commonhold association* of the *transfer* within 7 days beginning with the date on which the Land Registry gives notice to the new *unit-holder* or his representative[1] that the registration of the *transfer* has been completed. Forms 1 (*Transfer of commonhold unit*) and 2 (*Transfer of part only of a commonhold unit*) of Annex D or forms to the same effect must be used.

Leasing[2]

3. A *unit-holder* may not grant a tenancy in a *residential commonhold unit* for a term of more than 21 years.

4. A *unit-holder* may not grant—

   (a) a tenancy in a *commonhold unit*; or
   (b) a licence for consideration to occupy or use a *commonhold unit* for a period longer than 28 days

   unless it reserves the right for the *commonhold association* to carry out repair work in accordance with the provisions of this *commonhold community statement*. Any provision made in a tenancy agreement will be of no effect to the extent that it is inconsistent with this *commonhold community statement* or the *memorandum* or *articles of association* of the *commonhold association*.

5. A *unit-holder* must notify the *commonhold association* that a tenancy or a licence for a period longer than 28 days has been granted within 7 days from the date on which it was granted. Forms 3 or 4 respectively in Annex D or forms to the same effect must be used.

6. The *commonhold association* must maintain a register of *tenants* and enter in it—

[1] A representative includes, but is not limited to, a solicitor or licensed conveyancer.
[2] The restrictions on leasing apply to both fixed term and periodic leases.

(a) the postal address and unit number of the *commonhold unit*;
(b) the name(s) and address for service of the *unit-holder(s)*;
(c) the name(s) and address for service of the *tenant*; and
(d) the length of the tenancy or licence for a period longer than 28 days.

7. The *tenant* of a *commonhold unit* or part only of a *commonhold un*it must make payments to the *commonhold association* in discharge of payments which are due, in accordance with this *commonhold community statement*, to be made by the *unit-holder* or another *tenant* where the tenancy agreement imposes an obligation on the *tenant* to pay.

8. A *tenant* of a *commonhold unit* or part only of a *commonhold unit* is bound by the *rules* of this *commonhold community statement* which affect his occupancy.

B: Use, Insurance, repair and maintenanceUse

9. A *commonhold unit* may only be used in accordance with its permitted use as stated in Table 3.4 of Part II of this *commonhold community statement.*

10. *Limited use areas* may only be used by authorised persons and in a manner consistent with the authorised use specified in Table 4 of Part II of this *commonhold community statement.*

11. The *common parts* must not be used in such a way as to prevent reasonable access to a *commonhold unit* or which may prejudice the use of a *commonhold unit.*

12. A *unit-holder* must not make any alterations to the *common parts.*

13. A *commonhold unit* and the *common parts* must not be used in such a way as to cause a nuisance to other *unit-holders.*

14. A *unit-holder* must not act in any way that would be likely to prejudice the insurance cover of the *commonhold association* or other *unit-holders.*

15. A *unit-holder* must indemnify the *commonhold association* in respect of costs to put right any damage caused to the *common parts* by a licensee or invitee of the *unit-holder.*

Insurance

16. The *commonhold association* must take out and maintain public liability insurance in respect of the commonhold.

17. The *commonhold association* must take out and maintain buildings insurance in respect of the *common parts.*

18. The buildings insurance taken out and maintained by the *commonhold association* must cover—

(a) loss or damage by fire;

(b) full rebuilding and reinstatement costs of the property insured where the sum insured is—

  (i) based on the costs of rebuilding or reinstating the property assessed at a point 18 months in advance;
  (ii) properly calculated by a member of the Royal Institution of Chartered Surveyors; and
  (iii) index-linked;

(c) the cost of providing alternative accommodation in the event that a property is rendered incapable of use; and

may cover any other risk that the *commonhold association* considers appropriate.

19. An assessment of the reinstatement costs of the commonhold buildings must be carried out at least every five years for the purposes of buildings insurance.

Repair and maintenance

20. The *commonhold association* must keep the *common parts* in good repair.

21. In order to carry out work necessary to keep the *common parts* in good repair the *commonhold association* has a right to enter a *commonhold unit* where reasonable notice of the intention to enter has been given to the *unit-holder* save in an emergency when no notice is required.

22. The *commonhold association* must not alter the *common parts* unless a resolution is passed by the *commonhold association*.

C: Financial matters

Commonhold Assessment

23. The directors of the *commonhold association* must make an *annual estimate* and may make *occasional* and *emergency estimates* of income required to be raised from *unit-holders*[3] to meet the expenses of the *commonhold association*.

Annual estimate and occasional estimate

24. At least three calendar months before the first payment will be due the directors of the *commonhold association* must serve notices on each *unit-holder* specifying—

(a) the total amount of the *estimate*;
(b) the percentage that was allocated to his *commonhold unit* in Table 3.3 of Part II of this *commonhold community statement*; and

[3] For the purposes of Section C, '*unit-holder*' means the unit-holder, the tenant and any other tenants of the *commonhold unit* where a tenant is responsible for discharging payments in accordance with rule 7 and the tenancy agreement.

(c) the amount of the *estimate* allocated to his *commonhold unit*.

25. Within one calendar month beginning with the date on which the notice referred to in rule 24 was served, each *unit-holder* may make representations regarding the *estimate*, in writing, to the *commonhold association*.

26. Within one calendar month after the last day on which representations may be made under rule 25, the directors must make such adjustments, if any, to the *estimate* as they think fit, after considering any such representations, and must make a final *estimate* and serve further notices on the *unit-holders* specifying the payments required to be made by each *unit-holder* and the date on which each payment is due.

27. Subject to rule 28, the notice referred to in rule 26 must not specify a date for payment of any sum that is less than 1 calendar month after the date on which the notice was served.

Emergency estimate

28. The directors of the *commonhold association* must serve notices on each *unit-holder* specifying the amount of the *emergency estimate* that has been allocated to his *commonhold unit* and that the payment required to be made by each *unit-holder* must be made within 14 days of the date of the notice.

Payment of commonhold assessment and interest for late payments

29. Each *unit-holder* must make payments in respect of the percentage of any *estimate* that is allocated to his *commonhold unit* by the date(s) specified in any notice served in accordance with these *rules*.

30. Interest must be paid on any payment due in accordance with rule 29 that is late at the rate of 8 per cent. per annum for the period between the date on which the payment is due and the date on which the payment is made.

Reserve Fund

31. The directors of the *commonhold association* must commission a *reserve study* by an appropriate professional at least once in every 10 years.

32. The directors of the *commonhold association* must consider the results of the *reserve study* and, in particular, whether it is necessary in light of the findings in the *reserve study* to establish and maintain one or more *reserve funds* to finance the repair and maintenance of the *common parts*.

33. The directors of the *commonhold association* must set a levy from time to time in relation to the *reserve fund* ('the levy').

34. At least three calendar months before the first payment will be due the directors of the *commonhold association* must serve notices on each *unit-holder* specifying the amount of the levy that is to be allocated to his *commonhold unit*.

35. Within one calendar month beginning with the date on which the notice referred to in rule 34 was served, each *unit-holder* may make representations regarding the amount of the levy, in writing, to the *commonhold association*.

36. Within one calendar month after the last day on which representations may be made under rule 35, the directors must make such adjustments, if any, to the levy as they think fit, after considering such representations, and must make a final levy and serve further notices on the *unit-holders* specifying the payments required to be made by each *unit-holder* and the date on which each payment is due.

37. The notice referred to in rule 36 must not specify a date for payment that is less than 1 calendar month after the date on which the notice was served.

38. Each *unit-holder* must make payments in respect of the percentage of any levy that is allocated to his *commonhold unit* by the date(s) specified in the notice referred to in rule 36.

39. Interest must be paid on any payment due in accordance with rule 38 that is late at the rate of 8 per cent. per annum for the period between the date on which the payment is due and the date on which the payment is made.

40. In setting the levy the directors must endeavour to ensure that unnecessary reserves are not accumulated and where they do so accumulate they may be used for the general expenses of the commonhold.

D: Complaints and Default procedureGeneral Duties

41. In dealings between one *unit-holder* and another and in dealings between *unit-holders* and the *commonhold association*, each party has a duty not to be unreasonable when dealing with the other party and all aspects of a party's behaviour will be considered when assessing reasonableness.

Procedure for enforcement by unit-holder or tenant

42. A *unit-holder* or *tenant* (the "complainant") may seek to enforce a duty imposed on the *commonhold association* or a duty imposed on another *unit-holder* or *tenant* (the "defaulter") by serving a complaints notice on the *commonhold association*. Form 5 of Annex D or a form to the same effect must be used.

43. Where the defaulter is the *commonhold association* the Board of Directors may respond to the complaints notice by serving a reply notice within 21 days from the date on which the complaints notice was served. Form 6 of Annex D or a form to the same effect must be used.

44. Where the defaulter is a *unit-holder* or *tenant* the matter complained of will be considered by the Board of Directors who, having regard to the desirability of using arbitration, mediation or conciliation procedures including referral to the ombudsman instead of legal proceedings wherever possible, may—

(a) resolve the matter informally with the defaulter; or
(b) take no action; or
(c) serve a default notice on the defaulter and follow the procedure in *rules* 47 to 49.

45. Where a dispute remains between the complainant and the *commonhold association* regarding the matter complained of the complainant may refer the dispute to the ombudsman after at least 21 days have passed beginning with the date on which the complaints notice was served. Legal proceedings may not be brought until after the dispute has been referred to the ombudsman and he has notified the parties of his decision.

46. Where a duty is being enforced in an emergency the above procedure does not apply.

Procedure for enforcement by commonhold association

47. A *commonhold association* may seek to enforce a duty imposed on a *unit-holder* or *tenant* (the "defaulter") by serving a default notice on the defaulter. Form 7 of Annex D or a form to the same effect must be used.

48. The defaulter may respond to the default notice by serving a reply notice within 21 days from the date on which the default notice was served. Form 8 of Annex D or a form to the same effect must be used.

49. Where a dispute remains between the *commonhold association* and the defaulter, the *commonhold association* may refer the dispute to the ombudsman or bring legal proceedings after at least 21 days have passed beginning with the date on which the default notice was served.

50. Where a duty is being enforced in an emergency the above procedure does not apply.

51. Where a duty is enforced against a *tenant*, a copy of the default notice must be served on the *unit-holder* and the *tenant*. Where the duty being enforced relates to payment of the commonhold assessment or *reserve fund*, a copy of the default notice must also be served on any other tenants of the *commonhold unit*.

52. Where rule 7 applies, the *commonhold association* must first seek to enforce the duty against the *tenant* but may subsequently seek to enforce the duty against either the *unit-holder* or any other *tenant* of the *commonhold unit* who has been served with a copy of the default notice.

E: Termination

53. A *termination statement* must provide that where the *commonhold association* is entitled to become registered as the proprietor of the freehold estate in each *commonhold unit* following a termination application, a *unit-holder* may continue to occupy his *commonhold unit* until the *commonhold association* disposes of the *commonhold land.*

F: Amendment of the commonhold community statement

54. The *rules*, other than mandatory rules, contained in this *commonhold community statement* may be amended by resolution at a *general meeting* in accordance with the *articles of association* of the *commonhold association*.

55. A *unanimous* resolution is necessary to change the allocation of votes given to a *commonhold unit*.

56. *Special resolutions* are necessary to—

    (a) make a provision in place of a default provision;
    (b) with the consent of the *unit-holder*, change the permitted use of a *commonhold unit*;
    (c) change the percentage of the commonhold assessment or *reserve fund* levies allocated to a *commonhold unit*; and
    (d) change the restrictions on the *limited use areas*.

57. *Ordinary resolutions* are necessary to—

    (a) subject to rule 56(a), add, delete or amend any *rule* contained in the *default* or optional provisions of this *commonhold community statement*;
    (b) with the consent of the *unit-holder* and/or registered proprietor of any charge, change the size of a *commonhold unit* or the *common parts*;
    (c) alter the *common parts*; and
    (d) with the consent of the *developer*, amend the *development rights*.

58. Amendments to this *commonhold community statement* only take effect when the amended version is registered at the Land Registry.

59. An application to register an amended *commonhold community statement* must be accompanied by—

    (a) a certificate given by the directors of the *commonhold association* that the *rules* on amendment of this *commonhold community statement* have been complied with; and
    (b) where the amendment of the *commonhold community statement* changes the size of a *commonhold unit* or the *common parts*, the consent of the *unit-holder* or registered proprietor of any charge.

G: Notices

60. Any notice given by the *commonhold association* must contain the name of the *commonhold association*, its company number, the address of its registered office, an address for reply (if different) or the address for service (if different). In the event that the notice does not specify an address for reply or an address for service, any reply should be sent to the address of the registered office.

61. *Unit-holders, joint unit-holders and tenants* must provide at least one and up to three addresses for service to the *commonhold association* and notify the *commonhold association* of any change to an address for service. Any such address provided by a *unit-holder* or *joint unit-holders* will be the address at which notices are also sent to him in his capacity as a member of the commonhold association.

62. An address for service required by rule 61 must include at least one full postal address including postcode in the United Kingdom. The other addresses may be a combination of a postal address, a box number at a United Kingdom document exchange or an electronic address.

63. Any notice to be given under these r*ules* must be in writing.

64. Notices may be given—

    (a) personally; or
    (b) by leaving it at an address given as an address for service; or
    (c) by sending it by first class post in a prepaid envelope properly addressed to an address given as an address for service; or
    (d) where an electronic address has been provided as an address for service, by electronic communication to that address in accordance with any terms or conditions in connection with service by electronic communication as specified by the recipient.

65. Proof that an envelope containing a notice was properly addressed, prepaid and posted by first class post is conclusive evidence that it was given to a postal address. Electronic confirmation of receipt is conclusive evidence that a notice was given to an e-mail address.

66. A notice is deemed to be given—

    (a) immediately after it was handed to the recipient or left at the address for service;
    (b) at the expiration of 48 hours after it was posted to the recipient; or
    (c) at the expiration of 24 hours after it was transmitted by electronic communication.

ANNEX A: GLOSSARY

Annual estimate: Estimate made by the directors of the *commonhold association* of the income required to be raised from *unit-holders* to meet the expenses of the *commonhold association* for the next 12 months.

***Articles of association*:** The internal regulations for the management of the affairs of the company and the conduct of its business.

***Building*:** A physical entity within the commonhold land that is structurally independent.

***Common parts*:** Every part of the commonhold which is not for the time being a *commonhold unit* in accordance with the *commonhold community statement*.

***Commonhold association*:** A private company limited by guarantee the memorandum of which states that an object of the company is to exercise the functions of a commonhold association in relation to specified *commonhold land* and which specifies £1 as the amount of each member's guarantee.

***Commonhold community statement*:** A document which makes provision for the rights and duties of the *commonhold association* and the *unit-holders*, defines the extent of each *commonhold unit* and includes a plan of the commonhold.

***Commonhold land*:** A freehold estate which is registered as a freehold estate in commonhold land. The land must be specified in the *memorandum of association* of the *commonhold association* as the land in relation to which the commonhold association is to exercise its functions and it must be subject to the provisions of a *commonhold community statement*.

***Commonhold unit*:** One property of two or more within the *commonhold land* whose owner has a freehold title to the property. The extent of each commonhold unit will be defined in the *commonhold community statement* and shown on the plans. A commonhold unit may comprise the whole of a *building* or part of it and there may be more than one commonhold unit in a *building*.

***Developer*:** A person who makes an application to register a freehold estate in land as a freehold estate in *commonhold land,* or his successor in title who is treated as the developer, and who carries on *development business* on the *commonhold land.*

***Development business*:** The completion or execution of works on a commonhold or on land which is or may be added to a commonhold or land which has been removed from it; carrying out transactions in *commonhold units*; advertising or promoting transactions in *commonhold units*; adding land to or removing land from a commonhold; amending a *commonhold community statement* following development of the commonhold and appointing or removing the directors of a *commonhold association* are all classed as *development business*.

***Development rights*:** Rights given to the *developer* in the *commonhold community statement* to permit or assist him to carry out *development business*.

Emergency estimate: Estimate made by the directors of the *commonhold association* from time to time of income required to be raised from *unit-holders,* in addition to the *annual estimate,* in an emergency.

General meeting: General meetings of the members of the *commonhold association* held in accordance with the *articles of association* at which decisions about the running of the commonhold are made.

Joint unit-holder: One of two or more persons who are entitled to be registered as proprietors of the freehold estate in a *commonhold unit* (whether or not they are registered).

Limited use areas: Any part of the *common parts* which has restrictions on its use in the *commonhold community statement* such as the classes of person who may use the area or the kind of use to which it may be put.

Memorandum of association: The memorandum of association states the name, location of the registered office and objects of the *commonhold association.*

Non-residential commonhold unit: A *commonhold unit* which may not be used for residential purposes or for residential and other incidental purposes.

Occasional estimate: Estimate made by the directors of the *commonhold association* from time to time of income required to be raised from *unit-holders,* in addition to the *annual estimate,* which is not required in an emergency.

Ordinary Resolution: A resolution passed by a simple majority of such members as (being entitled to do so) vote in person or, where proxies are allowed, by proxy, at a general meeting of the *commonhold association.*

Reserve Fund: A fund set up by the directors of the *commonhold association* to which *unit-holders* contribute which finances the repair and maintenance of the *common parts* (and/or *commonhold units).*

Reserve Study: An inspection of all major assets, equipment, fixtures and fittings, including parts of the *common parts*, which are owned or maintained by the *commonhold association* and which have an estimated remaining life of less than 10 years. In respect of each item, its remaining life is estimated along with the cost of maintaining or replacing the item and the annual contribution that is required from *unit-holders* in respect of such costs. Any assets, equipment, fixtures or fittings that will need to be purchased within the following 10 year period are specified in the reserve study.

Residential commonhold unit: A *commonhold unit* which may only be used for residential purposes or for residential and other incidental purposes.

Rules: The rights and duties of the *commonhold association* and of the unit-holders contained in this *commonhold community statement.*

Special Resolution: A resolution passed by a majority of not less than 75 per cent. of such members as (being entitled to do so) vote in person or, where proxies are allowed, by proxy, at a general meeting of the *commonhold association* of which notice specifying the intention to propose the resolution as a special resolution has been given in accordance with the articles.

***Tenant*:** A person, other than a *unit-holder*, who has a right to occupy the *commonhold unit.*

***Termination statement*:** The *commonhold association's* proposals for the *transfer* of the *commonhold land* and for the distribution of the commonhold assets when the commonhold comes to an end.

***Transfer (of commonhold unit)*:** A transfer of the freehold estate in a *commonhold unit* whether or not for consideration, whether or not subject to any reservation or other terms, and whether or not by operation of law.

Unanimous Resolution: A resolution passed by 100% of the members who cast a vote.

Unit-holder: A person entitled to be registered as the proprietor of the freehold estate in a commonhold unit (whether or not he is registered).

ANNEX B: DEVELOPMENT RIGHTS

This Annex is optional and need only be included in a *commonhold community statement* if *development rights* are being granted.

Development Rights

ANNEX C: PLANS

ANNEX D: FORMS

1. Notice of transfer of commonhold unit
2. Notice of transfer of part only of a commonhold unit

3. Notice of tenancy
4. Notice of licence
5. Complaints notice
6. Reply to Complaints notice
7. Default notice
8. Reply to Default notice

(These forms have been omitted, but may be found, with the author's annotations, as forms 2.11, 2.12, 2.13, 2.14, 4.1, 4.3, 4.4 and 4.5.)

2.4 CERTIFICATE OF COMPLIANCE BY DIRECTORS OF COMMONHOLD ASSOCIATION ACCOMPANYING APPLICATION FOR REGISTRATION

Notes

(1) Paragraph 7 of Schedule 1 to the Act provides that an application for registration of a freehold estate in land as a freehold estate in commonhold land must be accompanied, among other documents, by a certificate given by the directors of the commonhold association confirming the information set out in this Form.

(2) In its Post-Consultation Report dated August 2003, the Department of Constitutional Affairs gave notice that it was intending that the Commonhold Regulations should prescribe a form of directors' certificate. In the absence thus far of any draft prescribed form, the text below sets out the authors' suggestions for the content of a suitable certificate.

(3) A registration obtained with an erroneous or otherwise invalid certificate will be liable to be altered by the court (section 6).

(4) Paragraph 2.19.3 of the text gives a full analysis of this topic.

COMMONHOLD

Certificate of compliance by directors of commonhold association

Commonhold and Leasehold Reform Act 2002 Schedule 1, paragraph 7

To the Chief Land Registrar

1. **Details of the freehold land the subject of the application to become commonhold ("the Land"):**

   Description:

   Title Number:

2. **Details of the commonhold association intended to exercise functions in relation to the Land ("the Association"):**

   Name:

   Company Registration Number:

3. **Details of the directors of the Association:**

Name:	*Name:*	*Name:*
Address:	*Address:*	*Address:*

4. Certificate

We, the undersigned directors of the Association, whose details appear in paragraph 3 above, certify that:

i. the memorandum and articles of association of the Association which accompany this Certificate comply with regulations under paragraph 2(1) of Schedule 3 to the Commonhold and Leasehold Reform Act 2002 ("the Act");
ii. the commonhold community statement which accompanies this Certificate satisfies the requirements of the Act;
iii. none of the Land is prohibited from being commonhold land by virtue of Schedule 2 to the Act;
iv. the Association has not traded; and
v. the Association has not incurred any liability which has not been discharged.

IMPORTANT

If this Certificate is inaccurate, any person who claims to be adversely affected by the registration of the Land may apply to court for a declaration under section 6 of the Act that the Land should not have been registered as a freehold estate in commonhold land.

Signed this ____ day of ____ 20 ____ by:

____	____	____
Director	Director	Director/Secretary

2.5 CERTIFICATE OF COMPLIANCE BY DIRECTORS OF COMMONHOLD ASSOCIATION ACCOMPANYING APPLICATION FOR REGISTRATION OF AMENDED COMMONHOLD COMMUNITY STATEMENT

Notes:

(1) The Consultation Paper issued by the Lord Chancellor's Department on 10 October 2002 proposes that a regulation be made under section 33 of the Act to the effect that, where a commonhold community statement is to be amended, the directors of the commonhold association must provide a certificate that the amended commonhold community statement satisfies the requirements of the Act. This requirement is repeated in rule 59 of the current (August 2003) version of the commonhold community statement.

(2) No prescribed form is proposed (although the Post-Consultation Report dated August 2003 suggests that a form will be prescribed for the Certificate dealt with in Form 2.4 above). The text set out below represents the authors' suggestions for the certificate.

(3) The Consultation Paper also proposes that the amended commonhold community statement should be signed by two directors or a director and secretary to confirm its authenticity.

(4) Rule 59 also provides that where the amendment of the commonhold community statement will change the size of a commonhold unit or the common parts, the consent of the unit-holder or registered proprietor of any charge must accompany the application to register an amended commonhold community statement.

(5) These requirements are discussed in the text at paragraph 2.18.5.

COMMONHOLD

Certificate of compliance by directors of commonhold association

Commonhold and Leasehold Reform Act 2002, section 33

To the Chief Land Registrar

1. Details of the commonhold land the subject of this application ("the Land"):

Description:

Title Number:

2. Details of the commonhold association exercising functions in relation to the Land ("the Association"):

Name:

Company Registration Number:

3. Details of the directors of the Association:

Name:	*Name:*	*Name:*
Address:	*Address:*	*Address:*

4. Certificate

We, the undersigned directors of the Association, whose details appear in paragraph 3 above, certify that the amended commonhold community statement of this Association, a signed copy of which accompanies this Certificate, satisfies the requirements of the regulations made under section 33 of the Commonhold and Leasehold Reform Act 2002 ("the Act").

IMPORTANT

If this Certificate is inaccurate, any unit-holder may apply to court for relief under section 40 of the Act.

Signed this ____ day of ____ 20 ____ by:

____	____	____
Director	Director	Director/Secretary

2.6 CERTIFICATE OF COMPLIANCE BY DIRECTORS OF COMMONHOLD ASSOCIATION ACCOMPANYING APPLICATION FOR REGISTRATION OF ALTERED MEMORANDUM OR ARTICLES OF ASSOCIATION

Notes

(1) Paragraph 3 of Schedule 3 to the Act provides that any alteration made to the memorandum or articles of association of a commonhold association will not have effect until the altered version is registered at the Land Registry.
(2) The application to the Land Registry must also be accompanied by a certificate given by the directors of the commonhold association that the altered memorandum or articles of association of the commonhold association complies with regulations (paragraph 3(3) of Schedule 3 to the Act).
(3) No form is prescribed for such a certificate, and the Form set out below represents the authors' views as to the appropriate text.
(4) This requirement is discussed further in paragraphs 2.14.2 and 2.14.4 of the text.

COMMONHOLD

Certificate of compliance by directors of commonhold association

Commonhold and Leasehold Reform Act 2002, Schedule 3, paragraph 3

To the Chief Land Registrar

1. **Details of the commonhold land the subject of this application ("the Land"):**

   Description:

   Title Number:

2. **Details of the commonhold association exercising functions in relation to the Land ("the Association"):**

   Name:

   Company Registration Number:

3. **Details of the directors of the Association:**

Name:	*Name:*	*Name:*
Address:	*Address:*	*Address:*

4. Certificate

We, the undersigned directors of the Association, whose details appear in paragraph 3 above, certify that the amended memorandum and/or articles of association of this Association, signed copies of which accompany this Certificate, satisfy the requirements of regulations made under paragraph 2(1) of Schedule 3 to the Commonhold and Leasehold Reform Act 2002 ("the Act").

IMPORTANT

If this Certificate is inaccurate, any unit-holder may apply to court for relief under section 40 of the Act.

Signed this ____ day of ____ 20 ____ by:

____	____	____
Director	Director	Director/Secretary

2.7 STATEMENT ACCOMPANYING APPLICATION FOR REGISTRATION REQUESTING SECTION 9 TO APPLY

Notes

(1) This statement is designed to be used where the applicant for a freehold estate to be registered as a freehold estate in commonhold land already has unit-holders who are entitled to be registered as owners of units in that estate.

(2) The Government is considering whether this document should be prescribed (ie made mandatory) by the Commonhold Regulations. The draft follows the illustrative document set out in the Consultation Paper published on 10 October 2002.

(3) This statement will accompany the application for registration (see Form 1.1 above). Once the Registrar is satisfied as to the application, he will register the commonhold association and the named unit-holders as the proprietors of the freehold estates respectively in the common parts and any unsold units, on the one hand, and in the units, on the other hand.

(4) This statement is discussed in paragraph 2.19.2 of the text.

COMMONHOLD

Section 9 Statement

Commonhold and Leasehold Reform Act 2002, section 9

To the Chief Land Registrar

1. **Details of the commonhold land the subject of this application ("the Land"):**

   Description:

   Title Number:

2. **Details of applicant:**

   Name:

   Address:

3. **Statement**

   I, the undersigned [director/authorised agent on behalf of the] applicant for registration of the Land as a freehold estate in commonhold land in accordance with section 2 of the Commonhold and Leasehold Reform Act 2002, request that section 9 of the Act should apply to my application.

4. **List of commonhold units required by section 9(2):**

UNITS	UNIT-HOLDERS
Unit 1 Postal Address Title Number (if registered)	Name Address Address for Service (if different) (*Repeat as necessary for joint unit-holders*)
Unit 2 Postal Address Title Number (if registered) *(Continue until all units and unit-holders have been detailed)*	Name Address Address for service (if different)

Signed this ____ day of ____ 20____ by:

2.8 LIST OF DATES OF REGISTRATIONS OF AMENDED COMMONHOLD DOCUMENTS

Notes

(1) The Act makes provision for the registration of an amended commonhold community statement or altered memorandum or articles of association (see section 33(3) and paragraph 3(1) of Schedule 3 to the Act, and Form 1.3 above).

(2) Such amendments may happen frequently, and it will therefore be good practice to keep a record of the dates of registration of the various amendments to provide a historical record, and so that the current version numbers of the relevant documents can be readily identified

(3) This topic is discussed in Sections 2.18 and 2.14 of the text.

COMMONHOLD

List of dates of registrations

Commonhold and Leasehold Reform Act 2002

[Name] Commonhold Association Limited

1. Details of the commonhold land the subject of this document ("the Land"):

Description:

Title Number:

2. Details of the commonhold association exercising functions in relation to the Land ("the Association"):

Name: [Name] Commonhold Association Limited

Company Registration Number:

3. List of dates of registrations

Document	**Version No.**	**Draft date**	**Reg date**	**Reason for change**
Commonhold community statement	V1			N/a
Memorandum and articles of association	V1			N/a
Commonhold community statement	V2			Addition of parking space 1 to common parts
. . .				

2.9 REGISTER OF MEMBERS

Notes

(1) This Form stems from the requirement in section 352 of the Companies Act 1985 that the commonhold association, in common with all limited companies, establish and maintain a register of its members. A failure to comply with these requirements may result in a fine (see section 352(5)).

(2) The form of this document is not currently prescribed by regulation, and the Department of Constitutional Affairs indicated in the Post-Consultation Report issued in August 2003 that it did not consider that prescription was necessary. If the form is not prescribed, this form may be modified provided that the commonhold association continues to satisfy the requirements of section 352.

(3) Paragraph 14 of Schedule 3 to the Act states that regulations may make provision about the performance of a commonhold association of its section 352 duty and, in particular, requiring entries in the register to be made within a specified period.

(4) Articles 4 and 5 of the articles of association provide that the particulars of the person entitled to be entered in the register of members must be entered by the commonhold association within 14 days of the occurrence of certain events; while the particulars must be removed within 14 days of the commonhold association becoming aware of the requisite facts.

(5) Paragraph 4.4.2 of the text discusses these requirements.

COMMONHOLD

Register of Members

Companies Act 1985 section 352

[Name] Commonhold Association Limited ("the Association")

Registered office address:

Company Registration Number:

Name of Member	Address	Date of membership	Date of resignation

IMPORTANT

This Register must be kept up to date.
The Association must enter the details of the individual unit-holders on this Register within 14 days from whichever of the following occurs first: (i) the receipt by the Association of the notification of either a transfer by the new unit-holder or the unit becoming commonhold land under section 9 of the Commonhold and Leasehold Reform Act 2002; or (ii) the directors becoming aware of the need to enter a new member on the Register.
If a member of the Association resigns by notice in writing to the Association, the Association must make the necessary entry on the Register within 14 days from receipt of the notice.
Failure to comply with these requirements may result in a fine being levied.

2.10 NOMINATION BY JOINT UNIT-HOLDERS OF ONE UNIT-HOLDER

Notes

(1) Paragraph 8 of Schedule 3 to the Act has the effect that joint unit-holders may choose that only one of them will be entered on the register of members of the commonhold association. Paragraph 8(3) provides that such a nomination must be made in writing to the commonhold association before the end of a period prescribed by regulation, failing which the person whose name appears first on the proprietorship register at the Land Registry is entitled to be entered on the register of members (paragraph 8(4)), unless a court orders otherwise (paragraph 8(5)).

(2) The Consultation Paper issued by the Lord Chancellor's Department on 10 October 2002 proposes that the period of time within which a nomination for one of two or more joint unit-holders to be entered on the register must be received should be 21 days from the date of transfer of the unit.

(3) There is currently no prescribed form for this document, and accordingly the Form that follows contains the authors' suggested content.

(4) Paragraph 2.15.5 of the text discusses this topic.

COMMONHOLD

Nomination by joint unit-holders of one unit-holder

Commonhold and Leasehold Reform Act 2002, Schedule 3, paragraph 8

To [Name] Commonhold Association Limited of [address]

1. Details of the unit ("the Unit") held by joint unit-holders:

Description/address:

Title Number:

2. Details of the joint unit-holders:

First joint unit-holder	Second joint unit-holder	Third joint unit-holder (if any)
Name:	*Name:*	*Name:*
Address:	*Address:*	*Address:*

If there are any more than three joint unit-holders, their details should also be given.

3. Nomination

We, the joint registered proprietors of the Unit whose details appear in paragraph 2 above, hereby nominate [name of joint unit-holder] to be entered in the register of members of the commonhold association which exercises functions in relation to the Unit, within the meaning of paragraph 8 of Schedule 3 to the Commonhold and Leasehold Reform Act 2002.

IMPORTANT

This nomination will only be effective if it is made in writing to the commonhold association before the end of the period of 21 days from the date of the transfer to the joint unit-holders. If the nomination is not made within this period, the joint unit-holder whose name appears first on the proprietorship register at the Land Registry is entitled to be entered on the register of members, unless a court orders otherwise (paragraph 8(5)).

Signed this ____ day of ____ 20 ____ by:

____	____	____
First joint unit-holder	Second joint unit-holder	Third joint unit-holder

2.11 NOTICE OF TRANSFER OF COMMONHOLD UNIT

Notes

(1) Section 15(3) of the Act provides that, on the transfer of a commonhold unit, the new unit-holder shall notify the commonhold association of the transfer.

(2) Section 15(3) of the Act provides that regulations may prescribe the form and content of the notice; the time by which notice must be given; and the sanction for failure to give a notice in time.

(3) The document that follows is the draft currently proposed as Form 1 in Annex D to the draft commonhold community statement supplied with the Post-Consultation Report from the Department of Constitutional Affairs in August 2003. This form, or one to the same effect, must be used.

(4) Rule 2 of the commonhold community statement requires that the notice should be given within 7 days of the date of notification by the Land Registry of registration of the transfer.

(5) Paragraphs 3.2.4 and 4.13.4 of the text give a full analysis of this topic.

FORM 1

NOTICE OF TRANSFER OF COMMONHOLD UNIT

This notice must be completed and sent to the commonhold association within 7 days from the date on which the Land Registry gives notice that the registration of the transfer has been completed. If you fail to do this the commonhold association will not register you as a member of the commonhold association and this will mean that you will not be entitled to vote or have any say in decisions relating to the running of the commonhold.

1. Details of commonhold unit transferred

Commonhold unit number: Title number:

Full postal address of commonhold unit (if available):

2. Details of unit-holders

Full name(s) and future address for service of correspondence (if known) of the former unit-holder(s) of the commonhold unit:

Full name(s) and address for service of correspondence (if different to the address of unit) of the new unit-holder(s) of the commonhold unit:

Please note: the address for service of correspondence must be a postal address, although in addition, a box number at a document exchange and/or an electronic address may be provided.

3. Notice of transfer

I/we give notice to ____ [*insert name of commonhold association*] that the above commonhold unit was transferred to me/us on ____ *(insert date of transfer)*.
I/we understand that we are liable to pay the debts of the former unit-holder(s) of the commonhold unit.

Signed: Dated:

Signed: Dated:

Please Note
Within 14 days of receiving this notice the commonhold association will register the person who is entitled to be entered in the register of members of the commonhold association.

A person is entitled to be entered in the register of members of the commonhold association if he becomes the sole unit-holder of a commonhold unit.

Where a unit is transferred to two or more persons only one of them may be registered as a member of the commonhold association. In this case, joint unit-holders may nominate one of themselves to be entitled to be registered as a member. Nominations must be sent in writing to the commonhold association **within 7 days** of the transfer. If no such nomination is received before the end of this period, the person whose name appears first in the proprietorship register held by HM Land Registry (this will be the first name that was entered in the transfer deed) will be entitled to become a member. However this may still be amended by applying to the court for an order that (one of) the other joint unit-holder(s) is registered as a member in place of the person who is entitled, or by submitting a late nomination.

If you are joint unit-holders you should submit your nomination within the next 7 days.

2.12 NOTICE OF TRANSFER OF PART ONLY OF COMMONHOLD UNIT

Notes

(1) Section 15(3) of the Act provides that on the transfer of a commonhold unit, the new unit-holder shall notify the commonhold association of the transfer.
(2) Section 15(3) of the Act provides that regulations may prescribe the form and content of the notice; the time by which notice must be given; and the sanction for failure to give a notice in time.
(3) This document is the draft currently proposed as Form 2 in Annex D to the draft commonhold community statement supplied with the Post-Consultation Report from the Department of Constitutional Affairs in August 2003. This form, or one to the same effect, must be used.
(4) Rule 2 of the commonhold community statement requires that the notice should be given within 7 days of the date of notification by the Land Registry of registration of the transfer.
(5) Paragraphs 3.2.4 and 4.13.4 of the text give a full analysis of this topic.

FORM 2

NOTICE OF TRANSFER OF PART ONLY OF A COMMONHOLD UNIT

This notice must be completed and sent to the commonhold association within 7 days from the date on which the Land Registry gives notice that the registration of the transfer has been completed. If you are a new unit-holder and you fail to do this, the commonhold association will not register you as a member of the commonhold association. This will mean that you will not be entitled to vote or have any say in decisions relating to the running of the commonhold.

1. Details of commonhold unit from which land is being transferred

Title number:

Full name of unit-holder(s) from which the land is being transferred:

Full postal address of commonhold unit from which land is being transferred:

2. Land becoming a new commonhold unit

Only complete this section if the land transferred is becoming a new commonhold unit, otherwise go to question 3.

Commonhold unit number:

Full postal address:

Full name of incoming registered proprietor(s) of new commonhold unit and address for service of correspondence (if different to the address of the unit):

3. Land being added to an existing commonhold unit

Commonhold unit number:

Full postal address:

Full name of registered proprietor of commonhold unit to which land is being added and address for service of correspondence (if different to the address of the unit):

Please note: the address for service of correspondence must be a postal address, although in addition, a box number at a document exchange and/or an electronic address may be provided.

4. Notice of transfer

I/we give notice to ____ [*insert name of commonhold association*] that ____ was registered at the Land Registry as a transfer of part of the above commonhold unit on ____ *(insert date of transfer)*.
I/we understand that we are liable to pay the debts of the former unit-holder(s) of the commonhold unit.

Signed: Dated:

Signed: Dated:

Please Note
Within 14 days of receiving this notice the commonhold association will register the person who is entitled to be entered in the register of members of the commonhold association.

A person is entitled to be entered in the register of members of the commonhold association if he becomes the sole unit-holder of a commonhold unit.

Where a unit is transferred to two or more persons only one of them may be registered as a member of the commonhold association. In this case, joint unit-holders may nominate one of themselves to be entitled to be registered as a member. Nominations must be sent in writing to the commonhold association **within 7 days** of the transfer. If no such nomination is received before the end of this period, the person whose name appears first in the proprietorship register held by HM Land Registry (this will be the first name that was entered in the transfer deed) will be entitled to become a member. However this may still be amended by applying to the court for an order that (one of) the other joint unit-holder(s) is registered as a member in place of the person who is entitled, or by submitting a late nomination.

If you are joint unit-holders you should submit your nomination within the next 7 days.

2.13 NOTICE OF TENANCY IN A COMMONHOLD UNIT

Notes

(1) Rule 5 of the commonhold community statement provides that a unit-holder must notify the commonhold association that a tenancy or a licence for a period longer than 28 days has been granted within 7 days from the date on which it was granted.

(2) This document is the draft currently proposed as Form 3 in Annex D to the draft commonhold community statement supplied with the Post-Consultation Report from the Department of Constitutional Affairs in August 2003. This form, or one to the same effect, must be used for notification of any such tenancy.

(3) Paragraph 4.13.7 of the text gives a full analysis of this topic.

FORM 3

NOTICE OF TENANCY IN A COMMONHOLD UNIT

This notice must be completed and sent to the commonhold association within 7 days from the date that the tenancy is granted. If you fail to do this, the commonhold association may bring proceedings to enforce the duty and you may be liable to pay their costs.

1. Details of commonhold unit

Title number:

Full postal address of commonhold unit:

2. Details of unit-holder(s) and tenant(s)

Full name(s) and address for service of correspondence (if different to the address of unit) of the tenant(s) of the commonhold unit:

Please note: the address for service of correspondence must be a postal address, although in addition, a box number at a document exchange and/or an electronic address may be provided.

3. Details of tenancy

Date tenancy granted:

Length of tenancy:

Fixed/periodic

Date tenancy commences:

I/we give notice to ____ [insert name of commonhold association] that a tenancy in the terms stated has been granted in the above commonhold unit [and that the tenant will be primarily responsible for the payment of the commonhold assessment]**delete if unit-holder remains responsible*

Signed: Dated:

Signed: Dated:

2.14 NOTICE OF LICENCE TO OCCUPY OR USE A COMMONHOLD UNIT

Notes

(1) Rule 5 of the commonhold community statement provides that a unit-holder must notify the commonhold association that a tenancy or a licence for a period longer than 28 days has been granted within 7 days from the date on which it was granted.

(2) This document is the draft currently proposed as Form 4 in Annex D to the draft commonhold community statement supplied with the Post-Consultation Report from the Department of Constitutional Affairs in August 2003. This form, or one to the same effect, must be used for notification of any such licence.

(3) Paragraph 4.13.9 of the text gives a full analysis of this topic.

FORM 4

NOTICE OF LICENCE TO OCCUPY OR USE A COMMONHOLD UNIT

This notice must be completed and sent to the commonhold association within seven days from the date that the licence is granted. If you fail to do this, the commonhold association may bring proceedings to enforce the duty and you may be liable to pay their costs.

1. Details of licensed commonhold unit

Title number:

Full postal address of commonhold unit:

2. Details of unit-holder(s) and licensees

Full name(s) and address for service of correspondence (if different to the address of unit) of the licensee(s) of the commonhold unit:

Please note: the address for service of correspondence must be a postal address, although in addition, a box number at a document exchange and/or an electronic address may be provided.

3. Details of licence

Length of licence:

Nature of licence:

Date of licence:

I/we give notice to ____ [insert name of commonhold association] that a licence in the terms stated has been granted in the above commonhold unit.

Signed: Dated:

Signed: Dated:

2.15 REGISTER OF TENANTS AND LICENSEES

Notes

(1) This Register is required by rule 6 of the commonhold community statement. The tenancies and licences required to be registered in it are those for terms longer than 28 days.
(2) The form of this document is not currently prescribed by regulation.
(3) Paragraph 4.4.8 of the text discusses this requirement.

COMMONHOLD

Register of Tenants and Licensees

Commonhold Community Statement, rule 6

[Name] Commonhold Association Limited ("the Association")

Unit address	Name and address of unit-holder	Name and address of tenant/licensee	Date and length of tenancy/licence	Date of notification of letting/ licence	Current tenant/licensee (if different)

IMPORTANT

This Register must be kept up to date.

The addresses supplied for the unit-holder and the tenant/licensee must be those at which documents may be served.

It is the obligation of the unit-holder to inform the commonhold association of any change in the identity of the tenant/licensee.

It is the obligation of the commonhold association to insert the details of any change in the identity of the tenant/licensee.

2.16 REGISTER OF DIRECTORS' INTERESTS

Notes

(1) This Register is required by article 63 of the articles of association.
(2) The interests required to be registered in it are those in any transaction or arrangement in which the commonhold association is otherwise interested.
(3) The form of this document is not currently prescribed by regulation.
(4) Paragraph 4.3.11 of the text discusses this requirement.

COMMONHOLD

Register of Directors' interests

Articles of association, article 63

[Name] Commonhold Association Limited ("the Association")

Name of director	Information received	Date of entry	Name of recipient

IMPORTANT

It is the obligation of the directors to inform the commonhold association of any interest in any transaction or arrangement in which the commonhold association is otherwise interested.

It is the obligation of the commonhold association to ensure that details of such interests are inserted in this Register.

<u>This Register must be kept up to date.</u>

2.17 RECORD OF POWERS DELEGATED BY DIRECTORS

Notes

(1) Article 58 of the articles of association provides that directors of the commonhold association may delegate their powers to a committee consisting of 2 or more people, the majority of whom are members of the association, or to any other executive director or managing agent.
(2) In the event of such delegation, article 58 requires a record to be kept.
(3) The form of this document is not currently prescribed by regulation. It sets out what the authors consider to be a suitable record.
(4) Paragraph 4.3.13 of the text discusses this requirement.

COMMONHOLD

Record of powers delegated by Directors

Articles of association, article 58

[Name] Commonhold Association Limited ("the Association")

Name of director	Powers delegated	Date of resolution for delegation	To whom delegated

IMPORTANT

Delegation of powers is ineffective unless sanctioned by ordinary resolution.
It is the obligation of the commonhold association to ensure that details of delegations are inserted in this Record.
Delegation does not absolve directors of responsibility for the performance of their duties.
This Record must be kept up to date.

2.18 NOTICE OF ANNUAL GENERAL MEETING OF COMMONHOLD ASSOCIATION

Notes

(1) It is a requirement of the Companies Act 1985 that a limited company should have an annual general meeting.

(2) Such a meeting will provide a valuable opportunity for the board of directors to present their proposals for management of the commonhold and its budget during the year ahead to the members.

(3) Notice of the meeting must be given, as discussed in paragraph 4.5.8 of the text.

[Name] Commonhold Association Limited

Notice of annual general meeting

Take notice that the annual general meeting of the members of [Name] Commonhold Association Limited ("the Association") will take place on [date] at [meeting place].

The purpose of the meeting is as follows:

1. Ordinary business

1.1 to receive and consider the report of the directors and the statement of accounts and the balance sheet of the company for the year ended . . . with the auditors' report;
1.2 to elect as directors the following who retire by rotation namely: (names of directors due to be re-elected);
1.3 to reappoint [Name] as auditors and authorise the directors to fix their remuneration;
1.4 any other business.

2. Special business

2.1 to consider, and if thought fit pass, the following resolutions as ordinary resolutions:

  2.1.1 that the budget for the year ending [ ] be approved.
  2.1.2 that the assessment of expenditure for the year ending and the proposed levies [ ] be approved.

2.2 to consider, and if thought fit pass, the following resolutions as special resolutions:

  2.2.1 . . .
  2.2.2 . . .

2.3 [any other special business].

It would assist with administration if you could let the Association Secretary know beforehand whether you will be able to attend.
Signed this ____ day of ____ 20 ____ by:

Association Secretary

Contact address:

Tel No:

2.19 PROXY NOTICE

Notes

(1) Article 38 of the articles of association provides that a member may vote at meetings of the commonhold association by proxy.
(2) Article 39 of the articles of association provides that the appointment of a proxy shall be in writing, executed by or on behalf of the appointor and shall be in the form set out below (or in a form to the same effect).
(3) This topic is discussed in paragraph 4.6.7 of the text.

[Name] Commonhold Association Limited

Proxy Notice

[I][We] ____, of ____, being [a] member/members of the above-named commonhold association, hereby appoint(s) ____ of ____, or failing him, ____ of ____, as my/our proxy to vote in my/our name(s) and on my/our behalf(ves) at the annual/interim general meeting of the commonhold association to be held on ____ 20__, and at any adjournment of it

Signed this ____ day of ____ 20 ____ by:

Contact address:

Tel No:

2.20 TARGETED PROXY NOTICE

Notes

(1) Article 38 of the articles of association provides that a member may vote at meetings of the commonhold association by proxy.
(2) Article 40 of the articles of association provides that members are to be given the opportunity of instructing the proxy how he shall act. The appointment of a proxy shall be in the following form (or in a form to the same effect).
(3) This topic is discussed in paragraph 4.6.7 of the text.

[Name] Commonhold Association Limited

Targeted Proxy Notice

[I][We] ____, of ____, being [a] member/members of the above-named commonhold association, hereby appoint(s) ____ of ____, or failing him, ____ of ____, as my/our proxy to vote in my/our name(s) and on my/our behalf(ves) at the annual/interim general meeting of the commonhold association to be held on ____ 20____, and at any adjournment of it.

This form is to be used in respect of the resolutions mentioned below as follows:

Resolution No.1 [for][against]

Resolution No.2 [for][against]

[Strike out whichever is not desired]

Unless otherwise instructed, the proxy may vote as he thinks fit or abstain from voting.

Signed this____ day of ____ 20____ by:

Contact address:

Tel No:

2.21 ENDURING PROXY NOTICE

Notes

(1) Article 38 of the articles of association provides that a member may vote at meetings of the commonhold association by proxy.

(2) Article 40 of the articles of association provides that members may be allowed to appoint such a proxy to vote for them in general meetings on more than one occasion. The form of appointment must be in writing, executed by or on behalf of the appointor, and must be in the form set out below (or in a form to the same effect).

(3) This topic is discussed in paragraph 4.6.7 of the text.

[Name] Commonhold Association Limited

Enduring Proxy Notice

[I][We] ____, of ____, being [a] member/members of the above-named commonhold association, hereby appoint(s) ____ of ____, or failing him, ____ of ____, as my/our proxy to vote in my/our name(s) and on my/our behalf(ves) in any special or ordinary resolution put to the vote at any of the annual and/or interim general meetings of the commonhold association held from ____ until further notice.

Signed this ____ day of ____ 20____ by:

Contact address:

Tel No:

PART 3. COMMONHOLD ASSESSMENT PROCEDURE

3.1 ANNUAL REPORT AND BUDGET

Notes

(1) The Companies Act 1985 requires a limited company to file annual accounts and its directors' report. The Act does not lay down any additional requirement in relation to a commonhold association.

(2) Formerly, rule 36 of the draft commonhold community statement appended to the Consultation Paper dated October 2002 provided that, in addition to and at the same time as providing the annual accounts and directors' report, the board of directors of the commonhold association should also circulate or lay before the members a written report comparing the results of the commonhold association against its estimated budget for the year and setting out an estimated budget for the forthcoming year. The mandatory nature of this proposal was removed by the Post-Consultation Report dated August 2003, although some commonhold associations will consider it good practice to provide such a report.

(3) No prescribed form for the annual report and budget are currently proposed, and the text below sets out the authors' suggestions for such a form.

(4) These requirements are discussed in paragraph 4.15.4 of the text.

COMMONHOLD

Annual Report and Budget

[Name] Commonhold Association Limited ("the Association")

1. Introduction

This document has been prepared for/by the directors of the Association. Its purpose is to review the income and expenditure of the Association during the current year, with the aims of:

(a) ascertaining whether the assessment made prior to the beginning of the year was appropriate;
(b) examining whether there are ways in which the administration of the business of the Association might be improved;
(c) investigating whether the Association needs to take any further measures to collect any overdue assessment sums;
(d) providing a guide to the likely level of the assessment for the Association for the forthcoming year;
(e) examining whether further provision needs to be made for the reserve fund.

This report will be discussed at the annual general meeting of the Association to be held on [ ].

2. Comparison of estimated with actual expenditure

The table below sets out:

(a) The estimated figures for this year's expenditure, based upon the assessment (see column (1)).
(b) The actual figures for this year's expenditure (see column (2)). Because this report has to be prepared before the end of 2004 financial year in order to prepare for the budget for the forthcoming year, not all the expenditure for the year has yet taken place, and some estimated figures (in *italics*) have been used instead. The estimated figures are based upon the assessed amounts for 2004, unless there is reason to believe that the assessment was an under- or over-estimate.
(c) The proposed budget figures for next year's expenditure are shown in column (3).

Item	(1) 2004 assessment (£)	(2) 2004 expenditure (£)	(3) 2005 budget (£)
1. Lift			
2. Roof works			
3. Plumbing			
4. Cleaning			
5. Gardening			
6. Surveyor's fees			
7. Buildings			
8. Public liability			
9. Electricity			
10. Gas			
11. Telecom			
12. Water rates			
13. Rates			
14. Waste disposal			
15. Fire precautions			

16. Cable/satellite			
17. Security			

Administration

18. Mgmt fees			
19. Office costs			
20. Audit			
21. Debt collection			
22. Legal			

Contingency

23. Contingency			

Extras

24. Flood works			

TOTAL			

3. Comments on 2004 expenditure

In general terms, the expenditure for 2004 has kept within the limits set by the 2004 assessment. The following items, however, call for special comment:

(a) Item 5: the gardening contractor went into liquidation in April and a new contractor was found at increased rates. No further assessment was needed because of the money saved during the period we were without a gardener. If the Association is to stay with the new contractor, however, then increased provision will need to be made in the assessment for 2005 (see paragraph 7(a) below).

(b) Item 24: a flood occurred in the common parts in March, and it was decided that the requisite remedial works should be carried out immediately. No provision had been made in the 2004 assessment for such a contingency, and accordingly a further assessment and levy were made, as shown against this item. The question whether increased contingency ought to be made for similar occurrence in 2005 is raised for discussion under paragraph 7(b) below;

(c) ...

4. Review of administration in 2004

The directors are pleased with the way in which the Association has been run in 2004. The following questions are, however, raised for consideration by members:

(a) Do the members feel that the service they receive from the management company is sufficiently prompt and effective?

(b) In the light of the letter received concerning pets (see annex A), do members think that a relaxation of the prohibition in rule * of the commonhold community statement would be appropriate?

(c) Are members content that matters of security should continue to be dealt with by a committee of members, or do they consider that it may be more appropriate for a security firm to be appointed to advise on such matters? A report on the subject which members may find interesting is attached at annex B.

(d) ...

5. Income

The Association has received rent for the spare garage in the sum of £*. This has been credited in the draft accounts (annex C), but is not reflected in the budget figures, there being no guarantee that the garage will be available in 2005.

6. Debt collection

The directors report that payment of levied assessment charges has for the most part been prompt, with 80% of levies being met within seven days, and all but one within three weeks. Prompt payers may wish the directors to apply sanctions to those who are less prompt in the form of interest demands; while the majority of members may wish further action to be taken in respect of the outstanding debt. The directors therefore raise the following questions for consideration by the members:

(a) What if any action do members wish to take to ensure prompter payment of the assessment levies?

(b) Do members approve the institution of dispute resolution procedures (culminating if necessary in litigation) against the non-payer?

7. The budget for 2005

The proposed expenditure for 2005 is shown in column (3) of the table in paragraph 2 above. The figures shown are drawn from the 2004 figures, with a 5% inflationary adjustment, save for:

(a) Gardening: members will note this charge is based upon the higher costs associated with the replacement contractor which was the only contractor the directors were able to obtain at short notice. More competitive quotations are being sought, and members will be updated on progress at the forthcoming meeting.
(b) Contingency: this has been increased to make more generous provision for unforeseen events such as the flood which occurred this year. An increased fund would lessen the need to make further (time-wasting and expensive) levies during the course of the year.
(c) Public liability insurance: the premium for this insurance is set to increase dramatically next year. The Association has achieved a modest discount in the past because it uses the same insurer for its building insurance. The directors have written to the Association's broker seeking other quotations, and should have the results in time for the meeting.
(d) . . .

These proposals and other suggestions the members of the Association may have to make will be discussed at the forthcoming annual general meeting, following which the directors will prepare a draft annual assessment estimate for 2005, which will be circulated for approval or further debate.

8. The reserve fund

All levies for 2004 have now been collected in, and the reserve fund stands in credit to the tune of £*. The directors are unaware of any circumstances suggesting that the reserve fund study carried out in [ ] needs to be reappraised, and they do not therefore propose that the levy for 2005 be altered.

9. Association contact

If you have any comments on this report which you would like the directors to take into account before the meeting, you should send them to the Association Secretary:

Address:

Tel No.:

Signed this ____ day of ____ 20____ by:

3.2 ANNUAL ASSESSMENT ESTIMATE

Notes

(1) Section 38(1)(a) of the Act provides that the commonhold community statement must make provision requiring the directors of the commonhold association to make an annual estimate of the income required to be raised by unit-holders to meet the expenses of the association.

(2) Section 38(1)(b) provides for the commonhold community statement to make provision enabling the directors to make further estimates from time to time of income required to be raised from unit-holders in addition to the annual estimate.

(3) Rule 23 of the current draft of the commonhold community statement follows this requirement by providing that the directors of the commonhold association must make an annual estimate of income required to be raised from unit-holders to meet the expenses of the commonhold association.

(4) The Consultation Paper issued by the Lord Chancellor's Department on 10 October 2002 proposed that, in determining the assessment estimate, the directors should take into consideration "any other income reasonably expected to accrue to the commonhold association in the next year". It also proposed that the estimate should include details of the expenditure from the previous year and the income received as well as a statement of the amounts due from defaulting unit-holders in the previous year. Although these proposals have not been pursued in the current draft of the statement, they are prudent, and should if possible be followed.

(5) The purpose of the Form is to give notice of the proposed expenditure to unit-holders, to enable any representations to be raised, and to pave the way for the annual assessment levy that will be required.

(6) This Form deals with the annual estimate and proposed levy, while Form 3.3 below deals with any further assessments that may be necessary or appropriate.

(7) These requirements are discussed in paragraph 4.15.3 of the text.

COMMONHOLD

draft Annual Assessment Estimate

Commonhold and Leasehold Reform Act 2002, section 38

Notes:

(1) This draft has been prepared by the directors taking into account the matters raised at the annual general meeting of the Association held on [ ] concerning the budget for 2005.

(2) If you have any comments on this draft which you would like the directors to take into account, you should send or give them to the Association Secretary:

Address:

Tel No.:

Signed this ____ day of ____ 20____ by:

A: Intended expenditure by [Name] Commonhold Association Limited for the year ending [date]

Fabric Repairs, Maintenance, Mechanical and Electrical

Site Maintenance	£
Roof Repairs	£
External Decoration and Ancillary Repairs	£
Access Control Maintenance	£
	£

Cleaning and Environmental

Cleaning Common Parts	£
Pest Control	£
Health and Safety	£
	£

Insurance

Buildings Insurance	£
Third Party Liability Insurance	£
	£

Administration

Audit Fees	£
Legal fees	£
Office expenses (postage, printing, photocopies)	£
Reserve Fund Study	£
	£

Energy

Electricity	£
Gas	£
Sundries	£
	£

Expense Total	£
Management Fee	£
GRAND TOTAL	£*

B: Income expected from other sources by [Name] Commonhold Association Limited for the year ending [date]

Rents received for use of communal garages	£**

C: Total assessment charge required by [Name] Commonhold Association Limited for the year ending [date] to meet shortfall of A over B:

£* expenditure less £** income:	£***

D: Apportionment of £*:**

	Percentage	**Proposed levy**
Unit 1	*%	£
Unit 2	*%	£
Unit 3	*%	£
Unit 4	*%	£
(*Insert any other units*)	*%	£
Totals	**100%**	**£**

3.3 EMERGENCY ASSESSMENT ESTIMATE

Notes

(1) Section 38(1)(b) of the Act provides that the commonhold community statement must make provision enabling the directors of the commonhold association to make estimates from time to time of income required to be raised from unit-holders to fund expenditure over and above that raised in response to the levy based upon the annual estimate (see Form 3.2 above).

(2) This Form should be used either where a shortfall has occurred in the commonhold association's income, or where an unplanned contingency has arisen, and funds are required to meet forthcoming liabilities.

(3) The purpose of the Form is both to give notice of the proposed expenditure to unit-holders and to require payment.

(4) The Form uses headings and some text that may be convenient in practice. The text in italics deals with a hypothetical situation requiring a further assessment.

(5) This topic is discussed further in paragraph 4.15.9 of the text.

COMMONHOLD

Emergency Assessment Estimate

Commonhold and Leasehold Reform Act 2002, section 38(1)(b)

[Name] Commonhold Association Limited ("the Association")

1. The annual estimate
On [date], an annual assessment estimate was produced on behalf of the Association for the purposes of calculating the annual assessment levy for the year ending [date].

2. The need for further expenditure
On [date], the stairwell in the common parts was flooded as a result of a broken pipe in the roof area, causing superficial damage to the decorations. The pipe has been repaired temporarily, but needs to be replaced, while the stairwell is now unsightly, and must be redecorated. The directors of the Association take the view that it would not be right to carry over the requisite works until next financial year, and consider that the works must be done as a matter of urgency.

3. The amount of the further expenditure
The cost of remedying the damage to the decorations and repairing the broken pipe has been estimated by the Association's surveyor to be £. This estimate is in line with tenders/quotations supplied by two building contractors who have visited the site.*

4. The need to raise a further levy
The annual estimate did not provide for any such expenditure. On current estimates, it would appear that the monies raised as a result of the levy following the annual estimate will be fully utilised on planned expenditure. The works proposed do not comprise long term repair or replacement of the Association's assets and it would therefore be inappropriate to use monies in the reserve fund for the works.

5. The total amount of the proposed levy
The directors propose that the sum of £* should be raised by way of a further levy. This sum should cover the anticipated cost of the works, professional fees, and contingencies.

6. The amount proposed to be payable by each unit-holder
Applying the percentages set out in the commonhold community statement to the amount proposed in paragraph 5 above produces the following proposed levy for each unit-holder:

APPORTIONMENT of £*	Percentage	Proposed levy
Unit 1	*%	£
Unit 2	*%	£
Unit 3	*%	£
Unit 4	*%	£
(*Insert any other units*)	*%	£
Totals	**100%**	**£**

Signed this ____ day of ____ 20____ by:

Address:

Tel No.:

3.4 ASSESSMENT LEVY

Notes

(1) Section 38(1)(e) of the Act provides that the commonhold community statement must make provision requiring the directors of the commonhold association to serve notices on unit-holders specifying payments required to be made by them to meet the expenses of the association and the date on which each payment is due.
(2) Neither the Consultation Paper issued by the Lord Chancellor's Department on 10 October 2002, nor the Post-Consultation Report dated August 2003, propose a prescribed form for such a notice. The authors' suggestion is therefore set out below.
(3) This Form may be adapted for use either as an annual assessment levy or as a further assessment levy.
(4) This topic is discussed in paragraph 4.15.7 of the text.

COMMONHOLD

Notice of Assessment Levy

Commonhold and Leasehold Reform Act 2002, section 38

[Name] Commonhold Association Limited ("the Association")

1. **The estimate**
   On [date] the directors of the Association made an annual estimate of the income required to be raised from unit-holders to meet the expenses of the Association for the financial year ending on [date].

[*If the levy is in respect of a further assessment rather than an annual assessment, then substitute the following for paragraph 1:*]

On [date] the directors of this commonhold association made an estimate of the extra income required to be raised from unit-holders to meet an extra cost of £* attributable to [*please specify*].

2. **The approval**
   The assessment was approved by the directors on [date] [when it was also resolved that, in the circumstances, payment should be required within 14 days, rather than the usual 28 days].

3. **Your percentage**
   Your specified percentage of the assessment is [*]% and your proportion of the levy is therefore [£*]. A formal invoice in enclosed.

4. **Payment**
   Please pay the amount of [£*] by sending a cheque made out in the name of [Name] Commonhold Association Limited to the following address by [date]:

   [Address of Association]

5. **[Payment by instalments**
   Should you find it difficult to pay the levy in one lump sum, you may instead pay by four equal instalments of £*, with each instalment being paid on the first days of (January, April, July and October 200*).]

6. **Non-payment**
   A failure to pay by the specified date may result in interest being payable on the full amount from the date of receipt of this Notice.

   Signed this ____ day of ____ 20____ by:

APPLICATION FOR PAYMENT

THIS IS NOT A TAX INVOICE

Unit Holder:

(Name)

(Address)

Premises:

Unit *

INTEREST MAY BE CHARGED ON LATE PAYMENT
Issue Date

Please return attached remittance advice with your cheque made payable to: [Name] Commonhold Association Limited at [address].

Due Date	**Detail**	**Amount Due**	**VAT Amount**

3.5 RESERVE FUND STUDY

Notes

(1) Section 39(1) of the Act provides that regulations may require a commonhold association to make provision requiring the directors of the commonhold association to establish and maintain one or more funds to finance the repair and maintenance of the common parts and the commonhold units.

(2) The Consultation Paper issued by the Lord Chancellor's Department on 10 October 2002 proposed that all commonholds should be required to establish and maintain a reserve fund.

(3) Rule 31 of the original draft commonhold community statement provided that, at least every 10 years, the board of directors of the commonhold association should prepare a written study (a) listing all its major wasting assets; (b) estimating the remaining life of each item; (c) estimating the cost of maintaining and replacing the item; and (d) estimating the annual contribution required to maintain such costs.

(4) However, in the Post-Consultation Report issued by the Department of Constitutional Affairs in August 2003, it was proposed that the requirement for a reserve fund should be left to the discretion of each commonhold association, although the proposal that commonhold associations should carry out a reserve fund study at least every 10 years would remain mandatory.

(5) There is currently no prescribed form for this purpose. Given the nature of the task, no one form will meet the requirements of the study. Accordingly this form sets out a number of suggested topics for the author of such a study to take into account.

(6) These requirements are discussed in more detail in paragraph 4.16.3 of the text.

COMMONHOLD

Reserve Fund Study

Commonhold and Leasehold Reform Act 2002, section 38

Introduction

1. This study has been prepared by [Mr X....... Y..... FRICS on behalf of] the board of directors of the [Name] Commonhold Association Limited with a view to [complying with rule* of its commonhold community statement, which provides that, at least every 10 years, the board of directors should prepare a written] study (a) listing all its major assets, equipment, fixtures or fittings with a remaining life of less than [ ] years; (b) estimating the remaining life of each item; (c) estimating the costs of maintaining and replacing the item; and (d) estimating the annual contribution required to maintain such costs.

2. In this Study:

   - "the Association" means the [Name] Commonhold Association Limited
   - "the Statement" is a reference to the commonhold community statement for the Association
   - "the Land" means the land registered as commonhold under title No. *
   - "the Common Parts" means the common parts of the Land, as defined in the Statement
   - "Unit *" is a reference to a particular Unit forming part of the commonhold

3. An inspection of the Land for the purposes of the Study was carried out on [date] by [ ].

4. [This Study updates a Study carried out for the board of directors on [date]].

The assets of the Association

5. The assets on the Land belonging to the Association which fall within the purview of this Study are shown in the table below, together with an estimate of the period until each asset will need major works or replacement. Where practical, a current day value for the works in question is also given, including the costs of any works necessary to maintain the asset in the meantime.

6. The attention of the Association is drawn to the Notes set out in paragraph 7 of this Study.

No.	Asset description	Estimated work date	Estimated cost of work(£)	Notes
1.	Roof over Block 1	20**	£*	See Note 1
2.	Car park resurfacing	20**	£*	See Note 2
3.				
. . .				

Notes

7. The following items in the table under paragraph 6 above require explanation:

   Note 1: The roof over Block 1 could conceivably be patch repaired to prolong its life for longer than the period stipulated. Having regard to the report prepared by [* Building Surveyors] on [date], however, the directors consider that it would be prudent to allow for total replacement.

   Note 2: The cost allows for a specification which will improve the drainage of the car parking area. Again, based on the advice received from [* FRICS] on [date], the directors consider that the cost should be allowed for.

   Note 3: . . .

Reserve fund contribution

8. In the light of the matters set out in paragraphs 6 and 7 above, my/our view is that [a reserve fund should be established and] an annual amount of £* should be paid into the reserve fund to cover the anticipated expenditure. This amount has been calculated by apportioning the total anticipated expenditure over the [ ] year period in accordance with the following calculation:

. . .

9. [The members of the Association are currently required to pay annual contributions totalling £* towards the reserve fund. Taking those contributions into account, together with the monies currently in the reserve fund, the future total annual contributions will need to be adjusted to £*.]

   Signed this ____ day of ____ 20____ by:

3.6 RESERVE FUND LEVY

Notes

(1) Section 39(2)(c) of the Act provides that the commonhold community statement must make provision requiring the directors of the commonhold association to serve notices on unit-holders specifying payments required to be made by them towards a reserve fund.

(2) The level of required contributions will have been calculated by a reserve fund study (see Form 3.5).

(3) The Consultation Paper issued by the Lord Chancellor's Department on 10 October 2002 does not propose a prescribed form for such a notice. The authors' suggestion follows.

(4) This topic is discussed in paragraph 4.16.9 of the text.

COMMONHOLD

Notice of Reserve Fund Levy

Commonhold and Leasehold Reform Act 2002, section 39

[Name] Commonhold Association Limited ("the Association")

1. The reserve fund study
On [date] the directors of the Association procured a study of the income required to be raised from unit-holders to meet the long term expenses of the Association which will be required for the repair and replacement of its assets.

2. The reserve fund estimate
The study estimated that the total annual contributions which should be required for this purpose are £*. The money collected will be put into a reserve fund in the names of the directors of the Association, and will not be drawn upon for the ordinary expenses of the Association, for which a separate levy is made.

3. Approval
This study was approved by a vote at a General Meeting of the Association held on [date].[1]

4. Your percentage
Your specified percentage of the assessment is [*]% and your proportion of the reserve fund levy is therefore [£*]. A formal invoice is enclosed.

5. Payment
Please pay the amount of [£*] by sending a cheque made out in the name of [Name] Commonhold Association Limited to the following address by [date]:
[**Address for Association**]

6. Non-payment
A failure to pay by the specified date may result in interest being payable on the full amount from the date of receipt of this Notice.

Signed this ____ day of ____ 20____ by:

[1] There is no requirement for this study to be approved by resolution but, given the importance of the subject matter, the commonhold association may consider that this course of action would be prudent.

APPLICATION FOR PAYMENT

THIS IS NOT A TAX INVOICE

Unit Holder:

(Name)

(Address)

Premises:

Unit *

INTEREST MAY BE CHARGED ON LATE PAYMENT
Issue Date

Please return attached remittance advice with your cheque made payable to: [Name] Commonhold Association Limited at [address].

Due Date	**Detail**	**Amount Due**	**VAT Amount**

PART 4. DISPUTE RESOLUTION FORMS

4.1 COMPLAINTS NOTICE

Notes

(1) Rules 42 to 52 of the commonhold community statement contain detailed provision for dispute resolution in a commonhold.
(2) Under the complaints procedure forming part of that dispute resolution provision, the unit-holder must, usually, try to resolve the difficulty with the offending party but, on failing to do so, may serve notice of the dispute on the commonhold association.
(3) Upon receipt of such a notice, the commonhold association should reply to the complainant in the form set out in Form 4.2 below.
(4) This form of notification is prescribed. The script in italics gives an example of a complaint. It should be noted that it will be insufficient to give general allegations of offending activity without also supplying details of the duty alleged to have been breached.
(5) The complaints procedure is discussed in Section 6.5 of the text.

FORM 5

COMPLAINTS NOTICE

1. Details of complainant

Full name(s): unit/holder(s)/tenant(s)

Full postal address:

Address for service (if different):

2. Details of defaulter

Full Name(s): commonhold association/unit-holder(s)/tenant(s)

Full postal address:

Address for service:

3. Commonhold community statement

Version Number:

Registered at Land Registry on:

4. Matter complained of

Give full details of the duty which it is alleged has not been complied with.

(a) *Details of complaint(s)*:

(i) *On or about [date], Tom ____, the unit-holder of [address or description of unit], acquired some stick insects. He allows them to wander around without restriction, despite the objections of a number of other unit-holders.*

(ii) *On or about [date], Rosie ____, the unit-holder of [address or description of unit], acquired a hamster called Daisy. While I have no particular objections to hamsters per se, Rosie stores large quantities of hamster food in the stairwell of the common parts, where it gives off unsavoury odours.*

(iii) *On or about [date], Ned ____, the unit-holder of [address or description of unit], acquired two large goldfish called Spitfire and Lancaster. Ned has placed the goldfish in the ornamental fountain in the entrance hall of the common parts together with a large quantity of weed, which is fouling the water.*

(b) *Details of commonhold community statement provision in breach*:

(i) *Rule * of the commonhold community statement, version 3, forbids the keeping of pets without the unanimous consent of all unit-holders.*

(ii) *Rule * of the same statement prevents any unit-holder from using any part of the common parts for their exclusive use, unless that part has been designated for exclusive use.*

(iii) *Rule * of the same statement prevents any unit-holder using any part of the common parts in such a way as to cause nuisance and annoyance to other unit-holders.*

(c) *Details of attempts to remedy breach:*

I have spoken to Rosie, Tom and Ned on a number of occasions, and have pointed out the terms of the commonhold community statement to them. I have also written to them in the same vein, asking them to comply with the terms of the commonhold community statement. My communications have fallen on deaf ears.

5. Action required to remedy matter complained of

(i) *I would like the commonhold association to require Tom to dispose of his insects, or at least to keep them safely inside his unit.*

(ii) *I would like the commonhold association to require Rosie to stop storing hamster food in the stairwell of the common parts.*

(iii) *I would like the commonhold association to require Ned to remove his goldfish and the weed from the fountain.*

Signed: **Dated:**

Signed: **Dated:**

The commonhold association may make representations about the matter complained of by serving a reply notice within 21 days from the date on which the complaints notice was served. If the commonhold association fails to respond, or the response is unsatisfactory, the matter may be referred to the ombudsman. The commonhold association will be required to comply with any order of the ombudsman.

4.2 ACKNOWLEDGEMENT OF COMPLAINT

Notes

(1) Rules 42 to 52 of the draft commonhold community statement contain detailed provision for dispute resolution in a commonhold.

(2) Under the complaints procedure forming part of that dispute resolution provision, the unit-holder must, usually, try to resolve the difficulty with the offending party but, on failing to do so, may serve notice of the dispute on the commonhold association. Form 4.1 above sets out the prescribed information, together with an example of a complaint.

(3) Upon receipt of such a notice, the board of directors of the commonhold association would be well advised to reply to the complainant.

(4) If the complaint is made against the commonhold association itself and a reply is thought to be appropriate, then the form of reply is prescribed, and is set out as Form 4.3 below.

(5) If the complaint is made against another unit-holder, then it would be appropriate for the commonhold association to acknowledge the complaint. There is no prescribed form for this purpose, and the form and content that follows contain the authors' suggestions as to the appropriate form for this notice, using as an example the sample complaints set out in Form 4.1.

(6) The complaints procedure is discussed in Section 6.5 of the text.

COMMONHOLD

Acknowledgment of complaint by unit-holder

Commonhold and Leasehold Reform Act 2002, section 37

---

1. This is a reply to your notification of complaint dated ____ regarding [the keeping of pets].

2. We now intend to send a default notice to [*Rosie, Tom and Ned*] enclosing a copy of the notification of complaint and inviting their comments and proposals within a period of 21 days [insert shorter period in case of urgency]. We enclose a copy of a draft of our intended default notice.

4. Once the period of 21 days [shorter period] has elapsed, we will then consider what further action to take in the light of any such comments and proposals that might by then have been received.

5. We shall keep you informed of any further action we take concerning your complaint.

6. If you are dissatisfied with this course of action, you may choose instead to refer your complaint to the ombudsman under the ombudsman scheme, details of which are set out in the commonhold community statement.

Signed this ____ day of ____ 20____ by:

4.3 REPLY NOTICE

Notes

(1) Rules 42 to 52 of the draft commonhold community statement contain detailed provision for dispute resolution in a commonhold.

(2) Under the complaints procedure forming part of that dispute resolution provision, the unit-holder must, usually, try to resolve the difficulty with the offending party but, on failing to do so, may serve notice of the dispute on the commonhold association. Form 4.1 above sets out the prescribed information, together with an example of a complaint.

(3) If the complaint is made against the commonhold association itself and a reply is thought to be appropriate, then the form of reply is prescribed, and is set out below.

(4) If the complaint is made against another unit-holder, then it would be appropriate for the commonhold association to acknowledge the complaint. There is no prescribed form for this purpose, and the authors' suggestions as to the appropriate form for this notice, using as an example the sample complaints set out in Form 4.1, are set out in Form 4.2 above.

(5) The complaints procedure is discussed in Section 6.5 of the text.

FORM 6

REPLY TO COMPLAINTS NOTICE

1. **Details of complainant**

   Commonhold unit number:

   Full name(s): unit/holder(s)/tenant(s)

   Full postal address:

   Address for service (if different):

2. **The commonhold association**

   Full Name:

   Address for service:

   Name and address of person to contact:

3. **Commonhold community statement**

   Version Number:

   Registered at Land Registry on:

   I [insert name] on behalf of the commonhold association named above acknowledge receipt of the complaints notice dated [ ] and state that the commonhold association—

   ☐ has complied with the duty

   ☐ will comply with the duty by

   ☐ disputes the matter complained of for the following reasons—

   Signed: **Dated:**

   Signed: **Dated:**

If the complainant is not satisfied with this response, the matter may be referred to the ombudsman.

4.4 DEFAULT NOTICE

Notes

(1) As part of the dispute resolution procedure set out under section 37 of the Act, the draft commonhold community statement makes provision for a notice of a default by any unit-holder to be served upon the alleged defaulting unit-holder. This may occur independently, or following notice of a complaint by another unit-holder to the commonhold association (see Form 4.1 above).

(2) Although this default notice is a prescribed form, the details prescribed are unsatisfactorily brief, and the commonhold association may wish to supplement those details with the notes set out in italic below, which do not form part of the prescribed form.

(3) The relevant procedure is described in Section 6.6 of the text.

FORM 7

DEFAULT NOTICE

---

1. **The commonhold association**

   Full Name:

   Address for service:

   Name and address of person to contact:

2. **Details of defaulter**

   Commonhold unit number:

   Full name(s): unit/holder(s)/tenant(s)

   Full postal address:

   Address for service (if different):

3. **Commonhold community statement**

   Version Number:

   Registered at Land Registry on:

4. **Matter complained of**

   Give full details of the duty which it is alleged has not been complied with.

5. **Action required to remedy matter complained of**

   Signed: **Dated:**

   Signed: **Dated:**

You may make representations about the matter complained of by serving a reply notice within 21 days from the date on which the default notice was served. If you fail to respond, or the response is unsatisfactory, the matter may be referred to the ombudsman or legal proceedings may be initiated.

Please note:

1. The internal complaints procedure of the Association

The Association has an internal complaints procedure for resolving disputes between unit-holders and between unit-holders and the Association without recourse to litigation (which is time consuming and expensive). Details of the procedure are contained in the common-hold community statement of the Association. This Notice, and the response it requires from you, formd part of that procedure.

2. What you are required to do

We require you within 21 days of the date of this notice to reply to us at the address shown below with any comments you have upon the matters set out in paragraph 1 above, and any proposals you have for remedying the breach referred to. We enclose a draft Form of Reply for your convenience.

3. If you do not reply

If you do not reply to this notice within the specified 21 day period, then we may decide to take further action. Such further action could include:

(a) the remedy of the breach followed by the recovery of the cost of remedy from you; or
(b) the reference of the dispute to an ombudsman; or
(c) the issue of proceedings.

4. Address for your reply

You should address your reply to this notice to:

The Directors of [Name] Commonhold Association Limited

[Address]

IMPORTANT

If you do not reply to this Notice, the directors may be left with no alternative but to take proceedings against you to remedy the breach referred to in this Notice, in which case they will also seek an order against you for the costs incurred in connection therewith.

4.5 NOTICE OF REPLY TO DEFAULT NOTICE

Notes

(1) Rules 42 to 52 of the draft commonhold community statement contain detailed provision for dispute resolution in a commonhold.

(2) Under the default procedure forming part of that dispute resolution procedure, the commonhold association may serve a default notice upon a unit-holder instancing a breach of the rules of the commonhold community statement or of a provision in the memorandum or articles of association of the commonhold association. Form 4.4 above provides the prescribed form of notice.

(3) Upon receipt of such a notice, the defaulting unit-holder should reply, giving his response and proposals.

(4) This form of notification is prescribed. The form and content set out below contain the authors' suggestions as to the appropriate form for this notice.

(5) The default procedure is discussed in Section 6.6 of the text.

FORM 8

REPLY TO DEFAULT NOTICE

1. Details of defaulter

Commonhold unit number:

Full name(s): unit/holder(s)/tenant(s)

Full postal address:

Address for service (if different):

2. The commonhold association

Full Name:

Address for service:

Name and address of person to contact:

3. Commonhold community statement

Version Number:

Registered at Land Registry on:

I/we [insert name(s)] acknowledge receipt of the complaints notice dated [ ] and state that I/we ____

have complied with the duty

will comply with the duty by

dispute the matter complained of for the following reasons—

Signed: **Dated:**

Signed: **Dated:**

If the commonhold association is not satisfied with this response, the matter may be referred to the Ombudsman or the court.

NOTE (NOT FORMING PART OF THE PRESCRIBED FORM):

Given the lack of space on the form for details of the response to the substantive complaint, respondents wishing to contest the complaint should consider inserting "see details on attached sheet", or "see overleaf", and then supplying the details separately.

A possible response to the complaint given in the example in Form 4.1 above would be:

1. *I accept that I have kept the pets referred to in the Notice.*

2. *I do not accept that the matters complained of are of sufficient importance to concern the association. Many other unit-holders keep pets and have not been singled out for this treatment. I have been complimented by my neighbours on how attractive my goldfish look.*

3. *My counter-proposals:*

(a) *I have nowhere to keep my goldfish, and do not intend to remove them. I am, however, prepared to keep the ornamental pond clean and free from excess weed.*

(b) *I do not intend to comply with the proposals for removing my pet, but I am prepared to meet a director of the commonhold association in an attempt to reach a negotiated solution to this complaint.*

4. *My contact details: [On the understanding that the details I provide will be kept confidential to officers of the Association,] I can be contacted in the following way:*

Correspondence address:

Tel:

Fax:

Email:

5. ***Confirmation of understanding of the internal complaints procedure:*** *I have read the information supplied by you concerning the internal complaints procedure of the Association, and I understand the procedures for resolving the dispute that has arisen. I will do my best to achieve a resolution.*

4.6 INDEMNITY NOTICE

Notes

(1) The commonhold community statement may provide that an indemnity notice may be served upon the commonhold association or any unit-holder who is in breach of any provision of the commonhold community statement itself or any statutory requirement.
(2) The service of an indemnity notice is part of the process of dispute resolution available to the directors of the commonhold association as an alternative or precursor to litigation.
(3) This topic is discussed further in paragraph 6.3.7 of the text.

COMMONHOLD

Indemnity Notice

Commonhold and Leasehold Reform Act 2002

To [name of unit-holder or commonhold association] of [address]

TAKE NOTICE that:

1. We, the undersigned directors of [Name] Commonhold Association Limited are of the opinion that [name of commonhold association or unit-holder] has incurred costs arising from a breach of rule * of the commonhold community statement which applies to this commonhold.
2. The breach consists of [brief details].
3. The costs arising from such breach are £*, being the cost of [insert brief details].
4. We require you to pay the amount of £* to [Name] Commonhold Association Limited or unit-holder] by [date].

IMPORTANT

If you do not pay the said amount by the said date, the directors reserve the right to take proceedings against you for recovery of the said amount and the costs incurred in connection therewith.

4.7 REFERENCE TO OMBUDSMAN

Notes

(1) Section 42 of the Act provides for the making of regulations to introduce a scheme which will enable unit-holders and the commonhold association to refer disputes between them to an ombudsman.

(2) The Commonhold Regulations provide (see Regulation 16) that commonhold associations will have to belong to an ombudsman scheme.

(3) Until further progress has been made with the regulations, however, it would be premature to form a view on the types of dispute which might be covered; whether such a referral would be voluntary or mandatory; and what powers the ombudsman would have to grant relief and enforce remedies.

(4) This topic is discussed further in Part 3 of Chapter 6 of the text.

COMMONHOLD

Referral to ombudsman

Commonhold and Leasehold Reform Act 2002

To the commonhold ombudsman

1. The commonhold association

Full Name:

Address for service:

Name and address of person to contact:

2. The person referring the matter to the Ombudsman (if not the commonhold association)

Commonhold unit number:

Full name(s): unit/holder(s)/tenant(s)

Full postal address:

Address for service (if different):

3. Commonhold community statement

Version Number:

Registered at Land Registry on:

4. Matter referred

Give full details of the dispute or other matter giving rise to the referral to the ombudsman. Copies of supporting documents should be attached.

5. Compliance with the internal complaints procedure

Give details of the attempts that have been made to comply with the internal complaints procedure of the commonhold association. Attach copies of the complaints notice and/or default notice as appropriate.

6. Details of steps taken or other response by the alleged defaulting party in response to the complaint

7. Reasons why the response is said to be unsatisfactory

8. Remedy sought by the complainant

I/we [insert name(s)] wish the ombudsman to consider the above matter.

Signed: **Dated:**

Signed: **Dated:**

Legal proceedings regarding this matter may not be brought until after the ombudsman has notified the parties of his decision.

PART 5. LITIGATION FORMS

Note

These Forms will comprise the sample applications and court orders set out below. Other Forms dealing with the procedure for termination of a commonhold association are set out in Part 6 below. Section 66(4) of the Act provides that rules of court or rules of procedure for a tribunal may make provision about proceedings. It is likely that the Civil Procedure Rules will be amended further to provide for the procedure to be followed and for the format of the proceedings. As soon as that has taken place, these Forms will be issued.

Form No	Description	Act ref
5.1	Application to court for order dispensing with requirement for consent to section 2 application.	s 3(2)(f)
5.2	Court order dispensing with requirement for consent to section 2 application (absolute or conditional, and making such other provision as the court thinks appropriate).	s 3(3)
5.3	Application to court for declaration that freehold estate should not have been registered as a freehold estate in commonhold land	s 6
5.4	Court order declaring that freehold estate should not have been registered as a freehold estate in commonhold land; and/or	s 6(3) s 6(5)
	(a) providing for the registration to be treated as valid for all purposes; and/or (b) providing for alteration of the register; and/or (c) providing for land to cease to be commonhold land; and/or (d) requiring a director or other specified officer of a commonhold association to take steps to alter or amend a document; and/or (e) requiring a director or other specified officer of a commonhold association to take specified steps; and/or	s 6(6)

Form No	Description	Act ref
	(f) making an award of compensation (whether or not contingent upon the occurrence or non-occurrence of a specified event) to be paid by one specified person to another; and/or (g) applying, disapplying or modifying a provision of Schedule 8 to the Land Registration Act 2002 (c 9) (indemnity).	
5.5	Application to court for an order in respect of an invalid lease	s 17(4)
5.6	Court order for invalid lease to have effect as if it provided for the creation of a term of years of a specified kind and/or for the return or payment of money and/or for such other provision as the court thinks appropriate.	s 17(4)
5.7	Application to court by commonhold association for an order dispensing with the requirement for consent by unit-holder to amendment to commonhold community statement to redefine extent of unit.	s 23(2)
5.8	Court order dispensing with requirement for consent by unit-holder to amendment to commonhold community statement to redefine extent of unit.	s 23(2)
5.9	Application to court by commonhold association for an order dispensing with the requirement for consent by chargee to amendment to commonhold community statement to redefine extent of unit.	s 24(3)
5.10	Court order dispensing with requirement for consent by chargee to amendment to commonhold community statement to redefine extent of unit.	s 24(3)
5.11	Application to court by commonhold association for an order dispensing with the requirement for consent by chargee to amendment to commonhold community statement to add land from unit to common parts.	s 30(3)
5.12	Court order dispensing with requirement for consent by chargee to amendment to commonhold community statement to add land from unit to common parts.	s 30(3)

Form No	Description	Act ref
5.13	Application to court for an order: (a) requiring compensation to be paid where a right is exercised in specified cases or circumstances; (b) requiring compensation to be paid where a duty is not complied with; (c) enabling recovery of costs where work is carried out for the purpose of enforcing a right or duty; (d) enabling recovery of costs where work is carried out in consequence of the failure to perform a duty; (e) permitting a unit-holder to enforce a duty imposed on another unit-holder, on a commonhold association or on a tenant; (f) permitting a commonhold association to enforce a duty imposed on a unit-holder or a tenant; (g) permitting a tenant to enforce a duty imposed on another tenant, a unit-holder or a commonhold association; (h) permitting the enforcement of terms or conditions to which a right is subject.	s 37(1)
5.14	Court order for exercise or enforcement of a right or duty imposed or conferred by or by virtue of the commonhold community statement, the memorandum and articles of association of the commonhold association or any provision under the Act.	s 37(1)
5.15	Application to court by a unit-holder for a declaration that: (a) the memorandum or articles of association of the commonhold association do not comply with regulations under paragraph 2(1) of Schedule 3; and/or (b) the commonhold community statement does not comply with a requirement imposed by or by virtue of the Act.	s 40(1) s 40(4)
5.16	Declaration by court that: (a) the memorandum or articles of association of the commonhold association do not comply with regulations under paragraph 2(1) of Schedule 3; and/or	s 40(2) s 40(3)

Form No	Description	Act ref
	(b) the commonhold community statement does not comply with a requirement imposed by or by virtue of the Act; and/or (c) requiring a director or other specified officer of a commonhold association to take steps to alter or amend a document; and/or (d) requiring a director or other specified officer of a commonhold association to take specified steps; and/or (e) making an award of compensation (whether or not contingent upon the occurrence or non-occurrence of a specified event) to be paid by the commonhold association to a specified person; and/or (f) making provision for land to cease to be commonhold land.	
5.17	Application to court by a unit-holder for an order requiring the directors to ensure that the commonhold association complies with regulations for approved ombudsman scheme.	s 42(4)
5.18	Court order requiring directors to ensure that the commonhold association complies with regulations for approved ombudsman scheme.	s 42(4)
5.19	Application by one of joint unit-holders for order that he is entitled to be entered in the register of members.	Sch 3, para 8(5)
5.20	Court order that one of joint unit-holders is entitled to be entered in the register of members.	Sch 3, para 8(5)

PART 6. TERMINATION FORMS

Note

These Forms will comprise the various documents which may be needed to terminate a commonhold, whether that termination be prompted by an insolvent liquidation or some other event, consensual or otherwise. The authors have drafted a proposed termination statement (see Form 6.4), and included drafts of a declaration of solvency (Form 6.1), minutes of directors meeting prepatory to winding-up (Form 6.2), a termination-statement resolution and winding-up resolution (Form 6.3), and a creditor's petition (Form 6.15). It is likely that the remainder of the forms will be prescribed by regulations made under the Act, under the Land Registration Act, under the Insolvency Rules or by new Civil Procedure Rules. Once that has taken place, the remainder of these Forms will be issued.

Form No	Description	Act ref
6.1	Declaration of solvency.	s 43
6.2	Minute of directors meeting preparatory to winding-up resolution.	s 43
6.3	Termination-statement resolution and winding-up resolution.	s 43
6.4	Termination statement.	s 47
6.5	Termination application by liquidator to land registry (100%), where liquidator content with termination statement.	s 44(2) s 47 s 48(3)
6.6	Termination application by others to land registry (100%).	s 44(3) s 47
6.7	Application by liquidator to court under section 112 Insolvency Act 1986 for order determining terms of termination statement.	s 48(3)
6.8	Application by liquidator to court for order determining terms of termination application and termination statement.	s 45(2)
6.9	Application by unit-holders or others to court for order determining terms of termination application and termination statement.	s 45(4)

Form No	Description	Act ref
6.10	Court order determining terms of termination application and termination statement.	s 45
6.11	Termination application by liquidator to land registry (80%).	s 45(3) s 47
6.12	Termination application by others to land registry following court order (80%).	s 45(4) s 47
6.13	Application by member of commonhold association for an order disapplying a provision of commonhold community statement regarding termination statement.	s 47(5)
6.14	Court order disapplying provision of commonhold community statement regarding termination statement.	s 47(4)
6.15	Petition to declare commonhold association insolvent.	s 50
6.16	Winding-up order.	s 125 IA s 53(3) s 53(4) s 54
6.17	Application to court for succession order.	s 51
6.18	Succession order.	s 51(4) s 52(4)
6.19	Notification by liquidator to land registry following winding-up order (no succession order)	s 54
6.20	Application for declaration that freehold estate should not have been registered as a freehold estate in commonhold land.	s 6
6.21	Court order providing for commonhold land to cease to be commonhold land.	s 6(6)(c)
6.23	Court order making provision in relation to liquidator.	s 55

6.1 DECLARATION OF SOLVENCY

Notes:

(1) Section 43(1) of the Act provides that any winding-up resolution by a commonhold association will be ineffective unless (among other things) the resolution is preceded by a declaration of solvency.
(2) A "declaration of solvency" is defined by the Act as "a directors' statutory declaration made in accordance with section 89 of the Insolvency Act 1986" (see section 43(2)).
(3) The Form set out below is a draft of such a declaration, based upon Form 4.70 of the Insolvency Rules 1986.
(4) This topic is discussed in paragraph 5.2.3 of the text.

S.89 (3)

Section 89(3) **The Insolvency Act 1986**
Members' Voluntary Winding Up
Declaration of Solvency Embodying
a Statement of Assets and Liabilities

Pursuant to section 89(3) of the Insolvency Act 1986

To the Registrar of Companies

For official use

Company Number

Name of company

(a) Insert full name of company

(a)

Limited

(b) Insert full name(s) and address(es)

I/We (b)

attach a declaration of solvency embodying a statement of assets and liabilities

Signed **Date**

Presenter's name, address and reference (if any)

For Official Use

Liquidation Section	**Post Room**

Section 89(3) **The Insolvency Act 1986**

Members' Voluntary Winding Up

Declaration of Solvency

Embodying a Statement of

Assets and Liabilities

Company number

____

Name of company

____

____ Limited

Presented by

____

Declaration of Solvency

(a) Insert names and addresses

We (a)

____

____

(b) Delete as applicable

being (b) [all the] the majority of the] directors of (c) do solemnly and sincerely declare that we have made a full inquiry into

(c) Insert name of company

the affairs of the company, and that, having done so, we have formed the opinion that this company will be able to pay its debts in full together with

(d) Insert a period of months not exceeding 12

interest at the official rate within a period of (d) ____ months, from the commencement of the winding up.

(e) Insert date

We append a statement of the company's assets and liabilities as at (e) ____, being the latest practicable date before the making of this declaration.

We make this solemn declaration, conscientiously believing it to be true, and by virtue of the provisions of the Statutory Declarations Act 1835.

Declared at ____

this ____ day of ____ 19____

Before me,

Solicitor or Commissioner of Oaths

Statement as at ____ showing assets at estimated realisable values and liabilities expected to rank

Assets and liabilities			Estimated to realise or to rank for payment to nearest £
			£
Assets:			
Balance at bank			
Cash in hand			
Marketable securities			
Bills receivable			
Trade debtors			
Loans and advances			
Unpaid calls			
Stock in trade			
Work in progress			
Freehold property			
Leasehold property			
Plant and machinery			
Furniture, fittings, utensils etc			
Patents, trade marks etc			
Investments other than marketable securities			
Other property, viz			
Estimated realisable value of assets £			
Liabilities			
Secured on specific assets, viz			£
Secured by floating charge(s)			
Estimated cost of liquidation and other expenses including interest accruing until payment of debts in full			
Unsecured creditors (amounts estimated to rank for payment)			
	£	£	
Trade accounts			
Bills payable			
Accrued expenses			
Other liabilities			
Contingent liabilities			
Estimated surplus after paying debts in full		£	

Remarks:

6.2 MINUTES OF DIRECTORS' MEETING PREPARATORY TO WINDING-UP RESOLUTION

Notes

(1) Section 43(1) of the Act provides that a winding-up resolution shall be of no effect unless it is preceded by a declaration of solvency and a termination statement resolution.

(2) The Form that follows is a draft of a minute providing for those antecedent steps to be taken.

(3) This topic is discussed in paragraph 5.2.2 of the text.

[Name] Commonhold Association Ltd ("the Association")

Minutes of a meeting of the board of directors of the Association held at [address] on [date]

PRESENT: [Name] (Chairman)

[Name]

[Name]

IN ATTENDANCE: [Name of accountant]

1. Financial report
[Name of accountant] produced to the meeting a report on the Association's financial position and the reasons it was considered advisable to wind up the Association. After deliberation the board resolved that the report be accepted.

2. Declaration of solvency
[Name of accountant] produced to the meeting a form of declaration of solvency which incorporated a statement of the Association's assets and liabilities as at [date]. After deliberation it was agreed that this was the latest practicable date as at which the statement could be prepared and it was resolved that:

2.1 all the directors present, being a majority of the directors, be authorised to make a statutory declaration verifying such declaration of solvency laid before the meeting; and

2.2 [Name of accountant] be instructed to file the statutory declaration with the registrar of companies.

3. Termination statement
[Name of accountant] produced to the meeting a form of termination statement which made proposals regarding the transfer of the land of the Association under Title No. *; proposals regarding the assets of the Association; and proposals regarding the rights of the members of the Association.

4. Extraordinary general meeting
There was produced to the meeting a notice convening an extraordinary general meeting for the purposes of considering and, if thought fit, passing the following resolutions of which the first and second would be proposed as special resolutions and the third as an ordinary resolution:

4.1. That the draft termination statement be approved.

4.2. That the Association be wound up voluntarily.

4.3. That [Name of accountant] of (address) be appointed liquidator for the purpose of such winding up.

The directors resolved that [Name of accountant] be instructed to issue the notice which was approved to all those persons entitled to notice of such a meeting.

5. Situation of registered office
It was resolved that the registered office of the Association be changed to [ ].

6. Any other business
There being no other business, the meeting then terminated.
The directors authorised the Chairman to sign these minutes forthwith as a true record of the proceedings.

(*signature*)

Chairman

6.3 TERMINATION-STATEMENT RESOLUTION AND WINDING-UP RESOLUTION

Notes

(1) Section 43(1) of the Act provides that any winding-up resolution by a commonhold association will be ineffective unless (among other things) the resolution is preceded by a termination-statement resolution.
(2) A "termination-statement resolution" is defined by the Act as a resolution approving the terms of a termination statement within the meaning of section 47 of the Act (see Form 6.4 below).
(3) The Form that follows records the forms both of the termination-statement resolution and of the winding-up resolution.
(4) This topic is discussed in paragraphs 5.2.4 and 5.2.5 of the text.

Termination-statement resolution:
There being at least 80% of the members present in favour, IT WAS RESOLVED that the draft termination statement be approved.

Winding-up resolution:
IT WAS RESOLVED that the Association be wound up voluntarily, and that [Name] of [address] be appointed liquidator for the purposes of such winding up and that the remuneration of the liquidator be . . .

6.4 TERMINATION STATEMENT

Notes

(1) Before a commonhold association can be wound up voluntarily, the members must pass a resolution agreeing a termination statement (see section 43 of the Act and Form 6.3 above).

(2) Section 47 of the Act sets out the ingredients for a termination statement. This Form sets out those ingredients.

(3) This topic is discussed in paragraph 5.2.4 of the text.

COMMONHOLD

Termination Statement

Commonhold and Leasehold Reform Act 2002, section 47

---

1. Details of the freehold land the subject of this statement ("the Land"):

Description:

Title Number:

2. Details of the commonhold association exercising functions in relation to the Land ("the Association"):

The [Name] Commonhold Association Limited

3. Proposals regarding transfer of the Land

Following the acquisition of the freehold estate in accordance with section 49(3) of the Commonhold and Leasehold Reform Act 2002, it is proposed that the Land will be transferred to . . .

4. Proposals regarding the assets of the Association

It is proposed that the assets will be distributed in the following manner:

(a) . . .
(b)

5. Proposals regarding the rights of unit-holders

It is proposed that the rights of the unit-holders on the Land will be dealt with in the following manner:

(a) . . .
(b)

Signed this ____ day of ____ 20____ by:

____ ____ ____

Director Director Director/Secretary

6.15 PETITION TO DECLARE COMMONHOLD ASSOCIATION INSOLVENT

Notes

(1) Section 50 of the Act introduces the procedure for the winding-up of an insolvent commonhold association. This procedure is governed by the Insolvency Act 1986, save where the Act stipulates otherwise.
(2) The first step in this process will be the service of a winding-up petition in the form set out below, which reproduces Form 4.2 of the Insolvency Rules 1986.
(3) This topic is discussed further in Section 5.3 of the text.

Winding-up Petition

[Name] Commonhold Association Ltd

(a) Insert title of court	To (a)
(b) Insert full name(s) and address(es) of petitioner(s)	The petition of (b)
(c) Insert full name of company subject to petition	1. (c) (hereinafter called "the company") was incorporated on
(d) Insert date of incorporation	(d) under the Companies Act 19
(e) Insert address of registered office	2. The registered office of the company is at (e)
	3. The nominal capital of the company is £ divided into shares of £ each. The amount of the capital paid up or credited as paid up is £ 4. The principal objects for which the company was established are as follows: and other objects stated in the memorandum of association of the company
(f) Set out the grounds on which a winding-up order is sought	5. (f)
	6. In the circumstances it is just and equitable that the company should be wound up The petitioner(s) therefore pray(s) as follows:– (1) that (c) may be wound up by the court under the provisions of the Insolvency Act 1986 or (2) that such other order may be made as the court thinks fit.

(g) If the company is the petitioner, delete "the company". Add the full name and address of any other person on whom it is intended to serve the petition

(h) Delete as applicable

(j) Insert name and address of court

(k) Insert name and address of District Registry

NOTE: It is intended to serve this petition on (g) [the company] [and]

Endorsement

This petition having been presented to the court on ____ will be heard at (h) Royal Courts of Justice, Strand, London WC2A 2LL [(j) ____ County Court ____]
[(k) ____ District Registry ____]
on:
Date ____
Time ____ hours____
(or as soon thereafter as the petition can be heard)
The solicitor to the petitioner is:-
Name ____
Address ____
____
Telephone no. ____
Reference ____
(h) [Whose London Agents are:–
Name ____
Address ____
____
Telephone no. ____
Reference ____]

PART D

STATUTORY AND OTHER MATERIALS

Commonhold and Leasehold Reform Act 2002

ARRANGEMENT OF SECTIONS

PART 1
COMMONHOLD

PART 3
SUPPLEMENTARY

SCHEDULES

PART I
COMMONHOLD
Nature of commonhold

Commonhold land

1.—(1) Land is commonhold land if—
- (a) the freehold estate in the land is registered as a freehold estate in commonhold land,
- (b) the land is specified in the memorandum of association of a commonhold association as the land in relation to which the association is to exercise functions, and
- (c) a commonhold community statement makes provision for rights and duties of the commonhold association and unit-holders (whether or not the statement has come into force).

(2) In this Part a reference to a commonhold is a reference to land in relation to which a commonhold association exercises functions.

(3) In this Part—
'commonhold association' has the meaning given by section 34,
'commonhold community statement' has the meaning given by section 31,
'commonhold unit' has the meaning given by section 11,
'common parts' has the meaning given by section 25, and
'unit-holder' has the meaning given by sections 12 and 13.

(4) Sections 7 and 9 make provision for the vesting in the commonhold association of the fee simple in possession in the common parts of a commonhold.

Commentary

Section 1 (which has been given two headings—"Nature of commonhold' and 'Commonhold land") performs a number of functions. First (subsections (1) and (2)), it provides a definition of the expressions 'commonhold land' and 'commonhold'. Although both expressions refer to the land which will have been registered as a freehold estate in commonhold land, the expression 'commonhold' can only properly be used to refer to the land once the commonhold association is functioning, whereas 'commonhold land' is a generic expression apt to refer to the land both before and after the commonhold association has begun to exercise its functions. Schedule 2 adds to this by stipulating land which may not be commonhold land.

Secondly, subsection (3) lists a number of the most important commonhold expressions, which are defined elsewhere in Part 1.

Thirdly (and perhaps a little miscellaneously) subsection (4) looks forward to the provisions dealing with the vesting of the proposed common parts of the commonhold (sic—surely commonhold land) in the commonhold association.

The expression 'exercises functions' is defined in section 8.
By virtue of section 69(3), the term 'land' has the meaning given to it by section 205(1)(ix) of the Law of Property Act 1925 and by section 132(1) of the Land Registration Act 2002 (reprinted at the end of this Act).

Registration

Application

2.—(1) The Registrar shall register a freehold estate in land as a freehold estate in commonhold land if—

(a) the registered freeholder of the land makes an application under this section, and

(b) no part of the land is already commonhold land.

(2) An application under this section must be accompanied by the documents listed in Schedule 1.

(3) A person is the registered freeholder of land for the purposes of this Part if—

(a) he is registered as the proprietor of a freehold estate in the land with absolute title, or

(b) he has applied, and the Registrar is satisfied that he is entitled, to be registered as mentioned in paragraph (a).

Commentary

This section and the four sections which follow deal with registration of a freehold estate as a freehold estate in commonhold land. Section 2 provides that such an estate must be registered by the Chief Land Registrar if three requirements are satisfied: (a) an application is made either by the registered freehold proprietor or by someone who would be entitled to be registered as such; (b) the application is accompanied by the documents listed in Schedule 1; and (c) no part of the land is already commonhold land.

The expression 'commonhold land' is defined in section 1.

By virtue of section 69(3), the expression 'land' has the meaning given to it by section 205(1)(ix) of the Law of Property Act 1925 and by section 132(1) of the Land Registration Act 2002.

The expression 'registered' is defined in section 67.

The expression 'the Registrar' means the Chief Land Registrar—see section 67.

This section is discussed in Sections 2.3 and 2.19 of the text.

Consent

3.—(1) An application under section 2 may not be made in respect of a freehold estate in land without the consent of anyone who—

(a) is the registered proprietor of the freehold estate in the whole or part of the land,

(b) is the registered proprietor of a leasehold estate in the whole or part of the land granted for a term of more than than 21 years,

(c) is the registered proprietor of a charge over the whole or part of the land, or

(d) falls within any other class of person which may be prescribed.

(2) Regulations shall make provision about consent for the purposes of this section; in particular, the regulations may make provision—

(a) prescribing the form of consent;

(b) about the effect and duration of consent (including provision for consent to bind successors);

(c) about withdrawal of consent (including provision preventing withdrawal in specified circumstances);

(d) for consent given for the purpose of one application under section 2 to have effect for the purpose of another application;
(e) for consent to be deemed to have been given in specified circumstances;
(f) enabling a court to dispense with a requirement for consent in specified circumstances.

(3) An order under subsection (2)(f) dispensing with a requirement for consent—
(a) may be absolute or conditional, and
(b) may make such other provision as the court thinks appropriate.

Commentary

This section prohibits the making of an application for registration of a freehold estate in commonhold land without the consent of what may loosely be called the owners of substantial legal interests in the land. Provision is also made for regulations to add to the list of those whose consent should be required; to deal with the form of consent; and for consent to be dispensed with by the court in certain circumstances. Section 6 deals with the effect of a failure to obtain any such consent.

Proposed regulations and forms for consent are set out in the Statutes etc and Forms and Precedents parts of this work.

The term 'court' means the High Court or a county court—see section 66.
By virtue of section 69(3), the term 'land' has the meaning given to it by section 205(1)(ix) of the Law of Property Act 1925 and by section 132(1) of the Land Registration Act 2002.
The terms 'prescribed' and 'regulations' are defined and explained by section 64.
The term 'registered' is defined in section 67.

This section is discussed in Sections 2.5, 2.9 and 6.14 of the text.

Land which may not be commonhold

4.—Schedule 2 (which provides that an application under section 2 may not relate wholly or partly to land of certain kinds) shall have effect.

Commentary

This section adds to the inclusionary definition of commonhold land in section 1 the list in Schedule 2 of types of land or interests in land (flying freeholds, agricultural land and land in which there are contingent interests) which may not be commonhold land. The contingent interests forming part of that list may be added to or subtracted from by regulation. No such regulation is currently proposed.

By virtue of section 69(3), the term 'land' has the meaning given to it by section 205(1)(ix) of the Law of Property Act 1925 and by section 132(1) of the Land Registration Act 2002.

This section is discussed in paragraphs 2.3.5 and 2.3.6 of the text.

Registered details

5.—(1) The Registrar shall ensure that in respect of any commonhold land the following are kept in his custody and referred to in the register—
(a) the prescribed details of the commonhold association;

(b) the prescribed details of the registered freeholder of each commonhold unit;
(c) a copy of the commonhold community statement;
(d) a copy of the memorandum and articles of association of the commonhold association.

(2) The Registrar may arrange for a document or information to be kept in his custody and referred to in the register in respect of commonhold land if the document or information—
(a) is not mentioned in subsection (1), but
(b) is submitted to the Registrar in accordance with a provision made by or by virtue of this Part.

(3) Subsection (1)(b) shall not apply during a transitional period within the meaning of section 8.

Commentary

This section sets out the documents and details prescribed by regulations which the Chief Land Registrar is required to keep in his custody and refer to in the register of title. See the end of this Part for details of the regulations in question which are proposed.

The expression 'commonhold association' is defined in section 34.
The expression 'commonhold land' is defined in section 1.
The term 'prescribed' means prescribed by regulations—see section 64.
The term 'register' is defined in section 67.
The expression 'the Registrar' means the Chief Land Registrar—see section 67.
The expression 'registered freeholder' is defined in section 2.

This section is discussed in Part 6 of Chapter 2 of the text.

Registration in error

6.—(1) This section applies where a freehold estate in land is registered as a freehold estate in commonhold land and—
(a) the application for registration was not made in accordance with section 2,
(b) the certificate under paragraph 7 of Schedule 1 was inaccurate, or
(c) the registration contravened a provision made by or by virtue of this Part.

(2) The register may not be altered by the Registrar under Schedule 4 to the Land Registration Act 2002 (c 9) (alteration of register).

(3) The court may grant a declaration that the freehold estate should not have been registered as a freehold estate in commonhold land.

(4) A declaration under subsection (3) may be granted only on the application of a person who claims to be adversely affected by the registration.

(5) On granting a declaration under subsection (3) the court may make any order which appears to it to be appropriate.

(6) An order under subsection (5) may, in particular—
(a) provide for the registration to be treated as valid for all purposes;
(b) provide for alteration of the register;
(c) provide for land to cease to be commonhold land;

(d) require a director or other specified officer of a commonhold association to take steps to alter or amend a document;
(e) require a director or other specified officer of a commonhold association to take specified steps;
(f) make an award of compensation (whether or not contingent upon the occurrence or non-occurrence of a specified event) to be paid by one specified person to another;
(g) apply, disapply or modify a provision of Schedule 8 to the Land Registration Act 2002 (c 9) (indemnity).

Commentary

This section sets out the consequences and possible remedies where a registration of commonhold land has been deficient in one of the ways specified.

See section 55 for the powers of the court and the liquidator where the court makes an order under section 6(6)(c) for all the land in relation to which the commonhold association exercises functions to cease to be commonhold land.

The expression 'commonhold association' is defined in section 34.
The expression 'commonhold land' is defined in section 1.
The term 'court' means the High Court or a county court—see section 66.
By virtue of section 69(3), the term 'director' has the meaning given to it by section 741(1) of the Companies Act 1985.
By virtue of section 69(3), the term 'document' has the meaning given to it by section 744 of the Companies Act 1985.
By virtue of section 69(3), the term 'land' has the meaning given to it by section 205(1)(ix) of the Law of Property Act 1925 and by section 132(1) of the Land Registration Act 2002.
The terms 'register' and 'registered' are defined in section 67.
The expression 'the Registrar' means the Chief Land Registrar—see section 67.

This section is discussed in Sections 2.27 and 6.14 of the text.

Effect of registration

Registration without unit-holders

7.—(1) This section applies where—
(a) a freehold estate in land is registered as a freehold estate in commonhold land in pursuance of an application under section 2, and
(b) the application is not accompanied by a statement under section 9(1)(b).

(2) On registration—
(a) the applicant shall continue to be registered as the proprietor of the freehold estate in the commonhold land, and
(b) the rights and duties conferred and imposed by the commonhold community statement shall not come into force (subject to section 8(2)(b)).

(3) Where after registration a person other than the applicant becomes entitled to be registered as the proprietor of the freehold estate in one or more, but not all, of the commonhold units—
(a) the commonhold association shall be entitled to be registered as the proprietor of the freehold estate in the common parts,

(b) the Registrar shall register the commonhold association in accordance with paragraph (a) (without an application being made),

(c) the rights and duties conferred and imposed by the commonhold community statement shall come into force, and

(d) any lease of the whole or part of the commonhold land shall be extinguished by virtue of this section.

(4) For the purpose of subsection (3)(d) 'lease' means a lease which—

(a) is granted for any term, and

(b) is granted before the commonhold association becomes entitled to be registered as the proprietor of the freehold estate in the common parts.

Commentary

This and the following three sections set out the substantive effect of registration on all those involved, including the registered proprietor of the commonhold land, the owners of the commonhold units, the commonhold association, and the owners of any extinguished leasehold interests. This section applies where, at the time of registration, there are not yet any unit-holders, and then goes on to deal with the situation when persons become unit-holders. Section 9 deals with the converse situation where, at the date of registration, there are already unit-holders in existence (ie persons entitled to be registered as the freehold proprietor of an estate in a unit—see section 12).

The expression 'common parts' is defined in section 25.
The expression 'commonhold association' is defined in section 34.
The expression 'commonhold community statement' is defined in section 31.
The expression 'commonhold land' is defined in section 1.
The expression 'commonhold unit' is defined in section 11.
The term 'register' is defined in section 67.
The expression 'the Registrar' means the Chief Land Registrar—see section 67.

This section is discussed in Section 2.22 of the text.

Transitional period

8.—(1) In this Part 'transitional period' means the period between registration of the freehold estate in land as a freehold estate in commonhold land and the event mentioned in section 7(3).

(2) Regulations may provide that during a transitional period a relevant provision—

(a) shall not have effect, or

(b) shall have effect with specified modifications.

(3) In subsection (2) 'relevant provision' means a provision made—

(a) by or by virtue of this Part,

(b) by a commonhold community statement, or

(c) by the memorandum or articles of the commonhold association.

(4) The Registrar shall arrange for the freehold estate in land to cease to be registered as a freehold estate in commonhold land if the registered proprietor makes an application to the Registrar under this subsection during the transitional period.

(5) The provisions about consent made by or under sections 2 and 3 and Schedule 1 shall apply in relation to an application under subsection (4) as they apply in relation to an application under section 2.

(6) A reference in this Part to a commonhold association exercising functions in relation to commonhold land includes a reference to a case where a commonhold association would exercise functions in relation to commonhold land but for the fact that the time in question falls in a transitional period.

Commentary

This section deals with the transitional period between registration of commonhold land without unit-holders, and the date upon which the land attracts the first person who becomes a unit-holder (ie entitled to be registered as the freehold proprietor of an estate in the unit—see section 12). During that period, the commonhold association is not operative, and this section provides for regulations to trigger the operation of certain provisions of the Act, the commonhold community statement or the memorandum or articles of association of the commonhold association. See the Statutes etc part of this work for details of the proposed regulations.

The expression 'commonhold association' is defined in section 34.
The expression 'commonhold community statement' is defined in section 31.
The expression 'commonhold land' is defined in section 1.
By virtue of section 69(3), the term 'land' has the meaning given to it by section 205(1)(ix) of the Law of Property Act 1925 and by section 132(1) of the Land Registration Act 2002.
The term 'register' is defined in section 67.
The expression 'the Registrar' means the Chief Land Registrar—see section 67.
The term 'regulations' is defined in section 64.

This section is discussed in Section 2.22 of the text.

Registration with unit-holders

9.—(1) This section applies in relation to a freehold estate in commonhold land if—

(a) it is registered as a freehold estate in commonhold land in pursuance of an application under section 2, and
(b) the application is accompanied by a statement by the applicant requesting that this section should apply.

(2) A statement under subsection (1)(b) must include a list of the commonhold units giving in relation to each one the prescribed details of the proposed initial unit-holder or joint unit-holders.

(3) On registration—

(a) the commonhold association shall be entitled to be registered as the proprietor of the freehold estate in the common parts,
(b) a person specified by virtue of subsection (2) as the initial unit-holder of a commonhold unit shall be entitled to be registered as the proprietor of the freehold estate in the unit,
(c) a person specified by virtue of subsection (2) as an initial joint unit-holder of a commonhold unit shall be entitled to be registered as one of the proprietors of the freehold estate in the unit,

(d) the Registrar shall make entries in the register to reflect paragraphs (a) to (c) (without applications being made),
(e) the rights and duties conferred and imposed by the commonhold community statement shall come into force, and
(f) any lease of the whole or part of the commonhold land shall be extinguished by virtue of this section.

(4) For the purpose of subsection (3)(f) 'lease' means a lease which—
(a) is granted for any term, and
(b) is granted before the commonhold association becomes entitled to be registered as the proprietor of the freehold estate in the common parts.

Commentary

This section deals with the converse situation to section 7—where, at the date of registration, there are already persons in existence who are entitled to be registered as unit-holders, and where the freeholder applicant has requested in his application that this section should apply. In those circumstances, the commonhold association and the unit-holders are entitled to be registered as proprietors of the freehold interests in the common parts and commonhold units respectively, and any leases are extinguished with the effects set out in section 10.

The expression 'commonhold association' is defined in section 34.
The expression 'commonhold community statement' is defined in section 31.
The expression 'commonhold land' is defined in section 1.
The expression 'commonhold unit' is defined in section 11.
The expression 'common parts' is defined in section 25.
The expression 'joint unit-holder' is defined in section 13.
The term 'prescribed' means prescribed by regulations—see section 64.
The terms 'register' and registered are defined in section 67.
The expression 'the Registrar' means the Chief Land Registrar—see section 67.
The term 'unit-holder' is defined in section 12.

This section is discussed in Section 2.22 of the text.

Extinguished lease: liability

10.—(1) This section applies where—
(a) a lease is extinguished by virtue of section 7(3)(d) or 9(3)(f), and
(b) the consent of the holder of that lease was not among the consents required by section 3 in respect of the application under section 2 for the land to become commonhold land.

(2) If the holder of a lease superior to the extinguished lease gave consent under section 3, he shall be liable for loss suffered by the holder of the extinguished lease.

(3) If the holders of a number of leases would be liable under subsection (2), liability shall attach only to the person whose lease was most proximate to the extinguished lease.

(4) If no person is liable under subsection (2), the person who gave consent under section 3 as the holder of the freehold estate out of which the extinguished lease was granted shall be liable for loss suffered by the holder of the extinguished lease.

Commentary

This section allocates liability for loss suffered by the holder of any lease extinguished as a result of the registration of land as commonhold land in the circumstances set out in section 7 or 9. That liability is borne by the most immediate landlord of the leaseholder in question who gave his consent under section 3 to the application for registration.

The expression 'commonhold land' is defined in section 1.
By virtue of section 69(3), the expression 'land' has the meaning given to it by section 205(1)(ix) of the Law of Property Act 1925 and by section 132(1) of the Land Registration Act 2002.

This section is discussed in Section 2.23 of the text.

Commonhold unit

Definition

11.—(1) In this Part 'commonhold unit' means a commonhold unit specified in a commonhold community statement in accordance with this section.

(2) A commonhold community statement must—
(a) specify at least two parcels of land as commonhold units, and
(b) define the extent of each commonhold unit.

(3) In defining the extent of a commonhold unit a commonhold community statement—
(a) must refer to a plan which is included in the statement and which complies with prescribed requirements,
(b) may refer to an area subject to the exclusion of specified structures, fittings, apparatus or appurtenances within the area,
(c) may exclude the structures which delineate an area referred to, and
(d) may refer to two or more areas (whether or not contiguous).

(4) A commonhold unit need not contain all or any part of a building.

Commentary

Section 11 and the 13 sections which follow it deal with the ingredients of a commonhold unit. This section deals with the physical description of a commonhold unit: it must be carefully defined by the commonhold community statement; it may consist simply of airspace or open land; and it may be made up of two or more geographically separated areas.

The expression 'commonhold community statement' is defined in section 31.
The term 'prescribed' means prescribed by regulations—see section 64.

This section is discussed in paragraph 2.17.6 of the text.

Unit-holder

12.—A person is the unit-holder of a commonhold unit if he is entitled to be registered as the proprietor of the freehold estate in the unit (whether or not he is registered).

Commentary

This section defines the expression 'unit-holder' by reference to entitlement to registration rather than registration itself.

The expression 'commonhold unit' is defined in section 11.
The term 'registered' is defined in section 67.

This section is discussed in paragraphs 2.15.4 and 2.15.5 of the text.

Joint unit-holders

13.—(1) Two or more persons are joint unit-holders of a commonhold unit if they are entitled to be registered as proprietors of the freehold estate in the unit (whether or not they are registered).

(2) In the application of the following provisions to a unit with joint unit-holders a reference to a unit-holder is a reference to the joint unit-holders together—
(a) section 14(3),
(b) section 15(1) and (3),
(c) section 19(2) and (3),
(d) section 20(1),
(e) section 23(1),
(f) section 35(1)(b),
(g) section 38(1),
(h) section 39(2), and
(i) section 47(2).

(3) In the application of the following provisions to a unit with joint unit-holders a reference to a unit-holder includes a reference to each joint unit-holder and to the joint unit-holders together—
(a) section 1(1)(c),
(b) section 16,
(c) section 31(1)(b), (3)(b), (5)(j) and (7),
(d) section 32(4)(a) and (c),
(e) section 35(1)(a), (2) and (3),
(f) section 37(2),
(g) section 40(1), and
(h) section 58(3)(a).

(4) Regulations under this Part which refer to a unit-holder shall make provision for the construction of the reference in the case of joint unit-holders.

(5) Regulations may amend subsection (2) or (3).

(6) Regulations may make provision for the construction in the case of joint unit-holders of a reference to a unit-holder in—
(a) an enactment,
(b) a commonhold community statement,
(c) the memorandum or articles of association of a commonhold association, or
(d) another document.

Commentary

This section seeks to be an exhaustive guide to the circumstances in the Act in which joint unit-holders are required to act jointly; may act individually; or are treated as jointly or severally liable. Provision is also made for regulations to perform the same function in relation to any other instrument, including the commonhold community statement and the memorandum and articles of association of the commonhold association.

The expression 'commonhold association' is defined in section 34.
The expression 'commonhold community statement' is defined in section 31.
The expression 'commonhold unit' is defined in section 11.
By virtue of section 69(3), the term 'document' has the meaning given to it by section 744 of the Companies Act 1985.
The term 'unit-holder' is defined in section 12.
The term 'registered' is defined in section 67.
The term 'regulations' is defined in section 64.
The term 'unit-holder' is defined in section 12.

This section is discussed in paragraph 2.15.5 of the text.

Use and maintenance

14.—(1) A commonhold community statement must make provision regulating the use of commonhold units.

(2) A commonhold community statement must make provision imposing duties in respect of the insurance, repair and maintenance of each commonhold unit.

(3) A duty under subsection (2) may be imposed on the commonhold association or the unit-holder.

Commentary

This deceptively short section is the gateway for the much more comprehensive regime governing the use, insurance, repair and maintenance of the commonhold units which must be set out in the commonhold community statement. It is the counterpart to section 26, which governs the common parts.

The expression 'commonhold association' is defined in section 34.
The expression 'commonhold community statement' is defined in section 31.
The expression 'commonhold unit' is defined in section 11.
The terms 'insure' and 'maintenance' are elaborated upon in section 69.
The term 'unit-holder' is defined in section 12.

This section and the relevant provisions of the commonhold community statement are discussed in Section 2.17 of the text.

Transfer

15.—(1) In this Part a reference to the transfer of a commonhold unit is a reference to the transfer of a unit-holder's freehold estate in a unit to another person—

(a) whether or not for consideration,
(b) whether or not subject to any reservation or other terms, and
(c) whether or not by operation of law.

(2) A commonhold community statement may not prevent or restrict the transfer of a commonhold unit.

(3) On the transfer of a commonhold unit the new unit-holder shall notify the commonhold association of the transfer.

(4) Regulations may—

(a) prescribe the form and manner of notice under subsection (3);

(b) prescribe the time within which notice is to be given;

(c) make provision (including provision requiring the payment of money) about the effect of failure to give notice.

Commentary

This section spells out the fundamental feature of commonhold that there are not to be any restrictions upon the transfer of a commonhold unit—however that transfer is to be achieved. Regulations may, however, provide for such matters as the notice of transfer to be given to the commonhold association.

The expression 'commonhold association' is defined in section 34.
The expression 'commonhold community statement' is defined in section 31.
The expression 'commonhold unit' is defined in section 11.
The term 'regulations' is defined in section 64.
The term 'unit-holder' is defined in section 12.

This section is discussed in Sections 3.2 and 4.13 of the text.

Transfer: effect

16.—(1) A right or duty conferred or imposed—

(a) by a commonhold community statement, or

(b) in accordance with section 20,

shall affect a new unit-holder in the same way as it affected the former unit-holder.

(2) A former unit-holder shall not incur a liability or acquire a right—

(a) under or by virtue of the commonhold community statement, or

(b) by virtue of anything done in accordance with section 20.

(3) Subsection (2)—

(a) shall not be capable of being disapplied or varied by agreement, and

(b) is without prejudice to any liability or right incurred or acquired before a transfer takes effect.

(4) In this section—

'former unit-holder' means a person from whom a commonhold unit has been transferred (whether or not he has ceased to be the registered proprietor), and

'new unit-holder' means a person to whom a commonhold unit is transferred (whether or not he has yet become the registered proprietor).

Commentary

The critical importance of this section is obscured by its opaque language. It deals with the effect of the transfer of a commonhold unit on outgoing and incoming unit-holders in this way: (a) an outgoing unit-holder does not acquire any further rights or incur any further liabilities under the commonhold community statement following transfer; while (b) the incoming unit-holder acquires the rights and becomes subject to the liabilities of the outgoing unit-holder under the commonhold community statement immediately following transfer.

The expression 'commonhold community statement' is defined in section 31.
The expression 'commonhold unit' is defined in section 11.
The term 'registered' is defined in section 67.
The term 'transfer' (of a commonhold unit) is defined in section 15.
The term 'unit-holder' is defined in section 12.

This section is discussed in paragraphs 3.2.5, 4.13.2 and 6.3.16 of the text.

Leasing: residential

17.—(1) It shall not be possible to create a term of years absolute in a residential commonhold unit unless the term satisfies prescribed conditions.

(2) The conditions may relate to—
(a) length;
(b) the circumstances in which the term is granted;
(c) any other matter.

(3) Subject to subsection (4), an instrument or agreement shall be of no effect to the extent that it purports to create a term of years in contravention of subsection (1).

(4) Where an instrument or agreement purports to create a term of years in contravention of subsection (1) a party to the instrument or agreement may apply to the court for an order—
(a) providing for the instrument or agreement to have effect as if it provided for the creation of a term of years of a specified kind;
(b) providing for the return or payment of money;
(c) making such other provision as the court thinks appropriate.

(5) A commonhold unit is residential if provision made in the commonhold community statement by virtue of section 14(1) requires it to be used only—
(a) for residential purposes, or
(b) for residential and other incidental purposes.

Commentary

This important section seeks to achieve the Government's objective of ensuring that the residential leasehold system does not become enshrined in commonhold. The section renders it impossible to create a residential lease which is not in accordance with regulations—currently a lease for a maximum term of seven years. Non-residential leases are not subject to the same constraints—see section 18.

The expression 'commonhold community statement' is defined in section 31.
The expression 'commonhold unit' is defined in section 11.
The term 'court' means the High Court or a county court—see section 66.
The term 'instrument' includes any document—see section 69.
The term 'prescribed' means prescribed by regulations—see section 64.

By virtue of section 69(3), the expression 'term of years absolute' has the meaning given to it by section 205(1)(xxvii) of the Law of Property Act 1925 and by section 132(1) of the Land Registration Act 2002.

This section is discussed in paragraph 4.13.6 and Section 3.3 of the text.

Leasing: non-residential

18.—An instrument or agreement which creates a term of years absolute in a commonhold unit which is not residential (within the meaning of section 17) shall have effect subject to any provision of the commonhold community statement.

Commentary

This section permits the leasing of a commonhold unit for a non-residential use, provided that such a use is sanctioned by the commonhold community statement.

The expression 'commonhold community statement' is defined in section 31.
The expression 'commonhold unit' is defined in section 11.
The term 'instrument' includes any document—see section 69.
By virtue of section 69(3), the expression 'term of years absolute' has the meaning given to it by section 205(1)(xxvii) of the Law of Property Act 1925 and by section 132(1) of the Land Registration Act 2002.

This section is discussed in paragraphs 2.17.13, 3.4.1 and 4.13.6 of the text.

Leasing: supplementary

19.—(1) Regulations may—
(a) impose obligations on a tenant of a commonhold unit;
(b) enable a commonhold community statement to impose obligations on a tenant of a commonhold unit.

(2) Regulations under subsection (1) may, in particular, require a tenant of a commonhold unit to make payments to the commonhold association or a unit-holder in discharge of payments which—
(a) are due in accordance with the commonhold community statement to be made by the unit-holder, or
(b) are due in accordance with the commonhold community statement to be made by another tenant of the unit.

(3) Regulations under subsection (1) may, in particular, provide—
(a) for the amount of payments under subsection (2) to be set against sums owed by the tenant (whether to the person by whom the payments were due to be made or to some other person);
(b) for the amount of payments under subsection (2) to be recovered from the unit-holder or another tenant of the unit.

(4) Regulations may modify a rule of law about leasehold estates (whether deriving from the common law or from an enactment) in its application to a term of years in a commonhold unit.

(5) Regulations under this section—
(a) may make provision generally or in relation to specified circumstances, and

(b) may make different provision for different descriptions of commonhold land or commonhold unit.

Commentary

This section introduces a radical but useful departure from traditional landlord and tenant law by providing for regulations to render a tenant of a commonhold unit liable for obligations in the commonhold community statement, whether or not the tenancy agreement so provides, and notwithstanding the fact that the tenant will not have subscribed to the commonhold community statement.

The expression 'commonhold association' is defined in section 34.
The expression 'commonhold community statement' is defined in section 31.
The expression 'commonhold land' is defined in section 1.
The expression 'commonhold unit' is defined in section 11.
The term 'regulations' is defined in section 64.
The term 'unit-holder' is defined in section 12.

This section is discussed in paragraphs 3.3.7 and 4.13.8 of the text.

Other transactions

20.—(1) A commonhold community statement may not prevent or restrict the creation, grant or transfer by a unit-holder of—
(a) an interest in the whole or part of his unit, or
(b) a charge over his unit.

(2) Subsection (1) is subject to sections 17 to 19 (which impose restrictions about leases).

(3) It shall not be possible to create an interest of a prescribed kind in a commonhold unit unless the commonhold association—
(a) is a party to the creation of the interest, or
(b) consents in writing to the creation of the interest.

(4) A commonhold association may act as described in subsection (3)(a) or (b) only if—
(a) the association passes a resolution to take the action, and
(b) at least 75 per cent of those who vote on the resolution vote in favour.

(5) An instrument or agreement shall be of no effect to the extent that it purports to create an interest in contravention of subsection (3).

(6) In this section 'interest' does not include—
(a) a charge, or
(b) an interest which arises by virtue of a charge.

Commentary

This section builds upon the prohibition in section 15 of any provisions in the commonhold community statement which prevent transfer of a commonhold unit, and extends that prohibition to the creation or dealing with any interest in the whole or part of the unit—but subject to the subsequent provisions of the section, including the restrictions on leasing in sections 17 to 19, and any other permitted restrictions in the commonhold community statement; and subject to section 21, which bans the creation of any interest (save for a permitted lease) in part only of a commonhold unit.

The expression 'commonhold association' is defined in section 34.
The expression 'commonhold community statement' is defined in section 31.
The expression 'commonhold unit' is defined in section 11.
The term 'instrument' includes any document—see section 69.
By virtue of section 69(3), the expression 'term of years absolute' has the meaning given to it by section 205(1)(xxvii) of the Law of Property Act 1925 and by section 132(1) of the Land Registration Act 2002.
The term 'transfer' (of a commonhold unit) is defined in section 15.
The term 'unit-holder' is defined in section 12.

This section is discussed in paragraphs 3.5.3 and 6.3.13 of the text.

Part-unit: interests

21.—(1) It shall not be possible to create an interest in part only of a commonhold unit.

(2) But subsection (1) shall not prevent—
  (a) the creation of a term of years absolute in part only of a residential commonhold unit where the term satisfies prescribed conditions,
  (b) the creation of a term of years absolute in part only of a non-residential commonhold unit, or
  (c) the transfer of the freehold estate in part only of a commonhold unit where the commonhold association consents in writing to the transfer.

(3) An instrument or agreement shall be of no effect to the extent that it purports to create an interest in contravention of subsection (1).

(4) Subsection (5) applies where—
  (a) land becomes commonhold land or is added to a commonhold unit, and
  (b) immediately before that event there is an interest in the land which could not be created after that event by reason of subsection (1).

(5) The interest shall be extinguished by virtue of this subsection to the extent that it could not be created by reason of subsection (1).

(6) Section 17(2) and (4) shall apply (with any necessary modifications) in relation to subsection (2)(a) and (b) above.

(7) Where part only of a unit is held under a lease, regulations may modify the application of a provision which—
  (a) is made by or by virtue of this Part, and
  (b) applies to a unit-holder or a tenant or both.

(8) Section 20(4) shall apply in relation to subsection (2)(c) above.

(9) Where the freehold interest in part only of a commonhold unit is transferred, the part transferred—
  (a) becomes a new commonhold unit by virtue of this subsection, or
  (b) in a case where the request for consent under subsection (2)(c) states that this paragraph is to apply, becomes part of a commonhold unit specified in the request.

(10) Regulations may make provision, or may require a commonhold community statement to make provision, about—
  (a) registration of units created by virtue of subsection (9);

(b) the adaptation of provision made by or by virtue of this Part or by or by virtue of a commonhold community statement to a case where units are created or modified by virtue of subsection (9).

Commentary

This section bans the creation of any interest (save for a permitted lease) in part only of a commonhold unit. Section 22 applies this prohibition expressly to charges over part only of an interest in a commonhold unit. The difference in the language between the sections ('an interest in part only of a commonhold unit'—section 21, cf 'part only of an interest in a commonhold unit'—section 22) appears to be accidental. At any rate, it is difficult to perceive any intended substantive change of content.

The expression 'commonhold association' is defined in section 34.
The expression 'commonhold community statement' is defined in section 31.
The expression 'commonhold land' is defined in section 1.
The expression 'commonhold unit' is defined in section 11.
The term 'instrument' includes any document—see section 69.
By virtue of section 69(3), the expressions 'land' and 'term of years absolute' have the meanings given to them by section 205(1) of the Law of Property Act 1925 and by section 132(1) of the Land Registration Act 2002.
The expressions 'prescribed' and 'regulations' are defined and explained by section 64.
The expression 'residential commonhold unit' is defined in section 17.
The term 'transfer' (of a commonhold unit) is defined in section 15.
The term 'unit-holder' is defined in section 12.

This section is discussed in paragraphs 3.2.6 and 3.5.1 of the text.

Part-unit: charging

22.—(1) It shall not be possible to create a charge over part only of an interest in a commonhold unit.

(2) An instrument or agreement shall be of no effect to the extent that it purports to create a charge in contravention of subsection (1).

(3) Subsection (4) applies where—
  (a) land becomes commonhold land or is added to a commonhold unit, and
  (b) immediately before that event there is a charge over the land which could not be created after that event by reason of subsection (1).

(4) The charge shall be extinguished by virtue of this subsection to the extent that it could not be created by reason of subsection (1).

Commentary

This section applies the prohibition in section 21 expressly to charges over part only of an interest in a commonhold unit. Where the whole of a unit has charged land added to it with the result that the charge then applies only to part of the enlarged unit, the charge is extinguished. The converse situation where uncharged land is added to a charged unit is dealt with by section 24.

The expression 'commonhold land' is defined in section 1.

The expression 'commonhold unit' is defined in section 11.
By virtue of section 69(3), the term 'land' has the meaning given to it by section 205(1)(ix) of the Law of Property Act 1925 and by section 132(1) of the Land Registration Act 2002.

This section is discussed in paragraph 3.5.2 of the text.

Changing size

23.—(1) An amendment of a commonhold community statement which redefines the extent of a commonhold unit may not be made unless the unit-holder consents—
(a) in writing, and
(b) before the amendment is made.

(2) But regulations may enable a court to dispense with the requirement for consent on the application of a commonhold association in prescribed circumstances.

Commentary

This section does not allow any amendment to the commonhold community statement which will change the size of a commonhold unit unless the unit-holder consents, or unless a court dispenses with the requirement for consent in circumstances which may be prescribed by regulations. There are no current plans to make any such regulations.

The expression 'commonhold association' is defined in section 34.
The expression 'commonhold community statement' is defined in section 31.
The expression 'commonhold unit' is defined in section 11.
The term 'court' means the High Court or a county court—see section 66.
The expressions 'prescribed' and 'regulations' are defined and explained by section 64.
The term 'unit-holder' is defined in section 12.

This section is discussed in paragraphs 2.24.2 and 3.2.6 of the text.

Changing size: charged unit

24.—(1) This section applies to an amendment of a commonhold community statement which redefines the extent of a commonhold unit over which there is a registered charge.

(2) The amendment may not be made unless the registered proprietor of the charge consents—
(a) in writing, and
(b) before the amendment is made.

(3) But regulations may enable a court to dispense with the requirement for consent on the application of a commonhold association in prescribed circumstances.

(4) If the amendment removes land from the commonhold unit, the charge shall by virtue of this subsection be extinguished to the extent that it relates to the land which is removed.

(5) If the amendment adds land to the unit, the charge shall by virtue of this subsection be extended so as to relate to the land which is added.

(6) Regulations may make provision—
(a) requiring notice to be given to the Registrar in circumstances to which this section applies;
(b) requiring the Registrar to alter the register to reflect the application of subsection (4) or (5).

Commentary

This section is the counterpart to section 22, which extinguishes a charge over land which has been added to a unit (because otherwise the charge would then relate only to part of the enlarged unit). Section 24, by contrast, deals with a charge over the unit itself, and avoids the section 22 result by providing for the chargee's consent to be obtained to any amendment to the commonhold community statement enlarging the unit, and then for the charge to extend to the whole of the enlarged unit. Where the unit is to have land taken away from it, on the other hand, then the chargee's consent is again required, and the charge is extinguished in relation to the land removed.

The expression 'commonhold association' is defined in section 34.
The expression 'commonhold community statement' is defined in section 31.
The expression 'commonhold unit' is defined in section 11.
By virtue of section 69(3), the term 'land' has the meaning given to it by section 205(1)(ix) of the Law of Property Act 1925 and by section 132(1) of the Land Registration Act 2002.
The expressions 'prescribed' and 'regulations' are defined and explained by section 64.
The term 'registered' is defined in section 67.
The expression 'the Registrar' means the Chief Land Registrar—see section 67.

This section is discussed in paragraphs 2.18.2 and 3.2.6 of the text.

Common parts

Definition

25.—(1) In this Part 'common parts' in relation to a commonhold means every part of the commonhold which is not for the time being a commonhold unit in accordance with the commonhold community statement.

(2) A commonhold community statement may make provision in respect of a specified part of the common parts (a 'limited use area') restricting—
(a) the classes of person who may use it;
(b) the kind of use to which it may be put.

(3) A commonhold community statement—
(a) may make provision which has effect only in relation to a limited use area, and
(b) may make different provision for different limited use areas.

Commentary

The draftsman of subsection (1) of this section is to be commended for his brevity in defining the common parts of a commonhold not by reference to any physical description, but simply as those parts of the commonhold which are not commonhold units.
Subsections (2) and (3) allow the commonhold community statement to treat specified parts of the common parts differently.

The expression 'a commonhold' is defined in section 1.
The expression 'commonhold community statement' is defined in section 31.
The expression 'commonhold unit' is defined in section 11.
The expression 'common parts' is defined in section 25.

This section is discussed in paragraph 2.17.4 of the text.

Use and maintenance

26.—A commonhold community statement must make provision—

(a) regulating the use of the common parts;
(b) requiring the commonhold association to insure the common parts;
(c) requiring the commonhold association to repair and maintain the common parts.

Commentary

This section imposes a comprehensive regime governing the use, insurance, repair and maintenance of the common parts by reference to provisions set out in the commonhold community statement. It is the counterpart to section 14, which governs each commonhold unit.

The expression 'commonhold association' is defined in section 34.
The expression 'commonhold community statement' is defined in section 31.
The expression 'common parts' is defined in section 25.
The terms 'insure' and 'maintenance' are expanded upon in section 69.

This section is discussed in Section 2.17 of the text.

Transactions

27.—(1) Nothing in a commonhold community statement shall prevent or restrict—

(a) the transfer by the commonhold association of its freehold estate in any part of the common parts, or
(b) the creation by the commonhold association of an interest in any part of the common parts.

(2) In this section 'interest' does not include—

(a) a charge, or
(b) an interest which arises by virtue of a charge.

Commentary

This section forbids the commonhold community statement from restricting dealings by the commonhold association with its interest in the common parts. It is therefore the counterpart to sections 15 to 20, which apply to dealings with any individual commonhold unit. There are, however, a number of important differences between the two: (a) leasing of the common parts is allowed in principle (subject to anything to the contrary in the commonhold community statement); (b) charging the common parts is expressly prohibited by section 28; (c) the creation of interests in part only of the common parts is allowed (subject again to anything to the contrary in the commonhold community statement).

The expression 'common parts' is defined in section 25.
The expression 'commonhold association' is defined in section 34.
The expression 'commonhold community statement' is defined in section 31.

This section is discussed in Section 3.5 of the text.

Charges: general prohibition

28.—(1) It shall not be possible to create a charge over common parts.

(2) An instrument or agreement shall be of no effect to the extent that it purports to create a charge over common parts.

(3) Where by virtue of section 7 or 9 a commonhold association is registered as the proprietor of common parts, a charge which relates wholly or partly to the common parts shall be extinguished by virtue of this subsection to the extent that it relates to the common parts.

(4) Where by virtue of section 30 land vests in a commonhold association following an amendment to a commonhold community statement which has the effect of adding land to the common parts, a charge which relates wholly or partly to the land added shall be extinguished by virtue of this subsection to the extent that it relates to that land.

(5) This section is subject to Section 29 (which permits certain mortgages).

Commentary

This section prohibits the charging of the common parts of a commonhold, and extinguishes any charge granted over the common parts before the registration of the commonhold association as proprietor, and any charge granted over land which is subsequently added to the common parts. One exception is made in the case of new legal mortgages approved by the commonhold association—see section 29 of the Act.

The expression 'common parts' is defined in section 25.
The expression 'commonhold association' is defined in section 34.
The expression 'commonhold community statement' is defined in section 31.
The term 'instrument' includes any document—see section 69.
By virtue of section 69(3), the term 'land' has the meaning given to it by section 205(1)(ix) of the Law of Property Act 1925 and by section 132(1) of the Land Registration Act 2002.
The term 'registered' is defined in section 67.

This section is discussed in paragraph 3.6.1 of the text.

New legal mortgages

29.—(1) Section 28 shall not apply in relation to a legal mortgage if the creation of the mortgage is approved by a resolution of the commonhold association.

(2) A resolution for the purposes of subsection (1) must be passed—
   (a) before the mortgage is created, and
   (b) unanimously.

(3) In this section 'legal mortgage' has the meaning given by section 205(1)(xvi) of the Law of Property Act 1925 (c 20) (interpretation).

Commentary

This section sets out the one permitted exception to the general prohibition in section 28 of the Act on the granting of charges over the common parts. New legal mortgages approved unanimously by the commonhold association will not be subject to the section 28 prohibition.

The expression 'commonhold association' is defined in section 34.

This section is discussed in paragraph 3.6.2 of the text.

Additions to common parts

30.—(1) This section applies where an amendment of a commonhold community statement—
 (a) specifies land which forms part of a commonhold unit, and
 (b) provides for that land (the 'added land') to be added to the common parts.

(2) The amendment may not be made unless the registered proprietor of any charge over the added land consents—
 (a) in writing, and
 (b) before the amendment is made.

(3) But regulations may enable a court to dispense with the requirement for consent on the application of a commonhold association in specified circumstances.

(4) On the filing of the amended statement under section 33—
 (a) the commonhold association shall be entitled to be registered as the proprietor of the freehold estate in the added land, and
 (b) the Registrar shall register the commonhold association in accordance with paragraph (a) (without an application being made).

Commentary

Subsections (1) and (2) provide that any addition of land to the common parts of a commonhold must receive the consent of the registered proprietor of any charge over it. The need for this separate stipulation is unclear, since the section deals only with land added from a commonhold unit; and the consent of the chargee of that unit would be required under section 24(2) of the Act in any event.

Subsection (3) provides for regulations to be made dispensing with consent in certain circumstances. No such regulations are currently envisaged.

Subsection (4) allows the Chief Land Registrar to register the commonhold association as proprietor of the extended land upon the filing of the amended commonhold community statement without any further formality.

The expression 'common parts' is defined in section 25.
The expression 'commonhold association' is defined in section 34.
The expression 'commonhold community statement' is defined in section 31.
The expression 'commonhold unit' is defined in section 11.
The term 'court' means the High Court or a county court—see section 66.
By virtue of section 69(3), the term 'land' has the meaning given to it by section 205(1)(ix) of the Law of Property Act 1925 and by section 132(1) of the Land Registration Act 2002.
The term 'registered' is defined in section 67.

The expression 'the Registrar' means the Chief Land Registrar—see section 67.
The term 'regulations' is explained in section 64.

This section is discussed in Section 3.7 of the text.

Commonhold community statement

Form and content: general

31.—(1) A commonhold community statement is a document which makes provision in relation to specified land for—

(a) the rights and duties of the commonhold association, and
(b) the rights and duties of the unit-holders.

(2) A commonhold community statement must be in the prescribed form.

(3) A commonhold community statement may—

(a) impose a duty on the commonhold association;
(b) impose a duty on a unit-holder;
(c) make provision about the taking of decisions in connection with the management of the commonhold or any other matter concerning it.

(4) Subsection (3) is subject to—

(a) any provision made by or by virtue of this Part, and
(b) any provision of the memorandum or articles of the commonhold association.

(5) In subsection (3)(a) and (b) 'duty' includes, in particular, a duty—

(a) to pay money;
(b) to undertake works;
(c) to grant access;
(d) to give notice;
(e) to refrain from entering into transactions of a specified kind in relation to a commonhold unit;
(f) to refrain from using the whole or part of a commonhold unit for a specified purpose or for anything other than a specified purpose;
(g) to refrain from undertaking works (including alterations) of a specified kind;
(h) to refrain from causing nuisance or annoyance;
(i) to refrain from specified behaviour;
(j) to indemnify the commonhold association or a unit-holder in respect of costs arising from the breach of a statutory requirement.

(6) Provision in a commonhold community statement imposing a duty to pay money (whether in pursuance of subsection (5)(a) or any other provision made by or by virtue of this Part) may include provision for the payment of interest in the case of late payment.

(7) A duty conferred by a commonhold community statement on a commonhold association or a unit-holder shall not require any other formality.

(8) A commonhold community statement may not provide for the transfer or loss of an interest in land on the occurrence or non-occurrence of a specified event.

(9) Provision made by a commonhold community statement shall be of no effect to the extent that—

(a) it is prohibited by virtue of section 32,
(b) it is inconsistent with any provision made by or by virtue of this Part,
(c) it is inconsistent with anything which is treated as included in the statement by virtue of section 32, or
(d) it is inconsistent with the memorandum or articles of association of the commonhold association.

Commentary

This and the next two sections legislate for the content of the commonhold community statement.

Subsection (1) defines the commonhold community statement.

Subsection (2) requires the commonhold community statement to be in a form prescribed by regulations. A draft has been produced and is included in the Forms and Precedents part of this work.

Subsection (3) provides for the imposition by the commonhold community statement of duties upon unit-holders and the commonhold association. Subsection (7) then provides that no further formality shall be required for such duties.

Subsection (4) stipulates that the duties that may be imposed by the commonhold community statement are subject to any contrary provision of the Act or the memorandum or articles of association of the commonhold association. Subsection (9) duplicates or adds to this by providing that any provision in the commonhold community statement shall be of no effect in so far as it is inconsistent with any provision of the Act or any regulations made under section 32 or any provision of the memorandum or articles of association of the commonhold association.

Subsection (5) sets out examples of the types of duty that may be imposed by the commonhold community statement.

Subsection (6) then provides for interest to be payable on any money required to be paid in performance of a duty imposed by the commonhold community statement.

Subsection (8) removes from the possible sanctions for breach of duty any penalty akin to forfeiture of an interest in land.

The expression 'commonhold association' is defined in section 34.
The expression 'commonhold unit' is defined in section 11.
The term 'prescribed' means prescribed by regulations—see section 64.
The term 'unit-holder' is defined in section 12.

This section is discussed in Section 2.16 and paragraph 6.2.2 of the text.

Regulations

32.—(1) Regulations shall make provision about the content of a commonhold community statement.

(2) The regulations may permit, require or prohibit the inclusion in a statement of—
(a) specified provision, or
(b) provision of a specified kind, for a specified purpose or about a specified matter.

(3) The regulations may—
(a) provide for a statement to be treated as including provision prescribed by or determined in accordance with the regulations;

(b) permit a statement to make provision in place of provision which would otherwise be treated as included by virtue of paragraph (a).

(4) The regulations may—

(a) make different provision for different descriptions of commonhold association or unit-holder;

(b) make different provision for different circumstances;

(c) make provision about the extent to which a commonhold community statement may make different provision for different descriptions of unit-holder or common parts.

(5) The matters to which regulations under this section may relate include, but are not limited to—

(a) the matters mentioned in sections 11, 14, 15, 20, 21, 25, 26, 27, 38, 39 and 58, and

(b) any matter for which regulations under section 37 may make provision.

Commentary

Although this section (which should be read together with the provisions regarding amendment in section 33) is grouped together with others dealing with the commonhold community statement, and although the greater part of it deals with the content of the commonhold community statement, the last subsection introduces a general rule-making power for commonhold going far beyond matters with which the commonhold community statement will be concerned.

Section 64 supplements the power to make regulations.

The expression 'common parts' is defined in section 25.
The expression 'commonhold association' is defined in section 34.
The expression 'commonhold community statement' is defined in section 31.
The expressions 'prescribed' and 'regulations' are defined and explained by section 64.
The term 'unit-holder' is defined in section 12.

This section is discussed in paragraph 2.16.3 of the text.

Amendment

33.—(1) Regulations under section 32 shall require a commonhold community statement to make provision about how it can be amended.

(2) The regulations shall, in particular, make provision under section 32(3)(a) (whether or not subject to provision under section 32(3)(b)).

(3) An amendment of a commonhold community statement shall have no effect unless and until the amended statement is registered in accordance with this section.

(4) If the commonhold association makes an application under this subsection the Registrar shall arrange for an amended commonhold community statement to be kept in his custody, and referred to in the register, in place of the unamended statement.

(5) An application under subsection (4) must be accompanied by a certificate given by the directors of the commonhold association that the amended commonhold community statement satisfies the requirements of this Part.

(6) Where an amendment of a commonhold community statement redefines the extent of a commonhold unit, an application under subsection (4) must be accompanied by any consent required by section 23(1) or 24(2) (or an order of a court dispensing with consent).

(7) Where an amendment of a commonhold community statement has the effect of changing the extent of the common parts, an application under subsection (4) must be accompanied by any consent required by section 30(2) (or an order of a court dispensing with consent).

(8) Where the Registrar amends the register on an application under subsection (4) he shall make any consequential amendments to the register which he thinks appropriate.

Commentary

This section makes provision for a commonhold community statement to be amended. Any such amendment will only take effect upon registration following an application accompanied by the requisite documents.

The expression 'common parts' is defined in section 25.
The expression 'commonhold association' is defined in section 34.
The expression 'commonhold community statement' is defined in section 31.
The expression 'commonhold unit' is defined in section 11.
By virtue of section 69(3), the term 'director' has the meaning given to it by section 741(1) of the Companies Act 1985.
The terms 'register' and 'registered' are defined in section 67.
The expression 'the Registrar' means the Chief Land Registrar—see section 67.
The term 'regulations' is explained in section 64.

This section is discussed in paragraph 2.18.5 of the text.

Commonhold association

Constitution

34.—(1) A commonhold association is a private company limited by guarantee the memorandum of which—

(a) states that an object of the company is to exercise the functions of a commonhold association in relation to specified commonhold land, and

(b) specifies £1 as the amount required to be specified in pursuance of section 2(4) of the Companies Act 1985 (c 6) (members' guarantee).

(2) Schedule 3 (which makes provision about the constitution of a commonhold association) shall have effect.

Commentary

This and the next two sections provide the framework for the structure and operation of the commonhold association. Section 34(1) requires the corporate structure to be that of a company limited by guarantee rather than any other mechanism.

Subsection (2) dictates the constitution of the commonhold association by reference to the detail regarding the memorandum and articles of association, members and other matters set out in Schedule 3.

The expression 'commonhold land' is defined in section 1.
The expression 'exercise functions' is defined in section 8.
The term 'object' is defined in section 69.
By virtue of section 69(3), the expression 'private company' has the meaning given to it by section 1(3) of the Companies Act 1985 (reprinted at the end of this Act).

This section is discussed in Sections 2.11 and 2.12 of the text.

Duty to manage

35.—(1) The directors of a commonhold association shall exercise their powers so as to permit or facilitate so far as possible—

(a) the exercise by each unit-holder of his rights, and
(b) the enjoyment by each unit-holder of the freehold estate in his unit.

(2) The directors of a commonhold association shall, in particular, use any right, power or procedure conferred or created by virtue of section 37 for the purpose of preventing, remedying or curtailing a failure on the part of a unit-holder to comply with a requirement or duty imposed on him by virtue of the commonhold community statement or a provision of this Part.

(3) But in respect of a particular failure on the part of a unit-holder (the 'defaulter') the directors of a commonhold association—

(a) need not take action if they reasonably think that inaction is in the best interests of establishing or maintaining harmonious relationships between all the unit-holders, and that it will not cause any unit-holder (other than the defaulter) significant loss or significant disadvantage, and
(b) shall have regard to the desirability of using arbitration, mediation or conciliation procedures (including referral under a scheme approved under section 42) instead of legal proceedings wherever possible.

(4) A reference in this section to a unit-holder includes a reference to a tenant of a unit.

Commentary

The title of this section is misleading. Instead of imposing a duty to manage upon the directors of the commonhold association, it sets out a code intended to balance a number of different objectives by satisfying the greatest number of unit-holders.

The expression 'commonhold association' is defined in section 34.
The expression 'commonhold community statement' is defined in section 31.
By virtue of section 69(3), the term 'director' has the meaning given to it by section 741(1) of the Companies Act 1985.
The term 'unit-holder' is defined in section 12.

This section is discussed in paragraph 4.3.18 of the text.

Voting

36.—(1) This section applies in relation to any provision of this Part (a 'voting provision') which refers to the passing of a resolution by a commonhold association.

(2) A voting provision is satisfied only if every member is given an opportunity to vote in accordance with any relevant provision of the memorandum or articles of association or the commonhold community statement.

(3) A vote is cast for the purposes of a voting provision whether it is cast in person or in accordance with a provision which—
   (a) provides for voting by post, by proxy or in some other manner, and
   (b) is contained in the memorandum or articles of association or the commonhold community statement.

(4) A resolution is passed unanimously if every member who casts a vote votes in favour.

Commentary

This section sets out three rules governing the way in which members of a commonhold association may pass a resolution: (a) every member must be given the opportunity to vote; (b) voting should be done either personally or in any other way stipulated in the memorandum and articles of association of the commonhold community statement; (c) a unanimous resolution means a resolution passed by every voting member (and not a resolution commanding 100 per cent support from those entitled to vote).

The expression 'commonhold association' is defined in section 34.
The expression 'commonhold community statement' is defined in section 31.

This section is discussed in Section 4.6 of the text.

Operation of commonhold

Enforcement and compensation

37.—(1) Regulations may make provision (including provision conferring jurisdiction on a court) about the exercise or enforcement of a right or duty imposed or conferred by or by virtue of—
   (a) a commonhold community statement;
   (b) the memorandum or articles of a commonhold association;
   (c) a provision made by or by virtue of this Part.

(2) The regulations may, in particular, make provision—
   (a) requiring compensation to be paid where a right is exercised in specified cases or circumstances;
   (b) requiring compensation to be paid where a duty is not complied with;
   (c) enabling recovery of costs where work is carried out for the purpose of enforcing a right or duty;
   (d) enabling recovery of costs where work is carried out in consequence of the failure to perform a duty;
   (e) permitting a unit-holder to enforce a duty imposed on another unit-holder, on a commonhold association or on a tenant;
   (f) permitting a commonhold association to enforce a duty imposed on a unit-holder or a tenant;
   (g) permitting a tenant to enforce a duty imposed on another tenant, a unit-holder or a commonhold association;
   (h) permitting the enforcement of terms or conditions to which a right is subject;

(i) requiring the use of a specified form of arbitration, mediation or conciliation procedure before legal proceedings may be brought.

(3) Provision about compensation made by virtue of this section shall include—
(a) provision (which may include provision conferring jurisdiction on a court) for determining the amount of compensation;
(b) provision for the payment of interest in the case of late payment.

(4) Regulations under this section shall be subject to any provision included in a commonhold community statement in accordance with regulations made by virtue of section 32(5)(b).

Commentary

This and the next two sections are the working parts of the Act in relation to the operation of a commonhold in practice. Section 37 provides for regulations to be made containing the means of enforcement between unit-holders and the commonhold association of rights and duties set out in the Act, the commonhold community statement and the memorandum and articles of association of the commonhold association. The sanction for breach of duty will be limited to a requirement to pay compensation and costs.

The expression 'commonhold association' is defined in section 34.
The expression 'commonhold community statement' is defined in section 31.
The term 'court' means the High Court or a county court—see section 66.
The term 'regulations' is explained in section 64.
The term 'unit-holder' is defined in section 12.

This section is discussed in Section 6.5 of the text.

Commonhold assessment

38.—(1) A commonhold community statement must make provision—
(a) requiring the directors of the commonhold association to make an annual estimate of the income required to be raised from unit-holders to meet the expenses of the association,
(b) enabling the directors of the commonhold association to make estimates from time to time of income required to be raised from unit-holders in addition to the annual estimate,
(c) specifying the percentage of any estimate made under paragraph (a) or (b) which is to be allocated to each unit,
(d) requiring each unit-holder to make payments in respect of the percentage of any estimate which is allocated to his unit, and
(e) requiring the directors of the commonhold association to serve notices on unit-holders specifying payments required to be made by them and the date on which each payment is due.

(2) For the purpose of subsection (1)(c)—
(a) the percentages allocated by a commonhold community statement to the commonhold units must amount in aggregate to 100;
(b) a commonhold community statement may specify 0 per cent in relation to a unit.

Commentary

This section (which should be read together with section 39) requires the commonhold community statement to provide for the mechanism by which the expenses of the commonhold association are to be met by the unit-holders.

The expression 'commonhold association' is defined in section 34.
The expression 'commonhold community statement' is defined in section 31.
By virtue of section 69(3), the term 'director' has the meaning given to it by section 741(1) of the Companies Act 1985 (reprinted at the end of this Act).
The term 'unit-holder' is defined in section 12.

This section is discussed in Section 4.15 and paragraph 2.17.18 of the text.

Reserve Fund

39.—(1) Regulations under section 32 may, in particular, require a commonhold community statement to make provision—
(a) requiring the directors of the commonhold association to establish and maintain one or more funds to finance the repair and maintenance of common parts;
(b) requiring the directors of the commonhold association to establish and maintain one or more funds to finance the repair and maintenance of commonhold units.

(2) Where a commonhold community statement provides for the establishment and maintenance of a fund in accordance with subsection (1) it must also make provision—
(a) requiring or enabling the directors of the commonhold association to set a levy from time to time,
(b) specifying the percentage of any levy set under paragraph (a) which is to be allocated to each unit,
(c) requiring each unit-holder to make payments in respect of the percentage of any levy set under paragraph (a) which is allocated to his unit, and
(d) requiring the directors of the commonhold association to serve notices on unit-holders specifying payments required to be made by them and the date on which each payment is due.

(3) For the purpose of subsection (2)(b)—
(a) the percentages allocated by a commonhold community statement to the commonhold units must amount in aggregate to 100;
(b) a commonhold community statement may specify 0 per cent in relation to a unit.

(4) The assets of a fund established and maintained by virtue of this section shall not be used for the purpose of enforcement of any debt except a judgment debt referable to a reserve fund activity.

(5) For the purpose of subsection (4)—
(a) 'reserve fund activity' means an activity which in accordance with the commonhold community statement can or may be financed from a fund established and maintained by virtue of this section,
(b) assets are used for the purpose of enforcement of a debt if, in particular, they are taken in execution or are made the subject of a charging order under section 1 of the Charging Orders Act 1979 (c 53), and

(c) the reference to a judgment debt includes a reference to any interest payable on a judgment debt.

Commentary

This section adds to section 38 by providing for regulations to be made which may require a commonhold association to make provision for reserve funds for the repair and maintenance of the common parts and commonhold units.

Section 56 provides for the release of the reserve fund where the commonhold association is wound-up, or the court makes an order under sections 6(6)(c) or 40(3)(d) terminating the commonhold (where a commonhold has been registered in contravention of the requirements of the Act or of provisions made under it, or where the memorandum or articles of association or the commonhold community statement do not comply with the requirements of the Act or the regulations: see also section 55).

The expression 'common parts' is defined in section 25.
The expression 'commonhold association' is defined in section 34.
The expression 'commonhold community statement' is defined in section 31.
The expression 'commonhold unit' is defined in section 11.
By virtue of section 69(3), the term 'director' has the meaning given to it by section 741(1) of the Companies Act 1985.
The term 'maintenance' is defined in section 69.
The term 'regulations' is explained in section 64.

This section is discussed in Section 4.16 and paragraph 2.17.19 of the text.

Rectification of documents

40.—(1) A unit-holder may apply to the court for a declaration that—
(a) the memorandum or articles of association of the relevant commonhold association do not comply with regulations under paragraph 2(1) of Schedule 3;
(b) the relevant commonhold community statement does not comply with a requirement imposed by or by virtue of this Part.

(2) On granting a declaration under this section the court may make any order which appears to it to be appropriate.

(3) An order under subsection (2) may, in particular—
(a) require a director or other specified officer of a commonhold association to take steps to alter or amend a document;
(b) require a director or other specified officer of a commonhold association to take specified steps;
(c) make an award of compensation (whether or not contingent upon the occurrence or non-occurrence of a specified event) to be paid by the commonhold association to a specified person;
(d) make provision for land to cease to be commonhold land.

(4) An application under subsection (1) must be made—
(a) within the period of three months beginning with the day on which the applicant became a unit-holder,
(b) within three months of the commencement of the alleged failure to comply, or
(c) with the permission of the court.

Commentary

This section has little to do with its overall group heading 'Operation of commonhold', but deals rather with non-compliance by the memorandum or articles of association of the commonhold association or the commonhold community statement with any provision of the Act. It should therefore be read together with sections 32 and 34.

In a case of non-compliance, the section gives any unit-holder the right to apply to court for an order for amendment of the offending document, providing the application is made within stipulated time limits (which the court may extend).

See section 55 for the powers of the court and the liquidator where the court makes an order under section 40(3)(d) for all the land in relation to which the commonhold association exercises functions to cease to be commonhold land.

The expression 'commonhold association' is defined in section 34.
The expression 'commonhold community statement' is defined in section 31.
The expression 'commonhold land' is defined in section 1.
The term 'court' means the High Court or a county court—see section 66.
By virtue of section 69(3), the term 'director' has the meaning given to it by section 741(1) of the Companies Act 1985.
By virtue of section 69(3), the term 'land' has the meaning given to it by section 205(1)(ix) of the Law of Property Act 1925 and by section 132(1) of the Land Registration Act 2002.
The term 'regulations' is explained in section 64.
The term 'unit-holder' is defined in section 12.

This section is discussed in paragraphs 2.18.7 and 6.14.5 of the text.

Enlargement

41.—(1) This section applies to an application under section 2 if the commonhold association for the purposes of the application already exercises functions in relation to commonhold land.

(2) In this section—
(a) the application is referred to as an 'application to add land', and
(b) the land to which the application relates is referred to as the 'added land'.

(3) An application to add land may not be made unless it is approved by a resolution of the commonhold association.

(4) A resolution for the purposes of subsection (3) must be passed—
(a) before the application to add land is made, and
(b) unanimously.

(5) Section 2(2) shall not apply to an application to add land; but the application must be accompanied by—
(a) the documents specified in paragraph 6 of Schedule 1,
(b) an application under section 33 for the registration of an amended commonhold community statement which makes provision for the existing commonhold and the added land, and
(c) a certificate given by the directors of the commonhold association that the application to add land satisfies Schedule 2 and subsection (3).

(6) Where sections 7 and 9 have effect following an application to add land—

(a) the references to 'the commonhold land' in sections 7(2)(a) and (3)(d) and 9(3)(f) shall be treated as references to the added land, and
(b) the references in sections 7(2)(b) and (3)(c) and 9(3)(e) to the rights and duties conferred and imposed by the commonhold community statement shall be treated as a reference to rights and duties only in so far as they affect the added land.

(7) In the case of an application to add land where the whole of the added land is to form part of the common parts of a commonhold—
(a) section 7 shall not apply,
(b) on registration the commonhold association shall be entitled to be registered (if it is not already) as the proprietor of the freehold estate in the added land,
(c) the Registrar shall make any registration required by paragraph (b) (without an application being made), and
(d) the rights and duties conferred and imposed by the commonhold community statement shall, in so far as they affect the added land, come into force on registration.

Commentary

Again, this section has little to do with its overall group heading 'Operation of commonhold', but deals rather with an application by an existing commonhold association to extend the commonhold land, either by adding land to the common parts, or by adding land that will form new commonhold units.

The expression 'common parts' is defined in section 25.
The expressions 'a commonhold' and 'commonhold land' are defined in section 1.
The expression 'commonhold association' is defined in section 34.
The expression 'commonhold community statement' is defined in section 31.
By virtue of section 69(3), the term 'director' has the meaning given to it by section 741(1) of the Companies Act 1985.
The expression 'exercises functions' is defined in section 8.
By virtue of section 69(3), the term 'land' has the meaning given to it by section 205(1)(ix) of the Law of Property Act 1925 and by section 132(1) of the Land Registration Act 2002.
The term 'registered' is defined in section 67.
The expression 'the Registrar' means the Chief Land Registrar—see section 67.

This section is discussed in Section 3.7 of the text.

Ombudsman

42.—(1) Regulations may provide that a commonhold association shall be a member of an approved ombudsman scheme.

(2) An 'approved ombudsman scheme' is a scheme which is approved by the Lord Chancellor and which—
(a) provides for the appointment of one or more persons as ombudsman,
(b) provides for a person to be appointed as ombudsman only if the Lord Chancellor approves the appointment in advance,
(c) enables a unit-holder to refer to the ombudsman a dispute between the unit-holder and a commonhold association which is a member of the scheme,

(d) enables a commonhold association which is a member of the scheme to refer to the ombudsman a dispute between the association and a unit-holder,
(e) requires the ombudsman to investigate and determine a dispute referred to him,
(f) requires a commonhold association which is a member of the scheme to cooperate with the ombudsman in investigating or determining a dispute, and
(g) requires a commonhold association which is a member of the scheme to comply with any decision of the ombudsman (including any decision requiring the payment of money).

(3) In addition to the matters specified in subsection (2) an approved ombudsman scheme—
(a) may contain other provision, and
(b) shall contain such provision, or provision of such a kind, as may be prescribed.

(4) If a commonhold association fails to comply with regulations under subsection (1) a unit-holder may apply to the High Court for an order requiring the directors of the commonhold association to ensure that the association complies with the regulations.

(5) A reference in this section to a unit-holder includes a reference to a tenant of a unit.

Commentary

This section provides for regulations to be made requiring the commonhold association to be a member of an approved ombudsman scheme. The Government considers that such a requirement would be beneficial, and such regulations will be made. This section was brought into force on 29 September 2003 by the Commonhold and Leasehold Reform Act 2002 (Commencement No 3) Order 2003.

The expression 'commonhold association' is defined in section 34.
By virtue of section 69(3), the term 'director' has the meaning given to it by section 741(1) of the Companies Act 1985.
The expressions 'prescribed' and 'regulations' are defined and explained by section 64.
The term 'unit-holder' is defined in section 12.

This section is discussed in Section 6.7 of the text.

Termination: voluntary winding-up

Winding-up resolution

43.—(1) A winding-up resolution in respect of a commonhold association shall be of no effect unless—
(a) the resolution is preceded by a declaration of solvency,
(b) the commonhold association passes a termination-statement resolution before it passes the winding-up resolution, and
(c) each resolution is passed with at least 80 per cent. of the members of the association voting in favour.

(2) In this Part—
'declaration of solvency' means a directors' statutory declaration made in accordance with section 89 of the Insolvency Act 1986 (c 45),
'termination-statement resolution' means a resolution approving the terms of a termination statement (within the meaning of section 47), and

'winding-up resolution' means a resolution for voluntary winding-up within the meaning of section 84 of that Act.

Commentary

Sections 43 to 49 and section 56 provide for the termination of a commonhold association by voluntary winding-up and the de-registration of the relevant land as commonhold. These provisions will most commonly be relevant where the members of the association wish to sell the land for redevelopment. They enable the land to revert to a single freehold title. Winding-up by the court is dealt with in sections 50 to 54.

Section 43(1) sets out the three preconditions for a voluntary winding-up of the association. The directors must have made a statutory declaration that the association is solvent. At least 80 per cent of the members must have passed a termination-statement resolution, specifying the association's proposals for (a) the transfer of the commonhold land and (b) the distribution of the association's assets.

Section 89 of the Insolvency Act 1986 sets out the requirements for a statutory declaration of solvency: (a) its prescribed contents; (b) the time limit following the passing of the resolution for winding-up during which it must be made; (c) the requirement to deliver it to the registrar of companies; and (d) the duties and liabilities of the directors in making the declaration.

The expression 'commonhold association' is defined in section 34.

This section is discussed in paragraphs 5.2.3 and 5.2.4 of the text.

100 per cent agreement

44.—(1) This section applies where a commonhold association—

(a) has passed a winding-up resolution and a termination-statement resolution with 100 per cent of the members of the association voting in favour, and

(b) has appointed a liquidator under section 91 of the Insolvency Act 1986 (c 45).

(2) The liquidator shall make a termination application within the period of six months beginning with the day on which the winding-up resolution is passed.

(3) If the liquidator fails to make a termination application within the period specified in subsection (2) a termination application may be made by—

(a) a unit-holder, or

(b) a person falling within a class prescribed for the purposes of this subsection.

Commentary

This section sets out the process for making an application to the Chief Land Registrar that all the land in relation to which the commonhold association exercises functions should cease to be commonhold land, where (a) all the members of the commonhold association have voted unanimously in favour of a winding-up resolution and a termination-statement resolution, and (b) a liquidator has been appointed.

Section 91(1) of the Insolvency Act 1986 provides that in a voluntary winding-up a liquidator shall be appointed by the company in general meeting. Section 91(2) of that Act provides that on the appointment of a liquidator all the powers of the directors cease, except so far as the company in general meeting or the liquidator sanctions their continuance.

The duties of a liquidator once a termination application has been made under section 44 are set out in section 48.

The expression 'commonhold association' is defined in section 34.
The term 'prescribed' means prescribed by regulations—see section 64.
The expression 'the Registrar' means the Chief Land Registrar—see section 67(1).
The expression 'termination application' is defined in section 46.
The expressions 'termination-statement resolution' and 'winding-up resolution' are defined in section 43.
The term 'unit-holder' is defined in section 12.

This section is discussed in paragraphs 5.2.5 to 5.2.8 of the text.

80 per cent agreement

45.—(1) This section applies where a commonhold association—
 (a) has passed a winding-up resolution and a termination-statement resolution with at least 80 per cent of the members of the association voting in favour, and
 (b) has appointed a liquidator under section 91 of the Insolvency Act 1986.

(2) The liquidator shall within the prescribed period apply to the court for an order determining—
 (a) the terms and conditions on which a termination application may be made, and
 (b) the terms of the termination statement to accompany a termination application.

(3) The liquidator shall make a termination application within the period of three months starting with the date on which an order under subsection (2) is made.

(4) If the liquidator fails to make an application under subsection (2) or (3) within the period specified in that subsection an application of the same kind may be made by—
 (a) a unit-holder, or
 (b) a person falling within a class prescribed for the purposes of this subsection.

Commentary

This section sets out the process and preconditions for making an application to the Chief Land Registrar that all the land in relation to which the commonhold association exercises functions should cease to be commonhold land, where (a) at least 80 per cent of the members of the commonhold association have voted in favour of a winding-up resolution and a termination-statement resolution, and (b) a liquidator has been appointed. In contrast to the position where all the members have unanimously approved such resolutions (see section 44), the liquidator must obtain the court's approval of the terms and conditions on which the association may be terminated: section 45(2). Approval by 80 per cent of the members is the minimum for effecting a voluntary winding-up: section 43(1)(c).

Section 91(1) of the Insolvency Act 1986 provides that in a voluntary winding-up a liquidator shall be appointed by the company in general meeting. Section 91(2) of that Act provides that on the appointment all the powers of the liquidator cease, except so far as the company in general meeting or the liquidator sanctions their continuance.

The duties of a liquidator once a termination application has been made under section 45 are set out in section 48.

The expression 'commonhold association' is defined in section 34.
The term 'court' means the High Court or a county court—see section 66.
The term 'prescribed' means prescribed by regulations—see section 64.
The expression 'termination application' is defined in section 46.
The requirements for the contents of a 'termination statement' are set out in section 47.
The expressions 'termination-statement resolution' and 'winding-up resolution' are defined in section 43.
The term 'unit-holder' is defined in section 12.

This section is discussed in paragraph 5.2.8 of the text.

Termination application

46.—(1) A 'termination application' is an application to the Registrar that all the land in relation to which a particular commonhold association exercises functions should cease to be commonhold land.

(2) A termination application must be accompanied by a termination statement.

(3) On receipt of a termination application the Registrar shall note it in the register.

Commentary

This section sets out the nature of a termination application. The process and time limits for the making of a termination application are set out in sections 44 (agreement by 100 per cent of members) and 45 (agreement by at least 80 per cent of members).

The expression 'commonhold association' is defined in section 34.
The expression 'commonhold land' is defined in section 1.
The expression 'exercises functions' is defined in section 8.
By virtue of section 69(3), the term 'land' has the meaning given to it by section 205(1)(ix) of the Law of Property Act 1925 and by section 132(1) of the Land Registration Act 2002.
The term 'register' is defined in section 67.
The expression 'the Registrar' means the Chief Land Registrar—see section 67(1).
The requirements for the contents of a 'termination statement' are set out in section 47.

This section is discussed in Section 5.2 of the text.

Termination statement

47.—(1) A termination statement must specify—

(a) the commonhold association's proposals for the transfer of the commonhold land following acquisition of the freehold estate in accordance with section 49(3), and

(b) how the assets of the commonhold association will be distributed.

(2) A commonhold community statement may make provision requiring any termination statement to make arrangements—

(a) of a specified kind, or

(b) determined in a specified manner,

about the rights of unit-holders in the event of all the land to which the statement relates ceasing to be commonhold land.

(3) A termination statement must comply with a provision made by the commonhold community statement in reliance on subsection (2).

(4) Subsection (3) may be disapplied by an order of the court—
  (a) generally,
  (b) in respect of specified matters, or
  (c) for a specified purpose.

(5) An application for an order under subsection (4) may be made by any member of the commonhold association.

Commentary

This section defines a termination statement, and sets out the requirements for its contents. A termination statement must accompany a termination application (an application to the Chief Land Registrar that the relevant land should cease to be commonhold land): section 46(2).

The general provisions as to the form and content of the commonhold community statement are contained in sections 31 and 32. Section 33 enables amendment of the commonhold community statement, which will be relevant where the original statement makes no, or unsatisfactory, provision for the termination of the association.

The expression 'commonhold association' is defined in section 34.
The expression 'commonhold community statement' is defined in section 31.
The expression 'commonhold land' is defined in section 1.
The term 'court' means the High Court or a county court—see section 66.
By virtue of section 69(3), the term 'land' has the meaning given to it by section 205(1)(ix) of the Law of Property Act 1925 and by section 132(1) of the Land Registration Act 2002.
The term 'unit-holder' is defined in section 12.

This section is discussed in paragraph 5.2.4 of the text.

The liquidator

48.—(1) This section applies where a termination application has been made in respect of particular commonhold land.

(2) The liquidator shall notify the Registrar of his appointment.

(3) In the case of a termination application made under section 44 the liquidator shall either—
  (a) notify the Registrar that the liquidator is content with the termination statement submitted with the termination application, or
  (b) apply to the court under section 112 of the Insolvency Act 1986 (c 45) to determine the terms of the termination statement.

(4) The liquidator shall send to the Registrar a copy of a determination made by virtue of subsection (3)(b).

(5) Subsection (4) is in addition to any requirement under section 112(3) of the Insolvency Act 1986.

(6) A duty imposed on the liquidator by this section is to be performed as soon as possible.

(7) In this section a reference to the liquidator is a reference—
 (a) to the person who is appointed as liquidator under section 91 of the Insolvency Act 1986, or
 (b) in the case of a members' voluntary winding up which becomes a creditors' voluntary winding up by virtue of sections 95 and 96 of that Act, to the person acting as liquidator in accordance with section 100 of that Act.

Commentary

This section sets out the duties of a liquidator once a termination application has been made under sections 44 to 46 (an application that the relevant land should cease to be commonhold land).

Section 48(3) to (5) makes particular provision for the case where the winding-up resolution and the termination-statement resolution have been unanimously passed by all the members of the association: see section 44. (Where such resolutions have been passed by at least 80 per cent, but fewer than 100 per cent, of members, section 45(2) requires the liquidator to apply to the court for an order determining (a) the terms and conditions on which a determination application may be made, and (b) the terms of the accompanying termination statement.)

Section 91(1) of the Insolvency Act 1986 provides that in a voluntary winding-up a liquidator shall be appointed by the company in general meeting. Section 91(2) of that Act provides that on the appointment all the powers of the liquidator cease, except so far as the company in general meeting or the liquidator sanctions their continuance.

Section 112(1) of the Insolvency Act 1986 gives power to the liquidator (and any contributory or creditor) to apply to the court (a) to determine any question arising in the winding up of a company, or (b) to exercise, as respects the enforcing of calls or any other matter, all or any of the powers which the court might exercise if the company were being wound up by the court. The court is given the power under section 112(2) to (a) accede wholly or partially to the application on such terms and conditions as it thinks fit, or (b) make such other order on the application as it thinks fit, provided that the court is satisfied that the determination of the question or the required exercise of power will be just and beneficial. Section 112(3) requires that if an order is made under section 112 staying the proceedings in the winding up, a copy of the order must forthwith be forwarded by the company to the registrar of companies (who must enter it in his records relating to the company).

The expression 'commonhold land' is defined in section 1.
The term 'court' means the High Court or a county court—see section 66.
The expression 'the Registrar' means the Chief Land Registrar—see section 67.
The expression 'termination application' is defined in section 46.
The requirements for the contents of a 'termination statement' are set out in section 47.

This section is discussed in Section 5.2 of the text.

Termination

49.—(1) This section applies where a termination application is made under section 44 and—
 (a) a liquidator notifies the Registrar under section 48(3)(a) that he is content with a termination statement, or

(b) a determination is made under section 112 of the Insolvency Act 1986 (c 45) by virtue of section 48(3)(b).

(2) This section also applies where a termination application is made under section 45.

(3) The commonhold association shall by virtue of this subsection be entitled to be registered as the proprietor of the freehold estate in each commonhold unit.

(4) The Registrar shall take such action as appears to him to be appropriate for the purpose of giving effect to the termination statement.

Commentary

This section provides that once the termination application has been made, and the liquidator has performed his relevant statutory duties, the commonhold association is entitled to be registered as the proprietor of the freehold estate in each commonhold unit. The Chief Land Registrar must also take appropriate action to give effect to the termination statement. This process will generally result in the land reverting to a single standard freehold title.

The expression 'commonhold association' is defined in section 34.
The expression 'commonhold unit' is defined in section 11.
The term 'registered' is defined in section 67.
The expression 'the Registrar' means the Chief Land Registrar—see section 67.
The expression 'termination application' is defined in section 46.
The requirements for the contents of a 'termination statement' are set out in section 47.

This section is discussed in Section 5.2 of the text.

Termination: winding-up by the court

Introduction

50.—(1) Section 51 applies where a petition is presented under section 124 of the Insolvency Act 1986 for the winding up of a commonhold association by the court.

(2) For the purposes of this Part—

(a) an 'insolvent commonhold association' is one in relation to which a winding-up petition has been presented under section 124 of the Insolvency Act 1986,

(b) a commonhold association is the 'successor commonhold association' to an insolvent commonhold association if the land specified for the purpose of section 34(1)(a) is the same for both associations, and

(c) a 'winding-up order' is an order under section 125 of the Insolvency Act 1986 for the winding up of a commonhold association.

Commentary

As a company limited by guarantee, a commonhold association may be compulsorily wound-up by the court in accordance with the provisions of Chapter VI of the Insolvency Act 1986. That is most likely to be relevant where the association is unable to pay its debts. Sections 122 and 123 of the Insolvency Act 1986 set out the circumstances in which a company may be wound-up by the court; section 124 deals with the application (by petition) for winding-up; and section 125 sets out the powers of the court on hearing the petition. Sections 50 to 54 of the 2002 Act contain additional provisions relating to the compulsory winding-up of a commonhold association. Sections 50 to 53 give the court an additional power to make a 'succession order', which allows a successor commonhold association to be registered as the freehold proprietor of the common parts, and take over their management. Section 54 provides for the termination of the commonhold where the court does not make a succession order.

Section 50 provides that the court has the power to make a succession order (under section 51) where a petition for the winding-up of a commonhold association is presented under section 124 of the Insolvency Act 1986.

Section 124 of the Insolvency Act 1986 provides for an application to the court for the winding-up of a company to be made by a petition presented by (a) the company; (b) the directors; (c) any creditor(s) (including any contingent or prospective creditor(s)); (d) any contributory(ies); (e) by all or any of such persons, together or separately; or (f) by the Secretary of State on grounds of public interest. Section 122 of the Insolvency Act 1986 provides that the circumstances in which a company may be wound-up by the court include where the company is unable to pay its debts, and where the court is of the opinion that it is just and equitable that the company should be wound-up.

Section 34(1)(a) requires the memorandum of a commonhold association to state that an object of the company is to exercise the functions of a commonhold association in relation to specified commonhold land.

The court also has power to wind-up a commonhold association where a commonhold has been registered in contravention of the requirements of the Act or of provisions made under it (see section 6, especially 6(5) and 6(6)(c), and section 55); and where the memorandum or articles of association or the community statement do not comply with the requirements of the Act or the regulations (see section 40, especially 40(2) and 40(3)(d), and section 55). Provision for a voluntary winding-up is made by sections 43 to 49 and section 56.

The expression 'commonhold association' is defined in section 34.

By virtue of section 69(3), the term 'land' has the meaning given to it by section 205(1)(ix) of the Law of Property Act 1925 and by section 132(1) of the Land Registration Act 2002.

This section is discussed in Section 6.17 of the text.

Succession order

51.—(1) At the hearing of the winding-up petition an application may be made to the court for an order under this section (a 'succession order') in relation to the insolvent commonhold association.

(2) An application under subsection (1) may be made only by—
(a) the insolvent commonhold association,
(b) one or more members of the insolvent commonhold association, or
(c) a provisional liquidator for the insolvent commonhold association appointed under section 135 of the Insolvency Act 1986.

(3) An application under subsection (1) must be accompanied by—
(a) prescribed evidence of the formation of a successor commonhold association, and

(b) a certificate given by the directors of the successor commonhold association that its memorandum and articles of association comply with regulations under paragraph 2(1) of Schedule 3.

(4) The court shall grant an application under subsection (1) unless it thinks that the circumstances of the insolvent commonhold association make a succession order inappropriate.

Commentary

A succession order allows a successor commonhold association to be registered as the freehold proprietor of the common parts, and take over their management, where the original commonhold association is compulsorily wound up by the court. This section sets out (a) who may apply for a succession order, (b) when they may do so (see also section 50(1)), (c) what documentation must be provided in support of such an application; and (d) when the court may refuse to make a succession order. The required contents of a succession order are set out in section 52(4).

The expression 'commonhold association' is defined in section 34.
The term 'court' means the High Court or a county court—see section 66.
By virtue of section 69(3), the term 'director' has the meaning given to it by section 741(1) of the Companies Act 1985.
The expression 'insolvent commonhold association' is defined in section 50(2)(a).
The expressions 'prescribed' and 'regulations' are defined and explained by section 64.
The expression 'successor commonhold association' is explained in sections 50, 51 and 52.

This section is discussed in Section 5.4 of the text.

Assets and liabilities

52.—(1) Where a succession order is made in relation to an insolvent commonhold association this section applies on the making of a winding-up order in respect of the association.

(2) The successor commonhold association shall be entitled to be registered as the proprietor of the freehold estate in the common parts.

(3) The insolvent commonhold association shall for all purposes cease to be treated as the proprietor of the freehold estate in the common parts.

(4) The succession order—

(a) shall make provision as to the treatment of any charge over all or any part of the common parts;

(b) may require the Registrar to take action of a specified kind;

(c) may enable the liquidator to require the Registrar to take action of a specified kind;

(d) may make supplemental or incidental provision.

Commentary

This section (a) provides for the successor commonhold association to be registered as the proprietor of the freehold estate in the common parts in place of the wound-up association; and (b) sets out the consequential provisions which the succession order should make.

Provision for succession to the management responsibilities of the association is made in section 53.

The expression 'common parts' is defined in section 25.
The expression 'commonhold association' is defined in section 34.
The expression 'insolvent commonhold association' is defined in section 50(2)(a).
The term 'registered' is defined in section 67.
The expression 'the Registrar' means the Chief Land Registrar—see section 67.
The expression 'succession order' is defined in section 51.
The expression 'successor commonhold association' is explained in sections 50, 51 and 52.
The expression 'winding-up order' is defined in section 50(2)(c).

This section is discussed in Section 5.4 of the text.

Transfer of responsibility

53.—(1) Where a succession order is made in relation to an insolvent commonhold association this section applies on the making of a winding-up order in respect of the association.

(2) The successor commonhold association shall be treated as the commonhold association for the commonhold in respect of any matter which relates to a time after the making of the winding-up order.

(3) On the making of the winding-up order the court may make an order requiring the liquidator to make available to the successor commonhold association specified—
  (a) records;
  (b) copies of records;
  (c) information.

(4) An order under subsection (3) may include terms as to—
  (a) timing;
  (b) payment.

Commentary

This section provides for the successor commonhold association to be treated as the commonhold association from the date of the order, and to take over the management responsibilities and the records of the wound-up association. Provision for succession to the proprietorship of the freehold estate in the common parts is made in section 52.

The expression 'commonhold association' is defined in section 34.
The term 'court' means the High Court or a county court—see section 66.
The expression 'insolvent commonhold association' is defined in section 50(2)(a).
The expression 'succession order' is defined in section 51.
The expression 'successor commonhold association' is explained in sections 50, 51 and 52.
The expression 'winding-up order' is defined in section 50(2)(c).

This section is discussed in paragraph 5.4.7 of the text.

Termination of commonhold

54.—(1) This section applies where the court—
  (a) makes a winding-up order in respect of a commonhold association, and
  (b) has not made a succession order in respect of the commonhold association.

(2) The liquidator of a commonhold association shall as soon as possible notify the Registrar of—
  (a) the fact that this section applies,
  (b) any directions given under section 168 of the Insolvency Act 1986 (c 45) (liquidator: supplementary powers),
  (c) any notice given to the court and the registrar of companies in accordance with section 172(8) of that Act (liquidator vacating office after final meeting),
  (d) any notice given to the Secretary of State under section 174(3) of that Act (completion of winding-up),
  (e) any application made to the registrar of companies under section 202(2) of that Act (insufficient assets: early dissolution),
  (f) any notice given to the registrar of companies under section 205(1)(b) of that Act (completion of winding-up), and
  (g) any other matter which in the liquidator's opinion is relevant to the Registrar.

(3) Notification under subsection (2)(b) to (f) must be accompanied by a copy of the directions, notice or application concerned.

(4) The Registrar shall—
  (a) make such arrangements as appear to him to be appropriate for ensuring that the freehold estate in land in respect of which a commonhold association exercises functions ceases to be registered as a freehold estate in commonhold land as soon as is reasonably practicable after he receives notification under subsection (2)(c) to (f), and
  (b) take such action as appears to him to be appropriate for the purpose of giving effect to a determination made by the liquidator in the exercise of his functions.

Commentary

This section provides for the termination of the commonhold where the court winds up a commonhold association but does not make a succession order under sections 50 to 53. Section 51(4) sets out when the court can refuse to make a succession order.

Sections 54(2) and (3) sets out the duties of the liquidator. Section 54(4) sets out the duties of the Chief Land Registrar.

Section 168(3) of the Insolvency Act 1986 gives the liquidator the power to apply to the court for directions in relation to any particular matter arising in the winding-up.

Section 172(8) of the Insolvency Act 1986 provides that where a final meeting has been held under section 146 of that Act (liquidator's duty to summon final meeting when winding up for practical purposes complete), the liquidator whose report was considered at the meeting must vacate office as soon as he has given notice to the court and the registrar of companies that the meeting has been held, and of the decisions (if any) of the meeting.

Section 174(3) of the Insolvency Act 1986 provides that if the official receiver while he is a liquidator gives notice to the Secretary of State that the winding-up is for practical purposes complete, he has his release with effect from such time as the Secretary of State determines.

Section 202(2) of the Insolvency Act 1986 provides that the official receiver may at any time apply to the registrar of companies for the early dissolution of a company if: (a) he is the liquidator of the company; and (b) it appears to him that (i) the realisable assets of the company are insufficient to cover the expenses of the winding-up, and that (ii) the affairs of the company do not require any further investigation.

Section 205(1)(b) deals with the receipt by the registrar of companies of a notice from the official receiver that the winding-up of a company by the court is complete.

The expression 'commonhold association' is defined in section 34.
The expression 'commonhold land' is defined in section 1.
The term 'court' means the High Court or a county court—see section 66.
The expression 'exercises functions' is defined in section 8.
By virtue of section 69(3), the term 'land' has the meaning given to it by section 205(1)(ix) of the Law of Property Act 1925 and by section 132(1) of the Land Registration Act 2002.
The term 'registered' is defined in section 67.
The expression 'the Registrar' means the Chief Land Registrar—see section 67.
The expression 'succession order' is defined in section 51.
The expression 'winding-up order' is defined in section 50(2)(c).

This section is discussed in Section 5.5 of the text.

Termination: miscellaneous

Termination by court

55.—(1) This section applies where the court makes an order by virtue of section 6(6)(c) or 40(3)(d) for all the land in relation to which a commonhold association exercises functions to cease to be commonhold land.

(2) The court shall have the powers which it would have if it were making a winding-up order in respect of the commonhold association.

(3) A person appointed as liquidator by virtue of subsection (2) shall have the powers and duties of a liquidator following the making of a winding-up order by the court in respect of a commonhold association.

(4) But the order of the court by virtue of section 6(6)(c) or 40(3)(d) may—
   (a) require the liquidator to exercise his functions in a particular way;
   (b) impose additional rights or duties on the liquidator;
   (c) modify or remove a right or duty of the liquidator.

Commentary

This section sets out the powers of the court and the liquidator where the court has decided to terminate the commonhold under section 6(6)(c) (where a commonhold has been registered in contravention of the requirements of the Act or of provisions made under it), or under section 40(3)(d) (where the memorandum or articles of association or the commonhold community statement do not comply with the requirements of the Act or the regulations).

The expression 'commonhold association' is defined in section 34.
The expression 'commonhold land' is defined in section 1.
The term 'court' means the High Court or a county court—see section 66.
The expression 'exercises functions' is defined in section 8.
By virtue of section 69(3), the term 'land' has the meaning given to it by section 205(1)(ix) of the Law of Property Act 1925 and by section 132(1) of the Land Registration Act 2002.
The expression 'winding-up order' is defined in section 50(2)(c).

This section is discussed in paragraph 2.27.3 of the text.

Release of reserve fund

56. Section 39(4) shall cease to have effect in relation to a commonhold association (in respect of debts and liabilities accruing at any time) if—

(a) the court makes a winding-up order in respect of the association,
(b) the association passes a voluntary winding-up resolution, or
(c) the court makes an order by virtue of section 6(6)(c) or 40(3)(d) for all the land in relation to which the association exercises functions to cease to be commonhold land.

Commentary

Section 39(4) provides that the assets of a reserve fund established under section 39 may not be used for the enforcement of any debt except a judgment debt referable to a reserve fund activity. This section provides that that restriction will no longer apply if the association is wound-up, or terminated in a similar way pursuant to sections 6(6)(c) or 40(3)(d). The court has power under sections 6(6)(c) or 40(3)(d) to terminate the commonhold where a commonhold has been registered in contravention of the requirements of the Act or of provisions made under it, or where the memorandum or articles of association or the commonhold community statement do not comply with the requirements of the Act or the regulations: see also the powers of the court under section 55.

The expression 'commonhold association' is defined in section 34.
The expression 'commonhold land' is defined in section 1.
The term 'court' means the High Court or a county court—see section 66.
The expression 'exercises functions' is defined in section 8.
By virtue of section 69(3), the term 'land' has the meaning given to it by section 205(1)(ix) of the Law of Property Act 1925 and by section 132(1) of the Land Registration Act 2002.
The expression 'winding-up order' is defined in section 50(2)(c).
The expression 'winding-up resolution' is defined in section 43.

This section is discussed in paragraphs 5.2.10 and 5.5.10 of the text.

Miscellaneous

Multiple site commonholds

57.—(1) A commonhold may include two or more parcels of land, whether or not contiguous.

(2) But section 1(1) of this Act is not satisfied in relation to land specified in the memorandum of association of a commonhold association unless a single commonhold community statement makes provision for all the land.

(3) Regulations may make provision about an application under section 2 made jointly by two or more persons, each of whom is the registered freeholder of part of the land to which the application relates.

(4) The regulations may, in particular—
(a) modify the application of a provision made by or by virtue of this Part;
(b) disapply the application of a provision made by or by virtue of this Part;
(c) impose additional requirements.

Commentary

This section deals with two quite separate topics. First (subsections (1) and (2)), it provides that the commonhold may include geographically separate areas of land (just as a commonhold unit may—see section 11(3)(d)), so long as one commonhold community statement covers all the areas.

Secondly (subsections (3 and (4)), it provides for regulations to make provision 'about' a joint application to register a freehold estate in commonhold land to be made in respect of land held in different ownerships. The Government's current intention, however, is to require any application for the registration of a multiple site commonhold to be preceded by an amalgamation of the titles affected.

The expression 'a commonhold' is defined in section 1.
The expression 'commonhold association' is defined in section 34.
The expression 'commonhold community statement' is defined in section 31.
By virtue of section 69(3), the term 'land' has the meaning given to it by section 205(1)(ix) of the Law of Property Act 1925 and by section 132(1) of the Land Registration Act 2002.
The term 'registered' is defined in section 67.
The expression 'registered freeholder' is defined in section 2.
The term 'regulations' is explained in section 64.

This section is discussed in paragraph 2.2.2 of the text.

Development rights

58.—(1) In this Part—

"the developer' means a person who makes an application under section 2, and
"development business' has the meaning given by Schedule 4.

(2) A commonhold community statement may confer rights on the developer which are designed—
(a) to permit him to undertake development business, or
(b) to facilitate his undertaking of development business.

(3) Provision made by a commonhold community statement in reliance on subsection (2) may include provision—
(a) requiring the commonhold association or a unit-holder to co-operate with the developer for a specified purpose connected with development business;
(b) making the exercise of a right conferred by virtue of subsection (2) subject to terms and conditions specified in or to be determined in accordance with the commonhold community statement;
(c) making provision about the effect of breach of a requirement by virtue of paragraph (a) or a term or condition imposed by virtue of paragraph (b);
(d) disapplying section 41(2) and (3).

(4) Subsection (2) is subject—
(a) to regulations under section 32, and
(b) in the case of development business of the kind referred to in paragraph 7 of Schedule 4, to the memorandum and articles of association of the commonhold association.

(5) Regulations may make provision regulating or restricting the exercise of rights conferred by virtue of subsection (2).

(6) Where a right is conferred on a developer by virtue of subsection (2), if he sends to the Registrar a notice surrendering the right—
   (a) the Registrar shall arrange for the notice to be kept in his custody and referred to in the register,
   (b) the right shall cease to be exercisable from the time when the notice is registered under paragraph (a), and
   (c) the Registrar shall inform the commonhold association as soon as is reasonably practicable.

Commentary

This section sets out the rights given to a developer of a commonhold community between (i) the creation of the commonhold and the sale of the first unit, and (ii) the sale of the last unit and the disengagement of the developer. The granting of such rights is intended to allow the developer some continued freedom and flexibility in completing the development. Section 59 deals with the development rights of a successor to the original developer.

The expression 'commonhold association' is defined in section 34.
The expression 'commonhold community statement' is defined in section 31.
The term 'register' is defined in section 67.
The expression 'the Registrar' means the Chief Land Registrar—see section 67.
The term 'regulations' is explained in section 64.
The term 'unit-holder' is defined in section 12.

This section is discussed in Section 2.19 of the text.

Development rights: succession

59.—(1) If during a transitional period the developer transfers to another person the freehold estate in the whole of the commonhold, the successor in title shall be treated as the developer in relation to any matter arising after the transfer.

(2) If during a transitional period the developer transfers to another person the freehold estate in part of the commonhold, the successor in title shall be treated as the developer for the purpose of any matter which—
   (a) arises after the transfer, and
   (b) affects the estate transferred.

(3) If after a transitional period or in a case where there is no transitional period—
   (a) the developer transfers to another person the freehold estate in the whole or part of the commonhold (other than by the transfer of the freehold estate in a single commonhold unit), and
   (b) the transfer is expressed to be inclusive of development rights,

   the successor in title shall be treated as the developer for the purpose of any matter which arises after the transfer and affects the estate transferred.

(4) Other than during a transitional period, a person shall not be treated as the developer in relation to commonhold land for any purpose unless he—

(a) is, or has been at a particular time, the registered proprietor of the freehold estate in more than one of the commonhold units, and
(b) is the registered proprietor of the freehold estate in at least one of the commonhold units.

Commentary

This section sets out the development rights (see section 58) of a successor to the original developer.

The expression 'commonhold land' is defined in section 1.
The expression 'commonhold unit' is defined in section 11.
The term 'developer' is defined in section 58.
The term 'registered' is defined in section 67.
The expression 'transitional period' is defined in section 8.

Development rights are discussed in Section 2.19 of the text.

Compulsory purchase

60.—(1) Where a freehold estate in commonhold land is transferred to a compulsory purchaser the land shall cease to be commonhold land.

(2) But subsection (1) does not apply to a transfer if the Registrar is satisfied that the compulsory purchaser has indicated a desire for the land transferred to continue to be commonhold land.

(3) The requirement of consent under section 21(2)(c) shall not apply to transfer to a compulsory purchaser.

(4) Regulations may make provision about the transfer of a freehold estate in commonhold land to a compulsory purchaser.

(5) The regulations may, in particular—
(a) make provision about the effect of subsections (1) and (2) (including provision about that part of the commonhold which is not transferred);
(b) require the service of notice;
(c) confer power on a court;
(d) make provision about compensation;
(e) make provision enabling a commonhold association to require a compulsory purchaser to acquire the freehold estate in the whole, or a particular part, of the commonhold;
(f) provide for an enactment relating to compulsory purchase not to apply or to apply with modifications.

(6) Provision made by virtue of subsection (5)(a) in respect of land which is not transferred may include provision—
(a) for some or all of the land to cease to be commonhold land;
(b) for a provision of this Part to apply with specified modifications.

(7) In this section 'compulsory purchaser' means—
(a) a person acquiring land in respect of which he is authorised to exercise a power of compulsory purchase by virtue of an enactment, and

(b) a person acquiring land which he is obliged to acquire by virtue of a prescribed enactment or in prescribed circumstances.

Commentary

This section sets out the consequences following from the compulsory purchase of commonhold land.

The expression 'commonhold association' is defined in section 34.
The expression 'commonhold land' is defined in section 1.
The expression 'commonhold unit' is defined in section 11.
The term 'court' means the High Court or a county court—see section 66.
By virtue of section 69(3), the term 'land' has the meaning given to it by section 205(1)(ix) of the Law of Property Act 1925 and by section 132(1) of the Land Registration Act 2002.
The expressions 'prescribed' and 'regulations' are defined and explained by section 64.
The expression 'the Registrar' means the Chief Land Registrar—see section 67.
The term 'unit-holder' is defined in section 12.

This section is discussed in Section 5.6 and paragraph 3.8.1 of the text.

Matrimonial rights

61. In the following provisions of this Part a reference to a tenant includes a reference to a person who has matrimonial home rights (within the meaning of section 30(2) of the Family Law Act 1996 (c 27) (matrimonial home)) in respect of a commonhold unit—
(a) section 19,
(b) section 35, and
(c) section 37.

Commentary

This gives the spouse of a tenant of a commonhold unit the like rights and obligations as the tenant. Section 19 deals with obligations imposed on the tenants of commonhold units by regulations or by the commonhold community statement. Section 35 deals with the directors' duty to manage, including the exercise of their powers in relation to tenants of commonhold units. Section 37 deals with the enforcement of rights or duties imposed by regulations, a commonhold community statement, or by the memorandum or articles of association.

The expression 'commonhold unit' is defined in section 11.

Advice

62.—(1) The Lord Chancellor may give financial assistance to a person in relation to the provision by that person of general advice about an aspect of the law of commonhold land, so far as relating to residential matters.

(2) Financial assistance under this section may be given in such form and on such terms as the Lord Chancellor thinks appropriate.

(3) The terms may, in particular, require repayment in specified circumstances.

Commentary

The expression 'commonhold land' is defined in section 1. This section was brought into force on 29 September 2003 by the Commonhold and Leasehold Reform Act 2002 (Commencement No 3) Order 2003.

The Crown

63. This Part binds the Crown.

General

Orders and regulations

64.—(1) In this Part 'prescribed' means prescribed by regulations.

(2) Regulations under this Part shall be made by the Lord Chancellor.

(3) Regulations under this Part—
- (a) shall be made by statutory instrument,
- (b) may include incidental, supplemental, consequential and transitional provision,
- (c) may make provision generally or only in relation to specified cases,
- (d) may make different provision for different purposes, and
- (e) shall be subject to annulment in pursuance of a resolution of either House of Parliament.

Commentary

This section adds to the regulation-making power in section 32. Such regulations are to be distinguished from the land registration rules which the Lord Chancellor is entitled to make under section 65, dealing with commonhold registration procedure.

A Consultation Paper seeking views on draft regulations was produced by the Lord Chancellor's Department 2 September 2002. The consultation period ended on 6 January 2003 and the Department of Constitutional Affairs (which has succeeded the Lord Chancellor's Department) produced a Post-Consultation Report in August 2003, which forecasts that regulations (now in draft form) will be made by the Lord Chancellor and laid before Parliament before the end of 2003. This section itself was brought into force on 29 September 2003 by the Commonhold and Leasehold Reform Act 2002 (Commencement No 3) Order 2003.

Registration procedure

65.—(1) The Lord Chancellor may make rules about—
- (a) the procedure to be followed on or in respect of commonhold registration documents, and
- (b) the registration of freehold estates in commonhold land.

(2) Rules under this section—
- (a) shall be made by statutory instrument in the same manner as land registration rules within the meaning of the Land Registration Act 2002 (c 9),
- (b) may make provision for any matter for which provision is or may be made by land registration rules, and

(c) may provide for land registration rules to have effect in relation to anything done by virtue of or for the purposes of this Part as they have effect in relation to anything done by virtue of or for the purposes of that Act.

(3) Rules under this section may, in particular, make provision—
 (a) about the form and content of a commonhold registration document;
 (b) enabling the Registrar to cancel an application by virtue of this Part in specified circumstances;
 (c) enabling the Registrar, in particular, to cancel an application by virtue of this Part if he thinks that plans submitted with it (whether as part of a commonhold community statement or otherwise) are insufficiently clear or accurate;
 (d) about the order in which commonhold registration documents and general registration documents are to be dealt with by the Registrar;
 (e) for registration to take effect (whether or not retrospectively) as from a date or time determined in accordance with the rules.

(4) The rules may also make provision about satisfaction of a requirement for an application by virtue of this Part to be accompanied by a document; in particular the rules may—
 (a) permit or require a copy of a document to be submitted in place of or in addition to the original;
 (b) require a copy to be certified in a specified manner;
 (c) permit or require the submission of a document in electronic form.

(5) A commonhold registration document must be accompanied by such fee (if any) as is specified for that purpose by order under section 102 of the Land Registration Act 2002 (c 9)(fee orders).

(6) In this section—
 "commonhold registration document' means an application or other document sent to the Registrar by virtue of this Part, and
 "general registration document' means a document sent to the Registrar under a provision of the Land Registration Act 2002.

Commentary

This section provides for rules to be made by statutory instrument concerning commonhold land registration procedure. These rules are to be distinguished from the regulations concerning commonhold generally which the Lord Chancellor is also entitled to make by statutory instrument (see section 64). A Consultation Paper seeking views on draft rules was produced by the Land Registry on 2 September 2002. The consultation period ended on 22 November 2002, and the draft rules, revised in the light of the responses received, were put in front of the Rules Committee at the end of March 2003. It is not expected that the rules will be made by the Minister and laid before Parliament until the commonhold regulations (see section 64 above) are more advanced.

This section was brought into force on 29 September 2003 by the Commonhold and Leasehold Reform Act 2002 (Commencement No 3) Order 2003.

The expression 'commonhold community statement' is defined in section 31.
The expression 'commonhold land' is defined in section 1.
The term 'court' means the High Court or a county court—see section 66.

The expression 'the Registrar' means the Chief Land Registrar—see section 67.

This section is discussed in paragraph 2.3.2 of the text.

Jurisdiction

66.—(1) In this Part 'the court' means the High Court or a county court.

(2) Provision made by or under this Part conferring jurisdiction on a court shall be subject to provision made under section 1 of the Courts and Legal Services Act 1990 (c. 41) (allocation of business between High Court and county courts).

(3) A power under this Part to confer jurisdiction on a court includes power to confer jurisdiction on a tribunal established under an enactment.

(4) Rules of court or rules of procedure for a tribunal may make provision about proceedings brought—

(a) under or by virtue of any provision of this Part, or

(b) in relation to commonhold land.

Commentary

This section deals with a number of matters to do with litigation of disputes under the Act.

First, subsections (1) and (2) explain that references in the Act to 'the court' are to both the High Court and the county courts, with the allocation between those courts depending upon the factors set out in section 1 of the Courts and Legal Services Act 1990. The High Court is given exclusive jurisdiction, uniquely, in relation to the unit-holders's right to seek the court's assistance with the ombudsman scheme under section 42(4).

Secondly, subsection (3) provides that the power to confer jurisdiction on a court may also be used to confer jurisdiction on a statutory tribunal (the obvious candidates for this post being the Lands Tribunal and the Leasehold Valuation Tribunal).

Thirdly, subsection (4) allows for rules of court or procedure to be made concerning proceedings regarding the Act or in relation to commonhold land. This section itself was brought into force on 29 September 2003 by the Commonhold and Leasehold Reform Act 2002 (Commencement No 3) Order 2003, but no such rules have yet been promulgated or formulated.

The expression 'commonhold land' is defined in section 1.

This section is discussed in Sections 6.18 and 6.19 of the text.

The register

67.—(1) In this Part—

'the register' means the register of title to freehold and leasehold land kept under section 1 of the Land Registration Act 2002,

'registered' means registered in the register, and

'the Registrar' means the Chief Land Registrar.

(2) Regulations under any provision of this Part may confer functions on the Registrar (including discretionary functions).

(3) The Registrar shall comply with any direction or requirement given to him or imposed on him under or by virtue of this Part.

(4) Where the Registrar thinks it appropriate in consequence of or for the purpose of anything done or proposed to be done in connection with this Part, he may—
  (a) make or cancel an entry on the register;
  (b) take any other action.

(5) Subsection (4) is subject to section 6(2).

Commentary

This section consolidates earlier references to the duties and powers of the Chief Land Registrar and introduces the regulation-making power which will be the source of those duties and powers. This section was brought into force on 29 September 2003 by the Commonhold and Leasehold Reform Act 2002 (Commencement No 3) Order 2003.

The term 'regulations' is explained in section 64.

This section is discussed in Part 6 of Chapter 2 of the text.

Amendments

68. Schedule 5 (consequential amendments) shall have effect.

Commentary

This section refers to a number of consequential amendments to sections of other statutes.

Interpretation

69.—(1) In this Part—

'instrument' includes any document, and

'object' in relation to a commonhold association means an object stated in the association's memorandum of association in accordance with section 2(1)(c) of the Companies Act 1985 (c 6).

(2) In this Part—
  (a) a reference to a duty to insure includes a reference to a duty to use the proceeds of insurance for the purpose of rebuilding or reinstating, and
  (b) a reference to maintaining property includes a reference to decorating it and to putting it into sound condition.

(3) A provision of the Law of Property Act 1925 (c 20), the Companies Act 1985 (c 6) or the Land Registration Act 2002 (c 9) defining an expression shall apply to the use of the expression in this Part unless the contrary intention appears.

Commentary

This section has three functions. First, subsection (1) defines 'instrument' to mean 'any document' (in contrast to the exclusionary definition in section 205(1)(viii) of the Law of Property Act 1925, which is potentially wider); and 'object' by reference to section 2(1)(c) of the Companies Act 1985 (reprinted at the end of this Act). The express definition of 'object' would appear to be superfluous in view of subsection (3).

Secondly, subsection (2) amplifies the ambit of the insurance and maintenance obligations.

Thirdly, subsection (3) assigns the original statutory meanings to expressions from the Law of Property Act 1925 and the Companies Act 1985 used in the Act, save where otherwise specified.

In so far as it relates to sections 42, 62, 64, 65, 66 and 67, this section was brought into force on 29 September 2003 by the Commonhold and Leasehold Reform Act 2002 (Commencement No 3) Order 2003.

The expression 'commonhold association' is defined in section 34.

Index of defined expressions

70. In this Part the expressions listed below are defined by the provisions specified.

Expression	**Interpretation provision**
Common parts	Section 25
A commonhold	Section 1
Commonhold association	Section 34
Commonhold community statement	Section 31
Commonhold land	Section 1
Commonhold unit	Section 11
Court	Section 66
Declaration of solvency	Section 43
Developer	Section 58
Development business	Section 58
Exercising functions	Section 8
Insolvent commonhold association	Section 50
Instrument	Section 69
Insure	Section 69
Joint unit-holder	Section 13
Liquidator (sections 44 to 49)	Section 44
Maintenance	Section 69
Object	Section 69
Prescribed	Section 64
The register	Section 67
Registered	Section 67
Registered freeholder	Section 2
The Registrar	Section 67
Regulations	Section 64
Residential commonhold unit	Section 17
Succession order	Section 51
Successor commonhold association	Section 50

Expression	Interpretation provision
Termination application	Section 46
Termination-statement resolution	Section 43
Transfer (of unit)	Section 15
Transitional period	Section 8
Unit-holder	Section 12
Winding-up resolution	Section 43

Commentary

This section collates for convenience the majority of the expressions which are defined for the purposes of Part 1 of the Act.

In so far as it relates to sections 42, 62, 64, 65, 66 and 67, this section was brought into force on 29 September 2003 by the Commonhold and Leasehold Reform Act 2002 (Commencement No 3) Order 2003.

. . .

PART 3
SUPPLEMENTARY

Commencement etc

181.—(1) Apart from section 104 and sections 177 to 179, the preceding provisions (and the Schedules) come into force in accordance with provision made by order made by the appropriate authority.

(2) The appropriate authority may by order make any transitional provisions or savings in connection with the coming into force of any provision in accordance with an order under subsection (1).

(3) The power to make orders under subsections (1) and (2) is exercisable by statutory instrument.

(4) In this section 'the appropriate authority' means—

(a) in relation to any provision of Part 1 or section 180 and Schedule 14 so far as relating to section 104, the Lord Chancellor, and

(b) in relation to any provision of Part 2 or section 180 and Schedule 14 so far as otherwise relating, the Secretary of State (as respects England) and the National Assembly for Wales (as respects Wales).

Commentary

This section provides for the Act to come into force by virtue of orders made by the Lord Chancellor and the Secretary of State by statutory instrument. In its Post Consultation Report dated August 2003, the Department of Constitutional Affairs (which has succeeded the Lord Chancellor's Department) indicated that it hoped to finalise the draft regulations by the end of 2003, with the aim of bringing them into force in Spring 2004.

The first Commencement Order relating to the commonhold provisions in Part I of the Act was made on 8 September 2003, bringing the regulation-making and other formal powers in sections 42, 62, 64, 65, 66, 67, 69 and 70 into force on 29 September 2003 (see the text of the Commonhold and Leasehold Reform Act 2002 (Commencement No 3) Order 2003 in the Statutory Instruments section at the end of this Part of the work).

Extent

182. This Act extends to England and Wales only.

Commentary

This section confines the territorial extent of the Act to England and Wales. Scotland already has its own system of shared land ownership.

Short title

183. This Act may be cited as the Commonhold and Leasehold Reform Act 2002.

SCHEDULES

SCHEDULE 1

APPLICATION FOR REGISTRATION: DOCUMENTS

Introduction

1. This Schedule lists the documents which are required by section 2 to accompany an application for the registration of a freehold estate as a freehold estate in commonhold land.

Commonhold association documents

2. The commonhold association's certificate of incorporation under section 13 of the Companies Act 1985 (c 6).

3. Any altered certificate of incorporation issued under section 28 of that Act.

4. The memorandum and articles of association of the commonhold association.

Commonhold community statement

5. The commonhold community statement.

Consent

6.—(1) Where consent is required under or by virtue of section 3—

(a) the consent,

(b) an order of a court by virtue of section 3(2)(f) dispensing with the requirement for consent, or

(c) evidence of deemed consent by virtue of section 3(2)(e).

(2) In the case of a conditional order under section 3(2)(f), the order must be accompanied by evidence that the condition has been complied with.

Certificate

7. A certificate given by the directors of the commonhold association that—

(a) the memorandum and articles of association submitted with the application comply with regulations under paragraph 2(1) of Schedule 3,

(b) the commonhold community statement submitted with the application satisfies the requirements of this Part,
(c) the application satisfies Schedule 2,
(d) the commonhold association has not traded, and
(e) the commonhold association has not incurred any liability which has not been discharged.

Commentary

This Schedule lists the documents which are required to accompany an application under section 2 for registration of land as a freehold estate in commonhold land. Section 6 gives the court power to deal with any deficiency in those documents.

The expression 'commonhold association' is defined in section 34.
The expression 'commonhold community statement' is defined in section 31.
The expression 'commonhold land' is defined in section 1.
The term 'court' means the High Court or a county court—see section 66.
By virtue of section 69(3), the term 'director' has the meaning given to it by section 741(1) of the Companies Act 1985.

This Schedule is discussed in paragraph 2.19.3 of the text.

SCHEDULE 2
LAND WHICH MAY NOT BE COMMONHOLD LAND

'Flying freehold'

(1) Subject to sub-paragraph (2), an application may not be made under section 2 wholly or partly in relation to land above ground level ('raised land') unless all the land between the ground and the raised land is the subject of the same application.

(2) An application for the addition of land to a commonhold in accordance with section 41 may be made wholly or partly in relation to raised land if all the land between the ground and the raised land forms part of the commonhold to which the raised land is to be added.

Agricultural land

An application may not be made under section 2 wholly or partly in relation to land if—
(a) it is agricultural land within the meaning of the Agriculture Act 1947 (c 48),
(b) it is comprised in a tenancy of an agricultural holding within the meaning of the Agricultural Holdings Act 1986 (c 5), or
(c) it is comprised in a farm business tenancy for the purposes of the Agricultural Tenancies Act 1995 (c 8).

Contingent title

(1) An application may not be made under section 2 if an estate in the whole or part of the land to which the application relates is a contingent estate.

(2) An estate is contingent for the purposes of this paragraph if (and only if)—
(a) it is liable to revert to or vest in a person other than the present registered proprietor on the occurrence or non-occurrence of a particular event, and

(b) the reverter or vesting would occur by operation of law as a result of an enactment listed in sub-paragraph (3).

(3) The enactments are—

(a) the School Sites Act 1841 (c. 38) (conveyance for use as school),

(b) the Lands Clauses Acts (compulsory purchase),

(c) the Literary and Scientific Institutions Act 1854 (c. 112) (sites for institutions), and

(d) the Places of Worship Sites Act 1873 (c. 50) (sites for places of worship).

(4) Regulations may amend sub-paragraph (3) so as to-

(a) add an enactment to the list, or

(b) remove an enactment from the list.

Commentary

This Schedule, which is introduced by section 4, defines three distinct categories of land which may not be commonhold land: flying freeholds, agricultural land and land in which there are contingent interests. The third category is restricted to contingencies occurring as a result of the operation of one of four listed statutes, but allows for additions to be made to that list by regulations.

The expression 'a commonhold' is defined in section 1.
By virtue of section 69(3), the term 'land' has the meaning given to it by section 205(1)(ix) of the Law of Property Act 1925 and by section 132(1) of the Land Registration Act 2002. The term 'regulations' is explained in section 64.

This Schedule is discussed in Section 2.3 of the text.

SCHEDULE 3

COMMONHOLD ASSOCIATION

PART 1 MEMORANDUM AND ARTICLES OF ASSOCIATION

Introduction

1. In this schedule—

(a) 'memorandum' means the memorandum of association of a commonhold association, and

(b) 'articles' means the articles of association of a commonhold association.

Form and content

2.—(1) Regulations shall make provision about the form and content of the memorandum and articles.

(2) A commonhold association may adopt provisions of the regulations for its memorandum or articles.

(3) The regulations may include provision which is to have effect for a commonhold association whether or not it is adopted under sub-paragraph (2).

(4) A provision of the memorandum or articles shall have no effect to the extent that it is inconsistent with the regulations.

(5) Regulations under this paragraph shall have effect in relation to a memorandum or articles—

(a) irrespective of the date of the memorandum or articles, but
(b) subject to any transitional provision of the regulations.

Alteration

3.—(1) An alteration of the memorandum or articles of association shall have no effect until the altered version is registered in accordance with this paragraph.

(2) If the commonhold association makes an application under this sub-paragraph the Registrar shall arrange for an altered memorandum or altered articles to be kept in his custody, and referred to in the register, in place of the unaltered version.

(3) An application under sub-paragraph (2) must be accompanied by a certificate given by the directors of the commonhold association that the altered memorandum or articles comply with regulations under paragraph 2(1).

(4) Where the Registrar amends the register on an application under sub-paragraph (2) he shall make any consequential amendments to the register which he thinks appropriate.

Disapplication of Companies Act 1985

4.—(1) The following provisions of the Companies Act 1985 (c 6) shall not apply to a commonhold association—
(a) sections 2(7) and 3 (memorandum), and
(b) section 8 (articles of association).

(2) No application may be made under paragraph 3(2) for the registration of a memorandum altered by special resolution in accordance with section 4(1) of the Companies Act 1985 (objects) unless—
(a) the period during which an application for cancellation of the alteration may be made under section 5(1) of that Act has expired without an application being made,
(b) any application made under that section has been withdrawn, or
(c) the alteration has been confirmed by the court under that section.

PART 2 MEMBERSHIP

Pre-commonhold period

5. During the period beginning with incorporation of a commonhold association and ending when land specified in its memorandum becomes commonhold land, the subscribers (or subscriber) to the memorandum shall be the sole members (or member) of the association.

Transitional period

6.—(1) This paragraph applies to a commonhold association during a transitional period.

(2) The subscribers (or subscriber) to the memorandum shall continue to be members (or the member) of the association.

(3) A person who for the time being is the developer in respect of all or part of the commonhold is entitled to be entered in the register of members of the association.

Unit-holders

7. A person is entitled to be entered in the register of members of a commonhold association if he becomes the unit-holder of a commonhold unit in relation to which the association exercises functions—

(a) on the unit becoming commonhold land by registration with unit-holders under section 9, or

(b) on the transfer of the unit.

Joint unit-holders

8.—(1) This paragraph applies where two or more persons become joint unit-holders of a commonhold unit—

(a) on the unit becoming commonhold land by registration with unit-holders under section 9, or

(b) on the transfer of the unit.

(2) If the joint unit-holders nominate one of themselves for the purpose of this sub-paragraph, he is entitled to be entered in the register of members of the commonhold association which exercises functions in relation to the unit.

(3) A nomination under sub-paragraph (2) must—

(a) be made in writing to the commonhold association, and

(b) be received by the association before the end of the prescribed period.

(4) If no nomination is received by the association before the end of the prescribed period the person whose name appears first in the proprietorship register is on the expiry of that period entitled to be entered in the register of members of the association.

(5) On the application of a joint unit-holder the court may order that a joint unit-holder is entitled to be entered in the register of members of a commonhold association in place of a person who is or would be entitled to be registered by virtue of sub-paragraph (4).

(6) If joint unit-holders nominate one of themselves for the purpose of this sub-paragraph, the nominated person is entitled to be entered in the register of members of the commonhold association in place of the person entered by virtue of—

(a) sub-paragraph (2),

(b) sub-paragraph (5), or

(c) this sub-paragraph.

Self-membership

9. A commonhold association may not be a member of itself.

No other members

10. A person may not become a member of a commonhold association otherwise than by virtue of a provision of this Schedule.

Effect of registration

11. A person who is entitled to be entered in the register of members of a commonhold association becomes a member when the company registers him in pursuance of its duty under section 352 of the Companies Act 1985 (c 6) (duty to maintain register of members).

Termination of membership

12. Where a member of a commonhold association ceases to be a unit-holder or joint unit-holder of a commonhold unit in relation to which the association exercises functions—
- (a) he shall cease to be a member of the commonhold association, but
- (b) paragraph (a) does not affect any right or liability already acquired or incurred in respect of a matter relating to a time when he was a unit-holder or joint unit-holder.

13. A member of a commonhold association may resign by notice in writing to the association if (and only if) he is a member by virtue of paragraph 5 or 6 of this Schedule (and not also by virtue of any other paragraph).

Register of members

14.—(1) Regulations may make provision about the performance by a commonhold association of its duty under section 352 of the Companies Act 1985 (c 6) (duty to maintain register of members) where a person—
- (a) becomes entitled to be entered in the register by virtue of paragraphs 5 to 8, or
- (b) ceases to be a member by virtue of paragraph 12 or on resignation.

(2) The regulations may in particular require entries in the register to be made within a specified period.

(3) A period specified under sub-paragraph (2) may be expressed to begin from—
- (a) the date of a notification under section 15(3),
- (b) the date on which the directors of the commonhold association first become aware of a specified matter, or
- (c) some other time.

(4) A requirement by virtue of this paragraph shall be treated as a requirement of section 352 for the purposes of section 352(5) (fines).

Companies Act 1985

15.—(1) Section 22(1) of the Companies Act 1985 (initial members) shall apply to a commonhold association subject to this Schedule.

(2) Sections 22(2) and 23 of that Act (members: new members and holding company) shall not apply to a commonhold association.

PART 3 MISCELLANEOUS

Name

16. Regulations may provide—
- (a) that the name by which a commonhold association is registered under the Companies Act 1985 must satisfy specified requirements;

(b) that the name by which a company other than a commonhold association is registered may not include a specified word or expression.

Statutory declaration

17. For the purposes of section 12 of the Companies Act 1985 (registration: compliance with Act) as it applies to a commonhold association, a reference to the requirements of that Act shall be treated as including a reference to a provision of or made under this Schedule.

Commentary

This Schedule makes provision for the constitution of a commonhold association. It is brought into effect by section 34.

Part 1 of this Schedule sets out provisions regarding the form, content and alteration of the memorandum and articles of association of the commonhold association, and disapplies certain provisions of the Companies Act 1985.

Part 2 of this Schedule lays down rules regarding those entitled to be members of a commonhold association.

Part 3 of this Schedule introduces further requirements regarding naming and company registration.

The expression 'commonhold land' is defined in section 1.
The expression 'commonhold unit' is defined in section 11.
The term 'court' means the High Court or a county court—see section 66.
The term 'developer' is defined in section 58.
By virtue of section 69(3), the terms 'director' and 'special resolution' have the meanings given to them respectively by sections 741(1) and 378(2) of the Companies Act 1985.
The expressions 'exercises functions' and 'transitional period' are defined in section 8.
The expression 'joint unit-holder' is defined in section 13.
By virtue of section 69(3), the term 'land' has the meaning given to it by section 205(1)(ix) of the Law of Property Act 1925 and by section 132(1) of the Land Registration Act 2002.
The expressions 'prescribed' and 'regulations' are defined and explained by section 64.
The terms 'register' and 'registered' are defined in section 67.
The term 'transfer' (of a commonhold unit) is defined in section 15.
The term 'unit-holder' is defined in section 12.

This Schedule is discussed in Parts 3 and 4 of Chapter 2 of the text.

SCHEDULE 4

DEVELOPMENT RIGHTS

Introductory

1. This Schedule sets out the matters which are development business for the purposes of section 58.

Works

2. The completion or execution of works on—

(a) a commonhold,

(b) land which is or may be added to a commonhold, or
(c) land which has been removed from a commonhold.

Marketing

3.—(1) Transactions in commonhold units.

(2) Advertising and other activities designed to promote transactions in commonhold units.

Variation

4. The addition of land to a commonhold.

5. The removal of land from a commonhold.

6. Amendment of a commonhold community statement (including amendment to redefine the extent of a commonhold unit).

Commonhold association

7. Appointment and removal of directors of a commonhold association.

Commentary

This schedule is brought into effect by section 58. It provides for the developer of a site that is intended to become a commonhold to be free to progress the development without being bound by rules in the commonhold community statement that would otherwise interfere with that progress.

The expression 'a commonhold' is defined in section 1.
The expression 'commonhold association' is defined in section 34.
The expression 'commonhold community statement' is defined in section 31.
The expression 'commonhold unit' is defined in section 11.
By virtue of section 69(3), the term 'director' has the meaning given to it by section 741(1) of the Companies Act 1985.
By virtue of section 69(3), the term 'land' has the meaning given to it by section 205(1)(ix) of the Law of Property Act 1925 and by section 132(1) of the Land Registration Act 2002.

This Schedule is discussed in Section 2.20 of the text.

SCHEDULE 5

COMMONHOLD: CONSEQUENTIAL AMENDMENTS

Law of Property Act 1922 (c 16)

1. At the end of paragraph 5 of Schedule 15 to the Law of Property Act 1922 (perpetually renewable leases) (which becomes sub-paragraph (1)) there shall be added—

'(2) Sub-paragraph (3) applies where a grant—
(a) relates to commonhold land, and
(b) would take effect by virtue of sub-paragraph (1) as a demise for a term of two thousand years or a subdemise for a fixed term.

(3) The grant shall be treated as if it purported to be a grant of the term referred to in sub-paragraph (2)(b) (and sections 17 and 18 of the Commonhold and Leasehold Reform Act 2002 (residential and non-residential leases) shall apply accordingly).'

Law of Property Act 1925 (c 20)

2. After section 101(1) of the Law of Property Act 1925 (mortgagee's powers) there shall be added—

'(1A) Subsection (1)(i) is subject to section 21 of the Commonhold and Leasehold Reform Act 2002 (no disposition of part-units).'

3. At the end of section 149 of that Act (90-year term in place of certain determinable terms) there shall be added—

'(7) Subsection (8) applies where a lease, underlease or contract—

(a) relates to commonhold land, and
(b) would take effect by virtue of subsection (6) as a lease, underlease or contract of the kind mentioned in that subsection.

(8) The lease, underlease or contract shall be treated as if it purported to be a lease, underlease or contract of the kind referred to in subsection (7)(b) (and sections 17 and 18 of the Commonhold and Leasehold Reform Act 2002 (residential and non-residential leases) shall apply accordingly).'

Limitation Act 1980 (c 58)

4. After section 19 of the Limitation Act 1980 (actions for rent) there shall be inserted—

'Commonhold

19A Actions for breach of commonhold duty

An action in respect of a right or duty of a kind referred to in section 37(1) of the Commonhold and Leasehold Reform Act 2002 (enforcement) shall not be brought after the expiration of six years from the date on which the cause of action accrued.'

Housing Act 1985 (c 68)

5. At the end of section 118 of the Housing Act 1985 (the right to buy) there shall be added—

'(3) For the purposes of this Part, a dwelling-house which is a commonhold unit (within the meaning of the Commonhold and Leasehold Reform Act 2002) shall be treated as a house and not as a flat.'

Insolvency Act 1986 (c 45)

6. At the end of section 84 of the Insolvency Act 1986 (voluntary winding-up) there shall be added—

'(4) This section has effect subject to section 43 of the Commonhold and Leasehold Reform Act 2002.'

Law of Property (Miscellaneous Provisions) Act 1994 (c 36)

7.—(1) Section 5 of the Law of Property (Miscellaneous Provisions) Act 1994 (discharge of obligations) shall be amended as follows.

(2) In subsection (1) for the words 'or of leasehold land' substitute 'of leasehold land or of a commonhold unit'.

(3) After subsection (3) insert—

'(3A) If the property is a commonhold unit, there shall be implied a covenant that the mortgagor will fully and promptly observe and perform all the obligations under the commonhold community statement that are for the time being imposed on him in his capacity as a unit-holder or as a joint unit-holder.'

(4) For subsection (4) substitute—

'(4) In this section—

(a) 'commonhold community statement', 'commonhold unit', 'joint unit-holder' and 'unit-holder' have the same meanings as in the Commonhold and Leasehold Reform Act 2002, and

(b) 'mortgage' includes charge, and 'mortgagor' shall be construed accordingly.'

Trusts of Land and Appointment of Trustees Act 1996 (c 47)

8. At the end of section 7 of the Trusts of Land and Appointment of Trustees Act 1996 (partition by trustees) there shall be added—

'(6) Subsection (1) is subject to sections 21 (part-unit: interests) and 22 (part-unit: charging) of the Commonhold and Leasehold Reform Act 2002.'

Commentary

This schedule is brought into effect by section 68. It sets out a number of consequential amendments to sections of other statutes.

The expression 'commonhold community statement' is defined in section 31.
The expression 'commonhold land' is defined in section 1.
The expression 'commonhold unit' is defined in section 11.
The term 'dwelling-house' is defined by section 183 of the Housing Act 1985 to mean a house or a flat, other than where the building containing the house or flat lies above the remainder of a structure.
The term 'flat' is defined by section 183 of the Housing Act 1985 to mean (in effect) a horizontally divided dwelling-house.
The expression 'joint unit-holder' is defined in section 13.
The term 'unit-holder' is defined in section 12.

Paragraph 4 of this Schedule is discussed in paragraph 6.20.2 of the text.

Commonhold and Leasehold Reform Act 2002 (Commencement No 3) Order 2003

(SI 2003 No 2377)

Made *8 September 2003*

1. This Order may be cited as the Commonhold and Leasehold Reform Act 2002 (Commencement No 3) Order 2003.

2. The following provisions of the Commonhold and Leasehold Reform Act 2002 shall come into force on 29th September 2003—

(a) section 42 (ombudsman);
(b) section 62 (advice);
(c) section 64 (orders and regulations);
(d) section 65 (registration procedure);
(e) section 66 (jurisdiction);
(f) section 67 (the register); and
(g) sections 69 (interpretation) and 70 (index of defined expressions) so far as they relate to those sections.

Explanatory Note

(This note is not part of the Order)

This Order brings into force on 29th September 2003 provisions in the Commonhold and Leasehold Reform Act 2002 (c. 15) relating to the ombudsman, the giving of advice and rule- and regulation-making powers. By section 42 of the Act the Lord Chancellor may approve an ombudsman scheme and by section 62 the Lord Chancellor may give financial assistance to a person in relation to that person providing general advice about an aspect of the law of commonhold land, so far as it relates to residential matters. Sections 64 to 67 allow the Lord Chancellor to make regulations on commonhold and for those regulations to confer functions on the Registrar, to make rules on the registration of freehold estates in commonhold land and to make rules of court or rules of procedure in relation to commonhold land. Section 69 defines a number of terms in the Act and section 70 lists where other expressions are defined.

Commentary

This instrument is the first commencement order to be made under the Act regarding the commonhold provisions set out in Part I.

Commonhold Regulations (Draft)

Note by the authors

No regulations have yet been fully formulated. On 10 October 2002, the Lord Chancellor's Department published a Consultation Paper seeking views on its policy proposals relating to the matters to be included in the commonhold regulations. The consultation period ended on 6 January 2003, and the Department of Constitutional Affairs (which has succeeded the Lord Chancellor's Department) produced a Post Consultation Report in August 2003, which forecasts that the regulations will be finalised by the end of the year and brought into force in spring 2004.

Act reference	**Proposed regulation**	**Status**	**Draft regulation reference**
s 3(1)(d)	Revision to classes of persons whose consent to commonhold should be required	Regulations drafted but not yet finalised	Reg 2
s 3(2)	Form and substance of consent to commonhold	Regulations drafted but not yet finalised; specimen document drafted	Regs 3 and 4
Sch 2, paras 3 and 4	Categories of contingent title which may not become commonhold land	No current proposals for regulations	Reg 5
s 5(1)	Prescribed details to be kept by Registrar	Regulations drafted but not yet finalised	
s 8(2)	Application of provisions to transitional period	No regulations yet proposed	
s 9(2)	Registration with unit-holders	Regulations drafted but not yet finalised; specimen document drafted	Reg 6
s 11(3)	Plan to show extent of commonhold unit	Regulations drafted but not yet finalised	Reg 8
s 13	"joint unit-holders"	Regulations proposed but not drafted	
s 15(4)	Form and effect of notice of transfer of unit	Regulations proposed and specimen document drafted	

Act reference	**Proposed regulation**	**Status**	**Draft regulation reference**
s 17(1)	Restrictions on lease of residential unit	Regulations drafted but not yet finalised	Reg 10
s 19	Obligations on tenant of unit	Regulations proposed but not drafted	
s 20(3)	Prescribed interests	Regulations proposed but not drafted	
s 21	Restrictions on lease of part of unit	No regulations yet proposed	
s 23(2)	Dispensing with consent of unit-holder to alteration of size of unit	No regulations proposed	
s 24(2)	Dispensing with consent of mortgagee to alteration of size of unit	No regulations proposed	
s 24(6)	Requiring notification of Land Registry of alteration in size of charged unit	Regulations drafted but not yet finalised	Reg 11
s 30(3)	Dispensing with consent of mortgagee to addition of part of unit to common parts	No regulations proposed	
s 31(2)	Form of commonhold community statement	Regulations drafted but not yet finalised; specimen document drafted—see Form 2.3	Reg 14
s 32	Content of commonhold community statement	Regulations drafted but not yet finalised; specimen document drafted—see Form 2.3	Reg 14
s 33	Amendment of a commonhold community statement	Regulations drafted but not yet finalised	Reg 14
Sch 3, para 2	Form and content of memorandum and articles of association	Regulations drafted but not yet finalised; specimen documents drafted—see Forms 2.1 and 2.2	Regs 12 and 13

Act reference	**Proposed regulation**	**Status**	**Draft regulation reference**
Sch 3, para 8	Nomination of one of joint unit-holders for membership of commonhold association	Regulations proposed but not drafted	
Sch 3, para 14	Requirement to keep Register of Members	Regulations proposed but not drafted	
Sch 3, para 16	Name of commonhold association	Regulations drafted but not yet finalised	Reg 15
s 37	Exercise or enforcement of right or duty in commonhold	Regulations drafted but not yet finalised	Reg 17
s 39(1)	Reserve fund requirements	Regulations proposed but not drafted	
s 42	Application of ombudsman scheme	Regulations proposed but not drafted	
s 44(3)	Persons entitled to make 100% termination application	Regulations drafted but not yet finalised	Reg 16
s 45(2)	Timing of termination application	Regulations drafted but not yet finalised	Reg 19
s 45(4)	Persons entitled to make 80% termination application	Regulations proposed but not drafted	
s 51(3)	Evidence of formation of successor commonhold association	No regulations yet proposed	
s 57	Application for registration of commonhold by separate freeholders	Regulations proposed but not drafted	
s 58(5)	Exercise of development rights	Regulations drafted but not yet finalised	Reg 18
s 60	Transfer to compulsory purchaser	No regulations yet proposed	
s 64	Making of regulations		
s 65	Registration procedure		

Act reference	**Proposed regulation**	**Status**	**Draft regulation reference**
s 66(4)	Rules of court and procedure	No regulations yet proposed	
s 67(2)	Functions of the Chief Land Registrar		

Commonhold Regulations (Draft)

Part I

General

Citation, commencement and interpretation

1.—(1) These Regulations may be cited as the Commonhold Regulations 2003 and shall come into force on [ ].

(2) In these Regulations, unless the context requires otherwise, a section or Schedule referred to by number alone means the section or Schedule so numbered in the Commonhold and Leasehold Reform Act 2002.

(3) In these Regulations, the 'model CCS' means the commonhold community statement contained in Schedule 3 to the Regulations.

Part II

Registration and Effects

Consents required prior to the creation of a commonhold additional to those required by section 3(1)(a) to (c)

2. An application under section 2 may not be made in respect of a freehold estate in land without the consent of anyone who is—

(a) the estate owner of any leasehold estate in the whole or part of the land granted for a term of more than 21 years which is not registered;

(b) the person entitled to the benefit of any charge over the whole or part of the land which is not registered; or

(c) the person entitled to the benefit of any interest over the whole or part of the land that is the subject of an entry in the register of title to the land or under the Land Charges Act 1972 which will be extinguished by virtue of section 21(5).

Details of consent

3.—(1) Consent must be given in the appropriate form prescribed in rule [X] to the Commonhold (Land Registration) Rules 2003.

(2) Consent is binding on the person giving consent only where the commonhold community statement and memorandum and articles of association accompanying the application are unchanged, or have undergone no material change, since the consent was given.

(3) Consent is deemed to have been given by persons deriving title from a person who has given consent and will be binding on a person deriving title to the same extent to which it would be binding on the person who gave consent.

(4) Consent will lapse if no application is made within a period of 12 months beginning with the date on which consent was given.

(5) Consent may not be withdrawn after the application has been submitted to the Registrar.

(6) Consent has effect for the purpose of a subsequent application ('the new application') only where the new application is submitted—
   (a) in place of a previous application which has been withdrawn, rejected or cancelled;
   (b) within a period of 12 months beginning with the date on which the previous application was submitted; and
   (c) where the commonhold community statement and memorandum and articles of association accompanying the new application are unchanged, or have undergone no material change, since the consent was given.

(7) Consent is deemed to have been given by the person or persons making the application where their consent would otherwise be required in accordance with section 3 or regulation 2.

(8) In this Regulation, 'consent' means consent in accordance with section 3.

Dispensing with a requirement for consent

4. The court may dispense with the requirement for consent if a person—
   (a) cannot be identified after all reasonable efforts have been made to ascertain the identity of the person required to give consent; or
   (b) cannot be traced after all reasonable efforts have been made to trace him; or
   (c) has been sent the request for consent and all reasonable efforts have been made to obtain a response but the person has not responded.

Details required by the Registrar for entry in the register

5. The Registrar must ensure that in respect of any commonhold land the following details are kept in his custody and referred to in the register—
   (a) in respect of the commonhold association, the association's—
      (i) name;
      (ii) company number given when registered in accordance with the Companies Act 1985; and
      (iii) address for service; and
   (b) in respect of the registered freeholder of each commonhold unit—
      (i) his name;
      (ii) his address for service;
      (iii) the unit number of the commonhold unit; and
      (iv) the postal address of the commonhold unit (if available).

Statement under section 9(1)(b): Registration with unit-holders

6. A statement under section 9(1)(b) which accompanies an application to register a freehold estate in commonhold land with the proposed initial unit-holder or joint unit-holders must state in relation to each commonhold unit—
   (a) the full name of the proposed initial unit-holder or if there are proposed joint unit-holders the full name of each of them;
   (b) the address for service of the proposed unit-holder or if there are proposed joint unit-holders the address for service of each of them; and
   (c) the unit number of the commonhold unit; and
   (d) the postal address of the commonhold unit (if available).

Multiple site commonholds

7. For the purposes of an application under section 2 made jointly by two or more persons, each of whom is the registered freeholder of part of the land to which the application relates ('a part site') section 11 is modified so that, in addition to complying with the requirements in section 11(3), in defining the extent of a commonhold unit the commonhold community statement must provide for the extent of each commonhold unit to be situated wholly upon one part site, and not situated partly on one part site and partly on one or more part sites.

PART III

COMMONHOLD UNIT

Requirements of a plan included in the commonhold community statement

8. A plan referred to in a commonhold community statement for the purposes of defining the extent of a commonhold unit must—

(a) be marked with the date and version number of the commonhold community statement to which it is attached;

(b) be no larger than A0 paper size;

(c) show any measurements in metric units;

(d) be to a scale of no less than 1/500 save that where the boundaries of individual commonhold units are clear a scale of no less than 1/1250 may be used;

(e) be based on an accurate survey, plotted to the chosen scale which must be shown on the plan;

(f) show the position of the commonhold in relation to the boundaries of the registered freeholder's title and the position of each commonhold unit in relation to the boundaries of the commonhold;

(g) where appropriate, identify the floor on which each commonhold unit is situated;

(h) show the boundaries of each commonhold unit including any non-contiguous areas, using a separate number or colour reference for each non-contiguous area comprised within the commonhold unit; and

(i) show the extent of the commonhold using a colour reference distinct from the colours used to denote the commonhold units.

Definition of commonhold unit

9.—(1) In defining the extent of a commonhold unit a commonhold community statement—

(a) may exclude the structure and exterior of a building where the building contains only one commonhold unit or part of one commonhold unit;

(b) must exclude the structure and exterior of a building where the building contains all or part of more than one commonhold unit.

(2) In this regulation—

'building' means a physical entity which is structurally independent;

'structure and exterior' includes the pipes, wires, drains, sewers and other service media in or serving the building but does not include any service media which are within and exclusively serving one commonhold unit.

Leasing of commonhold unit

10.—(1) A term of years absolute in a residential commonhold unit must not be granted for a term longer than twenty-one years or contain an option to renew.

(2) A commonhold community statement must impose on a tenant of a commonhold unit the provisions contained in rules 7 and 8 of the model CCS.

(3) A commonhold community statement must contain the provision in rule 52 of the model CCS.

(4) This regulation applies (with any necessary modifications) to a term of years absolute in part only of a commonhold unit.

Requirement to notify Registrar of amendment to extent of land

11.—(1) This regulation applies where an amendment to a commonhold community statement is made which redefines the extent of a commonhold unit over which there is a registered charge.

(2) The unit-holder of the commonhold unit to which the charge relates must submit notice of the alteration to the Registrar in the form prescribed in rule [X] of the Commonhold (Land Registration) Rules 2003.

(3) On receipt of such notification the Registrar must alter the register to reflect the amendment to the charge.

PART IV

GOVERNING DOCUMENTS

Memorandum of association

12. The memorandum of association of a commonhold association must be in the form contained in Schedule 1 to these Regulations or a form to the same effect and further clauses may be added.

Articles of association

13.—(1) Subject to the following paragraphs, the articles of association of a commonhold association must be in the form contained in Schedule 2 to these Regulations or a form to the same effect and each article will have effect for a commonhold association whether or not it is adopted under paragraph 2(2) of Schedule 3 except that a commonhold association may include a provision which is to have effect in place of articles 7, 12, 21, 27, 31, 32, 42, 44, 46, 52, 55(a) and (f), 59, 60, 61, 62, 65 to 75 and 78.

(2) Where a commonhold contains only non-residential units the commonhold association may include a provision which is to have effect in place of article 11.

(3) Article 16 has effect for a commonhold association where the commonhold contains less than six commonhold units except with—

(a) in paragraph (a) two members substituted for three members;
(b) in paragraph (b) three members substituted for four members; and
(c) in paragraph (c) four members substituted for five members

although a commonhold association may include a provision which is to have effect in place of this article except that no provision must be made in place of the words from 'Business' to the end of the sentence.

(4) Where a commonhold contains more than six commonhold units, article 44 must be altered to provide that at least one director must be a member of the commonhold association although the commonhold association may provide that more than one director should be a member.

(5) Where a commonhold contains less than six commonhold units, article 45 may be altered to provide that the minimum number of directors is one.

(6) A commonhold association may include provision which is to have effect in place of article 79 which provides for any surplus to be paid or distributed to members of the commonhold association in percentages other than those stated in article 79.

(7) In this Regulation an article referred to by number alone means the article so numbered in Schedule 2 to these Regulations.

Commonhold community statement

14.—(1) Subject to the following paragraphs, a commonhold community statement must be in the form contained in Schedule 3 to these Regulations or a form to the same effect and continuation pages may be added.

(2) The front page and glossary of a commonhold community statement must be in the form contained in the model CCS save that a commonhold association may omit 'or for residential and other incidental purposes' from the definition of 'residential commonhold unit' and may add definitions to the glossary.

(3) Table 3.3 of the model CCS may be amended as follows—

(a) column 3 may be omitted where a commonhold association does not establish a reserve fund; and

(b) column 4 may be omitted where a commonhold association does not make any provision in place of articles 31 or 32 of the articles of association in Schedule 2 to these Regulations.

(4) A commonhold community statement must contain the provisions in rules 1, 2, 4 to 6, 9 to 18, 20 to 29, 31, 32, 41 to 43, 45 to 51 and 54 to 66 of the model CCS.

(5) Where a commonhold contains one or more residential commonhold units the commonhold community statement must contain the provision in rule 3 of the model CCS.

(6) A commonhold community statement is treated as including the provisions in rules 19, 30, and 53 of the model CCS unless a provision is made in place of each of those provisions.

(7) Where the directors of a commonhold association establish and maintain one or more reserve funds a commonhold community statement must contain the provisions in rules 33 to 38 and 40 of the model CCS and will be treated as including the provision in rule 39 of the model CCS unless a provision is made in place of it.

(8) A commonhold community statement is treated as including the provision in rule 44 of the model CCS unless it contains the same provision as that contained in rule 44 with any committee or agency substituted for the Board of Directors.

(9) A commonhold community statement may contain, but is not limited to, provisions about the following matters—
 (a) dealings with the land;
 (b) use, insurance, repair and maintenance of a commonhold unit or common parts;
 (c) financial matters relating to the commonhold assessment or any reserve fund;
 (d) complaints and default procedure;
 (e) termination statement;
 (f) amendment of the commonhold community statement; and
 (g) notices.

PART V

OPERATION OF A COMMONHOLD

The name of the commonhold association

15.—(1) The name by which a commonhold association is registered under the Companies Act 1985 must include 'commonhold association limited' or, if the memorandum of association states that the commonhold association's registered office is to be situated in Wales, those words or their equivalent in Welsh ('Cymdeithas Cydradd-Ddaliad Cyfngedig').

(2) The name by which a company other than a commonhold association is registered may not include 'commonhold association limited' or the Welsh equivalent 'Cymdeithas Cydradd-Ddaliad Cyfngedig'.

Requirement to be a member of an approved ombudsman scheme

16. A commonhold association must be a member of an approved ombudsman scheme.

Enforcement and compensation

17.—(1) Jurisdiction is conferred on a county court to deal with the exercise or enforcement of a right or duty imposed by—
 (a) a commonhold community statement; or
 (b) the articles of association; or
 (c) Regulation 19;
 and the commonhold association must be a party to the proceedings.

(2) In proceedings for the exercise or enforcement of a right or duty the court may—
 (a) order compensation to be paid; and
 (b) provide for the payment of simple interest in the case of late payment of compensation for the period between the date on which the payment is due and the date on which the payment is made
 as the court thinks fit.

(3) Where work is carried out for the purpose of enforcing a right or duty the reasonable cost of such work may be recovered from the unit-holder or commonhold association against whom the right or duty is being enforced.

(4) Where work is carried out in consequence of the failure to perform a duty the reasonable cost of such work may be recovered from the unit-holder or commonhold association who has failed to perform the duty.

Development rights

18.—(1) Where a commonhold community statement confers development rights on the developer in accordance with section 58 it will be treated as including the following provisions unless a provision is made in place of it—

(a) the commonhold community statement must not be amended without the consent of the developer, in so far as the proposed amendment relates to development rights;

(b) section 41(3) does not apply where an application to add land to the commonhold is being made by the developer;

(c) subject to paragraph (6), the commonhold association must co-operate with the developer for the purposes of amending the commonhold community statement in the event that land is added to or removed from the commonhold or the extent of a commonhold unit is redefined;

(d) in the event of a breach of the requirement in sub-paragraph (c) a resolution of the commonhold association to amend the commonhold community statement will be deemed to have been passed; and

(e) the developer has rights of access to the commonhold units and common parts in order to facilitate his undertaking of development business.

(2) The rights conferred on the developer in a commonhold community statement are restricted or regulated in accordance with the following paragraphs.

(3) The developer must not unreasonably interfere with a unit-holder's quiet or peaceful enjoyment of the freehold interest in a commonhold unit.

(4) The developer must not reserve the right to remove parts of the common parts from the commonhold.

(5) The developer may not remove land from the commonhold that has been transferred to a unit-holder.

(6) The developer may not add land to the commonhold unless he reserved the right to add that land to the commonhold in the commonhold community statement.

(7) The developer must specify any major works in the commonhold community statement but this will not prevent unspecified major works being undertaken in an emergency.

(8) The developer must specify in the commonhold community statement the date on which the common parts will be completed and where major works on the common parts is specified in the commonhold community statement the developer must specify the date on which this will be completed.

(9) If in the commonhold community statement the developer reserves the right to use services available to the commonhold including, but not limited to, water, sewerage, drainage, gas, electricity, oil, rubbish disposal, air conditioning and telephone, or to install additional services, that right is subject to the developer making payment for the use of such services.

(10) The standard of materials, finishes and landscaping, and the height and density of buildings on land which is to be added to the commonhold must not be inferior to, or substantially different from those of the completed buildings in the

commonhold development, except to the extent set out in the development rights in the commonhold community statement (if any).

(11) The developer, in his capacity as such, must not use any part of the commonhold except to the extent necessary to carry out the permitted development or as specified in the development rights.

(12) Any damage to the common parts or a commonhold unit caused by the developer in the course of undertaking development business must—

(a) be put right by the developer; or

(b) the reasonable costs to put right the damage must be paid by the developer as soon as reasonably practicable.

(13) The developer must minimise the disruption to other occupants of the commonhold.

(14) The development rights expire five years from the date on which the first commonhold unit is transferred except that—

(a) where work has been commenced during the five year period it may be completed notwithstanding that the five year period has expired; and

(b) the developer may reserve the right to continue marketing the development until the last commonhold unit is sold.

(15) In this regulation 'major works' includes, but is not limited to, the construction of a new building, road or sewer or the demolition of, or structural changes to, an existing building, road or sewer.

PART VI

TERMINATION

Termination

19.—(1) The liquidator must, in accordance with section 45(2), apply to the court for an order determining—

(a) the terms and conditions on which a termination application may be made; and

(b) the terms of the termination statement to accompany a termination application within the period of 3 months beginning with the day on which the liquidator was appointed.

(2) An application under section 51(1) must be accompanied by the certificate of incorporation of the successor commonhold association given in accordance with section 13 of the Companies Act 1985 and any altered certificates of incorporation issued under section 28 of that Act.

Index